Econometric Modeling

Econometric Modeling

A Likelihood Approach

David F. Hendry
Bent Nielsen

PRINCETON UNIVERSITY PRESS

PRINCETON AND OXFORD

Copyright © 2007 by Princeton University Press

Published by Princeton University Press
41 William Street, Princeton, New Jersey 08540

In the United Kingdom: Princeton University Press
3 Market Place, Woodstock, Oxfordshire OX20 1SY

All Rights Reserved

Library of Congress Control Number 2006052859

ISBN-13: 978-0-691-13128-3
ISBN-10: 0-691-13128-7
ISBN-13: 978-0-691-13089-7 (pbk.)
ISBN-10: 0-691-13089-2 (pbk.)

British Library Cataloging-in-Publication Data is available

This book has been composed in LaTeX

The publisher would like to acknowledge the authors of this volume for
providing the camera-ready copy from which this book was printed.

Printed on acid-free paper. ∞

press.princeton.edu

Printed in the United States of America

10 9 8 7 6 5 4 3 2 1

Contents

Preface

This book provides a *likelihood*-based introduction to econometrics. In essence, the idea is to carefully investigate the sample variation in the data, then exploit that information to learn about the underlying economic mechanisms. The relative likelihood reflects how well different models of the data perform. We find this is a useful approach for both expository and methodological reasons.

The substantive context of econometrics is economics. Economic theory is concerned about how an economy might function and how agents in the economy behave, but not so much about a detailed description of the data variation that will be observed. Econometrics faces the methodological challenge that much of the observed economic data variability is due to factors outside of economics, such as wars, epidemics, innovations, and changing institutions. Consequently, we pursue a methodology where fairly general econometric models are formulated to capture the sample variation, with one or several economic theories being special cases that can be tested. This approach offers the possibility of falsifying that theory, by not imposing the structure of an economic theory at the outset. More constructively, it is possible to enhance the economic theory by also explaining important variations in the economy. An example is the theory of consumption smoothing. By looking at the variation in a quarterly time series, we will see that consumption is not smooth but in fact shows a large increase every Christmas, followed by a slump in the first quarter of the following year. It is then clear that a general theory of consumption would have to take this seasonal fluctuation into account.

We will use a maximum likelihood approach to analyze distributional models for the data. The models we consider have parameters that characterize features of the data: to learn about these parameters, each is accorded its most likely value. Within such a framework, it is then relatively easy to explain *why* we use the various econometric techniques proposed. The book is organized so as to develop empirical, as well as theoretical, econometric aspects in each chapter. Quite often the analysis of data sets is developed over a sequence of chapters. This continued data analysis serves as a constant reminder that in practice one has to be pragmatic, and there will be many situations where one has to make compromises. By developing a likelihood approach, it is easier to realize where compromises are made and decide on the best resolution.

The book is written to be self-contained. Most chapters have exercises at the end. A few are marked with an asterisk, *, indicating that they are more advanced, often trying to illustrate some definitions, but otherwise tangential to the flow of the text. Others are labeled Computer Tasks and are computer-based exercises. Monte Carlo methods can with advantage be used to illustrate the econometric methods from an early point. An introduction to Monte Carlo theory is, however, deferred to Chapter 18.

Throughout the book, references are given to books or articles with related material. These references are relatively few in number, given the large econometric literature. Chapter 22 therefore concludes the book by discussing a way ahead in the econometric literature beyond this book. At this point, however, it may be useful to highlight a few other econometric textbooks that can be consulted. An introduction to the likelihood approach can also be found in the political science textbook by King (1989). The book by Gujarati (2003) has approximately the same algebraic level as this book. It follows a least-squares approach rather than a likelihood approach, but may be a useful companion as it provides wider coverage. Maddala, Rao and Vinod (1992) is similar, but at a slightly lower level. Dougherty (2002) and in particular Verbeek (2000) follow the least-squares approach, with many empirical illustrations based on downloadable data. Another textbook at about the same algebraic level is Wooldridge (2006), which uses a method-of-moments motivation for the econometric theory rather than a likelihood approach. The style of Kennedy (2003) is idiosyncratic as a detailed introduction to econometrics, in that it largely avoids algebra. Our initial discussion of sample distributions is inspired by Goldberger (1991, 1998).

We are indebted to Swarnali Ahmed, Gunnar Bårdsen, Jennifer Castle, David Cox, Guillaume Chevillon, Jurgen Doornik, Katy Graddy, Vivien Hendry, Søren Johansen, Hans-Martin Krolzig, Marius Ooms, four anonymous referees, students, and class teachers for many helpful comments on an earlier draft, and for assistance with the data and programs that are such an essential component of empirical modeling. The book was typeset using MikTex. Illustrations and numerical computations have been done using R (see R Development Core Team, 2006) and OxMetrics (see Doornik, 2006). Lucy Day Werts Hobor of Princeton University Press kindly steered the preparation of the final version.

Data and software

We use a number of different data sets to illustrate and motivate the econometric theory. These can be downloaded from the Web page associated with the book:

http://press.princeton.edu/titles/8352.html.

These data sets and their sources are:

(1) *Sex of newborn babies in the UK.* This first data set simply records the numbers of girls and boys among newborn babies in 2003 and 2004. The information is taken from the printed population statistics: Office for National Statistics (2005, 2006), see also http://www.statistics.gov.uk.

(2) *US census data.* Individual-level data are typically not publicly available due to data protection issues. An exception is the Integrated Public Use Microdata Series at http://www.ipums.org. The data are 5% samples from the US censuses, which are held every 10 years. For the 1990 and 2000 censuses, the publicly available data have been perturbed, once again due to data protection issues. We will consider data from the 1980 census, from which we have drawn a 500th-part random subset, that is 0.01% of the population. Many variables are available for each individual, but we will focus on labor market issues for women of age 18 to 65 in the sample.

(3) *UK production,* 1700–2000. This is a long time series for "Output in Industry" compiled from several sources, primarily Crafts and Harley (1992, p. 725), Mitchell (1988, p. 846), and Central Statistical Office (1993) (see Hendry, 2001: the data were missing during the Second World War, so were linearly interpolated between 1938 and 1946).

(4) *Katy Graddy's data from the Fulton Fish Market.* From April to May 1992, Katy Graddy worked with a trader at the Fulton Fish Market in New York and collected an extensive data set of quantities and prices for trades of whiting, as documented in Graddy (1995) and Graddy (2006). A data set involving aggregated daily prices and quantities for the period December 1991 to May 1992 was also collected and analyzed by Angrist, Graddy and Imbens (2000). This data set will be used here.

(5) *UK money data.* This set of UK monetary data was collected quarterly for the period 1963:1–1989:2 and seasonally adjusted. These data were first documented in Hendry and Ericsson (1991b).

(6) *US GDP data.* This data set of US real GDP was collected quarterly for the period 1947:1 to 2006:1 measured in year 2000 US dollars. Its source is the Bureau of Economic Analysis, http://www.bea.gov.

(7) *UK consumption.* This set of UK consumption data was collected quarterly, but not seasonally adjusted, for the period 1957:1 to 1976:2. It has been documented and analyzed by Davidson, Hendry, Srba and Yeo (1978). An extension of this consumption data set is also provided, based on more recent records from the U.K. Office for National Statistics, http://www.statistics.gov.uk.

(8) *UK annual macroeconomic data,* 1875–2000 This set of annual macro variables for the UK has previously been analysed by Ericsson, Hendry and Prestwich (1998). It is an extension of the data analysed by Friedman and Schwartz (1982).

For carrying out the Computer Tasks, most econometric software packages could be used. Initially we introduce the OxMetrics system (Doornik, 2006) and STATA. Later exercises focus on OxMetrics, which includes the module PcGive for analyzing the data and building empirical models (Doornik and Hendry, 2006a), and the module PcNaive that is designed for Monte Carlo experiments (Doornik and Hendry, 2006d). A free version of the OxMetrics software with the above data sets pre-loaded, but without the possibility of loading other data sets, can be downloaded from the above-mentioned Web page.

Chapter One

The Bernoulli model

In this chapter and in Chapter 2, we will consider a data set recording the number of newborn girls and boys in the UK in 2004 and investigate whether the distribution of the sexes is even among newborn children. This question could be of interest to an economist thinking about the wider issue of incentives facing parents who are expecting a baby. Sometimes the incentives are so strong that parents take actions that actually change basic statistics like the sex ratio.

When analyzing such a question using econometrics, an important and basic distinction is between sample and population distributions. In short, the sample distribution describes the variation in a particular data set, whereas we imagine that the data are sampled from some population about which we would like to learn. This first chapter describes that distinction in more detail. Building on that basis, we formulate a model using a class of possible population distributions. The population distribution within this class, which is the one most likely to have generated the data, can then be found. In Chapter 2, we can then proceed to question whether the distribution of the sexes is indeed even.

1.1 SAMPLE AND POPULATION DISTRIBUTIONS

We start by looking at a simple demographic data set showing the number of newborn girls and boys in the UK in 2004. This allows us to consider the question whether the chance that a newborn child is a girl is 50%. By examining the frequency of the two different outcomes, we obtain a *sample distribution*. Subsequently, we will turn to the general population of newborn children from which the data set has been sampled, and establish the notion of a *population distribution*. The econometric tools will be developed with a view toward learning about this population distribution from a sample distribution.

1.1.1 Sample distributions

In 2004, the number of newborn children in the UK was 715996, see Office for National Statistics (2006). Of these, 367586 were boys and 348410 were girls. These data have come about by observing $n = 715996$ newborn children. This

i	sex	Y_i
1	boy	0
2	girl	1
$\vdots$	$\vdots$	$\vdots$
715996	boy	0

Table 1.1 Cross-sectional data set of the sex of children born in 2004

gives us a *cross-sectional* data set as illustrated in Table 1.1. The name cross-section data refers to its origins in surveys that sought to interview a cross section of society. In a convenient notation, we let $i = 1, \ldots, n$ be the child index, and for each child we introduce a *random variable Y_i*, which can take the numerical value 0 or 1 representing "boy" or "girl," respectively. While the data set shows a particular set of outcomes, or observations, of the random variables $Y_1, \ldots, Y_n$, the econometric analysis will be based on a *model* for the possible variation in the random variables $Y_1, \ldots, Y_n$. As in this example, random variables always take numerical values.

To obtain an overview of a data set like that reported Table 1.1, the number of cases in each category would be counted, giving a summary as in Table 1.2. This reduction of the data, of course, corresponds to the actual data obtained from the Office of National Statistics.

Y_i	0	1
count	367586	348410

Table 1.2 Sex of newborn children in the UK in 2004

The magnitudes of the numbers in the cells in Table 1.2 depend on the numbers born in 2004. We can standardize by dividing each entry by the total number of newborn children, with the result shown in Table 1.3.

y	0	1
$\widehat{f}(y)$	0.513	0.487

Table 1.3 Sample frequency of newborn boys and girls for 2004

Each cell of Table 1.3 then shows:

$$\widehat{f}(y) = \text{"frequency of sex } y \text{ among } n = 715996 \text{ newborn children."}$$

We say that Table 1.3 gives the frequency distribution of the random variables $Y_1, \ldots, Y_n$. There are two aspects of the notation $\widehat{f}(y)$ that need explanation. First, the argument y of the function $\widehat{f}$ represents the potential outcomes of child births, as opposed to the realization of a particular birth. Second, the function $\widehat{f}$, said as "f-hat", is an *observed*, or *sample*, quantity, in that it is computed from the observations $Y_1, \ldots, Y_n$. The notation $\widehat{f}$, rather than f, is used to emphasize the *sample* aspect, in contrast to the *population* quantities we will discuss later on.

The variables $Y_1, \ldots, Y_n$ (denoted Y_i in shorthand) take the values 0 or 1. That is, Y_i takes $J = 2$ distinct values for $j = 1, \ldots, J$. Thus, the sum of the cell values in Table 1.3 is unity:

$$\sum_{j=1}^{J} \widehat{f}(y_j) = 1.$$

1.1.2 Population distributions

We will think of a sample distribution as a random realization from a population distribution. In the above example, the sample is all newborn children in the UK in 2004, whereas the population distribution is thought of as representing the biological causal mechanism that determines the sex of children. Thus, although the sample here is actually the population of all newborn children in the UK in 2004, the population from which that sample is drawn is a hypothetical one.

The notion of a population distribution can be made a little more concrete with a coin-flipping example. The outcome of a coin toss is determined by the coin and the way it is tossed. As a model of this, we imagine a symmetric coin is tossed fairly such that there is an equal chance of the outcome being heads or tails, so the probability of each is $1/2$. It is convenient to think in terms of a random variable X describing the outcome of this coin-flipping experiment, so X takes values 0 and 1 if the outcome is tails and heads, respectively. The distribution of the outcomes can be described in terms of an underlying probability measure, P say, giving rise to the imagined population frequencies:

$$f(0) = P(X = 0) = 1/2 \quad \text{and} \quad f(1) = P(X = 1) = 1/2.$$

Here f appears without a "hat" as it is a population quantity, and $P(X = 0)$ is read as "the probability of the event $X = 0$". We think of the frequency f as related to the random variable X, although that aspect is suppressed in the notation. In contrast, the probability measure P is more generic. We could introduce a new random variable $Y = 1 - X$, which takes the value 0 and 1 for heads and tails, rather than tails and heads, and write $P(Y = 1) = P(X = 0) = 1/2$.

We can sample from this population distribution as many times as we want. If, for instance, we toss the coin $n = 27$ times, we may observe 12 heads, so the sample frequency of heads is $\widehat{f}(1) = 12/27$. In fact, when sampling an odd number of times, we can never observe that $\widehat{f}(1) = f(1) = 1/2$. One important difference between $f(x)$ and $\widehat{f}(x)$ is that f is a deterministic function describing the distribution of possible outcomes for a random variable X, whereas $\widehat{f}$ is a random function describing the observed frequency of the outcomes in a sample of random variables $X_1, \ldots, X_n$; another sample of tosses would lead to different values of $\widehat{f}$, but not f.

1.2 DISTRIBUTION FUNCTIONS AND DENSITIES

We need a structured way of thinking about distributions in order to build appropriate models. From probability theory, we can use the concepts of distribution functions and densities.

1.2.1 Distribution functions and random variables

Distribution theory is centered around *cumulative distribution functions* or just *distribution functions*. This is the function $F(x) = P(X \leq x)$, which is well defined regardless of the type of random variable. For the coin example, the distribution function is plotted in panel (a) of Figure 1.1. It has the defining property of any distribution function: it starts at zero on the far left and increases toward unity, reaching one at the far right. The probability is zero of observing an outcome less than zero, jumps to $1/2$ at 0 (tails), then to unity at 1 (heads), and stays there.

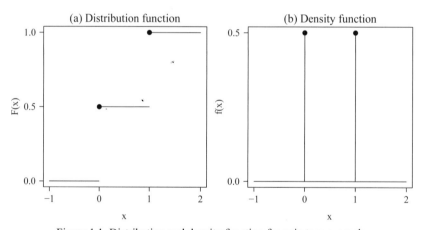

Figure 1.1 Distribution and density function for coin toss example

If we consider the inverse of the distribution function, we get the *quantiles* of a distribution. The 50% quantile, also called the median, is the smallest value of x such that $P(X \leq x) = 0.5$. For the coin-flipping example considered in Figure 1.1, the median is 0.

When dealing with two random variables X and Y that could, for instance, describe the outcomes of two coin tosses, we have the *joint distribution function*:

$$F(x, y) = P(X \leq x \text{ and } Y \leq y).$$

We get the *marginal distribution function* of Y by allowing X to take any value:

$$\mathsf{F}(y) = \mathsf{P}(Y \leq y) = \mathsf{P}(X < \infty \text{ and } Y \leq y).$$

For example, when X and Y refer respectively to whether the mother is young/old and the child is boy/girl, then the marginal distribution of the sex of the child is so called because it refers to the distribution in the margin of the 2×2 table of possible outcomes irrespective of the mother's age: see Table 4.2 below.

If we flip a coin twice and let X and Y describe the two outcomes, we do not expect any influence between the two outcomes, and hence obtain:

$$\mathsf{P}(X \leq x \text{ and } Y \leq y) = \mathsf{P}(X \leq x)\mathsf{P}(Y \leq y). \tag{1.2.1}$$

If so, we say that the variables X and Y are *independent*. More generally, the variables $X_1, \ldots, X_n$ are said to be independent if their joint distribution function equals the product of the marginal distribution functions:

$$\mathsf{P}(X_1 \leq x_1, \ldots, X_n \leq x_n) = \prod_{i=1}^{n} \mathsf{P}(X_i \leq x_i).$$

For example, the probability of 3 heads in a row is $\frac{1}{2} \times \frac{1}{2} \times \frac{1}{2} = \frac{1}{8}$.

1.2.2 Density functions

In an econometric analysis, it is often convenient to consider the rate of increase of the distribution function rather than the distribution function itself.

For the birth and the coin-flipping experiments, the jumps of the distribution function determine the distribution uniquely. This is generally the case for any distribution function that is piecewise constant and therefore associated with a *discrete* distribution. The jumps are the *probability mass function* or the *density*:

$$\mathsf{f}(x) = \mathsf{P}(X = x).$$

Since the distribution function is piecewise constant, we can find the size of the jump at a point x as the value of the distribution function at x minus the value immediately before x, which we could write as:

$$\mathsf{f}(x) = \mathsf{P}(X = x) = \mathsf{P}(X \leq x) - \lim_{h \downarrow 0} \mathsf{P}(X \leq x - h).$$

As an example, compare the distribution function and the corresponding density shown in Figure 1.1. Here it is seen that the density is 0.5 when $x = 0$ or $x = 1$ and otherwise 0.

We can recover the distribution function from the density by summation:

$$\mathsf{F}(x) = \mathsf{P}(X \leq x) = \sum_{\substack{z: \text{ possible value} \\ \text{for } X \text{ so } z \leq x}} \mathsf{f}(z).$$

In particular, the sum over all possible outcomes is always unity.

We can also work with joint densities. It follows from (1.2.1) that two discrete random variables X, Y are independent if and only if:

$$f(x, y) = \mathsf{P}(X = x \text{ and } Y = y) = \mathsf{P}(X = x)\mathsf{P}(Y = y) = f(x)f(y), \quad (1.2.2)$$

whereas the *marginal density* of X is:

$$f(x) = \mathsf{P}(X = x) = \mathsf{P}(X = x \text{ and } Y \leq \infty) = \sum_{y:\text{ possible values for }Y} f(x, y),$$

$$(1.2.3)$$

where the sum is taken over all possible outcomes for Y.

1.2.3 A discrete distribution: the Bernoulli distribution

If a variable X takes the values 0 and 1, as with the variable for sex, it is said to be binary or dichotomous. It then has what is called a *Bernoulli* . The probability of a unit outcome:

$$\theta = \mathsf{P}(X = 1)$$

is the *success probability*. The parameter θ takes a value in the range $[0, 1]$. It follows that the probability of a *failure* is $\mathsf{P}(X = 0) = 1 - \theta$. In short, we write $X \overset{D}{=} \text{Bernoulli}[\theta]$ to indicate that X is Bernoulli-distributed with parameter θ. Figure 1.1 shows the distribution function and the density for a Bernoulli distribution with success parameter $\theta = 0.5$. ·

The density for the Bernoulli distribution can be written in a compact form:

$$f(x) = \theta^x (1 - \theta)^{1-x} \qquad \text{for } x = 0, 1. \qquad (1.2.4)$$

In (1.2.4), it holds that $\mathsf{P}(X = 0) = f(0) = (1 - \theta)$ and $\mathsf{P}(X = 1) = f(1) = \theta$.

1.3 THE BERNOULLI MODEL

We are now ready to develop our first statistical model. Using the above distribution theory, a statistical model and its associated likelihood function can be defined for the birth data. The likelihood function can then be used to find the specific member of the statistical model that is most likely to have generated the observed data.

1.3.1 A statistical model

Reconsider the birth data summarized in Table 1.2, where we are interested in learning about the population frequency of girls among newborn children. To do this, we will build a simple *statistical model* for the sex of newborn children. The objective is to make a good description of the sample distribution, which will eventually allow us to make inferences about, in this case, the frequency of girl births in the population of possible births. Here we will concentrate on describing the distribution with a view toward checking any assumptions we make.

Let Y_i denote the sex for child i, and consider n random variables $Y_1, \ldots, Y_n$ representing the data. We will make four assumptions:

(i) *independence*: $Y_1, \ldots, Y_n$ are mutually independent;
(ii) *identical distribution*: all children are drawn from the same population;
(iii) *Bernoulli distribution*: $Y_i \overset{\mathrm{D}}{=} \mathrm{Bernoulli}[\theta]$;
(iv) *parameter space*: $0 < \theta < 1$, which we write as $\theta \in \Theta = (0, 1)$.

We need to think about whether these assumptions are reasonable. Could they be so wrong that all inferences we draw from the model are misleading? In that case, we say the model is mis-specified. For example, the assumptions of independence or an identical distribution could well be wrong. In cases of identical twins, the independence assumption (i) is indeed not correct. Perhaps young and old mothers could have different chances of giving birth to girls, which could be seen as a violation of (ii). Is that something to worry about? In this situation, no more data are available, so we either have to stick to speculative arguments, turn to an expert in the field, or find more detailed data. We will proceed on the basis that any violations are not so large as to seriously distort our conclusions. Assumption (iii), however, is not in question in this model as the Bernoulli distribution is the only available distribution for binary data. Assumption (iv) is also not problematic here, even though the parameter space is actually restrictive in that it is chosen as $0 < \theta < 1$ as opposed to $0 \leq \theta \leq 1$. The resolution is that since we have observed both girls and boys, it is not possible that $\theta = 0$ or $\theta = 1$. These two points can therefore be excluded.

1.3.2 The likelihood function

Based on the statistical model, we can analyze how *probable* different outcomes $y_1, \ldots, y_n$ of $Y_1, \ldots, Y_n$ are for any given choice of the parameter θ. This is done by writing down the joint density of $Y_1, \ldots, Y_n$. Using the notation $f_\theta (y_1, \ldots, y_n)$ for the joint density and the rules from §1.2.2, we get:

$$f_\theta (y_1, \ldots, y_n) = \prod_{i=1}^{n} f_\theta (y_i) \qquad [\ (i): \text{independence, see } (1.2.2)\ ]$$

$$= \prod_{i=1}^{n} \theta^{y_i} (1 - \theta)^{1 - y_i} \qquad [\ (ii, iii): \text{Bernoulli, see } (1.2.4)\ ]$$

This expression can be reduced further using the fact that:

$$\theta^a \theta^b = \theta^{a+b}, \qquad (1.3.1)$$

which is the functional equation for power functions. Then (1.3.1) implies that:

$$\prod_{i=1}^{n} \theta^{y_i} (1-\theta)^{1-y_i} = \theta^{\sum_{i=1}^{n} y_i} (1-\theta)^{\sum_{i=1}^{n}(1-y_i)}.$$

Introducing the notation $\overline{y}$ for the average $n^{-1}\sum_{i=1}^{n} y_i$, the joint density becomes:

$$f_\theta (y_1,\ldots,y_n) = \theta^{n\overline{y}} (1-\theta)^{n(1-\overline{y})} = \left\{ \theta^{\overline{y}} (1-\theta)^{(1-\overline{y})} \right\}^n. \qquad (1.3.2)$$

For known θ, we can calculate the density for any value of $\overline{y}$.

   In practice, however, the premises are turned around: we have observed a data set that is a realization of the random variables $Y_1,\ldots,Y_n$, while θ is unknown. The aim is now to find the most *likely* value of θ for this particular outcome. To that end, we define the *likelihood function*:

$$L_{Y_1,\ldots,Y_n} (\theta) = f_\theta (Y_1,\ldots,Y_n), \qquad (1.3.3)$$

where the argument becomes the parameter θ varying in the parameter space Θ, rather than the possible data outcomes. Inserting (1.3.2) for the joint density, but expressed in terms of Y, we get:

$$L_{Y_1,\ldots,Y_n} (\theta) = \left\{ \theta^{\overline{Y}} (1-\theta)^{(1-\overline{Y})} \right\}^n. \qquad (1.3.4)$$

Two steps have been taken:

   (1) y_i is replaced by Y_i to indicate that the likelihood function is based on the random variables representing the data;
   (2) the expression (1.3.4) is viewed as a function of θ rather than Y_i.

Figure 1.2 illustrates the link between the joint density and the likelihood function. In panel (a), rather than showing the joint density as a function of its n-dimensional argument, it is shown as a function of $\overline{y}$. This is done for three different choices of θ. Panel (b) shows the corresponding likelihood function as a function of θ for $\overline{Y} = 0.487$. The three marked points indicate how the three different densities link up with the likelihood function. What would happen if the likelihood function were not raised to the power $1/n$ as in the figure?

   Notice that the likelihood function depends only on the observations through $\overline{Y}$, so $\overline{Y}$ is said to be a *sufficient statistic* for θ. The summary statistics of Table 1.2 are therefore sufficient for our analysis, once it has been established that the model is not mis-specified.

1.3.3 Estimation

We will now seek to find the most likely parameter value by maximizing the likelihood function (1.3.4). The likelihood function has a product structure. Here, the

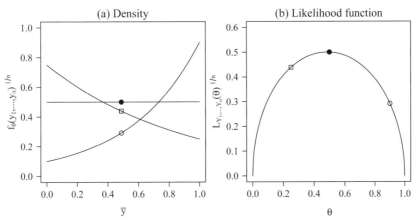

Figure 1.2 (a) Bernoulli densities as function of $\overline{y}$ given $\theta = 0.25, \; 0.5, \; 0.9$ for $\square, \bullet, \circ$, respectively. (b) Bernoulli likelihood given $\overline{Y} = 0.487$, where the points $\square, \bullet, \circ$ mark $\theta = 0.25, \; 0.5, \; 0.9$

product structure arises from the independence assumption, but we will later see, in Chapter 12, that such a structure can also arise in other ways. Since sums are much easier to deal with than products, it is convenient to linearize the likelihood function by applying the (natural) logarithm. The *log-likelihood function* is:

$$\ell_{Y_1,\ldots,Y_n}(\theta) \overset{\text{def}}{=} \log \mathsf{L}_{Y_1,\ldots,Y_n}(\theta) = \log\left[\left\{\theta^{\overline{Y}}(1-\theta)^{\left(1-\overline{Y}\right)}\right\}^n\right].$$

Due to the monotonicity of the log transformation, the maxima of L and ℓ occur at the same value of the parameter. The above expression can be simplified by noting that the (natural) logarithm satisfies the functional equation:

$$\log(ab) = \log(a) + \log(b). \qquad (1.3.5)$$

The log-likelihood function therefore reduces to:

$$\ell_{Y_1,\ldots,Y_n}(\theta) = \log \mathsf{L}_{Y_1,\ldots,Y_n}(\theta) = n\left\{\overline{Y}\log(\theta) + \left(1-\overline{Y}\right)\log(1-\theta)\right\}. \quad (1.3.6)$$

Figure 1.2(b) indicates that the likelihood function, and hence the log-likelihood function, has a unique maximum. To find this maximum, we differentiate with respect to θ:

$$\frac{\partial}{\partial\theta}\ell_{Y_1,\ldots,Y_n}(\theta) = n\left(\frac{\overline{Y}}{\theta} - \frac{1-\overline{Y}}{1-\theta}\right).$$

We set this expression equal to zero to find the value $\widehat{\theta}$ for which the likelihood takes its maximum:

$$n\left(\frac{\overline{Y}}{\widehat{\theta}} - \frac{1-\overline{Y}}{1-\widehat{\theta}}\right) = 0.$$

This first-order equation is called the *likelihood equation* for θ. Rearranging the likelihood equation:

$$\frac{\overline{Y}}{\widehat{\theta}} = \frac{1 - \overline{Y}}{1 - \widehat{\theta}} \qquad \Leftrightarrow \qquad \frac{\overline{Y}(1 - \widehat{\theta})}{\widehat{\theta}(1 - \widehat{\theta})} = \frac{(1 - \overline{Y})\widehat{\theta}}{\widehat{\theta}(1 - \widehat{\theta})} \qquad \Leftrightarrow \qquad \widehat{\theta} = \overline{Y}.$$

Thus, $\widehat{\theta}$ is the value, among all possible parameter values θ, that maximizes the likelihood function. Thus, the *maximum likelihood estimator* for θ is:

$$\widehat{\theta} = \overline{Y}.$$

Once again, the hat over θ is used to indicate that $\widehat{\theta}$ is a function of the observed random variables, and hence the sample version of the parameter θ that is a population quantity. The maximum for the log-likelihood function is then:

$$\max_{0 < \theta < 1} \ell_{Y_1,...,Y_n}(\theta) = \ell_{Y_1,...,Y_n}\left(\widehat{\theta}\right) = n\left\{\overline{Y}\log\left(\widehat{\theta}\right) + (1 - \overline{Y})\log\left(1 - \widehat{\theta}\right)\right\}.$$

In the above analysis, $\widehat{\theta}$ was found to be a unique maximum by appealing to Figure 1.2(b). This can alternatively be proved by checking the second derivative of the log-likelihood function:

$$\frac{\partial^2}{\partial\theta^2}\ell_{Y_1,...,Y_n}(\theta) = -n\left\{\frac{\overline{Y}}{\theta^2} + \frac{1 - \overline{Y}}{(1 - \theta)^2}\right\}.$$

Since $1 > \overline{Y} > 0$, this expression is negative for any value of $\theta \in \Theta$, so the log-likelihood function is concave with a unique maximum at $\widehat{\theta} = \overline{Y}$.

While an estimator is a random variable, a realization for a particular dataset is called an *estimate*. Thus, using the birth data, we estimate the chance of a newborn child being female by:

$$\widehat{\theta} = 0.4874 = 48.74\%, \tag{1.3.7}$$

while the log-likelihood function has its maximum value of:

$$\ell_{Y_1,...,Y_n}(\widehat{\theta}) = -496033.8.$$

It is worth noting that these numbers are numerical approximations and subject to rounding errors, so that the estimate 0.4874 is only an approximation to the fraction of 348410 divided by 715996. In Chapter 2, we will see that this rounding error is small compared to the more important sampling error, so we choose to apply the equality symbol even when numbers are subject to rounding error.

We could reparametrize the model in terms of the proportion of boys, η say, satisfying $\eta = 1 - \theta$. Going through everything above would deliver a new log-likelihood function $\widetilde{\ell}$ leading to the maximum likelihood estimator $\widehat{\eta} = 1 - \overline{Y}$, taking the value 51.26% in this case. We immediately see that the maximum likelihood estimators from these two parametrizations satisfy $\widehat{\eta} = 1 - \widehat{\theta}$, and the two likelihood functions have the same maximum value:

$$\max_{0<\theta<1} \ell_{Y_1,\ldots,Y_n}(\theta) = \max_{0<\eta<1} \widetilde{\ell}_{Y_1,\ldots,Y_n}(\eta).$$

This is no coincidence, but a fundamental equivariance property of likelihood theory, namely that a likelihood function has the same maximum value for all, but very abstract, one-one parametrizations of the parameter space.

1.3.4 Restricting the statistical model

The motivation for this particular data analysis is to consider whether the chance that a newborn child is a girl could possibly be 50%. To do this, we can compare the values of the likelihood function at the unrestricted estimate, $\widehat{\theta}$, found above, and at the hypothesized point $\theta = 50\%$. We formalize this analysis as follows.

The analysis above represents an unrestricted model, where the likelihood function is maximized over an unrestricted parameter space, which we will now denote $\Theta_U = (0,1)$, with maximum likelihood estimate $\widehat{\theta}_U = \overline{Y} = 48.74\%$. Our hypothesis is that $\theta = 50\%$, which restricts the parameter space to a single point $\Theta_R = \{0.5\}$. It is easy to maximize the likelihood function in the case of such a simple hypothesis, and we find:

$$\max_{\theta \in \Theta_R} \ell_{Y_1,\ldots,Y_n}(\theta) = \ell_{Y_1,\ldots,Y_n}(0.5) = -496290.6,$$

where, of course, the restricted maximum likelihood estimate is $\widehat{\theta}_R = 50\%$.

We now evaluate that restriction by comparing the relative likelihoods of the unrestricted maximum likelihood estimator $\widehat{\theta}_U$ and the restricted maximum likelihood estimator $\widehat{\theta}_R$, in terms of the ratio or quotient:

$$Q = \frac{\max_{\theta \in \Theta_R} \mathsf{L}_{Y_1,\ldots,Y_n}(\theta)}{\max_{\theta \in \Theta_U} \mathsf{L}_{Y_1,\ldots,Y_n}(\theta)},$$

satisfying $0 \leq Q \leq 1$. The closer Q is to unity, the more likely it is that θ could satisfy the restriction. In practice, we usually look at a transformation of Q called the *log-likelihood ratio test statistic* or simply the likelihood ratio test statistic:

$$\mathsf{LR} = -2\log Q = 2\left\{\max_{\theta \in \Theta_U} \ell_{Y_1,\ldots,Y_n}(\theta) - \max_{\theta \in \Theta_R} \ell_{Y_1,\ldots,Y_n}(\theta)\right\}.$$

This takes non-negative values, so $\mathsf{LR} \geq 0$, and the closer LR is to zero, the more likely it is that θ could satisfy the restriction.

In our example we have:

$$\mathsf{LR} = 2\left(-496033.8 + 496290.6\right) = 513.6.$$

The crucial question is whether this is a large or a small value. In the following chapter, we will learn that there is an easy criterion for judging this. We will find that it is actually very large indeed, which in turn will lead us to reject the hypothesis that there is an equal chance that a newborn child is a boy or a girl.

1.4 SUMMARY AND EXERCISES

Sample quantities	Population quantities
$\widehat{f}$ frequency	f density
$\widehat{\theta}$ estimator	θ parameter

Table 1.4 Sample and population quantities

Summary: Sample and population quantities were introduced. It is fundamental to distinguish between those. The former are computed from the data. The latter are related to a postulated population. The notation distinguishes the two concepts by using a hat for sample quantities (Table 1.4).

We think of observations as outcomes of random variables. The probability theory is set up in terms of distribution functions. The density is the rate of increase of a distribution function. For likelihood theory, the multiplicative decomposition of joint densities in the independence case is crucial.

A statistical model specifies a parametrized class of distributions, one of which could have generated the data. This is in contrast with most other subjects where the notion of a model is reserved for a single distribution or other generating mechanism. For each value of the parameters, the joint density describes how probable outcomes are. Interpreted as a likelihood function, the joint density describes how likely parameters are. The maximum likelihood estimator is the most likely parameter value.

Bibliography: Many texts give detailed introductions to probability theory. A favorite choice is Hoel, Port and Stone (1971). Maximum likelihood was first suggested by Thiele (1886), see Lauritzen (2002) for an English translation, but the proposal did not take off at the time. The idea is usually attributed to R. A. Fisher, who, apparently unaware of Thiele's work, rediscovered the idea in Fisher (1922). Fisher understood the general applicability of likelihood and this, along with his many other contributions, revolutionized the way statistics was done.

In our notation, we have not formally distinguished between a random variable and a realization of a random variable computed from the data. This would require a little more probability theory than we need, and such a notation would actually become a hindrance later on in the book. For the same reason, our definition of the likelihood function in (1.3.3) differs from that in many classical texts on statistical theory, such as that of Cox and Hinkley (1974), and our notation is the same for estimators and estimates.

Key questions:
- What is the difference between sample and population distributions?
- Describe the notion of independence.
- How are joint densities and likelihood functions related?
- What is a statistical model?
- Discuss the validity of the assumptions of the statistical model for the newborn children data.

Exercise 1.1. *Let Y_1 and Y_2 be independent* Bernoulli$[0.5]$-*distributed random variables. Find the possible outcomes, the density, and the distribution function for $\overline{Y} = (Y_1 + Y_2)/2$.*

Exercise 1.2. *Table 1.5 shows the number of newborn boys and girls in the UK in 2003 and 2004.*
(a) Set up a Bernoulli model for the 2003 data and estimate the success parameter.
(b) Consider a joint model for the data for 2003 and 2004, where the success parameters can be different for the two years, and where all observations are independent. Argue that the joint likelihood is found by multiplying the two marginal likelihoods for 2003 and for 2004. How would you estimate the success parameters in this model?

	boys	girls
2003	356578	338971
2004	367586	348410

Table 1.5 Sex of newborn children in the UK in 2003 and 2004. Sources: Office for National Statistics (2005, 2006)

Exercise 1.3. *Table 1.6 shows the number of newborn boys and girls in the US in 2002, measured in thousands. Set up a Bernoulli model for the data and estimate the success parameter.*

	boys	girls
2002	2058	1964

Table 1.6 Sex of newborn children in the US in 2002, measured in thousands. Source: Census Bureau (2005)

Exercise 1.4. * *Consider a pair of random variables X, Y taking values $(1,0)$, $(0,1)$, $(-1,0)$, $(0,-1)$ with equal probability.*
(a) Find the marginal distribution of X.
(b) Are X and Y independent?

Chapter Two

Inference in the Bernoulli model

In Chapter 1, we looked at the sample distribution of the data set for the sex of newborn children. We set up a statistical model and found the most likely population distribution. We considered the question whether there is an equal chance of a newborn being either a boy or a girl, and computed the relative likelihood of this restriction of the model. In the following, we will work toward evaluating whether the resulting statistic is large or small, in order to be able to draw inferences about the hypothesis of an equal chance of a newborn child being either a boy or a girl.

In this chapter, we describe the sampling variation of the likelihood statistics $\widehat{\theta}$ and LR found in Chapter 1. This will help us to infer whether the deviation of $\widehat{\theta} = 0.487$ from the hypothesized value of 0.5 is due to a small random variation or a more systematic deviation. We start by introducing the notions of expectation and variance. Moving on to the Law of Large Numbers and the Central Limit Theorem, we will be able to discuss the distribution of the likelihood statistics in a simple way and, in turn, use that distribution to conduct inference.

2.1 EXPECTATION AND VARIANCE

With the estimate at hand for the chance of a newborn child being a girl, the next issue is whether it can be said to be close to a 50% chance. To discuss this, we need to understand the sampling variation, or uncertainty, of the estimate. The probabilistic concepts of expectation and variance are therefore introduced, first in a sample context using the birth data, and next in a population context. Subsequently, the expectation and variance of $\widehat{\theta}$ can be derived.

2.1.1 Sample expectation and variance

The most intuitive quantity of interest is the average, or mean, of the individual outcomes Y_i. This we can compute in several ways. The first is simply to add the n outcomes as reported in Table 1.1 and then divide by n as in:

$$\widehat{\mathsf{E}}(Y) = \frac{1}{n} \sum_{i=1}^{n} Y_i = \overline{Y} = 0.487,$$

where the "hat" once again indicates that $\widehat{\mathsf{E}}(Y)$ is a sample version of what we will later call the expectation of Y. Note also that the maximum likelihood estimator found for the Bernoulli model equals this sample expectation. Now, the n outcomes fall in just $J = 2$ different categories, which were summarized in Tables 1.2 and 1.3. By using the latter table, the mean can instead be computed in terms of sample frequencies of the J possible sexes as:

$$\widehat{\mathsf{E}}(Y) = \sum_{j=1}^{J} y_j \widehat{\mathsf{f}}(y_j), \tag{2.1.1}$$

which amounts to:

$$\widehat{\mathsf{E}}(Y) = 0 \times 0.513 + 1 \times 0.487 = 0.487.$$

To get an idea of how much the data are dispersed around the sample mean, we often compute the *sample variance*, which measures the sample expectations of the quadratic deviations from the sample expectation:

$$\widehat{\mathsf{Var}}(Y) = \frac{1}{n} \sum_{i=1}^{n} (Y_i - \overline{Y})^2.$$

This expression can be simplified by completing the square:

$$\widehat{\mathsf{Var}}(Y) = \frac{1}{n} \sum_{i=1}^{n} Y_i^2 - 2\overline{Y} \frac{1}{n} \sum_{i=1}^{n} Y_i + \overline{Y}^2 \tag{2.1.2}$$

$$= \frac{1}{n} \sum_{i=1}^{n} Y_i^2 - \overline{Y}^2 \qquad \text{[Exercise 2.5]} \tag{2.1.3}$$

$$= \widehat{\mathsf{E}}(Y^2) - \left\{\widehat{\mathsf{E}}(Y)\right\}^2. \tag{2.1.4}$$

From Table 1.3, we get:

$$\widehat{\mathsf{Var}}(Y) = 0^2 \times 0.513 + 1^2 \times 0.487 - (0.487)^2 = 0.250.$$

Since the units of Y are measured in "success", the variance is measured in the squared units "success"×"success". Likewise, if Y had been a variable measured in Pounds, the units of the variance would be Pounds × Pounds. To measure the spread in the same units as Y, we take the square root of $\widehat{\mathsf{Var}}(Y)$ and thereby get the *sample standard deviation*: $\mathsf{sdv}(Y) = \{\widehat{\mathsf{Var}}(Y)\}^{1/2} = 0.500$.

When two sets of variables X_i and Y_i are available, we sometimes calculate the *sample covariance*, which is defined as:

$$\widehat{\mathsf{Cov}}(X,Y) = \frac{1}{n} \sum_{i=1}^{n} (X_i - \overline{X})(Y_i - \overline{Y}) = \frac{1}{n} \sum_{i=1}^{n} X_i Y_i - \overline{X}\,\overline{Y}.$$

This measures how X_i, Y_i vary together, hence the prefix "co" in covariance.

2.1.2 Population expectation, variance, and covariance

The *expectation* is the population version of the sample mean. Just as the sample average is computed using the sample frequency in (2.1.1), the expectation is computed from the density. Discrete densities are linked with their distribution function through differencing and summing. In the same way, the expectation of a discrete random variable, X say, is computed as in (2.1.1) as:

$$\mathsf{E}\left(X\right) = \sum_{x:\text{ possible values for } X} x\mathsf{f}\left(x\right). \tag{2.1.5}$$

The additivity property of sums implies that, for constants a, b:

$$\mathsf{E}\left(aX + b\right) = a\mathsf{E}\left(X\right) + b. \tag{2.1.6}$$

Further, if X and Y are random variables, and a and b are constants, then:

$$\mathsf{E}\left(aX + bY\right) = a\mathsf{E}\left(X\right) + b\mathsf{E}\left(Y\right). \tag{2.1.7}$$

If X and Y are independent, we saw above that the joint density is the product of the marginal densities, so correspondingly by (1.2.2):

$$\mathsf{E}\left(XY\right) = \sum_{x,y} xy\mathsf{f}(x,y) = \sum_{x,y} xy\mathsf{f}(x)\mathsf{f}(y) \qquad [\text{ independence }]$$
$$= \mathsf{E}\left(X\right)\mathsf{E}\left(Y\right) \tag{2.1.8}$$

The *variance* of a random variable X is now an easy generalization of the sample variance, that is:

$$\mathsf{Var}\left(X\right) = \mathsf{E}\left\{X - \mathsf{E}\left(X\right)\right\}^2 = \mathsf{E}\left(X^2\right) - \left\{\mathsf{E}\left(X\right)\right\}^2, \tag{2.1.9}$$

see Exercise 2.6. To get a spread measure in the same units as X, we again take the square root of $\mathsf{Var}\left(X\right)$. This is the *standard deviation* given by $\mathsf{sdv}\left(X\right) = \left\{\mathsf{Var}\left(X\right)\right\}^{1/2}$. The variance is a quadratic function rather than a linear function:

$$\mathsf{Var}\left(aX + b\right) = a^2\mathsf{Var}\left(X\right), \tag{2.1.10}$$
$$\mathsf{Var}\left(aX + bY\right) = a^2\mathsf{Var}\left(X\right) + b^2\mathsf{Var}\left(Y\right) + 2ab\mathsf{Cov}\left(X,Y\right), \tag{2.1.11}$$

where:

$$\mathsf{Cov}\left(X,Y\right) = \mathsf{E}\left[\left\{X - \mathsf{E}\left(X\right)\right\}\left\{Y - \mathsf{E}\left(Y\right)\right\}\right] = \mathsf{E}(XY) - \mathsf{E}(X)\mathsf{E}(Y) \tag{2.1.12}$$

is called the *covariance* of X and Y. If $\mathsf{Cov}\left(X,Y\right) = 0$, then X and Y are *uncorrelated*. Because of (2.1.8), independence implies uncorrelatedness:

$$X, Y \text{ independent } \Rightarrow X, Y \text{ uncorrelated,} \tag{2.1.13}$$

but the opposite implication does not necessarily hold (Exercise 2.8). If X and Y are uncorrelated, it follows from (2.1.11) that:

$$\text{Var}\,(aX + bY) = a^2\text{Var}\,(X) + b^2\text{Var}\,(Y) \qquad [\text{ uncorrelatedness }]. \quad (2.1.14)$$

Random variables need not have any variation. Then they have zero variance:

$$\text{Var}\,(X) = 0 \qquad \Leftrightarrow \qquad \text{P}\,\{X = \text{E}\,(X)\} = 1. \qquad (2.1.15)$$

This property implies that sample and population variances can be very different. As an example consider an even number of random variables where those in the first half, $Y_1, \ldots, Y_{n/2}$, are all equal to -1 with probability one, and those in the second half, $Y_{n/2+1}, \ldots, Y_n$, are all equal to 1. In that case we have:

$$\widehat{\text{E}}(Y) = 0 \qquad \text{and} \qquad \widehat{\text{Var}}(Y) = 1,$$

but, for any $i = 1, \ldots, n$ it holds $\text{Var}(Y_i) = 0$. This discrepancy comes about because the variables $Y_1, \ldots, Y_n$ are not identically distributed. However, sample and population variances will be closely related when the variables are independent and identically distributed. This is a consequence of the Law of Large Numbers, which will be introduced in §2.2.1.

2.1.3 Example: the Bernoulli distribution

The Bernoulli distribution was introduced in §1.2.3. If $X \overset{\text{D}}{=} \text{Bernoulli}[\theta]$ then X has expectation and variance:

$$\text{E}\,(X) = \theta \qquad \text{and} \qquad \text{Var}\,(X) = \theta\,(1 - \theta). \qquad (2.1.16)$$

The proof is left to Exercise 2.4.

2.1.4 Application to the Bernoulli model

We now have the tools to find the expectation and variance of the maximum likelihood estimator $\widehat{\theta} = \overline{Y}$ of the Bernoulli model in Chapter 1.

The role of the parameter θ in this context has to be established first. In the statistical model and the derivation of the likelihood function in §1.3 the parameter θ could take any value in the open unit interval $\Theta = (0, 1)$. This lead to the estimator $\widehat{\theta}$, which is a random variable. We are now interested in analyzing how probable different outcomes of $\widehat{\theta}$ are. We then choose a particular value of θ in Θ and discuss the properties of $\widehat{\theta}$, assuming that the data have been generated from a Bernoulli distribution with that parameter. Often, one will refer to such a value of θ as the population value or the "true value" and sometimes denote it by θ_0, said as "θ-naught".

First, the expectation of $\widehat{\theta}$ with respect to the distribution with population parameter θ is:

$$E(\widehat{\theta}) = E(\overline{Y}) = E\left(\frac{1}{n}\sum_{i=1}^{n}Y_i\right) = \frac{1}{n}\sum_{i=1}^{n}E(Y_i) \qquad [\text{ use } (2.1.7)]. \qquad (2.1.17)$$

Because $Y_i \stackrel{D}{=} \text{Bernoulli}[\theta]$, we get from the property (2.1.16) that $E(Y_i) = \theta$, so:

$$E(\widehat{\theta}) = \frac{1}{n}\sum_{i=1}^{n}\theta = \theta,$$

showing that the estimator gives the population parameter on average. This applies regardless of our choice of θ. We say $\widehat{\theta}$ is an *unbiased* estimator for θ. Thus, if a group of econometricians each studied different data on child births, sampled from the same Bernoulli-distributed population, and each estimated θ, then the average of their estimates would be close to the population value.

Second, the variance of $\widehat{\theta}$ can be found along the same lines, using (2.1.10):

$$Var(\widehat{\theta}) = Var\left(n^{-1}\sum_{i=1}^{n}Y_i\right) = n^{-2}Var\left(\sum_{i=1}^{n}Y_i\right).$$

Because of the independence assumption, the variables are uncorrelated as argued in (2.1.13), so, by (2.1.14):

$$Var(\widehat{\theta}) = n^{-2}\sum_{i=1}^{n}Var(Y_i).$$

Since the variables Y_i are identically distributed, this reduces further to:

$$Var(\widehat{\theta}) = n^{-1}Var(Y_1). \qquad (2.1.18)$$

Finally, since $Y_i \stackrel{D}{=} \text{Bernoulli}[\theta]$, with variance given in (2.1.16), we get:

$$Var(\widehat{\theta}) = \frac{\theta(1-\theta)}{n}.$$

The variation of $\widehat{\theta}$ around θ is seen to change with both the sample size n and the population parameter θ. The impact of θ is quadratic with maximal value for $\theta = 0.5$. Turning to the impact of n, we see that the larger the sample is, the smaller is the variance of $\widehat{\theta}$. In other words, the precision of the estimator increases with the sample size, provided of course that the statistical model is not mis-specified. The standard deviation of an estimator, like $\widehat{\theta}$, is called the *standard error*:

$$se(\widehat{\theta}) = \sqrt{Var(\widehat{\theta})} = \frac{\sqrt{\theta(1-\theta)}}{\sqrt{n}}.$$

This shows, for instance, that by enlarging the sample fourfold, the uncertainty is halved. The following large sample, or asymptotic, theory will facilitate a more precise discussion of the sampling distribution for the estimator $\widehat{\theta}$.

In the application to the birth data set, we can estimate the standard error of the maximum likelihood estimate $\widehat{\theta} = 0.4874$, noting that $n = 715996$ as:

$$\widehat{\text{se}}(\widehat{\theta}) = \frac{\sqrt{\widehat{\theta}(1 - \widehat{\theta})}}{\sqrt{n}} = 0.0006. \qquad (2.1.19)$$

2.2 ASYMPTOTIC THEORY

When working with sample averages like $\overline{Y}$, we can use large-sample, or asymptotic, theory to understand the sampling uncertainty. Two powerful probabilistic results, the Law of Large Numbers and the Central Limit Theorem, are available and form the basic mathematical underpinning of econometrics.

2.2.1 The Law of Large Numbers

The *Law of Large Numbers* shows that the sample average, $\overline{Y}$, of repeated trials is close to the population expectation, $\mathsf{E}(Y)$. More precisely, it says that the probability that they are close is higher the larger the sample. We have experience with this from coin-flipping experiments. Flipping a fair coin once, the outcome is either 0 or 1, quite far from $1/2$. Now, flip it 10 times, and the sample average would perhaps be $3/10$. Flipping a 100 times, the sample average would usually be closer to $1/2$.

Theorem 2.1. *Law of Large Numbers. Let $Y_1, \ldots, Y_n$ be independent random variables, all assumed to have the same distribution with expectation $\mathsf{E}(Y_i) = \theta$. Let $\overline{Y} = n^{-1} \sum_{i=1}^{n} Y_i$ be the sample average. Then, as $n \to \infty$:*

$$\mathsf{P}\left(\left|\overline{Y} - \theta\right| < \delta\right) \to 1, \qquad \text{for all } \delta > 0.$$

We often write $\overline{Y} \overset{\mathsf{P}}{\to} \theta$, read as "$\overline{Y}$ converges in probability to θ".

The interpretation of the result in Theorem 2.1 is as follows. One can think of a small distance, $\delta = 0.001$ say. Then for a sufficiently large sample, so n is large, the probability is close to unity that the distance from the sample expectation $\overline{Y}$ to the population expectation θ is less than $\delta = 0.001$.

The limiting value of the maximum likelihood estimator in the Bernoulli model can now be discussed. In the statistical model, the parameter θ can take any value in the parameter space $\Theta = (0, 1)$. In a distributional statement, we discuss for any one of these, θ say, the distribution of $\widehat{\theta}$, assuming that the data have been generated from a Bernoulli distribution with that population parameter. It then holds that:

$$\widehat{\theta} \overset{P}{\to} \theta.$$

This applies for all values of the population parameter θ. We say that $\widehat{\theta}$ is a *consistent* estimator for θ. The Central Limit Theorem presented below will make a more precise statement about the deviation of $\widehat{\theta}$ from θ.

For the Bernoulli distribution, the parameter θ is the probability of success. The Law of Large Numbers shows that we can give this probability a frequentist interpretation, in that θ is the limit in probability of a sequence of finite-sample frequencies $\overline{Y}$. The Law of Large Numbers also gives conditions ensuring that sample and population variances are in agreement.

When applying the Law of Large Numbers, we need to check its assumptions carefully. To illustrate this important point, consider an even number of independently Bernoulli-distributed observations, of which the first half, $Y_1, \ldots, Y_{n/2}$, and the second half, $Y_{n/2+1}, \ldots, Y_n$, have success probability $\theta_1 = 1/4$ and $\theta_2 = 3/4$, respectively. When we consider the full sample, $Y_1, \ldots, Y_n$, the assumptions of the Law of Large Numbers are violated and the Law of Large Numbers cannot be used. As explored in Exercise 2.10, the Law of Large Numbers can be applied to each of the two subsamples giving that $\overline{Y} \overset{P}{\to} 1/2$. This limiting value does not immediately relate to either θ_1 or θ_2, but is the average of the two.

2.2.2 The Central Limit Theorem

Having learned that $\overline{Y}$ is close to the common expectation $\mathsf{E}(Y_i) = \theta$ in large samples, the natural question is: How close is it? We know from (2.1.18) that $\overline{Y}$, and hence also $\overline{Y} - \theta$ (why?), has variance $\mathsf{Var}(\overline{Y}) = \sigma^2/n$, where $\sigma^2 = \mathsf{Var}(Y_i)$ is the common variance. Thus, as n increases, the variance of $\overline{Y}$ collapses to zero. This calculation indicates that it is natural to look at the normalized, or standardized, sample average:

$$Z = \frac{\overline{Y} - \mathsf{E}(\overline{Y})}{\sqrt{\mathsf{Var}(\overline{Y})}} = \frac{\overline{Y} - \theta}{\sqrt{\sigma^2/n}} = \frac{\sqrt{n}\left(\overline{Y} - \theta\right)}{\sqrt{\sigma^2}}. \tag{2.2.1}$$

This standardized average has expectation zero and variance of unity (why?).

The distribution function for the standardized average, Z, of Bernoulli$[0.5]$-distributed variables is explored in Figure 2.1. In panel (a) where $n = 1$, the figure is a reproduction of Figure 1.1(a). In panel (b) then $n = 2$, as in Exercise 1.1, whereas in panels (c,d) the distribution functions have been computed for $n = 4$ and $n = 25$, using the so-called binomial distribution. It is seen that as n increases, the distribution function takes a more and more regular form, so that in the last panel the distribution function is approximated quite well by a continuous curve.

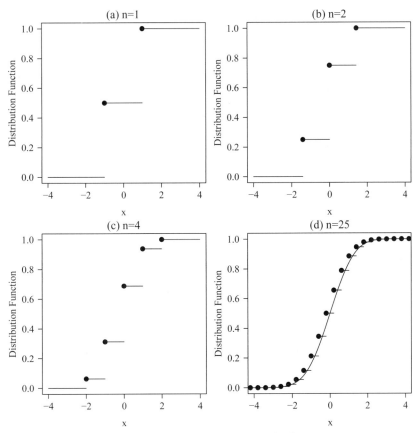

Figure 2.1 Distribution functions of averages of n Bernoulli$[0.5]$-distributed variables, where n equals 1, 2, 4, and 25 in the four panels. In the last panel the standard normal distribution function provides a continuous approximation

This continuous curve starts at zero and increases toward unity, and is therefore a distribution function. Quite remarkably, this distribution function is the same for all values of θ and is called the standard normal distribution. This result is fundamental for econometrics and is captured by the Central Limit Theorem, which will be presented below.

The distribution function for the normal distribution is complicated to work with analytically. Fortunately that is not needed in this book. For now, we will introduce the notation that $X \overset{D}{=} N[0, 1]$ if X is a standard normal variable. The parameters, 0, 1, in the normal distribution indicate that the expectation and variance of X are 0, 1, due to the standardization in (2.2.1). The Central Limit Theorem will then tell us that the distribution of the standardized sample average can be approximated by a standard normal distribution, which we write $Z \overset{D}{\approx} X$ or $Z \overset{D}{\approx} N[0, 1]$. The average itself can also be approximated by a normal distribution, albeit not a standard one. Indeed, we have $\overline{Y} \overset{D}{\approx} N[\theta, \sigma^2/n]$, where θ and σ^2/n are the expectation and variance parameters of the approximating distribution.

Theorem 2.2. *Central Limit Theorem.* *Let* $Y_1, \ldots, Y_n$ *be independent random variables, all assumed to have the same distribution with expectation* θ *and finite variance* σ^2. *Let* $\overline{Y} = n^{-1} \sum_{i=1}^{n} Y_i$ *be the sample average and let* $X \overset{D}{=} N[0,1]$. *Then, as* $n \to \infty$:

$$\mathsf{P}\left(\frac{\overline{Y} - \theta}{\sqrt{\sigma^2/n}} \le x\right) \to \mathsf{P}(X \le x), \qquad \text{for all } x \in \mathbb{R}.$$

We often write $\overline{Y} \overset{D}{\approx} N[\theta, \sigma^2/n]$, *which reads as "*$\overline{Y}$ *is asymptotically* $N[\theta, \sigma^2/n]$*-distributed".*

The Central Limit Theorem has broad applications since the assumptions cover not only Bernoulli distributions but a wide class of other distributions. Its assumptions can actually be relaxed considerably, which we will exploit in the time-series analysis introduced in Chapter 12. Although the theorem involves a statement that the sample size increases to infinity, $n \to \infty$, it actually works rather well in finite samples. Figure 2.1(d) shows how good the approximation can be when n is as small as 25. Thus we would expect the Central Limit Theorem to work extremely well in the birth example where $\widehat{\theta}$ is close to 0.5 and n is as large as 715996. A note of caution is that this close approximation is due to the symmetry of the underlying density function around $x = 0.5$ when $\theta = 0.5$. If θ were closer to 0 or 1, we would say that the underlying distribution is *skewed*, and the Central Limit Theorem would work less well.

The normal distribution has many important properties. For the inferential arguments in §2.3 below, it suffices to note that the distribution is symmetric, so that if a variable X is standard normal, $X \overset{D}{=} N[0,1]$, then $\mathsf{P}(X > x) = \mathsf{P}(X < -x)$. Its most important quantiles are tabulated in Table 2.1. Only a few values are listed, which are useful to remember even though most econometric software can compute probabilities $\mathsf{P}(X > x)$ for any x. More complete tables can also be found in many books; see, for instance, Table 5 of Lindley and Scott (1995).

x	1.03	1.645	1.960	2.576
$\mathsf{P}(X > x)$	0.15	0.05	0.025	0.005

Table 2.1 Upper quantiles for the standard normal distribution

As a simple consequence of Theorem 2.2, the distribution of the maximum likelihood estimator in the Bernoulli model can be approximated:

$$\frac{\sqrt{n}(\widehat{\theta} - \theta)}{\sqrt{\theta(1-\theta)}} \overset{D}{\approx} N[0,1]. \tag{2.2.2}$$

In the following, we will use this result to make inferences about the hypothesis that there is an equal chance that a newborn child is a boy or a girl. Note that the result in (2.2.2) is based on the assumption that the data-generating process is given by independent Bernoulli variables with parameter θ.

2.3 INFERENCE

It will now be shown how inference can be conducted using confidence intervals, or more formally through statistical testing.

2.3.1 Confidence intervals

In (2.2.2), we found the approximate distribution of the maximum likelihood estimator $\widehat{\theta}$ in the Bernoulli model. From the symmetry of the standard normal distribution and the quantiles of Table 2.1 we learn:

$$\mathsf{P}\left\{-2 \leq \frac{\sqrt{n}(\widehat{\theta} - \theta)}{\sqrt{\theta(1-\theta)}} \leq 2\right\} \approx 95\%,$$

or equivalently, by rearranging the inequalities, that:

$$\mathsf{P}\left\{\theta - 2\sqrt{\frac{\theta(1-\theta)}{n}} \leq \widehat{\theta} \leq \theta + 2\sqrt{\frac{\theta(1-\theta)}{n}}\right\} \approx 95\%. \qquad (2.3.1)$$

To be precise, this is a probability statement about $\widehat{\theta}$ for a particular value of θ stating the uncertainty of $\widehat{\theta}$ given we know θ. This is, therefore, not directly useful for making inference about the unknown θ, since we know $\widehat{\theta}$ but not θ.

In order to make use of the probability statement, we swap the sample and population values of θ in (2.3.1), and say that with 95% *confidence* the population parameter belongs to the interval:

$$\widehat{\theta} - 2\sqrt{\frac{\widehat{\theta}(1-\widehat{\theta})}{n}} \leq \theta \leq \widehat{\theta} + 2\sqrt{\frac{\widehat{\theta}(1-\widehat{\theta})}{n}}. \qquad (2.3.2)$$

Traditionally, confidence intervals are chosen to be of coverage 95%, as here. It does not make sense to ask for a 100% confidence interval, in that this would usually include all possible values of the parameter, which is not helpful. By choosing a 95% coverage, we accept that with 5% confidence we reach the false conclusion that the true parameter is not in the confidence interval. The magnitude of 95% of the confidence interval is somewhat arbitrarily set but is often chosen as the default value. When analyzing a small data set, a 90% coverage is sometimes chosen, and when analyzing a situation with nearly a million observations as in the birth data set, the coverage is often chosen to be 99% or even higher.

In the application to the birth data, the 95% confidence interval is:

$$0.4862 \leq \theta \leq 0.4886.$$

The value 0.5 is not included, which suggests that the chance of observing a girl is not the same as observing a boy. The same inference would also have been obtained from looking at a 99% confidence interval.

The trouble with confidence intervals is that, although they are useful, we cannot easily work with them using probability theory. A formal theory can instead be formulated for statistical tests, as we will see in the following discussion.

2.3.2 The likelihood ratio test

In §1.3.4 we looked at the likelihood ratio test statistic. This involved formulating a restricted model and considering the statistic:

$$\text{LR} = -2\log \text{Q} = 2\left\{ \max_{\theta \in \Theta_U} \ell_{Y_1,\dots,Y_n}(\theta) - \max_{\theta \in \Theta_R} \ell_{Y_1,\dots,Y_n}(\theta) \right\}.$$

A lengthy derivation (Exercise 2.11) shows that the log-likelihood ratio test statistic has the same asymptotic distribution as the square of the standardized unrestricted maximum likelihood estimator:

$$\text{LR} \overset{D}{\approx} \left\{ \frac{\sqrt{n}\left(\widehat{\theta} - \theta\right)}{\sqrt{\theta(1-\theta)}} \right\}^2. \tag{2.3.3}$$

Here $\widehat{\theta} = \overline{Y}$ is the unrestricted maximum likelihood estimator, and θ is the hypothesized value of the parameter. The Central Limit Theorem and (2.2.2) show that the distribution of the standardized unrestricted maximum likelihood estimator is approximately that of a standard normal variable X, so $X \overset{D}{=} \text{N}[0,1]$. The log-likelihood ratio test statistic therefore has approximately the same distribution as X^2, a squared standard normal, which we call a $\chi^2[1]$-distribution (read as "chi square with one degree of freedom"). Accordingly we write: $\text{LR} \overset{D}{\approx} \chi^2[1]$. From Table 2.1, we can immediately construct a table of the $\chi^2[1]$-distribution as reported in Table 2.2 by squaring the quantiles.

$\text{P}(\chi^2[1] > q)$	0.10	0.05	0.01
q	2.706	3.841	6.635

Table 2.2 Upper quantiles q for $\chi^2[1]$-distribution

A statistical test can now be constructed as a decision rule. If Q is (close to) unity, and correspondingly LR is small, the restricted maximum likelihood estimate would be (nearly) as likely as the unrestricted estimate, so in that case, we would fail to reject the hypothesis. We therefore choose a *critical value* $c > 0$, and reject the hypothesis if $\text{LR} > c$. More formally, since the log-likelihood ratio test statistic LR is a function of the data, we perform the likelihood ratio test by investigating if the data fall within the *critical region* ($\text{LR} > c$).

Note the usage of the term *fail to reject* rather than accept above. This is so, since the decision is based on the assumption that the statistical model is valid. In §1.3.1 we looked at the assumptions underlying the model and found them to be reasonable but possibly not entirely correct. An important consequence is that testing can be used for *falsifying* economic theories, but we can support an economic theory only insofar as we are not able to falsify it.

Since the test statistic LR is random, we can never get an absolutely certain answer by testing. We can make two types of incorrect decisions: *type I error*, by rejecting a true hypothesis; or *type II error*, by failing to reject a false hypothesis. We therefore imagine a series of repeated samples drawn from the same population and choose c such that if the hypothesis is true, then $P(\text{LR} > c)$ is equal to some *level*, for instance 5%. This ensures that the occurrence of type I errors is not too frequent among these repeated samples and provides a way of controlling how often we falsely refute our hypothesis. The 5% level is, of course, arbitrary. In small samples, we may choose the level a little higher and in larger samples a 1% level is often chosen.

In our application, we get c from the $\chi^2[1]$-distribution as tabulated in Table 2.2. The 95% quantile is about 4, giving the approximate critical region $(\text{LR} > 4)$. In §1.3.4 we learned that $\text{LR} = 513.6$. This is clearly much larger than 4, so we reject the hypothesis that there is an equal chance that a newborn child is a boy or a girl. Notice that we would reach the same conclusion from a test with a 1% level, which would be based on the 99% quantile of the $\chi^2[1]$-distribution (approximately 6.6). In fact, the p-*value* of the test, that is $P(\text{LR} > 513.6)$, is less than 0.01. In this example, we actually have a rather extreme rejection of the hypothesis, arising from the enormous information when observing nearly a million cases.

When making inference, one should bear in mind that the continuous outcome of the test statistic, LR, is translated into a test $(\text{LR} > c)$ with only two outcomes. Clearly, some information is lost in this process. If the observed test statistic, LR, is far from the critical value, c, this is fine, but when LR is close to c, any decision is going to be *marginal*. This is precisely the situation where there is not enough information in the data to make a firm decision. Alternative information, typically in terms of more data from either the same source, or from similar situations, would be helpful. It is hard to make general rules stating when a decision is marginal. If a 5% level is used, investigators should at least pay additional attention when p-values are in the range of 1% to 10%, corresponding to critical values of about 3 to 5 for tests based on the $\chi^2[1]$-distribution.

The opening paragraph of Chapter 1 mentioned that the incentives facing parents who are expecting a child can be studied by looking at sex ratios. These sex ratios are rather stable over time in a population. This is illustrated in the Exercises 1.2 and 2.3 where the sex ratios are investigated for 2003 and 2004 for the UK. Given the huge number of births considered, it is remarkable that one cannot reject the hypothesis that the sex ratios are the same in those two years.

2.4 SUMMARY AND EXERCISES

Summary: The distinction between population and sample averages continues to be important. See Table 2.3 for an example, and contrast Exercises 2.5 and 2.6.

Sample quantities		Population quantities	
$\widehat{\mathsf{E}}(Y) = \overline{Y}$	average	$\mathsf{E}(Y)$	expectation
$\widehat{\theta}$	estimator	$\mathsf{E}(\widehat{\theta})$	expectation of estimator

Table 2.3 More sample and population quantities

In order to conduct inference, we need to describe the sample variation of estimators and test statistics. When doing so we think of one particular value of the parameter, sometimes called the population parameter. The population expectations and variances can then be discussed. This was applied to sample averages.

The Law of Large Numbers and the Central Limit Theorem give approximate distribution theory for sample averages in terms of the normal distribution. This was applied to the maximum likelihood estimator for the Bernoulli model.

Inference can be conducted in terms of confidence intervals, or more formally in terms of statistical tests.

Bibliography: While the asymptotic results presented here are immensely useful, they are difficult to prove. A version of the Law of Large Numbers with slightly stronger assumptions can be proved fairly easily; see Hoel et al. (1971, §4.6). These authors also sketch the proof of the Central Limit Theorem and the Law of Large Numbers as stated here, whereas a full proof has to be found in a more advanced probability text.

Key questions:
- Compute the expectation and variance of a sample average.
- What assumptions were needed to justify your calculation?
- Find the approximate distribution of a sample average.
- How can you form a confidence interval?
- How can you form a likelihood ratio test?
- Discuss the distinction between a test statistic and a test.

Exercise 2.1. *Consider the application with children born in 2004.*
(a) Construct a 99% confidence interval for the estimator $\widehat{\theta}$.
(b) Find the 1% level likelihood ratio test for the hypothesis $\theta = 0.5$.

Exercise 2.2. *Consider the model for the sex of children born in the US in 2002 set up in Exercise 1.3. Construct a 99% confidence interval for the parameter. What is n?*

Exercise 2.3. *Consider the joint model for the sex of boys and girls in 2003 and 2004 set up in Exercise 1.2. We will construct a test for the hypothesis that the success parameter is the same in the two years.*
(a) *Consider the restricted model where the success parameter is the same in both years. Find the maximum likelihood estimate.*
(b) *Compute the log-likelihood ratio test statistic,* LR, *for the hypothesis.*
(c) *Test the hypothesis by comparing* LR *to a* $\chi^2[1]$*-distribution.*

Exercise 2.4. *Let X be Bernoulli-distributed. Find its expectation and variance. Choose a value for the success probability. Plot the density and distribution functions. What are the probabilities that X falls in the intervals* $\mathsf{E}(X) - \mathsf{sdv}(X) < X < \mathsf{E}(X) + \mathsf{sdv}(X)$ *and* $\mathsf{E}(X) - 2\mathsf{sdv}(X) < X < \mathsf{E}(X) + 2\mathsf{sdv}(X)$?

Exercise 2.5. (a) *Prove that $\sum_{i=1}^{n}(Y_i - \overline{Y}) = 0$.*
(b) *Prove that $\sum_{i=1}^{n}(Y_i - \overline{Y})^2 = \sum_{i=1}^{n} Y_i(Y_i - \overline{Y}) = \sum_{i=1}^{n} Y_i^2 - n\overline{Y}^2$.*

Exercise 2.6. *Show that $\mathsf{E}\{X - \mathsf{E}(X)\}^2 = \mathsf{E}(X^2) - \{\mathsf{E}(X)\}^2$.*

Exercise 2.7. *Prove that:*
$\mathsf{Cov}(X + Y, V + W) = \mathsf{Cov}(X, V) + \mathsf{Cov}(X, W) + \mathsf{Cov}(Y, V) + \mathsf{Cov}(Y, W)$.

Exercise 2.8. *Prove (2.1.13).*

Exercise 2.9. * *Recall the bivariate distribution introduced in Exercise 1.4. As a counterexample for the opposite implication in (2.1.13), show that X and Y are uncorrelated but not independent.*

Exercise 2.10. * *Consider an even number of independent Bernoulli-distributed observations, where the two subsamples $Y_1, \ldots Y_{n/2}$ and $Y_{n/2+1}, \ldots Y_n$ have success parameters $\theta_1 = 1/4$ and $\theta_2 = 3/4$, respectively.*
(a) *Use the Law of Large Numbers to show: $Z_1 = (2/n)\sum_{i=1}^{n/2} Y_i \overset{P}{\to} 1/4$ and $Z_2 = (2/n)\sum_{i=n/2+1}^{n} Y_i \overset{P}{\to} 3/4$.*
(b) *Combine the results in (a) to show that $\overline{Y} = (1/n)\sum_{i=1}^{n} Y_i \overset{P}{\to} 1/2$.*
(c) *Why can the Law of Large Numbers not be used for analyzing $\overline{Y}$ directly?*

Exercise 2.11. * *Prove (2.3.3) in the following steps:*
(a) *Argue* LR $= -2n[\overline{Y}\log(\theta/\overline{Y}) + (1 - \overline{Y})\log\{(1 - \theta)/(1 - \overline{Y})\}]$
(b) *Argue* LR $= -2n\{\overline{Y}\log(1 + x) + (1 - \overline{Y})\log(1 - y)\}$ *with $x = (\theta - \overline{Y})/\overline{Y}$ and $y = (\theta - \overline{Y})/(1 - \overline{Y})$*
(c) *Use the Taylor approximation:*

$$\log(1 + x) = x - x^2/2 + (x^*)^3/3 \text{ for } |x| < 1 \text{ and some } x^* \text{ so } |x^*| \le |x| \quad (2.4.1)$$

to show LR $= n(\theta - \overline{Y})^2/\{\overline{Y}(1 - \overline{Y})\} + Z^*$ *where Z^* is a function of $n(\theta - \overline{Y})^3$ and $\overline{Y}$.*
(d) *Use the Law of Large Numbers and Central Limit Theorem to argue (2.3.3).*

Chapter Three

A first regression model

We will now turn our focus to a data set of wages derived from the 1980 US census. Here we will be concerned with describing the distribution of wages and in particular the average wage. This would be one of several issues of interest to an economist working on the question of how the distribution of wages varies over time. In a broader analysis, one could, for instance, analyze data from different censuses and hence whether the distribution is changing in terms of a widening or narrowing inequality between high and low earners. This in turn could have implication for the macroeconomy. Later, in Chapters 5, 7, and 9 we will look at this data set again, and seek to link wages to the length of education and other variables.

In this chapter, the wage will be modeled as a continuous variable rather than a discrete variable. Apart from this difference, the methodology is very similar to what we have seen for the Bernoulli model. We start by giving a brief overview of the data in §3.1. This is then followed by a discussion of the theory of continuous distributions in §3.2. A statistical model for the data is set up and analyzed in §3.3, whereas inference is discussed in §3.4.

3.1 THE US CENSUS DATA

In the following, we will investigate a 0.01% subsample of the 1980 US census. From this subsample, we select all women of age 18 to 65 who are in the labor force, and who gave positive values in response to questions about weeks worked, usual hours worked per week, and wage income for the year 1979. This reduces the sample to 3877 observations. For the moment, we will focus on just one variable: wage income. For data protection reasons, wage income has been top–coded at US$ 75000 annually, meaning that any income higher than 75000 is truncated at that amount. As this truncation concerns only two women in the data, we will ignore it. We will look at the weekly wage, defined as the top-coded annual wage income divided by the number of weeks worked in 1979. Table 3.1 illustrates the outline of this data set.

The wage variable can take a near continuum of values, although in practice wages are rounded to the nearest cent. As a slight abstraction, we will think of the

Individual	Wage
1	192.40
2	67.05
⋮	⋮
3877	115.48

Table 3.1 US census sample

outcomes as continuous outcomes. The theory for continuous variables is therefore reviewed in the following section.

3.2 CONTINUOUS DISTRIBUTIONS

In §1.2.1 the notions of random variables and distribution functions were introduced. In short, a random variable X can take any real value, and its distribution function $\mathsf{F}(x) = \mathsf{P}(X \le x)$ could be any function that starts at zero on the far left and increases toward unity without ever falling, reaching one at the far right. We distinguish between *discrete* and *continuous* distributions as follows. The distribution function for a discrete random variable has jumps and is piecewise constant, while in the continuous case the distribution function is continuous. Examples are given in Figure 3.1(a,b) showing the distribution functions for a Bernoulli[0.5] distribution and for a standard normal $\mathsf{N}[0,1]$-distribution.

The discussion in §1.2.1 of multivariate distribution functions and of independence applies regardless of whether the distribution is discrete or continuous, or a mixture thereof for that matter. Density functions are, however, defined differently in the two cases. Densities are meant to capture the rate of increase of the distribution function, and we saw that in the discrete case the density is defined in terms of the jumps of the distribution function.

In the continuous case, the *density* is defined as the derivative of the distribution function:

$$\mathsf{f}(x) = \frac{\partial}{\partial x}\mathsf{P}(X \le x) = \frac{\partial}{\partial x}\mathsf{F}(x).$$

In this way, Figure 3.1(d) shows the normal density. Following from the definition of a continuous density, it holds for small values of h that:

$$\mathsf{P}(x < X \le x + h) \approx \mathsf{f}(x)\,h.$$

When sampling from a continuous distribution, we will therefore be able to evaluate the probability that an outcome falls in a certain interval, but not that it has a particular value, since, for h decreasing toward zero, we have $\mathsf{P}(X = x) = 0$ for all values of x.

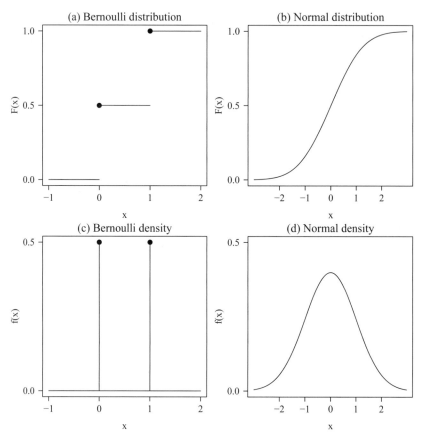

Figure 3.1 Distribution and density functions for coin-flipping example and for a (standard) normal distribution

We can get back to the distribution function by integrating:

$$F(x) = P(X \leq x) = \int_{-\infty}^{x} f(z)\, dz.$$

Differentiating (1.2.1) with respect to x and y, it follows that two continuous random variables X, Y are independent if and only if:

$$f(x, y) = \frac{\partial^2}{\partial x \partial y} P(X \leq x \text{ and } Y \leq y)$$

$$= \frac{\partial}{\partial x} P(X \leq x) \frac{\partial}{\partial y} P(Y \leq y) = f(x) f(y). \quad (3.2.1)$$

The *marginal* density of X is:

$$f(x) = \frac{\partial}{\partial x} P(X \leq x \text{ and } Y < \infty) = \int_{-\infty}^{\infty} f(x, y)\, dy. \quad (3.2.2)$$

Likewise, the expectation of a continuous random variable is given by an integral rather than a sum, as in (2.1.5), so:

$$E\left(X\right) = \int_{-\infty}^{\infty} x f\left(x\right) dx.$$

3.2.1 A continuous distribution: the normal distribution

The most frequently used continuous distribution in econometric models is the normal distribution. This can be motivated by the Central Limit Theorem when observations can be thought of as averages of many unrelated suboutcomes.

In §2.2.2 the distribution function of the standard normal distribution was discussed. While the analytic expression for the distribution function is complicated, the normal density is more straightforward. If X has a *standard normal distribution*, in shorthand $X \overset{D}{=} N[0, 1]$, then it has the density:

$$f\left(x\right) = \frac{1}{\sqrt{2\pi}} \exp\left(-\frac{1}{2}x^2\right),$$

where $\exp(x)$ rather than e^x is used for the exponential function for typographical convenience and $e \approx 2.72$ and $\pi \approx 3.14$ are the mathematical constants. This density, and the corresponding distribution function, which is often denoted $\Phi(x) = P(X \leq x)$, were plotted in Figure 3.1(d,b).

More generally, we say that a variable X is normally distributed with location μ and scale σ if it has the density:

$$f\left(x\right) = \frac{1}{\sqrt{2\pi\sigma^2}} \exp\left\{-\frac{1}{2\sigma^2}\left(x - \mu\right)^2\right\}. \tag{3.2.3}$$

The parameter μ can take any value, while σ^2 takes a positive value. We write $\mu, \sigma^2 \in \mathbb{R} \times \mathbb{R}_+$. In short hand, we often write $X \overset{D}{=} N[\mu, \sigma^2]$.

The interpretation of the parameters μ, σ^2 is as follows.

(1) $f\left(x\right)$ is symmetric around μ: inspect the density, replacing $x - \mu$ by $\mu - x$. Therefore, μ has an interpretation as a location parameter.
(2) The parameter σ has an interpretation as a scale parameter: if X measures income in dollars and σ_X has a value of 1, then $Y = 100X$ measures income in cents and $\sigma_Y = 100$.

Moreover, it can be proved that if $X \overset{D}{=} N[\mu, \sigma^2]$ then:

$$Z = \frac{X - \mu}{\sqrt{\sigma^2}} \overset{D}{=} N\left[0, 1\right]. \tag{3.2.4}$$

The variable Z is a *standardized* version of X, in that it has location at the origin and scale of unity. Figure 3.2 illustrates how scaling and location shifts change the normal density. While property (1) could be derived directly from the density, the proof of property (2) and (3.2.4) requires more probability theory than we need in this exposition.

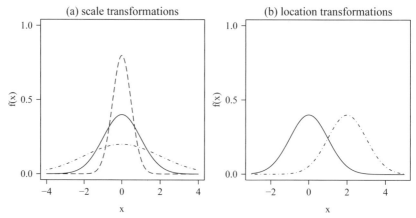

Figure 3.2 Scale and location transformations of density functions: (a) scaling: N$[0, 1]$ solid line, N$[0, 1/4]$ dashed line, N$[0, 4]$ dashed-dotted line; (b) location shifts: N$[0, 1]$ solid line, N$[2, 1]$ dashed line

The location parameter μ and the squared scale parameter σ^2 actually represent the expectation and the variance of the normal distribution. That is, if $X \overset{\text{D}}{=} \mathsf{N}[\mu, \sigma^2]$, then it can be shown that:

$$\mathsf{E}(X) = \mu \qquad \text{and} \qquad \mathsf{Var}(X) = \sigma^2. \qquad (3.2.5)$$

Since the normal distribution has only the two parameters μ, σ^2, we can therefore characterize a normal distribution by its expectation and variance, often called its first two moments.

3.3 REGRESSION MODEL WITH AN INTERCEPT

We are now ready to develop a statistical model for the distribution of wages.

3.3.1 The sample distribution

We start the empirical analysis by investigating the sample distribution of the data.

Figure 3.3(a,b) shows histograms of wages and of log wages. These histograms are constructed by dividing the first axis into a number of intervals, or "bins", and then counting how many observations fall in each bin. The presented histograms are normalized to integrate to unity like a density; and the ranges shown are needed to include all the observed outcomes. We see that log wages are much better described by a normal distribution than wages are. This comes about since the logarithmic function is non-linear with a dampening effect on large values. With economic data, we often have to search for an appropriate transformation in this way.

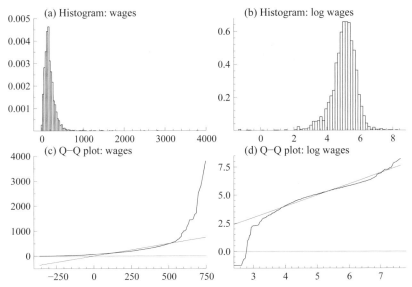

Figure 3.3 Histogram and Q-Q plots for weekly wages and log weekly wages

Sample distributions can alternatively be represented by *Quantile-Quantile-plots*, also called Q-Q plots as in Figure 3.3(c,d). The Q-Q plot graphs sample quantiles against the quantiles of the assumed reference distribution. In this case, the reference distribution is a normal distribution. If the sample distribution is also normal, we should observe a curve close to the $45°$ line. Note that Q-Q plots relate to distribution functions, rather than densities, and in contrast to the histograms, there is no need to distribute the observations in bins. From the scale of the Q-Q plot for wages, we see that the deviation is huge, whereas a more modest *s*-shape deviation from the $45°$ line appears for the log-transformed data.

Comparing the four plots, we see that the log transformation makes the distribution of wages more normal. For wages, the sample frequency is *skewed* to the right. In addition, the sample distribution is more peaked at the center of the distribution. We say that the sample distribution has *excess kurtosis* compared with the normal distribution. For log wages, the degree of excess kurtosis has been reduced somewhat, and the sample distribution is nearer to symmetry.

It will, of course, be important to develop tools for investigating whether the observed departure from normality for log wages is important for the inferences we would like to draw. For now we will assume that log wages are approximately normally distributed.

3.3.2 A statistical model

We will now build a simple statistical model that can be used to analyze log wages. Once again, the objective is to develop a good description of the sample distribution, which will allow us to make inference about, in this case, the expected wage. Here, we will concentrate on describing the distribution in such a way that we are able to check any assumptions we make.

Let the random variable Y_i represent the outcome for person i. In the application, Y_i is the log wage. Consider random variables $Y_1, \ldots, Y_n$ and define a statistical model for these through the four assumptions:

(i)   *independence*: $Y_1, \ldots, Y_n$ are mutually independent;
(ii) *identical distribution*: the interviewees are drawn from the same population;
(iii) *normality*: $Y_i \overset{\mathsf{D}}{=} \mathsf{N}[\beta, \sigma^2]$;
(iv) *parameter space*: $\beta \in \mathbb{R}$ and $\sigma^2 > 0$.

Apart from the normality assumption and the different parameter space, the setup is precisely as in the Bernoulli model. We have already seen that β can be interpreted as a location parameter as well as an expectation parameter. Thus, we have a parameter related to the expected wage in the population.

In the application, we need to think a little about whether these assumptions are reasonable. For the moment, we will not worry about assumption (i), but will return to it in §11.4, while assumption (ii) will be addressed in §9.3. As for assumption (iii), we have already attempted to test normality by graphical methods in §3.3.1, and it is clear that the normality assumption is more appropriate for log wages than for wages themselves. A formal test for normality will be introduced in §9.2. We will then see that the normality assumption is not entirely appropriate for the wage data: however, to reach that point, we need to fit the model to the data.

An equivalent formulation of the model is:

$$Y_i = \beta + u_i, \tag{3.3.1}$$

where $u_1, \ldots, u_n$ are independently $\mathsf{N}[0, \sigma^2]$-distributed. We will call this type of model a *regression model* where Y_i is called the regressand, or the dependent variable, while β is the *intercept* parameter. We could write β as $\beta \times 1$, where the number 1 is referred to as the *constant* or the *intercept*, and it is an example of a *regressor*. We can interpret β as a location parameter or an expectation parameter since $\mathsf{E}(Y_i) = \beta$. The equation (3.3.1) is called a *regression equation* or a *model equation*.

3.3.3 The likelihood function

Based on the statistical model, we can write down the joint density of $(Y_1, \ldots, Y_n)$ exactly as in §1.3.2. An operational expression is obtained in a few steps. The independence assumption (i) implies, due to (3.2.1):

$$f_{\beta,\sigma^2}(y_1, \ldots, y_n) = \prod_{i=1}^{n} f_{\beta,\sigma^2}(y_i).$$

The normality assumptions (ii), (iii) then imply:

$$f_{\beta,\sigma^2}(y_1, \ldots, y_n) = \prod_{i=1}^{n} \frac{1}{\sqrt{2\pi\sigma^2}} \exp\left\{-\frac{1}{2\sigma^2}(y_i - \beta)^2\right\}.$$

This expression can be reduced further using the fact that the functional equation for power functions, as in (1.3.1), implies:

$$\prod_{i=1}^{n} \exp\left\{-\frac{1}{2\sigma^2}(y_i - \beta)^2\right\} = \exp\left\{-\frac{1}{2\sigma^2}\sum_{i=1}^{n}(y_i - \beta)^2\right\},$$

$$\prod_{i=1}^{n} \frac{1}{\sqrt{2\pi\sigma^2}} = (2\pi\sigma^2)^{-n/2}.$$

Thereby the above expression for the joint density becomes:

$$f_{\beta,\sigma^2}(y_1, \ldots, y_n) = (2\pi\sigma^2)^{-n/2} \exp\left\{-\frac{1}{2\sigma^2}\sum_{i=1}^{n}(y_i - \beta)^2\right\}.$$

We do not know β, σ^2, which are the parameters we would like to learn about. The aim is now to find the most likely values of β, σ^2 when the random variables $Y_1, \ldots, Y_n$ have been observed. Thus, we form the likelihood function:

$$L_{Y_1,\ldots,Y_n}(\beta, \sigma^2) = f_{\beta,\sigma^2}(Y_1, \ldots, Y_n)$$

$$= (2\pi\sigma^2)^{-n/2} \exp\left\{-\frac{1}{2\sigma^2}\sum_{i=1}^{n}(Y_i - \beta)^2\right\}.$$

For estimation purposes, the log-likelihood function is again more useful:

$$\ell_{Y_1,\ldots,Y_n}(\beta, \sigma^2) = \log\left[(2\pi\sigma^2)^{-n/2} \exp\left\{-\frac{1}{2\sigma^2}\sum_{i=1}^{n}(Y_i - \beta)^2\right\}\right],$$

which by the functional equation for logarithms, as in (1.3.5), can be written as:

$$\ell_{Y_1,\ldots,Y_n}(\beta, \sigma^2) = -\frac{n}{2}\log(2\pi\sigma^2) - \frac{1}{2\sigma^2}\sum_{i=1}^{n}(Y_i - \beta)^2. \qquad (3.3.2)$$

3.3.4 Estimation by maximizing the likelihood

To maximize the log-likelihood function with respect to β, we need to *minimize* the *sum of squared deviations* in the last term of (3.3.2)—its only appearance—to find the value of β with the smallest *sum of squared deviations* from $Y_1, \ldots, Y_n$:

$$\text{minimize:} \quad \text{SSD}(\beta) = \sum_{i=1}^{n} (Y_i - \beta)^2. \tag{3.3.3}$$

This is a quadratic function in β. To find the minimum, we differentiate:

$$\frac{\partial}{\partial \beta} \sum_{i=1}^{n} (Y_i - \beta)^2 = -2 \sum_{i=1}^{n} (Y_i - \beta).$$

We set this equal to zero to find the likelihood equation for $\widehat{\beta}$, or the normal equation for $\widehat{\beta}$ as it is often called in a regression context:

$$-2 \sum_{i=1}^{n} \left(Y_i - \widehat{\beta} \right) = 0. \tag{3.3.4}$$

This equation is solved by:

$$\sum_{i=1}^{n} Y_i = n\widehat{\beta} \quad \Leftrightarrow \quad \widehat{\beta} = n^{-1} \sum_{i=1}^{n} Y_i = \overline{Y},$$

so the maximum likelihood estimator for β is:

$$\widehat{\beta} = \overline{Y}. \tag{3.3.5}$$

We see that a sample average can be a maximum likelihood estimator in different statistical models. In this particular model, we have minimized the squared deviations to estimate β, so we say that $\widehat{\beta}$ is an *ordinary least-squares* estimator, abbreviated to *OLS* estimator.

In general, likelihood equations can have several solutions. In this case, we have used the result that a quadratic function like (3.3.3) has a unique minimum. This can be made more explicit by looking at the second-order derivative:

$$\frac{\partial^2}{\partial \beta^2} \sum_{i=1}^{n} (Y_i - \beta)^2 = -2 \frac{\partial}{\partial \beta} \sum_{i=1}^{n} (Y_i - \beta) = 2n,$$

which is positive, showing that the sum of squared deviations is convex in β for all values of β.

Inserting $\widehat{\beta}$ in the model equation (3.3.1) and setting the *error term* u_i to zero (which is its expected value), we obtain the *predictor* for Y_i, which is $\widehat{Y}_i = \widehat{\beta}$.

Subtracting $\widehat{Y}_i$ from Y_i yields the *residual*:

$$\widehat{u}_i = Y_i - \widehat{Y}_i = Y_i - \widehat{\beta} = Y_i - \overline{Y}, \tag{3.3.6}$$

which is the variation in Y_i that we have not been able to explain.

The likelihood has now been maximized with respect to β, so:

$$\ell_{Y_1,\ldots,Y_n}(\widehat{\beta}, \sigma^2) = \max_{\beta \in \mathbb{R}} \ell_{Y_1,\ldots,Y_n}(\beta, \sigma^2)$$

$$= -\frac{n}{2} \log\left(2\pi\sigma^2\right) - \frac{1}{2\sigma^2} \sum_{i=1}^{n} (Y_i - \widehat{\beta})^2$$

$$= -\frac{n}{2} \log\left(2\pi\right) - \frac{n}{2} \log\left(\sigma^2\right) - \frac{1}{2\sigma^2} \sum_{i=1}^{n} \widehat{u}_i^2, \tag{3.3.7}$$

which is called the *profile likelihood*, or concentrated likelihood, for σ^2. To maximize with respect to σ^2, we differentiate with respect to σ^2—here the parameter σ^2 can be replaced by θ to avoid confusion about the powers—to obtain (by equivariance, one could use σ, but the calculations are more tedious):

$$\frac{\partial}{\partial \sigma^2} \ell_{Y_1,\ldots,Y_n}(\widehat{\beta}, \sigma^2) = -\frac{n}{2\sigma^2} + \frac{1}{2\left(\sigma^2\right)^2} \sum_{i=1}^{n} \widehat{u}_i^2 = -\frac{n}{2\sigma^4} \left(\sigma^2 - \frac{1}{n} \sum_{i=1}^{n} \widehat{u}_i^2\right). \tag{3.3.8}$$

The likelihood equation for σ^2 is then:

$$-\frac{n}{2\widehat{\sigma}^4} \left(\widehat{\sigma}^2 - \frac{1}{n} \sum_{i=1}^{n} \widehat{u}_i^2\right) = 0,$$

which is solved by:

$$\widehat{\sigma}^2 = \frac{1}{n} \sum_{i=1}^{n} \widehat{u}_i^2 = \frac{1}{n} \sum_{i=1}^{n} \left(Y_i - \overline{Y}\right)^2. \tag{3.3.9}$$

In Exercise 3.4, it is argued that $\widehat{\sigma}^2$ is a unique maximum point. Inserting the variance estimator in the likelihood function, we see that it has the maximum:

$$\max_{\beta,\sigma^2} \mathsf{L}_{Y_1,\ldots,Y_n}\left(\beta, \sigma^2\right) = \mathsf{L}_{Y_1,\ldots,Y_n}\left(\widehat{\beta}, \widehat{\sigma}^2\right) = \left(2\pi\widehat{\sigma}^2 e\right)^{-n/2}. \tag{3.3.10}$$

Here we have used the principle that a hill can be climbed in two stages: go half way up (i.e., find $\widehat{\beta}$), then climb the rest (i.e., find $\widehat{\sigma}^2$), so (3.3.10) is the top of the likelihood "hill".

3.3.5 Application to the wage data

In applications, we will typically use not the notation Y_i for the dependent variable, but rather a letter reflecting the variable name. We can for instance use W_i for wages and w_i for log wages following a convention of using lowercase letters for variables in logs. Using the available data, we can then compute:

$$\sum_{i=1}^{n} w_i = 19460.1, \qquad \sum_{i=1}^{n} w_i^2 = 99875.5, \qquad n = 3877,$$

and thus the maximum likelihood estimates of the parameters are:

$$\widehat{\beta} = 5.02, \quad \widehat{\sigma}^2 = 0.567 = (0.753)^2, \quad \ell(\widehat{\beta}, \widehat{\sigma}^2) = -4401.16. \qquad (3.3.11)$$

We will write the estimated regression equation as:

$$\widehat{w}_i = 5.02, \qquad \widehat{\sigma} = 0.753.$$

Here $\widehat{w}_i$ is the prediction from the regression. If we were to predict the log wage of an individual, with index $n + 1$ say, who is not in the sample, we would use the value $\widehat{w}_{n+1} = \widehat{\beta}$.

3.4 INFERENCE

We will now move on to discuss inference in the regression model. As in §2.3, we can use the Central Limit Theorem to conduct approximate inference. For the regression model, it is also possible to exploit properties of the normal distribution to make exact inference, as will be discussed subsequently. Exact inference is of interest as it reveals the structure of the regression model, but it is questionable how important it is in economic applications.

3.4.1 Approximate inference

Approximate inference can be carried out as in the Bernoulli model in §2.3. Since $\widehat{\beta} = \overline{Y}$ is an average of independent, identically distributed random variables according to the model assumptions (i), (ii), (iii), the Central Limit Theorem can be used directly. As in §2.1.4, and in particular formulas (2.1.17) and (2.1.18), the expectation and variance are given by:

$$\mathsf{E}\left(\widehat{\beta}\right) = \mathsf{E}\left(\overline{Y}\right) = \mathsf{E}\left(Y_1\right),$$
$$\mathsf{Var}\left(\widehat{\beta}\right) = \mathsf{Var}\left(\overline{Y}\right) = n^{-1}\mathsf{Var}\left(Y_1\right).$$

The formulas for the expectation and variance in normal distributions (3.2.5) imply:

$$\mathsf{E}\left(\widehat{\beta}\right) = \beta, \qquad \mathsf{Var}\left(\widehat{\beta}\right) = \frac{\sigma^2}{n},$$

so $\widehat{\beta}$ is an unbiased estimator of β. Using the Central Limit Theorem, the standardized estimator is then asymptotically standard normal:

$$\frac{\widehat{\beta} - \beta}{\sqrt{\sigma^2/n}} \overset{\mathsf{D}}{\approx} \mathsf{N}\left[0, 1\right]. \qquad (3.4.1)$$

In this expression, the variance of $\widehat{\beta}$ is based on the unknown parameter σ^2, but this we can replace by its maximum likelihood estimator $\widehat{\sigma}^2$. In general, $\widehat{\sigma}^2$ is different from σ^2, but it can be shown to be consistent (defined in §2.2.1), and thus asymptotic normality is preserved:

$$\frac{\widehat{\beta} - \beta}{\sqrt{\widehat{\sigma}^2/n}} \overset{\mathrm{D}}{\approx} \mathsf{N}\left[0, 1\right]. \tag{3.4.2}$$

The 95% confidence interval for the parameter β is then:

$$\widehat{\beta} - 2\widehat{\sigma}/\sqrt{n} \leq \beta \leq \widehat{\beta} + 2\widehat{\sigma}/\sqrt{n}, \tag{3.4.3}$$

that is, $5.00 \leq \beta \leq 5.04$. You may want to mark this 95% confidence interval in the top right panel of Figure 3.3. In this example, there are no obvious hypotheses to consider. Testing whether β, which is the expectation of log wages, is equal to zero, or 5 for that matter, does not have any particular economic interpretation.

3.4.2 Exact inference

In (3.4.1) the distribution of the standardized estimator was argued to be asymptotically standard normally distributed. This result actually holds exactly in the one-variable regression model due to the normality assumption. To see this, we need some further properties of the normal distribution.

It is a consequence of (2.1.6) and (2.1.10) that if $X \overset{\mathrm{D}}{=} \mathsf{N}[\mu, \sigma^2]$, then it holds that $\mathsf{E}(aX + b) = a\mu + b$ and $\mathsf{Var}(aX + b) = a^2\sigma^2$ (Exercise 3.6). In parallel with the property (3.2.4), it can actually be proved that $aX + b$ is normally distributed:

$$\text{If } X \overset{\mathrm{D}}{=} \mathsf{N}\left[\mu, \sigma^2\right], \text{ then } aX + b \overset{\mathrm{D}}{=} \mathsf{N}\left[a\mu + b, a^2\sigma^2\right]. \tag{3.4.4}$$

Furthermore, it can be shown that:

$$\text{If } X_1, X_2 \text{ are independent and normally distributed,}$$
$$\text{then } X_1 + X_2 \text{ is normally distributed.} \tag{3.4.5}$$

Therefore, with the formulas for the expectation and variance of sums, (2.1.7), (2.1.11):

$$\text{If } X_1 \overset{\mathrm{D}}{=} \mathsf{N}\left[\mu_1, \sigma_1^2\right], X_2 \overset{\mathrm{D}}{=} \mathsf{N}\left[\mu_2, \sigma_2^2\right], \text{ and } X_1, X_2 \text{ are independent,}$$
$$\text{then } X_1 + X_2 \overset{\mathrm{D}}{=} \mathsf{N}\left[\mu_1 + \mu_2, \sigma_1^2 + \sigma_2^2\right]. \tag{3.4.6}$$

In other words, the sum of independently, normally distributed random variables is normally distributed with expectation and variance parameters that are simply given as the sum of the individual expectations and variances, respectively.

Since $\widehat{\beta} = \overline{Y}$ is an average of independent variables that are normally distributed in the one-variable regression model, the above results imply that (3.4.1) holds exactly:

$$\frac{\widehat{\beta} - \beta}{\sqrt{\sigma^2/n}} \overset{\mathrm{D}}{=} \mathsf{N}\left[0, 1\right]. \qquad (3.4.7)$$

As noted above, this standardized statistic is not so useful in practice as it depends on the variance parameter σ^2. It turns out that when replacing the parameter with an estimator, exact distribution theory can still be carried out in this case. For such a purpose, it is a convention to consider a normalized version of the maximum likelihood estimator for σ^2, namely:

$$s^2 = \frac{n}{n-1}\widehat{\sigma}^2 = \frac{1}{n-1}\sum_{i=1}^{n}\widehat{u}_i^2.$$

The count $n - 1$ is the difference between the number of observations and the number of parameters characterizing the expectation, and is called the *degrees of freedom* of the model. It can be shown that inserting this estimator in the standardized estimator gives a statistic that is distributed according to what is called a t-distribution:

$$Z = \frac{\widehat{\beta} - \beta}{\sqrt{s^2/n}} \overset{\mathrm{D}}{=} \mathsf{t}\left[n - 1\right]. \qquad (3.4.8)$$

This version of the estimator is called a t-statistic.

Figure 3.4 shows the density of the $\mathsf{t}[n]$-distribution for various degrees of freedom along with a standard normal distribution. This is done on the usual scale as well as on a log scale, where the difference between the distributions is perhaps more easily seen. The expression for the normal density, as in (3.2.3), implies that the log density is a parabola. In comparison, the tails of the t-distribution bend outward. Standard econometric software can generate quantiles of the $\mathsf{t}[n]$-distribution, and printed tables can be found for instance in Table 10 of Lindley and Scott (1995). The confidence interval in (3.4.3) can therefore be improved using the tabulated 2.5% and 97.5% quantiles of the t-distribution rather than the coefficient 2. It is seen from Figure 3.4 that the t-distribution approaches the $\mathsf{N}[0, 1]$-distribution as $n \to \infty$, so except for very small degrees of freedom, $n < 10$ or so, the asymptotic values can be used without much loss of precision. While we will not delve into the derivation of the t-distribution, it is worth noting that its discovery by Gossett, published in Student (1908), was a major breakthrough for statistical theory.

Econometric software will typically report a t-statistic for the hypothesis that $\beta = 0$. In this application, that is:

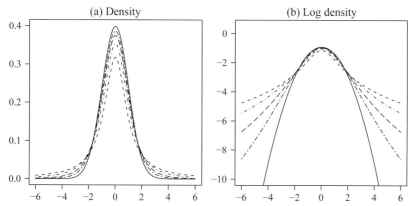

Figure 3.4 Densities for t-distributions and N $[0, 1]$-distribution, plotted on the usual scale and on a log scale: N$[0, 1]$ solid line, t$[1]$ dashed line, t$[2]$ dashed-dotted line, t$[4]$ long dashed line, t$[8]$ long dashed-dotted line

$$Z = \frac{5.02 - 0}{\sqrt{0.567/3877}} = 415.$$

Along with this, the p-value $\mathsf{P}(|Z| > 415) = 0.000$ is reported using the t$[3876]$-distribution. This probability is extremely small. As the hypothesis $\beta = 0$ has no economic interpretation, we will say more vaguely that the constant is a significant regressor.

In the same way as the $\chi^2 [1]$-distribution came about by squaring an N $[0, 1]$-distributed variable, we can consider the square of a t-distributed variable. This is said to be F-distributed:

$$F = Z^2 = \frac{\left(\widehat{\beta} - \beta\right)^2}{s^2/n} \overset{\mathsf{D}}{=} \mathsf{F}\,[1, n - 1]\,. \tag{3.4.9}$$

When the sample size is moderately large, so that $n - 1$ is larger than about 10, the F $[1, n - 1]$-distribution and the $\chi^2 [1]$-distribution are very close.

With s^2, we have two different estimators for σ^2 to choose from with different merits. On the one hand, s^2 is an unbiased estimate of σ^2, and hence $\widehat{\sigma}^2$ is not:

$$\mathsf{E}(\widehat{\sigma}^2) = \frac{n - 1}{n}\mathsf{E}(s^2) < \mathsf{E}(s^2) = \sigma^2,$$

but, on the other hand, $\widehat{\sigma}^2$ has a smaller variance:

$$\mathsf{Var}(\widehat{\sigma}^2) = \left(\frac{n - 1}{n}\right)^2 \mathsf{Var}(s^2) < \mathsf{Var}(s^2).$$

We, therefore, have a trade-off between bias and variation, which is sometimes weighted in terms of *mean square error*; see Exercise 3.11. Econometric software usually reports s^2 as the variance estimator rather than $\widehat{\sigma}^2$.

3.4.3 Robustness

While the exact distribution results discussed in §3.4.2 have a lot of mathematical beauty, they rely critically on the assumptions of the statistical model. The model assumes that the observations $Y_1, \ldots, Y_n$ are independently, identically normally distributed. In many applications, these assumptions will only be satisfied approximately. There are two types of issues. First, in the discussion of Figure 3.3, we saw that log wages are closer to normality than wages. However, we have not yet discussed whether the deviation from the $45°$ line in Figure 3.3(b) is significant; some skewness and excess kurtosis seem to remain, which we have not yet quantified. Second, if we did look at the US census sample in more detail, we would see that the observations of annual wages have a tendency to cluster at round numbers, which contradicts that they were drawn from a continuous distribution. Nonetheless, $\widehat{\beta}$ can be considered as a reasonable estimator for the expectation of the wage distribution. The Central Limit Theorem 2.2 and variants thereof certainly show that the approximate properties explored in §3.4.1 remain valid as long as assumptions $(i), (ii), (iii)$ hold up to an approximation. This shows that the inferences we draw are *robust* to some deviations from the assumptions. The quality of this approximation, or robustness, provided by the Central Limit Theorem, will however deteriorate with, for instance, increased skewness.

3.5 SUMMARY AND EXERCISES

Summary: Continuous distributions were introduced. The distribution function is a unified concept covering both discrete and continuous cases. Densities are defined differently. The rule for independence has the same appearance though.

The regression model with an intercept was introduced. Apart from replacing the Bernoulli distribution with a normal distribution, the analysis is the same as in Chapters 1 and 2. The approach is applicable to many other distributions like the Poisson distribution, analyzed in Exercise 3.12.

Bibliography: This chapter covers the three main approaches used in econometrics. In the *least-squares approach*, the sum of squared deviations is minimized as in (3.3.3). This is the basis for many popular expositions such as Gujarati (2003). The *method of moments* is based on estimation equations like (3.3.4), which can be written as $\sum_{i=1}^{n}\{Y_i - \mathsf{E}(Y_i)\} = 0$, so the sample expectation $\overline{Y}$ is equated to the corresponding population expectation β. This approach is followed by, for instance, Wooldridge (2006). The *likelihood approach* is followed here.

In the data we considered, the top-coding concerns only two observations and is therefore ignored. The *censored regression model* can be used in situations with more frequent censoring; see, for instance, Maddala (1983) or Wooldridge (2006).

The derivation of the exact distributions for regression estimators can be found in for instance Hoel et al. (1971). As such derivations are somewhat involved, it is often advantageous to investigate the finite sample distributions using Monte Carlo simulation. The module PcNaive for OxMetrics is designed with this in mind (Doornik and Hendry, 2006d). The underlying theory is set out in §§18.1 and 18.2, although the method is easy to use in practice.

Key questions:

- Compare the notion of distribution functions and densities for discrete and for continuous variables.
- Discuss the validity of assumptions of the statistical model for the wage data.

Exercise 3.1. *In section 3.3 we analyzed the log of wages. Have a look at wages themselves. The sum and sum of squares of wages are:*

$$\sum_{i=1}^{n} Y_i = 745938.5, \qquad \sum_{i=1}^{n} Y_i^2 = 242416457.1, \qquad n = 3877.$$

Derive the average, sample variance, and sample standard deviation. What are their units? Compare this average with $\exp(\widehat{\beta})$ where $\widehat{\beta}$ is the estimate in (3.3.11). What could explain why these values are so different?

Exercise 3.2. *Suppose $\widehat{\beta}$, $\widehat{\sigma}^2$ are as in (3.3.11). Compute the confidence intervals in (3.4.3), first, for $n = 100$ and then $n = 10000$. How do they vary with n?*

Exercise 3.3. *Suppose $Y_1, \dots, Y_n$ are independent and $\mathsf{N}[\beta x_i, \sigma^2]$-distributed for some non-random constants $x_1, \dots, x_n$.*
(a) Write down the corresponding likelihood.
(b) Show that the likelihood equation is $\sum_{i=1}^{n} \widehat{u}_i X_i = 0$ where $\widehat{u}_i = Y_i - \widehat{\beta} X_i$.
(c) Show that the maximum likelihood estimator for β is $\sum_{i=1}^{n} Y_i x_i / \sum_{i=1}^{n} x_i^2$.
(d) Find the maximum likelihood estimator for σ^2.

Exercise 3.4. * *Consider the profile likelihood for σ^2 in (3.3.7).*
(a) Look at the second-order condition for σ^2 to prove that $\widehat{\sigma}^2$ is a maximum point as expected.
(b) Reparametrize the likelihood in terms of $\theta = \log \sigma$. Show that $\widehat{\theta}$ is a global maximum point.

Exercise 3.5. * *Consider the log likelihood function in (3.3.2). Show that the partial derivative $\frac{\partial^2}{\partial \beta \partial \sigma^2} \ell_{Y_1, \dots, Y_n}(\beta, \sigma^2)$ is zero when evaluated at $\widehat{\beta}$, $\widehat{\sigma}^2$.*

Exercise 3.6. *Show that if* $X \overset{D}{=} \mathsf{N}[\mu, \sigma^2]$, *then* $\mathsf{E}(aX + b) = a\mu + b$ *and* $\mathsf{Var}(aX + b) = a^2\sigma^2$.

Exercise 3.7. *Show that if* $X_1 \overset{D}{=} \mathsf{N}[\mu_1, \sigma_1^2]$, $X_2 \overset{D}{=} \mathsf{N}[\mu_2, \sigma_2^2]$, *and* X_1, X_2 *are independent, then* $\mathsf{E}(X_1 + X_2) = \mu_1 + \mu_2$ *and* $\mathsf{Var}(X_1 + X_2) = \sigma_1^2 + \sigma_2^2$.

Exercise 3.8. *Consider Table 2.1 of the normal distribution.*
(*a*) *Suppose* $X \overset{D}{=} \mathsf{N}[0, 1]$. *Find the* p*-values* $\mathsf{P}(X \le 0)$, *and* $\mathsf{P}(X \le 2.58)$.
(*b*) *Suppose* $Y \overset{D}{=} \mathsf{N}[4, 4]$. *Find the* p*-value* $\mathsf{P}(Y \le 0)$ *and the 97.5% quantile.*

Exercise 3.9. *Robustness. The results in section 3.4 assumed that* $Y_1, \ldots, Y_n$ *are* (*i*) *independent and* (*ii*) *identically* $\mathsf{N}[\beta, \sigma^2]$-*distributed. For many results, weaker assumptions are sufficient. In this way, prove that:*
(*a*) *to show* $\mathsf{E}(\widehat{\beta}) = \beta$, *it suffices that* $\mathsf{E}(Y_i) = \beta$ *for all* i.
(*b*) *to show* $\mathsf{Var}(\widehat{\beta}) = \sigma^2/n$, *it suffices that* $Y_1, \ldots, Y_n$ *are uncorrelated with constant variance, that is* $\mathsf{Var}(Y_i) = \sigma^2$ *for all* i.

Exercise 3.10. *Return to Exercise 3.3. Find the distribution of* $\widehat{\beta}$.

Exercise 3.11. *Consider the mean square error* $\mathsf{MSE}(\widehat{\theta}) = \mathsf{E}(\widehat{\theta} - \theta)^2$.
(*a*) *Show* $\mathsf{MSE}(\widehat{\theta}) = \mathsf{Var}(\widehat{\theta}) + \{\mathsf{E}(\widehat{\theta}) - \theta\}^2$.
(*b*) *Compare* $\mathsf{MSE}(\widehat{\sigma}^2)$ *and* $\mathsf{MSE}(s^2)$ *for the model in section 3.3.2, taking the identity* $\mathsf{Var}\{\sum_{i=1}^{n}(Y_i - \overline{Y})^2\} = 2(n-1)\sigma^4$ *as given.*

Exercise 3.12. *Let* $Y_1, \ldots, Y_n$ *be discrete random variables with non-negative integer values. Suppose they are independently* $\mathsf{Poisson}[\lambda]$-*distributed so:*

$$\mathsf{f}_\lambda(y) = \frac{\lambda^y}{y!} \exp(-\lambda), \qquad for\ y \in \mathbb{N}$$

where the factorial function is defined by $y! = y(y-1)(y-2)\cdots 2 \cdot 1$ *for* $y > 0$ *and* $0! = 1$. *Such a Poisson model is often used for describing queuing problems like the arrival of telephone calls or patent applications. It can be shown that* $\mathsf{E}(Y_i) = \mathsf{Var}(Y_i) = \lambda$; *see Hoel et al. (1971).*
(*a*) *Write down the likelihood function.*
(*b*) *Show that the maximum likelihood estimator for* λ *is* $\widehat{\lambda} = \overline{Y}$.

Computing Task 3.13. *Introduction to OxMetrics and PcGive. Table 3.2 reports an index of total industrial output in the UK over 25-year periods. Open OxMetrics by clicking on its icon.*
(*a*) *Create a new data base by clicking the "New" icon (the first). Select "Annual or undated" with a start date of 1800 and 7 observations. Input data for two variables:* t *counting the period,* $1, 2, \ldots, 7$, *and* Y *giving the output. Change variable names by double-clicking on the variable names and typing* Y *and* t. *Save into your folder, e.g., as* indust.in7. *Load the data:* indust.in7.
(*b*) *Look at the data:*

Click "view", then "summary statistics" to describe the data in terms of means, standard deviations, minima, and maxima.

Click the "graph" icon, select Y, t *then "scatter plot" to cross plot Y on t.*

Double click on the graph to bring up the "Edit graph" dialog, and select "type" to switch from "symbols" to "line and symbols". Describe the functional relationship between Y and t.

Click the "graph" icon, deselect t, *so only* Y *is selected, then "All plot types", "Distribution" and finally "Plot" to graph the density of the variable.*

(c) *Run a regression using software:*

Open PcGive by clicking on "PcGive" in the "Module" list. Now, focus on the PcGive window.

Click "Category" then select "Models for cross-section data".

Click "Model" then select "Cross-section Regression using PcGive" and click "Formulate".

Double click Y. A model consisting of Y and a constant is then created. Note the Y flag on the Y-variable indicating that this is the regressand. Click "OK" twice. Discuss the output.

Click the "Test icon" and select "Graphic Analysis". Click "OK" twice to plot the fitted values and the residuals. Discuss.

(d) *Run a regression by hand:*

In OxMetrics, click "Algebra" icon. Type:

```
Ybar = mean(Y);
res = Y − Ybar;
```

You can save this algebra code by clicking "Save As". Run it by clicking "OK: Run". Look at the data base and discuss.

(e) *Create a new variable:* $y = \log(Y)$:

Click the "Calculator" icon. Highlight Y, *then click "log" and click "=" and name it* y. *Redo* (b), (c) *for* y, t.

Period	Total industrial output (index)
1800–1824	346
1825–1849	796
1850–1874	1878
1875–1899	3344
1900–1924	5089
1925–1949	8495
1950–1974	17237

Table 3.2 Total UK industrial output by 25-year periods from 1800 to 1974. *Sources: Crafts and Harley (1992, p. 725), Mitchell (1988, p. 846)*

Computing Task 3.14. *Introduction to STATA. Consider Table 3.2.*

Open STATA by clicking on its icon.

Start by changing Directory: type, e.g., cd u :

Open a log file by typing log using *"filename".*

(*a*) *Create a new data base by typing* edit *or use icon. Input data for two variables:* t *counting the period,* $1, 2, \ldots, 7$, *and* Y *giving the output. Change variable names by double-clicking on the variable names. Save into your folder, e.g., as* indust.dta. *Load the data:* use indust

(*b*) *Look at the data: Use the commands:*

describe	*describes the data*
sum	*computes mean, standard deviations, minima, maxima*
inspect	
tabulate	
graph Y t	*cross plots* Y *on* t
kdensity	*graph density of variable*

(*c*) *Run a regression using software:*

Use the command reg Y .

Create predicted values using predict Yp. *Graph predicted* Yp *against* Y.

(*d*) *Run a regression by hand by typing:*

     egen Ybar $=$ mean(Y)

     gen res $=$ Y $-$ Ybar

What is the difference between egen *and* gen?

(*e*) *Create a new variable,* $y = \log(Y)$, *by typing* gen y $=$ ln(Y). *Redo* (*b*), (*c*) *for* y, t.

Close the log file by log close. *Close STATA by* exit, clear.

Chapter Four

The logit model

In this chapter, we will look at the proportion of women participating in the labor market. In particular, we will investigate how participation rates change with the length of schooling, to see whether participation increases with schooling. Such information would be of interest when devising an economic policy addressing participation; hence this type of empirical analysis could be the start of a policy analysis. It would naturally lead to a more detailed study investigating the variation of participation with other individual characteristics, and ultimately to an analysis of the costs and benefits of increasing the length of education for all or just for targeted groups of the population.

The starting point of the analysis is to describe the marginal participation rate using the Bernoulli model developed in Chapters 1 and 2. We will describe variations in participation in terms of Bernoulli distributions, where the success parameter depends on the length of education. To do so, we introduce the notion of a *conditional distribution*, then formulate a conditional statistical model for participation given educational levels. Such a generalization of the Bernoulli model is known as the logistic model or, in short, the logit model.

4.1 CONDITIONAL DISTRIBUTIONS

We will now look at the 0.01% subsample of the 1980 US census sample introduced in §3.1, with a view to explaining labor force participation. Here, we simply select all women of age 18 to 65, including those who work as well as those who do not work. This gives a sample of 7184 women. Cross tabulation of the variables participation against education motivates the notion of *sample conditional distributions*, leading on to the corresponding population distributions.

4.1.1 Sample conditional distributions

We will focus on the issue of participation in the labor market and length of education measured in years. The original data for education is reported in number of years of finished education as $0, 1, \ldots, 20$. Due to data protection issues, the length of education has been top–coded by 20. The responses are captured by two discrete random variables, denoted Y_i and X_i for the ith individual. The participation variable Y is binary, with the convention that no/yes is coded as $0/1$. To get an overview of the data, we cross tabulate participation against education in Table 4.1, showing the number of cases in each category. For simplicity, the 21 possible values of the education variable have been grouped in just 7 categories.

	Elementary School		High School		College		
$Y \backslash X$	0–7	8	9–11	12	13–15	16–19	≥ 20
0	256	180	579	1228	463	219	7
1	143	127	560	1858	858	665	41

Table 4.1 Cross tabulation of participation against education

Because the magnitudes of the numbers in the cells in Table 4.1 depend on the overall number of individuals, n, we standardize by dividing by n as shown in Table 4.2 to get the joint sample frequency of the two variables. Each cell of Table 4.2 then has:

$$\widehat{f}(x,y) = \text{"frequency of 7184 women who reported } (X_i = x \text{ and } Y_i = y)\text{."}$$
(4.1.1)

The variable Y_j takes the values 0 and 1. That is, Y_j takes $J = 2$ distinct values for $j = 1, \ldots, J$. Correspondingly, X_i takes $K = 21$ distinct values x_k (for $k = 1, \ldots, K$), that is $(0, 1, \ldots, 20)$, reduced to $K = 7$ when the educational outcomes are grouped. Clearly, the sum of all cell values in Table 4.2 is unity, as:

$$\sum_{j=1}^{J} \sum_{k=1}^{K} \widehat{f}(y_j, x_k) = 1.$$

It does not matter whether we sum over columns before rows, so we also have:

$$\sum_{j=1}^{J} \sum_{k=1}^{K} \widehat{f}(y_j, x_k) = \sum_{k=1}^{K} \sum_{j=1}^{J} \widehat{f}(y_j, x_k) = 1.$$
(4.1.2)

$y \backslash x$	0–7	8	9–11	12	13–15	16–19	≥ 20
0	0.04	0.03	0.08	0.17	0.06	0.03	0.00
1	0.02	0.02	0.08	0.26	0.12	0.09	0.01

Table 4.2 Joint frequency distribution of participation and education

If we calculate row and column sums in Table 4.2, we get the marginal frequency distributions:

$$\widehat{f}(x) = \sum_{j=1}^{J} \widehat{f}(y_j, x) \quad \text{and} \quad \widehat{f}(y) = \sum_{k=1}^{K} \widehat{f}(y, x_k).$$
(4.1.3)

These are reported in the margin of Table 4.3. For example, 41% of the sample do not participate.

$y \backslash x$	0–7	8	9–11	12	13–15	16–19	≥ 20	$\widehat{f}(y)$
0	0.04	0.03	0.08	0.17	0.06	0.03	0.00	0.41
1	0.02	0.02	0.08	0.26	0.12	0.09	0.01	0.59
$\widehat{f}(x)$	0.06	0.04	0.16	0.43	0.18	0.12	0.01	1

Table 4.3 Marginal frequencies

Sometimes we are interested in conditional information: What is the participation rate for those with 12 years of education? This question is addressed by the *sample conditional distribution* or *conditional frequency*:

$$\widehat{f}(y \mid x) = \frac{\widehat{f}(y, x)}{\widehat{f}(x)}. \tag{4.1.4}$$

Inserting the figures from Table 4.1 we get:

$$\widehat{f}(y = 1 \mid x = 12) = \frac{1858/7184}{(1858 + 1228)/7184} = \frac{1858}{3086} \simeq 0.60.$$

In this calculation, the numbers have been rounded as indicated by the approximation sign. The complete set of conditional participation frequencies is reported in Table 4.4. These show that the conditional participation rate $\widehat{f}(y = 1|x)$ is increasing with the length of education.

x	0–7	8	9–11	12	13–15	16–19	≥ 20
$\widehat{f}(y = 0|x)$	0.64	0.59	0.51	0.40	0.35	0.25	0.15
$\widehat{f}(y = 1|x)$	0.36	0.41	0.49	0.60	0.65	0.75	0.85

Table 4.4 Conditional participation frequencies

In Table 4.4, each column adds up to 1. This is because women must either participate or not; or, more technically, the conditional frequency is simply a normalized version of the joint frequency, where the normalization ensures that the conditional frequencies add up to unity:

$$
\begin{aligned}
\sum_{j=1}^{J} \widehat{f}(y_j \mid x) &= \sum_{j=1}^{J} \frac{\widehat{f}(y_j, x)}{\widehat{f}(x)} && [\text{ use (4.1.4) }] \\
&= \frac{\sum_{j=1}^{J} \widehat{f}(y_j, x)}{\widehat{f}(x)} && [\text{ denominator constant in } j] \\
&= \frac{\widehat{f}(x)}{\widehat{f}(x)} = 1 && [\text{ use (4.1.3) }]
\end{aligned}
$$

Averaging the conditional frequencies over the conditioning variable gives the marginal frequencies:

$$\sum_{k=1}^{K} \widehat{\mathsf{f}}\,(y \mid x_k)\,\widehat{\mathsf{f}}\,(x_k) = \sum_{k=1}^{K} \widehat{\mathsf{f}}\,(x_k, y) \qquad [\text{ use } (4.1.4)\,]$$

$$= \widehat{\mathsf{f}}\,(y)\,. \qquad [\text{ use } (4.1.3)\,]$$

In this way:

$$\widehat{\mathsf{f}}\,(y = 1) = \sum_{k=1}^{K} \widehat{\mathsf{f}}\,(y = 1 \mid x_k)\,\widehat{\mathsf{f}}\,(x_k) = 0.36 \times 0.06 + \cdots = 0.59. \qquad (4.1.5)$$

For a binary variable like participation, conditional relationships can be explored further in terms of *odds*. For instance, for $X_i = 12$, we find the odds for participation to be:

$$\frac{\widehat{\mathsf{f}}\,(y_i = 1 | x_i = 12)}{\widehat{\mathsf{f}}\,(y_i = 0 | x_i = 12)} = \frac{1858}{1228} = 1.51,$$

so among women with 12 years of education there are 1.5 times as many with jobs as without jobs. The odds are collected in Table 4.5.

x	0–7	8	9–11	12	13–15	16–19	≥ 20
odds	0.56	0.71	0.97	1.51	1.85	3.04	5.86

Table 4.5 Odds of participation

In the literature, there is disagreement on terminology. While the term *odds ratio* is used by some authors instead of *odds*, we will follow bookmakers in reserving the notion *odds ratio* for ratios of odds.

Often, it is much easier to get an overview of econometric results like these using plots rather than tables. In this way, Figure 4.1 shows the sample odds and sample log odds as a function of education. The full information about the 21 possible lengths of education is used rather than the 7 groups of education used above, and therefore only the entries for 8 and 12 years are common for Table 4.5 and Figure 4.1. From Figure 4.1(b), we see that the log odds are close to a linear function of education. We will exploit this information shortly.

As explored in §2.1.1, the mean, or sample expectation, is given by:

$$\widehat{\mathsf{E}}\,(Y) = \sum_{j=1}^{J} y_j \widehat{\mathsf{f}}\,(y_j)\,,$$

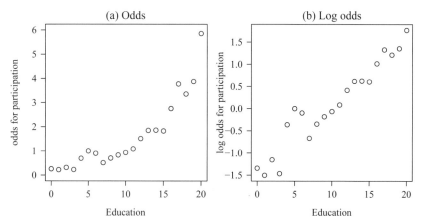

Figure 4.1 Odds and log odds for participation as a function of education

which, in the case of the binary variable participation, reduces to $\widehat{f}(1) = 0.59$. In the same way, we can compute the conditional sample expectation of participation given length of education:

$$\widehat{\mathsf{E}}(Y \mid X = x_k) = \sum_{j=1}^{J} y_j \widehat{f}(y_j \mid x_k) . \qquad (4.1.6)$$

Once again, due to the binary nature of the participation variable, this amounts to:

$$\widehat{\mathsf{E}}(Y \mid X = x) = 0 \times \widehat{f}(0 \mid x) + 1 \times \widehat{f}(1 \mid x) = \widehat{f}(1 \mid x) .$$

The mean of the full sample can be obtained by taking a weighted average of the conditional means, using what is known as the (sample) *Law of Iterated Expectations*:

$$\widehat{\mathsf{E}}(Y) = \sum_{j=1}^{J} y_j \widehat{f}(y_j) \qquad [\text{ use (2.1.1) }]$$

$$= \sum_{j=1}^{J} \sum_{k=1}^{K} y_j \widehat{f}(y_j, x_k) \qquad [\text{ use (4.1.3) }]$$

$$= \sum_{j=1}^{J} \sum_{k=1}^{K} y_j \widehat{f}(y_j \mid x_k) \widehat{f}(x_k) \qquad [\text{ use (4.1.4) }]$$

$$= \sum_{k=1}^{K} \widehat{\mathsf{E}}(Y \mid X = x_k) \widehat{f}(x_k) = \widehat{\mathsf{E}}\left\{ \widehat{\mathsf{E}}(Y \mid X) \right\} . \qquad [\text{ use (4.1.6) }]$$

Since participation is binary, this calculation reduces to that of (4.1.5):

$$\widehat{\mathsf{E}}(Y) = \sum_{k=1}^{K} \widehat{\mathsf{E}}(Y \mid X = x_k)\widehat{\mathsf{f}}(x_k) = \sum_{k=1}^{K}\widehat{\mathsf{f}}(y = 1 \mid x_k)\widehat{\mathsf{f}}(x_k) = 0.59.$$

4.1.2 Population distributions

Corresponding to the conditional sample frequency defined in (4.1.4), we can define the *conditional density* of Y given X as:

$$\mathsf{f}(y \mid x) = \frac{\mathsf{f}(y, x)}{\mathsf{f}(x)}, \tag{4.1.7}$$

which is a definition that applies both for discrete and continuous variables. Conditional densities are intimately linked with the independence concept; see (1.2.1) and (3.2.1). Two random variables, Y, X, discrete or continuous, are independent if their joint density satisfies:

$$\mathsf{f}(y, x) = \mathsf{f}(y)\mathsf{f}(x).$$

Therefore, if Y and X are independent, then the conditional density of Y given X equals the marginal density:

$$\text{independence} \qquad \Longleftrightarrow \qquad \mathsf{f}(y \mid x) = \mathsf{f}(y).$$

In other words, given independence, we do not learn any more about Y by knowing X. Likewise, expressed in terms of expectations we have:

$$\text{independence} \qquad \Longrightarrow \qquad \mathsf{E}(y \mid x) = \mathsf{E}(y).$$

The Law of Iterated Expectations also holds for population expectations:

$$\mathsf{E}(Y) = \mathsf{E}\{\mathsf{E}(Y|X)\}. \tag{4.1.8}$$

Note that the above properties hold for discrete as well as continuous distributions.

4.2 THE LOGIT MODEL

This preliminary analysis of participation and length of education indicates that these variables are related. In the following, we will set up an econometric model, with a focus on explaining the variation in participation by the length of education. We refer to this as an econometric, rather than just a statistical, model as the possible relationship has a basis in economic analysis. The basic ingredient will be the Bernoulli model of Chapter 1, which we will extend by allowing the success parameter to vary with education.

4.2.1 Econometric model

In order to describe the variation in the data, we need a joint model for all the observations. Assuming (i) that the pairs of observations are independent, we need to describe and parametrize the joint density of X_i, Y_i denoted $\mathsf{f}(x_i, y_i)$. The definition of conditional densities, as in (4.1.7), implies:

$$\mathsf{f}\left(x_i, y_i\right) = \mathsf{f}\left(y_i \mid x_i\right) \mathsf{f}\left(x_i\right).$$

A description of the joint distribution therefore comes about by describing (ii) the conditional distribution of participation given schooling, which is of primary interest; and (iii) the marginal distribution of the length of schooling, which is of less interest in this example. The opposite factorization, $\mathsf{f}\left(x_i|y_i\right) \mathsf{f}\left(y_i\right)$, is also possible, but of less interest, as schooling happened in the past relative to participation.

The *conditional sample frequencies* of Y_i given X_i were reported in Table 4.4, where a tendency to higher participation among women with longer education was observed. Since Y_i takes only two values, the conditional distribution of Y_i given X_i must be a Bernoulli distribution, but we can let the success parameter depend on the conditioning variable X_i so:

$$\mathsf{f}\left(y = 1 \mid x\right) = 1 - \mathsf{f}\left(y = 0 \mid x\right) = p\left(x\right),$$

where p is some function of x that takes values in the interval $[0, 1]$.

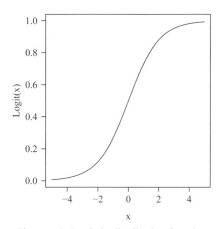

Figure 4.2 Logistic distribution function

For modeling purposes, we need to specify the success probability, $p(x)$. As a simplifying assumption, we will suppose that p rises from zero toward one as the length of education rises. This simplifying assumption therefore restricts our choice to the class of distribution functions. Modeling the success probability and the odds, or the log thereof, are equivalent:

$$\log\left\{\mathrm{odds}\left(x\right)\right\} = \log\left\{\frac{p\left(x\right)}{1 - p\left(x\right)}\right\} \stackrel{\mathrm{def}}{=} \mathrm{logit}\left\{p\left(x\right)\right\},$$

where the function $\mathrm{logit}(p) = \log\{p/(1-p)\}$ is called the *logistic function*, or simply the *logit function*. The logit formulation has the useful feature that the dependent variable can take any value, yet be consistent with $0 \le p(x) \le 1$. Figure 4.1(b) indicates that it may be reasonable to assume that log odds are a linear function of education:

$$\mathrm{logit}\{p\,(x)\} = \beta_1 + \beta_2 x.$$

Solving this equation for $p(x)$ gives:

$$\mathrm{f}\,(y = 1 \mid x) = p\,(x) = \frac{\exp\,(\beta_1 + \beta_2 x)}{1 + \exp\,(\beta_1 + \beta_2 x)}. \tag{4.2.1}$$

The function $\exp(x)/\{1 + \exp(x)\}$ is the inverse of the logit function and, perhaps confusingly, is called the *logistic distribution function*. The logistic distribution function is plotted in Figure 4.2. Can you show analytically that this function is a distribution function?

The parameters of this logit model can be interpreted in terms of odds and odds ratios. By construction, the log odds are modeled as linear in the parameters β_1, β_2 since:

$$\log\left\{\frac{\mathrm{f}\,(y_i = 1|x_i)}{\mathrm{f}\,(y_i = 0|x_i)}\right\} = \beta_1 + \beta_2 x_i. \tag{4.2.2}$$

The intercept parameter β_1 is therefore the log odds for an individual with no education, $x_i = 0$. The parameter β_2 relates to the change in log odds from an additional year of education. This can be seen from the log odds ratio:

$$\log\left\{\frac{\mathrm{f}\,(y_i = 1|x_i + 1)}{\mathrm{f}\,(y_i = 0|x_i + 1)} \Big/ \frac{\mathrm{f}\,(y_i = 1|x_i)}{\mathrm{f}\,(y_i = 0|x_i)}\right\} = \beta_2. \tag{4.2.3}$$

The logistic distribution function is very similar to the standard normal distribution function plotted in Figure 3.1, apart from in the extreme tails. That function could be used instead, to generate a so-called probit model, which would produce only slightly different outcomes.

The *marginal density* of education is much harder to describe. It would certainly require considerable institutional knowledge about the US school system prior to 1980 to provide a good description. Since our primary interest is the variation in participation, it is unappealing to undertake such a detailed study. We will, therefore, seek to avoid describing the marginal distribution of the conditioning, or explanatory, variables, and draw our inference exclusively from a model based on the conditional density.

The key question that arises from this decision is whether our inferences are affected by the lack of a description of the marginal density. There are two instances where we need such distributional assumptions. First, to write down the likelihood, and hence to derive estimators and test statistics. Second, to find the distributions of the estimators and other statistics in order to conduct inference. As for the first issue of writing down the likelihood, it suffices to look at the conditional likelihood if the parameters of the conditional and the marginal likelihood are unrelated. In the statistical literature, the explanatory variables are then called *ancillary*, whereas the literature on econometric time series uses the notion *strong exogeneity* (see §10.3.1). We will simply say that X is an *exogenous* variable, which therefore does not require to be modeled for the derivations of estimators and test statistics. The second issue, related to the distributions of the estimators, will be discussed in §10.1.2, and turns out not to be a problem in this model, whereas it is a more serious issue in time-series analysis. Since the distribution of X is left unspecified, we say that a conditional model is an *open model* as opposed to the *closed models* of the earlier chapters, where the joint distributions of all the variables were formulated.

In summary, we are assuming:

(*i*) *independence*: the pairs $(Y_1, X_1), \ldots, (Y_n, X_n)$ are mutually independent;
(*ii*) *conditional distribution*: $(Y_i \mid X_i) \overset{D}{=} \text{Bernoulli}\,[p(X_i)]$, where the success probability varies with X so $\text{logit}\{p(X_i)\} = \beta_1 + \beta_2 X_i$;
(*iii*) *exogeneity*: the conditioning variable X_i is exogenous;
(*iv*) *parameter space*: $\beta_1, \beta_2 \in \mathbb{R}^2 = \mathbb{R} \times \mathbb{R}$.

The discussion so far suggests that the logit assumption is not unreasonable. A formal test for this assumption will be presented in §4.4.3.

This model can also be formulated in terms of a model equation. The model equation cannot be written directly for the observed variables Y_i but requires that the construction involves a set of unobserved variables Y_i^*, satisfying:

$$Y_i^* = \beta_1 + \beta_2 X_i + u_i, \tag{4.2.4}$$

where the pairs $(u_1, X_1), \ldots, (u_n, X_n)$ are independently distributed according to a logistic distribution:

$$\mathsf{P}(u_i \leq v \mid X_i) = \text{logit}(v) = \frac{\exp(v)}{1 + \exp(v)}.$$

The observed binary variables arise from the unobserved variables Y_i^* by:

$$Y_i = 1_{(Y_i^* \geq 0)}. \tag{4.2.5}$$

Exercise 4.2 shows that this gives the desired distribution for Y_i. In this construction, the distribution of the observable variable Y_i is specified in terms of the unobserved variable Y_i^*. We say that Y_i^* is a *latent variable*, and refer to the model as a *discrete choice model*. Often Y_i^* can be given a behavioral interpretation.

4.2.2 The likelihood function

Based on the econometric model, we can write down the conditional density of $(Y_1, \ldots Y_n)$ given $(X_1, \ldots, X_n)$ and rewrite it in a few steps. The independence assumption (i) implies:

$$\mathsf{f}_{\beta_1,\beta_2}\left(y_1, \ldots, y_n | x_1, \ldots, x_n\right) = \prod_{i=1}^{n} \mathsf{f}_{\beta_1,\beta_2}\left(y_i | x_i\right).$$

Due to the assumption (ii) for the conditional distribution, this equals:

$$\prod_{i=1}^{n} \left\{ \frac{\exp\left(\beta_1 + \beta_2 x_i\right)}{1 + \exp\left(\beta_1 + \beta_2 x_i\right)} \right\}^{y_i} \left\{ \frac{1}{1 + \exp\left(\beta_1 + \beta_2 x_i\right)} \right\}^{1 - y_i}.$$

Finally, since a product of exponentials equals an exponential of sums, this equals:

$$\left[\prod_{i=1}^{n} \left\{ \frac{1}{1 + \exp\left(\beta_1 + \beta_2 x_i\right)} \right\} \right] \exp\left(\beta_1 \sum_{i=1}^{n} y_i + \beta_2 \sum_{i=1}^{n} y_i x_i \right).$$

In the econometric analysis, we observe $Y_1, \ldots, Y_n$ and $X_1, \ldots, X_n$ and wish to know how likely an outcome β_1, β_2 is, so turn to the likelihood function. As this is based on a conditional density, it is called a *conditional likelihood*:

$$\mathsf{L}_{Y_1,\ldots,Y_n | X_1,\ldots,X_n}\left(\beta_1, \beta_2\right) = \mathsf{f}_{\beta_1,\beta_2}\left(Y_1, \ldots, Y_n \mid X_1, \ldots, X_n\right)$$

$$= \left[\prod_{i=1}^{n} \left\{ \frac{1}{1 + \exp\left(\beta_1 + \beta_2 X_i\right)} \right\} \right] \exp\left(\beta_1 \sum_{i=1}^{n} Y_i + \beta_2 \sum_{i=1}^{n} Y_i X_i \right).$$

The corresponding conditional log-likelihood function is:

$$\ell_{Y_1,\ldots,Y_n | X_1,\ldots,X_n}\left(\beta_1, \beta_2\right)$$

$$= - \sum_{i=1}^{n} \log\left\{ 1 + \exp\left(\beta_1 + \beta_2 X_i\right) \right\} + \beta_1 \sum_{i=1}^{n} Y_i + \beta_2 \sum_{i=1}^{n} Y_i X_i.$$

According to assumption (iv), the parameters vary freely, so $\beta_1, \beta_2 \in \mathbb{R}^2$.

4.2.3 Estimation

The likelihood equations for the parameters β_1, β_2 are found by taking partial derivatives of the log-likelihood function:

$$\frac{\partial}{\partial \beta_1} \ell_{Y_1,\ldots,Y_n | X_1,\ldots,X_n}\left(\beta_1, \beta_2\right) = - \sum_{i=1}^{n} \frac{\exp\left(\beta_1 + \beta_2 X_i\right)}{1 + \exp\left(\beta_1 + \beta_2 X_i\right)} + \sum_{i=1}^{n} Y_i, \quad (4.2.6)$$

$$\frac{\partial}{\partial \beta_2} \ell_{Y_1,\ldots,Y_n | X_1,\ldots,X_n}\left(\beta_1, \beta_2\right) = - \sum_{i=1}^{n} \frac{\exp\left(\beta_1 + \beta_2 X_i\right)}{1 + \exp\left(\beta_1 + \beta_2 X_i\right)} X_i + \sum_{i=1}^{n} Y_i X_i.$$

$$(4.2.7)$$

Equating these to zero gives the likelihood equations for $\widehat{\beta}_1, \widehat{\beta}_2$:

$$\sum_{i=1}^{n} \frac{\exp(\widehat{\beta}_1 + \widehat{\beta}_2 X_i)}{1 + \exp(\widehat{\beta}_1 + \widehat{\beta}_2 X_i)} = \sum_{i=1}^{n} Y_i, \tag{4.2.8}$$

$$\sum_{i=1}^{n} \frac{\exp(\widehat{\beta}_1 + \widehat{\beta}_2 X_i)}{1 + \exp(\widehat{\beta}_1 + \widehat{\beta}_2 X_i)} X_i = \sum_{i=1}^{n} Y_i X_i. \tag{4.2.9}$$

In general, there is no analytic solution to these equations, since the first term of each equation involves logarithms of sums, so that the parameters β_1, β_2, and the *covariate* X_i cannot be disentangled. Apart from an exception discussed in Exercise 4.4, the only way to solve the likelihood equations is to use numerical methods that search for the maximum of the likelihood function. Fortunately, numerical maximization algorithms are included in most econometric software. Proving that there is a unique maximum is a little harder than in the previous models. This is done in Exercise 4.6.

4.2.4 Logit model for participation given schooling

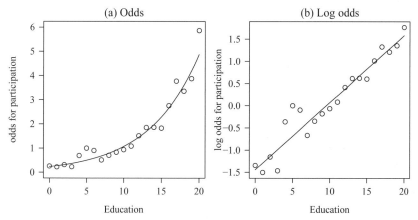

Figure 4.3 Odds and log odds for participation as a function of education, together with logit fit (for the odds, the shape is exponential, whereas it is linear for the log odds)

A logit model for participation given schooling can be fitted using ready-made maximization algorithms in econometric software. Using OxMetrics (see Doornik and Hendry, 2006c), we find the estimates:

$$\widehat{\beta}_1 = -1.4, \qquad \widehat{\beta}_2 = 0.15.$$

Figure 4.3 shows the sample log odds together with the fitted line. Recalling the expression for the log odds ratio in (4.2.3), this model suggests that one additional year of education increases the log odds for participation by $\widehat{\beta}_2 = 0.15$. The intercept of $\widehat{\beta}_1 = -1.4$ is interpreted as the log odds of participation for a woman without education. The corresponding empirical log odds of participation for a woman without education is $\log(12/46) = -1.34$. A more meaningful value of the intercept can be achieved by subtracting either the average of education or a value in the middle of the distribution of education, like 12, from education before fitting the logistic model. Figure 4.3(b) indicates that the fit is quite good in general for all values of education.

The maximum of the log-likelihood function is found to be:

$$\ell_{Y_1,\ldots,Y_n|X_1,\ldots,X_n}\left(\widehat{\beta}_1,\widehat{\beta}_2\right) = -4702.71. \qquad (4.2.10)$$

In Exercise 4.6, it is argued that the log-likelihood function indeed has a unique maximum. This can be illustrated by plotting profiles of the likelihood as a function of first one parameter and then the other (see Figure 4.4).

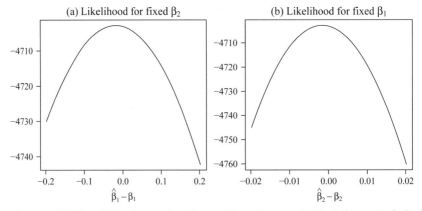

Figure 4.4 Log likelihood function evaluated around maximum. In the left panel, β_2 is fixed, whereas β_1 varies around $\widehat{\beta}_1$; and vice versa in the right panel

4.3 INFERENCE

We can now proceed to ask the question, Does education matter for labor force participation? This will be based on the assumption that the econometric model is correct, or at least not obviously wrong, which we will test in §4.4.

4.3.1 The likelihood ratio test

We will consider the hypothesis that labor force participation *does not* vary with education, that is, $\beta_2 = 0$. Imposing that restriction on the model reduces it to the Bernoulli model of Chapter 1 (also see Exercise 4.3). Reestimating the model delivers:

$$\widehat{\beta}_{1,R} = 0.37.$$

The estimate $\widehat{\beta}_{1,R}$ is the log odds for participation versus non-participation. The connection between the odds and the participation probability is:

$$\frac{\widehat{f}\,(y=1)}{\widehat{f}\,(y=0)} = \exp\left(\widehat{\beta}_{1,R}\right) = 1.45, \qquad \widehat{f}\,(y=1) = \frac{\exp\left(\widehat{\beta}_{1,R}\right)}{1 + \exp\left(\widehat{\beta}_{1,R}\right)} = 0.59.$$

Finally, we find the maximized restricted log-likelihood function to be:

$$\ell_{Y_1,\ldots,Y_n|X_1,\ldots,X_n}\left(\widehat{\beta}_{1,R}, 0\right) = -4857.61.$$

To test the hypothesis, we compute the log-likelihood ratio test statistic:

$$\mathsf{LR} = -2\log Q = -2\log\mathsf{L}\left(\widehat{\beta}_{1,R}, 0\right) + 2\log\mathsf{L}\left(\widehat{\beta}_1, \widehat{\beta}_2\right) = 310.$$

Once again, this statistic is approximately $\chi^2[1]$-distributed when the hypothesis is true. Comparing with the 5% level critical value of 3.84, from Table 2.2, or computing the p-value, $P(\mathsf{LR} > 310) < 0.001$, we reject the hypothesis that education does not matter for participation.

4.3.2 Interpreting the test result

When conducting a statistical test, the thought experiment is that our sample is drawn from some *hypothetical* population distribution that could have generated the data. Our sample is then compared with hypothetical samples drawn from that hypothetical population distribution. By choosing a level of 5%, we accept that in 5% of these samples a true hypothesis like that of $\beta_2 = 0$ is rejected by chance. This could possibly happen in our sample. In the present situation, however, the test statistic is so large that we do not find any support for the hypothesis that $\beta_2 = 0$ in the *hypothetical* population distribution. As the data are actually drawn from a concrete population, namely the US population of women of age 18 to 65 in 1980, it is tempting to extrapolate the result, to conclude that the result holds for the entire US population of women of age 18 to 65 in 1980.

From a policy viewpoint, one would be interested in whether education *causes* participation. If the whole population were given an additional year of education, by raising the school leaving age for example, would we then expect the log odds for participation to change by $\widehat{\beta}_2 = 0.15$? This will not necessarily be the case, in that the length of education is possibly a signal of taste for work, or ability, or perhaps a preference for studying rather than working, or a combination of these. The effect of an additional year of education could therefore be smaller or larger depending on the underlying causal mechanism. For such reasons, it is notoriously difficult to learn about causality from an econometric analysis, even though that may often be the objective of the analysis.

4.3.3 The signed likelihood ratio test

From the subject-matter viewpoint of economics, we would expect that length of education has a positive effect on participation rates. In other words, if β_2 is non-zero, we would expect it to have a positive sign. We can exploit such information for a more powerful test of the hypothesis that $\beta_2 = 0$. We then refer to $\beta_2 = 0$ as the null hypothesis and $\beta_2 > 0$ as the alternative hypothesis.

The likelihood ratio test is essentially based on the squared distance between $\widehat{\beta}_2$ and $\beta_2 = 0$, so the information about the sign of $\widehat{\beta}_2$ is lost. We can introduce the sign by looking at the square root of the likelihood ratio statistic, attributing the relevant sign. This signed likelihood ratio statistic is approximately normally distributed when the hypothesis is true:

$$\omega = \text{sign}(\widehat{\beta}_2)\sqrt{\text{LR}} \stackrel{D}{\approx} \text{N}\left[0, 1\right], \tag{4.3.1}$$

where the *sign function* is given by:

$$\text{sign}\left(x\right) = \begin{cases} +1 & \text{if } x \geq 0, \\ -1 & \text{if } x < 0. \end{cases}$$

We construct a test by comparing the test statistic ω to a critical value c. In cases where economic theory suggests that β_2 is non-negative, that is zero or positive, the test is given by the critical region $(\omega > c)$, where c is chosen so as to control the type I error of rejecting a true hypothesis. A test of 5% level comes about by choosing c as 1.65, according to Table 2.1, so $\text{P}(\omega > 1.65) = 5\%$ if the hypothesis is true. Vice versa, if economic theory suggests that β_2 is non-positive, the test is given by the critical region $(\omega < -c)$. If, however, the sign of β_2 suggested by economic theory differs from that of $\widehat{\beta}_2$, the interpretation of the test is confusing. An example will be given in §7.6.3.

The signed likelihood ratio statistic is easily computed in the present application. The unrestricted estimate, $\widehat{\beta}_2 = 0.15$, is positive in accordance with our economic reasoning, and the null hypothesis is that $\beta_2 = 0$, while $\text{LR} = 310$, so:

$$\omega = +\sqrt{310} = 17.6,$$

with $\text{p} = \text{P}(\text{LR} > 17.6) < 0.001$, using the $\text{N}[0, 1]$-distribution. The hypothesis is once again rejected using a 5% level test (with critical value of 1.65, see Table 2.1). Given the large sample, a 1% level test is perhaps more appropriate (with a critical value of 2.6), but even so, the hypothesis is rejected.

The signed likelihood ratio test is more powerful than the likelihood ratio test, at least if the hypothesis concerning the sign is correct. This comes about as follows. If the signed test statistic ω happens to fall in the region 1.65 to 2, for instance $\omega = 1.8$, then the likelihood ratio test accepts, since $\omega^2 = 3.24$ is smaller than 4, the 95% quantile of the $\chi^2\,[1]$-distribution, whereas the signed test, rejects since 1.8 is larger than 1.65. In this way, the signed, or *one-sided*, test rejects more often than the *two-sided* likelihood ratio test, so fewer type II errors of accepting a false hypothesis are made. One could decide, however, not to bother exploiting the difference between one- and two-sided tests, since the decision is rather marginal anyway if one rejects by one test and accepts by the other. As pointed out in §2.3.2, this would be a situation where more information is needed to draw firm inferences.

4.4 MIS-SPECIFICATION ANALYSIS

Once a logistic model has been fitted, one can investigate whether the assumptions of the model are supported by the data. A test of assumption (ii), the logistic distribution, can be done by comparing the fitted logistic model to a more general and more flexible distribution. In the following, a test statistic is derived at first, and then a discussion of χ^2-distributions follows to facilitate the construction of a test.

4.4.1 A mis-specification test statistic

The logistic model can be tested by comparing it to a more general model using a likelihood ratio test. We could, for instance, consider a model where the conditional participation probabilities given schooling vary freely, that is:

$$\mathsf{f}\,(y = 1 \mid x) = \pi\,(x)\,,$$

where the function $\pi\,(x)$ takes $J = 21$ different values depending on the length of education. In other words, the conditional participation probability is parametrized in terms of J unrestricted parameters rather than just two parameters, β_1, β_2. Following on from Exercise 4.3, since $j = 0, \ldots 20$, we can formulate this more flexible model using a saturated logistic specification as:

$$\text{logit}\{p\,(X_i)\} = \sum_{j=0}^{J-1} \pi_j 1_{(X_i=j)},$$

where the *indicator function* or *dummy variable* is given by:

$$1_{(X_i=j)} = \begin{cases} 1 & \text{if } X_i = j, \\ 0 & \text{if } X_i \neq j. \end{cases} \tag{4.4.1}$$

Note that this model does not include an intercept; a constant is implicitly included since the indicator functions satisfy $\sum_{j=0}^{J-1} 1_{(X_i=j)} = 1$.

Applying the saturated logistic specification to the data leads to the maximum of the log-likelihood function as:

$$\ell_{Y_1,\ldots,Y_n|X_1,\ldots,X_n}\,(\widehat{\pi}_0, \ldots, \widehat{\pi}_{J-1}) = -4688.92. \tag{4.4.2}$$

The likelihood ratio test statistic for the logistic distribution assumption is then found by comparing (4.4.2) with the value found in (4.2.10), that is:

$$\mathrm{LR} = -2\left\{\ell_{Y_1,\ldots,Y_n|X_1,\ldots,X_n}\left(\widehat{\beta}_1,\widehat{\beta}_2\right) - \ell_{Y_1,\ldots,Y_n|X_1,\ldots,X_n}\left(\widehat{\pi}_0,\ldots,\widehat{\pi}_{J-1}\right)\right\}$$
$$= -2\left(-4702.72 + 4688.92\right) = 27.59.$$

4.4.2 The χ^2-distribution

We have several times used the $\chi^2[1]$-distribution for testing. The family of χ^2-distributions is a generalization thereof, which can be used for testing more complicated hypotheses.

The general χ^2-distribution is defined as follows. Suppose $Z \stackrel{D}{=} \mathrm{N}[0,1]$. Then Z^2 is said to be $\chi^2[1]$-distributed as discussed in §2.3.2. If $Z_1,\ldots,Z_m$ are independently $\mathrm{N}[0,1]$-distributed, then $V_m = Z_1^2 + \cdots + Z_m^2$ is χ^2-distributed with m degrees of freedom, also written $\chi^2[m]$.

In a testing situation like §4.4.1, the likelihood ratio test statistic is approximately χ^2-distributed. The degrees of freedom are found from the number of parameter restrictions: that is, the number of parameters in the unrestricted model, which is 21, minus the number of parameters in the restricted model, which is 2, giving 19 degrees of freedom. Using asymptotic theory, which we will not pursue here, one can argue that the likelihood ratio test statistic can be represented as the sum of 19 approximately independent terms, each of which is $\chi^2[1]$-distributed.

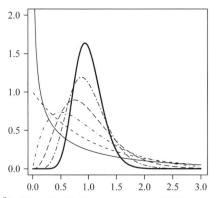

Figure 4.5 Densities for $\chi^2[m]/m$-distributions: $m = 1$ solid line, $m = 2$ dashed line, $m = 4$ dashed-dotted line, $m = 8$ long dashed line, $m = 16$ long dashed-dotted line, $m = 32$ bold solid line

Figure 4.5 shows $\chi^2[m]/m$-densities for various values of m. For large m, the density looks like a normal density. Most computer software can generate the quantiles of the χ^2-distribution, and, for instance, Table 8 of Lindley and Scott (1995) provides a printed table of the χ^2-distribution. A summary of quantiles is given in Table 4.6.

m versus $P(\chi^2[m] > q)$	0.10	0.05	0.01
1	2.7	3.8	5.0
2	4.6	6.0	7.4
3	6.3	7.8	9.3
4	7.8	9.5	11.1
$\vdots$			
17	24.8	27.6	33.4
18	26.0	28.9	34.8
19	27.2	30.1	36.2

Table 4.6 Upper quantiles q for $\chi^2[m]$-distributions

4.4.3 A goodness-of-fit test

As argued above, the likelihood ratio test statistic in §4.4.1, LR $= 27.59$, should be compared with a $\chi^2[19]$-distribution. Table 4.6 shows that the 95% quantile is 30.1, while a more accurate calculation gives the p-value of $P(LR > 27.59) = 9.2\%$, indicating that we cannot reject the logistic assumption by this test.

The principle of the test constructed in §4.4.1 is to *stratify* the individuals by education. That is, the individuals are divided into *strata* or groups with common characteristics. For each strata, the sample frequency is then compared with the probability predicted from the model. In the statistical literature, such tests are said to check the *goodness-of-fit* of the model. In econometrics, such a test is often said to check the *validity* of the model, with rejection suggesting it is not a valid model for the given data.

4.5 SUMMARY AND EXERCISES

Summary: Conditional distributions were introduced. Marginal densities and expectations can be found as weighted averages of conditional densities and expectations, respectively.

The logit model of participation given education is an open model. The log-odds variable is modeled as linear in education. Estimation is done using numerical methods. One-sided and two-sided likelihood ratio tests were introduced.

The validity of the model can be investigated using a goodness-of-fit test. This uses χ^2-distributions with several degrees of freedom.

Bibliography: More detailed introductions to theory, interpretation, and mis-specification analysis for the logit model can be found in Cramer (2003) and Hosmer and Lemeshow (2000). A related model is the *probit model*, in which the logistic distribution function in (4.2.1) is replaced by the standard normal distribution function, $\Phi(x)$; see §3.2.1. In many applications, analyses based on the logit model and the probit model will give the same substantive results. Train (2003) and Wooldridge (2006) give detailed treatments of the probit model.

Key questions:

- How are marginal densities and a conditional densities related?
- Compare the notions of open and closed models.
- Explain the difference between one-sided and two-sided tests.
- Discuss the validity of the assumptions of the statistical model for the participation data.

Exercise 4.1. *Consider the logit specification given in (4.2.1). What effect does a unit change in X have on the success probability? To answer this question, differentiate (4.2.1) with respect to X. Plot the derivative as a function of the success probability. Discuss the plot.*

Exercise 4.2. *Consider the logistic model as defined through (4.2.4) and (4.2.5). Show that $(Y_i \mid X_i) \stackrel{D}{=} \text{Bernoulli}[p(X_i)]$, where $\text{logit}\{p(X_i)\} = \beta_1 + \beta_2 X_i$.*

Exercise 4.3. *Bernoulli model as logit model. Consider the birth data for 2004, as well as the Bernoulli model discussed in Chapter 1.*
(a) Express the odds ratio and log-odds ratio in terms of θ, and estimate these quantities.
(b) Construct a logit model for the data, assuming that $\mathsf{P}(Y_i = 1) = \text{logit}(\beta)$. Estimate β and compare the result with the log odds ratio found in (a).
(c) We would like to test that the chance of having a girl is 50%. What does that imply about the odds ratio and the log-odds ratio? Impose that restriction on the logit model, and find the value of the log-likelihood function. Compute the likelihood ratio test statistic and test the hypothesis. Compare the result with section 2.3.

Exercise 4.4. *Consider the logit model of section 4.2, and suppose X_i is binary. Solve the likelihood equations (4.2.8) and (4.2.9).*

Exercise 4.5. *Show that the likelihood equations (4.2.8) and (4.2.9) can be written as the moment equations:*

$$\sum_{i=1}^{n}\{Y_i - \mathsf{E}(Y_i)\} = 0 \quad and \quad \sum_{i=1}^{n} X_i\{Y_i - \mathsf{E}(Y_i)\} = 0.$$

Exercise 4.6. * *Consider the partial derivatives of the likelihood in (4.2.6) and (4.2.7). Define $p_i = p(X_i)$.*

(a) *Show that the partial derivatives of the log-likelihood function are:*

$$\frac{\partial}{\partial \beta_1}\ell(\beta_1,\beta_2) = -\sum_{i=1}^{n} p_i + \sum_{i=1}^{n} Y_i, \quad \frac{\partial}{\partial \beta_2}\ell(\beta_1,\beta_2) = -\sum_{i=1}^{n} p_i X_i + \sum_{i=1}^{n} Y_i X_i.$$

(b) *Argue that, conditionally on the information set $\mathcal{I}$ given by the covariates $X_1,\ldots,X_n$, then $\mathsf{E}\{\frac{\partial}{\partial \beta_j}\ell(\beta_1,\beta_2)|\mathcal{I}\} = 0$ for $j = 1,2$.*

(c) *Show that the log-likelihood function has the second-order partial derivatives:*

$$\left\{ \begin{array}{cc} \frac{\partial^2}{\partial \beta_1^2}\ell(\beta_1,\beta_2) & \frac{\partial^2}{\partial \beta_1 \partial \beta_2}\ell(\beta_1,\beta_2) \\ \frac{\partial^2}{\partial \beta_2 \partial \beta_1}\ell(\beta_1,\beta_2) & \frac{\partial^2}{\partial \beta_2^2}\ell(\beta_1,\beta_2) \end{array} \right\}$$

$$= -\left\{ \begin{array}{cc} \sum_{i=1}^{n} p_i(1-p_i) & \sum_{i=1}^{n} p_i(1-p_i)X_i \\ \sum_{i=1}^{n} p_i(1-p_i)X_i & \sum_{i=1}^{n} p_i(1-p_i)X_i^2 \end{array} \right\} \stackrel{\text{def}}{=} -\mathcal{J}. \quad (4.5.1)$$

The matrix $\mathcal{J}$ is called the information matrix. In the following, we will argue that the matrix $-\mathcal{J}$ is negative definite for all values of β_1, β_2. This implies that the likelihood function has a unique maximum (Chapter 8 discusses the matrix algebra of regression).

(d) *Show that the diagonal elements are negative: $\frac{\partial^2}{\partial \beta_j^2}\ell(\beta_1,\beta_2) < 0$, for $j = 1,2$.*

(e) *Assume that not all covariates $X_1,\ldots,X_n$ are identical. Now show that the determinant is negative:*

$$\frac{\partial^2}{\partial \beta_1^2}\ell(\beta_1,\beta_2)\frac{\partial^2}{\partial \beta_2^2}\ell(\beta_1,\beta_2) - \frac{\partial^2}{\partial \beta_1 \partial \beta_2}\ell(\beta_1,\beta_2)\frac{\partial^2}{\partial \beta_2 \partial \beta_1}\ell(\beta_1,\beta_2) < 0.$$

Hint: Use the Cauchy–Schwarz inequality: $(\sum_{i=1}^{n} a_i b_i)^2 \leq (\sum_{i=1}^{n} a_i^2)(\sum_{i=1}^{n} b_i^2)$, noting that equality is achieved only if $a_i = b_i$ for all i, and with $a_i = \sqrt{p_i(1-p_i)}$ and $b_i = X_i a_i$. For a proof of the Cauchy–Schwarz inequality, see Exercise 5.7.

Exercise 4.7. *Poisson regression model. Recall the Poisson-distribution of Exercise 3.12. Now let $(Y_1,X_1),\ldots,(Y_n,X_n)$ be independent pairs of random variables so $(Y_i|X_i) \stackrel{\mathrm{D}}{=} \mathsf{Poisson}[\exp(\beta_1 + \beta_2 X_i)]$ with β_1, $\beta_2 \in \mathbb{R}^2$.*
(a) *Write down the likelihood function.*
(b) *Find the likelihood equations for β_1, β_2. Is there an exact solution? Hint: see Exercise 4.4.*
(c) * *Is there a unique solution? Hint: see Exercise 4.6.*

Computing Task 4.8. *Consider the data set for participation and the variables Part and Educ for participation and education.*
(a) *Reproduce the results presented in this chapter. When conducting the misspecification analysis of section 4.4, it is necessary to construct indicator variables for the each level of education. For OxMetrics this has been pre-coded in the algebra file* `part.alg`.
(b) *Do the same calculations using the larger data set* `census`. *Are all test results the same?*

Chapter Five

The two-variable regression model

We now return to the wage data that were analyzed in Chapter 3 to examine the association between wages and schooling. Economists have long had an interest in understanding the link between these variables with the central policy question being whether governments should provide more or fewer resources for education for the population as a whole. In the following, we look at wages and length of schooling. This analysis will give a first, but crude, answer to these questions, as no consideration is given to individuals' background and their ability to benefit from schooling. In Chapters 7 and 9, we will look at this data set again and seek to link wages with other variables in addition to education. In this book, we will not consider the question of ability. This is often modeled using the simultaneous equations techniques developed in Chapters 14 and 15.

In this chapter, we focus on developing a model for the association of one continuous variable like wages with another variable like education. In the same way as the logit model was developed from the Bernoulli model by allowing the success probability to vary with an explanatory variable, we will let the expectation parameter of the regression model in Chapter 3 vary with an explanatory variable. We start this development by giving an overview of the data and developing a conditional econometric model in §5.1 for the conditional distribution of wages given education. The maximum likelihood estimators are derived in §5.2, and a structural interpretation offered in §5.3. While the conditional formulation for wages given education hints at a causal relationship, correlations are introduced in §5.4 as a symmetric measure for the association between two variables. This feeds into a discussion of inference in §5.5.

5.1 ECONOMETRIC MODEL

As before, the data consist of $n = 3877$ observations of women for whom we have information about log wage and education. We now have an array of 2 observations for each of n individuals. We will seek to construct an appropriate description of the sample distribution. Following the approach of §4.2.1, the aim is to describe the joint density of two variables Y_i, X_i. Their density can be decomposed as:

$$\mathsf{f}\left(x_i, y_i\right) = \mathsf{f}\left(y_i \mid x_i\right) \mathsf{f}\left(x_i\right).$$

Our primary concern will be to describe the conditional density of log wages given education, while avoiding modeling the marginal distribution of education.

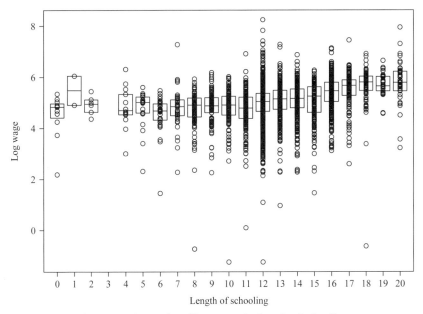

Figure 5.1 Cross plot of log wages by length of schooling

We start by looking at the conditional sample distribution using two plots. The first of these, Figure 5.1, has two features. It presents a *cross plot*, also called a scatterplot, of log wages by schooling, showing all the different outcomes of wage and schooling. In addition, for each level of schooling a *box plot* is given. Each box has three horizontal lines giving the quartiles, that is, the 25%, 50%, and 75% quantiles of the observations. From this figure, we can make two observations. First, by looking at the median, that is, the 50% quantile, we see that, apart from levels of schooling less than 6 years, there is a tendency for log wages to increase with the length of schooling. This dependency seems to be nearly linear. Second, while the range of outcome tends to be larger for levels of schooling with many observations, the sizes of the boxes do not vary much with schooling. This indicates that while the conditional expectation varies with schooling, the conditional variance varies much less with schooling. We can therefore attempt a model with constant variance, but varying expectation.

To explore the distributional variation further, we look at the conditional sample densities in Figure 5.2. The plots show the sample densities in terms of normalized histograms of log wages for the four schooling levels with most observations. Apart from a location shift, the distributions are rather similar. The density has the same general shape as seen in Figure 3.3(b). As in Chapter 3, we will approximate this distribution with a normal distribution.

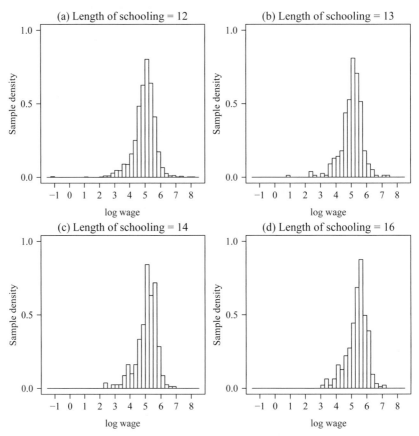

Figure 5.2 Conditional sample densities of log wages when length of schooling is 12, 13, 14, and 16 years, respectively

The analysis of the data through Figures 5.1 and 5.2 leads to assuming that the conditional distribution of log wages given schooling is normal with (conditional) expectation growing linearly with schooling and constant (conditional) variance:

$$(Y_i \mid X_i) \stackrel{\mathrm{D}}{=} \mathsf{N}\left[\beta_1 + \beta_2 X_i, \sigma^2\right].$$

The econometric model will, therefore, be based on the following assumptions:

(i) *independence*: the pairs $(X_1, Y_1), \ldots, (X_n, Y_n)$ are mutually independent;

(ii) *conditional normality*: $(Y_i \mid X_i) \stackrel{\mathrm{D}}{=} \mathsf{N}[\beta_1 + \beta_2 X_i, \sigma^2]$;

(iii) *exogeneity*: the conditioning variable X_i is exogenous;

(iv) *parameter space*: $\beta_1,\ \beta_2,\ \sigma^2 \in \mathbb{R}^2 \times \mathbb{R}_+$.

As for the simple regression model in §3.3.2, it is convenient to write assumptions (i) and (ii) in terms of a regression equation:

$$Y_i = \beta_1 + \beta_2 X_i + u_i, \tag{5.1.1}$$

where the pairs $(u_1, X_1), \ldots, (u_n, X_n)$ are independent, and $(u_i|X_i) \overset{D}{=} N[0, \sigma^2]$. The parameters β_1, β_2, also called *regression coefficients* can be interpreted using the conditional expectation:

$$E(Y_i \mid X_i) = \beta_1 + \beta_2 X_i.$$

The intercept β_1 is the conditional expectation of Y_i for an individual with explanatory variable $X_i = 0$. If $E(X_i) = 0$, it is also the marginal expectation $E(Y_i) = \beta_1$ due to the Law of Iterated Expectations, see (4.1.8). In that case, β_1 has the same interpretation as the intercept in the one-variable regression model. The parameter β_2 can be interpreted in terms of a partial derivative with respect to X_i, so:

$$\beta_2 = \frac{\partial}{\partial X_i} E(Y_i \mid X_i).$$

This means that when comparing two individuals for whom the values of X_i differ by one unit, then the conditional expectations of Y_i differ by β_2. As an example, consider a regression equation linking log wages, w, with length of schooling, S:

$$w_i = \beta_1 + \beta_2 S_i.$$

For a woman with no education, $S_i = 0$, the expected wage will be β_1. The intercept would have a more reasonable interpretation in a reparametrized model, where, for instance, the typical length of schooling (12 years) or the sample average $\overline{S}$, were subtracted from S_i. To interpret β_2 consider two women. If one has an additional year of education, her log wage will on average be β_2 higher.

To check the assumptions, we will not worry here about (i) concerning independence between individuals, but return to this in §11.4, whereas Figures 5.1 and 5.2 are an attempt to check (ii), with more formal tests being introduced in Chapter 9. The exogeneity assumption (iii) should ideally be checked by modeling the marginal distribution: although there is a chronological ordering in the present example, as individuals first get an education and then proceed into the labor market, the choice of educational level could depend on expected future wages.

5.2 ESTIMATION

We will argue that the maximum likelihood estimators for β_1, β_2 are given by:

$$\widehat{\beta}_1 = \overline{Y} - \widehat{\beta}_2 \overline{X}, \qquad \widehat{\beta}_2 = \frac{\sum_{i=1}^n Y_i (X_i - \overline{X})}{\sum_{j=1}^n (X_j - \overline{X})^2}. \tag{5.2.1}$$

This result is derived in two steps: first the likelihood function is found and then it is maximized. It is instructive to maximize the likelihood in two different ways: first, by using the likelihood equations directly; second, by reparametrizing the model to simplify the problem. Subsequently the estimator for the variance parameter σ^2 is discussed, and the results are applied to the census sample.

5.2.1 The likelihood function

The likelihood for the conditional model in which we are interested is based on the conditional density of $Y_1, \ldots, Y_n$ given $X_1, \ldots, X_n$. We derive an operational expression in a few steps. Due to the independence assumption (i), it holds:

$$f_{\beta_1, \beta_2, \sigma^2}(y_1, \ldots, y_n \mid x_1, \ldots, x_n) = \prod_{i=1}^{n} f_{\beta_1, \beta_2, \sigma^2}(y_i \mid x_i).$$

Based on the conditional normality assumption (ii), this can be rewritten as:

$$\prod_{i=1}^{n} \left(2\pi\sigma^2\right)^{-1/2} \exp\left\{ -\frac{1}{2\sigma^2}(y_i - \beta_1 - \beta_2 x_i)^2 \right\}.$$

Finally, since products of exponentials are exponentials of sums, this equals:

$$\left(2\pi\sigma^2\right)^{-n/2} \exp\left\{ -\frac{1}{2\sigma^2} \sum_{i=1}^{n} (y_i - \beta_1 - \beta_2 x_i)^2 \right\}.$$

The last line leads to the conditional likelihood:

$$\begin{aligned}
\mathsf{L}_{Y_1, \ldots, Y_n \mid X_1, \ldots, X_n}\left(\beta_1, \beta_2, \sigma^2\right) &= f_{\beta_1, \beta_2, \sigma^2}(Y_1, \ldots, Y_n \mid X_1, \ldots, X_n) \\
&= \left(2\pi\sigma^2\right)^{-n/2} \exp\left\{ -\frac{1}{2\sigma^2} \sum_{i=1}^{n} (Y_i - \beta_1 - \beta_2 X_i)^2 \right\}. \quad (5.2.2)
\end{aligned}$$

The corresponding log-likelihood function is:

$$\ell_{Y_1, \ldots, Y_n \mid X_1, \ldots, X_n}\left(\beta_1, \beta_2, \sigma^2\right) = -\frac{n}{2}\log\left(2\pi\sigma^2\right) - \frac{1}{2\sigma^2} \sum_{i=1}^{n} (Y_i - \beta_1 - \beta_2 X_i)^2.$$

5.2.2 Estimation using the original parameters

Maximizing the log-likelihood function with respect to β_1, β_2 is equivalent to minimizing the sum of squared deviations, as in §3.3.4:

$$\mathsf{SSD}(\beta_1, \beta_2) = \sum_{i=1}^{n} (Y_i - \beta_1 - \beta_2 X_i)^2.$$

This is a quadratic function of two arguments, and as such it will have a unique minimum. To find this minimum, we differentiate with respect to β_1 and β_2:

$$\frac{\partial}{\partial \beta_1} \sum_{i=1}^{n} (Y_i - \beta_1 - \beta_2 X_i)^2 = -2 \sum_{i=1}^{n} (Y_i - \beta_1 - \beta_2 X_i),$$

$$\frac{\partial}{\partial \beta_2} \sum_{i=1}^{n} (Y_i - \beta_1 - \beta_2 X_i)^2 = -2 \sum_{i=1}^{n} (Y_i - \beta_1 - \beta_2 X_i) X_i.$$

Equating these expressions to zero gives the likelihood equations:

$$-2\sum_{i=1}^{n}\left(Y_i - \widehat{\beta}_1 - \widehat{\beta}_2 X_i\right) = 0, \qquad (5.2.3)$$

$$-2\sum_{i=1}^{n}\left(Y_i - \widehat{\beta}_1 - \widehat{\beta}_2 X_i\right) X_i = 0. \qquad (5.2.4)$$

These two equations in two unknowns have to be solved simultaneously. To do so, take either of the two equations, for instance the first, (5.2.3). Solving for $\widehat{\beta}_1$ as a function of $\widehat{\beta}_2$ shows:

$$n\widehat{\beta}_1 = \sum_{i=1}^{n} Y_i - \widehat{\beta}_2 \sum_{i=1}^{n} X_i \qquad \text{hence} \qquad \widehat{\beta}_1 = \overline{Y} - \widehat{\beta}_2 \overline{X}.$$

Inserting this into the other equation, (5.2.4), gives:

$$\widehat{\beta}_2 \sum_{i=1}^{n} X_i^2 = \sum_{i=1}^{n} Y_i X_i - \widehat{\beta}_1 \sum_{i=1}^{n} X_i = \sum_{i=1}^{n} Y_i X_i - \left(\overline{Y} - \widehat{\beta}_2 \overline{X}\right) \sum_{i=1}^{n} X_i,$$

or equivalently, using Exercise 5.5:

$$\widehat{\beta}_2 \left(\sum_{i=1}^{n} X_i^2 - n\overline{X}^2\right) = \sum_{i=1}^{n} Y_i X_i - n\overline{Y}\,\overline{X} = \sum_{i=1}^{n} Y_i \left(X_i - \overline{X}\right).$$

Solving this for $\widehat{\beta}_2$ and inserting the result in the above equation for $\widehat{\beta}_1$ gives the solutions in (5.2.1).

If we compare these manipulations with those of the simple regression model in §3.3.4, it is clear that the algebraic complexity has increased. If a further regressor were introduced in the model, we would get three likelihood equations to solve, which would be even more cumbersome. The natural mathematical tool to address this issue is matrix algebra, which is exactly designed to solve such systems of linear equations, which we will explore in Chapter 6. Whether one uses matrix algebra or not, it is convenient to look at a reparametrization of the model to simplify the problem of deriving the estimators.

5.2.3 Orthogonalizing variables and reparametrizations

The complexity in the previous approach to maximizing the likelihood function comes from the fact that both expectation parameters β_1, β_2 appear in each of the two likelihood equations (5.2.3) and (5.2.4). In the following, we will show that the model can be reparametrized in such a way that two new likelihood equations emerge, each with just one unknown parameter. This will facilitate solving the likelihood equations, and also help the general interpretation and use of regression models.

To motivate a reparametrization of the model, we will begin by having a closer look at the maximum likelihood estimator for β_2 in (5.2.1). We start by giving the regressors more generic names: $X_{1,i} = 1$ for the constant and $X_{2,i} = X_i$ for the stochastic regressor. The variable $X_{2\cdot 1,i} = X_i - \overline{X}$ occurring in both the numerator and the denominator of $\widehat{\beta}_2$ in (5.2.1) can be thought of as the residual from regressing $X_{2,i}$ on $X_{1,i}$. The notation $X_{2\cdot 1,i}$ emphasizes that this variable is found by removing, or partialling out, information about $X_{2,i}$ also reflected in $X_{1,i}$, which is the level, or average, $\overline{X}$. We can now write:

$$\widehat{\beta}_2 = \frac{\sum_{i=1}^{n} X_{2\cdot 1,i} Y_i}{\sum_{i=1}^{n} X_{2\cdot 1,i}^2}. \tag{5.2.5}$$

Turning to the model equation (5.1.1), we rename the regressors likewise:

$$Y_i = \beta_1 + \beta_2 X_i + u_i = \beta_1 X_{1,i} + \beta_2 X_{2,i} + u_i.$$

This linear equation can be rewritten by decomposing $X_{2,i} = X_{2\cdot 1,i} + \widehat{X}_{2,i}$, where $X_{2\cdot 1,i} = X_i - \overline{X}$ is the residual and $\widehat{X}_{2,i} = \overline{X} = \overline{X} X_{1,i}$ is the predictor, respectively, from regressing X_i on a constant. Doing this transformation yields:

$$Y_i = \beta_1 X_{1,i} + \beta_2 \left(X_{2\cdot 1,i} + \widehat{X}_{2,i} \right) + u_i$$
$$= \left(\beta_1 + \beta_2 \overline{X} \right) X_{1,i} + \beta_2 X_{2\cdot 1,i} + u_i.$$

Rename the parameters:

$$\delta_1 = \beta_1 + \beta_2 \overline{X}, \qquad \delta_2 = \beta_2, \tag{5.2.6}$$

and insert these expressions to get a *reparametrized* model equation:

$$Y_i = \delta_1 X_{1,i} + \delta_2 X_{2\cdot 1,i} + u_i. \tag{5.2.7}$$

The regressors of this reparametrized model satisfy:

$$\sum_{i=1}^{n} X_{2\cdot 1,i} X_{1,i} = 0, \tag{5.2.8}$$

due to the normal equation (3.3.4). We say that the regressors $(X_{1,i}, X_{2\cdot 1,i})$ are *orthogonal*. The reparametrized model is therefore found by orthogonalizing X_i with respect to the constant.

The sum of squared deviations for the reparametrized model is:

$$\mathsf{SSD}(\delta_1, \delta_2) = \sum_{i=1}^{n} (Y_i - \delta_1 - \delta_2 X_{2\cdot 1,i})^2.$$

Differentiating gives, as in §5.2.2:

$$\frac{\partial}{\partial \delta_1} \sum_{i=1}^{n} (Y_i - \delta_1 - \delta_2 X_{2\cdot 1,i})^2 = -2 \sum_{i=1}^{n} (Y_i - \delta_1 - \delta_2 X_{2\cdot 1,i}),$$

$$\frac{\partial}{\partial \delta_2} \sum_{i=1}^{n} (Y_i - \delta_1 - \delta_2 X_{2\cdot 1,i})^2 = -2 \sum_{i=1}^{n} (Y_i - \delta_1 - \delta_2 X_{2\cdot 1,i}) X_{2\cdot 1,i}.$$

By exploiting the orthogonality property $\sum_{i=1}^{n} X_{2\cdot 1,i} = 0$, these reduce to:

$$\frac{\partial}{\partial \delta_1} \sum_{i=1}^{n} (Y_i - \delta_1 - \delta_2 X_{2\cdot 1,i})^2 = -2 \sum_{i=1}^{n} (Y_i - \delta_1),$$

$$\frac{\partial}{\partial \delta_2} \sum_{i=1}^{n} (Y_i - \delta_1 - \delta_2 X_{2\cdot 1,i})^2 = -2 \sum_{i=1}^{n} (Y_i - \delta_2 X_{2\cdot 1,i}) X_{2\cdot 1,i},$$

and hence result in the likelihood equations:

$$-2 \sum_{i=1}^{n} \left(Y_i - \widehat{\delta}_1 \right) = 0, \qquad -2 \sum_{i=1}^{n} \left(Y_i - \widehat{\delta}_2 X_{2\cdot 1,i} \right) X_{2\cdot 1,i} = 0.$$

These likelihood equations are easily solved by:

$$\widehat{\delta}_1 = \overline{Y}, \qquad \widehat{\delta}_2 = \frac{\sum_{i=1}^{n} Y_i X_{2\cdot 1,i}}{\sum_{j=1}^{n} X_{2\cdot 1,j}^2}.$$

We see that not only $\widehat{\delta}_2 = \widehat{\beta}_2$ as expected but that the estimator $\widehat{\delta}_1$ has the same expression as in the one-variable regression model; see (3.3.5). This means that adding to the one-variable regression model a regressor that is orthogonal to the constant, does not alter the regression estimate for the intercept parameter. The population version of this is that $E(X_i) = 0$, as discussed in connection with the interpretation of the regression in §5.1. We will return to this point in the empirical illustration below.

There is a one-one relation between the parameters of the original model (5.1.1) and those of the reparametrized model (5.2.7) given by (5.2.6), that is:

$$\beta_2 = \delta_2, \qquad \beta_1 = \delta_1 - \delta_2 \overline{X}. \tag{5.2.9}$$

Inserting the estimators $\widehat{\delta}_1, \widehat{\delta}_2$ gives the desired expressions for $\widehat{\beta}_1, \widehat{\beta}_2$ in (5.2.1). This is due to the equivariance property of the likelihood function also noted in §1.3.3. It follows that the predictions and the residuals from the original model and from the reparametrized model are the same:

$$\widehat{Y}_i = \widehat{\beta}_1 + \widehat{\beta}_2 X_i = \widehat{\delta}_1 + \widehat{\delta}_2 X_{2\cdot 1,i}, \tag{5.2.10}$$

$$\widehat{u}_i = Y_i - \widehat{Y}_i = Y_i - \overline{Y} - \widehat{\beta}_2 \left(X_i - \overline{X} \right) = Y_i - \widehat{\delta}_1 - \widehat{\delta}_2 X_{2\cdot 1,i}. \tag{5.2.11}$$

The interpretations of the parameters in the two models will, however, be somewhat different. While the slope parameters are the same, $\beta_2 = \delta_2$, the intercepts are different. The intercept in the original model, β_1, is the expected value of Y_i for an individual with $X_i = 0$. This could be an extreme value relative to the sample, whereas δ_1 is the expected value for an individual with an average value of X_i.

In this approach, $\widehat{\beta}_2$ was found by orthogonalizing $X_{2,i}$ with respect to $X_{1,i}$. The approach is generic, so interchanging the role of $X_{1,i}$ and $X_{2,i}$ gives an easy way of finding $\widehat{\beta}_1$. Denoting the residual from regressing $X_{1,i}$ on $X_{2,i}$, we get:

$$\widehat{\beta}_1 = \frac{\sum_{i=1}^n X_{1\cdot 2,i} Y_i}{\sum_{i=1}^n X_{1\cdot 2,i}^2}, \qquad \text{where} \qquad X_{1\cdot 2,i} = 1 - \frac{\sum_{j=1}^n X_j}{\sum_{j=1}^n X_j^2} X_i. \qquad (5.2.12)$$

This expression can also be found directly from (5.2.1); see Exercise 5.4.

5.2.4 The variance estimator

The variance parameter σ^2 is now estimated exactly as in §3.3.4. Inserting the residuals (5.2.11) in the log-likelihood function gives:

$$\ell_{Y_1,\ldots,Y_n|X_1,\ldots,X_n}\left(\widehat{\beta}_1,\widehat{\beta}_2,\sigma^2\right) = -\frac{n}{2}\log\left(2\pi\sigma^2\right) - \frac{1}{2\sigma^2}\sum_{i=1}^n \widehat{u}_i^2.$$

As in §3.3.4, the maximum likelihood estimator for σ^2 is therefore:

$$\widehat{\sigma}^2 = \frac{1}{n}\sum_{i=1}^n \widehat{u}_i^2, \qquad (5.2.13)$$

which in turn shows that the likelihood function has an overall maximum given by:

$$\max_{\beta_1,\beta_2,\sigma^2} \mathsf{L}_{Y_1,\ldots,Y_n|X_1,\ldots,X_n}\left(\beta_1,\beta_2,\sigma^2\right)$$
$$= \mathsf{L}_{Y_1,\ldots,Y_n|X_1,\ldots,X_n}\left(\widehat{\beta}_1,\widehat{\beta}_2,\widehat{\sigma}^2\right) = \left(2\pi\widehat{\sigma}^2 e\right)^{-n/2}. \qquad (5.2.14)$$

5.2.5 The wage-education regression

The two-variable model is now used for analyzing the relation between log wages, w_i, and the length of schooling, S_i. From the labor force data we can get:

$$\sum_{i=1}^n S_i = 48943, \qquad \sum_{i=1}^n w_i = 19460.1, \qquad n = 3877, \qquad (5.2.15)$$

$$\sum_{i=1}^n S_i^2 = 645663, \qquad \sum_{i=1}^n w_i^2 = 99876, \qquad \sum_{i=1}^n S_i w_i = 247775, \qquad (5.2.16)$$

from which we can compute:

$$\widehat{\beta}_1 = 4.06, \qquad \widehat{\beta}_2 = 0.076, \qquad \widehat{\sigma}^2 = 0.526 = (0.725)^2, \qquad (5.2.17)$$

$$\widehat{\delta}_1 = 5.02, \qquad \widehat{\delta}_2 = 0.076, \qquad \widehat{\ell} = -4254.3. \qquad (5.2.18)$$

Compare these with the values found in (3.3.11).

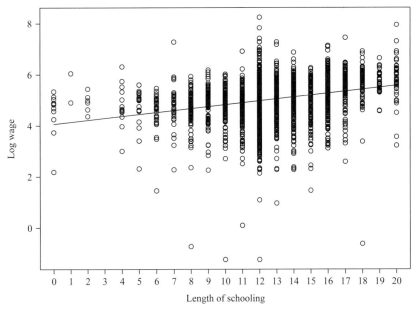

Figure 5.3 Cross plot of log wages by schooling with added regression line

Figure 5.3 shows the estimated regression line:

$$\widehat{w}_i = 4.06 + 0.076 S_i = 5.02 + 0.076 \left(S_i - \overline{S} \right). \qquad (5.2.19)$$

The interpretation of the intercept $\widehat{\beta}_1$ from the original parametrization is that it shows the estimated expected wage for individuals with no schooling at all. While there are some of those in the sample, most individuals have been to school, so $\widehat{\beta}_1$ focuses attention on an atypical situation. In contrast, the intercept $\widehat{\delta}_1$ from the orthogonalized parametrization is the estimated expected wage for someone with an average length of schooling, $\overline{S} = 12.6$. Nobody in the sample actually has that length of schooling, but at least it is a value in the middle of the range for the length of schooling.

The interpretation of the slope coefficient $\widehat{\beta}_2$ is as follows. Comparing two individuals where one has an additional year of education, we would expect a difference in log wages of about $\widehat{\beta}_1 = 0.076$.

It is interesting to compare the estimated two-variable regression in (5.2.19) with the result from the one-variable model, namely $\widehat{w}_i = 5.02$.

This intercept is the same as that of the orthogonalized two-variable regression, whereas it is different from the non-orthogonalized two-variable regression. An interpretation of this match is that the one-variable model concerns the marginal distribution of wages, while the two-variable model concerns the conditional distribution of wages given education. These will be different, unless they are made to be the same through an orthogonalization.

5.3 STRUCTURAL INTERPRETATION

It is natural to interpret a regression like (5.2.19) in the context of economic theory. We will start by discussing the notion of economic structure, and then move on to some specific structural interpretations of the regression (5.2.19).

5.3.1 Structure

The notion of structure has long been discussed in econometrics (see Hendry, 1995a, §2.3). We will think of structure as the set of basic, permanent features of the economic mechanism. The parameters of an economic structure may include those of agents' decision rules, but no presumption is made here that those rules are derived by intertemporal optimization. A structure is often specified up to some unknown coefficients, b varying in a set $\mathbb{B}$ say, which can be called structural parameters. Thus, $b \in \mathbb{B}$ defines a structure if it is invariant, in the sense of not changing with interventions to the economy, and if it directly characterizes the relations of the economy under analysis, in the sense of not being derived from more basic parameters.

A number of necessary conditions follow as consequences of this definition. A parameter of an econometric model can be structural only if it is:
   (1) constant, and so is invariant to an extension of the sample;
   (2) unaltered by changes elsewhere in the economy, and so is invariant to regime shifts; and
   (3) remains the same for extensions of the information set, and so is invariant to adding more variables to an analysis.

All of these aspects are open to scrutiny empirically, so necessary attributes of structure are testable. However, because structural relationships must not be derived ones, structure entails a correspondence between a model and reality that is not open to independent testing. Thus, a parameter need not be structural even when it is invariant to all three extensions of information, since it could be derived from more basic structural parameters, so there are no sufficient conditions. Nymoen (2002) analyzes the related notion of a "structural interpretation", versus a "structural representation", of an economy. He contrasts the first phrase denoting "derived from theory" as in Svensson, Houg, Solheim and Steigum (2002), with an operational concept based on the second which embodies not only theory content, but also "explanatory power, stability and robustness to regime shifts". In other words, "structure" is not guaranteed by a close connection with any specific theory-based analyses.

5.3.2 Elasticity and marginal return

Economic analysis, as in Mincer (1974), may lead to the idea that the log wage, w, and length of schooling, S, are linked through the log-linear equation:

$$w = b_1 + b_2 S, \tag{5.3.1}$$

where b_1, b_2 are structural parameters, and hence denoted by roman letters rather than Greek letters. The elasticity and the marginal return from schooling can be derived from this log-linear equation using the chain rule and the facts that $(\partial w / \partial W) = 1/W$ and $(\partial s / \partial S) = 1/S$, where $s = \log S$:

$$\frac{\partial (\log W)}{\partial (\log S)} = \frac{\partial w}{\partial s} = \left(\frac{\partial w}{\partial S}\right)\left(\frac{\partial S}{\partial s}\right) = b_2 S,$$

$$\frac{\partial W}{\partial S} = \left(\frac{\partial w}{\partial S}\right)\left(\frac{\partial W}{\partial w}\right) = b_2 W.$$

These formulas show that the elasticity increases with the length of schooling, while the marginal return increases with the level of the wage.

It is tempting to link the structural equation (5.3.1) to the estimated regression equation (5.2.19), and in particular to equate b_2 and $\widehat{\beta}_2$. This could be justified by the notion of Frisch (1934) that the structural equation is the exact economic relation, which would hold if data were perfectly measured. However, is invariance likely here?

5.3.3 Omitted variable bias

An economic analysis inspired by the theory of human capital as in Becker (1964) may include a notion of ability, A. This suggests a new structural equation:

$$w_i = b_1 + b_2 S_i + b_3 A_i + v_i. \tag{5.3.2}$$

In this equation, indices i are included to emphasize that the relation holds for all individuals. A random error v_i is also included and can be given a structural interpretation. In general it will not be directly linked to the error u_i in the statistical model equation (5.1.1), which describes the conditional sample distribution of u_i given S_i. A general discussion of the possible interpretations will be given in Chapter 11. For now, to make v_i more specific, we will assume that it is independent across individuals and satisfies $\mathsf{E}_s(v_i | S_i, A_i) = 0$, where the subscript s indicates that the expectation is taken with respect to the distribution of the structural model.

The structural parameters are now b_1, b_2, b_3. While the variable ability is recognized to be important in earnings models, it is generally unobservable and can only be described partially by measures based on, for instance, intelligence tests.

We can analyze the consequences of linking the estimated regression equation (5.2.19), to the structural equation (5.3.2) and in particular to relate $\widehat{\beta}_2$ to b_2. Manipulating the expression for $\widehat{\beta}_2$ in the context of the structural equation gives:

$$\widehat{\beta}_2 = \frac{\sum_{i=1}^n w_i \left(S_i - \overline{S}\right)}{\sum_{j=1}^n \left(S_j - \overline{S}\right)^2} \qquad [\,(5.2.1)\,]$$

$$= \frac{\sum_{i=1}^n \left(b_1 + b_2 S_i + b_3 A_i + v_i\right)\left(S_i - \overline{S}\right)}{\sum_{j=1}^n \left(S_j - \overline{S}\right)^2} \qquad [\,(5.3.2)\,]$$

$$= b_2 + b_3 \frac{\sum_{i=1}^n A_i \left(S_i - \overline{S}\right)}{\sum_{j=1}^n \left(S_j - \overline{S}\right)^2} + \frac{\sum_{i=1}^n v_i \left(S_i - \overline{S}\right)}{\sum_{j=1}^n \left(S_j - \overline{S}\right)^2}. \qquad [\text{ Exercise 2.5 }]$$

The conditional expectation of the last term given all the variables $S_1, \ldots, S_n$ and $A_1, \ldots A_n$ is zero when evaluated with respect to the structural distribution. Thus:

$$\mathrm{E}_s\left(\widehat{\beta}_2 \,\middle|\, S_1, \ldots, S_n, A_1, \ldots A_n\right) = b_2 + b_3 \frac{\sum_{i=1}^n A_i \left(S_i - \overline{S}\right)}{\sum_{j=1}^n \left(S_j - \overline{S}\right)^2}. \qquad (5.3.3)$$

In general, the conditional expectation of $\widehat{\beta}_2$ is different from the structural parameter b_2. If the statistical model had included ability as a regressor, the conditional expectation would be exactly b_2. In the context of the structural equation (5.3.2), we say that $\widehat{\beta}_2$, as an estimator for the structural parameter b_2, suffers from *omitted variable bias*. This bias would disappear either if $b_3 = 0$, or if ability and schooling were orthogonal, so that their sample covariance would be zero.

It is an open research question how best to deal with the omitted variable bias stemming from ability. One approach is to extend the structural model with another equation specifying how ability is determined by observable variables and then use the identification approach that will be introduced in Chapter 15. Ashenfelter, Harmon and Oosterbeek (1999) and Card (1999) provide overviews of recent research into earnings models.

5.4 CORRELATIONS

In the two-variable regression model, the estimator for the slope parameter $\widehat{\beta}_2$ can be written as:

$$\widehat{\beta}_2 = \frac{n^{-1} \sum_{i=1}^n \left(Y_i - \overline{Y}\right)\left(X_i - \overline{X}\right)}{n^{-1} \sum_{j=1}^n \left(X_j - \overline{X}\right)^2},$$

so it is the ratio of the sample covariance of Y_i and X_i to the sample variance of X_i. It is asymmetric, in that the regressand Y_i and the regressor X_i enter differently. In the following, we will look at correlations that represent a symmetric measure for the association between the variables.

5.4.1 Sample correlations

The *sample correlation* has the form:

$$r = \frac{\sum_{i=1}^{n} \left(X_i - \overline{X}\right)\left(Y_i - \overline{Y}\right)}{\sqrt{\sum_{j=1}^{n} \left(X_j - \overline{X}\right)^2 \sum_{k=1}^{n} \left(Y_k - \overline{Y}\right)^2}}. \tag{5.4.1}$$

It has the following properties.

(1) It is unit free: $r_{X,Y}^2 = r_{aX+c,bY+d}^2$, for $a, b \neq 0$.

Thus scaling does not matter, so the correlation of wages and education is the same whether wages are measured in dollars or cents. Further, a location shift does not matter either, so a correlation involving log wages is also invariant to whether wages are measured in dollars or cents. However, correlations are not invariant to non-linear transformations such as logarithms, so the correlations of education with wages and with log wages would be different.

(2) $r = 0$ if the sample covariance of X_i, Y_i is zero;

(3) $r^2 \leq 1$, with $r^2 = 1$ if and only if $Y_i = aX_i + c$ for all $i = 1, \ldots, n$.

The last statement follows from the inequality:

$$\{\widehat{\mathrm{Cov}}(X, Y)\}^2 \leq \widehat{\mathrm{Var}}(X)\widehat{\mathrm{Var}}(Y),$$

which arises from the Cauchy–Schwarz inequality (see Exercise 5.7).

In the log-wage–on–schooling example, $r^2 = 0.073 = (0.270)^2$.

5.4.2 Population correlations

The *population correlation* is defined as:

$$\rho_{X,Y} = \frac{\mathrm{Cov}\,(X, Y)}{\sqrt{\mathrm{Var}\,(X)\,\mathrm{Var}\,(Y)}}.$$

It has similar properties to the sample correlation:

(1) It is unit free: $\rho_{X,Y} = \rho_{aX+c,bY+d}$, for $a, b \neq 0$;

(2) $\rho_{X,Y} = 0$ if X, Y are uncorrelated;

(3) $\rho_{X,Y}^2 \leq 1$, with $\rho_{X,Y}^2 = 1$ if and only if $Y = aX + c$.

The notation distinguishing the sample and population correlations differs from the usual scheme used in this book. Here a Greek letter is used for the population correlation and the corresponding Roman letter for the sample version. This follows the tradition of Fisher (1915).

5.4.3 Sample correlations and the two-variable model

There are some interesting connections between the sample correlation r^2 and the estimators $\widehat{\beta}_2$ and $\widehat{\sigma}^2$. In particular, the link with the variance estimators turns out to be useful.

The connection between $\widehat{\beta}_2$ and r^2 comes about by considering both the regressions of Y_i on X_i and of X_i on Y_i given by:

$$Y_i = \beta_1 + \beta_2 X_i + u_i, \tag{5.4.2}$$
$$X_i = \gamma_1 + \gamma_2 Y_i + v_i. \tag{5.4.3}$$

Using the estimation results from §5.2, we can see that:

$$r^2 = \widehat{\beta}_2 \widehat{\gamma}_2, \tag{5.4.4}$$

where $\widehat{\beta}_2$ is the least-squares estimator from (5.4.2) and $\widehat{\gamma}_2$ is the least-squares estimator from (5.4.3). Since r^2 is smaller than unity when the equations are not exact, we have that $\widehat{\beta}_2 \widehat{\gamma}_2 < 1$, where one might perhaps have expected $\widehat{\beta}_2 \widehat{\gamma}_2$ to be unity since the two regression relations appear to be the inverses of each other.

The variance estimator $\widehat{\sigma}^2$ has an even more important relation to r^2. As argued in Exercise 5.9, the expression for the estimator given in (5.2.13) can be rewritten as:

$$\widehat{\sigma}^2 = \left(1 - r^2\right) \frac{1}{n} \sum_{i=1}^{n} \left(Y_i - \overline{Y}\right)^2. \tag{5.4.5}$$

The one-variable regression model explored in Chapter 3 can be viewed as a restriction of the present two-variable model where $\beta_2 = 0$. Thus, denoting the variance estimator from the one-variable model by $\widehat{\sigma}_R^2$, we get from (3.3.9):

$$\widehat{\sigma}_R^2 = \frac{1}{n} \sum_{i=1}^{n} \left(Y_i - \overline{Y}\right)^2.$$

The ratio of the two variance estimators is:

$$\frac{\widehat{\sigma}^2}{\widehat{\sigma}_R^2} = 1 - r^2, \tag{5.4.6}$$

so the squared sample correlation is a measure of how much the residual variance is reduced by including the regressor X_i in the model. It is interesting to note that this expression is symmetric in Y_i and X_i; so it is the same when we regress Y_i on X_i and vice versa.

In the log-wage–on–schooling example, $1 - r^2 = 0.937$. Compare that with the ratio of the variance estimates in (3.3.11) and (5.2.17).

There is one further connection between the variance estimators and the correlation. The restricted variance estimator $\widehat{\sigma}_R^2$ can be decomposed by adding and subtracting the predictor $\widehat{Y}_i = \widehat{\delta}_1 + \widehat{\delta}_2(X_i - \overline{X})$, which gives:

$$n\widehat{\sigma}_R^2 = \sum_{i=1}^n \{(Y_i - \widehat{Y}_i) + (\widehat{Y}_i - \overline{Y})\}^2 = \sum_{i=1}^n (Y_i - \widehat{Y}_i)^2 + \sum_{i=1}^n (\widehat{Y}_i - \overline{Y})^2, \quad (5.4.7)$$

because of the following orthogonality property, derived in Exercise 5.10:

$$\sum_{i=1}^n (Y_i - \widehat{Y}_i)(\widehat{Y}_i - \overline{Y}) = 0. \qquad (5.4.8)$$

The decomposition (5.4.7) can also be written as:

$$\text{TSS} = \text{RSS} + \text{ESS}, \qquad (5.4.9)$$

using the notation:

$$\text{explained sum of squares}: \qquad \text{ESS} = \sum_{i=1}^n (\widehat{Y}_i - \overline{Y})^2,$$

$$\text{residual sum of squares}: \qquad \text{RSS} = n\widehat{\sigma}^2 = \sum_{i=1}^n \widehat{u}_i^2,$$

$$\text{total sum of squares}: \qquad \text{TSS} = \sum_{i=1}^n (Y_i - \overline{Y})^2.$$

The sample correlation can therefore be written in terms of these sums of squares:

$$r^2 = 1 - \frac{\text{RSS}}{\text{TSS}} = \frac{\text{ESS}}{\text{TSS}}, \qquad (5.4.10)$$

see Exercise 5.11. Then (5.4.10) shows that r^2 can be interpreted as a measure of the proportion of the total variation of Y_i that is explained by the regressor X_i in the model (5.4.2). One could, therefore, say that r^2 is a measure of goodness-of-fit of the unrestricted model relative to the restricted model.

5.5 INFERENCE

As in earlier chapters, we will start by looking at confidence intervals, then turn our attention to the likelihood ratio test statistic and its asymptotic and exact distribution properties.

5.5.1 Confidence intervals

We can construct approximate confidence intervals for the estimators $\widehat{\beta}_1$ and $\widehat{\beta}_2$ in the same way as in §3.4.1. To do so, we need to find their distributions.

We start with the estimator $\widehat{\beta}_2$, recalling the notation of §5.2.3, so that:

$$\widehat{\beta}_2 = \frac{\sum_{i=1}^n X_{2\cdot1,i} Y_i}{\sum_{i=1}^n X_{2\cdot1,i}^2} = \frac{\sum_{i=1}^n X_{2\cdot1,i}(\beta_1 X_{1,i} + \beta_2 X_{2,i} + u_i)}{\sum_{i=1}^n X_{2\cdot1,i}^2},$$

where the model equation has been inserted. Since:

$$\sum_{i=1}^{n} X_{2\cdot1,i}X_{1,i} = 0, \qquad \sum_{i=1}^{n} X_{2\cdot1,i}X_{2,i} = \sum_{i=1}^{n} X_{2\cdot1,i}^2, \qquad (5.5.1)$$

of which the first is the equation (5.2.8), and the second stems from Exercise 2.5, the expression for $\widehat{\beta}_2$ reduces to:

$$\widehat{\beta}_2 = \beta_2 + \frac{\sum_{i=1}^{n} X_{2\cdot1,i}u_i}{\sum_{i=1}^{n} X_{2\cdot1,i}^2}.$$

Conditional on the information set $\mathcal{I}$ given by the regressors $X_1, \ldots, X_n$, the second term is a linear combination of the independently, normally distributed variables $u_1, \ldots, u_n$. Therefore $\widehat{\beta}_2$ is conditionally normally distributed. We only need to determine the conditional expectation and variance to get:

$$\left(\widehat{\beta}_2 \,\middle|\, \mathcal{I}\right) \overset{D}{=} \mathsf{N}\left[\beta_2, \frac{\sigma^2}{\sum_{i=1}^{n} X_{2\cdot1,i}^2}\right].$$

This expression is similar to that for the one-variable regression apart from the denominator, which has changed from n to $\sum_{i=1}^{n} X_{2\cdot1,i}^2$. Both will, however, have to be large to get precise estimates. Likewise, by interchanging the roles of $X_{1,i}$ and $X_{2,i}$, it is seen that:

$$\left(\widehat{\beta}_1 \,\middle|\, \mathcal{I}\right) \overset{D}{=} \mathsf{N}\left[\beta_1, \frac{\sigma^2}{\sum_{i=1}^{n} X_{1\cdot2,i}^2}\right].$$

Inserting the error variance estimator into these variance expressions and taking square roots yields the standard errors, for instance:

$$\widehat{\mathsf{se}}(\widehat{\beta}_2) = \sqrt{\widehat{\mathsf{Var}}\left(\widehat{\beta}_2 \,\middle|\, \mathcal{I}\right)} = \frac{\widehat{\sigma}^2}{\sum_{i=1}^{n} X_{2\cdot1,i}^2},$$

and the approximate 95% confidence intervals:

$$\widehat{\beta}_k - 2\widehat{\mathsf{se}}(\widehat{\beta}_k) \le \beta_k \le \widehat{\beta}_k + 2\widehat{\mathsf{se}}(\widehat{\beta}_k). \qquad (5.5.2)$$

In the log–wage–on–schooling application, we find the standard errors:

$$\widehat{\mathsf{se}}(\widehat{\beta}_1) = 0.056, \qquad \widehat{\mathsf{se}}(\widehat{\beta}_2) = 0.0043.$$

The approximate 95% confidence intervals for the estimates are, therefore:

$$3.95 \le \beta_1 \le 4.17 \qquad 0.067 \le \beta_2 \le 0.085.$$

Economic theory for wages suggests that wages should increase with the length of schooling. This seems to be the case here since $\widehat{\beta}_2$ is positive, and zero is not included in the confidence interval.

5.5.2 The likelihood ratio test

A formal test for the hypothesis that there is no association between schooling and log wages can easily be constructed. This is done by considering the likelihood ratio test for the restriction given by the hypothesis $\beta_2 = 0$.

The present two-variable model is the unrestricted model. An expression for the maximum of the likelihood function is given in terms of the variance estimator $\widehat{\sigma}^2$ in (5.2.14). The one-variable model of Chapter 3 represents the restricted model, with the restricted maximum of the likelihood function given in (3.3.10) in terms of the restricted variance estimator, which was then called $\widehat{\sigma}^2$, but is now called $\widehat{\sigma}_R^2$ to avoid confusion. Then the likelihood ratio test statistic is given by:

$$Q = \frac{\max_{restricted} \mathsf{L}_{Y_1,\ldots,Y_n|X_1,\ldots,X_n}\left(\beta_1,\beta_2,\sigma^2\right)}{\max_{unrestricted} \mathsf{L}_{Y_1,\ldots,Y_n|X_1,\ldots,X_n}\left(\beta_1,\beta_2,\sigma^2\right)} = \left(\frac{\widehat{\sigma}_R^2}{\widehat{\sigma}^2}\right)^{-n/2}.$$

As this statistic involves only the variance estimators, Fisher coined the phrase *analysis of variance*, or ANOVA , for such an analysis.

The log-likelihood ratio statistic is now:

$$\mathsf{LR} = -2\log Q = -n\log\left(\frac{\widehat{\sigma}^2}{\widehat{\sigma}_R^2}\right) = -n\log\left(1 - r^2\right),$$

due to the relation (5.4.6). Thus, when Y_i and X_i have a small squared sample correlation, then the test statistic is small. As for previous likelihood ratio tests, we have the asymptotic distributional result:

$$\mathsf{LR} \overset{\mathsf{D}}{\approx} \chi^2\left[1\right].$$

When one is concerned about the sign of the parameter in question, the signed likelihood ratio test developed in §4.3.3 can be used. This satisfies:

$$w = \text{sign}\left(\widehat{\beta}_2\right)\sqrt{\mathsf{LR}} \overset{\mathsf{D}}{\approx} \mathsf{N}\left[0,1\right].$$

A variant of the likelihood ratio test is the *Lagrange multiplier test* , also called the *score test*. In the regression context, this test is given in terms of the test statistic nr^2. When the null hypothesis is correct, then r^2 tends to be small, so the two test statistics are linked through a Taylor expansion, as in (2.4.1):

$$\mathsf{LR} = -n\log\left(1 - r^2\right) = nr^2 + \text{small terms}. \qquad (5.5.3)$$

It can be proved that nr^2 is also asymptotically χ^2-distributed:

$$nr^2 \overset{\mathsf{D}}{\approx} \chi^2\left[1\right]. \qquad (5.5.4)$$

In the log-wage–on–education application:

$$\text{LR} = -2\log Q = -3877 \log{(0.937)} = 294 = (17)^2,$$

with $p < 0.001$ using a $\chi^2[1]$-distribution. Thus, the hypothesis of no association between log wages and schooling is rejected. Economic theory indicates that we should have a positive association between wages and schooling and, indeed, $\widehat{\beta}_2$ is positive. We can therefore compute the one-sided, signed likelihood ratio test statistic $w = +\sqrt{\text{LR}} = 17$, with $p < 0.001$ using a $N[0, 1]$-distribution. Once again the hypothesis of no association is rejected.

5.5.3 Exact inference

As we saw in §3.4.2, exact distribution theory can be worked out for regression analysis. We start by computing the least-squares variance estimator:

$$s^2 = \frac{n}{n-2}\widehat{\sigma}^2 = \frac{1}{n-2}\sum_{i=1}^{n}\widehat{u}_i^2.$$

As the two-variable model has two expectation parameters, β_1, β_2, the count $n - 2$ is said to be the degrees of freedom of the model.

An exact confidence interval for β_2, or a one-sided test for a hypothesis on β_2, can be based on the t-test statistic:

$$Z = \frac{\widehat{\beta}_2 - \beta_2}{\widehat{\text{se}}(\widehat{\beta}_2)} \overset{D}{=} t[n-2] \qquad \text{where} \qquad \widehat{\text{se}}^2(\widehat{\beta}_2) = \frac{s^2}{\sum_{j=1}^{n}\left(X_j - \overline{X}\right)^2}.$$

The gain is limited though, since the $t[n]$-distribution is hardly distinguishable from the $N[0, 1]$-distribution when $n > 10$, let alone $n = 3877$. A two-sided test can be based on the squared t-statistic, which is the F-test statistic:

$$F = Z^2 \overset{D}{=} F[1, n-2].$$

The F-statistic for testing $\beta_2 = 0$ has some interesting connections with the expressions for sample correlation found in §5.4.3 in that it satisfies:

$$F = \frac{\left(\widehat{\sigma}_R^2 - \widehat{\sigma}^2\right)}{\widehat{\sigma}^2/(n-2)} = \frac{r^2/1}{(1-r^2)/(n-2)} = \frac{\text{ESS}/1}{\text{RSS}/(n-2)}. \qquad (5.5.5)$$

A similar approach can be applied to form a confidence interval for the intercept β_1, but it is rarely of interest to test hypotheses about the intercept in cross sections.

5.5.4 The role of the regressors when testing

The discussion of the distributional properties of estimators and test statistics in §5.5 gave conditional statements for fixed values of the regressors. This was done in accordance with assumption (iii) of the statistical model. A direct consequence is that any inference about, for instance, β_2 drawn from the sample would hold only for populations with exactly the same figuration of regressors. Fortunately, the results hold more generally than that.

In §5.5.1 the conditional expectation of $\widehat{\beta}_2$, given the information set $\mathcal{I}$ determined by the regressors, was found to be $\mathsf{E}(\widehat{\beta}_2|\mathcal{I}) = \beta_2$. By the Law of Iterated Expectations, displayed in (4.1.8), it follows that:

$$\mathsf{E}\left(\widehat{\beta}_2\right) = \mathsf{E}\left\{\mathsf{E}\left(\widehat{\beta}_2\middle|\mathcal{I}\right)\right\} = \beta_2.$$

This shows that $\widehat{\beta}_2$ will be unbiased not only in populations where the regressors have exactly the same characteristics as in the sample, but also in populations for which the observed set of regressors can be thought of as being representative.

Although the unconditional variance of $\widehat{\beta}_2$ does depend on the regressors, this dependence comes about so that the distributions of the standardized estimator, the t-statistic and the other test statistics, do not depend on the regressors. Therefore, it is not necessary to require that the different samples have exactly the same sets of regressors to reach any conclusion. In practice, one should, however, be careful when extrapolating to hypothetical sets of regressors with values that are outside the range of the original regressors.

5.6 SUMMARY AND EXERCISES

Summary: The simple regression model was extended to an open model, including a regressor in a conditional setup. The conditional likelihood is maximized using the same principles as before. The algebraic manipulations are more involved than before. The derivations can be simplified through a reparametrized model where the regressors are orthogonalized. The maximum of the likelihood function is invariant to this change.

Correlations describe the association between two variables in a regression context. In regression, the likelihood ratio test statistics can often, as here, be expressed in terms of correlations.

Bibliography: The terms "regression" and "co-relation" were defined and their links explored by F. Galton in a series of papers in the late 1880s, notably in Galton (1886) and Galton (1889). Both the logistic model and the two-variable regression model are open models, in contrast to the Bernoulli model and the one-variable regression model. Other regression-type models can be found by replacing the distributional assumption. In this way, Exercise 4.7 considers a Poisson regression. Maddala (1983) discusses that model along with other models for count data and truncated data.

Key questions:

- Explain the differences between and similarities of estimation using the original parameters as in §5.2.2 and estimation using orthogonalized regressors as in §5.2.3.
- How do correlations link with test statistics in the two-variable model?
- Discuss the validity of the assumptions of the econometric model for wages.

Exercise 5.1. *Suppose $X_1 \overset{D}{=} N[\mu_1, \sigma_1^2]$, $X_2 \overset{D}{=} N[\mu_2, \sigma_2^2]$ and their covariance is $\rho\sigma_1\sigma_2$. Find $E(X_1 + X_2)$ and $Var(X_1 + X_2)$.*

Exercise 5.2. *Reconsider Exercise 3.3. Compare the results with those obtained in section 5.2. When would one model be preferred to the other?*

Exercise 5.3. *Prove (5.2.10) and (5.2.11), showing that the predictors, $\widehat{Y}_i$, and hence the residuals, $\widehat{u}_i$, are the same in the two-variable model, as formulated in (5.1.1), and its reparametrized version in (5.2.7).*

Exercise 5.4. *Derive the expression (5.2.12) directly from (5.2.1).*

Exercise 5.5. *Show that:*
(a) $E[\{X - E(X)\}\{Y - E(Y)\}] = E[\{X - E(X)\}Y] = E(XY) - E(X)E(Y)$.
(b) $\sum_{i=1}^{n}(X_i - \overline{X})(Y_i - \overline{Y}) = \sum_{i=1}^{n}(X_i - \overline{X})Y_i = \sum_{i=1}^{n} X_iY_i - n\overline{X}\,\overline{Y}$.

Exercise 5.6. *Consider the data in Table 3.2.*
(a) Let $t = 1, \dots, 7$ represent the seven periods, and let Y_t be the output, with $y_t = \log(Y_t)$. Plot Y_t, y_t.
(b) Estimate the parameters for expectation and variance in the model:

$$y_t = \beta_1 + \beta_2 t + u_t.$$

Next, estimate the parameters in the reparametrized model:

$$y_t = \delta_1 + \delta_2 \left(t - \overline{t}\right) + u_t,$$

where $\overline{t} = \sum_{t=1}^{7} t/7$. What is the relation between the parameters β_1, β_2 and δ_1, δ_2? Predict log output for the period 1975–1999.

Exercise 5.7. * *The inequality $\{E(XY)\}^2 \leq E(X^2)E(Y^2)$ is known as the* **Cauchy–Schwarz inequality.** *Prove it in the following steps:*
(a) Argue that for any $a \in \mathbb{R}$ then $E\{(Y - aX)^2\} \geq 0$.
(b) Prove the inequality using $a = E(XY)/E(X^2)$.

Exercise 5.8. *Consider the two-variable regression model (5.1.1), and suppose that $\beta_2 = 0$ so that $(Y_i|X_i) \overset{D}{=} N[\beta_1, \sigma^2]$.*
(a) Show that the estimators $\widehat{\beta}$ in (3.3.5) and $\widehat{\beta}_1$ in (5.2.1) are both unbiased estimators for β_1.
(b) Show that $\mathsf{Var}(\widehat{\beta})$ in general is smaller than $\mathsf{Var}(\widehat{\beta}_1)$.
(c) When is $\mathsf{Var}(\widehat{\beta}) = \mathsf{Var}(\widehat{\beta}_1)$?
(d) * Show that the ratio $\mathsf{Var}(\widehat{\beta}_1)/\mathsf{Var}(\widehat{\beta})$ can be arbitrarily large.
*When comparing two unbiased estimators we typically prefer the one with least variance, which is then said to be **efficient**.*

Exercise 5.9. *Derive the expression (5.4.5) directly from (5.2.13).*

Exercise 5.10. *Derive (5.4.8) using (5.2.10). It is convenient to use the orthogonal parametrization.*

Exercise 5.11. *Prove the two identities in (5.4.10) using (5.4.6) and (5.4.9).*

Exercise 5.12. *Prove the identities in (5.5.5) in the following steps.*
(a) For the first identity, establish that $n(\widehat{\sigma}_R^2 - \widehat{\sigma}^2) = \widehat{\beta}_2 \sum_{i=1}^n X_{2\cdot 1,i}^2$.
(b) For the last two identities use (5.4.6) and (5.4.10).

Exercise 5.13. ** Prove that a two-sided t-test is equivalent to an F-test; that is: exactly the same decision are made using the two tests for any outcome.*

Exercise 5.14. *Return to Exercise 5.6. Find r^2 for the model, and derive the one-sided and the two-sided t-tests for $\beta_2 = 0$. Next, derive the F-test for $\beta_2 = 0$.*

Computing Task 5.15. *Consider the data in Table 3.2.*
(a) Regress Y on t and a constant and create fitted values.
Store the fitted values from the regression using the test menu.
Graph fitted output against period.
Graph output and fitted output against period.
Predict the output for the period 1975–1999.
How accurate was your result when in fact $Y = 246813$?
(b) Construct $y = \log(Y)$, name it y. Redo (a).
(c) Orthogonalized parametrization: Regress t on just a constant. Keep the residuals, $tres$ say.
What is the theoretical expression for $tres$?
Regress y on a constant and $tres$. Compare with the outcome in (b).
(d) Create a variable t^2 and estimate the parameters in the model:

$$y_t = \beta_1 + \beta_2 t + \beta_3 t^2 + u_t.$$

Would you expect $\beta_3 = 0$?

Chapter Six

The matrix algebra of two-variable regression

The manipulations of regression analysis are intimately linked with matrix algebra. As we have seen in Chapters 3 and 5, there is a pattern in the derivations of estimators and their distribution for different regression models. This structure can be explored systematically using matrix algebra. Matrix algebra is, however, an investment. For the purpose of this book, this chapter could be avoided; nevertheless, for a continued study of econometrics beyond this book, matrix algebra is certainly worth the effort. In this chapter, we will look at the matrix algebra that is relevant for the two-variable regression model and expand on that theory in Chapter 8.

We start by an introductory example in terms of the two-variable regression model without an intercept. A section on matrix algebra then follows, and finally its application to the unrestricted two-variable regression model is discussed.

6.1 INTRODUCTORY EXAMPLE

The two-variable regression model without intercept was discussed in Exercise 3.3. The data consist of the pairs $(Y_1, X_1), \ldots, (Y_n, X_n)$, and the econometric model is that of the two-variable regression model of §5.1, but excluding the intercept:

   (i) *independence*: the pairs (X_i, Y_i) are mutually independent;
   (ii) *conditional normality*: $(Y_i \mid X_i) \overset{\mathrm{D}}{=} \mathsf{N}[\beta X_i, \sigma^2]$;
   (iii) *exogeneity*: the conditioning variable is exogenous;
   (iv) *parameter space*: $\beta, \sigma^2 \in \mathbb{R} \times \mathbb{R}_+$.

In Exercise 3.3, we found the maximum likelihood estimators:

$$\widehat{\beta} = \left(\sum_{i=1}^{n} X_i^2 \right)^{-1} \left(\sum_{i=1}^{n} X_i Y_i \right), \tag{6.1.1}$$

$$\widehat{\sigma}^2 = \frac{1}{n} \left\{ \left(\sum_{i=1}^{n} Y_i^2 \right) - \left(\sum_{i=1}^{n} Y_i X_i \right) \left(\sum_{i=1}^{n} X_i^2 \right)^{-1} \left(\sum_{i=1}^{n} X_i Y_i \right) \right\}. \tag{6.1.2}$$

Note that the usual fractions of estimators are written as products where the denominators are raised to the power -1. We will see that this is an important feature of the matrix algebra. We will now write these expressions in matrix form.

Arrange the variables $Y_1, \ldots, Y_n$ and $X_1, \ldots, X_n$ as n-dimensional *vectors*:

$$\mathbf{Y} = \begin{pmatrix} Y_1 \\ \vdots \\ Y_n \end{pmatrix}, \qquad \mathbf{X} = \begin{pmatrix} X_1 \\ \vdots \\ X_n \end{pmatrix}.$$

While vectors are columns, matrices are arrays with k columns. A vector is therefore a matrix with one column. As a typographical convention in this book, vectors and matrices are typeset with bold font. A more important convention is that vectors are always vertical rather than horizontal. Along the same line we will arrange the scalar β in an 1-dimensional vector:

$$\boldsymbol{\beta} = (\beta).$$

The term $\sum_{i=1}^{n} X_i Y_i$ can be thought of as the inner product of $\mathbf{X}$ and $\mathbf{Y}$. This means that we first transpose $\mathbf{X}$ giving:

$$\mathbf{X}' = (X_1, \ldots, X_n).$$

The prime on $\mathbf{X}$ indicates that this is a transposed vector and therefore horizontal. We then perform a matrix product:

$$\mathbf{X}'\mathbf{Y} = (X_1, \ldots, X_n) \begin{pmatrix} Y_1 \\ \vdots \\ Y_n \end{pmatrix} = \left(\sum_{i=1}^{n} X_i Y_i \right),$$

by multiplying first elements of the two vectors, second elements, and so on, and then adding everything up. We will think of $\mathbf{X}'\mathbf{Y}$ as a 1×1 matrix. In the same way:

$$\mathbf{X}'\mathbf{X} = \sum_{i=1}^{n} X_i^2.$$

The next step is to invert the matrix $(\mathbf{X}'\mathbf{X})^{-1} = (\sum_{i=1}^{n} X_i^2)^{-1}$. Finally, we multiply the matrices $(\mathbf{X}'\mathbf{X})^{-1}$ and $\mathbf{X}'\mathbf{Y}$ to get a more compact expression for (6.1.1):

$$\widehat{\boldsymbol{\beta}} = (\mathbf{X}'\mathbf{X})^{-1} \mathbf{X}'\mathbf{Y}.$$

Using similar manipulations, we can express $\widehat{\sigma}^2$ in a form like (6.1.2) as:

$$\widehat{\sigma}^2 = \frac{1}{n} \left\{ \mathbf{Y}'\mathbf{Y} - \mathbf{Y}'\mathbf{X} (\mathbf{X}'\mathbf{X})^{-1} \mathbf{X}'\mathbf{Y} \right\}.$$

When introducing more regressors, $\mathbf{X}$ becomes an $(n \times k)$-matrix but otherwise all the steps use the same notation. The step that is most difficult to generalize is the inversion of the $(k \times k)$-matrix $\mathbf{X}'\mathbf{X}$. This is essentially the step where we solve k equations with k unknown.

6.2 MATRIX ALGEBRA

We will first define matrices, and then show how to add and multiply matrices.

6.2.1 Matrices

A *matrix* is an array of numbers with n rows and k columns. For $n = 3$, $k = 2$, an example is the (3×2) matrix:

$$\mathbf{A} = \begin{pmatrix} 1 & 4 \\ 2 & 5 \\ 3 & 6 \end{pmatrix}.$$

If the matrix has only one column, it is a *vector*. We write $\mathbf{A}_{32}$ if we are particularly interested in the element in the 3rd row and 2nd column, so $\mathbf{A}_{32} = 6$. The *transpose* of $\mathbf{A}$ is an $(n \times m)$ matrix mirror imaged along the diagonal from the top-left corner toward the bottom right. For $\mathbf{A}$, the diagonal line comprises the elements $\mathbf{A}_{11} = 1$, $\mathbf{A}_{22} = 5$, so:

$$\mathbf{A}' = \begin{pmatrix} 1 & 2 & 3 \\ 4 & 5 & 6 \end{pmatrix}.$$

A matrix with as many rows as columns is a *square matrix*. Some examples:

$$\begin{pmatrix} 1 & 2 \\ 4 & 5 \end{pmatrix}, \quad \begin{pmatrix} 1 & 2 \\ 2 & 3 \end{pmatrix}, \quad \begin{pmatrix} 1 & 0 \\ 0 & 3 \end{pmatrix}.$$

A square matrix that is equal to its transpose is said to be *symmetric*. The first of the above matrices is not symmetric, whereas the next two are. The last one is even a *diagonal* matrix with zero elements outside the top-left to bottom-right diagonal.

6.2.2 Addition of matrices

Consider two matrices with the same dimensions:

$$\mathbf{A} = \begin{pmatrix} 1 & 4 \\ 2 & 5 \\ 3 & 6 \end{pmatrix}, \quad \mathbf{B} = \begin{pmatrix} 7 & 10 \\ 8 & 11 \\ 9 & 12 \end{pmatrix}.$$

Matrix addition is defined by element-wise addition:

$$\mathbf{A} + \mathbf{B} = \begin{pmatrix} 1+7 & 4+10 \\ 2+8 & 5+11 \\ 3+9 & 6+12 \end{pmatrix} = \begin{pmatrix} 8 & 14 \\ 10 & 16 \\ 12 & 18 \end{pmatrix}.$$

The *zero matrix* has zero elements, so:

$$\mathbf{A} + \mathbf{0} = \begin{pmatrix} 1 & 4 \\ 2 & 5 \\ 3 & 6 \end{pmatrix} + \begin{pmatrix} 0 & 0 \\ 0 & 0 \\ 0 & 0 \end{pmatrix} = \begin{pmatrix} 1 & 4 \\ 2 & 5 \\ 3 & 6 \end{pmatrix} = \mathbf{A}.$$

Addition satisfies a *commutative law* so $\mathbf{A} + \mathbf{B} = \mathbf{B} + \mathbf{A}$. We can also subtract matrices from each other: If $\mathbf{A} + \mathbf{B} = \mathbf{C}$, then $\mathbf{C} - \mathbf{A} = \mathbf{B}$.

6.2.3 Multiplication of matrices

Two types of multiplication are relevant for matrices. A matrix can be multiplied by a scalar, and two matrices can be multiplied.

In *scalar multiplication* a matrix is multiplied by a scalar by multiplying each element with that scalar:

$$\text{if } \mathbf{A} = \begin{pmatrix} 1 & 4 \\ 2 & 5 \\ 3 & 6 \end{pmatrix} \text{ then } 2\mathbf{A} = \begin{pmatrix} 2 \times 1 & 2 \times 4 \\ 2 \times 2 & 2 \times 5 \\ 2 \times 3 & 2 \times 6 \end{pmatrix} = \begin{pmatrix} 2 & 8 \\ 4 & 10 \\ 6 & 12 \end{pmatrix}.$$

Matrix multiplication involving two matrices is, in contrast, based on inner products as we saw in §6.1. We therefore need to consider the inner product of two vectors. For two vectors of the same length:

$$\mathbf{a} = \begin{pmatrix} 1 \\ 2 \end{pmatrix}, \qquad \mathbf{b} = \begin{pmatrix} 3 \\ 4 \end{pmatrix},$$

the *inner product* of the vectors $\mathbf{a}$ and $\mathbf{b}$ is defined by element-wise multiplication and then adding up the terms, that is, $1 \times 3 + 2 \times 4 = 11$. Using $\mathbf{a}' = (1, 2)$, we write the inner product as $\mathbf{a}'\mathbf{b}$.

Consider now two matrices where the number of columns of the first matrix equals the number of rows of the second:

$$\mathbf{A} = \begin{pmatrix} 1 & 4 \\ 2 & 5 \\ 3 & 6 \end{pmatrix}, \qquad \mathbf{C} = \begin{pmatrix} 7 & 9 \\ 8 & 10 \end{pmatrix}.$$

We can write $\mathbf{A}$ as a vector of transposed vectors:

$$\mathbf{A} = \begin{pmatrix} \mathbf{a}'_1 \\ \mathbf{a}'_2 \\ \mathbf{a}'_3 \end{pmatrix} \text{ where } \mathbf{a}_1 = \begin{pmatrix} 1 \\ 4 \end{pmatrix}, \ \mathbf{a}_2 = \begin{pmatrix} 2 \\ 5 \end{pmatrix}, \ \mathbf{a}_3 = \begin{pmatrix} 3 \\ 6 \end{pmatrix},$$

and $\mathbf{C}$ as a transposed vector of vectors:

$$\mathbf{C} = (\mathbf{c}_1, \mathbf{c}_2) \text{ where } \mathbf{c}_1 = \begin{pmatrix} 7 \\ 8 \end{pmatrix}, \ \mathbf{c}_2 = \begin{pmatrix} 9 \\ 10 \end{pmatrix}.$$

The *matrix product* of $\mathbf{A}$ and $\mathbf{C}$ is the matrix of inner products:

$$\mathbf{AC} = \begin{pmatrix} \mathbf{a}_1'\mathbf{c}_1 & \mathbf{a}_1'\mathbf{c}_2 \\ \mathbf{a}_2'\mathbf{c}_1 & \mathbf{a}_2'\mathbf{c}_2 \\ \mathbf{a}_3'\mathbf{c}_1 & \mathbf{a}_3'\mathbf{c}_2 \end{pmatrix}$$

$$= \left\{ \begin{array}{ll} (1 \times 7) + (4 \times 8) & (1 \times 9) + (4 \times 10) \\ (2 \times 7) + (5 \times 8) & (2 \times 9) + (5 \times 10) \\ (3 \times 7) + (6 \times 8) & (3 \times 9) + (6 \times 10) \end{array} \right\} = \begin{pmatrix} 39 & 49 \\ 54 & 68 \\ 69 & 87 \end{pmatrix}.$$

The product $\mathbf{AC}$ has the same number of rows as $\mathbf{A}$ and the same number of columns as $\mathbf{C}$. The order of the matrices is important. In this case it makes *no* sense to multiply $\mathbf{C}$ with $\mathbf{A}$, since $\mathbf{C}$ has two columns and $\mathbf{A}$ has three rows, so the relevant inner products cannot be formed.

It is useful to note that $(\mathbf{AC})' = \mathbf{C}'\mathbf{A}'$, so transposition of a product is the product of the transposed matrices in the opposite order. Prove this for these particular matrices, noting that $\mathbf{a}_i'\mathbf{c}_j = \mathbf{c}_j'\mathbf{a}_i$ as both are the same scalar.

For the usual product of scalars, we have a commutative law, for instance: $2 \times 3 = 3 \times 2 = 6$. It is important to realize that there is *no commutative law* for matrix multiplication. As an example, consider two square matrices $\mathbf{D}$ and $\mathbf{E}$ of the same dimension, so that we can form both of the matrix products $\mathbf{DE}$ and $\mathbf{ED}$. In general, $\mathbf{DE} \neq \mathbf{ED}$. As an example let:

$$\mathbf{D} = \begin{pmatrix} 0 & 1 \\ -1 & 0 \end{pmatrix}, \qquad \mathbf{E} = \begin{pmatrix} 0 & 1 \\ 1 & 0 \end{pmatrix}.$$

These matrices do not commute since:

$$\mathbf{DE} = \begin{pmatrix} 1 & 0 \\ 0 & -1 \end{pmatrix} \neq \begin{pmatrix} -1 & 0 \\ 0 & 1 \end{pmatrix} = \mathbf{ED}.$$

For the usual product of scalars, the number 1 plays a special role. Multiplying by 1 does not change anything, for instance: $2 \times 1 = 2$. For matrix multiplication the *identity matrix* plays the same role. Identity matrices are square matrices with ones along the diagonal and zero everywhere else. In the two-dimensional case the identity matrix is the diagonal matrix with diagonal elements of unity:

$$\mathbf{I}_2 = \begin{pmatrix} 1 & 0 \\ 0 & 1 \end{pmatrix}.$$

Check that $\mathbf{EI}_2 = \mathbf{I}_2\mathbf{E} = \mathbf{E}$. Having an identity matrix, we can define *matrix inversion*. If $\mathbf{F}$ is an $n \times n$ square matrix, and there exists a matrix $\mathbf{F}^{-1}$ of the same dimensions so $\mathbf{FF}^{-1} = \mathbf{I}_n$, we say $\mathbf{F}^{-1}$ is the inverse of $\mathbf{F}$. The matrices $\mathbf{F}$ and $\mathbf{F}^{-1}$ do commute so $\mathbf{F}^{-1}\mathbf{F} = \mathbf{I}_n$.

6.2.4 How to find the inverse of a matrix

Having defined what we mean by the inverse of a matrix, the next question concerns how we actually invert a matrix. Here we will focus on (2×2)-matrices, starting with diagonal matrices, and progressing to general matrices.

Diagonal matrices are square matrices, with zeros outside the diagonal. They are very easy to invert as we just invert the diagonal elements. Some examples:

$$\mathbf{G} = \begin{pmatrix} 2 & 0 \\ 0 & 3 \end{pmatrix}, \qquad \mathbf{G}^{-1} = \begin{pmatrix} 2^{-1} & 0 \\ 0 & 3^{-1} \end{pmatrix},$$

$$\mathbf{H} = \begin{pmatrix} a & 0 \\ 0 & b \end{pmatrix}, \qquad \mathbf{H}^{-1} = \begin{pmatrix} a^{-1} & 0 \\ 0 & b^{-1} \end{pmatrix}.$$

Check that $\mathbf{G}\mathbf{G}^{-1} = \mathbf{I}_2 = \mathbf{G}^{-1}\mathbf{G}$. It is important that all diagonal elements are different from zero as one cannot divide by zero. If a diagonal matrix has any zero diagonal elements, it is not invertible.

For a general (2×2)-matrix we have the formula:

$$\mathbf{K} = \begin{pmatrix} a & c \\ d & b \end{pmatrix}, \qquad \mathbf{K}^{-1} = \frac{1}{ab - cd} \begin{pmatrix} b & -c \\ -d & a \end{pmatrix}, \qquad (6.2.1)$$

Check that $\mathbf{K}\mathbf{K}^{-1} = \mathbf{I}_2 = \mathbf{K}^{-1}\mathbf{K}$. Note the division by $ab - cd$, which is the *determinant* of the matrix $\mathbf{K}$. We write $\det(\mathbf{K}) = ab - cd$. Since we cannot divide by zero, it is a condition for invertibility that $\det(\mathbf{K}) \neq 0$. Synonymously with the adjective invertible, the terms *full-rank* and *regular* are used. Examples of *non-invertible* matrices, or *reduced-rank* matrices, or *singular* matrices, are:

$$\begin{pmatrix} 1 & 1 \\ 1 & 1 \end{pmatrix}, \qquad \begin{pmatrix} 1 & 0 \\ 0 & 0 \end{pmatrix}, \qquad \begin{pmatrix} 0 & 0 \\ 0 & 0 \end{pmatrix}.$$

For a product of square matrices, $\mathbf{G}$, $\mathbf{H}$, we have: $(\mathbf{G}\mathbf{H})^{-1} = \mathbf{H}^{-1}\mathbf{G}^{-1}$. This matches the formula for taking the transpose of a product of matrices.

A matrix that is equal to its transpose, $\mathbf{K} = \mathbf{K}'$, is said to be *symmetric*, and will be a square matrix. The inversion of symmetric matrices is intimately linked with regression analysis. For a symmetric (2×2)-matrix, so $c = d$:

$$\mathbf{K} = \begin{pmatrix} a & c \\ c & b \end{pmatrix},$$

we can form an upper *triangular* matrix:

$$\mathbf{L} = \begin{pmatrix} 1 & -cb^{-1} \\ 0 & 1 \end{pmatrix}, \qquad \text{so} \qquad \mathbf{L}\mathbf{K}\mathbf{L}' = \begin{pmatrix} a - cb^{-1}c' & 0 \\ 0 & b \end{pmatrix}. \qquad (6.2.2)$$

The matrix $\mathbf{LKL}'$ is diagonal and easy to invert. Using the rule for the inverse of matrix products, we can then compute:

$$\mathbf{K}^{-1} = \mathbf{L}' \left(\mathbf{LKL}'\right)^{-1} \mathbf{L}. \tag{6.2.3}$$

Computing this expression yields the formula in 6.2.1; check for yourself.

6.3 MATRIX ALGEBRA IN REGRESSION ANALYSIS

We will reconsider the two-variable model without an intercept from §6.1. First, we will show how the formula (6.2.2) underpins the regression estimators and, second, turn to the likelihood function and derive the maximum likelihood estimators using matrix algebra. Finally, we will discuss the notion of orthogonal regressors that was introduced for the general two-variable model.

6.3.1 Matrix expressions for the regression estimators

Reconsider the two-variable model without an intercept in §6.1. Put $\mathbf{Y}$ and $\mathbf{X}$ together as an $(n \times 2)$-matrix:

$$(\mathbf{Y}, \mathbf{X}) = \begin{pmatrix} Y_1 & X_1 \\ \vdots & \vdots \\ Y_n & X_n \end{pmatrix}.$$

Next, perform the matrix product:

$$(\mathbf{Y}, \mathbf{X})' (\mathbf{Y}, \mathbf{X}) = \begin{pmatrix} \mathbf{Y}' \\ \mathbf{X}' \end{pmatrix} (\mathbf{Y}, \mathbf{X}) = \begin{pmatrix} \mathbf{Y}'\mathbf{Y} & \mathbf{Y}'\mathbf{X} \\ \mathbf{X}'\mathbf{Y} & \mathbf{X}'\mathbf{X} \end{pmatrix}.$$

This is a symmetric matrix since the off-diagonal elements satisfy $(\mathbf{Y}'\mathbf{X})' = \mathbf{X}'\mathbf{Y}$. We can capture the idea of regression analysis by following (6.2.2) and compute:

$$\begin{pmatrix} 1 & -\mathbf{Y}'\mathbf{X}(\mathbf{X}'\mathbf{X})^{-1} \\ 0 & 1 \end{pmatrix} \begin{pmatrix} \mathbf{Y}'\mathbf{Y} & \mathbf{Y}'\mathbf{X} \\ \mathbf{X}'\mathbf{Y} & \mathbf{X}'\mathbf{X} \end{pmatrix} \begin{pmatrix} 1 & 0 \\ -(\mathbf{X}'\mathbf{X})^{-1}\mathbf{X}'\mathbf{Y} & 1 \end{pmatrix}$$
$$= \begin{pmatrix} \mathbf{Y}'\mathbf{Y} - \mathbf{Y}'\mathbf{X}\left(\mathbf{X}'\mathbf{X}\right)^{-1}\mathbf{X}'\mathbf{Y} & 0 \\ 0 & \mathbf{X}'\mathbf{X} \end{pmatrix},$$

or in the notation of the regression model:

$$\begin{pmatrix} 1 & -\widehat{\beta}' \\ 0 & 1 \end{pmatrix} \begin{pmatrix} \mathbf{Y}'\mathbf{Y} & \mathbf{Y}'\mathbf{X} \\ \mathbf{X}'\mathbf{Y} & \mathbf{X}'\mathbf{X} \end{pmatrix} \begin{pmatrix} 1 & 0 \\ -\widehat{\beta} & 1 \end{pmatrix} = \begin{pmatrix} n\widehat{\sigma}^2 & 0 \\ 0 & \mathbf{X}'\mathbf{X} \end{pmatrix}.$$

This result contains all the main elements of regression analysis; the matrix $\mathbf{X}'\mathbf{X}$, called the *information matrix*, appears in the expression for the variance of $\widehat{\beta}$.

6.3.2 Likelihood analysis

The model equation for the two-variable model without intercept is $Y_i = X_i\beta + u_i$. These n individual equations can be stacked as:

$$\begin{pmatrix} Y_1 \\ \vdots \\ Y_n \end{pmatrix} = \begin{pmatrix} X_1 \\ \vdots \\ X_n \end{pmatrix} \beta + \begin{pmatrix} u_1 \\ \vdots \\ u_n \end{pmatrix}$$

or in more compact matrix notation:

$$\mathbf{Y} = \mathbf{X}\beta + \mathbf{u}. \tag{6.3.1}$$

The (conditional) log-likelihood function of §5.2.1 then becomes:

$$\ell_{\mathbf{Y}|\mathbf{X}} \left(\beta, \sigma^2\right) = -\frac{n}{2} \log(2\pi\sigma^2) - \frac{1}{2\sigma^2} \left(\mathbf{Y} - \mathbf{X}\beta\right)' \left(\mathbf{Y} - \mathbf{X}\beta\right).$$

We now wish to maximize the log likelihood with respect to β. As previously, this is equivalent to minimizing the sum of squared deviations, $(\mathbf{Y} - \mathbf{X}\beta)'(\mathbf{Y} - \mathbf{X}\beta)$, with respect to β. There exists a matrix differentiation calculus that could be used; see Magnus and Neudecker (1999), but here it suffices to simply show that the minimum is at $\widehat{\beta} = (\mathbf{X}'\mathbf{X})^{-1}\mathbf{X}'\mathbf{Y}$. To do that, it is convenient to rewrite the model equation by adding and subtracting $\mathbf{X}\widehat{\beta}$:

$$\mathbf{u} = \mathbf{Y} - \mathbf{X}\beta = \mathbf{Y} - \mathbf{X}\widehat{\beta} + \mathbf{X}\widehat{\beta} - \mathbf{X}\beta = \left(\mathbf{Y} - \mathbf{X}\widehat{\beta}\right) + \mathbf{X}\left(\widehat{\beta} - \beta\right).$$

The matrix $\mathbf{X}$ and the residual $\widehat{\mathbf{u}} = \mathbf{Y} - \mathbf{X}\widehat{\beta}$ are *orthogonal*, in the sense that $\mathbf{X}'\widehat{\mathbf{u}} = \mathbf{0}$, see Exercise 6.3, and compare with Exercise 3.3. The sum of squared deviations therefore satisfies:

$$(\mathbf{Y} - \mathbf{X}\beta)' (\mathbf{Y} - \mathbf{X}\beta) = \widehat{\mathbf{u}}\widehat{\mathbf{u}}' + \left(\widehat{\beta} - \beta\right)' \mathbf{X}'\mathbf{X} \left(\widehat{\beta} - \beta\right). \tag{6.3.2}$$

This is a sum of two non-negative terms, with β only entering in the second term. The second term is zero precisely when $\widehat{\beta} = \beta$, achieving the minimum.

6.3.3 The two-variable regression model

The two-variable regression model has model equation $Y_i = \beta_1 + \beta_2 X_i + u_i$. This can be written in the form (6.3.1), that is, $\mathbf{Y} = \mathbf{X}\beta + \mathbf{u}$, if we define:

$$\mathbf{Y} = \begin{pmatrix} Y_1 \\ \vdots \\ Y_n \end{pmatrix}, \quad \mathbf{X} = \begin{pmatrix} 1 & X_1 \\ \vdots & \vdots \\ 1 & X_n \end{pmatrix}, \quad \beta = \begin{pmatrix} \beta_1 \\ \beta_2 \end{pmatrix}, \quad \mathbf{u} = \begin{pmatrix} u_1 \\ \vdots \\ u_n \end{pmatrix}.$$

To compute the estimator $\widehat{\beta} = (\mathbf{X}'\mathbf{X})^{-1}\mathbf{X}'\mathbf{Y}$, we first find the matrix products:

$$\mathbf{X}'\mathbf{X} = \begin{pmatrix} \sum_{i=1}^{n} 1^2 & \sum_{i=1}^{n} X_i \\ \sum_{i=1}^{n} X_i & \sum_{i=1}^{n} X_i^2 \end{pmatrix}, \quad \mathbf{X}'\mathbf{Y} = \begin{pmatrix} \sum_{i=1}^{n} Y_i \\ \sum_{i=1}^{n} X_i Y_i \end{pmatrix}. \tag{6.3.3}$$

We could then use the formula (6.2.1) to compute $(\mathbf{X}'\mathbf{X})^{-1}$ and then multiply it with $\mathbf{X}'\mathbf{Y}$. This will give the estimators found in (5.2.1); see Exercise 6.4.

In §5.2.3 we spent some effort orthogonalizing the regressors. This is easy using matrix algebra. To orthogonalize X_i with respect to the intercept, partition $\mathbf{X}$ as $(\mathbf{X}_1, \mathbf{X}_2)$ where $\mathbf{X}_1$ is the vector of ones and $\mathbf{X}_2$ is the vector of X_is. For the orthogonalization define the lower triangular matrix:

$$\mathbf{L} = \begin{pmatrix} 1 & 0 \\ -\mathbf{X}_2'\mathbf{X}_1(\mathbf{X}_1'\mathbf{X}_1)^{-1} & 1 \end{pmatrix},$$

where the off-diagonal element is the (transposed) regression coefficient from regressing $\mathbf{X}_2$ on $\mathbf{X}_1$. We can then form the orthogonalized regressors:

$$\mathbf{Z} = \mathbf{X}\mathbf{L} = \begin{pmatrix} 1 & X_1 - \overline{X} \\ \vdots & \\ 1 & X_n - \overline{X} \end{pmatrix} \quad \text{with} \quad \mathbf{Z}'\mathbf{Z} = \begin{pmatrix} n & 0 \\ 0 & \sum_{i=1}^n (X_i - \overline{X})^2 \end{pmatrix}.$$

These regressors are orthogonal precisely because $\mathbf{Z}'\mathbf{Z}$ is a diagonal matrix, with off-diagonal element $\mathbf{Z}_1'\mathbf{Z}_2 = \mathbf{0}$, as in (5.2.8). Now, rewrite the model equation as:

$$\mathbf{Y} = \mathbf{X}\mathbf{L}\mathbf{L}^{-1}\boldsymbol{\beta} + \mathbf{u} = \mathbf{Z}\boldsymbol{\delta} + \mathbf{u}, \qquad (6.3.4)$$

where the new regression parameter is defined by $\boldsymbol{\delta} = \mathbf{L}^{-1}\boldsymbol{\beta}$; see (5.2.6) and (5.2.7). Since $\mathbf{Z}'\mathbf{Z}$ is diagonal it can easily be inverted, so $\widehat{\boldsymbol{\delta}} = (\mathbf{Z}'\mathbf{Z})^{-1}\mathbf{Z}'\mathbf{Y}$ can be computed with modest effort; see Exercise 6.5. We can then compute $\widehat{\boldsymbol{\beta}}$ as $\widehat{\boldsymbol{\beta}} = \mathbf{L}\widehat{\boldsymbol{\delta}}$.

6.4 SUMMARY AND EXERCISES

Summary: Matrix algebra was introduced and developed for the two-variable regression model. Regression analysis is nearly synonymous with matrix inversion. Chapter 8 will take this theme a little further.

Bibliography: See §8.4.

Exercise 6.1. *Suppose we observed $Y_1 = 1$, $Y_2 = 2$, $Y_3 = 3$, and $X_1 = 1$, $X_2 = 1$, $X_3 = 1$ and fitted the model in section 6.1. Derive $\widehat{\boldsymbol{\beta}}$ and $\widehat{\sigma}^2$ using the matrix algebraic formulas.*

Exercise 6.2. *Let $\mathbf{Y} = (1, 2, 3, 4)'$ and $\mathbf{X} = (\mathbf{X}_1, \mathbf{X}_2)$, with $\mathbf{X}_1 = (1, 1, 1, 1)'$ and $\mathbf{X}_2 = (1, -1, 1, -1)'$.*
(a) Find $(\mathbf{X}'\mathbf{X})^{-1}\mathbf{X}'\mathbf{Y}$.

(b) Why does it not make sense to write "$\mathbf{X}'\mathbf{Y}(\mathbf{X}'\mathbf{X})^{-1}$" or "$\dfrac{\mathbf{X}'\mathbf{Y}}{\mathbf{X}'\mathbf{X}}$?"

Exercise 6.3. *Consider either the one-variable model or the two-variable model. Check that* $\mathbf{X}\widehat{\mathbf{u}} = \mathbf{0}$.

Exercise 6.4. *Consider the expressions for* $\mathbf{X}'\mathbf{X}$, $\mathbf{X}'\mathbf{Y}$ *in (6.3.3).*
(*a*) *Compute* $\widehat{\boldsymbol{\beta}} = (\mathbf{X}'\mathbf{X})^{-1}\mathbf{X}'\mathbf{Y}$.
(*b*) *Derive the expressions in (5.2.1).*

Exercise 6.5. *Consider the orthogonal two-variable model equation in (6.3.4).*
(*a*) *Compute* $(\mathbf{Z}'\mathbf{Z})^{-1}$ *and* $\mathbf{Z}'\mathbf{Y}$. *Derive* $\widehat{\boldsymbol{\delta}}$.
(*b*) *Derive* $\widehat{\boldsymbol{\beta}}$ *using the formula* $\widehat{\boldsymbol{\beta}} = \mathbf{L}\widehat{\boldsymbol{\delta}}$.

Exercise 6.6. *Write down* $\mathbf{Y}, \mathbf{X}$ *and compute* $\mathbf{X}'\mathbf{Y}$, $\mathbf{X}'\mathbf{X}$, $(\mathbf{X}'\mathbf{X})^{-1}$, *and* $\widehat{\boldsymbol{\beta}}$ *for each of the econometric models given by the model equations:*
(*a*) $Y_i \overset{D}{=} \mathsf{N}[\beta, \sigma^2]$.
(*b*) $Y_i \overset{D}{=} \mathsf{N}[\beta X_i, \sigma^2]$.
(*c*) $Y_i \overset{D}{=} \mathsf{N}[\beta_1 + \beta_2 X_i, \sigma^2]$.
(*d*) $Y_i \overset{D}{=} \mathsf{N}[\beta_1 + \beta_2 X_i, \sigma^2]$, *where* $\overline{X} = 0$.

Chapter Seven

The multiple regression model

In Chapter 5, we looked at the association between wages and education. From an economic viewpoint, we would expect wages to vary with other individual characteristics than with schooling alone. Theory would suggest a diminishing return to education, which we could seek to capture by including the square of education as an additional regressor. We will therefore extend the two-variable regression model to a model with several regressors. Here it will be done without involving matrix algebra, and then redone with matrix algebra in Chapter 8. In the subsequent Chapter 9, we will turn to a more detailed discussion of the specification analysis of regression models. Substantive interpretations of the regression results will be developed in Chapters 10 and 11.

When extending the two-variable regression model to a regression with three or more variables, most of the concepts and ideas presented so far carry through. The only additional conceptual issue is that we have to think about how the regressors interact with each other. The new concepts of partial correlations and multiple correlations will help us in doing so.

7.1 THE THREE-VARIABLE REGRESSION MODEL

The *three-variable regression model* is an extension of the two-variable model to the situation with two explanatory variables, $X_{2,i}$ and $X_{3,i}$. The data now consist of the triplets $(Y_i, X_{2,i}, X_{3,i})$ measured for all individuals, $i = 1, \ldots, n$. The statistical model is based on the following assumptions:

(i) *independence*: the triplets $(Y_i, X_{2,i}, X_{3,i})$ are independent across i;

(ii) *conditional distribution*: $(Y_i \mid X_{2,i}, X_{3,i}) \overset{\mathrm{D}}{=} \mathsf{N}[\beta_1 + \beta_2 X_{2,i} + \beta_3 X_{3,i}, \sigma^2]$;

(iii) *exogeneity*: the explanatory variables $X_{2,i}, X_{3,i}$ are exogenous;

(iv) *parameter space*: β_1, β_2, β_3, $\sigma^2 \in \mathbb{R}^3 \times \mathbb{R}_+$.

Alternatively, assumptions (i) and (ii) can be formulated as a regression equation:

$$Y_i = \beta_1 + \beta_2 X_{2,i} + \beta_3 X_{3,i} + u_i, \qquad (7.1.1)$$

where the triplets $(u_i, X_{2,i}, X_{3,i})$ are independent and $(u_i \mid X_{2,i}, X_{3,i}) \overset{\mathrm{D}}{=} \mathsf{N}[0, \sigma^2]$.

The parameters β_1, β_2, β_3 can be interpreted in terms of the conditional expectation:

$$\mathsf{E}(Y_i \mid X_{2,i}, X_{3,i}) = \beta_1 + \beta_2 X_{2,i} + \beta_3 X_{3,i}.$$

The intercept β_1 is the conditional expectation of Y_i for an individual with explanatory variables $X_{2,i} = X_{3,i} = 0$. If $\mathsf{E}(X_{2,i}) = \mathsf{E}(X_{3,i}) = 0$, then β_1 is the marginal expectation of Y_i. This is relevant when $X_{2,i}$, $X_{3,i}$ have been orthogonalized with respect to the constant. The other parameters can be interpreted in terms of partial derivatives with respect to the regressors, so for instance:

$$\beta_3 = \frac{\partial}{\partial X_{3,i}} \mathsf{E}(Y_i \mid X_{2,i}, X_{3,i}),$$

assuming that $X_{2,i}$ does not vary with $X_{3,i}$. This means that when comparing two individuals with the same value of $X_{2,i}$, but for whom the values of $X_{3,i}$ differ by one unit, then the conditional expectations of Y_i differ by β_3. As an example, consider a regression equation linking log wages, w, with length of schooling, S, and age, A:

$$w_i = \beta_1 + \beta_2 S_i + \beta_3 A_i + u_i.$$

For a woman with no education and age 0, the expected wage will be β_1. Since the sample includes only women of age 18 to 65, the intercept parameter would have a more reasonable interpretation in a reparametrized model, where, for instance, 18 was subtracted from A_i. Alternatively the average age could be subtracted, which would correspond to an orthogonalization of A_i with respect to the constant. If two women have the same age, but one has an additional year of education, her log wage will on average be β_2 higher; whereas if they have the same length of schooling, but one is a year older, her log wage will on average be β_3 higher. This type of interpretation breaks down when $X_{3,i}$ is a function of $X_{2,i}$. As an example, a non-linear relationship between log wages and schooling could be captured in the regression:

$$w_i = \beta_1 + \beta_2 S_i + \beta_3 S_i^2 + u_i.$$

In that situation, it is not possible to fix the second regressor S_i while varying the third regressor S_i^2.

7.2 ESTIMATION

We will argue that the maximum likelihood estimators for β_1, β_2, β_3 are:

$$\widehat{\beta}_1 = \frac{\sum_{i=1}^n Y_i X_{1 \cdot 2,3,i}}{\sum_{j=1}^n X_{1 \cdot 2,3,j}^2}, \quad \widehat{\beta}_2 = \frac{\sum_{i=1}^n Y_i X_{2 \cdot 1,3,i}}{\sum_{j=1}^n X_{2 \cdot 1,3,j}^2}, \quad \widehat{\beta}_3 = \frac{\sum_{i=1}^n Y_i X_{3 \cdot 1,2,i}}{\sum_{j=1}^n X_{3 \cdot 1,2,j}^2}.$$

$$(7.2.1)$$

As in §5.2.3, the notation for the X-variables indicates that these are residuals. For instance, $\widehat{\beta}_3$ is expressed in terms of $X_{3\cdot1,2,i}$, which arises as the residual from the two-variable regression of $X_{3,i}$ on $X_{1,i} = 1$ and $X_{2,i}$. One could say that $X_{3,i}$ has been orthogonalized with respect to $X_{1,i}$, $X_{2,i}$, or that $X_{1,i}$, $X_{2,i}$ have been partialled out. Sometimes the regression estimators are therefore called partial regression estimators. This result is in line with the interpretation of the three-variable model put forward in the previous section, where for instance β_3 is interpreted as the partial effect from varying $X_{3,i}$ for a fixed value of $X_{2,i}$ when $X_{1,i} = 1$.

7.2.1 The likelihood function

The starting point for the derivation of the estimators is the conditional likelihood for Y_i given $X_{2,i}, X_{3,i}$:

$$\mathsf{L}_{Y_1,\dots,Y_n|X_{2,1},\dots X_{2,n},X_{3,1},\dots,X_{3,n}}(\beta_1,\beta_2,\beta_3,\sigma^2)$$

$$= (2\pi\sigma^2)^{-n/2}\exp\left\{-\frac{1}{2\sigma^2}\sum_{i=1}^n(Y_i - \beta_1 - \beta_2 X_{2,i} - \beta_3 X_{3,i})^2\right\}. \quad (7.2.2)$$

The maximum likelihood estimators for the parameters β_1, β_2, β_3 are found by minimizing the sum of squared deviations:

$$\mathsf{SSD}(\beta_1,\beta_2,\beta_3) = \sum_{i=1}^n(Y_i - \beta_1 - \beta_2 X_{2,i} - \beta_3 X_{3,i})^2. \quad (7.2.3)$$

As in the two-variable regression model, (7.2.3) will have a unique minimum.

A derivation of the maximum likelihood estimators using the original parameters would involve solving three linear equations each with three unknown parameters, whereas with a derivation using orthogonalized regressors, three linear equations each with only one unknown parameter have to be solved. The expressions for the regression estimators in (7.2.1) indicate that it is natural to derive them by orthogonalizing the regressors along the lines of §5.2.3.

7.2.2 Orthogonalizing variables and reparametrizations

We will start by deriving an orthogonalized regression equation. As in §5.2.3 the variable $X_{2,i}$ is regressed on $X_{1,i} = 1$ giving the decomposition:

$$X_{2,i} = X_{2\cdot1,i} + \widehat{X}_{2,i}, \quad (7.2.4)$$

where $X_{2\cdot1,i} = X_{2,i} - \widehat{X}_{2,i}$ and $\widehat{X}_{2,i} = \overline{X}_2$. In the same fashion $X_{3,i}$ is regressed on both $X_{1,i}, X_{2,i}$. If we use expression (5.2.11), this gives the decomposition:

$$X_{3,i} = X_{3\cdot1,2,i} + \widehat{X}_{3,i}, \quad (7.2.5)$$

where $X_{3\cdot1,2,i} = X_{3,i} - \widehat{X}_{3,i}$ and $\widehat{X}_{3,i} = \overline{X}_3 + aX_{2,i}$, with

$$a = \frac{\sum_{j=1}^{n}(X_{3,j} - \overline{X}_3)(X_{2,j} - \overline{X}_2)}{\sum_{k=1}^{n}(X_{2,k} - \overline{X}_2)^2} = \frac{\sum_{j=1}^{n}X_{3\cdot1,j}X_{2\cdot1,j}}{\sum_{k=1}^{n}X_{2\cdot1,k}^2}. \qquad (7.2.6)$$

By construction, the variables $X_{1,i}$, $X_{2\cdot1,i}$, and $X_{3\cdot1,2,i}$ are orthogonal:

$$\sum_{i=1}^{n}1 \cdot X_{2\cdot1,i} = 0, \quad \sum_{i=1}^{n}1 \cdot X_{3\cdot1,2,i} = 0, \quad \sum_{i=1}^{n}X_{2\cdot1,i} \cdot X_{3\cdot1,2,i} = 0. \qquad (7.2.7)$$

To achieve the orthogonalized equation, replace $X_{2,i}$ and $X_{3,i}$ in the model equation (7.1.1) by the decompositions (7.2.4) and (7.2.5), respectively, giving:

$$Y_i = \beta_1 + \beta_2\left(X_{2\cdot1,i} + \widehat{X}_{2,i}\right) + \beta_3\left(X_{3\cdot1,2,i} + \widehat{X}_{3,i}\right) + u_i.$$

Rearranging this equation and introducing the new parameters:

$$\delta_1 = \beta_1 + \beta_2\overline{X}_2 + \beta_3\overline{X}_3, \qquad \delta_2 = \beta_2 + a\beta_3, \qquad \delta_3 = \beta_3, \qquad (7.2.8)$$

leads to the reparametrized model equation:

$$Y_i = \delta_1 + \delta_2 X_{2\cdot1,i} + \delta_3 X_{3\cdot1,2,i} + u_i, \qquad (7.2.9)$$

which has orthogonal regressors as shown in (7.2.7).

7.2.3 The estimators

Using the orthogonalized model equation the sum of squared deviations (7.2.3) can be written in terms of the orthogonalized parameters as:

$$\mathsf{SSD}(\delta_1, \delta_2, \delta_3) = \sum_{i=1}^{n}(Y_i - \delta_1 - \delta_2 X_{2\cdot1,i} - \delta_3 X_{3\cdot1,2,i})^2.$$

Differentiating this expression with respect to any of $\widehat{\delta}_1, \widehat{\delta}_2$ and $\widehat{\delta}_3$, exploiting the orthogonal relationship in (7.2.7) and equating to zero, gives rise to linear likelihood equations, each with a single unknown parameter. For instance, the derivative with respect to δ_3 is:

$$\frac{\partial}{\partial\delta_3}\mathsf{SSD}(\delta_1, \delta_2, \delta_3) = -2\sum_{i=1}^{n}(Y_i - \delta_1 - \delta_2 X_{2\cdot1,i} - \delta_3 X_{3\cdot1,2,i})X_{3\cdot1,2,i}.$$

Using the orthogonal relationship in (7.2.7) and equating to zero leads to the linear likelihood equation:

$$\sum_{i=1}^{n}(Y_i - \widehat{\delta}_3 X_{3\cdot1,2,i})X_{3\cdot1,2,i} = 0, \qquad (7.2.10)$$

which is easily solved for $\widehat{\delta}_3$. Similarly, the likelihood equations for δ_1, δ_2 are:

$$\sum_{i=1}^{n}(Y_i - \widehat{\delta}_1 X_{1,i})X_{1,i} = 0 \text{ and } \sum_{i=1}^{n}(Y_i - \widehat{\delta}_2 X_{2\cdot 1,i})X_{2\cdot 1,i} = 0, \quad (7.2.11)$$

so the full set of maximum likelihood estimators is:

$$\widehat{\delta}_1 = \overline{Y}, \qquad \widehat{\delta}_2 = \frac{\sum_{i=1}^{n} Y_i X_{2\cdot 1,i}}{\sum_{j=1}^{n} X_{2\cdot 1,j}^2}, \qquad \widehat{\delta}_3 = \frac{\sum_{i=1}^{n} Y_i X_{3\cdot 1,2,i}}{\sum_{j=1}^{n} X_{3\cdot 1,2,j}^2}. \qquad (7.2.12)$$

It is immediately seen from (7.2.8) that $\widehat{\beta}_3 = \widehat{\delta}_3$, as suggested in (7.2.1).

The estimators for β_1, β_2 could be derived from those of δ_1, δ_2, δ_3 using (7.2.8). However, it is far easier to derive them simply by interchanging the roles of the regressors $X_{1,i} = 1$, $X_{2,i}$, $X_{3,i}$. In this way, the expression for $\widehat{\beta}_2$ in (7.2.1) is given in terms of the residuals from the two-variable regression of $X_{2,i}$ on $X_{1,i} = 1$ and $X_{3,i}$, that is:

$$X_{2\cdot 1,3,i} = (X_{2,i} - \overline{X}_2) - \frac{\sum_{j=1}^{n}(X_{2,j} - \overline{X}_2)(X_{3,j} - \overline{X}_3)}{\sum_{k=1}^{n}(X_{3,k} - \overline{X}_3)^2}(X_{3,i} - \overline{X}_3). \quad (7.2.13)$$

Likewise, the estimator $\widehat{\beta}_1$ is given in terms of the residuals from the two-variable regression of $X_{1,i}$ on $X_{2,i} = 1$ and $X_{3,i}$, that is:

$$X_{1\cdot 2,3,i} = X_{1\cdot 3,i} - \frac{\sum_{j=1}^{n} X_{1\cdot 3,j} X_{2\cdot 3,j}}{\sum_{k=1}^{n} X_{2\cdot 3,k}^2} X_{2\cdot 3,i}, \qquad (7.2.14)$$

where:

$$X_{1\cdot 3,i} = X_{1,i} - \frac{\sum_{j=1}^{n} X_{1,j} X_{3,j}}{\sum_{k=1}^{n} X_{3,k}^2} X_{3,i}, \qquad X_{2\cdot 3,i} = X_{2,i} - \frac{\sum_{j=1}^{n} X_{2,j} X_{3,j}}{\sum_{k=1}^{n} X_{3,k}^2} X_{3,i}.$$

Thus, the calculations for the regression of Y on X_2 and X_3 themselves involve regressing X_2 on X_3 (or vice versa).

The predictor for the conditional mean is the same for both parametrizations:

$$\widehat{Y}_i = \widehat{\beta}_1 + \widehat{\beta}_2 X_{2,i} + \widehat{\beta}_3 X_{3,i} = \widehat{\delta}_1 + \widehat{\delta}_2 X_{2\cdot 1,i} + \widehat{\delta}_3 X_{3\cdot 1,2,i}. \qquad (7.2.15)$$

This gives rise to the residuals $\widehat{u}_i = Y_i - \widehat{Y}_i$ as well as the residual sum of squared deviations:

$$\text{RSS} = \min_{\beta_1,\beta_2,\beta_3} \text{SSD}(\beta_1, \beta_2, \beta_3) = \min_{\delta_1,\delta_2,\delta_3} \text{SSD}(\delta_1, \delta_2, \delta_3) = \sum_{i=1}^{n} \widehat{u}_i^2.$$

In particular, using the orthogonalized parametrization, RSS is:

$$\text{RSS} = \sum_{i=1}^{n}(Y_i - \widehat{\delta}_1)^2 - \widehat{\delta}_2^2 \sum_{i=1}^{n} X_{2\cdot 1,i}^2 - \widehat{\delta}_3^2 \sum_{i=1}^{n} X_{3\cdot 1,2,i}^2 \qquad (7.2.16)$$

(see Exercise 7.5). The maximum likelihood estimator for σ^2 is in turn:

$$\widehat{\sigma}^2 = n^{-1}\mathsf{RSS},$$

whereas an unbiased estimator for σ^2 is found as $s^2 = (n-3)^{-1}\,\mathsf{RSS}$.

7.2.4 Application to the wage data

In §5.2.5 a two-variable model was used to explain log weekly wages, w_i, by the length of schooling, S_i. With the idea of diminishing returns to education in mind, it is natural to include the square of the length of schooling, S_i^2, as an additional regressor and to investigate the sign of its coefficient. Fitting the three-variable model to the data gives:

$$\widehat{w}_i = 4.79 - 0.050S_i + 0.0051S_i^2, \qquad (7.2.17)$$

$$= 5.02 + 0.076X_{S\cdot1,i} + 0.0051X_{S^2\cdot1,S,i}, \qquad (7.2.18)$$

$$\widehat{\sigma} = 0.7213 \qquad \widehat{\ell} = -4233.1. \qquad (7.2.19)$$

The orthogonalized fit in (7.2.18) is based on the residual $X_{S\cdot1,i}$ from regressing S_i on a constant and the residual $X_{S^2\cdot1,S,i}$ from regressing S_i^2 on S_i and a constant as regressors. The two parametrizations give rise to the same predictions, as argued in (7.2.15). Figure 7.1 shows this quadratic prediction combined with the cross plot and box plots of Figure 5.1. It is seen that the fitted curve largely stays within the conditional quartiles indicated by the box plots. The curve is decreasing for small values of schooling and increasing for large values of schooling. It is interesting to note that the sign of the linear term is different in (7.2.17) and (7.2.18). An explanation for this apparent sign change will be discussed in §7.3.1.

The elasticity associated with the fit (7.2.17) is found as in §5.3.2. Differentiate log wages, $w = \beta_1 + \beta_2 S + \beta_3 S^2$, with respect to log length of schooling, $s = \log S$, and use the chain rule to obtain:

$$\frac{\partial\,(\log W)}{\partial\,(\log S)} = \frac{\partial w}{\partial s} = \left(\frac{\partial w}{\partial S}\right)\left(\frac{\partial S}{\partial s}\right) = (\beta_2 + 2\beta_3 S)\frac{1}{S} = \frac{\beta_2}{S} + 2\beta_3.$$

Inserting the estimated values, the elasticity is found to be positive for most values of S. For instance, for the median value $S = 12$ we get an elasticity of $-0.050/12 + 0.0051 = 0.001$, increasing to $-0.050/20 + 0.0051 = 0.003$ for $S = 20$. This finding contradicts the theory of diminishing returns to schooling (Card, 1999) but it is consistent with recent findings of Belzil and Hansen (2002) and Söderbom, Teal, Wambugu and Kahyarara (2004). A first reaction is to check whether the estimate for the quadratic effect is significantly different from zero. The analysis in §7.6.3 will show this is actually the case. Rather than rejecting the theory outright, we will continue the econometric analysis of this aspect in Chapter 9, and in particular in §9.6.3, in order to understand this apparent inconsistency between theory and application.

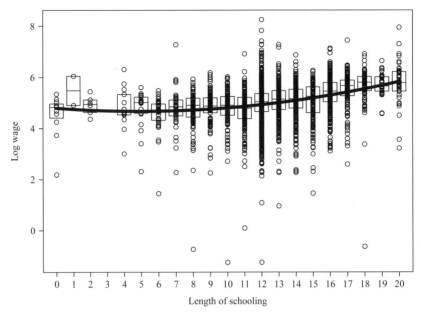

Figure 7.1 Cross plot of log wages by length of schooling showing the prediction from the regression (7.2.17)

7.3 PARTIAL CORRELATIONS

Correlations were introduced in §5.4 as standardized measures of the linear association between two variables. When dealing with three variables, it is natural to look at partial correlations. These measure the partial association between two variables given a third variable.

7.3.1 Sample partial correlations

The *partial correlation* between two variables Y_i and $X_{3,i}$ given a third variable $X_{2,i}$ is found as follows. Let $\widehat{u}_{y\cdot2,1,i}$ and $\widehat{u}_{3\cdot2,1,i}$ be the residuals of Y_i and $X_{3,i}$, respectively, regressed on $X_{2,i}$ and a constant. The sample correlation between $\widehat{u}_{y\cdot2,1,i}$ and $\widehat{u}_{3\cdot2,1,i}$ is then the sample partial correlation of Y_i and $X_{3,i}$ given $X_{2,i}$ and the constant:

$$r_{y,3\cdot1,2} = \frac{\sum_{i=1}^{n} \widehat{u}_{y\cdot2,1,i}\widehat{u}_{3\cdot2,1,i}}{\left(\sum_{i=1}^{n} \widehat{u}_{y\cdot2,1,i}^2\right)^{1/2}\left(\sum_{i=1}^{n} \widehat{u}_{3\cdot2,1,i}^2\right)^{1/2}}.$$

When $\widehat{u}_{y\cdot2,1,i}$ and $\widehat{u}_{3\cdot2,1,i}$ have a sample covariance of zero, then $r_{y,3\cdot1,2} = 0$. The partial correlation can also be expressed in terms of the pairwise correlations (see Exercise 7.6):

$$r_{y,3\cdot1,2} = \frac{r_{y,3\cdot1} - r_{y,2\cdot1}r_{2,3\cdot1}}{\left(1 - r_{y,2\cdot1}^2\right)^{1/2}\left(1 - r_{2,3\cdot1}^2\right)^{1/2}}. \tag{7.3.1}$$

Usually, intercepts are included when computing (partial) correlations, in which case the "·1" can be dropped from the notation. This is done immediately below.

Recalling the labor force survey, and in particular using the variables log wage, schooling and age, we find the following sample correlations:

$$r_{w,S} = 0.270, \qquad r_{w,A} = 0.115, \qquad r_{S,A} = -0.139.$$

Formula (7.3.1) then leads to the partial sample correlations:

$$r_{w,S \cdot A} = 0.291, \qquad r_{w,A \cdot S} = 0.161.$$

We see that age explains $r^2_{w,A \cdot S} = 0.161^2 = 3.0\%$ of the variation in log wages for individuals with the same length of education. In this situation, the partial correlations are slightly bigger than the simple correlations, for instance, $r^2_{w,A \cdot S} > r^2_{w,A}$, because age and education happen to be negatively correlated, and both have a positive effect on log wage. This means that we get more explanatory power from age in conjunction with log wage than when using it alone.

Sometimes the correlation of two variables and the partial correlation of the same two variables given a third may even have different sign. This is, for example, the case when $r_{y,2}$, $r_{y,3}$ and $r_{3,2}$ are all positive, but $r_{y,2} < r_{y,3}r_{3,2}$. As an illustration, consider the variables log wage, schooling, and its square for the census data:

$$r_{w,S} = 0.270, \qquad r_{w,S^2} = 0.286, \qquad r_{S,S^2} = 0.976.$$

In this case, the correlation between log wage and education changes sign when correcting for squared education:

$$r_{w,S \cdot S^2} = -0.040.$$

This explains the different signs to schooling in the two- and three-variable regressions in §§5.2.5 and 7.2.4.

7.3.2 Population partial correlations

For the corresponding population partial correlation, it holds that if Y and X_2 are independent given X_3, that is, if:

$$f_{Y,X_2|X_3}(y, x_2 \mid x_3) = f_{Y|X_3}(y \mid x_3)f_{X_2|X_3}(x_2 \mid x_3),$$

then the partial correlation of Y and X_2 given X_3 is $\rho_{y,2 \cdot 3} = 0$.

7.3.3 Collinearity

The formulas for the regression estimators in the three-variable model can be formulated in terms of partial correlation coefficients. For example, as proved in

Exercise 7.7:

$$\left\{ \frac{\sum_{i=1}^{n}(X_{2,i} - \overline{X}_2)^2}{\sum_{i=1}^{n}(Y_i - \overline{Y})^2} \right\}^{1/2} \widehat{\beta}_2 = \left(\frac{1 - r_{y,3\cdot1}^2}{1 - r_{2,3\cdot1}^2} \right)^{1/2} r_{y,2\cdot1,3} = \frac{r_{y,2\cdot1} - r_{y,3\cdot1}r_{3,2\cdot1}}{1 - r_{2,3\cdot1}^2}.$$

(7.3.2)

It is seen that the signs of the regression estimator $\widehat{\beta}_2$ and the partial correlation $r_{y,2\cdot1,3}$ are the same. Signs of estimators are therefore only interpretable in the context of a given set of estimators.

When $r_{2,3\cdot1} = 0$, then the expression in (7.3.2) reduces to the same expression as for a regression estimator in a two-variable model (see §5.4.3). This is the situation where the regressors X_2 and X_3 have a sample correlation of zero and are therefore orthogonal.

If $r_{2,3\cdot1}^2 = 1$, we would be dividing by zero in expression (7.3.2), which must be avoided. This situation is called perfect *collinearity* between X_2 and X_3. This essentially means that the two variables offer exactly the same explanation, so one should be omitted from the regression. In practice, perfect collinearity arises only as a result of an over-specified model. For example, when regressing on indicator variables for men and for women as well as a constant, each regressor can be obtained as a linear combination of the other two, so one of the three regressors can be omitted without loss of generality.

In practice, it is more of a problem if $r_{2,3\cdot1}^2$ is close to unity but differs slightly from one. That situation is called *near collinearity*. An example of near collinearity was given in §7.3.1, where the correlation between schooling and its square was found to be 0.976. Near collinearity potentially implies numerical problems in the computation of the regression estimators, as well as their variances being large (see §7.5 below). It is important to realize that near collinearity is a consequence of the chosen parametrization, and it can be avoided by orthogonalizing the regressors resulting in the reparametrized model:

$$Y_i = \beta_1 + \beta_2 X_{2,i} + \beta_3 X_{3,i} + u_i = \delta_1 + \delta_2 X_{2\cdot1,i} + \delta_3 X_{3\cdot1,2,i} + u_i,$$

as discussed in §7.2. When the squared sample correlation $r_{2,3\cdot1}^2$ is high, there can be numerical problems in computing the estimators $\widehat{\beta}_1, \widehat{\beta}_2$ and $\widehat{\beta}_3$. The near collinearity will not be a problem when estimating δ_1, δ_2, but some numerical problems remain for $\widehat{\delta}_3$. Due to the near collinearity, the importance of the regressor $X_{3\cdot1,2,i}$ will typically be modest. Near collinearity, however, has little consequence for finding the predictor $\widehat{Y}_i$ of Y_i, the residuals $\widehat{u}_i$, the variance estimator $\widehat{\sigma}^2$, and the maximum likelihood value $\max L$. The problem in estimating the original parameters β_1, β_2, β_3 remains, since β_1, β_2, β_3 are all functions of δ_3. If β_1, β_2, β_3 are indeed the *parameters of economic interest*, a solution could be to find different variables which carry the same economic interpretation but are less collinear. In a k-variable model, orthogonalization may help to detect problematic variables.

Orthogonalization requires a hierarchy of the regressors to determine which regressors should be orthogonalized with respect to which. In most applications, econometric models will have a richer structure than theory models. Such a framework could suggest that a hierarchy.

It is important to note that the degree of near collinearity is not unique to a model but depends on the choice of explanatory variables. Orthogonalizing the regressors does not change the model and the likelihood, but it eliminates the near collinearity. In contrast to this situation, perfect collinearity is unique to the model and cannot be eliminated by orthogonalization.

7.4 MULTIPLE CORRELATIONS

Another generalization of the sample correlation is the multiple correlation. This is also known as the coefficient of determination, and it is often used to judge how a regression model describes the variation of the dependent variable.

7.4.1 The sample multiple correlation

The squared *multiple correlation* R^2 generalizes the squared correlation as used in equation (5.4.10). Recall the following quantities:

$$\text{explained sum of squares}: \quad \text{ESS} = \sum_{i=1}^{n} (\widehat{Y}_i - \overline{Y})^2,$$

$$\text{residual sum of squares}: \quad \text{RSS} = \sum_{i=1}^{n} (Y_i - \widehat{Y}_i)^2 = \sum_{i=1}^{n} \widehat{u}_i^2,$$

$$\text{total sum of squares}: \quad \text{TSS} = \sum_{i=1}^{n} (Y_i - \overline{Y})^2,$$

where, in a three-variable model, Y_i is predicted by $\widehat{Y}_i = \widehat{\beta}_1 + \widehat{\beta}_2 X_{2,i} + \widehat{\beta}_3 X_{3,i}$ but the residuals are still $\widehat{u}_i = Y_i - \widehat{Y}_i$. We will call the ratio:

$$R^2 = \frac{\text{ESS}}{\text{TSS}} \tag{7.4.1}$$

the squared *sample multiple correlation*. In the two-variable model, this expression reduces to the usual squared *sample correlation*.

The multiple correlation satisfies an intriguing product relation with correlations and partial correlations (see Exercise 7.8):

$$(1 - R^2) = (1 - r_{y,3\cdot 1,2}^2)(1 - r_{y,2\cdot 1}^2). \tag{7.4.2}$$

We have the orthogonality property:

$$\sum_{i=1}^{n}(Y_i - \widehat{Y}_i)(\widehat{Y}_i - \overline{Y}) = 0, \qquad (7.4.3)$$

just as in (5.4.8) for the two-variable model, and therefore:

$$\mathsf{TSS} = \mathsf{ESS} + \mathsf{RSS}. \qquad (7.4.4)$$

This relation ensures that R^2 lies in the interval 0 to 1, and it is often interpreted as the proportion of variation that is explained by the model. When used in this way, it is called the *coefficient of determination*.

It is worth noting that R^2 is not unique for a given model, but depends on the choice of dependent variable. Subtracting a regressor once on both sides of a regression equation does not change the model and the likelihood, but it can change R^2 considerably. A first example will be given in §7.6.7 below.

In the census data, we find that R^2 increases from 5.7% when regressing log wage on education to 8.5% when including age in the regression model. While both of these numbers show that most of the variation in the data is left unexplained, the increase in explanation is relatively large. One could get the idea of developing this into an automatic model selection strategy of searching for variables that make a high contribution to R^2. This would be considered a specific-to-general approach to modeling. It could be difficult to work with in practice, because, among other reasons, the sequence of adding variables matters when variables are correlated. An alternative automatic model section approach, using a general-to-specific approach, is discussed in Chapter 19.

7.4.2 Multiple correlations and the three-variable model

Just as correlations are related to error variance estimators in two-variable models, multiple correlations are related to them in three-variable models.

The error variance estimator in the three-variable model is $\widehat{\sigma}^2 n = \mathsf{RSS}$. First, by using the relation (7.4.4) and then the definition of R^2 in (7.4.1):

$$\widehat{\sigma}^2 n = \mathsf{TSS} - \mathsf{ESS} = \left(1 - \frac{\mathsf{ESS}}{\mathsf{TSS}}\right)\mathsf{TSS} = \left(1 - R^2\right)\mathsf{TSS}. \qquad (7.4.5)$$

Due to the relation (7.4.2), this can again be rewritten as:

$$\widehat{\sigma}^2 n = (1 - r_{y,3\cdot1,2}^2)(1 - r_{y,2\cdot1}^2)\mathsf{TSS}. \qquad (7.4.6)$$

Here the term $(1 - r_{y,2\cdot1}^2)\mathsf{TSS}$ is the variance, $\widehat{\sigma}_{\beta_3=0}^2$ say, in a two-variable model where Y_i is regressed on $X_{2,i}$. The partial correlation coefficient, or rather the difference $(1 - r_{y,3\cdot1,2}^2)$, therefore represents the reduction in residual variance by adding a regressor to a two-variable model.

7.5 PROPERTIES OF ESTIMATORS

The distributions of the estimators are closely related to what we found for the two-variable model in §5.5. The maximum likelihood estimators in the original model, $\widehat{\beta}_k$, or the orthogonalized estimators $\widehat{\delta}_k$ for that matter, are all of the form:

$$\widehat{\theta} = \frac{\sum_{i=1}^{n} w_{k,i} Y_i}{\sum_{i=1}^{n} w_{k,i}^2}$$

for a weight function depending only on the information set $\mathcal{I}$ given by the regressors $X_{2,i}, X_{3,i}$ for $i = 1, \ldots n$. The conditional distribution of $\widehat{\theta}$ given $\mathcal{I}$ is in turn of the form:

$$\left(\widehat{\theta} \,\middle|\, \mathcal{I} \right) \overset{D}{=} \mathsf{N} \left[\theta, \frac{\sigma^2}{\sum_{i=1}^{n} w_{k,i}^2} \right].$$

For a specific estimator like $\widehat{\beta}_3$, the derivation is exactly as in §5.5: Replace Y_i by the model equation and exploit the orthogonality:

$$\widehat{\beta}_3 = \frac{\sum_{i=1}^{n} X_{3\cdot 1,2,i} \left(\beta_1 X_{1,i} + \beta_2 X_{2,i} + \beta_3 X_{3,i} + u_i \right)}{\sum_{i=1}^{n} X_{3\cdot 1,2,i}^2} = \beta_3 + \frac{\sum_{i=1}^{n} X_{3\cdot 1,2,i} u_i}{\sum_{i=1}^{n} X_{3\cdot 1,2,i}^2}.$$

Using the properties of the error distribution and of $X_{3\cdot 1,2,i}$, we then get:

$$\left(\widehat{\beta}_3 \,\middle|\, \mathcal{I} \right) \overset{D}{=} \mathsf{N} \left[\beta_3, \frac{\sigma^2}{\sum_{i=1}^{n} X_{3\cdot 1,2,i}^2} \right].$$

The covariances of the estimators can also be described. Starting with the orthogonal parametrization $\delta_1, \delta_2, \delta_3$ is easiest. In this case the weights are $w_{1,i} = X_{1,i} = 1$, $w_{2,i} = X_{2\cdot 1,i}$, and $w_{3,i} = X_{3\cdot 1,2,i}$, which are orthogonal:

$$\sum_{i=1}^{n} X_{1,i} X_{2\cdot 1,i} = 0, \qquad \sum_{i=1}^{n} X_{1,i} X_{3\cdot 1,2,i} = 0, \qquad \sum_{i=1}^{n} X_{2\cdot 1,i} X_{3\cdot 1,2,i} = 0.$$

$$(7.5.1)$$

As a consequence, the associated estimators are uncorrelated:

$$\mathsf{Cov}\left(\widehat{\delta}_1, \widehat{\delta}_2 \right) = \mathsf{Cov}\left(\widehat{\delta}_1, \widehat{\delta}_3 \right) = \mathsf{Cov}\left(\widehat{\delta}_2, \widehat{\delta}_3 \right) = 0. \qquad (7.5.2)$$

In general, the estimators $\widehat{\beta}_1, \widehat{\beta}_2, \widehat{\beta}_3$ will be correlated. As an example, the covariance between $\widehat{\beta}_2$ and $\widehat{\beta}_3$ can be found as follows. Noting from (7.2.8) that $\widehat{\beta}_2 = \widehat{\delta}_2 - a\widehat{\delta}_3$ and $\widehat{\beta}_3 = \widehat{\delta}_3$ it follows that:

$$\mathsf{Cov}\left(\widehat{\beta}_2, \widehat{\beta}_3 \right) = \mathsf{Cov}\left(\widehat{\delta}_2, \widehat{\delta}_3 \right) - a\mathsf{Var}\left(\widehat{\delta}_3 \right) = -a\mathsf{Var}\left(\widehat{\delta}_3 \right). \qquad (7.5.3)$$

The case of near collinearity described in §7.3.3 is of some practical interest. This is the situation where the square of the sample correlation between $X_{2,i}$ and $X_{3,i}$ is close to unity. To illustrate what happens, we will express the variances of $\widehat{\beta}_2$ and $\widehat{\beta}_3$ in terms of $r_{2,3\cdot1}$:

$$\text{Var}\left(\widehat{\beta}_3\right) = \frac{\sigma^2}{\sum_{j=1}^n X_{3\cdot1,2,j}^2} = \frac{\sigma^2}{(1 - r_{2,3\cdot1}^2)\sum_{j=1}^n X_{3\cdot1,j}^2}, \qquad (7.5.4)$$

$$\text{Var}\left(\widehat{\beta}_2\right) = \frac{\sigma^2}{\sum_{j=1}^n X_{2\cdot1,3,j}^2} = \frac{\sigma^2}{(1 - r_{2,3\cdot1}^2)\sum_{j=1}^n X_{2\cdot1,j}^2}, \qquad (7.5.5)$$

whereas their covariance satisfy:

$$\text{Cov}\left(\widehat{\beta}_2,\widehat{\beta}_3\right) = -a\text{Var}\left(\widehat{\delta}_3\right) = \frac{-\sigma^2 r_{2,3\cdot1}}{(1 - r_{2,3\cdot1}^2)\sqrt{\sum_{j=1}^n X_{2\cdot1,j}^2 \sum_{j=1}^n X_{3\cdot1,j}^2}}.$$

In the case of near collinearity, $r_{2,3\cdot1}^2$ will be close to unity, and hence $1 - r_{2,3\cdot1}^2$ appearing in the dominator will be close to zero. Both variances and the correlation will then be large, indicating considerable uncertainty. In the orthogonalized parametrization, the collinearity problem will be concentrated on δ_3, whereas δ_2 will be better estimated with a more modest variance.

The distribution of the error-variance estimator can be shown to be:

$$\widehat{\sigma}^2 \overset{\text{D}}{=} \frac{\sigma^2}{n}\chi^2\left[n - 3\right].$$

Recall the definition of the $\chi^2[m]$-distribution in §4.4.2 as a sum of m independent $\chi^2[1]$-variables. The result for $\widehat{\sigma}^2$ therefore comes about since it is the sum of squared residuals, and the residuals $\widehat{u}_i$ are each normally distributed, but satisfy the three constraints arising from the likelihood equations in (7.2.10) and (7.2.11).

7.6 INFERENCE

The principles for inference in the three-variable regression model are as discussed for the two-variable model in §5.5. While the likelihood ratio test statistics for the two-variable model are formulated in terms of sample correlations, now partial and multiple correlations are involved.

7.6.1 The likelihood ratio test

In the three-variable model, there are three types of hypotheses of interest. In each case, the likelihood ratio statistic is approximately χ^2-distributed, but the statistics will be computed in different ways using the partial correlations, the sample correlations, and the multiple correlation coefficient.

The general appearance of the likelihood ratio test statistic in the three-variable model is just as in §5.5.2. The likelihood ratio test statistic itself is:

$$Q = \frac{\max_{restricted} L_{Y_1,\ldots,Y_n|X_{2,1},\ldots,X_{2,n},X_{3,1},\ldots,X_{3,n}}(\beta_1,\beta_2,\beta_3,\sigma^2)}{\max_{unrestricted} L_{Y_1,\ldots,Y_n|X_{2,1},\ldots,X_{2,n},X_{3,1},\ldots,X_{3,n}}(\beta_1,\beta_2,\beta_3,\sigma^2)} = \left(\frac{\widehat{\sigma}_R^2}{\widehat{\sigma}^2}\right)^{-n/2},$$

whereas the corresponding log-likelihood ratio statistic satisfies:

$$LR = -2\log Q = -n\log\left(\frac{\widehat{\sigma}^2}{\widehat{\sigma}_R^2}\right) \overset{D}{\approx} \chi^2[m],$$

where the degrees of freedom m reflect the number of restrictions imposed.

The first hypothesis of interest is to restrict one of the parameters to be zero, for instance, $\beta_3 = 0$, which reduces the model to the two-variable model in Chapter 5. Due to the expression for the variance estimators in the three-variable model and the two-variable model found in (7.4.6) and (5.4.5) respectively, the log-likelihood ratio statistic satisfies:

$$LR_{\beta_3=0} = -n\log(1 - r_{y,3\cdot1,2}^2) \overset{D}{\approx} \chi^2[1].$$

A second hypothesis is to restrict the parameters of both the regressors to zero, so $\beta_2 = \beta_3 = 0$, which reduces the model to the one-variable regression model of Chapter 3. Using the variance expressions (7.4.5) and (3.3.9), the test statistic for this hypothesis against the three-variable model is found to be:

$$LR_{\beta_2=\beta_3=0} = -n\log(1 - R^2) \overset{D}{\approx} \chi^2[2].$$

A model like the three-variable model is often reduced in a step-wise procedure. This will be discussed further below. Here we simply note that if the hypothesis $\beta_3 = 0$ is true, the second hypothesis, $\beta_2 = \beta_3 = 0$, could be tested within the two-variable model studied in §5.5.2:

$$LR_{\beta_2=0|\beta_3=0} = -n\log(1 - r_{y,2\cdot1}^2) \overset{D}{\approx} \chi^2[1].$$

The three test statistics above are related by:

$$LR_{\beta_2=\beta_3=0} = LR_{\beta_3=0} + LR_{\beta_2=0|\beta_3=0}.$$

This comes about either by using the logarithm of the formula (7.4.2) or simply by writing out the error variance estimates:

$$-n\log\left(\frac{\widehat{\sigma}^2}{\widehat{\sigma}_{\beta_2=\beta_3=0}^2}\right) = -n\log\left(\frac{\widehat{\sigma}^2}{\widehat{\sigma}_{\beta_3=0}^2}\right) - n\log\left(\frac{\widehat{\sigma}_{\beta_3=0}^2}{\widehat{\sigma}_{\beta_2=\beta_3=0}^2}\right).$$

Moreover, within the three-variable regression model the test statistics $LR_{\beta_3=0}$ and $LR_{\beta_2=0|\beta_3=0}$ are independent. Their degrees of freedom therefore add to the degrees of freedom of the overall test statistic $LR_{\beta_2=\beta_3=0}$.

This idea opens the possibility of testing the joint hypothesis $\beta_2 = \beta_3 = 0$ in one or two steps. One should bear in mind, though, that the levels, or type I errors, add up when conducting multiple tests. To see this, let c_α be the critical value of a $\chi^2[1]$-test at level α, which would be about 4 for a 5%-level test. Due to their independence, the probability of not rejecting using both tests is:

$$P\left(LR_{\beta_3=0} < c\right) P\left(LR_{\beta_2=0|\beta_3=0} < c\right) \approx (1 - \alpha)^2 \approx 1 - 2\alpha, \qquad (7.6.1)$$

where the first approximation refers to the usage of asymptotic distributions, and the second to an expansion of the power function for small values of α. If the individual tests are at the 5% level, the overall test will be 10%. When only two tests are involved, the practical difference between levels of 5% and 10% is marginal (see also the discussion in §2.3.2). However, if more than just a couple of tests were performed, $k = 10$ say, the effect on the overal test significance level would be noticeable. Our general advice would be to split overall hypotheses into subhypotheses that have substantive interpretations and choose the levels accordingly.

7.6.2 Multiple testing

Up to this point, the underlying idea has been that the statistical model is correct. The distributions for estimators and test statistics would be normal or χ^2 under this assumption. In practice, models will not be correct, and in particular the discussion in §7.6.1 above points to a multiple testing approach with a possible accumulation of inferential errors. How will conductng a number of tests affect inference?

While we will never know whether a statistical model is correct, we should do our best to test whether it could be refuted, as well as to corroborate it with previous empirical and theoretical knowledge. Indeed, in the next chapter, a series of mis-specification tests will be introduced with the purpose of enhancing the possibility of rejecting models. Models constructed in this way, if not correct, will at least not be implausible. This suggests that we can adopt a "conditional interpretation" of statistical models, where we act as if the models are correct, and conduct inference using normal or χ^2-distributions. A schematic representation of this viewpoint is a three-variable model where a test for $\beta_3 = 0$ is conducted first using $LR_{\beta_3=0}$, and if that is accepted, then testing $\beta_2 = 0$ using $LR_{\beta_2=0|\beta_3=0}$. With this "conditional interpretation" a χ^2-distribution would apply for both tests.

An important prerequisite in §7.6.1 is that β_3 *is* zero when performing the second test. In practice, one would not know if $\beta_3 = 0$. In fact, the hypothesis $\beta_2 = 0$ would be considered only if testing supports *setting* β_3 to zero. If $LR_{\beta_3=0}$, is close to zero, then β_3 is unlikely to be far from zero, suggesting that only small errors will arise from acting as if $\beta_3 = 0$. When $\text{LR}_{\beta_3=0}$ is close to the critical value, however, there will be great uncertainty over the true value of β_3, raising a question over a "conditional interpretation" of the subsequent test for $\beta_2 = 0$. The use of χ^2-inference could introduce large errors in that case, and it would perhaps be more appropriate to use a so-called "pre-test distribution" reflecting the multiple testing being undertaken.

Extensive research has been conducted in this area indicating that one can go seriously wrong by applying the χ^2-distribution for the second test. Some of this literature, and some more specific evidence, will be discussed in the context of automatic model selection in Chapter 19. These studies suggest, however, that the errors in applying the χ^2-distribution are small in the important case where there is firm evidence for setting β_3 to zero, whereas the largest discrepancies come when the test for the restriction $\beta_3 = 0$ is marginal. This indicates that the errors in applying a "conditional interpretation" of the restricted model are modest. The exception is the marginal cases where inferences are bound to be uncertain, and should be done cautiously as pointed out in §2.3.2.

A similar discussion can be made for estimators. Here, the issue in question is the distribution of the estimator for β_2, which will be computed from a two-variable regression if the test for $\beta_3 = 0$ is not rejected, and otherwise from the three-variable regression. The problem is a little more complicated since regressors will in general be correlated, giving an additional dependence structure. If both the correlation of the regressors is modest and the test for $\beta_3 = 0$ does not give strong evidence against the restriction, the impact is modest, whereas in the case of either collinearity or a marginal test, the impact can be large, which is referred to variously as "pre-test bias", "selection bias", or "post-model selection bias". Orthogonalizing the regressor $X_{3,i}$ with respect to $X_{2,i}$ remedies the problem, by forcing the same interpretation and the same estimation for the parameter β_2 in the two-variable model and in the three-variable model. This argument is in parallel with the discussion of omitted variable bias in §5.3.3.

7.6.3 Example: likelihood statistics and partial correlations

To illustrate the connection between the likelihood ratio test statistic and partial correlations, we will return to the regression linking log wage with a quadratic specification in schooling in §7.2.4. The coefficient, β_3 say, for the square of schooling was found to be positive. Using a likelihood ratio test, it can be investigated whether it is significantly different from zero. To do this, we compare the likelihood values for the three-variable regression in (7.2.19) and the two-variable regression in 5.2.5 giving:

$$\text{LR} = -2(4254.3 + 4233.1) = 42.4,$$

with $p < 0.001$ using a $\chi^2[1]$-distribution indicating that the hypothesis should be rejected even at a 1% level. This is an instance where the signed likelihood ratio test statistic introduced in §4.3.3 is less convincing in use since we expect the sign of β_3 to be non-positive and find that $\widehat{\beta}_3$ is positive.

	coefficient	standard error	t-value	t-prob	partial R^2
constant	4.79	0.12	38.4	0.000	0.2754
schooling	-0.050	0.020	-2.52	0.012	0.0016
schooling^2	0.00515	0.00079	6.53	0.000	0.0109
$\widehat{\sigma} = 0.7212$	RSS = 2015.49		$R^2 = 0.083$	$\widehat{\ell} = -4233$	

Table 7.1 Three-variable model for log weekly wages

Econometric packages will typically give a little more information than simply the estimates and the likelihood value. Table 7.1 reports a more complete regression analysis for the three-variable model than reported in §7.2.4. In particular, the partial correlation between log wages and the square of education given the other variables is reported. The likelihood ratio test statistic for testing that the coefficient of the square of schooling is zero can then be computed as:

$$\text{LR} = -n \log \left(1 - r_{w,S^2 \cdot S,1}^2 \right) = -3877 \log(1 - 0.0109) = 42.4.$$

7.6.4 Example: higher dimensional multiple regressions

The discussion in §7.6.1 carries through to multiple regression models with more than three variables. To illustrate the ideas involved, we will regress log wage on schooling, the square of schooling, and the log of usual hours worked per week in 1979. For the unrestricted model, the output is given in Table 7.2, whereas Table 7.1 reported results when hours worked is omitted. In the four-variable model, the multiple correlation satisfies a formula like (7.4.1), while the partial correlations are obtained by correcting for three variables, one of which could be the intercept.

	coefficient	standard error	t-value	t-prob	partial R^2
constant	1.98	0.14	13.9	0.000	0.0476
schooling	-0.038	0.018	-2.17	0.030	0.0012
schooling^2	0.00460	0.00070	6.55	0.000	0.0109
log hours	0.783	0.025	31.6	0.000	0.2054
$\widehat{\sigma} = 0.6430$	RSS = 1601.53		$R^2 = 0.271$	$\widehat{\ell} = -3787$	

Table 7.2 Four-variable model for log weekly wages including hours worked

If we want to test the hypothesis that hours worked is irrelevant, we can form the test statistic in various ways. The log-likelihood ratio test statistic can be found by comparing the two log-likelihood values or using the partial correlation:

$$\text{LR} = 2(-3787 + 4233) = -3877 \log(1 - 0.2054) = 891,$$

with $p < 0.001$ using a $\chi^2[1]$-distribution. The hypothesis is rejected. It is not surprising that hours worked has an impact on the weekly wage. What is more surprising is that hours worked has by far the largest partial correlation with the log wage. In §7.6.7 we will return to this model and consider whether the coefficient of hours worked could be unity.

7.6.5 Exact inference

Exact tests come about just as in §§3.4.2, 5.5.3. The least-squares error variance estimator in the $k = 3$ variable model is given by:

$$s^2 = \frac{n}{n-k}\widehat{\sigma}^2 = \frac{1}{n-k}\sum_{i=1}^{n}\widehat{u}_i^2.$$

An exact confidence interval, for instance, for β_3, or a one-sided test for a hypothesis on β_3, can be based on the t-test statistic:

$$Z = \frac{\widehat{\beta}_3 - \beta_3}{\widehat{se}(\widehat{\beta}_3)} \overset{D}{=} t\,[n-k] \qquad \text{where} \qquad \widehat{se}^2(\widehat{\beta}_3) = \frac{s^2}{\sum_{j=1}^{n} X_{3\cdot1,2}^2}.$$

When testing $m = 1, 2,$ or 3 linear restrictions in the $k = 3$ variable model, an F-test is used. This is given by:

$$F = \frac{(\widehat{\sigma}_R^2 - \widehat{\sigma}^2)/m}{\widehat{\sigma}^2/(n-k)} = \frac{(\text{RSS}_R - \text{RSS})/m}{\text{RSS}/(n-k)} \overset{D}{=} F\,(m, n-k)\,, \qquad (7.6.2)$$

where $\text{RSS}_R = \text{TSS}$ when testing that all parameters except the intercept are zero.

As an example, we revisit §7.6.4 and the hypothesis that hours worked is irrelevant. The F-test statistic is given by:

$$F = \frac{(2015.49 - 1601.53)/1}{1601.53/3877} = 1002.$$

Under the null hypothesis, this statistic is $F[1, 3873]$-distributed. Due to the large degrees of freedom of the unrestricted model, this distribution is close to the $\chi^2[1]$-distribution, and has a 95% quantile of 3.84. The test statistic is large compared to that value so we conclude that the hypothesis is rejected. A one-sided test can be formed from the t-test statistic. From the regression output of Table 7.2, we see that the t-statistic is 31.6. By comparing the 5% quantile of the $t[3873]$-distribution, which is 1.65, it is once again concluded that the hypothesis that hours worked is irrelevant is rejected.

7.6.6 Testing linear hypotheses involving several parameters

A linear restriction like $\beta_2 = \beta_3$ has 1 degree of freedom but involves two parameters. Such linear restrictions arise in connection with testing purchasing-power parity. To derive the test statistic, it is convenient to reparametrize the model and test that a single coefficient is zero. This could, for example, be done by testing $\delta_3 = \beta_3 - \beta_2 = 0$ in the model:

$$Y_i = \beta_1 + \beta_2 X_{2,i} + \beta_3 X_{3,i} + u_i = \underbrace{\beta_1}_{\delta_1} + \underbrace{\beta_2}_{\delta_2} \underbrace{(X_{2,i} + X_{3,i})}_{Z_{2,i}} + \underbrace{(\beta_3 - \beta_2)}_{\delta_3} \underbrace{X_{3,i}}_{Z_{3,i}} + u_i.$$

$$(7.6.3)$$

It is now clear that the likelihood ratio test statistic is based on $r_{y,z_3 \cdot z_2,1}$, which is the sample partial correlation of Y_i and $Z_{3,i} = X_{3,i}$ given the new regressor $Z_{2,i} = X_{2,i} + X_{3,i}$ and (of course) an intercept.

Regression software usually allows easy imposition of linear restrictions.

7.6.7 Testing affine hypotheses

A hypothesis like $\beta_3 = 1$ is an affine hypothesis, rather than a linear hypothesis, since the parameter of interest is not set to zero but to some other value. An example is the regression reported in Table 7.2, where it was of interest to test whether the coefficient of hours worked could be unity. This hypothesis can also be tested in a regression framework. To do so for a three-variable model, reparametrize the model as:

$$\underbrace{Y_i - X_{3,i}}_{W_i} = \underbrace{\beta_1}_{\delta_1} + \underbrace{\beta_2}_{\delta_2} X_{2,i} + \underbrace{(\beta_3 - 1)}_{\delta_3} \underbrace{X_{3,i}}_{Z_{3,i}} + u_i$$

and test that $\delta_3 = 0$. The likelihood ratio test statistic is based on $r_{w,z_3 \cdot z_2,1}$, which is the sample partial correlation of W_i and $Z_{3,i}$ given $Z_{2,i}$ and (as usual) an intercept.

	coefficient	standard error	t-value	t-prob	partial R^2
constant	1.98	0.14	13.9	0.000	0.0476
education	-0.038	0.018	-2.17	0.030	0.0012
education^2	0.00460	0.00070	6.55	0.000	0.0109
log hours	-0.217	0.025	-8.77	0.000	0.0195
$\hat{\sigma} = 0.6430$	RSS $= 1601.53$		$R^2 = 0.111$	$\hat{\ell} = -3787$	

Table 7.3 Unrestricted model for hourly log wages

In this way, Table 7.3 represents a reparametrization of Table 7.2, where log hours per week has been subtracted from the log weekly wage, so the regressand becomes the log hourly wage. Note that nearly all reported figures are the same in the two tables. One of the few differing quantities is the regression estimate for log hours, but not its standard error. The t-statistics are different, but also test different hypotheses. Likewise, the partial correlation of hourly wages with hours is different from that of weekly wages with hours. The overall multiple correlation, R^2, is

	coefficient	standard error	t-value	t-prob	partial R^2
constant	1.20	0.11	10.7	0.000	0.0287
education	-0.035	0.018	-1.97	0.048	0.0010
education^2	0.00445	0.00071	6.27	0.000	0.0101
$\widehat{\sigma} = 0.6493$	RSS $= 1633.33$		$R^2 = 0.093$	$\widehat{\ell} = -3826$	

Table 7.4 Restricted model for hourly log wages

also different, demonstrating that R^2 is not invariant to changes of the regressand, whereas the maximum likelihood value is invariant to reparametrizations.

Table 7.4 reports the restricted model, where the coefficient of hours in Table 7.3 is now set to zero, corresponding to a coefficient of unity in the original regression in Table 7.2. The log-likelihood ratio test statistic for the hypothesis is:

$$LR = 2(-3725 + 3762) = 76,$$

with p < 0.001 using a $\chi^2[1]$-distribution. Thus, the hypothesis that the coefficient of hours worked is unity is not supported. Interestingly, the coefficient is between 0 and 1, indicating that hourly wages fall with hours worked.

A hypothesis like $\beta_2 + \beta_3 = 1$ is also an affine hypothesis. This is perhaps a situation where the name is more fitting, since the line $\beta_3 = 1 - \beta_2$ does not pass through the origin. An example of this restriction arises in connection with Cobb–Douglas production functions. A standard Cobb–Douglas production function for output, capital, and labor is:

$$output = e^{\beta_1} (capital)^{\beta_2} (labor)^{\beta_3} . \tag{7.6.4}$$

According to a hypothesis of constant returns to scale, the elasticities add up to unity: $\beta_2 + \beta_3 = 1$. Taking logarithms to linearize (7.6.4), we have:

$$y_i = \beta_1 + \beta_2 k_i + \beta_3 \ell_i,$$

where $y = \log$ output, $k = \log$ capital, and $\ell = \log$ labor. This hypothesis can also be tested in a regression framework. For a three-variable regression model, this is done by testing $\delta_3 = 0$ in:

$$\underbrace{Y_i - X_{3,i}}_{W_i} = \underbrace{\beta_1}_{\delta_1} + \underbrace{\beta_2}_{\delta_2} \underbrace{(X_{2,i} - X_{3,i})}_{Z_{2,i}} + \underbrace{(\beta_3 + \beta_2 - 1)}_{\delta_3} \underbrace{X_{3,i}}_{Z_{3,i}} + u_i. \tag{7.6.5}$$

Most regression software programs provide direct tests of both linear and affine hypotheses of interest, avoiding the need to actually reparametrize an equation for every test. This approach is referred to as restricted least squares estimation. It is discussed in Exercises 7.12 and 7.13. However, the above explanation applies to all such tests.

7.7 SUMMARY AND EXERCISES

Summary: A multiple regression model can have many regressors. Here we restricted attention to the three-variable regression model. That model illustrates the main principles, while the estimation algebra is still not too complicated.

The main difference from the two-variable model is the notion of partial effects. These are highlighted through partial correlation coefficients. The multiple correlation coefficient is another generalization of correlations, measuring the association between one variable on the one hand and multiple variables on the other hand.

Bibliography: Multiple regression and partial correlation are natural generalizations of their bivariate counterparts and have been widely studied for more than a century.

Key questions:

- Explain the difference between simple, partial, and multiple correlations.
- Discuss the validity of the assumptions of the statistical model for wages.

Exercise 7.1. *Give a detailed derivation of the conditional likelihood in (7.2.2), showing how the assumptions are used.*

Exercise 7.2. *Use (7.2.8) and (7.2.12) to verify the weight functions:*
(a) (7.2.13) for the estimator $\widehat{\beta}_2$,
(b) (7.2.14) for the estimator $\widehat{\beta}_1$.

Exercise 7.3. *Estimation without orthogonalizing regressors. Consider the sum of squared deviations (7.2.3). Find the partial derivatives with respect to $\beta_1, \beta_2, \beta_3$. Equate these to zero. Solve these likelihood equations for $\beta_1, \beta_2, \beta_3$ directly and show that the solutions equal those listed in (7.2.1).*

Exercise 7.4. *Frisch–Waugh Theorem. Define variables $\widehat{u}_{y\cdot 1,2,i}$ and $X_{3\cdot 1,2,i}$ as the residuals from regressing Y_i and $X_{3,i}$ on a constant and $X_{2,i}$. Show that the least-squares estimator of γ in the regression $\widehat{u}_{y\cdot 1,2,i} = \gamma X_{3\cdot 1,2,i} + v_i$ equals $\widehat{\beta}_3$ as given by (7.2.1).*
This result was proved by Frisch and Waugh (1933) who looked at two time series Y_i and $X_{3,i}$, where $X_{2,i}$ was a linear deterministic time trend.

Exercise 7.5. *Derive the formula (7.2.16) by exploiting (7.2.7).*

Exercise 7.6. *Derive the formula (7.3.1) by inserting the expressions for $\widehat{u}_{y\cdot 1,2,i}$ and $\widehat{u}_{3\cdot 1,2,i}$ and dividing both numerator and denominator by the square roots of $\sum_{i=1}^{n}(Y_i - \overline{Y})^2$ and $\sum_{i=1}^{n}(X_{3,i} - \overline{X}_3)^2$.*

Exercise 7.7. *Derive the formula (7.3.2). Note first that:*

$$\widehat{\beta}_2 = \frac{S_{y2\cdot 1,3}}{S_{22\cdot 1,3}} = \left(\frac{S_{yy\cdot 1,3}}{S_{22\cdot 1,3}}\right)^{1/2} \frac{S_{y2\cdot 1,3}}{(S_{yy\cdot 1,3}S_{22\cdot 1,3})^{1/2}}$$

where:

$$S_{y2\cdot 1,3} = \sum_{i=1}^{n} \widehat{u}_{y\cdot 1,3,i}\widehat{u}_{2\cdot 1,3,i}, \quad S_{yy\cdot 1,3} = \sum_{i=1}^{n} \widehat{u}_{y\cdot 1,3,i}^2, \quad S_{22\cdot 1,3} = \sum_{i=1}^{n} \widehat{u}_{2\cdot 1,3,i}^2,$$

then apply (7.3.1) and (5.4.5).

Exercise 7.8. *Prove the identity (7.4.2) in the following steps:*

(a) Use (7.2.16), (7.4.1) to argue: $R^2 = \dfrac{\widehat{\delta}_2^2 \sum_{i=1}^{n} X_{2\cdot 1,i}^2 + \widehat{\delta}_3^2 \sum_{i=1}^{n} X_{3\cdot 1,2,i}^2}{\sum_{i=1}^{n} \widehat{u}_{y\cdot 1}^2}$

(b) Argue that: $r_{y,2\cdot 1}^2 = \widehat{\delta}_2^2 \sum_{i=1}^{n} X_{2\cdot 1,i}^2 / \sum_{i=1}^{n} \widehat{u}_{y\cdot 1}^2.$

(c) Argue that: $r_{y,3\cdot 1,2}^2 = \widehat{\delta}_3^2 \sum_{i=1}^{n} X_{3\cdot 1,2,i}^2 / \sum_{i=1}^{n} \widehat{u}_{y\cdot 1,2}^2.$

(d) Argue that: $\sum_{i=1}^{n} \widehat{u}_{y\cdot 1,2}^2 / \sum_{i=1}^{n} \widehat{u}_{y\cdot 1}^2 = 1 - r_{y,2\cdot 1}^2.$

(e) Finish the proof, by combining the results (a)–(d).

Exercise 7.9. *Derive the formula (7.4.3) using (7.2.15). It is convenient to use the orthogonal parametrization and (7.2.7).*

Exercise 7.10. *Consider the three-variable model given by (7.1.1). Use (7.4.1) to show that the F-test statistic for the hypothesis $\beta_2 = \beta_3 = 0$ satisfies:*

$$F = \frac{R^2/2}{(1 - R^2)/(n - 3)}. \qquad (7.7.1)$$

This hypothesis, where all the regressors apart from the constant are excluded, is called the hypothesis of **overall significance** *of the regressors. It is part of the standard regression output from software, although the hypothesis is usually rejected.*

Exercise 7.11. **Three-variable regression model without intercept**:

$$Y_i = \beta_1 X_{1,i} + \beta_2 X_{2,i} + u_i.$$

(a) Orthogonalize $X_{2,i}$ with respect to $X_{1,i}$.

(b) Derive $\widehat{\beta}_2$.

(c) Find the distribution of $\widehat{\beta}_2$, assuming that the explanatory variables are fixed.

(d) What would the corresponding results be for β_1?

Exercise 7.12. **Testing equality of two regression coefficients**. *Consider the three-variable regression model (7.1.1). The hypothesis $\beta_2 = \beta_3$ can be tested using a t-test statistic for $\delta_3 = 0$ in the reparametrized model (7.6.3).*

(a) Write down an expression for this t-statistic in terms of the observations.

An alternative interpretation of that test statistic can be derived as follows.
(b) Write $\widehat{se}(\hat{\beta}_2 - \hat{\beta}_3)$ in terms of the observations. Hint: use:

$$\widehat{se}(\hat{\beta}_2 - \hat{\beta}_3) = \{\widehat{Var}(\hat{\beta}_2) + \widehat{Var}(\hat{\beta}_3) - 2\widehat{Cov}(\hat{\beta}_2, \hat{\beta}_3)\}^{1/2}.$$

(c) Show that the t-test statistic for $\delta_3 = 0$ equals $(\hat{\beta}_2 - \hat{\beta}_3)/\widehat{se}(\hat{\beta}_2 - \hat{\beta}_3)$.

Exercise 7.13. *Restricted least squares*. *Consider the three-variable regression model (7.1.1) . The hypothesis $\beta_2 + \beta_3 = 1$ can be tested using a t-statistic for $\delta_3 = 0$ in the reparametrized model (7.6.5).*
(a) Write down an expression for this t-statistic in terms of the observations.
An alternative interpretation of that test statistic can be derived as follows.
(b) Compute $\widehat{se}(\hat{\beta}_2 + \hat{\beta}_3)$. Hint: see Exercise 7.12.
(c) Show that the t-test statistic for $\delta_3 = 0$ equals $(\hat{\beta}_2 + \hat{\beta}_3 - 1)/\widehat{se}(\hat{\beta}_2 + \hat{\beta}_3)$.

Exercise 7.14. *Consider the model*

$$Y_i = \alpha + \beta X_i + \gamma Z_i + \varepsilon_i \qquad for\ i = 1, \dots, n,$$

Now, suppose wage data are available for a sample of n_1 men and n_2 women and that it has been established for given education level

$$log\ wage \overset{D}{=} N(\alpha_m + \beta educ, \sigma^2) \qquad for\ men,$$
$$log\ wage \overset{D}{=} N(\alpha_w + \beta educ, \sigma^2) \qquad for\ women.$$

(a) How would you use the above model to test the hypothesis $\alpha_m = \alpha_w$?
(b) Would you use a one-sided or a two-sided test?

Chapter Eight

The matrix algebra of multiple regression

In Chapter 6, the matrix algebra of the two-variable regression model was introduced. Building on that we will now elaborate on the matrix algebra for the multiple regression model. As pointed out in Chapter 6, the matrix algebra is not necessary for the rest of this book, but it will come in handy for further studies of econometrics.

The key to regression analysis is inversion of symmetric matrices. We will therefore elaborate on matrix inversion at first and then discuss how it underpins multiple regression, now with k regressors. Finally, we will briefly discuss some of the numerical aspects for the computer implementation of matrix inversion.

8.1 MORE ON INVERSION OF MATRICES

There are at least four approaches to inverting symmetric matrices of higher dimension. *First*, we could mimic the algorithm for solving two equations with two unknown parameters. *Second*, we could work with determinants, generalizing the idea in (6.2.1). The determinant approach to matrix inversion is also called Cramer's rule. This is used for regression analysis by for instance Gujarati (2003, §§B.4, B.5). *Third*, we could partition a $(k \times k)$-matrix into a (2×2)-block matrix and then generalize the idea in (6.2.2). We will briefly discuss this approach in this section, as it reveals some of the structures in regression analysis. *Finally*, a so-called QR-decomposition is useful for computer implementations, as will be discussed in §8.3.

A (3×3)-matrix can be partitioned as a (2×2)-block matrix:

$$\begin{pmatrix} \mathbf{m}_{11} & \mathbf{m}_{12} & \mathbf{m}_{13} \\ \mathbf{m}_{21} & \mathbf{m}_{22} & \mathbf{m}_{23} \\ \mathbf{m}_{31} & \mathbf{m}_{32} & \mathbf{m}_{33} \end{pmatrix} = \left(\begin{array}{c|cc} \mathbf{m}_{11} & \mathbf{m}_{12} & \mathbf{m}_{13} \\ \mathbf{m}_{21} & \mathbf{m}_{22} & \mathbf{m}_{23} \\ \mathbf{m}_{31} & \mathbf{m}_{32} & \mathbf{m}_{33} \end{array} \right).$$

In a similar way, any $(k \times k)$-matrix can be partitioned as a (2×2)-block matrix:

$$\mathbf{M} = \left(\begin{array}{c|c} \mathbf{M}_{11} & \mathbf{M}_{12} \\ \hline \mathbf{M}_{21} & \mathbf{M}_{22} \end{array} \right),$$

where $\mathbf{M}_{12} = \mathbf{M}'_{21}$. As in (6.2.2), we can define an upper triangular matrix:

$$\mathbf{L} = \begin{pmatrix} \mathbf{I} & -\mathbf{M}_{12}\mathbf{M}_{22}^{-1} \\ \mathbf{0} & \mathbf{I} \end{pmatrix} \quad \text{so} \quad \mathbf{LML}' = \begin{pmatrix} \mathbf{M}_{11\cdot 2} & \mathbf{0} \\ \mathbf{0} & \mathbf{M}_{22} \end{pmatrix},$$

where $\mathbf{M}_{11\cdot 2} = \mathbf{M}_{11} - \mathbf{M}_{12}\mathbf{M}_{22}^{-1}\mathbf{M}_{21}$. In the (3×3)-dimensional example above, $\mathbf{M}_{11\cdot 2}$ will be a scalar, while $\mathbf{M}_{22}$ is a (2×2)-matrix, which can be inverted using the techniques in §6.2.4, so we can invert a (3×3)-matrix. In particular, as in (6.2.3), it holds that:

$$\mathbf{M}^{-1} = \mathbf{L}' \left(\mathbf{LML}' \right)^{-1} \mathbf{L}, \tag{8.1.1}$$

so we can compute an expression for the inverse of $\mathbf{M}$. This is done in Exercise 8.1. Knowing how to invert matrices of dimension (2×2), we can invert a (4×4)-matrix, etc. In this way we have a recursive system for inverting symmetric matrices of any dimension.

8.2 MATRIX ALGEBRA OF MULTIPLE REGRESSION ANALYSIS

In the following we will first introduce the multiple regression model in matrix notation, then discuss the likelihood function, estimators, and their distribution.

8.2.1 The econometric model

The general multiple regression model has the model equation:

$$Y_i = \beta_1 + \beta_2 X_{2,i} + \cdots + \beta_k X_{k,i} + u_i$$

and satisfies the assumptions:

(i) *independence*: the k-vectors $(u_i, X_{2,i}, \ldots, X_{k,i})$ are independent across i;

(ii) *normality*: $(u_i \mid X_{2,i}, \ldots, X_{k,i}) \overset{\mathrm{D}}{=} \mathsf{N}[0, \sigma^2]$;

(iii) *exogeneity*: the explanatory variables $X_{2,i}, \ldots, X_{k,i}$ are exogenous;

(iv) *parameter space*: $\beta_1, \ldots, \beta_k, \sigma^2 \in \mathbb{R}^k \times \mathbb{R}_+$.

The n individual model equations can be stacked as:

$$\begin{pmatrix} Y_1 \\ \vdots \\ Y_n \end{pmatrix} = \begin{pmatrix} 1 & X_{2,1} & \cdots & X_{k,1} \\ \vdots & \vdots & & \vdots \\ 1 & X_{2,n} & \cdots & X_{k,n} \end{pmatrix} \begin{pmatrix} \beta_1 \\ \vdots \\ \beta_k \end{pmatrix} + \begin{pmatrix} u_1 \\ \vdots \\ u_n \end{pmatrix},$$

or in more compact notation, with dimension indicated below, as:

$$\underbrace{\mathbf{Y}}_{n \times 1} = \underbrace{\mathbf{X}}_{n \times k} \underbrace{\beta}_{k \times 1} + \underbrace{\mathbf{u}}_{n \times 1}. \tag{8.2.1}$$

8.2.2 Estimators and likelihood function

The formulas for estimators and the analysis of the likelihood function described in §6.3 apply directly. In particular, using the model equation (8.2.1) we have:

$$\widehat{\beta} = \left(\mathbf{X}'\mathbf{X}\right)^{-1}\mathbf{X}'\mathbf{Y}$$

$$= \left(\mathbf{X}'\mathbf{X}\right)^{-1}\mathbf{X}'\left(\mathbf{X}\beta + \mathbf{u}\right) = \beta + \left(\mathbf{X}'\mathbf{X}\right)^{-1}\mathbf{X}'\mathbf{u}, \qquad (8.2.2)$$

$$n\widehat{\sigma}^2 = \mathbf{Y}'\mathbf{Y} - \mathbf{Y}'\mathbf{X}\left(\mathbf{X}'\mathbf{X}\right)^{-1}\mathbf{X}'\mathbf{Y} = \widehat{\mathbf{u}}'\widehat{\mathbf{u}}, \qquad (8.2.3)$$

where $\widehat{\mathbf{u}}$ are the residuals, which in Exercise 8.2 are shown to satisfy:

$$\widehat{\mathbf{u}} = \{\mathbf{I}_n - \mathbf{X}\left(\mathbf{X}'\mathbf{X}\right)^{-1}\mathbf{X}'\}\mathbf{Y} = \{\mathbf{I}_n - \mathbf{X}\left(\mathbf{X}'\mathbf{X}\right)^{-1}\mathbf{X}'\}\mathbf{u}. \qquad (8.2.4)$$

8.2.3 Expectation of $\widehat{\beta}$

First of all, we need a definition for the expectation of vectors:

$$\mathsf{E}\left(\widehat{\beta}\right) = \mathsf{E}\begin{pmatrix} \widehat{\beta}_1 \\ \vdots \\ \widehat{\beta}_k \end{pmatrix} \overset{\text{def}}{=} \begin{pmatrix} \mathsf{E}(\widehat{\beta}_1) \\ \vdots \\ \mathsf{E}(\widehat{\beta}_k) \end{pmatrix}.$$

Due to the linear algebra for vectors and the linearity of expectations:

$$\mathsf{E}\left(\underbrace{\mathbf{a}}_{m \times k}\underbrace{\widehat{\beta}}_{k \times 1} + \underbrace{\mathbf{b}}_{m \times 1}\right) = \underbrace{\mathbf{a}}_{m \times k}\mathsf{E}\left(\widehat{\beta}\right)\underbrace{}_{k \times 1} + \underbrace{\mathbf{b}}_{m \times 1}.$$

As a consequence of this formula we find $\mathsf{E}(\mathbf{u}|\mathbf{X}) = \mathbf{0}$, hence:

$$\mathsf{E}\left(\widehat{\beta}\,\Big|\,\mathbf{X}\right) = \beta.$$

8.2.4 Variance of $\widehat{\beta}$

The variance of a vector is defined as the matrix of variances and covariances:

$$\mathsf{Var}\left(\widehat{\beta}\right) \overset{\text{def}}{=} \begin{pmatrix} \mathsf{Var}(\widehat{\beta}_1) & \mathsf{Cov}(\widehat{\beta}_1, \widehat{\beta}_2) & \cdots & \mathsf{Cov}(\widehat{\beta}_1, \widehat{\beta}_k) \\ \mathsf{Cov}(\widehat{\beta}_2, \widehat{\beta}_1) & \mathsf{Var}(\widehat{\beta}_2) & \ddots & \vdots \\ \vdots & \ddots & \ddots & \mathsf{Cov}(\widehat{\beta}_{k-1}, \widehat{\beta}_k) \\ \mathsf{Cov}(\widehat{\beta}_k, \widehat{\beta}_1) & \cdots & \mathsf{Cov}(\widehat{\beta}_k, \widehat{\beta}_{k-1}) & \mathsf{Var}(\widehat{\beta}_k) \end{pmatrix}.$$

The quadratic rule for variances of scalars can then be generalized to:

$$\mathsf{Var}\left(\underbrace{\mathbf{a}}_{m \times k}\underbrace{\widehat{\beta}}_{k \times 1} + \underbrace{\mathbf{b}}_{m \times 1}\right) = \underbrace{\mathbf{a}}_{m \times k}\mathsf{Var}\left(\widehat{\beta}\right)\underbrace{}_{k \times k}\underbrace{\mathbf{a}'}_{k \times m}.$$

As a consequence of this formula we find $\text{Var}(\mathbf{u}|\mathbf{X}) = \sigma^2 \mathbf{I}_n$, hence:

$$\text{Var}\left(\widehat{\beta}\,\Big|\,\mathbf{X}\right) = \left(\mathbf{X}'\mathbf{X}\right)^{-1}\mathbf{X}'\sigma^2\mathbf{I}_n\mathbf{X}\left(\mathbf{X}'\mathbf{X}\right)^{-1} = \sigma^2\left(\mathbf{X}'\mathbf{X}\right)^{-1}.$$

8.2.5 Relation between $\widehat{\beta}$ and residuals

According to (8.2.2) and (8.2.3), the regression estimator and the residuals are:

$$\widehat{\beta} - \beta = \left(\mathbf{X}'\mathbf{X}\right)^{-1}\mathbf{X}'\mathbf{u}, \qquad \widehat{\mathbf{u}} = \{\mathbf{I}_n - \mathbf{X}\left(\mathbf{X}'\mathbf{X}\right)^{-1}\mathbf{X}'\}\mathbf{u}.$$

Using the techniques for expectations and variances stated above, we then have:

$$\mathsf{E}\left(\widehat{\beta} - \beta\right) = \mathbf{0}, \qquad \mathsf{E}\left(\widehat{\mathbf{u}}\right) = \mathbf{0}, \qquad \mathsf{Cov}\left(\widehat{\beta} - \beta, \widehat{\mathbf{u}}\right) = \mathbf{0}.$$

Thus, regression separates the information given in the dependent-variable vector $\mathbf{Y}$ into two unrelated parts: the explained part given by the estimator $\mathbf{X}\widehat{\beta}$ and the unexplained part given by the residuals $\widehat{\mathbf{u}}$, that is, $\mathbf{Y} = \mathbf{X}\widehat{\beta} + \widehat{\mathbf{u}}$. It is possible to argue that $\widehat{\beta} - \beta$ and $\widehat{\mathbf{u}}$ are not only uncorrelated, but also independent.

The independence result can be elaborated a little further for the partial regression model:

$$\mathbf{Y} = \mathbf{X}_1\beta_1 + \mathbf{X}_2\beta_2 + \mathbf{u},$$

with hypothesis $\beta_2 = \mathbf{0}$. Let LR denote the log-likelihood ratio test statistic for the hypothesis, and $\widehat{\mathbf{u}}_U$ the residuals in the unrestricted model, while $\widehat{\mathbf{u}}_R$, $\widehat{\beta}_{1,R}$, and $\widehat{\sigma}_R^2$ are the residuals and estimators in the restricted model without $\mathbf{X}_2$. By the same argument as above, it holds that $\mathbf{X}_1\widehat{\beta}_{1,R}$, $\widehat{\mathbf{u}}_R - \widehat{\mathbf{u}}_U$, and $\widehat{\mathbf{u}}_U$ are uncorrelated and independent. This independence sustains the exact distribution theory for F- and t-tests. Further, $\widehat{\beta}_{1,R}$, $\widehat{\sigma}_R^2$, and LR are independent, implying that we can separate the information about testing and about estimating the restricted model. This idea underpins the discussion in §7.6.2.

We can write $\mathbf{X}\widehat{\beta} = \mathbf{P}\mathbf{Y}$, where $\mathbf{P} = \mathbf{X}(\mathbf{X}'\mathbf{X})^{-1}\mathbf{X}'$. The square matrix $\mathbf{P}$ is idempotent: $\mathbf{PP} = \mathbf{P}$, and symmetric: $\mathbf{P} = \mathbf{P}'$, and is said to be an orthogonal projection matrix. Likewise $\widehat{\mathbf{u}} = \mathbf{QY}$, where $\mathbf{Q} = \mathbf{I}_n - \mathbf{P}$ is also an orthogonal projection matrix. If the regression analysis can be written in terms of orthogonal projections, the important orthogonality formula (7.4.3) is then a consequence of the property that $\mathbf{PQ} = \mathbf{0}$. Likewise, the formula TSS = ESS + RSS in (7.4.4) is a variant of Pythagoras' Theorem. Ruud (2000) presents regression analysis that way.

8.3 NUMERICAL COMPUTATION OF REGRESSION ESTIMATORS

Regression analysis is nearly synonymous with the problem of inverting matrices. We have seen that, except for diagonal matrices, it is actually hard to do inversions.

In the same way, it is difficult to compute the inverses of matrices numerically on computers; see Golub and Van Loan (1996) for a detailed exposition. Software like PcGive therefore avoids computing the inverse of matrices but instead uses a *QR decomposition*. We will briefly sketch this approach.

It can be proved that any $(n \times k)$-matrix, $\mathbf{X}$ can be decomposed as:

$$\mathbf{X} = \mathbf{QR}, \tag{8.3.1}$$

where, for $k \leq n$, the matrix $\mathbf{Q}$ is $(n \times k)$-dimensional, while $\mathbf{R}$ is of dimension $(k \times k)$. The matrix $\mathbf{Q}$ has orthogonal columns that are normalized, so $\mathbf{Q'Q} = \mathbf{I}_k$. The matrix $\mathbf{R}$ is upper-triangular so all elements below the diagonal are zero. Importantly, the QR-algorithm and the inversion of the matrix $\mathbf{R}$ can be implemented numerically on computers with efficiency and high accuracy.

We can compute the regression estimators using (8.3.1) as:

$$\widehat{\beta} = \left(\mathbf{X'X}\right)^{-1}\mathbf{X'Y} = \left(\mathbf{R'Q'QR}\right)^{-1}\mathbf{R'Q'Y} = \mathbf{R}^{-1}\mathbf{Q'Y},$$

so the only inversion involved is of the upper-triangular matrix $\mathbf{R}$. In numerical implementations, this inversion is also avoided by solving the triangular equation $\mathbf{R}\widehat{\beta} = \mathbf{Q'Y}$ recursively. For the variance estimator, we get in a similar way:

$$n\widehat{\sigma}^2 = \mathbf{Y'Y} - \mathbf{Y'X}\left(\mathbf{X'X}\right)^{-1}\mathbf{X'Y} = \mathbf{Y'Y} - \mathbf{Y'QQ'Y},$$

which does not require any inversions at all.

A more refined version of the QR-decomposition is the *singular value decomposition*. Computationally it is slower in use than the QR-decomposition, but is convenient for so-called reduced-rank regression problems, which we will introduce in §14.2.3; see Doornik and O'Brien (2002). It can be proved that any $(n \times k)$-matrix $\mathbf{X}$ can be decomposed as:

$$\mathbf{X} = \mathbf{UWV'}, \tag{8.3.2}$$

where, for $k \leq n$, the matrix $\mathbf{U}$ is $(n \times k)$-dimensional, while $\mathbf{W}, \mathbf{V}$ are of dimension $(k \times k)$. The matrices $\mathbf{U}, \mathbf{V}$ have orthogonal columns that are normalized, so $\mathbf{U'U} = \mathbf{I}_k$ and $\mathbf{V'V} = \mathbf{I}_k = \mathbf{VV'}$. The matrix $\mathbf{W}$ is diagonal with non-negative diagonal elements called the singular values. In the special case where $\mathbf{X}$ is symmetric, so $\mathbf{X} = \mathbf{X'}$ and therefore $n = k$, the singular values are called *eigenvalues* and $\mathbf{U} = \mathbf{V}$ is the matrix of *eigenvectors*. When all eigenvalues of symmetric matrix $\mathbf{X}$ are positive, then $\mathbf{X}$ is said to be *positive definite*. Using the singular value decomposition, the regression estimators can be rewritten as:

$$\widehat{\beta} = \mathbf{VW}^{-1}\mathbf{U'Y}, \qquad n\widehat{\sigma}^2 = \mathbf{Y'Y} - \mathbf{Y'UU'Y},$$

so the only inversion involved is of the diagonal matrix $\mathbf{W}$.

8.4 SUMMARY AND EXERCISES

Summary: Matrix algebra has been developed further for the multiple regression model. Regression analysis is nearly synonymous with matrix inversion.

Bibliography: Hendry (1995a, Appendix A1) gives a brief overview of matrix algebra, including topics not covered here. Golub and Van Loan (1996) provide an introduction to the numerical implementation of matrix algebra. Magnus and Neudecker (1999) is a standard reference for matrix algebra and its use in econometrics and statistics.

Exercise 8.1. *Consider a block-matrix*

$$\mathbf{M} = \left(\begin{array}{cc} \mathbf{M}_{11} & \mathbf{M}_{12} \\ \mathbf{M}_{21} & \mathbf{M}_{22} \end{array} \right)$$

(a) *Use (8.1.1) to argue:*

$$\mathbf{M}^{-1} = \left(\begin{array}{cc} \mathbf{M}_{11\cdot 2}^{-1} & -\mathbf{M}_{11\cdot 2}^{-1}\mathbf{M}_{12}\mathbf{M}_{22}^{-1} \\ -\mathbf{M}_{22}^{-1}\mathbf{M}_{21}\mathbf{M}_{11\cdot 2}^{-1} & \mathbf{M}_{22}^{-1} + \mathbf{M}_{22}^{-1}\mathbf{M}_{21}\mathbf{M}_{11\cdot 2}^{-1}\mathbf{M}_{12}\mathbf{M}_{22}^{-1} \end{array} \right),$$

where:

$$\mathbf{M}_{11\cdot 2} = \mathbf{M}_{11} - \mathbf{M}_{12}\mathbf{M}_{22}^{-1}\mathbf{M}_{21}, \qquad \mathbf{M}_{22\cdot 1} = \mathbf{M}_{22} - \mathbf{M}_{21}\mathbf{M}_{11}^{-1}\mathbf{M}_{12}.$$

(b) *Prove that* $\mathbf{M}_{22\cdot 1}^{-1} = \mathbf{M}_{22}^{-1} + \mathbf{M}_{22}^{-1}\mathbf{M}_{21}\mathbf{M}_{11\cdot 2}^{-1}\mathbf{M}_{12}\mathbf{M}_{22}^{-1}.$

Exercise 8.2. *Prove (8.2.4) by replacing* $\mathbf{Y}$ *using the model equation.*

Exercise 8.3. *Consider the model given by:* $Y_i = \beta_1 + \beta_2 X_{2,i} + \beta_3 X_{3,i} + u_i$. *Derive the estimator for* β_3 *using matrix algebra.*

Exercise 8.4. *Numerical issues of matrix inversion. Consider the matrices:*

$$\left(\begin{array}{cc} 1 & 1 \\ 1 & 1.1 \end{array} \right), \qquad \left(\begin{array}{cc} 1 & 1 \\ 1 & 1.00001 \end{array} \right), \qquad \left(\begin{array}{cc} 1 & 1 \\ 1 & 1.000000001 \end{array} \right).$$

Show that all three matrices are invertible and find their inverses. Now imagine calculating these numbers using a pocket calculator or computer. Suppose the calculator can remember only 8 digits in each step. What do you think will happen? Most econometric software packages compute using about 13–15 digits, depending on the complexity of the calculations: comment.

Chapter Nine

Mis-specification analysis in cross sections

Until now, we have mainly postulated statistical or econometric models. That is, we have formulated distributional assumptions and then analyzed the corresponding likelihood. It is an important part of any econometric analysis to test the assumptions of the statistical model. All inferences we draw from the model are conditional on those assumptions. Thus, if the assumptions are not, at least approximately, correct, the conclusions cannot be trusted. While graphical methods have mainly been used to justify cross-sectional regression models so far, we now introduce formal tests for the specification.

9.1 THE CROSS-SECTIONAL REGRESSION MODEL

The cross-sectional k-variable regression model is intended for analysis of an array $(Y_i, X_{2,i}, \ldots, X_{k,i})$ for $i = 1, \ldots, n$. The model equation is:

$$Y_i = \beta_1 + \beta_2 X_{2,i} + \cdots + \beta_k X_{k,i} + u_i, \tag{9.1.1}$$

and the statistical model is defined by the assumptions:

 (i) *independence*: the vectors $(Y_i, X_{2,i}, \ldots, X_{k,i})$ are mutually independent;
 (ii) *conditional normality*: $(u_i \mid X_{2,i}, \ldots, X_{k,i}) \overset{\mathrm{D}}{=} \mathrm{N}[0, \sigma^2]$;
 (iii) *exogeneity*: the conditioning variables $X_{2,i}, \ldots, X_{k,i}$ are exogenous;
 (iv) *parameter space*: $\beta_1, \ldots, \beta_k, \sigma^2 \in \mathbb{R}^k \times \mathbb{R}_+$.

The independence assumption is typically not questioned for cross sections. Tests for conditional normality will be presented in the next section, based on distributional shape. Next, we consider testing the assumption of identical distributions by examining the constancy of the error variance σ^2, and then we turn to the functional form of the expectation. We leave a consideration of exogeneity till the next chapter and consider the constancy of the parameters in Chapters 11 and 13. The tests will be illustrated by the wage–education example.

Most of the tests presented are not likelihood ratio tests, which we have emphasized above. Likelihood ratio tests are well suited for making inferences about restrictions on a well-specified model, where we are able, and willing, to maximize the likelihood function in the unrestricted model as well as the restricted model.

When testing for mis-specification, we typically do not have a precise alternative model in mind, so the tests presented sometimes have an ad hoc motivation.

9.2 TEST FOR NORMALITY

For the one-variable regression model, normality was justified using Figure 3.3. This presented quantile-quantile plots and histograms for wages and log wages. Normality was found to be more plausible for log wages than wages themselves. For the two-variable regression model, Figures 5.1 and 5.2 showed conditional box plots and conditional histograms for wages given schooling. Once again, these gave some justification for a normality assumption. While, these graphical methods are typically implemented without confidence bands in software, formal tests for normality are now presented to ensure better-based answers.

9.2.1 The Jarque–Bera test

To construct a test, we have to think about alternative specifications to test against. Various types of departure from normality are shown in Figure 9.1. The top panels show some symmetric distributions with *kurtosis* (essentially fat tails) different from the normal distribution, while the bottom panels show some distributions with *skewness*.

In Figure 9.1, all distributions have been standardized. That is, a random variable X with a given distribution is standardized as $Y = \{X - \mathsf{E}(X)\}/\mathrm{sdv}(X)$, which has zero expectation and unit variance. Then $\kappa_3 = \mathsf{E}(Y^3)$ is the *skewness*, $\mathsf{E}(Y^4)$ is the *kurtosis*, and $\kappa_4 = \mathsf{E}(Y^4) - 3$ is the *excess kurtosis*. We have seen in (3.2.4) that if X is normally distributed, then Y is standard normal distributed. Further, it can be proved that $\kappa_3 = \kappa_4 = 0$ for the standard normal distribution, so these will be our null hypotheses. A test for normality can then be constructed using the sample analogues of these population quantities:

(1) obtain residuals $\widehat{u}_i$ from model (9.1.1);

(2) compute sample skewness $\widehat{\kappa}_3$ and sample excess kurtosis $\widehat{\kappa}_4$, and then the test statistics:

$$\chi^2_{\mathsf{skew}} = n\frac{\widehat{\kappa}_3^2}{6}, \quad \chi^2_{\mathsf{kurt}} = n\frac{\widehat{\kappa}_4^2}{24}, \quad \text{or jointly} \quad \chi^2_{\mathsf{norm}} = \chi^2_{\mathsf{skew}} + \chi^2_{\mathsf{kurt}}.$$

Construct tests by comparing these statistics to χ^2-distributions with 1, 1, and 2 degrees of freedom, respectively.

The tests were introduced by Thiele (1886) and later reintroduced by Pearson (1902). The joint test is often referred to as the *Jarque–Bera test*, since Jarque and Bera (1987) gave a more formal likelihood-based motivation.

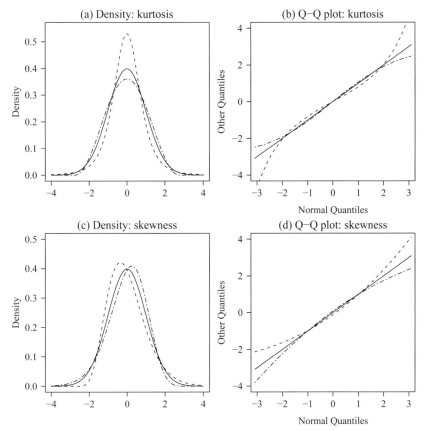

Figure 9.1 standardized distributions compared with normal distribution, solid line. Top panels: *Kurtosis.* t[4] dashed and Beta[7/2, 7/2] dot-dashed. Bottom panels: *Skewness.* $\chi^2[16]$ dashed and $\chi^2[32]$ dot-dashed

9.2.2 Application to wage-education models

For the regression of log wage on a constant as in §3.3 we get:

$$\widehat{\kappa}_3 = -1.335, \qquad \widehat{\kappa}_4 = 7.024, \qquad n = 3877,$$

so that the normality test statistics are:

$$\chi^2_{\text{skew}} = 1151, \qquad \chi^2_{\text{kurt}} = 7970, \qquad \chi^2_{\text{norm}} = 9121.$$

These statistics are all very large compared with the $\chi^2[1]$ and $\chi^2[2]$ critical values. Thus, the quantile-quantile plot in Figure 5.1 should be taken as an indication of departure from normality.

Applying the test to the more general model of regressing log wage on education in §5.2.5, we obtain similar results:

$$\widehat{\kappa}_3 = -1.522, \qquad \widehat{\kappa}_4 = 8.045, \qquad n = 3877.$$

The test statistics are now considerably larger:

$$\chi^2_{\text{skew}} = 1497, \qquad \chi^2_{\text{kurt}} = 10445, \qquad \chi^2_{\text{norm}} = 11952,$$

although the substantive difference is not so large when comparing these to χ^2-distributions.

9.2.3 Mending mis-specification problems

There are a number of ways to address the normality problems observed in §9.2.2.

Look at the data. A first step is to have a closer look at the data base. We discover that the left-hand tail of the distribution is quite long. This is clear from the histogram in Figure 3.3. The five smallest observations are those with a negative log wage. These few observations make a huge contribution to skewness and kurtosis. Removing those changes these statistics to:

$$\widehat{\kappa}_3 = -0.791, \qquad \widehat{\kappa}_4 = 2.534, \qquad n = 3872,$$

so that the test statistics are reduced to:

$$\chi^2_{\text{skew}} = 404, \qquad \chi^2_{\text{kurt}} = 1036, \qquad \chi^2_{\text{norm}} = 1440.$$

This finding indicates that our analysis is potentially heavily influenced by these few observations, so one way forward would be to look into the way the data set was constructed: Are these observations due to recording errors? Has the weekly wage variable been constructed wrongly? Do these observations have an important influence on the regression results?

Change the distributional assumption. If the normality assumption appears entirely unreasonable, normality could be replaced by a different distributional assumption. A wealth of other classes of distributions could be used as alternatives to the normal distribution. Figure 9.2 indicates what one should be looking for. This plots a smoothed version of the log histogram for log wages. To obtain a sufficiently smooth curve, the plot has been based on a 0.125% census sample with 48179 observations rather than the usual 3877 observations. In the case of normality, this should look like a parabola. There are several distinctive features. The density is clearly skew, as we already knew from $\widehat{\kappa}_3$. Further, the tails do not appear to follow a parabola. In particular, the left tail appears to be very different, perhaps closer to a line or even bending outward.

By choosing a different distributional assumption, the likelihood function would change, and maximum likelihood estimation would not be equivalent to least-squares estimation. There are, for instance, classes of distributions leading to *least absolute deviation* (LAD) estimators, thus putting less weight on the outlying observations than least squares estimators do. The maximum likelihood estimator

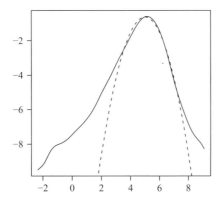

Figure 9.2 Smoothed log histogram for log wage, and the log density of a fitted normal distribution

is then found at the median rather than at the average (see Ruud, 2000, Chapter 13). For the log wage, based on the 0.125% census sample, the median is 5.09 as compared to the mean of 5.00, which is a relatively small difference. The gain from applying the correct distribution for the econometric analysis is mainly in the description of the variance, and thus for inference. The 2.5% and 97.5% quantiles of the sample distribution are 3.23 and 6.19 as compared to 3.53 and 6.48 for the fitted normal distribution.

Check the robustness of the method. From the Central Limit Theorem 2.2, we know that a sample average is asymptotically normal so long as the error terms are identically distributed. Thus we could continue to use least-squares estimators even though normality fails. Potentially this leads to a loss in efficiency of the inference compared to a likelihood approach, and less awareness of the assumptions underlying the econometric analysis, but it may still be valid. This idea is followed up with the method of moments approach as advocated by, for instance, Wooldridge (2006).

The reported problem with the normality assumption is commonly found for log wages and is often attributed to a heterogeneity that is not easily picked up by regression. Other cross-sectional variables like consumption appear to be much closer to normality; see Blundell and Stoker (2005) for a discussion.

9.3 TEST FOR IDENTICAL DISTRIBUTION

The assumption of identical distribution of the error terms, u_i, implies that the conditional variances of error terms given regressors are the same for all individuals, so $\text{Var}(u_i|X_{2,i}, \ldots X_{k,i}) = \sigma^2$. If the variance is not constant over i, the error terms are said to be *heteroskedastic*. The assumption about identical distribution of the error terms across the sample can be checked graphically by plotting the conditional distribution of the regressands given the regressors (Figure 5.1). A formal test will be introduced in the following section.

9.3.1 White's test for heteroskedasticity

The long word heteroskedasticity, loved by econometricians, means that the variance changes over the sample, as opposed to homoskedasticity (constant variance). A formal test for the null hypothesis of homoskedasticity was suggested by White (1980). Having a two-variable model in mind for simplicity, so $k = 2$ in (9.1.1), we consider whether $\text{Var}(u_i|X_i)$ varies with X_i. The absence of a quadratic dependence like $\text{Var}(u_i|X_i) = \alpha_1 + \alpha_2 X_i + \alpha_3 X_i^2$ could be tested using an auxiliary regression. The procedure is as follows:

(1) obtain residuals $\widehat{u}_i$ from the model (9.1.1);

(2) obtain R^2_{het} from the auxiliary regression:

$$\widehat{u}_i^2 = \alpha_1 + \alpha_2 X_i + \alpha_3 X_i^2 + v_i, \qquad (9.3.1)$$

and test $\alpha_2 = \alpha_3 = 0$ using $nR^2_{\text{het}} \overset{D}{\approx} \chi^2[2]$.

The regression arising from equation (9.3.1) is referred to as an *auxiliary regression* since it does not represent a statistical model with normal errors but rather generates some statistics that can be used as test statistics. Even if $\alpha_2 = \alpha_3 = 0$, the error term v_i in (9.3.1) will not be normally distributed but, since the regressand is the squared residual, it will have a distribution more like a χ^2-distribution. Its expectation is, therefore, not zero, so the constant term in (9.3.1) is crucial.

In a model with k regressors, there are several possible extensions:

(1) regress $\widehat{u}_i^2$ on all regressors and their squares, resulting in a test with $m = k$ degrees of freedom;

(2) regress $\widehat{u}_i^2$ on all regressors, their squares and their cross products, creating a test with $m = k(k + 1)/2$ degrees of freedom.

Since the residuals already satisfy k restrictions from the original regression in (9.1.1), and a further $m+1$ parameters arise in the auxiliary regression, the number of observations, n, has to exceed $k + m + 1$ to carry out the auxiliary regression.

Often White's test is reported as an F-type form rather than the χ^2-form. The background for this transformation is that when n is larger than, but not much larger than, $k + m + 1$, then the χ^2-approximation to the distribution of the test statistic nR^2_{het} is poor. Inspired by the expression in Exercise 7.10, we can instead calculate the F-type test statistic:

$$F_{\text{het}} = \frac{R^2_{\text{het}}/m}{\left(1 - R^2_{\text{het}}\right)/(n - m)}.$$

When n is large and R^2_{het} is small, as it would be in the absence of heteroskedasticity, then $R^2_{\text{het}} \approx mF_{\text{het}}$, so mF_{het} would be approximately $\chi^2[m]$-distributed. While F_{het} will not be exactly $\mathsf{F}[m, n - m]$-distributed, there is some evidence that the $\mathsf{F}[m, n - m]$-distribution gives a more accurate approximation than the $\chi^2[m]/m$-distribution when n is small (see Kiviet, 1986, Hendry and Krolzig, 2005).

9.3.2 Application to a wage-schooling model

Applying White's test to the two-variable model of regressing log wage on the length of schooling in §5.2.5 gives the result:

$$F_{\text{het}}[2, 3872] = 1.565 \quad [\text{p} = 0.21].$$

Thus, homoskedasticity cannot be rejected. This is consistent with the conditional box plots, shown in Figure 5.1, which indicate that the conditional variance does not vary much with schooling.

9.3.3 Application to a wage-hours model

Another example would be a regression of log wages on the logarithm of the usual hours worked. This yields the regression result:

$$\widehat{w}_i = \underset{(0.09)}{2.23} + \underset{(0.03)}{0.79}\,h_i, \qquad \widehat{\sigma} = 0.68,$$

where standard errors are reported under the estimates, and h denotes log hours. Applying White's heteroskedasticity test gives

$$F_{\text{het}}[2, 3872] = 19.5 \quad [\text{p} < 0.001].$$

This test gives a strong indication that the conditional variance of log wages given log hours varies with log hours.

It is not so obvious how this model can be improved. The consequence of the heteroskedasticity is that standard errors are misleading, which can distort inferences. The setup for White's heteroskedasticity test does not give much guidance toward more appropriate alternative models. An easy way out is to keep the model and replace the standard errors by the heteroskedasticity corrected standard errors (HCSE) suggested by White (1980); also see Greene (2003, §10.3). The HCSE calculations assume that the heteroskedasticity is due to changes in the error variance, which are reflected in the squared regressors, rather than say, to the wrong conditional mean specification. If such robust standard errors are roughly equal to the usual standard errors, there is not much practical gain from using them. If the difference is large, it is questionable how valid such robust standard errors actually are. Thus, it is often beneficial to search for a more appropriate empirical model, to gain a better understanding of the data. An exploratory analysis is then needed.

An analysis of the sample distribution of the hours variable reveals that 55% of the individuals usually work 40 hours per week, and the rest of the observations are spread over the range 1 to 99 hours. Moreover, the code book for the census indicates that the lower values of this variable may be somewhat unreliable, which raises the issue as to whether it is meaningful to use these hourly wage data. A more detailed analysis of the conditional distribution of log wages reveals that the heteroskedasticity relates mainly to individuals with the most extreme values of the hours variable (see Computer Task 9.3). The exploratory analysis indicates that it could be more appropriate to model the conditional variance of the error terms in terms of a function of the regressors $h(X)$, say. A model of the form:

$$Y_i = \beta_1 + \beta_2 X_i + h(X_i)u_i,$$

might then be used, where the error terms u_i are independently $N[0, \sigma^2]$-distributed. Such a model can be estimated by the *generalized least-squares* approach; see, for instance, Greene (2003, Chapter 11).

9.4 TEST FOR FUNCTIONAL FORM

A third concern with a regression model is whether the chosen functional form for the conditional expectation is correct. While the regression equation provides a linear link between a regressand Y_i and regressor X_i, it is common to consider applying transformations to the original data, using logarithms or taking squares or inverses. The logarithm is often used for variables that are intrinsically positive, whereas the other transformations are more typically used for situations where the suggestions from economic theory are vague, such as an unspecified monotone or convex relationship. In Chapter 5 we linked log wages with schooling, whereas in Chapter 7 we included the square of schooling as a regressor to capture a possibly convex relation. Since it will not necessarily be clear from economic theory that a quadratic form is appropriate, a test for functional form is useful.

9.4.1 Ramsey's regression specification error test

This test was introduced by Ramsey (1969) and is referred to by the acronym RESET (from *regression specification error test*). For simplicity, consider once again the two-variable regression model, so $k = 2$ in (9.1.1). The idea is to investigate whether squares and cubes of the predicted variable $\widehat{Y}_i$ can help to explain Y_i: under the null of a correct functional form, such added variables should not matter. The test statistic is based on a two-step procedure:

(1) obtain the predicted variables $\widehat{Y}_i$ from the model (9.1.1);

(2) obtain the partial correlation, r^2_{RESET} say, of Y_i and $\widehat{Y}_i^2$ given X_i from the auxiliary regression:

$$Y_i = \alpha_1 + \alpha_2 X_i + \alpha_3 \widehat{Y}_i^2 + v_i, \tag{9.4.1}$$

and test $\alpha_3 = 0$ using $nr^2_{\text{RESET}} \overset{D}{\approx} \chi^2[1]$.

The RESET test is often reported in an F-type form in the same way as White's heteroskedasticity test (see §9.3.1).

9.4.2 Application to wage-education models

Applying the RESET test to the two-variable model of regressing log wage on schooling in §5.2.5 gives the result:

$$F_{\text{reset}}[1, 3874] = 42.6 \quad [\text{p} < 0.001].$$

This outcome strongly suggests that a simple linear relationship between log wages and schooling is inappropriate. Indeed, the idea of diminishing returns to schooling led us to consider a quadratic specification in §7.2.4 and to reject the assumption that the conditional expectation of log wages given schooling is linear in schooling.

Consider instead the three-variable model in §7.2.4, regressing log wage on schooling and squared schooling. Application of the RESET test delivers:

$$F_{\text{reset}}[1, 3873] = 0.078 \quad [\text{p} = 0.78],$$

consistent with the quadratic specification.

9.5 SIMULTANEOUS APPLICATION OF MIS-SPECIFICATION TESTS

In many applications, investigators apply several mis-specification tests simultaneously. There is then a question as to how these tests interact. This issue is complementary to that of multiple testing discussed in §7.6.2.

Often, each test would be conducted at a 5% level. When using $k = 3$, say, tests simultaneously, the overall level is higher than the level of the individual tests. If we assume that the k test statistics are independent, and the model is not mis-specified, the overall level can be computed according to the formula:

$$\text{P (not reject any test)} = \prod_{i=1}^{k} \text{P (not reject test } i) \qquad [\text{ independence }]$$

$$= (1 - \alpha)^k \approx 1 - k\alpha, \qquad (9.5.1)$$

where α denotes the common level of each of the $k = 3$ individual tests. The overall level is then $k\alpha$. Thus, an overall level of 5% for not falsely rejecting the model could be achieved by conducting the individual tests at a level in the range 1%–2%. The assumption of independence has been proved by Jarque and Bera (1980) between the normality test statistic and the heteroskedasticity test statistic.

Table 9.1 cumulates the results for the linear model linking log wage with education. It is seen that both the normality test and the RESET test fail. In this situation, one should bear in mind that the reported distributional assumptions, and hence the reported p-values, are valid only when the model is not mis-specified. It is, therefore, a possibility that normality fails but the functional form is correct.

Table 9.2 shows that including the square of education as a regressor appears to solve the functional form problem, whereas the normality problem remains.

$$\widehat{w}_i = 4.06 + 0.076\,S_i, \qquad \widehat{\sigma} = 0.73$$
$$\text{se} \quad (0.06) \quad (0.004)$$

$$\chi^2_{\text{norm}}[2] = 11952 \quad [p<0.01]$$
$$F_{\text{het}}[2, 3872] = 1.565 \quad [p=0.21] \qquad F_{\text{reset}}[1, 3874] = 42.6 \quad [p<0.01]$$

Table 9.1 Wage model that is linear in schooling

$$\widehat{w}_i = 4.78 - 0.050\,S_i + 0.0051\,S_i^2, \qquad \widehat{\sigma} = 0.72$$
$$\text{se} \quad (0.12) \quad (0.020) \quad (0.0008)$$

$$\chi^2_{\text{norm}}[2] = 12800 \quad [p<0.01]$$
$$F_{\text{het}}[3, 3870] = 0.40 \quad [p=0.75] \qquad F_{\text{reset}}[1, 3873] = 0.08 \quad [p=0.78]$$

Table 9.2 Wage model that is quadratic in schooling

9.6 TECHNIQUES FOR IMPROVING REGRESSION MODELS

In previous sections, we have seen how formal mis-specification tests can be used to investigate the validity of model assumptions. The quadratic specification of the wage-schooling association seemed to give a better fit than most of the other models, although normality remained a problem. Nevertheless, the model remains surprising, if not unsatisfactory, from an economic viewpoint, in that the sign of the quadratic term is positive (see also §7.2.4). In the following discussion, three techniques for improving regressions will be explored: adding variables, orthogonalization, and stratification.

9.6.1 Adding a variable

Economic theory and experience from applied work can often be helpful in suggesting variables that could be added to the model. Thereby the information set available for the analysis would be extended. Such an extension is best done at the start of an empirical analysis, rather than in mid-stream, to avoid using ad hoc "corrections".

In the wage-schooling context, other characteristics of individuals could be of interest. The census collects information on hundreds of questions, so it could be tempting to try a range of these. Age might be included as a proxy for tenure in the job, whereas occupation or geographical information could also be important determinants of wages. Economic theory suggests that "ability" is important for determining wages, but this elusive variable is not measured directly, so other variables, thought of as "proxies", might be tried.

9.6.2 Orthogonalization

Regressors will often carry somewhat related information and thereby be correlated to some extent, or even near collinear (see §7.3.3). An orthogonalization of the regressors can help in separating the information. The operation does not change the likelihood value and the fit, but it will change the coefficient estimates. Such an orthogonalization requires an ordering, which can be based on the statistical properties of the variables or on the substantive context. In Chapter 17, we will discuss cointegration analysis of time series, which is an example of the former. The wage-schooling relation gives an example of the latter, with the levels and squares of schooling being highly correlated. Given the context, it seems more natural to orthogonalize the square with respect to the linear term, than vice versa.

9.6.3 Stratification

In the standard regression formulation, the variation in Y with the regressors is linear for all values of the regressors. It is possible that this linear dependence could be different for different subgroups, or *strata*, of the data. The strata could be chosen using an excluded variable like marital status, or by different types of schooling.

The wage-schooling cross plot in Figure 7.1 indicates that the dependence is possibly not quadratic in the way suggested. For those with the lowest levels of schooling, there seems little variation with education, whereas the effect of diminishing returns to education can be discerned among those with the highest levels of education. It may, therefore, be reasonable to introduce three strata: those with less than 10 years of education, those with 10–14 years of education, and those with at least 15 years of education. In practice we can do that by introducing three dummies, or indicator variables, see (4.4.1):

$$D_{1,i} = 1_{(S_i \leq 9)}, \qquad D_{2,i} = 1_{(10 \leq S_i \leq 14)}, \qquad D_{3,i} = 1_{(15 \leq S_i)}.$$

Interacting the three regressors, namely intercept, S_i, and S_i^2, with these dummies results in a model with nine regressors as presented in Table 9.3. This model has the same specification quality as the previous models. The log-likelihood ratio test statistic for the quadratic specification in §7.2.4 against this more general model is:

$$\text{LR} = -2\,(-4233.06 + 4226.47) = 13.18,$$

with p $= 0.04$ using a $\chi^2[6]$-distribution. Thus, the restriction to the quadratic specification would be a marginal decision at the 5% level.

Alternatively, we can impose a specification, which is first constant, then linear, and finally quadratic, as specified in Table 9.4. Comparing the likelihoods of the restricted model in Table 9.4 and the unrestricted model in Table 9.3 gives:

$$\text{LR} = -2\,(-4227.63 + 4226.47) = 2.32,$$

$$\widehat{w}_i = \{\underset{(0.19)}{4.72} - \underset{(0.07)}{0.03}\,S_i + \underset{(0.006)}{0.005}\,S_i^2\}D_{1,i} + \{\underset{(1.4)}{2.5} + \underset{(0.23)}{0.32}\,S_i - \underset{(0.01)}{0.01}\,S_i^2\}D_{2,i}$$
$$\text{se}$$
$$+\{\underset{(3.7)}{-5.9} + \underset{(0.43)}{1.18}\,S_i - \underset{(0.01)}{0.03}\,S_i^2\}D_{3,i}$$

$$\widehat{\sigma} = 0.72, \qquad \widehat{\ell} = -4226.47$$

$\chi^2_{\text{norm}}[2]$	$=$	909.4	$[\text{p}<0.01]$	$F_{\text{het}}[11, 3856] = 0.39 \quad [\text{p}=0.96]$
$F_{\text{reset}}[1, 3867]$	$=$	1.03	$[\text{p}=0.31]$	$F_{\text{hetX}}[14, 3853] = 0.49 \quad [\text{p}=0.94]$

Table 9.3 Wage model that is quadratic in schooling and stratified by level of schooling

$$\widehat{w}_i = \underset{(0.04)}{4.75}\,D_{1,i} + \{\underset{(0.18)}{3.93} + \underset{(0.014)}{0.084}S_i\}D_{2,i} + \{\underset{(3.7)}{-5.9} + \underset{(0.43)}{1.18}\,S_i - \underset{(0.012)}{0.030}S_i^2\}D_{3,i}$$
$$\text{se}$$
$$\widehat{\sigma} = 0.72, \qquad \widehat{\ell} = -4227.63$$

Table 9.4 Wage model that is quadratic in schooling and stratified by level of schooling

with $\text{p} = 0.51$ using a $\chi^2[3]$-distribution. In this specification, there is no attempt to link the functions for the three different strata. Had the regressors been continuous, such linking would typically be easier to interpret. This could be done using *spline functions* or, more flexibly, using *non-parametric regression*; for an introduction, see Greene (2003, §7.2.5, 16.4.2).

The quadratic model of §7.2.4 and the restricted stratified model in Table 9.4 can both be viewed as valid reductions of the unrestricted stratified model in Table 9.3, although the reduction to Table 9.4 is more comfortable. In terms of its interpretation, the specification in Table 9.4 is perhaps preferable. It shows a log-linear return to schooling for individuals with a high school level of schooling, combined with a diminishing return to education for higher levels of schooling.

9.7 SUMMARY AND EXERCISES

Summary: Mis-specification tests that are applicable to checking some of the key assumptions of the linear regression model were presented. We focused on testing normality, homoskedasticity, and the linear functional form, and obtained tests of all three possible departures. Because such tests generalize the initial model, they are often not based on likelihood ratio statistics.

The use of several such tests and the interpretation of test outcomes were also addressed. Possible methods for improving a baseline model were noted.

Bibliography: Mis-specification testing and model evaluation date back to the early days of statistics, and a vast array of tests now exists. We return to the choice of hypotheses to test in Chapter 11.

Key questions:

- Discuss the difficulty that a mis-specification test may reject for reasons other than the one being tested (e.g., heteroskedasticity rejects because the functional form was incorrect).
- Can one infer the source of a rejection from a test outcome, or is there a problem of multiple interpretations of any reject outcome?
- Is it legitimate to calculate many mis-specification tests?

Computing Task 9.1. *Estimate the log wage-schooling model of section 5.2.5. Store residuals and predictions.*
(*a*) *What is the sample average of the residuals?*
(*b*) *Construct the test for no skewness of section 9.2 in the following steps. Compute the standardized residuals. Compute the third power of these. Cumulate, then take squares. Multiply by* $n/6$.
(*c*) *Construct White's test for heteroskedasticity using the auxiliary regression in (9.3.1).*
(*d*) *Construct the RESET test using the auxiliary regression in (9.4.1).*

Computing Task 9.2. *It is generally easier to reject a model in a large sample than in a small sample. To illustrate this, select a small subsample of the wage data set and rerun the mis-specification tests:*
(*a*) *Sort the observations by the uniform random variable* ran.
(*b*) *Regress log wage on a constant using the full sample and find the tests for mis-specification presented in this chapter.*
(*c*) *Regress log wage on a constant using the first 100 observations. Conduct the mis-specification tests presented in this chapter. Compare the results with the full sample results.*

Computing Task 9.3. *Consider the wage-hours application in section 9.3.3.*
(*a*) *Regress log wage on log hours and conduct mis-specification tests. Discuss the results.*
(*b*) *Sort the observations by hours.*
(*c*) *Regress log wage on log hours for individuals who usually work 32–48 hours per week. Conduct mis-specification tests. Discuss the results.*

Chapter Ten

Strong exogeneity

The logistic model introduced in Chapter 4 and the regression models discussed in Chapters 5 and 7 are examples of open models. These models are based on the conditional distributions of a dependent variable given one or more explanatory variables. In each case, we made the loose assumption that the explanatory variables were "exogenous". Three issues arise when analyzing conditional models. The first relates to estimation: when does maximizing the conditional likelihood give the same result as maximizing a joint likelihood? The second relates to inference: when do features of the joint distribution need to be specified to justify the asymptotic theory? The third issue relates to the causal interpretation: when can the resulting conditional model be taken to represent a causal relation? The first two issues can be explored systematically, which we will do in this chapter, whereas the third issue is more complex, and we will return to it in Chapter 11.

In this chapter, we will first introduce a formal definition of exogeneity that facilitates conditional estimation. The argument requires the formulation of a statistical model for the joint distribution of the regressand and the regressors, so a multivariate distribution is needed. We will introduce the bivariate normal distribution and show how exogeneity can be discussed naturally for two-variable regression models in this context. Finally, inference in the presence of conditional variables is revisited.

10.1 STRONG EXOGENEITY

The notion of strong exogeneity is introduced. We will consider its impact on estimation and inference in turn.

10.1.1 Estimation in the presence of strong exogeneity

The data we have in mind is an array $\mathbf{X}_1, \ldots, \mathbf{X}_n$ given as n repetitions of a bivariate vector:

$$\mathbf{X}_i = \left(\begin{array}{c} Y_i \\ Z_i \end{array} \right).$$

As it is convenient to use the notation $\mathbf{X}$ for a vector of variables, the variable we will condition on is now denoted Z_i instead of X_i. For the time being, we will assume that the conditional distribution of Y_i given Z_i and the marginal distribution of Z_i are given by some densities $f_\psi(y|z)$ and $f_\lambda(z)$. The conditional density could, for instance, be Bernoulli, as in Chapter 4, or normal, as in Chapters 5 and 7. This results in a statistical model under the assumptions:

 (i) *independence*: $\mathbf{X}_1, \ldots, \mathbf{X}_n$ are mutually independent;
 (ii) *conditional distribution*: Y_i given Z_i has density $f_\psi(y|z)$;
 (iii) *marginal distribution*: Z_i has density $f_\lambda(z)$;
 (iv) *parameter space*: $\psi, \lambda \in \Theta$ for some space Θ.

It follows from (4.1.7) that the joint density of Y_i, Z_i is $f_{\psi,\lambda}(y, z) = f_\psi(y|z)f_\lambda(z)$.

The joint density of $\mathbf{X}_1, \ldots, \mathbf{X}_n$ can be written as:

$$f_{\psi,\lambda}(\mathbf{x}_1, \ldots, \mathbf{x}_n) = \prod_{i=1}^{n} f_{\psi,\lambda}(\mathbf{x}_i) \qquad [\ (i): \text{independence}\ ]$$

$$= \prod_{i=1}^{n} f_\psi(y_i \mid z_i)f_\lambda(z_i) \qquad [\ (ii), (iii): \text{distribution}\ ]$$

$$= f_\psi(y_1, \ldots, y_n \mid z_1, \ldots, z_n)f_\lambda(z_1, \ldots, z_n). \qquad [\ (i): \text{independence}\ ]$$

Correspondingly, the likelihood function for ψ, λ can be decomposed as:

$$\mathsf{L}_{\mathbf{X}_1,\ldots,\mathbf{X}_n}(\psi, \lambda) = \mathsf{L}_{Y_1,\ldots,Y_n|Z_1,\ldots,Z_n}(\psi)\, \mathsf{L}_{Z_1,\ldots,Z_n}(\lambda).$$

The first component $\mathsf{L}_{Y_1,\ldots,Y_n|Z_1,\ldots,Z_n}(\psi)$ is a conditional likelihood like those we have been analyzing in Chapters 4, 5, and 7.

In general, the conditional maximum likelihood estimator of ψ, maximizing the conditional likelihood $\mathsf{L}_{Y_1,\ldots,Y_n|Z_1,\ldots,Z_n}(\psi)$ for the parameter space $\psi \in \Psi$ say, will be different from the joint likelihood estimator of ψ based on the joint likelihood $\mathsf{L}_{\mathbf{X}_1,\ldots,\mathbf{X}_n}(\psi, \lambda)$. These maximized likelihoods will satisfy the inequality:

$$\max_{\psi,\lambda \in \Theta} \mathsf{L}_{\mathbf{X}_1,\ldots,\mathbf{X}_n}(\psi, \lambda) \geq \left\{ \max_{\psi \in \Psi} \mathsf{L}_{Y_1,\ldots,Y_n|Z_1,\ldots,Z_n}(\psi) \right\} \left\{ \max_{\lambda \in \Lambda} \mathsf{L}_{Z_1,\ldots,Z_n}(\lambda) \right\}.$$

In some important situations, however, we will have the equality:

$$\max_{\psi,\lambda \in \Theta} \mathsf{L}_{\mathbf{X}_1,\ldots,\mathbf{X}_n}(\psi, \lambda) = \left\{ \max_{\psi \in \Psi} \mathsf{L}_{Y_1,\ldots,Y_n|Z_1,\ldots,Z_n}(\psi) \right\} \left\{ \max_{\lambda \in \Lambda} \mathsf{L}_{Z_1,\ldots,Z_n}(\lambda) \right\}.$$
$$(10.1.1)$$

When the equality in (10.1.1) is satisfied, maximum likelihood estimators for ψ based on the joint likelihood and on the conditional likelihood are identical. If only the parameter ψ of the conditional model is of interest, it then suffices to maximize the conditional likelihood alone. A sufficient condition for the equality (10.1.1) is that there are no cross restrictions linking ψ, λ, like $\psi = \lambda$. Another way to express this is that the parameter space Θ is a product space, $\Psi \times \Lambda$ so:

$$(\psi, \lambda) \in \Theta \qquad \Leftrightarrow \qquad (\psi \in \Psi \quad \text{and} \quad \lambda \in \Lambda), \qquad (10.1.2)$$

where Ψ and Λ are the conditional and marginal parameter spaces. Following Engle, Hendry and Richard (1983), we then say that Z_i is *strongly exogenous* for the parameter ψ when the parameter space is a *product space*, $\Theta = \Psi \times \Lambda$, as in (10.1.2). Thereby, we have a precise way of thinking about the exogeneity assumed in the two-variable regression model in §5.1. Strong exogeneity would fail if we were to impose a cross restriction like $\psi = \lambda$: in that case, important information about ψ would be missed if we ignored λ. In the following, we will introduce the bivariate normal distribution to allow a more specific discussion of these issues.

10.1.2 Inference in the presence of strong exogeneity

In order to conduct inference, we need to think about the sampling distributions of estimators and test statistics. Strong exogeneity is helpful in that context.

For the cross-sectional models that we have considered, estimators and test statistics have been derived from the conditional likelihood of $Y_1, \ldots, Y_n$ given the regressors, $Z_1, \ldots, Z_n$, say. The distributions of these statistics conditionally on the regressors were then discussed. When the regressors are strongly exogenous, these arguments go hand in hand.

In §5.5.4 it was pointed out that the conditional distribution of a statistic given the regressors may not in fact depend on the regressors, in which case the resulting distribution is also the marginal distribution. This argument does not actually require a full specification of the distribution of the regressors, merely that conditioning on the full set of regressors is valid. This aspect of exogeneity will not apply so easily when it comes to time series (see §12.7).

10.2 THE BIVARIATE NORMAL DISTRIBUTION

The bivariate normal distribution is now introduced, along with its most important properties.

10.2.1 Definition

Consider random variables Y and Z arranged as a bivariate random vector:

$$\mathbf{X} = \begin{pmatrix} Y \\ Z \end{pmatrix}.$$

We can define the expectation of the random vector $\mathbf{X}$ simply by arranging the marginal expectations of Y and Z in a vector as in §8.2.3:

$$\boldsymbol{\mu} = \mathsf{E}\left(\mathbf{X}\right) = \mathsf{E}\begin{pmatrix} Y \\ Z \end{pmatrix} = \begin{pmatrix} \mathsf{E}\left(Y\right) \\ \mathsf{E}\left(Z\right) \end{pmatrix} = \begin{pmatrix} \mu_y \\ \mu_z \end{pmatrix}.$$

Correspondingly, the variance of the random vector $\mathbf{X}$ is defined as a matrix:

$$\boldsymbol{\Sigma} = \mathsf{Var}\left(\mathbf{X}\right) = \begin{pmatrix} \mathsf{Var}(Y) & \mathsf{Cov}(Y,Z) \\ \mathsf{Cov}(Z,Y) & \mathsf{Var}(Z) \end{pmatrix} = \begin{pmatrix} \sigma_{yy} & \sigma_{yz} \\ \sigma_{zy} & \sigma_{zz} \end{pmatrix},$$

where $\sigma_{yz} = \sigma_{zy}$ while σ_{yy} and σ_{zz} are the marginal variances of Y and Z respectively. The correlation coefficient is:

$$\rho = \mathsf{Corr}\left(Y, Z\right) = \frac{\sigma_{yz}}{\sqrt{\sigma_{yy}\sigma_{zz}}}.$$

We will say that $\mathbf{X}$ has a bivariate normal distribution, $\mathbf{X} \overset{\mathsf{D}}{=} \mathsf{N}_2[\boldsymbol{\mu}, \boldsymbol{\Sigma}]$, when $\mathbf{X}$ has the joint density:

$$\mathsf{f}(\mathbf{x}) = \frac{1}{2\pi\sqrt{\sigma_{yy}\sigma_{zz}(1-\rho^2)}} \exp\left(-\frac{w^2}{2}\right), \qquad (10.2.1)$$

where $\mathbf{x} = (y, z)'$ and:

$$w^2 = \frac{1}{1-\rho^2}\left\{\left(\frac{y-\mu_y}{\sqrt{\sigma_{yy}}}\right)^2 + \left(\frac{z-\mu_z}{\sqrt{\sigma_{zz}}}\right)^2 - 2\rho\left(\frac{y-\mu_y}{\sqrt{\sigma_{yy}}}\right)\left(\frac{z-\mu_z}{\sqrt{\sigma_{zz}}}\right)\right\}.$$

This, of course, requires that marginal variances are positive, $\sigma_{yy} > 0$ and $\sigma_{zz} > 0$, and that the variables are not collinear, that is, $\rho^2 < 1$. When Y and Z are uncorrelated, so $\rho = 0$, the density in (10.2.1) reduces to $\mathsf{f}(\mathbf{x}) = \mathsf{f}(y)\mathsf{f}(z)$, showing that y and z are independent.

To draw a picture of the bivariate normal density, a three-dimensional plot is needed; Figure 10.1 shows the density of the distribution:

$$\begin{pmatrix} X \\ Y \end{pmatrix} \overset{\mathsf{D}}{=} \mathsf{N}_2\left[\begin{pmatrix} 1 \\ 2 \end{pmatrix}, \begin{pmatrix} 2 & 1 \\ 1 & 1 \end{pmatrix}\right]. \qquad (10.2.2)$$

10.2.2 Conditioning and marginalizing

An important property of the bivariate normal distribution is that both conditioning and marginalization preserve normality. The conditional distribution of Y given Z, and the marginal distribution of Z are, respectively:

$$Y|Z \overset{\mathsf{D}}{=} \mathsf{N}\left[\beta_1 + \beta_2 Z, \sigma^2\right] \qquad \text{and} \qquad Z \overset{\mathsf{D}}{=} \mathsf{N}\left[\mu_z, \sigma_{zz}\right], \qquad (10.2.3)$$

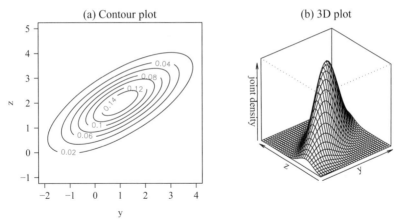

Figure 10.1 Bivariate normal density: contour plot and 3D plot

where the parameters β_1, β_2, σ^2 are defined by:

$$\beta_1 = \mu_y - \beta_2 \mu_z, \qquad \beta_2 = \frac{\sigma_{yz}}{\sigma_{zz}}, \qquad \sigma^2 = \sigma_{yy} - \frac{\sigma_{yz}^2}{\sigma_{zz}} = \sigma_{yy}\left(1 - \rho^2\right). \quad (10.2.4)$$

Given the constraints on $\boldsymbol{\mu}$, $\boldsymbol{\Sigma}$, these parameters satisfy β_1, β_2, $\sigma^2 \in \mathbb{R}^2 \times \mathbb{R}_+$ as in the two-variable regression model of Chapter 5. The proof of this central property is given in Exercise 10.1.

10.2.3 Some further properties

The bivariate normal distribution has many other useful properties. We will mention a few.

(1) If Y and Z have a bivariate normal distribution, then it holds that:

$$Y, Z \text{ are uncorrelated} \qquad \Leftrightarrow \qquad Y, Z \text{ are independent.}$$

The implication from right to left in (1) holds generally; see (2.1.13). The implication from left to right was shown in §10.2.1 in that $\sigma_{yz} = 0$ implies $\rho = 0$. When $\rho = 0$, then (10.2.1) reduces to $f(\mathbf{x}) = f(y)f(z)$, showing independence. The equivalence between uncorrelatedness and independence relies on the joint normality assumption, and Exercise 2.8 shows that it does not hold in general.

(2) It can be proved that the parameters $\boldsymbol{\mu}$ and $\boldsymbol{\Sigma}$ are the expectation and variance of $\mathbf{X}$ as indicated above.

(3) If Y and Z have a bivariate normal distribution, then a linear combination of Y and Z is also normally distributed:

$$aY + bZ + c \overset{\mathrm{D}}{=} \mathsf{N}\left[a\mu_y + b\mu_z + c, a^2\sigma_{yy} + 2ab\sigma_{yz} + b^2\sigma_{zz}\right].$$

Moreover, two linear combinations, $a_1 Y + b_1 Z + c_1$ and $a_2 Y + b_2 Z + c_2$, will be jointly normally distributed.

Property (3) is a generalization of (3.4.6). This follows from property (1).

10.3 THE BIVARIATE NORMAL MODEL

We will now define a model based on the bivariate normal distribution and show how the parameters can be estimated using the techniques of the one-variable model of Chapter 3 and the two-variable regression model of Chapter 5.

The data we have in mind is an array $\mathbf{X}_1, \ldots, \mathbf{X}_n$ given as n repetitions of a bivariate vector:

$$\mathbf{X}_i = \begin{pmatrix} Y_i \\ Z_i \end{pmatrix}.$$

The bivariate normal model is then based on the assumptions:

   (i) *independence*: $\mathbf{X}_1, \ldots, \mathbf{X}_n$ are mutually independent;

   (ii) *normality*: $\mathbf{X} \overset{\mathrm{D}}{=} \mathsf{N}_2[\boldsymbol{\mu}, \Sigma]$ with parameters:

$$\boldsymbol{\mu} = \begin{pmatrix} \mu_y \\ \mu_z \end{pmatrix}, \qquad \Sigma = \begin{pmatrix} \sigma_{yy} & \sigma_{yz} \\ \sigma_{zy} & \sigma_{zz} \end{pmatrix};$$

   (iii) *parameter space*: $\mu_y,\ \mu_z,\ \sigma_{yz},\ \sigma_{yy},\ \sigma_{zz} \in \mathbb{R}^3 \times \mathbb{R}_+^2$ so that $\sigma_{yy}\sigma_{zz} > \sigma_{yz}^2$.

Alternatively, assumptions (i) and (ii) can be formulated in equation form as:

$$Y_i = \mu_y + u_{y,i},$$
$$Z_i = \mu_z + u_{z,i},$$

where the pairs $u_{y,i},\ u_{z,i}$ are independent over i and $\mathsf{N}_2[0, \Sigma]$-distributed.

10.3.1 Strong exogeneity

Strong exogeneity has to be established in order to justify the conditional analysis of Chapter 5. The analysis in §10.2.2 shows that $(Y_i|Z_i) \overset{\mathrm{D}}{=} \mathsf{N}[\beta_1 + \beta_2 Z_i, \sigma^2]$ and $Z_i \overset{\mathrm{D}}{=} \mathsf{N}[\mu_z, \sigma_{zz}]$. The conditional and marginal parameters satisfy:

$$\boldsymbol{\psi} = (\beta_1, \beta_2, \sigma^2) \in \Psi = \mathbb{R}^2 \times \mathbb{R}_+, \qquad \boldsymbol{\lambda} = (\mu_z, \sigma_{zz}) \in \Lambda = \mathbb{R} \times \mathbb{R}_+,$$

where the conditional parameters are defined in terms of the original parameters as in (10.2.4). In an equation format, we could write this bivariate model as:

$$Y_i = \beta_1 + \beta_2 Z_i + u_{y \cdot z, i}, \qquad (10.3.1)$$
$$Z_i = \mu_z + u_{z,i}. \qquad (10.3.2)$$

Assumptions (i) and (ii) then translate into independence of the pairs $(u_{y \cdot z, i}, Z_i)$ so $(u_{y \cdot z, i}|Z_i) \overset{\mathrm{D}}{=} \mathsf{N}[0, \sigma^2]$. This in turn implies that the errors $u_{y \cdot z, i}$ and $u_{z,i}$ are independent.

Two issues remain. First, Z_i is strongly exogenous for Y_i if we can establish that the parameters ψ and λ vary freely; see (10.1.2). Second, the original model formulated above was parametrized in terms of:

$$\boldsymbol{\theta} = (\mu_y,\ \mu_z,\ \sigma_{yz},\ \sigma_{yy},\ \sigma_{zz}) \in \Theta = \left(\mathbb{R}^3 \times \mathbb{R}^2_+ \text{ where } \sigma_{yy}\sigma_{zz} > \sigma^2_{yz}\right),$$

so it needs to be established that there is a one-one mapping between the original parameter space Θ and the reparametrized parameter space $\Psi \times \Lambda$, in order to ensure that the apparent strong exogeneity is not achieved by a restriction of the original model.

The first issue is easy. The parameters ψ and λ vary in the spaces Ψ and Λ. If we do not introduce any cross restrictions on ψ and λ, they will vary in a product space $\Psi \times \Lambda$ as required.

The second issue is more convoluted. From the construction of ψ and λ, it follows that for any $\boldsymbol{\theta} \in \Theta$ we can find $\psi, \lambda \in \Psi \times \Lambda$. Thus, we need to establish that for any $\psi, \lambda \in \Psi \times \Lambda$ we can find a $\boldsymbol{\theta} \in \Theta$. It is clear that μ_z, σ_{zz} satisfy their constraints, so we can focus on:

$$\mu_y = \beta_1 + \beta_2\mu_z, \qquad \sigma_{yy} = \sigma^2 + \beta_2^2\sigma_{zz}, \qquad \sigma_{yz} = \beta_2\sigma_{zz}. \qquad (10.3.3)$$

There are two binding constraints that need to be satisfied. First, the variance parameter σ_{yy} is positive, since it is a sum of a positive term, σ^2, and a non-negative term $\beta_2^2\sigma_{zz}$. Second, the covariance satisfies the constraint $\sigma^2_{yz} < \sigma_{zz}\sigma_{yy}$ as required, since:

$$\sigma^2_{yz} = \beta_2^2\sigma^2_{zz} = \sigma_{zz}\left(\beta_2^2\sigma_{zz}\right) < \sigma_{zz}\left(\sigma^2 + \beta_2^2\sigma_{zz}\right) = \sigma_{zz}\sigma_{yy}.$$

Thus, we can recover the original joint distribution parameters, despite treating the parameters of the conditional and marginal distributions separately.

10.3.2 The likelihood analysis

The likelihood analysis of the bivariate normal model in (10.3.1) and (10.3.2) can now be carried out with ease. From the considerations in §10.3.1, it follows that the likelihood is:

$$\mathsf{L}_{\mathbf{x}_1,\ldots,\mathbf{x}_n}(\boldsymbol{\theta}) = \mathsf{L}_{\mathbf{x}_1,\ldots,\mathbf{x}_n}(\psi,\lambda) = \mathsf{L}_{Y_1,\ldots,Y_n|Z_1,\ldots,Z_n}(\psi)\,\mathsf{L}_{Z_1,\ldots,Z_n}(\lambda),$$
$$(10.3.4)$$

so that there is a one-one mapping between $\boldsymbol{\theta}$ and (ψ,λ), and the latter vary in a product space. The conditional likelihood of Y_i given Z_i is then maximized as in Chapter 5, whereas the marginal likelihood of Z_i is maximized as in Chapter 3. The maximum likelihood estimator for ψ is therefore given by:

$$\widehat{\beta}_1 = \overline{Y} - \widehat{\beta}_2\overline{Z}, \qquad \widehat{\beta}_2 = \frac{\sum_{i=1}^n \left(Y_i - \overline{Y}\right)\left(Z_i - \overline{Z}\right)}{\sum_{i=1}^n \left(Z_i - \overline{Z}\right)^2},$$

and:

$$\widehat{\sigma}^2 = \frac{1}{n} \sum_{i=1}^{n} \left(Y_i - \overline{Y} \right)^2 - \frac{\left\{ \frac{1}{n} \sum_{i=1}^{n} \left(Y_i - \overline{Y} \right) \left(Z_i - \overline{Z} \right) \right\}^2}{\frac{1}{n} \sum_{i=1}^{n} \left(Z_i - \overline{Z} \right)^2},$$

whereas the maximum likelihood estimator for λ is given by:

$$\widehat{\mu}_z = \overline{Z}, \qquad \widehat{\sigma}_{zz} = \frac{1}{n} \sum_{i=1}^{n} \left(Z_i - \overline{Z} \right)^2.$$

The maximum likelihood estimator of the original parameter θ then follows immediately using (10.3.3):

$$\widehat{\mu} = \begin{pmatrix} \widehat{\mu}_y \\ \widehat{\mu}_z \end{pmatrix} = \begin{pmatrix} \overline{Y} \\ \overline{Z} \end{pmatrix},$$

$$\widehat{\Sigma} = \begin{pmatrix} \widehat{\sigma}_{yy} & \widehat{\sigma}_{yz} \\ \widehat{\sigma}_{zy} & \widehat{\sigma}_{zz} \end{pmatrix}$$

$$= \left\{ \begin{array}{cc} \frac{1}{n} \sum_{i=1}^{n} \left(Y_i - \overline{Y} \right)^2 & \frac{1}{n} \sum_{i=1}^{n} \left(Y_i - \overline{Y} \right) \left(Z_i - \overline{Z} \right) \\ \frac{1}{n} \sum_{i=1}^{n} \left(Y_i - \overline{Y} \right) \left(Z_i - \overline{Z} \right) & \frac{1}{n} \sum_{i=1}^{n} \left(Z_i - \overline{Z} \right)^2 \end{array} \right\}.$$

Following on from this, the two-variable *sample regression* function of §5.2:

$$\widehat{\beta}_1 + \widehat{\beta}_2 Z_i = \left(\widehat{\mu}_y - \frac{\widehat{\sigma}_{yz}}{\widehat{\sigma}_{zz}} \widehat{\mu}_z \right) + \frac{\widehat{\sigma}_{yz}}{\widehat{\sigma}_{zz}} Z_i$$

is maximum likelihood estimator for the conditional expectation of Y_i given Z_i:

$$\mathsf{E}(Y_i \mid Z_i) = \beta_1 + \beta_2 Z_i = \left(\mu_y - \frac{\sigma_{yz}}{\sigma_{zz}} \mu_z \right) + \frac{\sigma_{yz}}{\sigma_{zz}} Z_i,$$

which we call the *population regression*. Correspondingly, the conditional variance of Y_i given Z_i has the maximum likelihood estimator:

$$\widehat{\mathsf{Var}(Y_i|Z_i)} = \sigma_{yy} - \frac{\widehat{\sigma_{yz}^2}}{\sigma_{zz}} = \widehat{\sigma}_{yy} - \frac{\widehat{\sigma}_{yz}^2}{\widehat{\sigma}_{zz}}.$$

10.3.3 Application to wage-schooling

To illustrate the bivariate normal model, we apply it to log wages and schooling. The marginal distributions for these variables are estimated as in Chapter 3:

$$\widehat{w}_i = \underset{(0.01)}{5.02}, \quad \widehat{\sigma}_{ww} = 0.753, \quad \widehat{\ell}_w = -4401.2, \quad \chi^2_{\mathsf{norm}}[2] = 9121 \; [\text{p}<0.001],$$

$$\widehat{S}_i = \underset{(0.04)}{12.62}, \quad \widehat{\sigma}_{SS} = 2.68, \quad \widehat{\ell}_S = -9320.7, \quad \chi^2_{\mathsf{norm}}[2] = 913 \;\; [\text{p}<0.001].$$

In passing, we note that the normality assumption is rejected for both log wages and schooling. Nonetheless we persevere with these variables as an illustration. Estimating the joint bivariate normal model gives the above results along with information about the correlation of the errors:

$$\widehat{\rho}_{wS} = 0.270, \qquad \widehat{\ell}_{w,S} = -13575.0.$$

The sum of the individual likelihood values is $\widehat{\ell}_w + \widehat{\ell}_S = -13722$. Comparing that with the overall likelihood value yields a likelihood ratio test statistic:

$$\mathsf{LR}_{independence} = -2\left(\widehat{\ell}_w + \widehat{\ell}_S - \widehat{\ell}_{w,S}\right) = 294,$$

which is, in fact, a test for independence of the errors of the marginal equations, that is for $\rho = 0$. The test statistic is large compared with a $\chi^2[1]$-distribution, thereby indicating that the hypothesis of independence can be rejected.

Rather than looking upon this model as a system, one could think of it in terms of the conditional model of w_i given S_i, and the marginal model of S_i. As discussed above, this leads to two separate single-equation models with independent errors. The conditional model was considered in Chapter 5 and gives:

$$\underset{(0.06)}{\widehat{w}_i = 4.06} + \underset{(0.004)}{0.076\,S_i}, \qquad \widehat{\sigma}_{w\cdot S} = 0.725, \qquad \widehat{\ell}_{w|S} = -4254.3,$$

whereas the estimated marginal model for S_i was reported above. Combining the likelihoods of the conditional model and of the marginal model yields exactly the joint likelihood:

$$\widehat{\ell}_{w|S} + \widehat{\ell}_S = \widehat{\ell}_{w,S}. \tag{10.3.5}$$

Correspondingly, the sample correlation of the conditional and marginal residuals is exactly zero. The standard error of the conditional equation of u_i given S_i is somewhat reduced as compared to that of the marginal equation of S_i because of the additional explanatory variable.

Figure 10.2 illustrates the above findings. Panel (a) shows a scatterplot of the marginal residuals. The 95% sampling region of the estimated bivariate normal distribution is indicated with an ellipsoid that is rotated due to the non-zero correlation. Panel (b) shows a scatterplot of the conditional residuals along with marginal residuals for S_i. The estimated 95% sampling region is no longer rotated since the residuals are uncorrelated. In both cases, the estimated residuals appear to be skewed toward the right, both in the wage and the schooling dimensions. This is consistent with the non-normality found above.

10.3.4 Seemingly unrelated regressions

Strong exogeneity is needed to justify conditional plus marginal analysis, instead of joint analysis, of the variables involved. If exogeneity fails, maximizing the

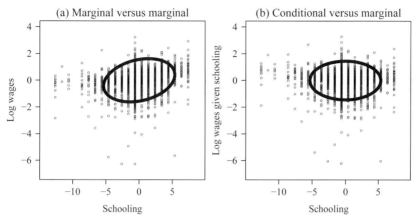

Figure 10.2 Scatterplot of the residuals: (a) using the marginal w_i and S_i equations, (b) using the conditional equation of w_i given S_i along with the marginal equation for S_i (in each plot, the estimated 95% sampling regions are indicated)

conditional likelihood and the marginal likelihood will typically not lead to an overall maximum of the joint likelihood. This, in turn, may lead to inefficient, and sometimes to biased, estimators.

As an example, consider the bivariate model again, with the restriction that $\mu_y = 0$ where μ_z is the parameter of interest. As before, we can write the joint likelihood as:

$$\mathsf{L}_{\mathbf{X}_1,\ldots,\mathbf{X}_n}(\boldsymbol{\theta}) = \mathsf{L}_{\mathbf{X}_1,\ldots,\mathbf{X}_n}(\boldsymbol{\psi},\boldsymbol{\lambda}) = \mathsf{L}_{Y_1,\ldots,Y_n|Z_1,\ldots,Z_n}(\boldsymbol{\psi})\,\mathsf{L}_{Z_1,\ldots,Z_n}(\boldsymbol{\lambda}).$$

The restriction $\mu_y = 0$ relates to both the conditional and the marginal equation, (10.3.1) and (10.3.2), and is therefore referred to as a *cross-equation restriction*. The parameters $\boldsymbol{\psi},\boldsymbol{\lambda}$ no longer vary in a product space since $\mu_y = \beta_1 + \beta_2\mu_z = 0$, where β_1, β_2 are functions of $\boldsymbol{\psi}$, while μ_z is a function of $\boldsymbol{\lambda}$, so that Z_i is not strongly exogenous for Y_i.

The marginal likelihood for Z_i corresponds to a simple regression as in Chapter 3. Thus, maximizing the marginal likelihood must lead to the estimator:

$$\widetilde{\mu}_z = \overline{Z}.$$

Due to the lack of strong exogeneity, this estimator is unlikely to be the maximum likelihood estimator in the joint model. In Exercise 10.5, it is shown that maximizing the joint likelihood gives:

$$\widehat{\mu}_z = \frac{\sum_{i=1}^n w_{1\cdot Y,i} Z_i}{\sum_{j=1}^n w_{1\cdot Y,j}^2} \qquad \text{where} \qquad w_{1\cdot Y,i} = 1 - \frac{\sum_{j=1}^n Y_j}{\sum_{k=1}^n Y_k^2} Y_i, \qquad (10.3.6)$$

This result comes about by conditioning Z_i on Y_i instead of Y_i on Z_i, and noting that Y_i actually is strongly exogenous for Z_i.

The issue that is observed here has two somewhat different aspects to it. First, in the above setup where Y_i is conditioned on Z_i, the error terms $u_{y \cdot z, i}$ and $u_{z,i}$ are independent. The restriction $\mu_y = 0$ is a cross-equation restriction across the parameters of the two unrelated equations and leads to a violation of strong exogeneity. Second, focusing on the two marginal models for Y_i and for Z_i, we note that the error terms $u_{y,i}$ and $u_{z,i}$ have covariance σ_{zy}. The restriction $\mu_y = 0$ is a *single-equation restriction* on the model for Y_i but has an impact on estimating the model for Z_i, due to the covariance σ_{zy}. The marginal models for Y_i and Z_i are therefore referred to as *seemingly unrelated regressions* (*SUR*). In general, numerical routines for maximizing functions are needed to maximize the likelihood for such seemingly unrelated regressions.

The estimators $\widetilde{\mu}_z$ and $\widehat{\mu}_z$ can be compared through their distributions. In Exercise 10.6, it is argued that both estimators are unbiased so $\mathsf{E}(\widetilde{\mu}_z) = \mathsf{E}(\widehat{\mu}_z) = \mu_z$, but their distributions are different:

$$\widetilde{\mu}_z \overset{D}{=} \mathsf{N}\left[\mu_z, n^{-1}\sigma_{zz}\right], \qquad \widehat{\mu}_z \overset{D}{\approx} \mathsf{N}\left[\mu_z, n^{-1}\sigma_{z\cdot y}^2\right]. \tag{10.3.7}$$

Comparing the two unbiased estimators $\widetilde{\mu}_z$ and $\widehat{\mu}_z$, we will typically prefer the latter, which is asymptotically efficient in that its variance is smaller: $\sigma_{z\cdot y}^2 = \sigma_{zz} - \sigma_{zy}^2/\sigma_{yy} \leq \sigma_{zz}$, unless $\sigma_{zy} = 0$. When $\sigma_{zy} = 0$ then of course the marginal models for Y_i and Z_i are unrelated and the issue disappears.

10.4 INFERENCE WITH EXOGENOUS VARIABLES

In §5.5.4 we explored the role of regressors when testing in the context of a regression model. This can now be discussed more precisely. In addition to the absence of links between the parameters of the conditional and marginal distributions, a key result for validating conditional inference with strongly exogenous variables is the separation of the joint density:

$$\mathsf{f}_\theta(\mathbf{x}_1, \ldots, \mathbf{x}_n) = \mathsf{f}_\psi(y_1, \ldots, y_n \mid z_1, \ldots, z_n)\mathsf{f}_\lambda(z_1, \ldots, z_n),$$

as in (10.3.4). Since the expression for the conditional distribution of $Y_1, \ldots, Y_n$ given $Z_1, \ldots, Z_n$ is available, we can work out the distribution of estimators and test statistics based on the conditional model. To simplify the algebra, we consider a bivariate regression without an intercept:

$$Y_i = \beta_2 Z_i + u_{y \cdot z, i}, \tag{10.4.1}$$
$$Z_i = u_{z,i}. \tag{10.4.2}$$

The estimator $\widehat{\beta}_2$ can be reformulated using the model equation (10.4.1):

$$\widehat{\beta}_2 = \frac{\sum_{i=1}^n Y_i Z_i}{\sum_{i=1}^n Z_i^2} = \beta_2 + \frac{\sum_{i=1}^n Z_i u_{y \cdot z, i}}{\sum_{i=1}^n Z_i^2}.$$

The earlier assumptions are maintained, with Z_i being strongly exogenous for β_2. In particular, $u_{y \cdot z, 1}, \ldots, u_{y \cdot z, n}$ are independent of the information set $\mathcal{I}$ given by $(Z_1 \ldots Z_n)$, so we get:

$$\mathsf{E}\left(\widehat{\beta}_2 - \beta_2 \middle| \mathcal{I}\right) = \mathsf{E}\left(\frac{\sum_{i=1}^n Z_i u_{y \cdot z, i}}{\sum_{i=1}^n Z_i^2} \middle| \mathcal{I}\right) = \frac{\sum_{i=1}^n Z_i \mathsf{E}\left(u_{y \cdot z, i} | \mathcal{I}\right)}{\sum_{i=1}^n Z_i^2} = 0,$$

since the independence implies $\mathsf{E}(u_{y \cdot z, i} \mid \mathcal{I}) = \mathsf{E}(u_{y \cdot z, i}) = 0$. By the Law of Iterated Expectations (see 4.1.8), $\widehat{\beta}_2$ is also unconditionally unbiased for β_2 under strong exogeneity:

$$\mathsf{E}\left(\widehat{\beta}_2 - \beta_2\right) = \mathsf{E}\left\{\mathsf{E}\left(\widehat{\beta}_2 - \beta_2 \middle| \mathcal{I}\right)\right\} = \mathsf{E}\left(0\right) = 0.$$

In the same way, the conditional variance of $\widehat{\beta}_2$ is:

$$\begin{aligned}
\mathsf{Var}\left(\widehat{\beta}_2 \middle| \mathcal{I}\right) &= \mathsf{E}\left(\frac{\sum_{i=1}^n Z_i u_{y \cdot z, i}}{\sum_{i=1}^n Z_i^2} \middle| \mathcal{I}\right)^2 = \mathsf{E}\left\{\frac{\sum_{i=1}^n \sum_{j=1}^n Z_i u_{y \cdot z, i} u_{y \cdot z, j} Z_j}{\left(\sum_{i=1}^n Z_i^2\right)^2} \middle| \mathcal{I}\right\} \\
&= \frac{\sum_{i=1}^n \sum_{j=1}^n Z_i \mathsf{E}\left(u_{y \cdot z, i} u_{y \cdot z, j} | \mathcal{I}\right) Z_j}{\left(\sum_{i=1}^n Z_i^2\right)^2} \\
&= \frac{\sum_{i=1}^n Z_i \mathsf{E}\left(u_{y \cdot z, i} u_{y \cdot z, i}\right) Z_i}{\left(\sum_{i=1}^n Z_i^2\right)^2} = \frac{\sigma^2}{\sum_{i=1}^n Z_i^2}.
\end{aligned}$$

Thus, the conditional distribution of $(\sum_{i=1}^n Z_i^2 / \sigma^2)^{1/2} \widehat{\beta}_2$ is standard normal and does not depend on the information set $\mathcal{I}$.

10.5 SUMMARY AND EXERCISES

Summary: The bivariate normal model is closely linked to both the one- and two-variable models analyzed previously. Strong exogeneity ensures that two-variable regression estimates are maximum likelihood within a bivariate normal framework. This implication breaks down, for instance, in the presence of cross-equation restrictions.

Key questions:

- Discuss the connection between, on the one hand, the bivariate normal model and, on the other hand, the one- and two-variable regression models.
- What is the role of strong exogeneity?
- Discuss situations where strong exogeneity does not hold.

Exercise 10.1. *Suppose* $\mathbf{X} \overset{\mathrm{D}}{=} \mathsf{N}_2[\boldsymbol{\mu}, \boldsymbol{\Sigma}]$. *Show (10.2.3) in the following steps:*
(*a*) *Show that:*

$$w^2 = \frac{(z - \mu_z)^2}{\sigma_{zz}} + \frac{(y - \beta_1 - \beta_2 z)^2}{\sigma^2}.$$

(b) Write $f(y, z) = g(y, z)h(z)$, where $g(y, z)$ is the density of the $N[\beta_1 + \beta_2 z, \sigma^2]$-distribution and $h(z)$ is the density of the $N[\mu_z, \sigma_{zz}^2]$-distribution.
(c) Show that $h(z) = \int_{-\infty}^{\infty} f(y, z) dy$.
(d) Argue that $h(z)$ is the marginal density for Z, and that this completes the proof.

Exercise 10.2. Let $\mathbf{X} \stackrel{D}{=} N_2[\boldsymbol{\mu}, \boldsymbol{\Sigma}]$ as in section 10.2.1. Define the variable $V = Y - \sigma_{yz}\sigma_{zz}^{-1}Z$.
(a) Find the distribution of V.
Hint: note that V is a linear combination of Y and Z and use section 10.2.3.
(b) Show that $\text{Cov}(V, Z) = 0$.

Exercise 10.3. Find $E(X|Y)$ and $E(Y|X)$ for the bivariate normal distribution (10.2.2).
Plot the functions in the contour plot in Figure 10.1.

Exercise 10.4. Strong exogeneity is based on the condition of variation freeness in (10.1.2). For a function taking the value xy on some domain $\mathbb{D}$ and zero otherwise, this corresponds to the condition:

$$\max_{(x,y) \in \mathbb{D}} xy = \left\{ \max_{x \text{ so } (x,y) \in \mathbb{D}} x \right\} \left\{ \max_{y \text{ so } (x,y) \in \mathbb{D}} y \right\} \tag{10.5.1}$$

(a) Suppose $\mathbb{D}$ is given by $0 \le x \le 1$ and $0 \le y \le 1$. Show that (10.5.1) holds.
(b) Suppose $\mathbb{D}$ is given by $0 \le x \le 1$, $0 \le y \le 1$, and $x + y = 1$. Show that (10.5.1) fails.

Exercise 10.5. Consider the model in section 10.3.4, so $\mathbf{X} \stackrel{D}{=} N_2[\boldsymbol{\mu}, \boldsymbol{\Sigma}]$, with the restriction $\mu_y = 0$.
(a) Write down the conditional model for $(Z_i \mid Y_i)$ and the marginal model for Y_i.
(b) Argue that Y_i is strongly exogenous for Z_i.
(c) Show that the estimator $\widehat{\mu}_z$ in (10.3.6) is the maximum likelihood estimator for the joint model.

Exercise 10.6. * Consider the estimator $\widehat{\mu}_z$ in (10.3.6).
(a) Argue that the conditional distribution of $\widehat{\mu}_z$ given $Y_1, \ldots, Y_n$ is $N[\mu_z, \omega^2]$, where $\omega^2 = \sigma_{z \cdot y}^2 / \sum_{i=1}^{n} w_{1 \cdot Y, i}^2$.
(b) Show that the marginal distribution of $(\sum_{i=1}^{n} w_{1 \cdot Y, i}^2)^{1/2}(\widehat{\mu}_z - \mu_z)$ is $N[0, \sigma_{z \cdot y}^2]$.
(c) Use the Law of Large Numbers to argue that $\sum_{i=1}^{n} w_{1 \cdot Y, i}^2 \approx 1$.
(d) Establish the results in (10.3.7).

Exercise 10.7. Consider the simple regression model of Chapter 3 with $n = 2$.
(a) Argue that:

$$\mathbf{Y} = \begin{pmatrix} Y_1 \\ Y_2 \end{pmatrix} \stackrel{D}{=} N_2 \left[\begin{pmatrix} \beta_1 \\ \beta_2 \end{pmatrix}, \begin{pmatrix} \sigma^2 & 0 \\ 0 & \sigma^2 \end{pmatrix} \right].$$

(b) *Find the joint distribution of* $Z_1 = Y_1 + Y_2$ *and* $Z_2 = Y_1 - Y_2$

(c) *Argue that* $\widehat{\beta}$ *and* $\widehat{\sigma}^2$, *as defined in (3.3.5), (3.3.9), are independent.*

(d) *Show that the* t*-statistic* Z *in (3.4.8) satisfies* $Z = N/D$ *where* $D^2 = s^2/\sigma^2$ *and* $N = (n/\sigma^2)^{1/2}(\widehat{\beta} - \beta)$, *still with* $n = 2$.

(e) *Argue that* N *and* D *are independent, that* $N \overset{\mathrm{D}}{=} \mathsf{N}[0,1]$, *and that* $D^2 \overset{\mathrm{D}}{=} \chi^2[1]$. *The result in* (e) *implies that* $Z \overset{\mathrm{D}}{=} \mathsf{t}[1]$; *see Hoel et al. (1971, section 6.6). These results can be developed more generally for any* n *and for the multiple regression model. They form the basis for the exact distribution theory for regression estimators; see Greene (2003, section 4.7).*

Exercise 10.8. **Matrix formulation of the bivariate normal distribution**. *Let* $\mathbf{X} \overset{\mathrm{D}}{=} \mathsf{N}_2[\boldsymbol{\mu}, \boldsymbol{\Sigma}]$. *If* $\mathbf{A} \in \mathbb{R}^{2 \times 2}$ *so* $\mathbf{A\Sigma A}'$ *is invertible and* $\mathbf{B} \in \mathbb{R}^2$, *then it holds that*

$$\mathbf{AX} + \mathbf{B} \overset{\mathrm{D}}{=} \mathsf{N}_2[\mathbf{A\mu} + \mathbf{B}, \mathbf{A\Sigma A}'].$$

Now, let

$$\mathbf{X} = \left(\begin{array}{c} Y \\ Z \end{array} \right), \qquad \mathbf{A} = \left(\begin{array}{cc} 1 & -\sigma_{yz}\sigma_{zz}^{-1} \\ 0 & 1 \end{array} \right).$$

(a) *Compute the coordinates of* $\mathbf{AX}$.

(b) *Compute the distribution of* $\mathbf{AX}$.

(c) *Argue that the coordinates of* $\mathbf{AX}$ *are independent.*

(d) * *Use the above results to find the distribution of* $(Y \mid Z)$.

Chapter Eleven

Empirical models and modeling

In the development so far, we have been concerned with statistical models for cross-sectional data. In the subsequent Chapters 12 to 17, in a similar way we will develop and analyze statistical models for time-series data. First, however, it is useful to consider some broader aspects of econometric modeling.

Initially, we will discuss the main motivation for econometric modeling, leading to a definition of empirical models. We can then proceed to a more detailed analysis of the possible interpretations of regression models. Finally, the notions *congruence* and *encompassing* are introduced to describe the aims of econometric modeling.

11.1 ASPECTS OF ECONOMETRIC MODELING

To account for the empirical evidence obtained in economics, economists treat observed data outcomes as the realizations of random variables that have been generated by economic behavior. The distribution function $F(x) = P(X \leq x)$ fully characterizes the properties of the random variable X, but F is typically unknown. Consequently, we formulate statistical models, which are families of possible distributions, indexed by a vector parameter θ. In the context of economic theory, we consider particular distributions, rather than families of distributions, with parameters denoted θ_0 that arise from the solutions of decision problems by economic agents: e.g., the marginal propensity to save (about 0.1 on average) is selected by agents when maximizing lifetime utility. As discussed in previous chapters, estimators of unknown parameters can be based on the observed data, derived from the likelihood function $L_X(\theta)$. Because data are realizations of random variables, such estimators have sampling distributions (so take different values in different samples), as do test statistics for hypotheses relevant to economics. Derivations of estimators and their distributions can be obtained in principle once we know which probability model, $F_{\theta_0}(x)$ say, generated the data. There are five important practical difficulties, however, which we now address.

First, until economists have a complete understanding about how economies function, researchers cannot know what the relevant class of statistical models should be. If an investigator "guesses" the wrong statistical model, he or she will derive an inappropriate estimator, which may be badly biased for the actual problem. Thus, economists have to proceed as in any empirical science: postulate a class of possible distributions and associated statistical models; derive appropriate estimators and their properties, assuming that the statistical model is correct; then see how well these models describe the relevant economic data. When mismatches appear, revise the statistical model, and restart. Thus, empirical research is a process, not a one-off event—hopefully a progressive process leading to increased understanding over time. We too will proceed in this way. We have considered a number of potentially relevant statistical models in earlier chapters, and in each case we have obtained estimators and test statistics and then considered their properties: these tools will prove essential in applied work.

Second, econometric models are often complicated, and the distributions of estimators and tests can be derived only for large samples (asymptotic distribution theory). Such results are useful but potentially limited. However, numerical simulation on computers, called Monte Carlo experimentation, can elucidate the operational properties of methods in finite samples of the size usually encountered in economics. This has been a standard approach for more than a century, and such simulations will be applied in Chapter 18 to experiments that mimic the empirical models under analysis.

Third, economics generally deals with joint distributions, often involving hundreds of variables—far too many to tackle at once. Conditional and marginal distributions are therefore often derived and analyzed. For conditioning to be valid, appropriate exogeneity conditions must be satisfied, and we have to discuss exogeneity more precisely in relation to making conditional inferences, conditional forecasts, and conditional policy analyses.

Fourth, macroeconomic data are usually time-series observations, so both the analysis and selection of dynamic models must be addressed. Dynamic reactions by economic agents complicate the econometric methods themselves, thus making analyses of such methods harder still. While we will develop methods for doing this, computer simulations of "pretend economies" to see how methods perform become even more valuable. It is also useful to investigate the practical consequences of applying econometric methods and tests to actual economic time-series data. Further, we must consider the implications of time for the analyses of cross-sectional microeconomic data we have discussed so far.

Finally, economies seem to be non-stationary processes where the data moments (such as means and variances) in fact vary over time. Indeed, an economy today is quite unlike that of a century ago, so constant expectations and variances over time (stationarity) are not a tenable assumption for the levels of economic variables. It is much harder to theorize about and study an object that continually changes than if the object stays the same. Nevertheless, we cannot ignore such a key feature. Modern macro-econometrics, therefore, investigates dynamic systems, which are called equilibrium-correction models, applicable to such non-stationary processes.

Consequently, the main ingredients of most econometric studies are:

(1) an economic theory model of the phenomenon of interest;

(2) a statistical model of the data to be analyzed;

(3) an estimation method for the unknown parameters;

(4) the sample of data to be used;

(5) evaluation procedures for the adequacy of the fitted model;

(6) a revision process if any mismatch occurs;

(7) an analysis of the properties of the procedures used.

The above listing is not intended to entail the order in which the ingredients must be developed: sometimes, (4) will come first, then (1), (2), (3) and (5)–(7). Above, we often adopted the order (2), (3), (7), (5), (4), (1), and (6). However, it is convenient, and indeed conventional, to follow the order in our list.

An economic theory suggests which variables are interrelated and in what ways, which parameters are of interest, possibly the functional forms of some of the relationships, and sometimes the dynamic responses and interactions. However, such theory is usually an abstract model of the behavior of economic agents, often in a "steady state", often non-stochastic, and always requiring many *ceteris paribus* clauses, both implicit and explicit. Thus, while distinctly helpful, economic analysis is the starting point, not the conclusion, for any empirical study, leaving many aspects to be "data determined", especially dynamics and special factors (seasonality, institutions, regime shifts, etc.).

A statistical model is also a theory, but about how the data to be analyzed are generated. The empirical econometric problem is that we do not have complete and correct stochastic economic theories from which to derive "correct" statistical models, so we do not know the actual relationship between the *data-generating process* (DGP) and the postulated statistical model.

Since data are neither perfectly accurate nor precise, we also do not know the relationship of the sample of measured data to the "true data" assumed in the economic analysis. Measurement errors are pervasive in econometrics and should always be considered as a possible complication. Like many of the other difficulties, their potential impact can be examined using simulation methods. Such methods will be explored in Chapter 18.

Fortunately, there are many theories about the behavior of economic agents which suggest potential statistical models, and plenty of statistical tools to test those ideas, so at least we can easily learn when models are wrong. Thus, although we do not know how the data were really generated, by postulating various classes of statistical models that could in principle generate appropriate data, by estimating their parameters assuming the models are correct, and then by evaluating the outcomes to check for mismatches, we can learn from our mistakes and develop improved models for the next round.

We will now discuss empirical econometric models, and some of the key concepts needed to interpret estimated equations. We then sketch four different but closely related linear equations, any one of which may have resulted from the empirical analysis. We then conclude by discussing the role of the exogeneity assumption in cross-sectional settings.

11.2 EMPIRICAL MODELS

To illustrate the discussion of empirical models, we consider a long-run time series, namely annual real industrial output, Y_t, in the UK since 1700. In contrast to cross-sectional data where characteristics are observed for unrelated individuals, a time series is a set of observations on a single variable developing over time. The index t rather than i indicates that we are working with a time series rather than with individuals. Likewise, the sample length is denoted T rather than n. The log of output $y_t = \log Y_t$ is shown in Figure 11.1(a). A simple theory is that the growth rate is constant on average:

$$\mathsf{E}\left(\Delta y_t\right) \stackrel{\text{def}}{=} \mathsf{E}\left(y_t - y_{t-1}\right) = b. \tag{11.2.1}$$

In order to link this with the data, we postulate two simple models for y_t.

First, solving $\Delta y_t = b$ in (11.2.1) for y_t gives a linear trend, which we augment with an error term to represent deviations from the average:

$$y_t = \alpha_1 + \alpha_2 t + u_t, \qquad u_t \stackrel{\mathsf{D}}{=} \mathsf{IN}[0, \sigma_u^2], \tag{11.2.2}$$

where the notation IN indicates that the errors u_t are assumed to be independently normal distributed. Panel (b) shows the least squares fit of the postulated trend line. Notice that u_t has the same units as y_t; and that σ_u has the same units as u_t, and therefore of y_t. For small values of σ_u, the use of logs makes σ_u into a proportion of Y_t: recalling that $\partial \log Y / \partial Y = 1/Y$ so:

$$\frac{\partial Y_t}{\partial u_t} = \left(\frac{\partial Y_t}{\partial y_t}\right)\left(\frac{\partial y_t}{\partial u_t}\right) = \frac{\partial y_t}{\partial u_t}Y_t,$$

we see that small errors change Y_t proportionally. Thus, if $\widehat{\sigma}_u = 0.05$, then one standard error change of $y_t = \log Y_t$ results in a 5% change of Y_t. This is assumed constant for all values of Y in (11.2.2). Similarly, α_1 is the rate of growth, so 0.025 would be 2.5% per annum, since the data are annual. However, the units of α_0 are arbitrary and depend on how we choose to measure Y_t. Nominal output could be measured in millions or billions of pounds, while the price index used for deflating nominal output could be normalized at unity in 1750, or 1950. The deviations from the fitted line in (11.2.2) are shown in Figure 11.1(b). It can be seen at a glance that the successive values of $\widehat{u}_t$ are not independent: a positive value is much more likely to be followed by a positive than a negative value. Thus, the simple trend is not an adequate statistical model because the outcome contradicts the postulated generating process in (11.2.2). Models with no trend term would do even worse, however. Just as for the cross-sectional models we have seen, note how easy it is to criticize an empirical model using evidence of mismatches between the claimed properties and the outcomes, although it is usually much harder to fix any problem. This dichotomy of destructive and constructive applications of econometrics is a recurring theme.

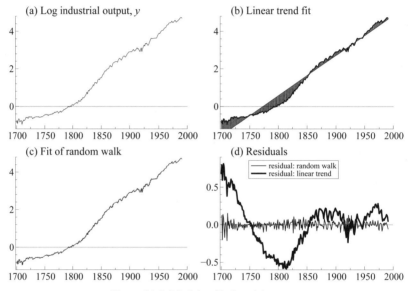

Figure 11.1 Models of industrial output

Second, we postulate the "constant change" relation by adding an error to $\Delta y_t = b$ before solving for y_t:

$$y_t = \gamma_1 + y_{t-1} + v_t, \qquad v_t \stackrel{\mathrm{D}}{=} \mathrm{IN}[0, \sigma_v^2], \tag{11.2.3}$$

so σ_v is again a proportion of Y. Figure 11.1(c) is the fit of this "random walk", or constant change, model. In (11.2.3), γ_1 is the rate of growth (so again 0.025 would be 2.5% per annum, since the data are annual), and $\widehat{\gamma}_1$ is the mean growth rate:

$$\widehat{\gamma}_1 = \frac{1}{T} \sum_{t=1}^{T} \Delta y_t = \frac{1}{T} (y_T - y_0).$$

This estimator uses only the first and the last observation. Nevertheless, when the process is generated by (11.2.3), then:

$$\widehat{\gamma}_1 = \frac{1}{T} \sum_{t=1}^{T} (\gamma_1 + v_t) = \gamma_1 + \frac{1}{T} \sum_{t=1}^{T} v_t,$$

so we have, just as for the regression model in Chapter 3:

$$\mathsf{E}\left(\widehat{\gamma}_1\right) = \gamma_1 \qquad \text{and} \qquad \mathsf{Var}\left(\widehat{\gamma}_1\right) = \frac{\sigma_v^2}{T}.$$

Here, the fit of (11.2.3) is vastly better than (11.2.2): Figure 11.1(d) contrasts the two sets of residuals on a common scale. Although both statistical models correspond to the simple theory that the growth rate is constant, in practice they behave quite differently. Thus, a given theory can have several statistical implementations.

The models in (11.2.2) and (11.2.3) above are usually given a "causal" interpretation, in that the data are assumed to be generated by the equation in question. Thus, for example, (11.2.3) entails that the next value of y_t is generated from the previous value by adding $\gamma_1 + v_t$ where γ_1 is a fixed (albeit unknown) constant and $v_t \overset{\mathsf{D}}{=} \mathsf{IN}\left[0, \sigma_v^2\right]$. Causal statements are difficult to test, however, as macroeconomists mainly get observational, or non-experimental, data, where there are many uncontrolled events. In principle, the effects of uncontrolled variables can be removed by partialling them out using techniques like multiple regression, as we have explained above. Unfortunately, not all relevant uncontrolled effects are known, and some may not even be measured. Thus, a major objective of empirical econometric analysis is to determine which factors are indeed relevant. Moreover, any assumption that our models are generating equations is thereby cast into doubt.

In an experiment, changes in outputs are caused by changes in inputs: by construction, the experiment is the mechanism that generates the data. Thus, experimenters conceive of the data-generating process as:

$$\underset{\text{output}}{Y_i} \quad = \quad \underset{\text{input}}{f(Z_i)} \quad + \quad \underset{\text{perturbation}}{u_i} \tag{11.2.4}$$

where Y_i is the observed outcome of the experiment when Z_i is the experimental input, $f(\cdot)$ is the mapping from input to output, and u_i is a small, random perturbation which varies between experiments conducted at the same Z. Thus, providing other factors are controlled, the same inputs Z_i generate essentially the same outputs. Thus, the experiment is repeatable, and causation is from the right-hand side to the left-hand side in (11.2.4) in that changing Z_i changes Y_i. Inadequately controlled experiments are prone to misleading interpretations, since changes in Y_i then derive from changes in the uncontrolled factors but are mistakenly attributed to changes in Z_i.

In economics, data are not generated as if the economy is a controlled experiment. The consequences of having "passive" data or *observational data*, often collected as an incidental part of an administrative process, are profound. Econometric equations may look like (11.2.4), but with a fundamental difference, which we express as:

$$Y_i \;\;\; = \;\;\; g\left(Z_i\right) \;\;\; + \;\;\; v_i$$
$$\text{observed} \quad\quad \text{explained} \quad\quad \text{remainder} \tag{11.2.5}$$

so the left-hand side is determining the right. Equation (11.2.5) describes all empirical economic models, since Y_i can always be decomposed into two components, namely the explained part, $g\left(Z_i\right)$, and the unexplained part, v_i. Such a split is feasible even when Y_i depends on completely different factors, $h\left(X_i\right)$ say, and not on $g\left(Z_i\right)$. Thus, v_i in (11.2.5) is what is left over from Y_i after extracting $g\left(Z_i\right)$ so:

$$v_i = Y_i - g\left(Z_i\right). \tag{11.2.6}$$

Hence, v_i is a derived variable that reflects the measurement errors in Y_i and the choice of Z_i, as well as everything that enters the data generation process for Y_i but is omitted from the model. Since Z_i is not controlled, it is easy to reach misleading interpretations if in fact Y_i does depend on $h(Z_i)$.

The formulation in (11.2.5) is generic: empirical econometric models are really decompositions of observed data rather than causal entities. At first sight, this may be thought to be destructive of the econometric enterprise, but we can nevertheless construct a viable approach to analyzing data in a non-experimental world. For example, changing Z_i in (11.2.5) need not change Y_i, but when it does so systematically (e.g., in economic policy), we can have much greater confidence in the model. Likewise, if adding X_i to (11.2.5) does not alter v_i, then we can exclude the possibility that it determines Y_i; and so on. Conversely, if the residuals depart from the assumptions made about v_i, or are correlated, heteroskedastic, etc., then we have evidence of an incomplete model, with the obvious danger that omitted factors may be inducing the observed problems with the residuals. Indeed, as already noted, rejection of inadequate models is rather easier than establishing adequacy, although we will show that both are feasible.

We call the entity $Y_i = g\left(Z_i\right) + v_i$ an *empirical model*, as its properties depend on those of the observed data. Both (11.2.2) and (11.2.3) are examples of empirical models, respectively "decomposing" measured industrial output into either a constant and a linear trend, or a constant and the lagged value, with very different residuals. In fact, industrial output is generated by humans working on machines transforming raw materials and energy into final goods, and not at all by a trend or the lagged value, so neither model could be the DGP. Thus, the status, properties, and evaluation procedures for empirical models must be investigated, but first we clarify an issue of interpretation of linear equations before proceeding.

11.3 INTERPRETING REGRESSION MODELS

The regression models we have worked with can be described as examples of linear models. In the following, we will first introduce this notion, and then provide four interpretations of such linear models.

11.3.1 Linear models

A linear equation is one that is invariant under linear transformations. Consider, for example:

$$Y_i = \sum_{j=1}^{k} \beta_j Z_{j,i} + u_i, \qquad (11.3.1)$$

which would have the same appearance if $\sum_{j=1}^{k} \alpha_j Z_{j,i}$ were added on both sides. A specific example is given below. In (11.3.1) one "dependent" variable Y_i is related to a set of k "independent" or "explanatory" variables denoted $Z_{j,i}$ for individual i, with a "disturbance" u_i. The coefficients β_j of the relation are assumed constant across individuals, and the impact of the Zs on Y is additive. These assumptions could be invalid empirically and need evaluation, as we have shown in earlier chapters. Also, such assumptions are not sufficient to fully describe the relationship; we also need to formulate the relation of the $Z_{j,i}$ to u_i, and state the stochastic properties of u_i. We will assume that $u_i \stackrel{D}{=} \mathsf{IN}[0, \sigma_u^2]$. Finally, we need an exogeneity assumption for the variables $Z_{j,i}$.

In the special case that $k = 2$, we typically let $Z_{1,i} = 1$ be an intercept, and then denote $Z_{2,i}$ by Z_i. The data set is then (Y_i, Z_i), so (11.3.1) becomes:

$$Y_i = \beta_1 + \beta_2 Z_i + u_i. \qquad (11.3.2)$$

This equation is linear, because for any three known real numbers α_1, α_2, and α_3:

$$Y_i - \alpha_1 - \alpha_2 Z_i = \{\beta_1 - \alpha_1 + (\beta_2 - \alpha_2)\,\alpha_3\} + (\beta_2 - \alpha_2)\,(Z_i - \alpha_3) + u_i, \qquad (11.3.3)$$

so that we can reparametrize (11.3.2) as:

$$Y_i^* = \delta_1 + \delta_2 Z_i^* + u_i, \qquad (11.3.4)$$

using $Y_i^* = Y_i - \alpha_1 - \alpha_2 Z_i$ and $Z_i^* = (Z_i - \alpha_3)$. Then (11.3.4) is the same equation as (11.3.2): it has the same disturbance process, u_i, and the same exogeneity properties. Notice from (11.3.3) that the definition of the dependent variable is not unique for a given model, so, as remarked in §7.4.1, the coefficient of determination, R^2, is not a unique measure of "fit" for a model, only for one choice of the dependent variable. Also, the correlations between the regressors are not unique, as these also differ between (11.3.2) and (11.3.3), as remarked in §7.3.3 concerning near collinearity. However, σ_u^2 is unaltered, and remains in the same units as the original Y. An important property of maximum likelihood estimates is that if we estimate β_1 and β_2 in (11.3.2) and transform them to δ_1 and δ_2, or estimate δ_1 and δ_2 directly in (11.3.4), we get identical answers. Thus, we can choose which model formulation best suits a given situation, a property we have actually used above.

In addition to this large class of admissible linear transformations of (11.3.4), four interpretations of such linear equations must be distinguished, namely, a regression, a linear least-squares approximation, a contingent plan, and a behavioral model. Without further information, a linear equation may sustain any one of these interpretations, but the meaning and status of its parameters will differ according to which type is valid.

11.3.2 Regression and conditional expectation

A regression equation is the conditional expectation of one variable Y_i given a second set of variables $Z_{j,i}$. In the bivariate case with $Z_{1,i} = 1$:

$$\mathsf{E}\left(Y_i \mid Z_i\right) = \beta_1 + \beta_2 Z_i. \tag{11.3.5}$$

From (11.3.5) it follows:

$$Y_i = \mathsf{E}(Y_i \mid Z_i) + u_i. \tag{11.3.6}$$

The remainder term u_i satisfies $\mathsf{E}(u_i|Z_i) = 0$, which is seen by taking conditional expectations with respect to Z_i in (11.3.6). This decomposition matches (11.2.5). Regression is a generic construct, and the regression function $\mathsf{E}(Y_i|Z_i) = g\left(Z_i\right)$ will only yield be linear as in (11.3.5) for certain joint distributions of (Y_i, Z_i).

The best-known distribution leading to linear regression is the bivariate normal distribution (see §10.2). In this case, (11.3.5) is the population regression function as in §10.3.2. Further, in Exercise 11.1 it is argued that $\mathsf{E}(Y_i|Z_i)$ is the minimum-variance unbiased predictor of Y_i as a function of Z_i with error variance $\sigma_u^2 = \sigma_{yy} - \sigma_{yz}^2 \sigma_{zz}^{-1}$, so no other equation fits better on the given information set. There are many joint distributions for which regressions, in the meaning of conditional expectations, are not linear. For example, when $y_i = \log Y_i$ and $z_i = \log Z_i$ are normal and linearly related, then Y_i and Z_i are not.

11.3.3 Linear least-squares approximation

When the data-generating process is that $Y_i = f\left(Z_i\right) + v_i$ where $v_i \overset{\mathsf{D}}{=} \mathsf{IN}[0, \sigma_v^2]$, a linear approximation to $f(Z_i)$ is given by:

$$f\left(Z_i\right) \approx \gamma_1 + \gamma_2 Z_i, \tag{11.3.7}$$

where a remainder term depending on Z_i is ignored. The coefficients γ_1, γ_2 in (11.3.7) can be selected to minimize the least-squares criterion:

$$\underset{(\gamma_1,\gamma_2)}{\mathrm{argmin}} \sum_{i=1}^{n} \left(Y_i - \gamma_1 - \gamma_2 Z_i\right)^2. \tag{11.3.8}$$

As explored in §5.2, the minimum defines the values of γ_1, γ_2 in (11.3.7). Note the decomposition of Y_i into $\gamma_1 + \gamma_2 Z_i$ and an error term $w_i = Y_i - \gamma_1 - \gamma_2 Z_i$, and that the "errors" w_i are not structural, but derived by the linear approximation. Also, (11.3.7) is not a linear Taylor-series approximation to the function $f(\cdot)$ at all values of Z_i, unless $f(Z_i)$ is linear, since the remainder term depends on Z_i and is ignored. Further, unless $f(\cdot)$ is linear, the coefficients (γ_1, γ_2) can change as the sample size n changes.

Figure 11.2 illustrates this using a quarterly time series of US constant-price GDP for the period 1947:1 to 2006:1. The trend model of (11.2.2) is fitted to three different subsamples, which are increasing in length. As the sample grows, the slope of the best-fitting line shifts markedly. Further, the residuals are highly correlated in each subsample and overall.

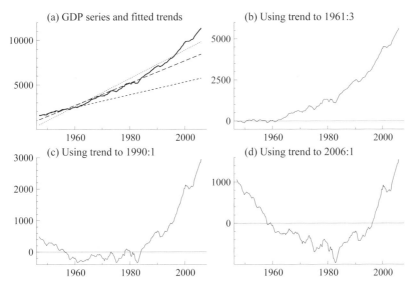

Figure 11.2 Least-squares trend approximations to US constant-price GDP. (a) bold line is data series; short-dashed line is based on subsample to 1961:3; long-dashed line is based on subsample to 1990:1; dotted line is based on full sample to 2006:1. (b)/(c)/(d) show the residuals and forecast errors using lines for first/second/full subsample.

11.3.4 Contingent plan

A contingent plan is one that is implemented by an economic agent after observing the outcome of a conditioning variable Z_i so:

$$Y_i^p = a_1 + a_2 Z_i, \qquad (11.3.9)$$

where the superscript p denotes an agent's plan, and a_1, a_2 are the structural parameters of interest. Equation (11.3.9) assumes the agent does not control Z_i, but tries to control Y_i as a linear function of Z_i. If agents act rationally in planning, they should achieve their aims on average, so:

$$E\left(Y_i \mid Y_i^p\right) = Y_i^p, \tag{11.3.10}$$

and hence:

$$Y_i = Y_i^p + e_i \qquad \text{where} \qquad e_i \overset{D}{=} \mathsf{IN}\left[0, \sigma_e^2\right]. \tag{11.3.11}$$

Taking conditional expectations with respect to Y_i^p in (11.3.11) and using (11.3.10) shows that $E(e_i|Y_i^p) = 0$, which in turn by (11.3.9) implies $E(e_i|Z_i) = 0$. Thus, the assumption (11.3.10) is not innocuous, but entails that the distribution of e_i is unaffected by the outcome of the contingent variables.

When the plan is linear in Z_i, as in (11.3.9), the assumption (11.3.10) then leads to a derived regression function:

$$E\left(Y_i \mid Z_i\right) = E\left(Y_i^p \mid Z_i\right) = a_1 + a_2 Z_i, \tag{11.3.12}$$

which coincides with the regression model (11.3.5). Thus, if Y_i, Z_i are also jointly normal, contingent plan parameters coincide with regression coefficients, and a contingent plan can be estimated using regression methods. However, the error on a contingent plan need not be normal.

11.3.5 Behavioral model

The fourth interpretation is as a behavioral model derived from an expectations-based plan:

$$Y_i^p = b_1 + b_2 Z_i^e, \tag{11.3.13}$$

where b_1, b_2 are structural parameters of interest. The agent's plan depends on the expected value Z_i^e of Z_i: agents are again assumed not to control Z_i, but they no longer know its value at the time the plan is implemented. However, (11.3.11) is assumed to hold.

To "complete" the model, a rule needs to be specified for how expectations Z_i^e of Z_i are formed. Often rational expectations are assumed, but care is required in defining "rational" when forming an expectation, since Z_i^e is an instrument in implementing the plan, not an end in itself. The expectation must then be based on an information set, represented by a variable X_i, say:

$$Z_i^e = E\left(Z_i \mid X_i\right), \tag{11.3.14}$$

so the agent must know X_i, and also how X_i enters the conditional expectation in (11.3.14). We can then decompose Z_i as follows:

$$Z_i = Z_i^e + u_i, \tag{11.3.15}$$

where u_i has the property:

$$E(u_i \mid X_i) = 0. \qquad (11.3.16)$$

This is seen by taking conditional expectations with respect to X_i in (11.3.15), and using the definition (11.3.14). To make this more explicit, we will assume that $(u_i \mid X_i) \overset{D}{=} N[0, \sigma_u^2]$, where $\sigma_u^2 \neq 0$ when agents do not know Z_i.

This construction of the expectations variable Z_i^e has some consequences. We will show that u_i has the property $E(u_i \mid Z_i) \neq 0$. First, note that the variables u_i and Z_i^e are uncorrelated. Following Exercise 11.2 then (11.3.16) implies $E(u_i) = 0$, so we just need to analyze the expectation of its product with Z_i^e:

$$
\begin{aligned}
E(Z_i^e u_i) &= E\{E(Z_i^e u_i \mid X_i)\} && [\,(4.1.8)\,] \\
&= E\{Z_i^e E(u_i \mid X_i)\} && [\, Z_i^e \text{ is a function of } X_i \,] \\
&= 0. && [\,(11.3.16)\,] \qquad (11.3.17)
\end{aligned}
$$

Second, this implies that u_i and Z_i must be correlated, since:

$$
\begin{aligned}
E(Z_i u_i) &= E(Z_i^e u_i) + E(u_i^2) && [\,(11.3.15)\,] \\
&= 0 + \sigma_u^2 \neq 0. && [\,(11.3.17)\, \& \text{ assumption on } u_i \,] \qquad (11.3.18)
\end{aligned}
$$

Finally, these imply that $E(u_i \mid Z_i) \neq 0$, since its negation, that $E(u_i \mid Z_i) = 0$, would imply:

$$
\begin{aligned}
E(Z_i u_i) &= E\{E(Z_i u_i \mid Z_i)\} && [\,(4.1.8)\,] \\
&= E\{Z_i E(u_i \mid Z_i)\} = 0, && [\text{ negation of } E(u_i \mid Z_i) \neq 0 \,]
\end{aligned}
$$

which contradicts (11.3.18). We can make this property more explicit by assuming:

$$E(u_i \mid Z_i) = c_1 + c_2 Z_i, \qquad (11.3.19)$$

where at least one of c_1, c_2 is different from zero.

The econometrician will typically not observe Z_i^e, so in an empirical analysis, might perhaps attempt to analyze Y_i using Z_i. Substituting (11.3.13) and (11.3.15) into (11.3.11) yields:

$$Y_i = b_1 + b_2 Z_i + v_i, \qquad (11.3.20)$$

where $v_i = e_i - b_2 u_i$. If we assume that the perturbation to the plan is independent of the outcome for Z_i, so $E(e_i \mid Z_i) = 0$, but $E(u_i \mid Z_i) \neq 0$, then $E(v_i \mid Z_i) \neq 0$, so equation (11.3.20) is not a regression equation. To derive a proper regression equation, we will need the conditional expectation of Y_i given Z_i:

$$
\begin{aligned}
E(Y_i \mid Z_i) &= E(Y_i^p \mid Z_i) + E(e_i \mid Z_i) && [\,(11.3.11)\,] \\
&= E(b_1 + b_2 Z_i^e \mid Z_i) + 0 && [\,(11.3.13)\, \& \, E(e_i \mid Z_i) = 0\,] \\
&= b_1 + b_2 E(Z_i - u_i \mid Z_i) && [\,(11.3.15)\,] \\
&= b_1 + b_2 Z_i - b_2(c_1 + c_2 Z_i). && [\,(11.3.19)\,]
\end{aligned}
$$

This results in the regression equation:

$$Y_i = \mathsf{E}\left(Y_i \mid Z_i\right) + w_i = \pi_1 + \pi_2 Z_i + w_i, \qquad (11.3.21)$$

where $\mathsf{E}(w_i|Z_i) = 0$ by construction, with $\pi_1 = b_1 - b_2 c_1$ and $\pi_2 = b_2(1 - c_2)$. From (11.3.21), the structural parameters b_1, b_2 are not delivered by the regression coefficients π_1, π_2: regression gives the wrong answer. Nevertheless, (11.3.21) is well defined, and it will fit better than (11.3.20), but its "parameters" depend on c_1, c_2, which are the parameters of the expectations process. Should those parameters change, then so would the coefficients of the model for Y_i. In other words, the multiple regression approach is not helpful as the structural parameters b_1, b_2 cannot be obtained. The approach discussed in Chapter 15 could address this issue. Some aspects of the practical implementation are discussed in §20.4.

Four interpretations of linear equations like (11.3.1) have been demonstrated: a regression, a linear least-squares approximation, a contingent plan, and a behavioral model. Without additional knowledge as to which is correct, a given linear equation may correspond to any one of the four, although the properties of its parameters differ accordingly. In particular, the coefficients of the equation may be functions of "deeper" parameters of the underlying behavior of the economic agents, as in (11.3.21).

11.4 CONGRUENCE

Because many data features are not explained by economic theory, it is essential to "match" the theoretical framework to the observations, rather than simply estimate a pre-specified theory model. This matching activity is called *econometric modeling*. In §11.2, empirical econometric models were shown to be a "decomposition" into explained and unexplained components. Because that decomposition can be done in many ways, all models are not born equal, so we seek those which are useful for understanding economic behavior, for testing economic theories, for forecasting the future, and for analyzing economic policy. Achieving these four objectives requires discovering sustainable relationships, and rejecting models that lack these desirable characteristics, respectively construction and destruction. It is easiest to commence with the latter—evaluating a given empirical claim—since §11.2 also demonstrated that destruction was all too feasible. The constructive aspect is harder in practice, but certainly possible, as we will discuss.

Conceptually, partition the data used in modeling into two information sets, namely regressand and regressors. Additional information includes economic theory, measurement, and the data used in rival models. Evaluation proceeds by formulating a null hypothesis, then testing against relevant alternatives. For cross-sectional data, the following null hypotheses correspond to the six main classes of information:

(1) homoskedastic, independent errors;

(2) strongly exogenous conditioning variables for the parameters of interest;

(3) constant, invariant parameters of interest;

(4) theory-consistent, identifiable structures;

(5) data-admissible formulations on accurate observations; and

(6) encompassing rival models.

The first three conditions relate to the sample distribution of the data. These will be satisfied for a well-specified statistical model. In econometric modeling, we also need to "match" the substantive context. Thus, *a congruent model* is one that satisfies the first five conditions: by analogy with one triangle matching another, the model matches the evidence in all measured respects; a failure on any condition is, therefore, sufficient to reject a congruency claim. Thus, even though empirical models correspond to "decompositions" rather than "experimental designs", the criteria for a congruent model allow stringent empirical evaluation of proposed models. We now consider these conditions in turn.

First, to "match" the regressand, a model's fit should deviate from the observations by small amounts (low $\hat{\sigma}$) that are not systematic (consistent with being independent) and do not behave differently for different values of the exogenous variables (hence are homoskedastic). Tests for heteroskedasticity were described in §9.3, whereas independence has to be discussed in terms of the type of data and its method of collection, an issue to which we return when discussing (3).

Second, to "match" the regressors, these should be exogenous—determined outside the model under consideration (see Chapter 10). Unfortunately, exogeneity is not a straightforward concept. All economic variables are endogenous— determined inside the model—since the world economy generates them all. In a given model, some must remain endogenous; but some need not. Textbooks often define exogenous as meaning "uncorrelated with the errors on the equation", but that is unsatisfactory, as seen from the example in §11.3.5, where Z_i was correlated with the error on the behavioral equation (11.3.20), but not with that on the "look-alike" reformulated equation (11.3.21). Thus, (11.3.20) delivered the "parameters of interest" characterizing the agents' behavior, whereas (11.3.21) had composite coefficients mixed with the parameters from the equation generating Z_i. So b_1, b_2 were of interest, but were not delivered by the regression coefficients π_1, π_2 where:

$$\text{E}\left(Y_i \mid Z_i\right) = \left(b_1 - b_2 c_1\right) + b_2 \left(1 - c_1\right) Z_i = \pi_1 + \pi_2 Z_i. \qquad (11.4.1)$$

There are two requirements for exogeneity, as defined in §10.1: that the parameters of interest can be obtained uniquely from the conditional model; and that they are not related to the parameters of the model for Z_i. Both fail for (11.4.1).

Third, to "match" in predictions, the parameters of interest must be constant across individuals and invariant to the values of the regressors. The constancy requirement is obvious, as predictions would fail if parameters changed. This aspect of a model is fundamental, and is one reason why we have always stressed assumptions about parameter spaces (another fundamental aspect is exogeneity).

Invariance means that the conditional relation of Y_i given Z_i does not change when Z_i changes. The "changes" can be expressed either in terms of varying parameters or in terms of an additional variable. First, in terms of parameters, we have that the π_j-parameters in (11.4.1) would alter, and therefore not be invariant, if the c_j-parameters of the Z_i variables given in (11.3.19) changed. This would hold even if the b_j-parameters stay constant. Second, in terms of an additional variable, W_i, we say the conditional relation of Y_i given Z_i is invariant to W_i if:

$$(Y_i|Z_i, W_i) \overset{\text{D}}{=} (Y_i|Z_i). \tag{11.4.2}$$

This is, of course, of substantial interest only if Z_i varies with W_i. Strong exogeneity of Z_i plus invariance with respect to W_i is called *super exogeneity*, a notion put forward by Engle et al. (1983), and is needed to sustain economic policy. The formulation in (11.4.2) can be operationalized in the context of a regression like $Y_i = \beta_1 + \beta_2 Z_i + \beta_3 W_i + u_i$, by testing that $\beta_3 = 0$.

An example is the suppressed time effect in cross-sectional analysis. A sample is usually collected on a given day, or over a brief period. This provides information that is conditional on whatever happened in that period. In the context of wages and schooling, the analysis ignored how relative wages of, for instance, skilled and unskilled workers evolved over time, how education patterns changed, and how these variables varied with other economic factors. There could be some common factors, like the stage of the business cycle, or the level of inflation, that influence everybody. Thus, the independence assumptions in the statistical models presented above are really about conditional independence given the sample period, so conclusions based on a cross section are not necessarily easily transferable over time or to other samples.

The invariance requirement also relates to the critique put forward by Lucas (1976). This will be discussed further in §20.4 below. Similarly, invariance has a bearing on conclusions about *causality*. If, indeed, the conditional relationship between Y_i and Z_i is invariant to changes in Z_i, then Z_i is deemed to cause the resultant changes in Y_i. In effect, nature creates an experimental design. The power of any test to detect changes in π_1, π_2 when c_1, c_2 alter depends on the magnitude of the change in the latter and is a practical matter, which does not raise any issue of principle: when changes in c_1, c_2 are large and often, without affecting π_1, π_2, it seems reasonable to conclude that Z_i causes Y_i. A similar notion underpins the causality theory put forward by Heckman (2005).

Fourth, to "match" theory information, a model must be consistent with that theory, and have identifiable parameters related to that theory. For example, the b_j-parameters are not identifiable from (11.4.1). This aspect will be discussed further in general terms in Chapter 15 on identification of structural models and more specifically in §20.4.

Fifth, to "match" measurement information, the observations must be accurate, and the model formulation "data admissible", so it cannot generate impossible outcomes, such as negative wages, or unemployment above 100%.

Sixth, an encompassing model is one that can explain the results of other models. Consider attempting to test between two models of the consumption function. The first is denoted M_1: consumption depends on income, versus M_2: consumption depends on wealth. Such a proliferation of rival empirical explanations is common, but at least one of them must be wrong. If M_1 claims to explain the data, then M_1 also ought to be able to explain the results of M_2 (see Davidson et al., 1978, although their study used time-series data). Encompassing is explained more fully in the next section, §11.5.

Once an investigator has developed a congruent, encompassing model, then no evidence remains in conflict with the empirical findings. This provides a viable basis for further progressive research.

11.5 ENCOMPASSING

We will now consider encompassing in more detail for three models: M_0, M_1, and M_2. The model M_0 is to be thought of as the general unrestricted model, and both M_1 and M_2 are special cases of M_0. We will discuss the properties of encompassing as a way of comparing the models M_1 and M_2, and describe some of its properties.

11.5.1 Comparing non-nested models

Consider three variables such as log wages, Y_i, length of schooling, $X_{1,i}$, and tenure in the job, $X_{2,i}$. By analogy with the bivariate normal distribution introduced in §10.3, the variables $(Y_i, X_{1,i}, X_{2,i})$ are assumed to satisfy a trivariate normal distribution. For simplicity, we assume all variables have zero expectations, so $E(Y_i) = E(X_{1,i}) = E(X_{2,i}) = 0$. The general model is denoted M_0, and is given by the conditional relation $E(Y_i|X_{1,i}, X_{2,i})$ assumed linear, that is:

$$M_0: \quad Y_i = \beta_1 X_{1,i} + \beta_2 X_{2,i} + \epsilon_i, \tag{11.5.1}$$

where $(\epsilon_i|X_{1,i}, X_{2,i}) \overset{D}{=} \mathsf{IN}[0, \sigma_\epsilon^2]$, and β_1, β_2, $\sigma_\epsilon^2 \in \mathbb{R}^2 \times \mathbb{R}_+$ are constant.

We will first consider an investigator who represents $E(Y_i|X_{1,i})$ by:

$$M_1: \quad Y_i = \alpha X_{1,i} + v_i, \tag{11.5.2}$$

and assumes $(v_i|X_{1,i}) \overset{D}{=} \mathsf{IN}[0, \sigma_v^2]$. The model M_1 is nested in M_0, in that it can be found by imposing $\beta_2 = 0$ in (11.5.1).

In the general case where β_2 is unrestricted, the parameter α of M_1 will be a function of β_1, β_2 of M_0. To find this relationship, we need to find the conditional expectation of Y_i with respect to $X_{1,i}$. Taking iterated expectations this is:

$$
\begin{aligned}
\mathsf{E}(Y_i \mid X_{1,i}) &= \mathsf{E}\{\mathsf{E}(Y_i \mid X_{1,i}, X_{2,i}) \mid X_{1,i}\} && [\,(4.1.8)\,] \\
&= \mathsf{E}(\beta_1 X_{1,i} + \beta_2 X_{2,i} \mid X_{1,i}) && [\,(11.5.1)\,] \\
&= \beta_1 X_{1,i} + \beta_2 \mathsf{E}(X_{2,i} \mid X_{1,i}).
\end{aligned}
$$

Exploiting that $X_{1,i}$, $X_{2,i}$ are assumed to have a joint normal distribution with zero expectation, then we have from §10.2.2 that $\mathsf{E}(X_{2,i}|X_{1,i}) = b_{21}X_{1,i}$, defining $b_{21} = m_{21}m_{11}^{-1}$ and $m_{jk} = \mathsf{E}(X_{j,i}X_{k,i})$. Therefore

$$
\mathsf{E}(Y \mid X_{1,i}) = \alpha X_{1,i}, \qquad \text{where} \qquad \alpha = \beta_1 + \beta_2 b_{21}, \tag{11.5.3}
$$

which is a population version of the orthogonalized parametrization in (5.2.6).

The implication of relation (11.5.3), showing how the parameter α of the model M_1 can be derived from the parameters of the general model M_0, is that the latter model explains the former. For example, (11.5.3) might account for why α had the opposite sign to that anticipated for β_1, a situation that could arise when β_2 was negative but b_{21} positive. In such a setting, knowledge of M_0 explains M_1, and we say that M_0 *encompasses* M_1, writing that in shorthand as $M_0 \; \mathcal{E} \; M_1$.

Consider a second conditional model of Y_i, denoted M_2, which postulates that $\mathsf{E}(Y_i|X_{2,i})$ is:

$$
M_2: \quad Y_i = \delta X_{2,i} + u_i, \tag{11.5.4}
$$

where its proprietor assumes $(u_i|X_{2,i}) \overset{\mathsf{D}}{=} \mathsf{IN}[0, \sigma_u^2]$. By an equivalent argument to that leading to (11.5.3):

$$
\delta = \beta_2 + \beta_1 b_{12}, \tag{11.5.5}
$$

where $b_{12} = m_{12}m_{22}^{-1}$. The models M_1 and M_2 are said to be *non-nested*, in that neither model is a special case of the other, unless there is a perfect correlation between $X_{1,i}$ and $X_{2,i}$, a case we exclude. Confronted with two such models, we are interested in the question whether, for instance, model M_1 could explain model M_2, so that $M_1 \; \mathcal{E} \; M_2$.

We assume M_1 views her model as correct and complete, namely, she believes it is really $\mathsf{E}(Y_i|X_{1,i}, X_{2,i})$ where the restriction $\beta_2 = 0$ is valid. Both modelers should agree on the estimated values for b_{12} and b_{21}, as these do not depend on their theories of wage formation, just on the data correlations between the unmodeled variables $X_{1,i}$ and $X_{2,i}$.

Since the proprietor of M_1 believes that $\alpha = \beta_1$ and $\beta_2 = 0$, she must also believe that $\delta = \alpha b_{12}$ in (11.5.5). Thus, she could derive an estimate of δ from her model as equal to αb_{12}, which we denote by δ_α being the value of δ derived from α in (11.5.3). Consequently, the proprietor of M_1 indirectly believes $\delta = \delta_\alpha$. She will be correct only if $\beta_2 = 0$, in which case $M_1 \; \mathcal{E} \; M_2$, but will be wrong otherwise. Thus, a sufficient condition for M_1 to account for the results of M_2 is that $\beta_2 = 0$, which entails that indeed $\alpha = \beta_1$ from (11.5.3). In that case, M_1 coincides with M_0, and since M_0 can explain δ, then M_1 can as well, so both predict δ to be $\beta_1 b_{12} = \alpha b_{12}$.

Moreover, since M_1 coincides with M_0 when $\beta_2 = 0$, then $M_1 \; \mathcal{E} \; M_0$ as a model can always explain its own results. Now we have the interesting outcome that the smaller model (11.5.2) can explain the results of the larger (11.5.1), which is called *parsimonious encompassing* .

Conversely, when $\beta_2 \neq 0$, then M_1 should fail to explain the value of δ found by M_2: the predicted value δ_α remains αb_{12}, whereas the actual value is $\delta = \beta_2 + \beta_1 b_{12}$, so $\delta \neq \delta_\alpha$. Thus, we can test the hypothesis that $M_1 \; \mathcal{E} \; M_2$ in two ways: either by testing $\beta_2 = 0$ in the unrestricted model M_0, or by testing directly $\delta = \delta\alpha$ using the restricted models M_1 and M_2 only. Tests for these hypotheses are introduced in the next section and are shown to be equivalent.

11.5.2 Tests for encompassing

Two types of tests for encompassing are discussed. In the first set of tests, the models M_1 and M_2 are compared directly. This approach is useful in situations where it is inconvenient to construct the joint model M_0. The second test is based on testing the models M_1 and M_2, respectively, as restrictions of the joint model M_0.

A test for the encompassing hypothesis $M_1 \; \mathcal{E} \; M_2$, based directly on estimators for the parameters $\delta, \delta\alpha$ is now presented. The encompassing difference $\delta - \delta_\alpha$ is estimated by:

$$\widehat{\delta} - \widehat{\alpha}\widehat{b}_{12} = \frac{\sum_{i=1}^n X_{2,i} Y_i}{\sum_{i=1}^n X_{2,i}^2} - \left(\frac{\sum_{i=1}^n X_{1,i} Y_i}{\sum_{i=1}^n X_{1,i}^2} \right) \left(\frac{\sum_{i=1}^n X_{2,i} X_{1,i}}{\sum_{i=1}^n X_{2,i}^2} \right).$$

This can be rewritten as:

$$\widehat{\delta} - \widehat{\alpha}\widehat{b}_{12} = \frac{\sum_{i=1}^n X_{2\cdot1,i} Y_i}{\sum_{i=1}^n X_{2,i}^2}, \tag{11.5.6}$$

using the notation $X_{2\cdot1,i} = X_{2,i} - \widehat{b}_{21} X_{1,i}$ for the residuals from regressing $X_{2,i}$ on $X_{1,i}$. Inserting the model equation (11.5.1) for Y_i, under the hypothesis $\beta_2 = 0$, then $\widehat{\delta} - \widehat{\alpha}\widehat{b}_{12} = (\sum_{i=1}^n X_{2,i}^2)^{-1} \sum_{i=1}^n X_{2\cdot1,i}\epsilon_i$. Under that hypothesis, and conditionally on the regressors, we can deduce that $\widehat{\delta} - \widehat{\alpha}\widehat{b}_{12}$ is normally distributed with conditional expectation and variance given by:

$$\mathsf{E}\left(\widehat{\delta} - \widehat{\alpha}\widehat{b}_{12}\right) = 0, \qquad \mathsf{Var}\left(\widehat{\delta} - \widehat{\alpha}\widehat{b}_{12}\right) = \frac{\sigma_\epsilon^2 \sum_{i=1}^n X_{2\cdot 1,i}^2}{\left(\sum_{i=1}^n X_{2,i}^2\right)^2}.$$

Thus, a t-test can be formed.

The derived test for $\delta = \delta\alpha$ is now shown to be equivalent to a test for $\beta_2 = 0$ in the joint model M_0, which checks if the regressor $X_{2,i}$ is indeed irrelevant. This second form of testing is one of model simplification, or parsimonious encompassing. Both forms of encompassing test will prove useful in Chapter 19, so we establish their relationship here. The regressors in (11.5.1) can be orthogonalized by adding and subtracting $\widehat{b}_{21}X_{1,i}$, giving:

$$Y_i = (\beta_1 + \beta_2\widehat{b}_{21})X_{1,i} + \beta_2 X_{2\cdot 1,i} + \epsilon_i. \tag{11.5.7}$$

As seen in Exercise 7.11, and using (11.5.6), estimation delivers:

$$\widehat{\beta}_2 = \frac{\sum_{i=1}^n X_{2\cdot 1,i} Y_i}{\sum_{i=1}^n X_{2\cdot 1,i}^2} = \left(\widehat{\delta} - \widehat{\alpha}\widehat{b}_{12}\right)\frac{\sum_{i=1}^n X_{2,i}^2}{\sum_{i=1}^n X_{2\cdot 1,i}^2},$$

so that the estimators $\widehat{\beta}_2$ and $\widehat{\delta} - \widehat{\alpha}\widehat{b}_{12}$ are proportional, with the scaling factor depending only on the regressors. As a consequence:

$$\frac{\widehat{\beta}_2}{\sqrt{\mathsf{Var}\left(\widehat{\beta}_2\right)}} = \frac{\widehat{\delta} - \widehat{\alpha}\widehat{b}_{12}}{\sqrt{\mathsf{Var}\left(\widehat{\delta} - \widehat{\alpha}\widehat{b}_{12}\right)}}.$$

so that the t-test statistics for $\beta_2 = 0$ and $\delta = \delta\alpha$ are equal, and the tests are also equivalent to the likelihood ratio test for $\beta_2 = 0$ in the unrestricted model M_0.

A necessary condition for $M_1 \, \mathcal{E} \, M_2$ is that M_1 fits better than M_2 when $\beta_1 \neq 0$, that is, $\sigma_v^2 < \sigma_u^2$ (see Exercise 11.4). Such a test can be carried out by comparing the estimates $\widehat{\sigma}_v^2$ and $\widehat{\sigma}_u^2$, or the associated R^2-values, or likelihood values. Pesaran (1974) suggested that such tests could be based on statistics first proposed by Cox (1961). A more detailed discussion can be found in Hendry (1995a, Chapter 14).

11.5.3 Application to the wage data

In Chapter 5, log wages were related to schooling. We will look at two extensions of this model. In the first model, M_1, reported in Table 11.1, the square of schooling, S_i^2, is added to give a more flexible relationship. This model could be criticized on the ground that the return to schooling is not diminishing. An alternative model, M_2, reported in Table 11.2, arises by including age, A_i, as a regressor instead.

$$\widehat{w}_i = 4.78 - 0.050\,S_i + 0.0051\,S_i^2$$
standard error   (0.12)   (0.020)   (0.0008)
$$\widehat{\sigma} = 0.721, \quad \widehat{\ell} = -4233.06, \quad n = 3877$$

$\chi^2_{\text{norm}}[2] = 903$ [p<0.001]	$F_{\text{het}}[3, 3870] = 0.40$ [p = 0.75]
$F_{\text{reset}}[1, 3873] = 0.08$ [p = 0.78]	$F_{\text{hetX}}[4, 3869] = 0.31$ [p = 0.87]

Table 11.1 M_1: model with S_i^2 as regressor

$$\widehat{w}_i = 3.66 + 0.082\,S_i + 0.0090\,A_i$$
standard error   (0.07)   (0.004)   (0.0009)
$$\widehat{\sigma} = 0.716, \quad \widehat{\ell} = -4203.67, \quad n = 3877$$

$\chi^2_{\text{norm}}[2] = 935$ [p<0.001]	$F_{\text{het}}[4, 3869] = 0.88$ [p = 0.48]
$F_{\text{reset}}[1, 3873] = 28.0$ [p<0.001]	$F_{\text{hetX}}[5, 3868] = 0.76$ [p = 0.58]

Table 11.2 M_2: model with A_i as regressor

We note that both models are mis-specified, failing on the normality tests and, in the case of the second model, also on the RESET test. Even though the rival models are not congruent, we will proceed to compare them through encompassing tests, as reported in Table 11.3. It appears that neither model is able to explain the other model. It is, therefore, not possible to resolve any dispute over increasing returns to education versus an age-related effect using these models alone. Another interpretation is that both models are invalid reductions of the general model, including both S_i^2 and A_i as regressor. A way forward could be to work with the general model. However, doing so may not resolve the issue of the sign on S_i^2, which was part of the motivation for looking at the second model. An alternative approach would be to allow for an even more flexible specification of schooling as in §9.6.

$M_1 \, \mathcal{E} \, M_2$	$M_2 \, \mathcal{E} \, M_1$
$F_{\text{encomp}}[1, 3873] = 87.9$ [p<0.001]	$F_{\text{encomp}}[1, 3873] = 28.3$ [p<0.001]

Table 11.3 Encompassing tests

11.6 SUMMARY AND EXERCISES

Summary: The links between econometric models and economic models were discussed. Empirical models were introduced as decompositions of observed variables into explanations and remainder terms. Four interpretations of regression models were proposed. The notions of congruence and encompassing were introduced to describe the aims of econometric modeling. Two encompassing tests were developed and applied.

Key questions:

- Discuss the difference between a data-generating process like (11.2.4) and an econometric equation like (11.2.5).
- Discuss the four interpretations of regression models.
- Discuss the five conditions of congruence
- What would be needed to establish causality?

Exercise 11.1. *Prove that* $E(Y_i|Z_i)$ *is the minimum-variance unbiased predictor of* Y_i *as a function of* Z_i. *That is, for any predictor* $f(Z_i)$, *that is a function of* Z_i *and unbiased so* $E\{f(Z_i)\} = E(Y_i)$, *then* $Var\{Y_i - E(Y_i|Z_i)\} \leq Var\{Y_i - f(Z_i)\}$. *Use the following steps.*
(a) Argue $E\{Y_i - E(Y_i|Z_i)\}$ *and* $E\{Y_i - f(Z_i)\}$ *are both zero.*
(b) Argue $Var\{Y_i - f(Z_i)\} = E[\{Y_i - E(Y_i|Z_i)\}^2]$.
(c) Expand the variance using $Y_i - E(Y_i|Z_i) = \{Y_i - f(Z_i)\} + \{f(Z_i) - E(Y_i|Z_i)\}$.
(d) Complete by arguing $E[\{Y_i - f(Z_i)\}\{f(Z_i) - E(Y_i|Z_i)\}] = 0$ *using (4.1.8).*

Exercise 11.2. *Suppose* $E(Y \mid X) = 0$.
(a) Show that $E(Y) = 0$ *using (4.1.8).*
(b) Show that $E(YX) = 0$ *using (4.1.8). Hence* $Cov(Y, X) = 0$.

Exercise 11.3. * *Consider the setup in section 11.3.3. Explain why the coefficients* γ_1, γ_2 *can change as the sample size* n *changes when* $f(Z_i)$ *is non-linear. As an example, let* $Y_i = Z_i^2 + v_i$ *where* $v_i \overset{D}{=} IN[0, \sigma_v^2]$ *and use the following steps.*
(a) Find the estimators $\widehat{\gamma}_1, \widehat{\gamma}_2$ *of (11.3.8).*
(b) Suppose $Z_i \overset{D}{=} IN[\mu_z, \sigma_z^2]$. *Show that* $\widehat{\gamma}_1, \widehat{\gamma}_2$ *are consistent using the Law of Large Numbers in Theorem 2.1.*
(c) Suppose $Z_i = i$. *Show that* $\widehat{\gamma}_1, \widehat{\gamma}_2$ *are not consistent using the Law of Large Numbers in Theorem 2.1 and the approximation* $\sum_{i=1}^{n} i^{k-1} \approx n^k/k$ *for* $k > 1$.

Exercise 11.4. *Prove that the error variance* $\sigma_v^2 = Var(Y_i - \alpha X_{1,i})$ *in (11.5.2) for model* M_1 *must be bounded by* $\sigma_u^2 = Var(Y_i - \delta X_{2,i})$ *in (11.5.4) for model* M_2, *if* $M_1 \, \mathcal{E} \, M_2$. *Hint: follow the steps of Exercise 11.1*

Chapter Twelve

Autoregressions and stationarity

Until now, we have mainly been looking at cross-sectional data, where outcomes have been observed for unrelated individuals. Another type of data common in economics is time-series data, where one variable, such as price, is followed over time. For many time series of prices, a dominating feature is that prices today are close to prices yesterday. The basic tool in modeling such dependent observations is an autoregression, which is introduced here. The next four chapters then turn to time-series versions of topics that we have seen for cross-sectional data such as mis-specification testing, bivariate models, and structural modelling in Chapters 13, 14, and 15 respectively.

A time series for the price of fish is presented in §12.1, and tools for assessing the temporal dependence are presented in §12.2. The autoregressive model and its estimation are discussed in §§12.3, 12.4, and 12.5. An autoregressive model can generate a wide range of different types of data processes. The stationary case will be discussed in §12.6, while inference in that situation is discussed in §12.7.

12.1 TIME-SERIES DATA

As an example of a time series, we will look at a data set collected from the Fulton Fish Market in New York by Kathryn Graddy. Graddy (1995) used this data set to estimate a demand and supply system, as will be discussed in Chapter 15. The full data set consists of all trades of whiting sold from one particular wholesale dealer in the 111 trading days in the period 2 December 1991 to 8 May 1992. We will look at the aggregated daily price series constructed by Angrist et al. (2000).

The price series is an example of a time series, in that one random variable is observed repeatedly over time. The individual observations of the price series are denoted P_t where the index t rather than i indicates that we are working with a time series. We can learn a lot about a time series by plotting it as in Figure 12.1(a). Looking at the vertical axis, it is seen that prices move considerably in the range of US$0.33 to US$1.94, a factor of more than fivefold. For econometric analysis, the volatility can be dampened somewhat by taking the (natural) logarithm as shown in panel (b). The log price series is denoted p_t, following the convention that log

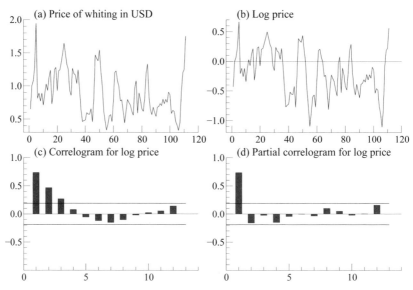

Figure 12.1 Daily prices for whiting in the Fulton Fish Market

variables are written with a lowercase letter. Two important features of the series are that (a) the price at a given time t is often closely related to the price in the previous period; and (b) that the price often reverts to an average level of about US\$0.88. We will see that these characteristics can be captured effectively using an autoregressive model.

12.2 DESCRIBING TEMPORAL DEPENDENCE

The price series has the feature that the price at time t is related to the price in the previous period. Such temporal dependence would violate the independence assumption in the models we have studied until now. The two main concepts for describing temporal dependence are autocorrelation and partial autocorrelation.

12.2.1 Autocorrelation

The simplest way of describing temporal dependence is the sample correlation between today's value of the time series and values s periods earlier, called *autocorrelations*. When the observations are indexed $Y_1, \ldots, Y_T$, this yields:

$$r_{0,s} = \frac{\sum_{t=s+1}^{T}(Y_t - \overline{Y}_{1+s}^{T})(Y_{t-s} - \overline{Y}_{1}^{T-s})}{\sqrt{\sum_{t=s+1}^{T}(Y_t - \overline{Y}_{1+s}^{T})^2 \sum_{t=s+1}^{T}(Y_{t-s} - \overline{Y}_{1}^{T-s})^2}},$$

where $\overline{Y}_{1+s}^{T}$ and $\overline{Y}_{1}^{T-s}$ are the averages of the observations $Y_{1+s}, \ldots, Y_T$ and the lagged observations $Y_1, \ldots, Y_{T-s}$, respectively. The sequence $(r_{0,0}, r_{0,1}, r_{0,2}, \ldots)$

of sample autocorrelations is called the sample autocorrelation function . Plotting this function gives a sample correlogram. Often, $r_{0,s}$ is just denoted r_s.

Although correlograms are simple to compute, econometric software often computes scaled sample autocovariances instead:

$$g_{0,s} = \frac{\sum_{t=s+1}^{T}(Y_t - \overline{Y}_1^T)(Y_{t-s} - \overline{Y}_1^T)}{\sum_{t=1}^{T}(Y_t - \overline{Y}_1^T)^2},$$

where $\overline{Y}_1^T$ is the average of all the observations $Y_1, \ldots, Y_T$, and the denominator does not vary with s. Confusingly, these are often referred to as correlograms, although they are rather covariograms (see Nielsen, 2006). In many instances, the functions $r_{0,s}$ and $g_{0,s}$ are quite close, so we will make no further point in distinguishing the two. One exception, though, is the application to the levels of trending time series where the two functions can be very different—as will be discussed in §16.1.

Figure 12.1(c) shows the sample correlogram for the price series. The covariogram can be used to test the hypothesis of temporal independence. It can be shown that under temporal independence, $Tr_{0,s}^2 \overset{D}{\approx} \chi^2[1]$ in line with (5.5.4), whereas $\sqrt{T}g_{0,s} \overset{D}{\approx} N[0,1]$. The horizontal lines at $\pm 2/\sqrt{T}$ with $T = 111$, therefore, provide critical values for testing independence at a 5% level. Hence, the correlogram indicates temporal dependence.

12.2.2 Partial autocorrelation

The covariogram in Figure 12.1(c) indicates that both Y_{t-1} and Y_{t-2} are correlated with Y_t. To investigate whether Y_{t-2} and Y_t are related when correcting for Y_{t-1}, we consider the *partial autocorrelation*. Using the identity (7.3.1), that partial autocorrelation is given by:

$$r_{0,2\cdot1} = \frac{r_{0,2} - r_{0,1}r_{1,2}}{(1 - r_{0,1}^2)^{1/2}(1 - r_{1,2}^2)^{1/2}}.$$

The sequence of sample partial correlations, namely $(r_{0,1}, r_{0,2\cdot1}, r_{0,3\cdot1,2}, \ldots)$, is called the sample partial autocorrelation function, and the plot of this function is the sample partial correlogram .

As pointed out in §7.3, the population partial correlation of Y_t and Y_{t-2} given Y_{t-1} is zero if Y_t and Y_{t-2} are conditionally independent given Y_{t-1}. That is:

$$\mathsf{Corr}(Y_t, Y_{t-2} \mid Y_{t-1}) = 0,$$

if it holds that:

$$\mathsf{f}(y_t, y_{t-2} \mid y_{t-1}) = \mathsf{f}(y_t \mid y_{t-1})\,\mathsf{f}(y_{t-2} \mid y_{t-1}). \tag{12.2.1}$$

This has the important implication that the conditional distribution of Y_t given (Y_{t-1}, Y_{t-2}) does not depend on Y_{t-2}. To see that, use (4.1.7) to rewrite the joint density of (Y_t, Y_{t-2}) given Y_{t-1} as:

$$\mathsf{f}(y_t, y_{t-2} \mid y_{t-1}) = \mathsf{f}(y_t \mid y_{t-1}, y_{t-2}) \, \mathsf{f}(y_{t-2} \mid y_{t-1}) \qquad (12.2.2)$$

Equating (12.2.1) and (12.2.2) then shows:

$$\mathsf{f}(y_t \mid y_{t-1}, y_{t-2}) = \mathsf{f}(y_t \mid y_{t-1}).$$

If the more general property that the conditional distribution of Y_t given the entire past $Y_{t-1}, Y_{t-2}, \ldots$ depends only on the immediate past Y_{t-1}, the time series is said to be a Markov process.

Just as software packages tend to report covariograms instead of correlograms, their partial correlograms are also different. For instance, the partial autocovariance $a_{0,2\cdot1} = (g_{0,2} - g_{0,1}^2)/(1 - g_{0,1}^2)$ is reported rather than $r_{0,2\cdot1}$.

Figure 12.1(d) shows the sample partial correlogram for the price series. The horizontal lines at $\pm 2/\sqrt{T}$ indicate critical values for testing conditional independence of p_t and p_{t-s} given the observations in between. The partial correlogram indicates dependence of at least first order. The second-order partial autocorrelation is marginal, whereas higher-order conditional independence cannot be rejected. For the moment, we will ignore the possible second-order dependence, and assume that the time series satisfies the Markov property. We will revisit this issue in §13.3.

12.3 THE FIRST-ORDER AUTOREGRESSIVE MODEL

The basic tool for describing a time series like the price series p_t is an autoregression. The partial covariogram for the price series was studied in §12.2.2 and indicated a first-order dependence, in that the first partial correlation $r_{0,1}$ was large, but the second partial correlation $r_{0,2\cdot1}$ was small. This is consistent with a Markov property and will be an important feature of a first-order autoregression.

The setup of the autoregressive model is similar to that of the two-variable regression model for cross-sectional data. The time-series data are represented by random variables Y_t, which are conveniently indexed $t = 0, \ldots, T$, so the total number of observations is $T + 1$. The statistical model is formulated in terms of conditional distributions. The first formulation is as follows:

(i) *conditional independence*: $(Y_t \mid Y_0, \ldots, Y_{t-1}) \overset{\mathrm{D}}{=} (Y_t \mid Y_{t-1})$;

(ii) *conditional distribution*: $(Y_t \mid Y_{t-1}) \overset{\mathrm{D}}{=} \mathsf{N}[\beta_1 + \beta_2 Y_{t-1}, \sigma^2]$ for $t \geq 1$;

(iii) *parameter space*: $\beta_1,\ \beta_2,\ \sigma^2 \in \mathbb{R}^2 \times \mathbb{R}_+$.

There are two differences from the usual two-variable regression model. First, the distribution of the initial observation Y_0 is not modeled, so the model is formulated conditional on Y_0; and, second, the regressor is the time-lagged time series, also called the *lagged dependent variable*.

An alternative and equivalent formulation is given in terms of the equation:

$$Y_t = \beta_1 + \beta_2 Y_{t-1} + \epsilon_t, \qquad \text{for } t = 1, \ldots, T. \qquad (12.3.1)$$

In a time-series context the error terms ϵ_t are often called *innovations*. The assumptions about the conditional distribution of $\epsilon_1, \ldots, \epsilon_T$ given Y_0 are:

(i') $\epsilon_1, \ldots, \epsilon_T$ are independent;

(ii') $\epsilon_t \overset{D}{=} \mathsf{N}[0, \sigma^2]$.

The partial correlogram gives a graphical test of assumption (i). Assumption (ii) concerning the conditional distribution of Y_t given Y_{t-1}, or equivalently the marginal distribution of the innovation ϵ_t, cannot be tested immediately. To undertake such a test, the model has to be estimated, and tests can then be applied to the residuals $\widehat{\epsilon}_t$. This will be discussed in §12.5 and in Chapter 13.

12.4 THE AUTOREGRESSIVE LIKELIHOOD

To analyze the autoregressive model, we need the joint density of $(Y_1, \ldots, Y_T)$ conditional on the initial value of Y_0. This in turn leads to a conditional likelihood given the initial observation. The derivation is closely related to that of the two-variable regression model.

The first argument in the derivation is new, in that it deals with the dependence structure of the data. The purpose is to move from dealing with the joint density of $(Y_1, \ldots, Y_T)$ given Y_0 to a product of conditional densities of single observations Y_t given their past $Y_{t-1}, \ldots, Y_0$. This is achieved using a recursive argument. In the first step, a conditional argument, as in (4.1.7), yields:

$$\mathsf{f}(y_T, y_{T-1}, \ldots, y_1 \mid y_0) = \mathsf{f}(y_T \mid y_{T-1}, \ldots, y_1, y_0)\mathsf{f}(y_{T-1}, \ldots, y_1 \mid y_0).$$

The first term on the right-hand side is of the desired form. If we use this trick once again for the second term, we find:

$$\mathsf{f}(y_{T-1}, \ldots, y_1 \mid y_0) = \mathsf{f}(y_{T-1} \mid y_{T-2}, \ldots, y_0)\mathsf{f}(y_{T-2}, \ldots, y_1 \mid y_0).$$

Repeating this argument in total T times results in the desired decomposition:

$$\mathsf{f}(y_T, \ldots, y_1 \mid y_0) = \prod_{t=1}^{T} \mathsf{f}(y_t \mid y_{t-1}, \ldots, y_0). \qquad (12.4.1)$$

Note that this formula holds generally, as no assumptions have been used. It is often referred to as a *prediction decomposition*.

The conditional density of $(Y_1, \ldots, Y_T)$ given Y_0 can now be derived as for the two-variable model. If we let $\mathbf{y}$ denote $y_1, \ldots, y_T$, start from (12.4.1) and use the Markov property assumption (i) this is:

$$f_{\beta_1,\beta_2,\sigma^2}(\mathbf{y} \mid y_0) = \prod_{t=1}^{T} f_{\beta_1,\beta_2,\sigma^2}(y_t \mid y_{t-1}, \ldots, y_0) = \prod_{t=1}^{T} f_{\beta_1,\beta_2,\sigma^2}(y_t \mid y_{t-1}).$$

If we insert the conditional normality assumed in (ii) this is:

$$f_{\beta_1,\beta_2,\sigma^2}(\mathbf{y} \mid y_0) = \prod_{t=1}^{T} \left(2\pi\sigma^2\right)^{-1/2} \exp\left\{ -\frac{1}{2\sigma^2}(y_t - \beta_1 - \beta_2 y_{t-1})^2 \right\}.$$

Finally, using that products of exponentials equal the exponential of the sum:

$$f_{\beta_1,\beta_2,\sigma^2}(\mathbf{y} \mid y_0) = \left(2\pi\sigma^2\right)^{-T/2} \exp\left\{ -\frac{1}{2\sigma^2} \sum_{t=1}^{T} (y_t - \beta_1 - \beta_2 y_{t-1})^2 \right\}.$$

Inserting our particular observations, we obtain the likelihood function, which strictly speaking is a conditional likelihood given Y_0:

$$L_{Y_1,\ldots,Y_T \mid Y_0}(\beta_1, \beta_2, \sigma^2) = (2\pi\sigma^2)^{-T/2} \exp\left\{ -\frac{1}{2\sigma^2} \sum_{t=1}^{T} (Y_t - \beta_1 - \beta_2 Y_{t-1})^2 \right\}.$$

$$(12.4.2)$$

12.5 ESTIMATION

The likelihood function (12.4.2) has exactly the same structure as the two-variable likelihood function given in (5.2.2), in that the arguments β_1, β_2, σ^2 enter in the same way. We therefore get from §5.2 that the maximum likelihood estimators are:

$$\widehat{\beta}_1 = \overline{Y} - \widehat{\beta}_2 \overline{Y}_{(-)}, \qquad \widehat{\beta}_2 = \frac{\sum_{t=1}^{T} Y_t \{Y_{t-1} - \overline{Y}_{(-)}\}}{\sum_{s=1}^{T} \{Y_{s-1} - \overline{Y}_{(-)}\}^2}, \qquad (12.5.1)$$

where $\overline{Y} = T^{-1}\sum_{t=1}^{T} Y_t$ and $\overline{Y}_{(-)} = T^{-1}\sum_{t=1}^{T} Y_{t-1}$ (see Exercise 12.1). The predictions from the model are $\widehat{Y}_t = \widehat{\beta}_1 + \widehat{\beta}_2 Y_{t-1}$, the residuals are $\widehat{\epsilon}_t = Y_t - \widehat{Y}_t$, and the maximum likelihood estimator for σ^2 is $\widehat{\sigma}^2 = T^{-1}\sum_{t=1}^{T} \widehat{\epsilon}_t^2$.

$$\begin{aligned}
\widehat{p}_t &= -0.039 + 0.76\,p_{t-1} \\
\text{standard error} &\quad (0.027) \quad (0.06)
\end{aligned}$$

$$\widehat{\sigma} = 0.25, \qquad \widehat{\ell} = -4.48, \qquad T = 110$$

Table 12.1 Autoregressive model for price of whiting, p_t

A first-order autoregressive fit to the price series for whiting is reported in Table 12.1. In §12.7, it will be argued that the estimators are approximately normally distributed in the usual way. Since the estimated autoregressive coefficient of 0.76 is larger than twice the standard error, $2 \times 0.06 = 0.12$, it is seen that the lagged dependent variable is indeed significant.

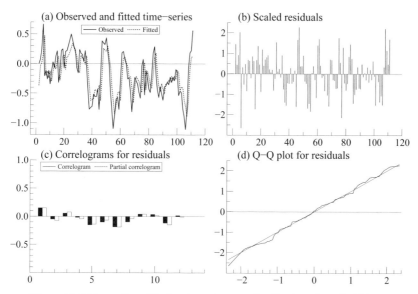

Figure 12.2 Properties of first-order autoregression for the price of whiting, p_t

Figure 12.2 reports various characteristics of the fit of this model. Panel (a) shows the observed time series p_t together with the fitted, or predicted, time series $\widehat{p}_t$. There is a tendency for the fitted time series to lag one step behind the observed time series p_t, so $\widehat{p}_t$ is closely related to p_{t-1}. This is in line with the estimated equation reported in Table 12.1 saying that the predictor $\widehat{p}$ equals $0.76p_{t-1}$ plus the intercept. Panel (b) shows the residuals standardized by the estimated innovation standard deviation $\widehat{\sigma}$, while panel (c) shows the correlogram and partial correlogram of the residuals. Comparing these with Figure 12.1(a,c,d), it is seen that the residuals $\widehat{\epsilon}_t$ from the first-order autoregression show considerably less time dependence than the original price series p_t. Figure 12.2(d) compares the sample distribution of the residuals with a standard normal distribution. The graph is close to the $45°$ line, so the normality assumption of this statistical model is more appropriate than any we have seen earlier in the book.

12.6 INTERPRETATION OF STATIONARY AUTOREGRESSIONS

In order to understand the type of processes an autoregressive equation can generate, we first look at the simplest autoregressive equation without an intercept. If we consider a time series $X_0, \ldots X_T$, this equation is:

$$X_t = \alpha X_{t-1} + \epsilon_t, \qquad \text{for } t = 1, \ldots, T. \qquad (12.6.1)$$

As before, the innovations are assumed to satisfy, conditional on X_0:

(a) $\epsilon_1, \ldots, \epsilon_T$ are independent;

(b) $\epsilon_t \overset{D}{=} \mathsf{N}[0, \sigma^2]$.

First, equation (12.6.1) is solved recursively. Next, we look at the marginal distribution of X_t and the population autocorrelation function. These quantities depend on the value of α. In this section, we consider the case when:

(c) $|\alpha| < 1$,

which we will refer to as the stationary case. The *unit-root* case (when $\alpha = 1$) is of considerable importance for the analysis of economic time series and will be discussed in Chapter 16.

12.6.1 Solving the autoregressive equation

The difference equation (12.6.1) can be solved recursively. In the first step, replace t by $t-1$ in (12.6.1) to see that $X_{t-1} = \epsilon_{t-1} + \alpha X_{t-2}$. Now, in (12.6.1) replace X_{t-1} with this expression so that:

$$X_t = \epsilon_t + \alpha X_{t-1} = \epsilon_t + \alpha(\epsilon_{t-1} + \alpha X_{t-2}) = \epsilon_t + \alpha\epsilon_{t-1} + \alpha^2 X_{t-2}.$$

Applying this idea once again to X_{t-2} shows:

$$X_t = \epsilon_t + \alpha\epsilon_{t-1} + \alpha^2(\epsilon_{t-2} + \alpha X_{t-3}) = \epsilon_t + \alpha\epsilon_{t-1} + \alpha^2\epsilon_{t-2} + \alpha^3 X_{t-3}.$$

Repeating this trick in total T times then delivers:

$$X_t = \epsilon_t + \alpha\epsilon_{t-1} + \alpha^2\epsilon_{t-2} + \cdots + \alpha^{t-1}\epsilon_1 + \alpha^t X_0 = \sum_{j=0}^{t-1} \alpha^j \epsilon_{t-j} + \alpha^t X_0. \quad (12.6.2)$$

Thus, X_t is expressed as a sum of independent, normally distributed variables. Due to the normality, we only need to find the expectation and variance of X_t to characterize the distribution of X_t.

12.6.2 The marginal distribution of an autoregressive process

The distribution of the process X_t generated by the simple autoregressive equation (12.6.1) depends on α. In the case where $|\alpha| < 1$, we will show that:

$$X_t \overset{D}{\approx} \mathsf{N}\left[0, \frac{\sigma^2}{1 - \alpha^2}\right], \quad (12.6.3)$$

which is an unconditional statement. Since the expectation and variance of X_t and the form of the distribution are the same at different points in time, such a process is said to be stationary (i.e., does not move over time, like a train standing in a station).

Since X_t is expressed as a sum of independent normally distributed variables in (12.6.2), we only need to derive the expectation and variance of X_t. The conditional expectation of X_t given X_0 is simply:

$$E(X_t \mid X_0) = \sum_{j=0}^{t-1} \alpha^j E\left(\epsilon_{t-j} \mid X_0\right) + \alpha^t X_0$$

$$= \alpha^t X_0. \qquad\qquad [\ (b)\colon E(\epsilon_t \mid X_0) = 0\ ]$$

Turning to the variance of X_t, we have:

$$Var(X_t \mid X_0) = \sum_{j=0}^{t-1} \alpha^{2j} Var(\epsilon_{t-j} \mid X_0) \qquad\qquad [\ (a)\colon \text{independence}\ ]$$

$$= \sigma^2 \sum_{j=0}^{t-1} \alpha^{2j}, \qquad\qquad [\ (b)\colon Var(\epsilon_{t-j} \mid X_0) = \sigma^2\ ]$$

which is a geometric series.

The geometric series in the variance formula has a closed-form expression:

$$S_t = \sum_{j=0}^{t-1} \alpha^{2j} = \frac{1 - \alpha^{2t}}{1 - \alpha^2}, \qquad\qquad (12.6.4)$$

whenever $\alpha^2 \neq 1$ and in particular under assumption (c) that $|\alpha| < 1$. To prove this, write out the sums S_t and $\alpha^2 S_t$ as:

$$S_t = 1 + \alpha^2 + \alpha^4 + \cdots + \alpha^{2(t-1)},$$
$$\alpha^2 S_t = \quad \alpha^2 + \alpha^4 + \cdots + \alpha^{2(t-1)} + \alpha^{2t}.$$

Subtracting the two equations from each other, we get:

$$(1 - \alpha^2)S_t = 1 - \alpha^{2t}.$$

As long as $\alpha^2 \neq 1$, we can divide through by $1 - \alpha^2$ to obtain (12.6.4).

Combining the expressions for expectation and variance delivers the conditional distribution of X_t given X_0 as:

$$(X_t \mid X_0) \overset{D}{=} N\left[\alpha^t X_0, \sigma^2 \frac{1 - \alpha^{2t}}{1 - \alpha^2}\right].$$

Under assumption (c), that $|\alpha| < 1$, then $\alpha^t \to 0$ as $t \to \infty$. This means that $E(X_t|X_0)$ is moving toward zero regardless of the initial value X_0. One could say that as time goes by, the time series forgets where it started. The expectation is therefore approximately *stationary* around zero regardless of the initial value X_0. Correspondingly, the variance is moving toward $\sigma^2/(1 - \alpha^2)$. We, therefore, have the desired approximate result stated in (12.6.3).

12.6.3 Autocorrelation

The population autocorrelation function for the simple autoregression (12.6.1) has a neat expression. We start by deriving the covariance of today's value and the value s periods back. To do this, rewrite the recursive solution (12.6.2) slightly as:

$$X_t = \sum_{j=0}^{s-1} \alpha^j \epsilon_{t-j} + \alpha^s X_{t-s}.$$

Since the innovations $\epsilon_t, \ldots, \epsilon_{t-s+1}$ are uncorrelated with the past represented by X_{t-s}, it is easy to find the covariance of X_t and X_{t-s}. The conditional covariance given X_0 is:

$$\mathsf{Cov}\left(X_t, X_{t-s} \mid X_0\right) = \mathsf{Cov}\left(\sum_{j=0}^{s-1} \alpha^j \epsilon_{t-j}, X_{t-s} \,\middle|\, X_0\right) + \alpha^s \mathsf{Var}\left(X_{t-s} \mid X_0\right).$$

Using assumption (a) of independence, we rewrite this as:

$$\mathsf{Cov}\left(X_t, X_{t-s} \mid X_0\right) = \alpha^s \mathsf{Var}(X_{t-s} \mid X_0).$$

The conditional population correlation of X_t and X_{t-s} given X_0, which is the sth autocorrelation, then satisfies:

$$\begin{aligned}
\rho_s = \mathsf{Corr}(X_t, X_{t-s} \mid X_0) &= \frac{\mathsf{Cov}(X_t, X_{t-s}|X_0)}{\{\mathsf{Var}(X_t|X_0)\mathsf{Var}(X_{t-s}|X_0)\}^{1/2}} \\
&= \alpha^s \left\{ \frac{\mathsf{Var}(X_{t-s}|X_0)}{\mathsf{Var}(X_t|X_0)} \right\}^{1/2}.
\end{aligned}$$

Assumption (c) that $|\alpha| < 1$ then entails that $\alpha^t \to 0$ as $t \to \infty$, while the ratio of variances above converges to unity. Thus, for large t, the autocorrelation function is exponentially decreasing:

$$\rho_s = \mathsf{Corr}(X_t, X_{t-s} \mid X_0) \approx \alpha^s.$$

In this argument, the conditioning on the initial value is not crucial. The same type of argument also shows that the unconditional covariance satisfies:

$$\mathsf{Cov}(X_t, X_{t-s}) = \alpha^s \mathsf{Var}(X_{t-s}).$$

In the time-series literature, it is often assumed at this point that the marginal variance of the time series is constant over time, so:

(d) $\mathsf{Var}(X_t) = \mathsf{Var}(X_{t-s})$ for all s, t.

When this is the case, the autocorrelation equals the normalized autocovariance:

$$\text{Corr}(X_t, X_{t-s}) = \frac{\text{Cov}(X_t, X_{t-s})}{\{\text{Var}(X_t)\text{Var}(X_{t-s})\}^{1/2}}$$

$$= \frac{\text{Cov}(X_t, X_{t-s})}{\text{Var}(X_{t-s})} = \alpha^s. \qquad [\text{ assumption } (d) \text{ }]$$

When econometric packages plot covariograms, $g_{0,s}$, under the heading correlograms as discussed in §12.2, they implicitly make assumption (d). While assumption (d) may be valid for the whiting price series p_t, it is problematic for many economic time series, which often exhibit non-stationary behavior. We will return to this issue in Chapter 16.

12.6.4 Definition of stationary processes

In §12.6.2, the concept of stationarity was used somewhat casually. The concept originates in the probability literature. The precise definition is that a process is stationary if the joint distribution of a block of data $(X_{t+1}, \ldots, X_{t+s})$ of length s does not depend on t.

Stationarity holds up to an approximation under assumption (c) that $|\alpha| < 1$. In that case, the conditional expectation, variance and autocorrelation satisfy:

$$\text{E}(X_t \mid X_0) \approx 0, \quad \text{Var}(X_t \mid X_0) \approx \frac{\sigma^2}{(1 - \alpha^2)}, \quad \text{Corr}(X_t, X_{t-s} \mid X_0) \approx \alpha^s.$$

The econometric analysis is based on the conditional distribution of $X_1, \ldots, X_T$ given X_0. This leads to the approximate expression for the marginal distribution of X_t given in (12.6.3). We could complement this with the assumption that X_0 has the distribution given in (12.6.3):

(d') $X_0 \overset{\text{D}}{=} \text{N}[0, \sigma^2/(1 - \alpha^2)]$,

It is shown in Exercise 12.4 that this implies that the unconditional expectation, variance, and autocorrelation are:

$$\text{E}(X_t) = 0, \qquad \text{Var}(X_t) = \frac{\sigma^2}{(1 - \alpha^2)}, \qquad \text{Corr}(X_t, X_{t-s}) = \alpha^s. \quad (12.6.5)$$

In particular, the distributional result (12.6.3) holds with equality rather than as an approximation. This result shows that assumption (d') implies assumption (d).

In the modeling approach taken here, we avoid making assumption (d'). There are two reasons for this. First, assumption (d') makes sense only under assumption (c). Often it is of interest to test that the autoregressive parameter is unity, so $\alpha = 1$, which would violate (c). Second, assumption (d') concerns a single observation, which makes it hard to test in a satisfactory way. Given that we will not be worried about assumption (d'), we will somewhat casually refer to assumption (c) that $|\alpha| < 1$ as the *stationary case*, although formally assumption (d') is needed to ensure stationarity.

12.6.5 The role of the intercept

We will now revisit the original autoregressive equation (12.3.1) with intercept β_1, and investigate the properties of that process. In line with assumption (c) above, assume:

(iv) $|\beta_2| < 1$.

In that case, equation (12.3.1) can be written as:

$$Y_t = \beta_1 \frac{1 - \beta_2}{1 - \beta_2} + \beta_2 Y_{t-1} + \epsilon_t,$$

or, equivalently, rewritten as:

$$\underbrace{\left(Y_t - \overbrace{\frac{\beta_1}{1 - \beta_2}}^{\mu_Y} \right)}_{X_t} = \underbrace{\beta_2}_{\alpha} \underbrace{\left(Y_{t-1} - \frac{\beta_1}{1 - \beta_2} \right)}_{X_{t-1}} + \epsilon_t.$$

We, therefore, get immediately from the results in §§12.6.2, 12.6.3 that:

$$\mathsf{E}(Y_t \mid Y_0) = \mathsf{E}\left(X_t \mid X_0 \right) + \mu_Y \approx \mu_Y = \frac{\beta_1}{1 - \beta_2}, \qquad (12.6.6)$$

$$\mathsf{Var}(Y_t \mid Y_0) = \mathsf{Var}(X_t \mid X_0) \approx \frac{\sigma^2}{1 - \beta_2^2} \overset{\text{def}}{=} \sigma_Y^2,$$

$$\mathsf{Corr}(Y_t, Y_{t-s} \mid Y_0) = \mathsf{Corr}(X_t, X_{t-s} \mid X_0) = \beta_2^s.$$

We say that μ_Y and σ_Y^2 are the unconditional expectation and variance of Y_t, noticing that the approximation improves as t increases. Since $|\beta_2| < 1$, we have $\sigma_Y^2 \geq \sigma^2$, so the autocorrelation amplifies the innovation variance.

As an example, recall the autoregressive model for the price of whiting reported in Table 12.1:

$$\widehat{p}_t = -0.039 + 0.76 p_{t-1}. \qquad (12.6.7)$$

The coefficient $\widehat{\beta}_1 = -0.039$ can be interpreted as a short-run mean of p_t when $p_{t-1} = 0$. The unconditional expectation is given by:

$$\widehat{\mu}_p = \frac{\widehat{\beta}_1}{1 - \widehat{\beta}_2} = \frac{-0.039}{1 - 0.76} = -0.16. \qquad (12.6.8)$$

This is actually not far from the sample average, $\overline{p} = T^{-1} \sum_{t=1}^{T} p_t$. Returning to (12.6.7), on average $p_{t-1} = -0.16$ here, so $\mathsf{E}(\widehat{p}_t) = -0.039 - 0.76 \times 0.16 =$

-0.16, matching (12.6.8). While $\widehat{\mu}_p$ is the maximum likelihood estimator for the unconditional expectation, it can be shown that the sample average will also estimate the unconditional expectation consistently.

12.7 INFERENCE FOR STATIONARY AUTOREGRESSIONS

We are now well placed to discuss inference in the autoregressive model with an intercept, as defined in §12.3. In the stationary case, where assumption (iv) that $|\beta_2| < 1$ holds, approximate inference is just as easy as in the two-variable regression model discussed in Chapter 5. Exact inference results are much more involved than those in §5.5.3, and have not been addressed fully in the literature. For most practical purposes, it suffices to use approximate results: the applicability of these for any given sample size can be checked by Monte Carlo simulation.

Recall the first-order autoregressive equation of (12.3.1) which is:

$$Y_t = \beta_1 + \beta_2 Y_{t-1} + \epsilon_t.$$

The log-likelihood ratio test statistic for the hypothesis that $\beta_2 = 0$ is easily derived, as in §5.5.2:

$$\mathsf{LR} = -T\log(1 - r_{0,1}^2) = Tr_{0,1}^2.$$

Under assumption (iv) and the null hypothesis, this statistic is once again approximately $\chi^2[1]$-distributed. Just as discussed in connection with the correlograms in §12.2.1, a one-sided test can be based on the statistic:

$$\omega = \text{sign}(\widehat{\beta}_2)\sqrt{\mathsf{LR}} \approx T^{1/2} r_{0,1},$$

which is approximately standard $\mathsf{N}[0,1]$-distributed.

Turning to the price series p_t, the estimated restricted model where $\beta_2 = 0$ is reported in Table 12.2. The restricted model is the one-variable model of Chapter 3. It is not based on all 111 observations since the initial observation Y_0 is ignored to match the autoregressive likelihood function of §12.4.

$\widehat{p}_t$	$= -0.191$	
standard error	(0.037)	
$\widehat{\sigma} = 0.38,$	$\widehat{\ell} = -50.01,$	$T = 110$

Table 12.2 Restricted model for price of whiting, p_t

The likelihood ratio test statistic is:

$$\mathsf{LR} = 2\{-4.48 - (-50.01)\} = 91.1,$$

with $\mathsf{p} < 0.001$ using a $\chi^2[1]$-distribution. This highlights once again the dependence structure in the data.

The likelihood ratio test is essentially the same test as that arising from the correlogram in Figure 12.1(c). The scaled first-order autocovariance is $r_{0,1} = 0.750$, leading to the two-sided test statistic $Tr_{0,1}^2 = 62$, and the one-sided test statistic $T^{1/2}r_1 = 7.9$. Comparing these with $\chi^2[1]$- and $N[0,1]$-distributions, respectively, once again leads to a rejection of the hypothesis $\beta_2 = 0$.

The exact distribution of the estimator $\widehat{\beta}_2$ is hard to derive. In the cross-sectional setup, we would condition on the set of regressors, $Y_0, \ldots, Y_{T-1}$, but that is not attractive here as it is the set of lagged dependent variables. While it can be shown that $E(\widehat{\beta}_2|Y_0)$ is different from β_2, so $\widehat{\beta}_2$ is a biased estimator, it still holds that $\widehat{\beta}_2$ is consistent, so $\widehat{\beta}_2 \xrightarrow{P} \beta_2$ (see also §2.2.1). Likewise, the variance of $\widehat{\beta}_2$ is not given by an expression like $\sigma^2 / \sum_{j=1}^{T}(Y_{j-1} - \overline{Y}_{(-)})^2$. Nonetheless, the econometric literature refers to:

$$\widehat{se}(\widehat{\beta}_2) = \left\{ \frac{\widehat{\sigma}^2}{\sum_{t=1}^{T}(Y_{t-1} - \overline{Y}_{(-)})^2} \right\}^{1/2} \tag{12.7.1}$$

as the standard error of $\widehat{\beta}_2$ as reported in Tables 12.1, 12.2. Similarly, the statistic:

$$\frac{\widehat{\beta}_2 - \beta_2^\circ}{\mathsf{se}(\widehat{\beta}_2)}$$

is referred to as the t-statistic for testing $\beta_2 = \beta_2^\circ$. While it is *not* t-distributed, it has approximately a standard normal distribution in the stationary case, $|\beta_2| < 1$. This will be illustrated using Monte Carlo simulation methods in §18.3.2 below.

In the stationary case, inferences about β_1 can be made in exactly the same way as for β_2. The standard error reported in Table 12.1 indicates that the hypothesis $\beta_1 = 0$ cannot be rejected. This suggests that the unconditional mean is not far from US$1, noting that there is no substantial interpretation to such this hypothesis.

12.8 SUMMARY AND EXERCISES

Summary: Time-series data often show temporal dependence. This dependence can be investigated using correlograms and partial correlograms. The basic tool in modeling such dependence is the autoregression.

A first-order autoregressive model is simply a two-variable regression model with the lagged dependent variable as regressor. The likelihood function is derived using the decomposition (12.4.1). It has the same form as the likelihood of the two-variable regression.

The autoregression is interpreted by solving the autoregressive equation recursively. Here, we considered the stationary case where the key autoregressive parameter is less than one in absolute value. Then estimators and test statistics have the same approximate normal or χ^2-distributions as seen before.

Bibliography: George Udny Yule, who will play an important role in later chapters, first formulated autoregressive processes in 1927: see Yule (1927). At approximately the same time, Eugene Slutsky formulated moving-average models, of which (12.6.2) is a special case, though his paper was published in English only in Slutsky (1937). Since then, both classes of model, and generalizations thereof, have played key roles in the econometric analysis of time series.

Key questions:

- Why would we expect temporal dependence in time-series data?
- Derive the decomposition (12.4.1).
- Discuss the validity of the assumptions of the statistical models for the whiting price series.

Exercise 12.1. *Show that* $\widehat{\beta}_1$, $\widehat{\beta}_2$ *in (12.5.1) are maximum likelihood estimators.*

Exercise 12.2. *Consider the simple autoregression (12.6.1). Plot the population correlograms for* $s = 0, 1, 2, \ldots, 5$ *when* $\alpha = -0.9, -0.5, 0, 0.5, 0.9$. *Comment on how the shape of the correlogram alters with* α.

Exercise 12.3. *Consider the simple autoregression (12.6.1).*
(a) Derive the likelihood function (conditional on X_0).
(b) Derive the maximum likelihood estimator for α.

Exercise 12.4. *Consider the simple autoregression (12.6.1). Suppose assumption (d') giving the distribution of X_0 is satisfied. Show that the unconditional distribution of X_t is normal, and satisfies (12.6.5).*

Chapter Thirteen

Mis-specification analysis in time series

To trust inferences drawn from econometric analyses, one must check that the underlying assumptions are satisfied. For autoregressive models, this can be done using the general methods presented for cross sections in Chapter 9. One major difference, though, is the time element, which gives a natural way to stratify, or order, the data. It is therefore easier, and perhaps also more important, to test the independence assumption. Likewise, we can use recursive analysis along the time dimension of the data to check parameter constancy.

In this chapter, we will first consider the mis-specification tests known from Chapter 9, along with a few new tests. These methods will be illustrated using the first-order autoregression for the price series for whiting at the Fulton Fish Market. Subsequently, we will use these methods to develop an econometric model for an associated time series of quantities of whiting sold at the Fulton Fish Market.

13.1 THE FIRST-ORDER AUTOREGRESSIVE MODEL

We will consider a first-order autoregressive equation for a time series $Y_0, \ldots, Y_T$:

$$Y_t = \beta_1 + \beta_2 Y_{t-1} + \epsilon_t \qquad \text{for } t = 1, \ldots, T. \tag{13.1.1}$$

The conditional statistical model of $Y_1, \ldots, Y_T$ given Y_0 is defined by the following assumptions:

(i) *independence*: the innovations $\epsilon_1, \ldots, \epsilon_T$ are independent;

(ii) *conditional normality*: $\epsilon_t \overset{D}{=} N[0, \sigma^2]$;

(iii) *parameter space*: $\beta_1, \beta_2, \sigma^2 \in \mathbb{R} \times \mathbb{R} \times \mathbb{R}_+$.

In the following, we will discuss tests for assumptions (i) and (ii). We will start by looking at the tests for normality, identical distribution, and functional form that were presented in Chapter 9. Subsequently some tests that exploit the time dimension as a means of stratification are presented.

13.2 TESTS FOR BOTH CROSS SECTIONS AND TIME SERIES

We will show how the tests for normality, identical distribution and functional form introduced in Chapter 9 can be used in a time series context.

13.2.1 Test for normality

In §9.2, tests for normality were presented, based on the skewness and excess kur-tosis of the residuals. These tests can also be applied to the residuals of autore-gressions. This has been argued by Kilian and Demiroglu (2000) in the context of stationary and unit root processes, so $-1 < \beta_2 \leq 1$. Engler and Nielsen (2007) go one step further and show that the tests are applicable for all values of the pa-rameters, β_1, β_2, σ^2. Thus, the normality aspect of the autoregressive model can be tested before making inference about the parameters. Similarly, it is possible to construct confidence bands for Q-Q plots that apply across the parameter space.

Example: price of whiting. Applying the normality test to the residuals of the price series, we obtain:

$$\widehat{\kappa}_3 = -0.071, \qquad \widehat{\kappa}_4 = -0.258, \qquad T = 110.$$

These numbers are much better than for the wage example, in line with the satis-factory quantile-quantile plot reported in Figure 12.2(d). The test statistics are:

$$\chi^2_{\text{skew}} = 0.09, \qquad \chi^2_{\text{kurt}} = 0.30, \qquad \chi^2_{\text{norm}} = 0.39,$$

which are all small when compared to χ^2-distributions with 1, 1, and 2 degrees of freedom respectively, so the normality hypothesis is not rejected.

13.2.2 Test for identical distribution

In §9.3 White's test for heteroskedasticity was presented. This test can also be applied to the residuals of autoregressions under certain assumptions. For the first-order autoregression, the test is applicable when $|\beta_2| \leq 1$, but not when $|\beta_2| > 1$; see Caceres and Nielsen (2007). The case $|\beta_2| < 1$ is the stationary case, as dis-cussed in §12.6, the case $\beta_2 = 1$ is the unit-root case, which will be discussed in Chapter 16, whereas the explosive case $|\beta_2| > 1$ is not discussed in this book. Since the test is valid only in the non-explosive case, the test should in principle be used simultaneously with inference about the autoregressive parameter: in or-der to know whether the series is non-explosive, we need to conduct inference on the autoregressive parameter, but in order to conduct valid inference on the autore-gressive parameter, the model assumptions need to be justified. This indicates that White's test for heteroskedasticity is more problematic than some of the other tests presented here. The only practical way to use the test is to maintain the belief that the time series being analyzed cannot be explosive.

Example: price of whiting. Applying White's test for heteroskedasticity to the residuals of the price series, we get:

$$F_{\text{het}}[2, 105] = 1.06 \qquad [\text{p} = 0.35].$$

Thus, we cannot reject the validity of the model based on this test.

13.2.3 Test for functional form

In §9.4 the regression specification test (RESET) was presented. It is often used for autoregressive models, although its properties do not appear to have been studied in that context.

Example: price of whiting. Applying the RESET test to the residuals of the price series, we find:

$$F_{\text{reset}}[1, 107] = 0.12 \qquad [\text{p} = 0.74].$$

Thus, we cannot reject the validity of the model based on this test.

13.3 TEST FOR INDEPENDENCE

The issue of independence is often a problem in time-series analysis. In a cross-section analysis based on a survey, it may not be a crucial issue, depending on how and when the survey was undertaken. For time series, correlograms provide a graphical means of evaluating independence (see §12.2). Tests against two types of dependence are reviewed here.

13.3.1 Test for autoregressively dependent innovations

The hypothesis of independence of the innovations in the first-order autoregression (13.1.1) is consistent with the hypothesis $\beta_3 = 0$ in the more general second-order model:

$$Y_t = \beta_1 + \beta_2 Y_{t-1} + \beta_3 Y_{t-2} + \epsilon_t,$$

where $\epsilon_1, \ldots, \epsilon_T$ are independently $N[0, \sigma^2]$-distributed. In this second-order autoregression, two initial values are needed, so one will have to sacrifice one more observation to be able to fit the model. The likelihood ratio test statistic for $\beta_3 = 0$ is given by:

$$\text{LR} = -T \log(1 - r_{0,2\cdot1}^2),$$

where $r_{0,2\cdot1}$ is the sample partial correlation $r_{0,2\cdot1}$, as discussed in §7.6. It can be proved that when $\beta_3 = 0$, then $\text{LR} \overset{D}{\approx} \chi^2[1]$ for an autoregression for any value of the parameters, β_1, β_2, σ^2 (see Nielsen, 2007). As for the normality test, this test can therefore be used before making inferences about the parameters. Equivalently, the test can be formulated in terms of the test statistic, $T r_{0,2\cdot1}^2$.

A version of this test can be implemented in terms of an auxiliary regression, as with White's test for heteroskedasticity. The idea is then to obtain R_{ar}^2 from the auxiliary regression:

$$\widehat{u}_t = \alpha_1 + \alpha_2 Y_{t-1} + \alpha_3 \widehat{u}_{t-1} + v_t \tag{13.3.1}$$

and test $\alpha_2 = \alpha_3 = 0$ using $TR^2_{\text{ar}} \overset{D}{\approx} \chi^2[1]$. Note that Y_{t-1} is needed in the auxiliary regression, but does not count toward the degrees of freedom of the test, as it was entered unrestrictedly in (13.1.1).

If there is cyclical behavior in the data, the residuals may have partial autocorrelations of higher order, but not of order one. Often the first-order model is therefore tested against a model of higher order than two.

Example: price of whiting. The partial correlogram for the residuals was plotted in Figure 12.2(c) and has numerical values:

$$r_{0,2\cdot1} = 0.20, \qquad r_{0,3\cdot1,2} = -0.004,$$

giving test statistics for first-order, second-order, and up to second-order autocorrelation in the residuals:

$$Tr^2_{0,2\cdot1} = 4.2, \qquad Tr^2_{0,3\cdot1,2} = 0.002, \qquad T(r^2_{0,2\cdot1} + r^2_{0,3\cdot1,2}) = 4.2.$$

Compared with χ^2-distributions with 1, 1, and 2 degrees of freedom, respectively, these test statistics result in p-values of 0.04, 0.96, and 0.12. This indicates that there is a slight problem with residual autocorrelation of first order. If we only applied the joint test for first- and second-order autocorrelation, we would not detect the first-order autocorrelation. This is an example of the general problem that when testing too many restrictions in one step, we are sometimes led to erroneous non-rejection decisions.

13.3.2 Test for temporally dependent innovation variances

Another departure from the model of independent innovations could be temporal dependence of the variances of a model. Engle (1982) proposed such a model for autoregressive conditional heteroskedasticity (ARCH). It has since become an important ingredient in the financial econometrics literature, and Engle was awarded the Nobel Prize in Economics for this contribution in 2003. Here our concern is to test against this form of dependence.

The idea is that the variance could change over the sample, by following an autoregressive structure where $\mathsf{Var}(\epsilon_t|\epsilon_{t-1}) = \alpha_1 + \alpha_2\epsilon^2_{t-1}$. The hypothesis of constant variance, $\alpha_2 = 0$, is tested as follows:

(1) Obtain residuals $\widehat{\epsilon}_t$ from the model (13.1.1).

(2) Obtain R^2_{arch} from the auxiliary regression :

$$\widehat{\epsilon}^2_t = \alpha_1 + \alpha_2\widehat{\epsilon}^2_{t-1} + v_t, \tag{13.3.2}$$

and test $\alpha_2 = 0$ using $TR^2_{\text{arch}} \overset{D}{\approx} \chi^2[1]$.

As for White's test for heteroskedasticity (see §9.3) the intercept α_1 in the auxiliary regression (13.3.2) is important. Higher-order lags of the residuals, such as $\widehat{\epsilon}_{t-2}$ and $\widehat{\epsilon}_{t-3}$, are sometimes included in the auxiliary regression, giving a multivariate hypothesis to be tested. Often the test is reported in an F-type form. The properties of this test have mainly been studied in the stationary case, $|\widehat{\beta}_2| < 1$.

Example: price of whiting. Applying the test for autoregressive conditional heteroskedasticity to the residuals of the price series, we get:

$$F_{\text{arch}(1)}[1, 106] = 2.63 \qquad [\text{p} = 0.11].$$

13.3.3 Improving a model with temporal dependence

A failure of a test for temporal independence of the innovations can often be remedied by reconsidering the specification of the model. Two attempts at doing so will be discussed, based on adding a potentially important variable. However, one must always remember that an apparent problem, such as residual autocorrelation, could have other causes than error autocorrelation, so it is worth investigating alternative sources, such as incorrect functional form (which was tested for above), or parameter non-constancy (which we will test in §13.4).

One approach to improving the model is to add a second lag of prices to the model. The resulting model is reported in Table 13.1. The test against autocorrelation in the residuals now accepts, as expected from the previous analysis, while the test for autoregressive conditional heteroskedasticity gives a marginal decision when testing at the 5% level. This analysis suggests that simply adding lags to the model is not quite the right way to get a well-specified model in this case, so a second way to improve the model would be to include a new variable in the analysis. In many situations, such a variable may be difficult to find, and one could then take a pragmatic view that since both the first-order model and the second-order model are only marginally rejected, we choose one of those models. The first-order model is obviously the simpler model—we say that it is more parsimonious—so we could have a slight preference for that model. Note that two initial values are needed for the second-order autoregression so the effective sample length is reduced to $T = 109$. The likelihood values in Tables 12.1 and 13.1 are therefore not directly comparable.

$\widehat{p}_t$	$= -0.05 + 0.91\,p_{t-1} - 0.20\,p_{t-2}$
standard error	(0.03) (0.10) (0.10)

$\widehat{\sigma} = 0.24, \qquad \widehat{\ell} = -1.74, \qquad T = 109$

$F_{\text{ar}(1-2)}[2, 104] = 0.7\,[\text{p} = 0.50] \qquad F_{\text{arch}(1)}[1, 104] = 4.2\,[\text{p} = 0.04]$

Table 13.1 Second-order autoregressive model for prices of whiting, p_t

A better approach is to find variables of subject-matter interest that can explain the apparent temporal dependence. To find such variables is part of the art of empirical econometric modeling. We are fortunate that Angrist et al. (2000) have analyzed the data before us, so we can seek inspiration there. A central variable in their analysis is the weather at sea, the point being that when it is stormy at sea, fewer fishing boats are out and so fewer fish are caught, which in turn influences the price. They constructed a dichotomous variable *stormy* taking the value unity when the average wave height and the average wind speed in the three days prior to time t exceeded 4.5 feet and 18 knots respectively, and zero otherwise. By that definition, it is stormy in 31 of the observed 110 days. The time lag is included to allow for the time it takes to bring the fish to market. This variable is plotted in Figure 13.2(d). Table 13.2 shows the fitted model when including *stormy* in the specification. It is seen that it explains the variation in the data that is reflected in the tests for temporal dependence in both first- and second-order autoregressions.

$$\widehat{p}_t = -0.10 + 0.70\,p_{t-1} + 0.19\,stormy_t$$
$$\text{standard error} \quad (0.03) \quad (0.06) \quad (0.05)$$

$$\widehat{\sigma} = 0.24, \qquad \widehat{\ell} = 1.41, \qquad T = 110$$

$$F_{ar(1-2)}[2, 105] = 1.6\,[\text{p} = 0.21] \qquad F_{arch(1)}[1, 105] = 1.4\,[\text{p} = 0.23]$$

Table 13.2 First-order autoregressive model for prices of whiting, p_t, with weather dummy

If, however, the autocorrelation in the residuals is not removed, standard errors will be misleading, which can distort inferences. In §9.3.3, it was mentioned that in the presence of heteroskedasticity the standard errors could be replaced by heteroskedasticity corrected standard errors. In the same way, heteroskedasticity and autocorrelation corrected standard errors (HACSE) have been suggested by Newey and West (1987). Once again, if the usual and the robust standard errors are very different, it is questionable how valid the robust standard errors actually are (Computer Task 14.4). Thus, it is often beneficial to search for better empirical models through an exploratory analysis.

13.4 RECURSIVE GRAPHICS

Recursive graphics can be used to check how constant the model's parameter estimates are over time. Figure 13.1 gives some examples of such recursive graphs.

Panels (a) and (b) report recursive estimates of β_2 and β_1 respectively from the model in Table 12.1. Here the x-axis runs from $M = 27$ to $T = 110$. For each value m on the x-axis, the sample $Y_0, \ldots, Y_m$ has been considered, giving a forward recursion as the samples become larger with m. For each sample, the parameters are estimated and reported together with plus and minus twice the estimated standard errors for that sample. Note that, as m increases, the information increases, so the standard error bands narrow. The idea is to look at the bands as

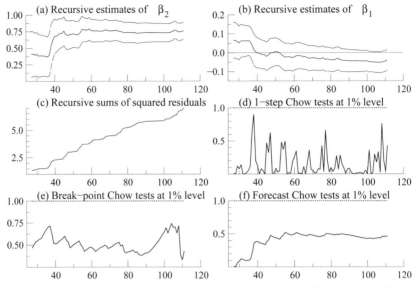

Figure 13.1 Recursive graphics in first-order autoregressive model for prices of whiting, p_t

a "tunnel" and ask whether one can see through it from one end to the other. In both cases, this is indeed just possible. At the time of the observations 36 to 41 corresponding to 23 to 29 January 1992, the graph for $\widehat{\beta}_2$ makes a shift upward. Going back to the graph of the time series p_t itself in Figure 12.2(b), this is seen to be associated with a few large downward movements in p_t.

Panel (c) reports forward recursive estimates of the residual sum of squares, RSS_m. In other words, for each sample $Y_0, \ldots, Y_m$, an autoregression is fitted and the panel reports the sum of squared residuals. When divided by the sample length m, this gives an estimate for the innovation variance σ^2, and therefore the RSS_m graph is expected to grow linearly, which it does approximately.

Panel (d) reports a 1-step Chow test, which is also a forward recursive test (see Chow, 1960). For each sample $Y_0, \ldots, Y_m$, it is tested whether the last observation comes from the same model as $Y_0, \ldots, Y_{m-1}$. The idea is to see whether the model based on $Y_0, \ldots, Y_{m-1}$ is good at forecasting Y_m for every feasible m. The unrestricted model is therefore:

$$\begin{cases} Y_t = \beta_1 + \beta_2 Y_{t-1} + \epsilon_t & \text{for } t = 1, \ldots, m-1, \\ Y_m \text{ is unrestricted}, \end{cases}$$

whereas the restricted model is that the autoregression governs the full sample including observation m. The unrestricted residual sum of squares is thus RSS_{n-1}, while the restricted residual sum of squares is RSS_m. These can then be used to compute an F-type statistic:

$$\frac{\text{RSS}_m - \text{RSS}_{m-1}}{\text{RSS}_{m-1}/\{(m-1) - 2\}}.$$

This statistic is approximately $\chi^2[1]$-distributed. The test statistics are normalized by the 1% critical value, so the horizontal line at 1 gives the critical value. Given that about 100 tests are done, which are only slightly dependent, at least two or three rejections would be needed to reject the model based on this type of test. For the price series, the test does actually not reject for any value of m.

Panel (e) reports a break-point Chow test. This is a variation of the 1-step Chow test. The idea is to see whether a model based on $Y_0, \ldots, Y_{m-1}$ is good at forecasting all the remaining variables $Y_m, \ldots, Y_T$. The forecast horizon $N = T - m + 1$ therefore decreases with m. The unrestricted residual sum of squares is thus RSS_{m-1}, while the restricted residual sum of squares is RSS_T, and hence the tests are based on the F-type statistic:

$$\frac{(\text{RSS}_T - \text{RSS}_{m-1})}{\text{RSS}_{m-1}/\{(m-1)-2\}},$$

which is approximately $\chi^2[T - m + 1]$-distributed. The outcomes for this test also support the price model.

Panel (f) reports a forecast Chow test. Here the idea is to see if a model based on the shortest sample $Y_0, \ldots, Y_{M-1}$ can forecast $Y_M, \ldots, Y_m$ where m increases from M to T. The unrestricted residual sum of squares is thus RSS_{M-1}, while the restricted residual sum of squares is RSS_m, and hence the tests are based on the F-type statistic:

$$\frac{(\text{RSS}_m - \text{RSS}_{M-1})}{\text{RSS}_{M-1}/\{(M-1)-2\}},$$

which are asymptotically $\chi^2[m - M + 1]$-distributed. The outcomes again support the model.

The last three tests are computed for many possible values, so they might by chance exceed their critical values, which are based on doing only one such test. There are corrections available in the literature (see Savin, 1984), but as no rejections occurred here, such an issue does not arise.

13.5 EXAMPLE: FINDING A MODEL FOR QUANTITIES OF FISH

For the price series p_t, it was rather easy to find a well-specified or *congruent* model, in the terminology of §11.4. In many instances, this will not be the case. In the following, another time series is studied to illustrate how mis-specification tests and graphics can help in building a well-specified model.

The data set of Graddy (1995) also has the daily aggregated quantities of whiting sold for the period from 2 December 1991 to 8 May 1992. Figure 13.2(a) reports the quantities, Q_t, in pounds, whereas panel (b) reports the corresponding

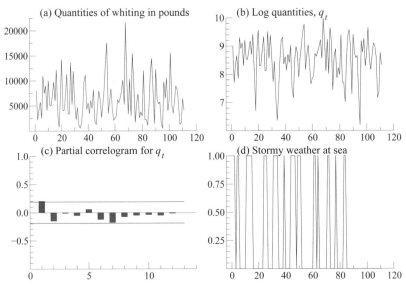

Figure 13.2 Daily quantities of whiting at the Fulton Fish Market

log quantities, q_t. The time series and the partial correlogram in panel (c) indicate that the quantities show less temporal dependence than the price series shown in Figure 12.1.

$$\widehat{q_t} = \underset{(0.8)}{6.8} + \underset{(0.09)}{0.20}\, q_{t-1}$$
standard error

$\widehat{\sigma} = 0.73, \qquad \widehat{\ell} = -120.67, \qquad T = 110$

$\chi^2_{\text{norm}}[2]$	=	5.0	[p= 0.08]	$F_{\text{ar}(1-2)}[2, 106] = 2.0$	[p= 0.14]
$\chi^2_{\text{skew}}[1]$	=	5.0	[p= 0.03]	$F_{\text{arch}(1)}[1, 106] = 2.0$	[p= 0.16]
$\chi^2_{\text{kurt}}[1]$	=	0.02	[p= 0.87]	$F_{\text{het}}[2, 105] = 3.6$	[p= 0.03]
				$F_{\text{reset}}[1, 107] = 0.1$	[p= 0.72]

Table 13.3 Autoregressive model for quantities of whiting, q_t, with mis-specification tests

As a model, a first-order autoregression is fitted to the quantity series. Table 13.3 reports the fitted autoregression and the associated mis-specification tests, whereas Figure 13.3 reports mis-specification graphics. The first hunch that q has less temporal dependence than p_t seems to be confirmed by the estimated autoregressive parameter. However, we cannot really make that inference until it has been shown that the model is congruent.

The overall mis-specification test for normality is just accepted. Breaking down this test for skewness and kurtosis shows hints of some skewness. The Q-Q plot in Figure 13.3(d) points to the same conclusion of skewness rather than kurtosis, when compared with Figure 9.1(d). The test for heteroskedasticity also indicates that the model is somewhat weak. Sometimes it is argued that mis-specification tests should be conducted at a 1% level, which would save the model here, but still it would be worth looking into the source of these issues.

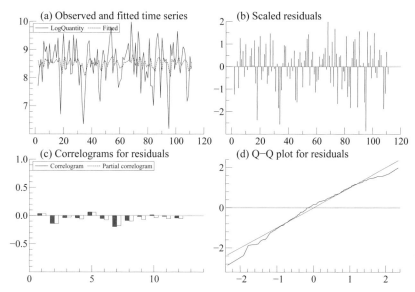

Figure 13.3 Properties of first-order autoregression for quantities of whiting, q_t, reported in Table 13.3

In order to improve the model, we will once again use the dichotomous variable $stormy_t$ which is plotted in Figure 13.2(d), as bad weather at sea is very likely to affect the supply of fish to the market. Comparing panels (b) and (d) shows that there is tendency for quantities to fall when it is stormy. Including the variable $stormy_t$ in the model changes the picture somewhat. Table 13.4 shows how the model and the formal mis-specification tests alter.

$$\widehat{q}_t = 7.0 + 0.19\, q_{t-1} - 0.36\, stormy_t$$
$$\text{standard error} \quad (0.8) \quad (0.09) \quad (0.15)$$

$$\widehat{\sigma} = 0.72, \qquad \widehat{\ell} = -117.82, \qquad T = 110$$

$\chi^2_{norm}[2]$	$= 6.9$	$[p= 0.03]$	$F_{ar(1-2)}[2, 106] = 0.9$	$[p= 0.40]$
$\chi^2_{skew}[1]$	$= 6.8$	$[p= 0.01]$	$F_{arch(1)}[1, 106] = 1.4$	$[p= 0.24]$
$\chi^2_{kurt}[1]$	$= 0.04$	$[p= 0.84]$	$F_{het}[3, 103] = 2.0$	$[p= 0.12]$
			$F_{reset}[1, 106] = 1.8$	$[p= 0.18]$

Table 13.4 Autoregressive model for quantities of whiting, q_t, with weather dummy

Comparing Tables 13.3 and 13.4, we see that $stormy_t$ explains some of the heterogeneity in the former model, in that the heteroskedasticity test is not significant in the latter model. The normality test, however, still indicates some problems, which are addressed in the following.

The graphical mis-specification analysis for the model including the variable $stormy_t$ is not given here, as it is not very different from that in Figure 13.3. In panel Figure 13.3(b), there are three large negative residuals, which are driving the skewness. Figure 13.3(a) suggests three days with the least turnover. The first two days can be identified as public holidays, whereas the third is close to Easter:

Observation 18:   Thursday, 26 December 1991:   Boxing Day.
Observation 34:   Monday, 20 January 1992:   Martin Luther King Day.
Observation 95:   Wednesday, 15 April 1992:   Easter week.

The fact that the first two days are public holidays when the market is open explains the reduced turnover, whereas the third day has a weaker explanation. Although only two of the three days are clearly explained, a dummy variable, hol_t, taking the value one for observations 18, 34, 95 and zero otherwise, is introduced into the model. The results from that model are given in Table 13.5. Now the autoregressive parameter is insignificant and the quantities fall below average when there is a stormy period or a holiday. Figure 13.4 reports graphical mis-specification tests.

$$\hat{q}_t = 7.9 + 0.09\,q_{t-1} - 0.36\,stormy_t - 2.05\,hol_t$$

standard error   (0.7)   (0.08)   (0.14)   (0.38)

$$\hat{\sigma} = 0.64, \qquad \hat{\ell} = -104.64, \qquad T = 110$$

$\chi^2_{norm}[2]$	$=$	3.6	$[p = 0.17]$	$F_{ar(1-2)}[2,104] = 0.1$	$[p = 0.89]$
$\chi^2_{skew}[1]$	$=$	2.6	$[p = 0.11]$	$F_{arch(1)}[1,104] = 1.2$	$[p = 0.27]$
$\chi^2_{kurt}[1]$	$=$	0.9	$[p = 0.32]$	$F_{het}[4,101] = 0.7$	$[p = 0.62]$
				$F_{reset}[1,105] = 2.4$	$[p = 0.12]$

Table 13.5   Autoregressive model for quantities of whiting, q_t, with dummies for weather and public holidays

13.6 MIS-SPECIFICATION ENCOMPASSING

Encompassing is a general principle explained in §11.5, wherein a given model is evaluated by deriving its implications for other existing models and checking that such implications are not rejected. As in Table 11.3, we have compared two models on their respective specifications: can M_1 explain the reported results of M_2, or vice versa? A more far-reaching approach is to use M_1 to deduce mis-specifications in M_2, of which the proprietor of M_2 may not even be aware. This is called mis-specification encompassing. For example, if M_1 involved a variable $z_{k,t}$ (say) that experienced a large location shift in-sample, but M_2 excluded that variable, then M_1 should predict a structural break in M_2 at the time $z_{k,t}$ shifted. If no such shift occurred in M_2, that is evidence against M_1, whereas if the predicted shift did occur, that is evidence in favor of M_1 and against M_2. We will reconsider that argument in §20.5 when discussing the Lucas critique.

As an empirical example, we now compare the second-order autoregressive model for prices of whiting, p_t, in Table 13.1, viewed as M_2, with the first-order

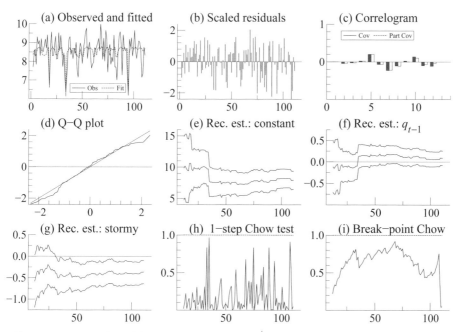

Figure 13.4 Properties of first-order autoregression for quantities of whiting, including dummies $stormy_t$ and hol_t as in Table 13.5

autoregressive model that included the weather dummy $stormy_t$ in Table 13.2, denoted M_1. The former exhibited residuals with autoregressive conditional heteroskedasticity, which the latter might predict would occur when $stormy_t$ was omitted. Indeed, the test for autoregressive conditional heteroskedasticity is insignificant in M_1. To date, however, no formal mis-specification encompassing test has been developed for that case. On a specification encompassing test, we find the results in Table 13.6, where the additional regressor in each model is tested for significance in the other. The evidence is consistent with (13.2) being able to explain the model with autoregressive conditional heteroskedastic residuals.

$M_1 \ \mathcal{E} \ M_2$	$M_2 \ \mathcal{E} \ M_1$
$F_{encomp}[1, 105] = 3.1 \ [p = 0.08]$	$F_{encomp}[1, 105] = 9.42 \ [p = 0.003]$

Table 13.6 Encompassing tests of models with $stormy$ or p_{t-2}

13.7 SUMMARY AND EXERCISES

Summary: A range of formal tests for mis-specifications is introduced. Most can be applied to both cross-sectional regressions and time-series regressions. For time-series regressions, the natural time ordering of data can in addition be used to more powerfully investigate temporal independence and construct recursive plots.

Bibliography: The first formal tests for residual autocorrelation were introduced in the 1940s and 1950s. The most famous was due to James Durbin and Geoffrey Watson, and is still often reported today, although it is only applicable to regression models without lagged dependent variables.

Key questions:

- Why are mis-specification tests important?
- How many mis-specification tests should one conduct? Show why a smaller number than you propose would miss testing important assumptions of the statistical model, but why a larger number would add little extra insight.
- Discuss the relative advantages and disadvantages of cross-section and time-series data for investigating model mis-specifications.

Computing Task 13.1. *Estimate the model for the price of whiting of Table 12.1. Store the residuals.*
(a) Construct a test of no autocorrelation using the auxiliary regression in (13.3.1).
(b) Construct a test of no autoregressive conditional heteroskedasticity using the auxiliary regression in (13.3.2).

Chapter Fourteen

The vector autoregressive model

In Chapters 12 and 13, we analyzed univariate time series for prices, p_t, and quantities, q_t, of whiting sold at the Fulton Fish Market. Demand and supply theory suggests that prices and quantities are determined simultaneously. We will, therefore, develop an econometric model for the bivariate system consisting of prices and quantities. This is done in two steps. In this chapter, we will set up a bivariate autoregressive model along the lines of the bivariate normal model introduced in §10.3. In Chapter 15, we will then show how a theoretical model, like a demand and supply model, can be identified from the econometric model of the data.

The bivariate normal model was developed as a multivariate generalization of the one-variable model. The vector autoregressive model is a similar extension for time series. Estimation follows along the same lines, except the notion of strong exogeneity will be adapted slightly to weak exogeneity.

14.1 THE VECTOR AUTOREGRESSIVE MODEL

The bivariate normal model developed for cross-sectional data in §10.3 can easily be adapted to a time-series model. The data are now $\mathbf{X}_0, \mathbf{X}_1, \ldots \mathbf{X}_T$, where $\mathbf{X}_t$ is the bivariate vector:

$$\mathbf{X}_t = \begin{pmatrix} Y_t \\ Z_t \end{pmatrix}.$$

The model is then given in terms of the equations:

$$Y_t = \varphi_y + \varphi_{yy} Y_{t-1} + \varphi_{yz} Z_{t-1} + \epsilon_{y,t}, \qquad (14.1.1)$$
$$Z_t = \varphi_z + \varphi_{zy} Y_{t-1} + \varphi_{zz} Z_{t-1} + \epsilon_{z,t}, \qquad (14.1.2)$$

with the lagged dependent vector, $\mathbf{X}_t$, appearing in each equation. Extensions where several lags of $\mathbf{X}_t$ enter as explanatory variables are possible. Denoting the vector of $\epsilon_{y,t}$ and $\epsilon_{z,t}$ by ϵ_t:

$$\epsilon_t = \begin{pmatrix} \epsilon_{y,t} \\ \epsilon_{z,t} \end{pmatrix},$$

the vector autoregressive model is defined by the assumptions:

(i) *independence*: $\epsilon_1, \ldots, \epsilon_T$ are mutually independent;

(ii) *normal distribution*: $\epsilon_t \overset{\text{D}}{=} N_2[0, \Sigma]$;

(iii) *parameter space*: $\varphi_y, \varphi_{yy}, \varphi_{yz}, \varphi_z, \varphi_{zy}, \varphi_{zz}, \sigma_{yz}, \sigma_{yy}, \sigma_{zz} \in \mathbb{R}^7 \times \mathbb{R}_+^2$ so $\sigma_{yz}^2 < \sigma_{yy}\sigma_{zz}$.

At a given point in time, t, the past values of the time series, like $\mathbf{X}_{t-1}$, are known, and $\mathbf{X}_t$ has a bivariate normal distribution. We can, therefore, find the conditional distribution of Y_t given Z_t and the past values of the time series using the results in §10.2.2. Then the conditional distribution of Y_t given Z_t and the past satisfies the equation:

$$Y_t = \beta_1 + \beta_y Y_{t-1} + \beta_z Z_{t-1} + \delta Z_t + \epsilon_{y \cdot z, t}. \tag{14.1.3}$$

Here, the parameters β_1, β_y, β_z, δ and the variance σ^2 of $\epsilon_{y \cdot z, t}$ are some function of the original parameters, in line with the discussion for the cross-sectional situation (Exercise 14.1). The conditional model based on equation (14.1.3) is called an *autoregressive distributed-lag model* (ADL), and is a natural generalization of both autoregressive and regression models.

First, however, we consider estimation of the first-order vector autoregressive model itself, for which we need the joint density of $\mathbf{X}_1, \ldots, \mathbf{X}_T$ given $\mathbf{X}_0$:

$$f(\mathbf{x}_1, \ldots, \mathbf{x}_T \mid \mathbf{x}_0)$$

$$= \prod_{t=1}^{T} f(\mathbf{x}_t \mid \mathbf{x}_{t-1}, \ldots, \mathbf{x}_0) \qquad\qquad [\,(12.4.1)\,]$$

$$= \prod_{t=1}^{T} f(\mathbf{x}_t \mid \mathbf{x}_{t-1}) \qquad\qquad [\,(i): \text{Markov property}\,]$$

$$= \prod_{t=1}^{T} f(y_t \mid z_t, \mathbf{x}_{t-1}) f(z_t \mid \mathbf{x}_{t-1}) \qquad\qquad [\,(4.1.7)\,]$$

$$= \left\{ \prod_{t=1}^{T} f(y_t \mid z_t, \mathbf{x}_{t-1}) \right\} \left\{ \prod_{t=1}^{T} f(z_t \mid \mathbf{x}_{t-1}) \right\}. \qquad [\,\text{collect products}\,]$$

The likelihood function therefore satisfies:

$$L_{\mathbf{X}_1, \ldots, \mathbf{X}_T \mid \mathbf{X}_0} \left(\varphi_y, \varphi_z, \varphi_{yy}, \varphi_{yz}, \varphi_{zy}, \varphi_{zz}, \Sigma \right)$$

$$= \left\{ \prod_{t=1}^{T} L_{Y_t \mid Z_t, \mathbf{X}_{t-1}} \left(\beta_1, \beta_y, \beta_z, \delta, \sigma^2 \right) \right\} \left\{ \prod_{t=1}^{T} L_{Z_t \mid \mathbf{X}_{t-1}} \left(\mu_z, \varphi_{zy}, \varphi_{zz}, \sigma_{zz} \right) \right\}.$$

The first term is now referred to as a *partial likelihood*, rather than a conditional likelihood, in that it is based on a product of conditional densities, rather than a single conditional density. The second term is usually referred to as a marginal likelihood, although, strictly speaking, it is also a partial likelihood.

The likelihood can be analyzed in parallel with the strong exogeneity argument in §10.1. So far we have not imposed restrictions on the parameters and therefore the parameters:

$$\boldsymbol{\psi} = \left(\beta_1, \beta_y, \beta_z, \delta, \sigma^2\right), \qquad \boldsymbol{\lambda} = \left(\mu_z, \varphi_{zy}, \varphi_{zz}, \sigma_{zz}\right)$$

vary in a product space, $\Psi \times \Lambda$. This condition ensures that:

$$\max_{\psi, \lambda \in \Theta} \mathsf{L}_{\mathbf{X}_1, \ldots, \mathbf{X}_T | \mathbf{X}_0} (\psi, \lambda)$$

$$= \left\{ \max_{\psi \in \Psi} \prod_{t=1}^{T} \mathsf{L}_{Y_t | Z_t, \mathbf{X}_{t-1}} (\psi) \right\} \left\{ \max_{\lambda \in \Lambda} \prod_{t=1}^{T} \mathsf{L}_{Z_t | \mathbf{X}_{t-1}} (\lambda) \right\}. \quad (14.1.4)$$

Following Engle et al. (1983), we say Z_t is *weakly exogenous* for the parameters of interest ψ. Comparing (14.1.4) with (10.1.1), we see that the temporal dependence prevents us from directly modeling all Y-variables conditional on all Z-variables in one go, hence the weak, rather than strong, notion of exogeneity. Many papers of interest are reprinted in Ericsson and Irons (1994).

Equation (14.1.4) shows that we can maximize the likelihood function for an unrestricted vector autoregression using two multiple regressions. For the partial likelihood of Y_t given $Z_t, \mathbf{X}_{t-1}$, a four-variable regression is needed, while the "marginal" likelihood of Z_t given $\mathbf{X}_{t-1}$ can be analyzed using a three-variable regression. An empirical illustration is provided in the next section.

The notion of super exogeneity introduced in (11.4.2) also applies in the time-series situation. We would have that the conditional relation of Y_t given Z_t and the past is invariant to a variable W_t if:

$$(Y_t \mid Z_t, W_t, \mathbf{X}_{t-1}) \overset{\mathrm{D}}{=} (Y_t \mid Z_t, \mathbf{X}_{t-1}), \quad (14.1.5)$$

which, again, is only of substantial interest if the distribution of $(Z_t | W_t, \mathbf{X}_{t-1})$ depends on W_t. If the invariance in (14.1.5) holds and (Z_t, W_t) are weakly exogenous then Z_t is said to be *super exogenous* for the conditional model of Y_t given Z_t with respect to the intervention W_t.

14.2 A VECTOR AUTOREGRESSIVE MODEL FOR THE FISH MARKET

In Chapters 12 and 13, we developed single-equation models for prices and quantities of whiting sold at the Fulton Fish Market. We will now model these variables simultaneously using the vector autoregressive model. This will facilitate a discussion of a demand and supply model in Chapter 15. First, an unrestricted vector autoregressive model is proposed, and subsequently two types of restrictions will be made, one that preserves the weak exogeneity structure of (14.1.4), and a cross-equation restriction that violates weak exogeneity.

14.2.1 The unrestricted model

The first issue is to consider which regressors to include in the model. The single-equation model for prices in Table 12.1 had a constant and lagged prices p_{t-1} as regressors, whereas the most congruent model for quantities in Table 13.5 had a constant, lagged quantities q_{t-1}, and the dummy variables $stormy_t$ and hol_t as regressors. Initially, all these regressors will be included in both equations. In addition, another weather dummy, $mixed_t$, will be used. This variable, also taken from Angrist et al. (2000), takes the value one when the wave height is greater than 3.8 feet, the wind speed greater than 13 knots, provided $stormy_t$ takes the value 0. By these definitions, it is stormy 31 days and mixed 34 days of the 110 observed days. We will use the notation s_t, m_t, h_t for the three dummy variables.

$$\widehat{p}_t = \underset{(0.28)}{0.10} + \underset{(0.07)}{0.65\,p_{t-1}} - \underset{(0.03)}{0.03\,q_{t-1}} + \underset{(0.06)}{0.25\,s_t} + \underset{(0.05)}{0.14\,m_t} + \underset{(0.14)}{0.09\,h_t}$$
$$\text{se}$$

$$\widehat{q}_t = \underset{(0.72)}{7.63} + \underset{(0.17)}{0.44\,p_{t-1}} + \underset{(0.09)}{0.15\,q_{t-1}} - \underset{(0.15)}{0.57\,s_t} - \underset{(0.14)}{0.25\,m_t} - \underset{(0.37)}{2.02\,h_t}$$
$$\text{se}$$

$$\sqrt{\widehat{\sigma}_{pp}} = 0.24, \quad \sqrt{\widehat{\sigma}_{qq}} = 0.62, \quad \widehat{\rho} = -0.44, \quad \widehat{\ell}_0 = -83.11, \quad T = 110$$

Table 14.1 Model M_0: vector autoregressive model for prices, p_t, and quantities, q_t, of whiting with indicators for weather and public holidays as regressors

Test	$\widehat{p}$	$\widehat{q}$	Test	$(\widehat{p}, \widehat{q})$
$\chi^2_{\text{norm}}[2]$	4.6 [p=0.10]	2.2 [p=0.33]	$\chi^2_{\text{norm}}[4]$	6.9 [p=0.14]
$\chi^2_{\text{skew}}[1]$	4.2 [p=0.04]	2.2 [p=0.14]		
$\chi^2_{\text{kurt}}[1]$	0.4 [p=0.53]	0.0 [p=0.87]		
$F_{\text{ar}(1-2)}[2, 102]$	1.1 [p=0.34]	0.7 [p=0.52]	$F_{\text{ar}(1-2)}[8, 198]$	1.1 [p=0.37]
$F_{\text{arch}(1)}[1, 102]$	0.4 [p=0.54]	1.4 [p=0.23]		
$F_{\text{het}}[6, 97]$	0.5 [p=0.78]	1.0 [p=0.45]	$F_{\text{het}}[18, 269]$	0.7 [p=0.80]

Table 14.2 Mis-specification tests for the vector autoregressive model in Table 14.1

The fitted unrestricted model is reported in Table 14.1 along with formal tests for mis-specification in Table 14.2 and graphical mis-specification analysis in Figure 14.1. In Table 14.2 and Figure 14.1, the only slight problem is some skewness of the residuals in the price equation: the vector versions of the tests reported below are documented in Doornik and Hendry (2006b, §11.9.2). Following the discussion in §9.5, it is appropriate to conduct these tests at a 1% level given the many tests that are performed. This single weak point can, therefore, be ignored, so the model is considered congruent. Similarly, one rejection on each of the 1-step Chow tests in Figure 14.1 is not a cause for concern.

Given the congruence of the model, we can now confidently interpret the equations reported in Table 14.1. Once again, we see that prices today, p_t, are positively correlated with prices yesterday, p_{t-1}, as found in Chapter 12. Today's quantities, q_t, are also positively correlated with lagged prices, p_{t-1}, so if whiting was dear yesterday, there will be a tendency to a larger turnover today. In both equations, lagged quantities, q_{t-1}, are insignificant, and public holidays do not seem to have a significant influence on prices. A more complicated feature is that the ratios of the coefficients for *stormy_t* and *mixed_t* are about the same in both equations. In §14.2.2, these features will be explored in further detail.

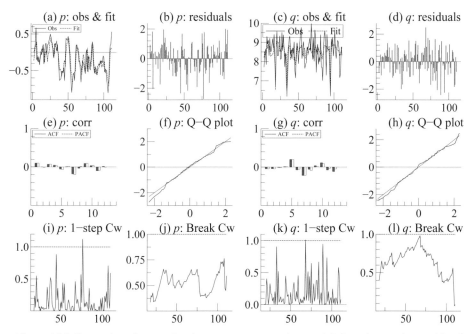

Figure 14.1 Properties of unrestricted vector autoregressive model for prices and quantities from Table 14.2

In §§10.3 and 14.1, it was demonstrated that the likelihood for a bivariate model can be maximized by analyzing the conditional and marginal equations separately; however, it is not enough to analyze the two marginal equations. To emphasize this point, note that the overall maximum of the joint likelihood function is $\widehat{\ell}_0 = -83.11$. The marginal likelihoods associated with the individual equations are:

$$\widehat{\ell}_p = -(T/2)\log(2\pi\widehat{\sigma}_{pp}^2 e) = 5.54,$$
$$\widehat{\ell}_q = -(T/2)\log(2\pi\widehat{\sigma}_{qq}^2 e) = -100.34.$$

Comparing the sum of these with the overall likelihood yields the test statistic:

$$\text{LR}_{independence} = -2\left(\widehat{\ell}_p + \widehat{\ell}_q - \widehat{\ell}_0\right) = 23.38,$$

with p < 0.001 using a $\chi^2[1]$-distribution. This can be viewed as a test for the hypothesis of independence of the innovations in the marginal processes, that is,

$\rho = 0$. This hypothesis can therefore be rejected. Note that the test statistic can be approximated in terms of the squared correlation, $\mathsf{LR} \approx T\widehat{\rho}^2 = 21.3$, as in (5.5.3).

The correlation can be taken into account by looking at, for instance, the conditional model of q_t given p_t, along with the marginal model of p_t. As discussed in §10.3.2, this leads to two separate single-equation models with independent errors, and likelihoods satisfying $\widehat{\ell}_{q|p} + \widehat{\ell}_p = \widehat{\ell}_0$, as in (10.3.5). The estimates of the conditional model are reported in Table 14.3; which is an autoregressive distributed-lag

model with added dummies. The standard error of the conditional equation of q_t given p_t in Table 14.3 is somewhat reduced as compared to that of the marginal equation of q_t in Table 14.1, because of the additional explanatory variable, p_t.

$$\underset{\text{se}}{\widehat{q}_t} = \underset{(0.65)}{7.75} - \underset{(0.23)}{1.15}\,p_t + \underset{(0.08)}{0.11}\,q_{t-1} + \underset{(0.22)}{1.20}\,p_{t-1} - \underset{(0.15)}{0.28}\,s_t - \underset{(0.13)}{0.09}\,m_t - \underset{(0.34)}{1.91}\,h_t$$

$$\sqrt{\widehat{\sigma}^2_{q\cdot p}} = 0.56, \quad \widehat{\ell}_{q|p} = -88.66, \quad T = 110$$

Table 14.3 Conditional autoregressive model for quantities, q_t, of whiting given prices, with indicators for weather and public holidays as regressors

$\chi^2_{\text{norm}}[2]$	$=$	5.1	[p=0.08]	$F_{\text{arch}(1)}[1, 101]$	$=$ 0.1	[p=0.77]
$\chi^2_{\text{skew}}[1]$	$=$	4.8	[p=0.03]	$F_{\text{ar}(1-2)}[2, 102]$	$=$ 1.5	[p=0.22]
$\chi^2_{\text{kurt}}[1]$	$=$	0.3	[p=0.58]	$F_{\text{het}}[8, 94]$	$=$ 1.2	[p=0.30]

Table 14.4 Mis-specification tests for the conditional autoregressive model in Table 14.3.

As a further check on congruency, Table 14.4 shows mis-specification tests for the conditional model. These indicate a potential problem with skewness in the residuals [p = 0.03]. By now, 21 formal tests of the vector autoregressive model have been carried out, of which this outcome is the most extreme. Given the large number of tests, the appropriate testing level is 1%, or even lower, as discussed in §9.5. Thus, we do not take such a finding as evidence against the model.

To illustrate the correlation issue further, Figure 14.2 shows scatterplots of the residuals. Panel (a) shows the residuals from the p_t and q_t equations in Table 14.1, while (b) shows the residuals from the conditional equation for q given p_t in Table 14.3 versus the p_t residuals. The 95% confidence regions are ellipsoids in both cases. In the first case, the axes are a little tilted precisely because of the correlation of the marginal residuals. Ideally about 5–6 observations should fall outside these regions. We see that there are a few more residuals outside these regions than expected, and they tend to be on the left side, which is consistent with the slight skewness observed above.

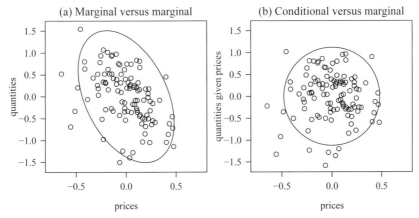

Figure 14.2 Scatterplots of the residuals: (a) using the marginal q_t and p_t equations; (b) using the conditional equation of q_t given p_t and the marginal equation for p_t. In each plot, the estimated 95% confidence regions are indicated

14.2.2 Imposing system restrictions

In the following discussion, system restrictions are considered. The idea is to impose restrictions on the system as a whole by eliminating regressors from all equations in the system. Maximum likelihood analysis is, therefore, still least-squares based.

$$\widehat{p}_t = \underset{(0.04)}{-0.17} + \underset{(0.06)}{0.67}\,p_{t-1} + \underset{(0.06)}{0.25}\,s_t + \underset{(0.05)}{0.14}\,m_t + \underset{(0.14)}{0.12}\,h_t$$
se

$$\widehat{q}_t = \underset{(0.11)}{+8.88} + \underset{(0.17)}{0.37}\,p_{t-1} - \underset{(0.15)}{0.56}\,s_t - \underset{(0.14)}{0.24}\,m_t - \underset{(0.37)}{2.16}\,h_t$$
se

$$\sqrt{\widehat{\sigma}_{pp}} = 0.24, \quad \sqrt{\widehat{\sigma}_{qq}} = 0.63, \quad \widehat{\rho} = -0.45 \quad \widehat{\ell}_1 = -84.74, \quad T = 110$$

Table 14.5 Model M_1: restricted vector autoregressive model, without q_{t-1}

We will first impose the restrictions that the lagged quantity, q_{-1}, is redundant in the system, by eliminating it from each of the marginal equations. Table 14.5 reports the estimated restricted model. The likelihood ratio test statistic is:

$$\mathsf{LR}_{01} = -2\left(\widehat{\ell}_1 - \widehat{\ell}_0\right) = 3.2,$$

with $\mathsf{p} = 0.20$ using a $\chi^2[2]$-distribution, so the restriction cannot be rejected.

Weak exogeneity divides a system into two subsystems, which we can analyze separately. Taking the conditional model of q_t given p_t and the marginal model of p_t as an example, we have by construction that the residuals from these models are uncorrelated, so the two subsystems form unrelated systems. We can, therefore, impose separate restrictions on each of them. Restrictions across the two sets of parameters would violate the weak exogeneity property, in which case we

$$\hat{q}_t = 8.68 - 1.18\,p_t + 1.16\,p_{t-1} - 0.27\,s_t - 0.08\,m_t - 2.01\,h_t$$
$$\text{se} \quad (0.11) \quad (0.23) \quad (0.22) \quad (0.15) \quad (0.13) \quad (0.33)$$

$$\sqrt{\hat{\sigma}_{q\cdot p}^2} = 0.56, \quad \hat{\ell}_{1,q|p} = -89.76, \quad T = 110$$

Table 14.6 Model $M_{1,q|p}$: restricted conditional autoregressive model, without q_{t-1}

$$\hat{p}_t = -0.17 + 0.67\,p_{t-1} + 0.25\,s_t + 0.14\,m_t + 0.12\,h_t$$
$$\text{se} \quad (0.04) \quad (0.06) \quad (0.06) \quad (0.05) \quad (0.14)$$

$$\sqrt{\hat{\sigma}_p^2} = 0.24, \quad \hat{\ell}_{1,p} = 5.03, \quad T = 110$$

Table 14.7 Model $M_{1,p}$: restricted marginal autoregressive model, without q_{t-1}

would need to analyze the full system when maximizing the likelihood. The above hypothesis of eliminating q_{t-1} from both equations has 2 degrees of freedom. We could break it down to two hypotheses of 1 degree of freedom by imposing the restriction on each of the marginal and conditional models. In Table 14.6 this is done for the conditional model. Comparison with the likelihood value for the unrestricted conditional model in Table 14.4 gives:

$$\text{LR}_{01,q|p} = -2\left(\hat{\ell}_{1,q|p} - \hat{\ell}_{q|p}\right) = 2.2,$$

with p $= 0.14$ using a $\chi^2[1]$-distribution, so the hypothesis is not rejected. In Table 14.7 the same has been done for the marginal model, giving:

$$\text{LR}_{01,p} = -2\left(\hat{\ell}_{1,p} - \hat{\ell}_p\right) = 1.0,$$

with p $= 0.32$ using a $\chi^2[1]$-distribution, so this hypotheses cannot be rejected either. This test could be interpreted as a test for strong exogeneity (why?).

Due to weak exogeneity, the likelihood ratio statistics add up: $\text{LR}_{01} = \text{LR}_{01,q|p} + \text{LR}_{01,p}$. If the joint test is conducted at a 5% level, the individual tests should be done at a 2.5% level to be comparable; see (7.6.1).

$$\hat{q}_t = 8.56 - 1.33\,p_t + 1.18\,p_{t-1} - 2.00\,h_t$$
$$\text{se} \quad (0.06) \quad (0.21) \quad (0.22) \quad (0.33)$$

$$\sqrt{\hat{\sigma}_{q\cdot p}^2} = 0.57, \quad \hat{\ell}_{3,q|p} = -91.44, \quad T = 110$$

Table 14.8 Model $M_{3,q|p}$: restricted conditional autoregressive model, without q_{t-1}, s_t, m_t

In Tables 14.6 and 14.7, we see that while the coefficients to the weather variables $stormy_t$, $mixed_t$ are significant in the marginal equation, they appear insignificant in the conditional equation. Due to the weak exogeneity, we can test for the absence of the weather variables in the conditional model. This gives the model reported in Table 14.8. Compared with the conditional model reported in Table 14.6 we then get:

$$\text{LR}_{13,q|p} = -2 \left(\widehat{\ell}_{3,q|p} - \widehat{\ell}_{1,q|p} \right) = 3.3,$$

with $p = 0.19$ using a $\chi^2[2]$-distribution. We can also compute the overall test against the unrestricted conditional model reported in Table 14.3, giving:

$$\text{LR}_{03,q|p} = -2 \left(\widehat{\ell}_{3,q|p} - \widehat{\ell}_{q|p} \right) = 5.6,$$

with $p = 0.14$ using a $\chi^2[3]$-distribution, since the variables q_{t-1}, s_t, m_t have been eliminated. A likelihood for a joint system can also be computed. Due to the weak exogeneity the (conditional) partial likelihood is simply added to the marginal likelihood. Choosing to combine with the marginal model, $\text{M}_{1,p}$, where q_{t-1} is eliminated gives a system where q_{t-1} is eliminated from the entire system and the weather variables $stormy_t$, $mixed_t$ are eliminated from the conditional model, $\text{M}_{3,q|p}$. This gives the model, M_3, reported in Table 14.9, with likelihood:

$$\widehat{\ell}_3 \overset{\text{def}}{=} \widehat{\ell}_{3,q|p} + \widehat{\ell}_{1,p} = -91.44 + 5.03 = -86.41. \qquad (14.2.1)$$

$$\underset{\text{se}}{\widehat{q}_t} = \underset{(0.21)}{-1.33}p_t + \underset{(0.06)}{8.56} + \underset{(0.22)}{1.18}p_{t-1} \qquad\qquad\qquad \underset{(0.33)}{-\ 2.00}h_t$$

$$\underset{\text{se}}{\widehat{p}_t} = \qquad\qquad \underset{(0.04)}{-\ 0.17} + \underset{(0.06)}{0.67}p_{t-1} + \underset{(0.06)}{0.25}s_t + \underset{(0.05)}{0.14}m_t + \underset{(0.14)}{0.12}h_t$$

$$\sqrt{\widehat{\sigma}^2_{q \cdot p}} = 0.57, \quad \sqrt{\widehat{\sigma}^2_p} = 0.24, \quad \widehat{\rho} = 0, \quad \widehat{\ell}_3 = -86.41$$

Table 14.9 Model M_3: restricted joint model, constructed by combining partial model, $\text{M}_{3,q|p}$, for q_t given p_t with marginal model, $\text{M}_{1,p}$, for p_t

14.2.3 Imposing cross-equation restrictions

We noted earlier that the ratios of the coefficients for $stormy_t$ and $mixed_t$ are about the same in the marginal equations in, for instance, Table 14.5. This hypothesis can be tested through a cross-equation restriction. In order to formulate that hypothesis, it is convenient to denote the relevant parameters by $\gamma_{p,s}$, $\gamma_{p,m}$, $\gamma_{q,s}$, $\gamma_{q,m}$ where the indices p and q refer to the price and quantity equations, while s and m refer to the regressors $stormy_t$ and $mixed_t$. The hypothesis of interest can then be expressed in three equivalent ways as:

$$\frac{\gamma_{p,s}}{\gamma_{p,m}} = \frac{\gamma_{q,s}}{\gamma_{q,m}} \quad \text{or} \quad \gamma_{p,s}\gamma_{q,m} = \gamma_{q,s}\gamma_{p,m} \quad \text{or} \quad a = \frac{\gamma_{q,s}}{\gamma_{p,s}} = \frac{\gamma_{q,m}}{\gamma_{p,m}}.$$

In the parlance of matrix algebra, this restriction is called a reduced-rank restriction. To see this, arrange the parameters in a matrix:

$$\mathbf{\Gamma} = \begin{pmatrix} \gamma_{p,s} & \gamma_{p,m} \\ \gamma_{q,s} & \gamma_{q,m} \end{pmatrix} = \begin{pmatrix} \gamma_{p,s} & \gamma_{p,m} \\ a\gamma_{p,s} & a\gamma_{p,m} \end{pmatrix}. \tag{14.2.2}$$

In this way, the restriction can be written as a reduced-rank matrix product:

$$\mathbf{\Gamma} = \begin{pmatrix} 1 \\ a \end{pmatrix} (\gamma_{p,s} \ \gamma_{p,m}).$$

Similarly, the determinant of the matrix $\mathbf{\Gamma}$ is zero (see §6.2.4), namely $\det(\mathbf{\Gamma}) = 0$.

$\widehat{p}_t = \underset{(0.04)}{-0.17} + \underset{(0.06)}{0.67\,p_{t-1}} +$ se	$(\underset{(0.06)}{0.25\,s_t} + \underset{(0.05)}{0.13\,m_t}) + \underset{(0.14)}{0.12\,h_t}$
$\widehat{q}_t = \underset{(0.11)}{+8.89} + \underset{(0.17)}{0.37\,p_{t-1}} - \underset{(0.59)}{2.20} \times$ se	$(\underset{(0.06)}{0.25\,s_t} + \underset{(0.05)}{0.13\,m_t}) - \underset{(0.37)}{2.16\,h_t}$
$\sqrt{\widehat{\sigma}_{pp}} = 0.24, \quad \sqrt{\widehat{\sigma}_{qq}} = 0.62, \quad \widehat{\rho} = -0.44 \quad \widehat{\ell}_2 = -84.88, \quad T = 110$	

Table 14.10 Model M_2: restricted vector autoregressive model, without q_{t-1}, and with a cross-equation restriction on the weather dummies

This reduced-rank hypothesis is a cross-equation restriction that links the parameters of the two equations together. The weak exogeneity property in (14.1.4) therefore fails. The model equations are often said to be *seemingly unrelated regressions* (SUR). Maximum likelihood estimates for this restricted model cannot be obtained by least-squares regression. Instead, a reduced-rank regression technique could be used, although we will not discuss it explicitly here, or a general maximum likelihood numerical optimization could be used as done by PcGive. Table 14.10 shows the estimated model with the reduced-rank restriction imposed. The log-likelihood ratio test statistic against the model of Table 14.5 is:

$$\mathsf{LR}_{12} = -2\left(\widehat{\ell}_2 - \widehat{\ell}_1\right) = 0.3, \tag{14.2.3}$$

with $\mathsf{p} = 0.60$ when compared with a $\chi^2[1]$-distribution.

$\widehat{q}_t = +8.77 + 0.85 p_{t-1} - 1.49 \times (0.25 s_t + 0.13 m_t) - 2.07 h_t + 0.71 p_t$
$\widehat{p}_t = -0.17 + 0.67 p_{t-1} + \qquad (0.25 s_t + 0.13 m_t) + 0.12 h_t$
$\sqrt{\widehat{\sigma}_{q \cdot p}} = 0.56, \quad \sqrt{\widehat{\sigma}_{pp}} = 0.24, \quad \widehat{\rho} = 0 \quad \widehat{\ell}_2 = -84.88, \quad T = 110$

Table 14.11 Model M_2 reformulated (note that this model is not estimated by least squares)

Although the weak exogeneity is lost by the reduced-rank restriction, a conditional model can still be formed. The estimation cannot be done by least-squares regression, but could for instance be computed from the model M_2 in Table 14.10 by subtracting $\widehat{\kappa} = (\widehat{\sigma}_{qq}/\widehat{\sigma}_{pp})^{1/2}\widehat{\rho} = -0.71$ times the marginal p_t equation from the marginal q_t equation as in Exercise 10.8. This gives the results reported in Table 14.11. Weak exogeneity would then be reestablished if the weather dummies s_t, m_t could be eliminated from the partial equation for q_t given p_t, which would in effect make p_t super exogenous for q_t with respect to the variables s_t, m_t. This is precisely what was done in model M_3. Using the likelihood value in (14.2.1) leads to the test statistic:

$$\mathsf{LR}_{23} = -2\left(\widehat{\ell}_3 - \widehat{\ell}_2\right) = 3.1, \tag{14.2.4}$$

with $\mathsf{p} = 0.08$ using a $\chi^2[1]$-distribution. Thus, the joint hypothesis of weak exogeneity and reduced rank cannot be rejected, but the decision is marginal.

14.3 AUTOREGRESSIVE DISTRIBUTED-LAG MODELS

In the presence of weak exogeneity, the system can be separated into a conditional system and a marginal system, as was done for model M_3 in Table 14.9. This is of particular interest when only the parameters of the conditional system are of interest. The situation where the conditional systems is of dimension one, as above, has received special attention in the econometric literature. This gives rise to the autoregressive distributed-lag model first discussed in (14.1.3).

The autoregressive distributed-lag model has the form:

$$Y_t = \beta_1 + \beta_2 Z_t + \beta_3 Y_{t-1} + \beta_4 Z_{t-1} + \epsilon_t, \tag{14.3.1}$$

with the assumptions:

(i) *independence*: $\epsilon_1, \ldots, \epsilon_T$ are mutually independent;
(ii) *normal distribution*: $\epsilon_t \stackrel{\mathsf{D}}{=} \mathsf{IN}[0, \sigma_\epsilon^2]$;
(iii) *weak exogeneity*: Z_t is weakly exogenous;
(iv) *parameter space*: β_1, β_2, β_3, β_4, $\sigma^2 \in \mathbb{R}^4 \times \mathbb{R}_+$.

Equation (14.3.1) has an autoregressive component Y_{t-1} and a distributed-lag component Z_t and Z_{t-1}, so is summarized as ADL(1, 1), where the indices in parentheses refer to the maximum lags of Y and Z respectively. The ADL(1, 1) class generalizes to ADL(r, s) with maximum lags of r and s on Y_t and Z_t. This can be generalized to situations with more than two variables. Nine special cases of ADL(1, 1) dominate the empirical literature, as noted in Doornik and Hendry (2006a).

The error ϵ_t on (14.3.1) is an innovation against the available information, and this serial independence is part of the definition of an ADL($\cdot$) model. Models with autoregressive errors, therefore, are a restriction of the class, and not a generalization (Exercise 14.2). The normality and homoskedasticity assumptions are for convenience. However, weak exogeneity is important if a single-equation partial model is to be the basis for inference. Thus, we briefly address the consequences of a failure of weak exogeneity.

In fact, a weak exogeneity failure does not have a unique implication and can vary from experiencing a small loss of information, when the conditional model can be consistently estimated, to inducing non-constant parameters. The former occurs in a context where the conditional expectation coincides with the estimated regression, but it happens that knowledge of the value of a parameter in the marginal model could have yielded an improved estimate of a related parameter in the conditional model. For example, β_2 in (14.3.1) might also happen to be a parameter of the marginal model, which violates weak exogeneity, but ignoring that link simply leads to a loss of efficiency in estimating β_2. The latter occurs when the conditioning variable is in fact endogenous and has a non-constant marginal distribution, which then contaminates the parameters of the conditional model. For example, Z_t in (14.3.1) might be endogenous because of contemporaneous feedback from Y_t, and its process could well have undergone a shift, in which case the conditional model would also shift. Such a failure is related to the Lucas critique discussed in §20.5. Hendry (1995b) provides several illustrations.

14.4 STATIC SOLUTIONS AND EQUILIBRIUM-CORRECTION FORMS

When a bivariate stochastic process (Y_t, Z_t) is stationary, it has a static, or long-run, solution that corresponds to its expected value (rather than to a long run of time). Rewrite (14.3.1) as:

$$Y_t - \beta_3 Y_{t-1} = \beta_1 + (\beta_2 Z_t + \beta_4 Z_{t-1}) + \epsilon_t. \tag{14.4.1}$$

Under stationarity, let $\mathsf{E}(Z_t) = z^*$ and $\mathsf{E}(Y_t) = y^*$ for all t. These are both constant over time, so taking expectations in (14.4.1):

$$(1 - \beta_3)\,\mathsf{E}(Y_t) = \beta_1 + (\beta_2 + \beta_4)\,\mathsf{E}(Z_t). \tag{14.4.2}$$

Thus, (14.4.2) implies (for $|\beta_3| < 1$):

$$y^* = \frac{\beta_1}{1 - \beta_3} + \left(\frac{\beta_2 + \beta_4}{1 - \beta_3}\right) z^* = \kappa_1 + \kappa_2 z^*. \tag{14.4.3}$$

Autoregressive distributed-lag models are seen to have linear static solutions with proportionality between y^* and z^* if $\kappa_1 = 0$. Many economic theories have log-linear long-run equilibrium solutions, so we can mimic those in the autoregressive distributed-lag class. The concept of equilibrium in (14.4.3) is that of "no inherent tendency to change", so any deviation $(y^* - \kappa_1 - \kappa_2 z^*) \neq 0$ is a disequilibrium, which should induce a change in the process Y_t in a later time period.

A one–one transformation of (14.3.1), which highlights the long-run behavior arising from the lag structure, is to reexpress that equation in terms of growth rates of Y_t and Z_t along with an equilibrium relation involving the lagged levels of the process. This is derived in a few steps. First, subtracting Y_{t-1} from both sides of (14.3.1) and using $\Delta Y_t = (Y_t - Y_{t-1})$ for the growth rate of Y_t yields:

$$\Delta Y_t = \beta_1 + \beta_2 Z_t + (\beta_3 - 1)\,Y_{t-1} + \beta_4 Z_{t-1} + \epsilon_t.$$

Next, adding and subtracting $\beta_2 Z_{t-1}$ on the right-hand side gives:

$$\Delta Y_t = \beta_1 + \beta_2 \Delta Z_t + (\beta_3 - 1) Y_{t-1} + (\beta_2 + \beta_4) Z_{t-1} + \epsilon_t. \qquad (14.4.4)$$

Under the assumption that $\beta_3 \neq 1$, we can collect the level terms as follows:

$$\begin{aligned}
\Delta Y_t &= \beta_2 \Delta Z_t + (\beta_3 - 1) \left(Y_{t-1} + \frac{\beta_1}{\beta_3 - 1} + \frac{\beta_2 + \beta_4}{\beta_3 - 1} Z_{t-1} \right) + \epsilon_t \\
&= \beta_2 \Delta Z_t + (\beta_3 - 1) (Y_{t-1} - \kappa_1 - \kappa_2 Z_{t-1}) + \epsilon_t. \qquad (14.4.5)
\end{aligned}$$

From the last line of (14.4.5), the immediate impact of a change in Z_t on Y_t is β_2. Even when ϵ_t and ΔZ_t are zero for a prolonged period, then ΔY_t will differ from zero until $Y_t = \kappa_1 + \kappa_2 Z_t$, matching the earlier interpretation of $(y^* - \kappa_1 - \kappa_2 z^*)$ as a disequilibrium. How rapidly ΔY_t converges to zero, which is the equilibrium outcome under stationarity, depends on the magnitude of $(\beta_3 - 1)$. The formulation (14.4.5) is sometimes said to be in error-correction form, however, the notion *equilibrium-correction form* describes the correction of disequilibriums more aptly.

When the process (Y_t, Z_t) is non-stationary, the relation $Y_t - \kappa_1 - \kappa_2 Z_t$ can still have an interpretation as a long-run relation between Y_t and Z_t. This is important in many macroeconomic applications and will be explored further in Chapter 17.

As an example, we could look at the conditional model for quantities given prices, $\mathsf{M}_{3,q|p}$, in Table 14.8. The equilibrium-correction form is:

$$\Delta q_t = \underset{(0.21)}{-1.33} \Delta p_t - (q_{t-1} - \underset{(0.15)}{0.15} p_{t-1} - \underset{(0.06)}{8.56}) - \underset{(0.33)}{2.00} h_t, \qquad \widehat{\sigma}_{q\cdot p} = 0.57,$$

where the new standard errors have been obtained by reestimating the model with Δp_t replacing p_{t-1} as regressor. The insignificance of p_{t-1} suggests that prices are only relevant for quantities in the short run.

14.5 SUMMARY AND EXERCISES

Summary: The vector autoregressive model is a generalization of the bivariate normal model to a time-series context. As economic models often involve several "endogenous" variables, such a system approach is often useful. Weak exogeneity was presented as the time-series equivalent of strong exogeneity. It ensures that a conditional regression remains maximum likelihood within a bivariate normal framework. Such a correspondence breaks down with cross-equation restrictions.

Bibliography: Reduced-rank regression can be expressed effectively only in terms of matrix algebra: derivations can be found in inter alia Anderson (1984, Chapter 12) or Johansen (1995, Chapter 6). The development of this technique dates back to Hotelling (1936) and Bartlett (1938), while Anderson (1951) derived the asymptotic theory for the estimators in the cross-sectional case.

Key questions:

- What is the role of weak exogeneity?
- Discuss situations where weak exogeneity does not hold.
- Contrast the notions of system restrictions and cross-equation restrictions.
- Discuss the validity of the assumptions of the various models presented.

Exercise 14.1. *Consider the conditional equation (14.1.3). Express the parameters in terms of the parameters of the vector autoregressive equations (14.1.1), (14.1.2). Hint: use the arguments of either of Exercises 10.1 or 10.8.*

Exercise 14.2. *Consider the regression equation $Y_t = \alpha_1 + \alpha_2 Z_t + u_t$ with autocorrelated errors $u_t = \rho u_{t-1} + \epsilon_t$ where $\epsilon_t \overset{D}{=} \mathrm{IN}[0, \sigma_\epsilon^2]$. Show that the equation can be written on the form (14.3.1), but where the parameters of (14.3.1) are not unrestricted.*

Computing Task 14.3. *Reproduce the empirical results given in this chapter. Use the "time-series" category of PcGive for "multiple equation dynamic model":*
(a) For Tables 14.1 to 14.8 estimate as "unrestricted system" and click "test summary" in the test menu. Store residuals using the test menu for Figure 14.2.
(b) For Table 14.10, estimate a "constrained simultaneous equations model" and enter the restriction (14.2.2) in the restrictions menu.
(c) Compute Table 14.11 by hand as PcGive does not implement covariance restrictions.

Computing Task 14.4. *Apply the model $q_t = \alpha_1 + \alpha_2 p_t + u_t$ for the Fulton Fish Market data.*
(a) Estimate the model using PcGive and consider the mis-specification tests.
(b) The heteroskedasticity and autocorrelation corrected standard errors discussed in section 13.3.3 can be found by choosing the option "further output" in the "test menu".
(c) Discuss the outcome and validity of this approach in the light of the models estimated in this chapter as well as Exercise 14.2.

Chapter Fifteen

Identification of structural models

Economic theory provides models developed from general principles of economic behavior, which are mainly concerned with entities that are not observable. While an overview of behavioral models was given in §11.3.5, we will now work more actively at analyzing such behavioral models econometrically. We will focus on the classic *demand and supply* model.

The demand and supply model describes how prices and quantities are settled according to the buyers' demand curve and the dealer's supply curve. In reality, we will observe the actual trades where buyers and sellers have agreed on a price and a quantity, but rarely (outside of an experimental setting) the demand curves and supply curves themselves. If we want to learn about a demand curve, therefore, we must match the economic model with the econometric model. A key aspect of this match is known as the *identification problem*, where we have to identify the parameters of an economic model (often called *structural*) from those of an econometric model (often called a *reduced form*).

In Chapter 14, we derived a two-equation model for prices and quantities of whiting at the Fulton Fish Market. This model will now serve as a reduced-form model. We will list a few structural models and discuss to what extent we can identify the demand functions of these models from the reduced-form model. Three different variations of the model are considered in order to introduce the notions of *under-identified, exactly-identified* and *over-identified* structural equations. At first, the exposition focuses on the principles of identifying structural parameters from a reduced-form system; then single-equation approaches are discussed. The choice of language here is historical but far from optimal, as the so-called reduced-form system can be more general than the simultaneous model from which it is supposedly derived. Thus, the simultaneous model is often obtained by reductions imposed on the (reduced-form) system.

15.1 UNDER-IDENTIFIED STRUCTURAL EQUATIONS

In the following, a simple demand and supply model is introduced as an illustration of a model where we cannot identify the demand function.

15.1.1 The structural model

We will consider a *demand function* where the log quantity, q_d, which specifies buyers' demand, is a linear function of possible log prices. In a similar way, the *supply function* specifies that the dealer's supplied log quantity, q_s, is a linear function of possible log prices, p. These functions are behavioral equations of the form:

Demand function: $q_d = b_d + a_d p$,   where $a_d < 0$,

Supply function: $q_s = b_s + a_s p$,   where $a_s > 0$.   (15.1.1)

The structural parameters are denoted by Roman letters b_d, a_d, b_s, a_s, reserving the usual Greek letters for reduced-form models. We interpret the intercepts as the quantities demanded and supplied at a zero price, while the slopes indicate the decrease and the increase, respectively, for a unit increase in price. Buyers and dealers will need to agree on the price and quantity at which they are willing to transact. This gives the equilibrium, or clearing, condition:

Equilibrium condition : $q_d = q_s$.

In formulating this structural model, we make the following type of assumptions:

(a) the correct variables are included in the model (15.1.1);

(b) the functional form is linear;

(c) market clearing occurs;

(d) the parameters of (15.1.1) are constants.

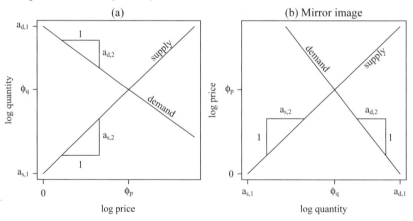

Figure 15.1 Linear demand and supply functions: quantities versus prices and vice versa

Given the values of the a-parameters, the equilibrium can be found by solving the above three linear equations. The clearing, or equilibrium, price, φ_p, and equilibrium quantity, φ_q, are therefore:

$$\varphi_p = \frac{b_s - b_d}{a_d - a_s}, \qquad \varphi_q = \frac{a_d b_s - b_d a_s}{a_d - a_s}.$$ (15.1.2)

Figure 15.1 illustrates the demand and supply functions and the equilibrium point.

In most situations, we cannot observe these demand and supply functions, but only the actual trades that occur when dealers and buyers agree on price and quantity. While trades will provide information about the equilibrium price, φ_p, and quantity, φ_q, the relations in (15.1.2) show that φ_p and φ_q are complicated functions of the structural parameters b_d, a_d, b_s, and a_s. If we knew the structural parameters, we would be able to compute φ_p and φ_q, but knowing φ_p and φ_q does not enable us to compute the structural parameters. Thus, the parameters φ_p and φ_q are onto, or surjective, functions of the structural parameters. The demand and supply functions of this model, therefore, cannot be *identified* uniquely from observations made at the fish market, and we say that they are *under-identified*. This lack of identification occurs even though the model is non-stochastic.

Another way of realizing that the structural equations are under-identified is the following. This argument focuses on the conditions $a_d < 0$ and $a_s > 0$, which are insufficient for identification. To see this, multiply the supply equation by a positive number λ, and add this new equation to the demand equation, giving:

$$(1 + \lambda)q = (b_d + \lambda b_s) + (a_d + \lambda a_s)p.$$

We can choose λ so that the new slope coefficient $a_d + \lambda a_s$ is negative. The equation then satisfies the conditions set up for demand equations above. In this way the demand and supply model can be manipulated to give a continuum of different functions with negative slope, so we are unable to identify one particular function as *the* demand function.

15.1.2 A stochastic extension

If the structural model above were to be taken to data like the whiting data set, with observations $(p_1, q_1), \ldots (p_T, q_T)$, it would be reasonable to make a stochastic extension of the model. This could come about by including a demand shock u_d and a supply shock u_s, giving the equations:

Demand function:	$q_{d,t} = b_d + a_d p_t + u_{d,t},$	where $a_d < 0$,
Supply function:	$q_{s,t} = b_s + a_s p_t + u_{s,t},$	where $a_s > 0$,
Equilibrium condition:	$q_{d,t} = q_{s,t}.$	

Due to the temporal element we modify the structural assumption (c) as:

(c') market clearing occurs in each period;

and add a distributional assumption for the shocks: $u_{d,t}$, $u_{s,t}$ like:

(e) the shocks are independently, normally distributed: $(u_{d,t}, u_{s,t}) \stackrel{D}{=} \mathsf{IN}_2[\mathbf{0}, \mathbf{\Omega}]$.

As above, these extended model equations can be solved to find equations for p, q:

$$p_t = \varphi_p + \epsilon_{p,t},$$
$$q_t = \varphi_q + \epsilon_{q,t}.$$

These equations describe the distributions of the observed equilibrium values of p_t and q_t resulting from actual trades. Since the structural equations are not directly described by these equations, they are said to define a *reduced-form* model. As its parameters are unrestricted it is also referred to as an *unrestricted reduced-form* model.

The equilibrium (φ_p, φ_q) was found in (15.1.2), while the shocks satisfy:

$$\epsilon_{p,t} = \frac{u_{s,t} - u_{d,t}}{a_d - a_s}, \qquad\qquad \epsilon_{q,t} = \frac{a_d u_{s,t} - u_{d,t} a_s}{a_d - a_s}, \qquad (15.1.3)$$

$$u_{d,t} = \epsilon_{q,t} - a_d \epsilon_{p,t}, \qquad\qquad u_{s,t} = \epsilon_{q,t} - a_s \epsilon_{p,t}. \qquad (15.1.4)$$

It is seen that the stochastic extension does not alter the under-identified nature of the structural model formulation.

Taking this reduced-form model to a data set like the fish data set, with observations $(p_1, q_1), \ldots (p_T, q_T)$, we would make assumptions like:

(i)   *independence*: $(\epsilon_{p,1}, \epsilon_{q,1}), \ldots, (\epsilon_{p,T}, \epsilon_{q,T})$ are mutually independent;

(ii) *normal distribution*: $(\epsilon_{p,t}, \epsilon_{q,t}) \overset{\mathrm{D}}{=} \mathsf{N}_2[\mathbf{0}, \boldsymbol{\Sigma}]$;

(iii) *parameter space*: $\varphi_p, \varphi_q \in \mathbb{R}^2$ and $\boldsymbol{\Sigma}$ is an unrestricted covariance matrix.

The reduced-form assumptions are implied by the structural assumptions, so that if the reduced-form assumptions fail, the structural assumptions fail. The reduced-form assumptions are testable as laid out in Chapters 9 and 13. If, for instance, the normality assumption fails, then the structural normality assumption (e) would fail. Even if the reduced-form assumptions were satisfied, however, we would still not be able to test the structural assumptions (a)–(e) directly.

15.1.3 Analysis using matrix algebra

Matrix algebra is rather helpful for thinking about identification. The structural model in §15.1.2 can be written in matrix form as:

$$\begin{pmatrix} -a_d & 1 \\ -a_s & 1 \end{pmatrix} \begin{pmatrix} p_t \\ q_t \end{pmatrix} = \begin{pmatrix} b_d \\ b_s \end{pmatrix} + \begin{pmatrix} u_{d,t} \\ u_{s,t} \end{pmatrix},$$

or in matrix notation:

$$\mathbf{A}\mathbf{Y}_t = \mathbf{B} + \mathbf{u}_t.$$

The reduced-form model is then given by:

$$\mathbf{Y}_t = \mathbf{A}^{-1}(\mathbf{B} + \mathbf{u}_t),$$

and the above expression is then calculated, noting that by (6.2.1):

$$\mathbf{A}^{-1} = \frac{1}{\det(\mathbf{A})} \begin{pmatrix} 1 & -1 \\ a_s & -a_d \end{pmatrix} \qquad \text{where} \qquad \det(\mathbf{A}) = a_s - a_d.$$

15.1.4 Empirical example

A well-specified unrestricted reduced-form model for the Fulton Fish Market data was reported in Table 14.5. It is reproduced in Table 15.1.

$$
\begin{aligned}
p_t &= \underset{(0.04)}{-0.17} + \underset{(0.06)}{0.67\,p_{t-1}} + \underset{(0.06)}{0.25\,s_t} + \underset{(0.05)}{0.14\,m_t} + \underset{(0.14)}{0.12\,h_t}, \\[-2pt]
\text{se}& \\[4pt]
q_t &= \underset{(0.11)}{+8.88} + \underset{(0.17)}{0.37\,p_{t-1}} - \underset{(0.15)}{0.56\,s_t} - \underset{(0.14)}{0.24\,m_t} - \underset{(0.37)}{2.16\,h_t} \\[-2pt]
\text{se}&
\end{aligned}
$$

Table 15.1 M_1: reduced-form model taken from Table 14.5

Since the reduced-form model in Table 15.1 contains the additional variables p_{t-1}, s_t, m_t, h_t, the assumptions of the structural model in §15.1.2 cannot be satisfied. We will therefore have to extend the structural model to make progress:

$$q_t = b_d + a_d p_t + b_{d,p} p_{t-1} + b_{d,s} s_t + b_{d,m} m_t + b_{d,h} h_t + u_{d,t}, \qquad (15.1.5)$$
$$q_t = b_s + a_s p_t + b_{s,p} p_{t-1} + b_{s,s} s_t + b_{s,m} m_t + b_{s,h} h_t + u_{s,t}, \qquad (15.1.6)$$

where clearing has been imposed so $q_{d,t} = q_{s,t} = q_t$, and the signs of the slopes are $a_d < 0$, $a_s > 0$. In formulating this structural model, we make the following type of assumptions:

(a) the correct variables are included in the model (15.1.5), (15.1.6);

(b) the functional form is linear;

(c) market clearing occurs in each period;

(d) the parameters are constant;

(e) the shocks are independently, normal: $(u_{d,t},\ u_{s,t}) \overset{\mathsf{D}}{=} \mathsf{N}_2[\mathbf{0}, \mathbf{\Omega}]$;

(f) the regressors s_t, m_t, h_t are weakly exogenous for the parameters.

Since the demand and supply functions are not directly observable, the assumptions of type (a)–(d) for the structural model are untestable. Given these assumptions, then (e) matches the normality assumption of the reduced-form model. The exogeneity assumption (f) can be addressed at least within the reduced-form model, which is a conditional model, given the dummy variables s_t, m_t, h_t. These variables are very likely to be strongly exogenous, and hence also weakly exogenous: the weather and the public holidays are most unlikely to be influenced by the buyers and the dealer. The assumptions (a)–(f) are untestable; only the derived assumptions for the reduced-form model can be tested.

Although the shocks in the model given by (15.1.5), (15.1.6) have the same names as in the model in §15.1.2, they are somewhat different. The demand shocks in (15.1.5) are assumed normal. If the dummy variables, s_t, m_t, h_t were absorbed into the shocks as in $\widetilde{u}_{d,t} = b_{d,s} s_t + b_{d,m} m_t + b_{d,h} h_t + u_{d,t}$, the demand equation would have the same appearance as in §15.1.2. Due to the binary nature of the dummy variables, the shocks $\widetilde{u}_{d,t}$ cannot be normally distributed; hence, they are different from the shocks in §15.1.2.

The reduced-form model derived from the extended structural model is:

$$p_t = \varphi_p + \varphi_{p,p} p_{t-1} + \gamma_{p,s} s_t + \gamma_{p,m} m_t + \gamma_{p,h} h_t + \epsilon_{p,t}, \qquad (15.1.7)$$

$$q_t = \varphi_q + \varphi_{q,p} p_{t-1} + \gamma_{s,s} s_t + \gamma_{s,m} m_t + \gamma_{s,h} h_t + \epsilon_{q,t}, \qquad (15.1.8)$$

which matches the form of the empirical, congruent model. The parameters of these equations are functions of the parameters of the structural equations. The intercept parameters φ_p and φ_q and the reduced-form errors $\epsilon_{p,t}$ and $\epsilon_{q,t}$ relate to b_d, a_d, b_s, a_s, and $u_{d,t}$ and $u_{s,t}$ *exactly* as described in (15.1.2) and (15.1.3). Corresponding relations can be found for the remaining parameters. By the same argument as in §15.1.1 the demand and supply functions are both under-identified. To find the reduced-form model using matrix algebra as in §15.1.3, use the same $\mathbf{A}$ and $\mathbf{u}$, and let $\mathbf{B}$ denoted the (2×5)-matrix of b-parameters in (15.1.5), (15.1.6).

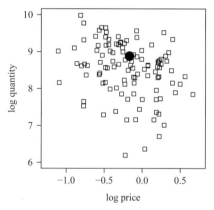

Figure 15.2 Quantities and prices with estimated equilibrium point

While the demand and supply functions are both under-identified, the equilibrium point is directly estimated by the reduced-form model. Due to the lagged dependent variable, p_{t-1}, and the weakly exogenous variables s_t, m_t, h_t, the equilibrium point will move around from day to day. For a day where these variables are zero, the equilibrium point can be estimated by the two intercepts: $(\widehat{\varphi}_p, \widehat{\varphi}_q) = (-0.17, 8.88)$. Figure 15.2 shows a scatterplot of the observed quantities and prices along with the observed equilibrium point.

The extension of the structural model to include lagged prices is important for the above analysis. In that way, we are able to match the temporal dependence found in the data, so we know that the structural model is not directly contradicted by the data. It does, however, complicate the interpretation of the structural model. We will return to that point in the next section.

15.2 EXACTLY-IDENTIFIED STRUCTURAL EQUATIONS

A structural model for which we can identify the demand function can be constructed by working more actively with the parameters of the additional regressors in the structural equations (15.1.5) and (15.1.6).

15.2.1 The structural model

A plausible modification of the simple deterministic structural model in §15.1.1 is that the weather at sea where the fish are caught will directly affect only the supply function and not the demand function. For simplicity, we will measure the weather by a binary variable w taking the value zero if the weather at sea is fair and unity if it rough. This gives:

Demand function:	$q_d = b_d + a_d p,$
Supply function:	$q_s = b_s + a_s p + b_{s,w} w,$
Equilibrium condition:	$q_d = q_s,$

with the parameters satisfying $a_d < 0$, $a_s > 0$ as before, while $b_{s,w} < 0$, so rough weather at sea has a negative impact on supply. Comparing with the earlier models, two additional assumptions are needed:

(g) the supply function shifts parallel to q_s by $b_{s,w} \neq 0$ if the weather changes;
(h) the demand function does not change with the weather.

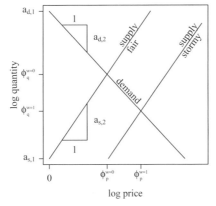

Figure 15.3 Linear demand and supply functions: the supply function now depends on the weather

As illustrated in Figure 15.3, the new model has two equilibrium points depending on the weather at sea. When the weather is fair, the equilibrium is given by $\varphi_p^{w=0}$, $\varphi_q^{w=0}$; and when it is rough, it changes to $\varphi_p^{w=1}$, $\varphi_q^{w=1}$. Since two points on the linear demand function are now known, the demand parameters b_d and a_d can be uniquely determined by the line going through the two points. We will be able to identify these points. The structural assumption that the curve going through these points is linear, and indeed the demand function, will, however, remain untestable.

In fair weather, $w = 0$, the model reduces to the model in §15.1.1, so:

$$\varphi_p^{w=0} = \varphi_p, \qquad \varphi_q^{w=0} = \varphi_q,$$

defines the equilibrium point, where (φ_p, φ_q) are the coordinates calculated in (15.1.2). When the weather is rough, $w = 1$, the model has the same appearance as in §15.1.1, but with b_s replaced by $b_s + b_{s,w}$. This implies:

$$\varphi_p^{w=1} = \varphi_p + \gamma_{p,w}, \qquad \varphi_q^{w=1} = \varphi_q + \gamma_{q,w},$$

where the formula (15.1.2), with b_s replaced by $b_s + b_{s,w}$ gives:

$$\gamma_{p,w} = \frac{b_{s,w}}{a_d - a_s}, \qquad \gamma_{q,w} = \frac{a_d b_{s,w}}{a_d - a_s}. \tag{15.2.1}$$

These are both non-zero under the above assumptions about a_d, a_s, $b_{s,w}$.

We can now find the line going through these points. Its slope, as a function of p, is given by the ratio $\delta = \gamma_{q,w}/\gamma_{p,w}$, as $\gamma_{p,w} \neq 0$, whereas the intercept is given by $\varphi_q - \delta\varphi_p$. As we are assuming that this *is* the demand function, we say that the demand function has been *identified*.

Indeed, we find that:

$$a_d = \frac{\gamma_{q,w}}{\gamma_{p,w}}, \qquad b_d = \varphi_q - a_d\varphi_p. \tag{15.2.2}$$

The inclusion of the variable w in the structural model with a zero restriction in the demand function is instrumental for the identification. Thus, w is said to be an *instrument* for identifying the demand function. The changes in w translate into changes in the equilibrium price and quantity. In such a situation, there is a uniquely defined line through the equilibrium points, and we say the demand function is *exactly-identified*. The supply function of this model is under-identified as before. While the binary nature of the instrument is expositionally convenient, the same argument could be made for continuous variables.

15.2.2 Estimating an exactly-identified demand function

In the empirical analysis, we will work with the reduced-form system from Table 15.1. As pointed out before, this is a congruent model.

The theory derived above allows for a single variable as an instrument, although a more flexible theory will be introduced in §15.3 below. There are actually two weather-related variables, $stormy_t$ and $mixed_t$, in the reduced-form system, so we will have to make a choice. In the first instance, $stormy_t$ is chosen as the instrument, since the effect on supply is likely to be most important when the weather is worst. The other weather variable, $mixed_t$, is left as an unrestricted regressor. We will therefore impose the identifying restriction $b_{d,s} = 0$ on the demand function (15.1.5). The structural model given by (15.1.5), (15.1.6) then becomes:

$$q_t = b_d + a_d p_t + b_{d,p} p_{t-1} \qquad\qquad + b_{d,m} m_t + b_{d,h} h_t + u_{d,t}, \tag{15.2.3}$$

$$q_t = b_s + a_s p_t + b_{s,p} p_{t-1} + b_{s,s} s_t + b_{s,m} m_t + b_{s,h} h_t + u_{s,t}, \tag{15.2.4}$$

where again $a_d < 0$, $a_s > 0$, $b_{s,w} < 0$. Structural assumptions of the types (a)–(h) listed in §§15.1.4 and 15.2.1 are assumed to hold.

Solving the structural equations for q_t and p_t yields the reduced-form model:

$$p_t = \varphi_p + \varphi_{p,p} p_{t-1} + \gamma_{p,s} s_t + \gamma_{p,m} m_t + \gamma_{p,h} h_t + \epsilon_{p,t}, \qquad (15.2.5)$$
$$q_t = \varphi_q + \varphi_{q,p} p_{t-1} + \gamma_{s,s} s_t + \gamma_{s,m} m_t + \gamma_{s,h} h_t + \epsilon_{q,t}, \qquad (15.2.6)$$

from which we will be able to identify the demand function (15.2.3). First, however, it is important to note that this reduced-form model is identical to the reduced-form model (15.1.7), (15.1.8), which we derived from the under-identified structural model, so the estimates of the above reduced-form model are once again those of Table 15.1. From an empirical point of view, we are therefore not able to distinguish between the under-identified model given by (15.1.5), (15.1.6) and the model with an exactly-identified demand function given by (15.2.3), (15.2.4). A choice between those two structural models has to be based on an economic theory-based belief about which model is right.

Turning to the issue of identifying the demand function, we can use the approach of §15.2.1. Using the formulas in (15.2.2), we have:

$$a_d = \frac{\gamma_{q,s}}{\gamma_{p,s}}, \qquad b_d = \varphi_q - a_d \varphi_p, \qquad (15.2.7)$$

and correspondingly:

$$b_{d,p} = \varphi_{q,p} - a_d \varphi_{p,p}, \quad b_{d,m} = \gamma_{q,m} - a_d \gamma_{p,m}, \quad b_{d,h} = \gamma_{q,h} - a_d \gamma_{p,h}. \quad (15.2.8)$$

The variance of the demand equation can also be identified through a somewhat tedious calculation in Exercise 15.4. Inserting the estimates from Table 15.1, we get, for instance, the demand slope $\widehat{a}_{d,p} = (-0.56)/(0.25) = -2.2$. The overall estimated demand equation is reported in Table 15.2.

$\widehat{q}_t =$	8.50	$- 2.24\, p_t$	$+ 1.87\, p_{t-1}$	$+ 0.07\, m_t$	$- 1.88\, h_t,$	$\sqrt{\widehat{\omega}_{dd}} = 0.61$
se	(0.08)	(0.60)	(0.48)	(0.13)	(0.37)	

Table 15.2 Estimated demand function of exactly-identified model: based on M_1

The estimators of this equation are maximum likelihood estimators, as they are derived from the maximum likelihood estimators of the reduced-form system. The demand slope estimate, for instance, comes about in the following steps. Defining the residuals $X_{(s \cdot 1, p, m, h), t}$ from regressing s_t on p_{t-1}, h_t, m_t and an intercept, we can compute the least-squares estimators:

$$\widehat{\gamma}_{p,w} = \frac{\sum_{t=1}^{T} p_t X_{(s \cdot 1, p, m, h), t}}{\sum_{t=1}^{T} X_{(s \cdot 1, p, m, h), t}^2}, \qquad \widehat{\gamma}_{q,w} = \frac{\sum_{t=1}^{T} q_t X_{(s \cdot 1, p, m, h), t}}{\sum_{t=1}^{T} X_{(s \cdot 1, p, m, h), t}^2}.$$

The maximum likelihood estimator for the demand slope is then:

$$\widehat{a}_{d,p} = \frac{\widehat{\gamma}_{q,w}}{\widehat{\gamma}_{p,w}} = \frac{\sum_{t=1}^{T} q_t X_{(s \cdot 1, p, m, h), t}}{\sum_{t=1}^{T} p_t X_{(s \cdot 1, p, m, h), t}}, \qquad (15.2.9)$$

which is not a least-squares estimator, but is referred to as an *indirect least-squares* (ILS) estimator (see §15.5.3). It can be shown that the t-statistics found from dividing estimators by their standard errors will not be exactly t-distributed. The estimators are approximately normal distributed with a complicated formula for the standard errors. These are, however, readily available from econometric software (see §15.5.2). In finite samples, the normal approximation can be poor. This applies in particular in the case where the denominator in (15.2.9) is close to zero. Normalized by T, this denominator is approximately the conditional covariance of the instrumented endogenous variable p_t and the instrument s_t given the other variables. When that covariance is close to zero, we say s_t is a *weak instrument*.

$$\underset{\text{se}}{\widehat{\Delta q_t}} = -(q_{t-1} + \underset{(0.21)}{0.37} p_{t-1} - \underset{}{8.50}) - \underset{(0.60)}{2.24} \Delta p_t + \underset{(0.13)}{0.07} m_t - \underset{(0.37)}{1.88} h_t$$

Table 15.3 Exactly-identified demand function in equilibrium-correction form

For the interpretation of the demand equation in Table 15.2, it is convenient to write it in equilibrium-correction form as in §14.4. This results in the demand function reported in Table 15.3. The long-run relation, $q = 8.50 - 0.37 p_t$, shows that the long-run demand is inelastic since 1% rise in the price level only gives a 0.4% fall in the quantity demanded. This long-run inelasticity could be real or it could be an artefact of the data, in that no alternative goods are included, and with the data running from December to May only half an annual cycle is covered, and any seasonal variation is not addressed. In the short run, the demand is elastic since a 1% change in prices results in a 2.2% fall in demand. This elasticity is just about significantly different from unity. The negative impact on Δq from a holiday is substantial at -1.88. The coefficients to $mixed_t$ and the lagged price p_{t-1} do not appear significant. We will return to that issue in §15.3. Figure 15.4 shows the demand function for a day where the regressors p_{t-1}, m_t, h_t are all set to zero, so that the slope matches the short-run elasticity of -2.2.

Although the assumptions underlying the structural model cannot be tested, it is certainly worth thinking about them. It is perhaps easiest to consider assumptions (g)–(h) concerning the instruments. The importance of the weather at sea can hardly be in doubt: serious storms at sea reduce catches. A major question will be whether the instrument is valid in the sense of entering the supply function but not the demand function. We could attempt a counter story that the weather at sea is closely related to the weather on the shore, which in turn affects the demand. If that story were true, the changes in weather at sea would move both the demand function and the supply of fish, and we would not be able to identify the demand

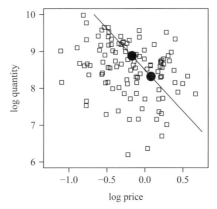

Figure 15.4 Quantity and price with estimated demand function

function. It is then up to economic judgment whether there could be some associ-ation between the weather and demand. Compared with other studies of structural models, that association is probably rather weak, which in turn suggests that in this situation Graddy (1995) and Angrist et al. (2000) have found a good instrument.

15.2.3 Identification using matrix algebra

To find the reduced-form model using matrix algebra as in §15.1.3, use the same $\mathbf{A}$ and $\mathbf{u}$, and let $\mathbf{B}$ denote the (2×5)-matrix of b-parameters in (15.2.3), (15.2.4), and let $\mathbf{X}_t$ be the five exogenous variables: $(1, p_{t-1}, s_t, m_t, h_t)'$, including the intercept with a slight abuse of terminology. The structural equation then becomes $\mathbf{A}\mathbf{Y}_t = \mathbf{B}\mathbf{X}_t + \mathbf{u}_t$. Multiplying through by $\mathbf{A}^{-1}$, we note that:

$$\mathbf{\Gamma}_s = \begin{pmatrix} \gamma_{p,s} \\ \gamma_{s,s} \end{pmatrix} = \mathbf{A}^{-1} \begin{pmatrix} 0 \\ b_{s,s} \end{pmatrix} = \frac{-1}{\det(\mathbf{A})} \begin{pmatrix} 1 \\ a_d \end{pmatrix} b_{s,s},$$

showing that a_d can be identified from $\mathbf{\Gamma}_s$. The other demand parameters can be identified as follows. Let $\mathbf{\Gamma} = \mathbf{A}^{-1}\mathbf{B}$ be the matrix of φ- and γ-parameters. Then the demand parameters satisfy $\mathbf{B}_d = (1,0)\mathbf{B} = (1,0)\mathbf{A}\mathbf{\Gamma}$. Since $(1,0)\mathbf{A}$ is identified, the demand function is identified.

15.3 OVER-IDENTIFIED STRUCTURAL EQUATIONS

Rather than working with one instrument, such as *stormy* or *mixed*, models can be constructed with several instruments. This can lead to over-identification, which can be used for testing structural models.

15.3.1 The structural model

Allowing two weather dummies, s, m, instead of just one, w, extends the structural model of §15.2.1 to:

Demand function:	$q_{d,t} = b_d + a_d p_t \qquad\qquad + u_{d,t},$
Supply function:	$q_{s,t} = b_s + a_s p_t + b_{s,s} s + b_{s,m} m + u_{s,t},$
Equilibrium condition:	$q_{d,t} = q_{s,t}.$

The assumptions of this model are of the same type as we have seen before.

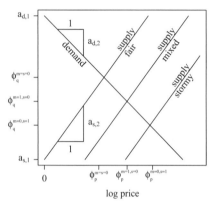

Figure 15.5 Linear demand and supply functions: the supply function now depends on whether the weather at sea is fair, mixed, or stormy

Figure 15.5 illustrates that this model has three different equilibrium points depending on the weather. The equilibrium points have the coordinates:

fair :	$\varphi_p^{m=s=0} = \varphi_p,$		$\varphi_q^{m=s=0} = \varphi_q,$
mixed :	$\varphi_p^{m=1,s=0} = \varphi_p + \gamma_{p,m},$		$\varphi_q^{m=1,s=0} = \varphi_q + \gamma_{q,m},$
stormy :	$\varphi_p^{m=0,s=1} = \varphi_p + \gamma_{p,s},$		$\varphi_q^{m=0,s=1} = \varphi_q + \gamma_{q,s},$

where the parameters φ_p, φ_q were defined in (15.1.2) and the γ-parameters are defined as in (15.2.1) as:

$$\gamma_{p,s} = \frac{b_{s,s}}{a_d - a_s}, \qquad \gamma_{p,m} = \frac{b_{s,m}}{a_d - a_s},$$

$$\gamma_{q,s} = \frac{a_d b_{s,s}}{a_d - a_s}, \qquad \gamma_{q,m} = \frac{a_d b_{s,m}}{a_d - a_s}.$$

Note, that the γ-parameters satisfy the restriction:

$$a_d = \frac{\gamma_{q,s}}{\gamma_{p,s}} = \frac{\gamma_{q,m}}{\gamma_{p,m}}. \qquad (15.3.1)$$

This restriction arises from the linearity assumption of the demand function. As we need only two points to determine a line, but have three points, we say that the demand function is *over-identified*, since we now have two instruments, s and m, for the demand function. In the empirical analysis, this results in a testable restriction, which was formulated as a reduced-rank restriction in §14.2.3:

$$\mathbf{\Gamma}_{s,m} = \begin{pmatrix} \gamma_{p,s} & \gamma_{p,m} \\ \gamma_{q,s} & \gamma_{q,m} \end{pmatrix} = \begin{pmatrix} \gamma_{p,s} & \gamma_{p,m} \\ a_d\gamma_{p,s} & a_d\gamma_{p,m} \end{pmatrix} = \begin{pmatrix} 1 \\ a_d \end{pmatrix} (\gamma_{p,s}, \gamma_{p,m}).$$

Over-identification does, however, not entail a unique identification. We saw in §15.2.2 that two different structural models can have the same reduced-form model. The examples of two such structural models were an under-identified model and a model with an exactly-identified demand function. In the same way, we can find an under-identified model that has precisely the same reduced-form as the above over-identified model:

Demand function: $q_{d,t} = b_d + a_d p_t + c\,(b_s s + b_m m) + u_{d,t},$

Supply function: $q_{s,t} = b_s + a_s p_t + \ \ (b_s s + b_m m) + u_{s,t},$

Equilibrium condition: $q_{d,t} = q_{s,t}.$

The interpretation is that the demand and the supply function respond proportionally to the weather, as illustrated in Figure 15.6. When $c = 0$, the over-identified model arises, and we say that s and m are *valid instruments*. The reduced-form model once again has a reduced-rank restriction:

$$\mathbf{\Gamma}_{s,m} = \begin{pmatrix} \gamma_{p,s} & \gamma_{p,m} \\ \gamma_{q,s} & \gamma_{q,m} \end{pmatrix} = \begin{pmatrix} 1 - c \\ a_d - a_s c \end{pmatrix} (\gamma_s, \gamma_m).$$

It is not possible to test the restriction $c = 0$ and in this way uniquely identify the model. Although the test for the hypothesis that the reduced-form parameter $\mathbf{\Gamma}_{s,m}$ has reduced rank is referred to as a test for over-identifying restrictions, it can be used for refuting both of the above models, but not for distinguishing between the over-identified and the under-identified model.

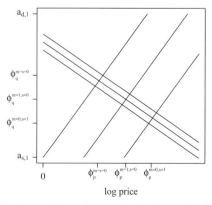

Figure 15.6 Linear demand and supply functions: both the demand and the supply function respond
proportionally to the weather at sea

15.3.2 Estimating an over-identified demand function

A restricted reduced-form model for the Fulton Fish Market data was reported in Table 14.10. It is reproduced in Table 15.4. Here the reduced-rank restriction is imposed. The unrestricted model was shown to be well specified in §14.2, whereas the test for the reduced-rank restriction reported in (14.2.3) could not be rejected.

$$p_t = \underset{(0.04)}{-0.17} + \underset{(0.06)}{0.67} p_{t-1} + \underset{(0.14)}{0.12} hol_t + \qquad (\underset{(0.06)}{0.25} s_t + \underset{(0.05)}{0.13} m_t),$$
$$\underset{\mathrm{se}}{}$$

$$q_t = \underset{(0.11)}{+8.89} + \underset{(0.17)}{0.37} p_{t-1} - \underset{(0.37)}{2.16} hol_t - \underset{(0.59)}{2.20} \times (\underset{(0.06)}{0.25} s_t + \underset{(0.05)}{0.13} m_t)$$
$$\underset{\mathrm{se}}{}$$

Table 15.4 M_2: Restricted reduced-form model taken from Table 14.10

A natural stochastic extension of the structural model of §15.3.1 is therefore:

$$q_t = b_d + a_d p_t + b_{d,p} p_{t-1} + b_{d,p} h_t \qquad\qquad + u_{d,t}, \quad (15.3.2)$$
$$q_t = b_s + a_s p_t + b_{s,p} p_{t-1} + b_{s,p} h_t + b_{s,s} s_t + b_{s,m} m_t + u_{s,t}, \quad (15.3.3)$$

where $a_d < 0$, $a_s > 0$, $a_{s,s} < a_{s,m}$ and $a_{s,s} < 0$, and structural assumptions of the types (a)–(h) listed in §15.1.4 and §15.2.1 are assumed to hold. Solving the structural equations delivers the desired reduced-form system:

$$p_t = \varphi_p + \varphi_{p,p} p_{t-1} + \quad (\gamma_{p,s} s_t + \gamma_{p,m} m_t) + \gamma_{p,h} h_t + \epsilon_{p,t}, \quad (15.3.4)$$
$$q_t = \varphi_q + \varphi_{q,p} p_{t-1} + \alpha(\gamma_{p,s} s_t + \gamma_{p,m} m_t) + \gamma_{q,h} h_t + \epsilon_{q,t}. \quad (15.3.5)$$

which matches the empirical model above. The demand slope is the ratio of the coefficients of the instruments in the two reduced-form equations, thus:

$$a_d = \alpha. \qquad\qquad (15.3.6)$$

The other demand parameters are then identified precisely as in (15.2.7), (15.2.8):

$$b_d = \varphi_q - \alpha\varphi_p, \quad b_{d,p} = \varphi_{q,p} - \alpha\varphi_{p,p}, \quad b_{d,h} = \gamma_{q,h} - \alpha\gamma_{p,h}. \qquad (15.3.7)$$

The maximum likelihood estimate for the demand function is reported in Table 15.5 and rewritten in equilibrium-correction form in Table 15.6. The estimated demand function is rather similar to what was found in the exactly-identified case.

The over-identification imposes a reduced-rank restriction on the reduced-form system. By testing that reduced-rank, or over-identifying, restriction we have a possibility of falsifying the model. In (14.2.3) the likelihood ratio test statistic for this over-identifying restriction was found to be LR = 0.3 with p = 0.60, showing that the over-identified model cannot be rejected. Had it been rejected this would have been evidence against the structural model, which has two, rather than just one, instruments to identify the demand equation. The likelihood ratio test is often approximated by the Sargan (1964) specification test.

$$q_t = \underset{(0.07)}{8.52} - \underset{(0.59)}{2.20} p_t + \underset{(0.48)}{1.84} p_{t-1} - \underset{(0.36)}{1.89} h_t, \qquad \sqrt{\widehat{\omega}_{dd}} = 0.61$$
se

Table 15.5 Estimated demand function of over-identified model: based on M_2

$$\widehat{\Delta q_t} = -(q_{t-1} + \underset{(0.21)}{0.36} p_{t-1} - 8.52) - \underset{(0.07)}{2.20} \Delta p_t - \underset{(0.59)}{1.89} hol_t$$
se

Table 15.6 Over-identified demand function in equilibrium-correction form

Figure 15.7 shows the three equilibrium prices for fair, mixed, and stormy weather, for a day where $hol_t = 0$ and $p_{t-1} = 0$. In general, three points will not lie on a straight line, but the over-identifying reduced-rank restriction imposes that they do, and the resulting straight line is the estimated demand function.

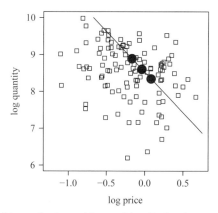

Figure 15.7 Quantities and prices with over-identified estimate of demand function

15.4 IDENTIFICATION FROM A CONDITIONAL MODEL

In the previous sections we identified the structural model from the reduced-form system. In special cases, however, it is possible to identify a structural equation, like the demand equation, directly from a conditional model. Super exogeneity of p_t is needed to get that property. In the following we will first follow the super exogeneity argument through and then discuss the so-called simultaneity bias, which arises when estimating from a conditional model in the absence of super exogeneity.

15.4.1 Super exogeneity and identification

A model for the conditional distribution of quantities given prices can be derived from the reduced-form system, such as the one given by (15.3.4), (15.3.5), in the over-identified case. This will facilitate a discussion of weak exogeneity and, hence, of super exogeneity.

Recalling that reduced-form errors were assumed $\mathsf{N}_2[\mathbf{0}, \Sigma]$-distributed, or:

$$\begin{pmatrix} \epsilon_{p,t} \\ \epsilon_{q,t} \end{pmatrix} \overset{\mathsf{D}}{=} \mathsf{N}_2 \left[\begin{pmatrix} 0 \\ 0 \end{pmatrix}, \begin{pmatrix} \sigma_{pp} & \sigma_{pq} \\ \sigma_{qp} & \sigma_{qq} \end{pmatrix} \right],$$

we find the conditional equation as in §10.2.2 or Exercise 10.8 by subtracting $\kappa = \sigma_{qp}/\sigma_{pp}$ times the p_t equation from the q_t equation giving the transformed system:

$$q_t = \varphi_{q \cdot p} + \varphi_{q \cdot p, p} p_{t-1} + (\alpha - \kappa)(\gamma_{p,s} s_t + \gamma_{p,m} m_t) + \varphi_{q \cdot p, h} h_t + \kappa p_t + \epsilon_{q \cdot p, t},$$

$$p_t = \varphi_p + \varphi_{p,p} p_{t-1} + \quad\quad (\gamma_{p,s} s_t + \gamma_{p,m} m_t) + \quad \gamma_{p,h} h_t + \epsilon_{p,t},$$

where the errors $\epsilon_{q \cdot p, t}, \epsilon_{p,t}$ are independent because of the conditioning, and:

$$\varphi_{q \cdot p} = \varphi_q - \kappa \varphi_p, \quad \varphi_{q \cdot p, p} = \varphi_{q,p} - \kappa \varphi_{p,p}, \quad \varphi_{q \cdot p, h} = \varphi_{q,h} - \kappa \varphi_{p,h}. \quad (15.4.1)$$

In this rewritten system p_t is not weakly exogenous for the conditional model, since the parameters $\gamma_{p,s}, \gamma_{p,m}$ enter both equations. Weak exogeneity can, however, be obtained by the restriction $\kappa = \alpha$, in which case the system reduces to:

$$q_t = \varphi_{q \cdot p} + \varphi_{q \cdot p, p} p_{t-1} \quad\quad\quad\quad\quad + \varphi_{q \cdot p, h} h_t + \kappa p_t + \epsilon_{q \cdot p, t}, \quad (15.4.2)$$

$$p_t = \varphi_p + \varphi_{p,p} p_{t-1} + \gamma_{p,s} s_t + \gamma_{p,m} m_t + \quad \gamma_{p,h} h_t + \epsilon_{p,t}. \quad (15.4.3)$$

The parameters of these equations are freely varying, so p_t is weakly exogenous for the parameters of the conditional model for q_t given p_t. This argument can be made formally along the lines of §10.1. Moreover, the parameters of the demand function are precisely those of the conditional equation: the slope parameter q_t equals α as in (15.3.6), and also the other structural parameters can be found directly from the conditional equation, which is seen by comparing (15.4.1) and (15.3.7). Since p_t is weakly exogenous, it will also be super exogenous for the demand function with respect to the intervention given by the instruments s_t, m_t; see (14.1.5).

The super exogeneity hypothesis, $\kappa = \alpha$, was investigated, empirically, in §14.2.3. The restricted model given by (15.4.2), (15.4.3) was then called M_3. The likelihood ratio test for the super exogeneity hypothesis was reported in (14.2.4), that is:

$$\mathsf{LR}_{23} = -2\left(\widehat{\ell}_3 - \widehat{\ell}_2\right) = 3.1,$$

with $p = 0.08$ using a $\chi^2[1]$-distribution, showing that the hypothesis cannot be rejected, although the decision is marginal. This likelihood ratio test is often approximated by the so-called Hausman (1978) specification test, building on Durbin (1954). A regression form of that test includes the residuals $\widehat{\epsilon}_{p,t}$ from the reduced-form equation (15.4.3) in the conditional equation (15.4.2), and it is then tested whether these residuals can be omitted.

The restricted conditional model with super exogeneity imposed was reported in Table 14.8 and reformulated in equilibrium-correction form in Table 15.7. The coefficient of Δp_t is quite different from what was previously seen, and in particular it is no longer significantly different from unity. We will return to this issue in the discussion of simultaneity bias in §15.4.2 below. Indeed eliminating p_{-1} and restricting the coefficient to Δp_t to unity, as reported in Table 15.8, is not rejected using the test statistic:

$$\mathsf{LR}_{34,q|p} = -2 \left(\widehat{\ell}_{4,q|p} - \widehat{\ell}_{3,q|p} \right) = 2.7,$$

with p $= 0.26$ using a $\chi^2[2]$-distribution.

$$\underset{\text{se}}{\widehat{\Delta q_t}} = -(q_{t-1} + \underset{(0.15)}{0.15}\,p_{t-1} - \underset{}{8.56}) - \underset{(0.21)}{1.33}\,\Delta p_t - \underset{(0.33)}{2.00}\,h_t$$

$$\sqrt{\widehat{\sigma}^2_{q\cdot p}} = 0.57, \quad \widehat{\ell}_{3,q|p} = -91.44, \quad T = 110$$

Table 15.7 $\mathsf{M}_{3,q|p}$: model of Table 14.8 in equilibrium-correction form

$$\underset{\text{se}}{\widehat{\Delta q_t}} = -(q_{t-1} - \underset{(0.05)}{8.58}) - \Delta p_t - \underset{(0.33)}{2.05}\,h_t$$

$$\sqrt{\widehat{\sigma}^2_{q\cdot p}} = 0.57, \quad \widehat{\ell}_{3,q|p} = -92.78, \quad T = 110$$

Table 15.8 $\mathsf{M}_{4,q|p}$: equilibrium-correction model with coefficients of p_{t-1} and Δp_t restricted

15.4.2 Simultaneity bias

In §15.4.1 we saw that a structural equation can be estimated from a conditional model if the endogenous variables are weakly exogenous. If weak exogeneity fails, standard regression analysis will lead to biased estimates. This is referred to as *Simultaneity bias*

Estimating a conditional model like (15.4.2) will, under general assumptions, provide a consistent estimate for the conditional relationship of quantities given prices and the information set $\mathcal{I}_t$ representing the variables p_{t-1}, h_t, s_t, m_t, and the intercept. In particular, the estimator $\widehat{\kappa}$ will be consistent for the parameter:

$$\kappa = \frac{\sigma_{qp}}{\sigma_{pp}} = \frac{\mathsf{Cov}\,(q_t, p_t \mid \mathcal{I}_t)}{\mathsf{Var}\,(p_t \mid \mathcal{I}_t)},$$

which is the population regression coefficient from regressing quantities on prices given the various regressors. Replacing q_t by the demand equation (15.3.2) gives:

$$\kappa = \frac{\mathsf{Cov}\,(b_d + a_d p_t + b_{d,p} p_{t-1} + b_{d,h} h_t + u_{d,t}, p_t \mid \mathcal{I}_t)}{\mathsf{Var}\,(p_t \mid \mathcal{I}_t)}.$$

Apart from p_t and $u_{d,t}$, all terms are constant given $\mathcal{I}_t$, so this reduces to:

$$\kappa = a_d + \frac{\mathsf{Cov}\,(u_{d,t}, p_t \mid \mathcal{I}_t)}{\mathsf{Var}\,(p_t \mid \mathcal{I}_t)} = a_d + \frac{\mathsf{Cov}\,(u_{d,t}, \epsilon_{p,t} \mid \mathcal{I}_t)}{\mathsf{Var}\,(\epsilon_{p,t} \mid \mathcal{I}_t)},$$

where the second term arises by inserting the reduced-form expression for prices in (15.3.4). If prices are uncorrelated with the (unobserved) demand shocks, the second terms vanish, so we are left with κ being equal to the demand slope a_d, and regression will be consistent. If prices are correlated with the demand shocks, we would perhaps expect this correlation to be negative since larger quantities supplied should lead to lower prices.

To get more of a handle on the bias term in the demand and supply model, we can insert the expression for the demand shock in (15.1.4) giving:

$$\frac{\mathsf{Cov}\,(u_{d,t}, \epsilon_{p,t} \mid \mathcal{I}_t)}{\mathsf{Var}\,(\epsilon_{p,t} \mid \mathcal{I}_t)} = \frac{\mathsf{Cov}\,(\epsilon_{q,t} - a_d \epsilon_{p,t}, \epsilon_{p,t} \mid \mathcal{I}_t)}{\mathsf{Var}\,(\epsilon_{p,t} \mid \mathcal{I}_t)}$$

$$= \frac{\sigma_{qp} - a_d \sigma_{pp}}{\sigma_{pp}} = \frac{\kappa \sigma_{pp} - a_d \sigma_{pp}}{\sigma_{pp}} = \kappa - a_d.$$

We see that there is no simultaneity bias if p_t is weakly exogenous.

In the study of the Fulton Fish Market, we saw, precisely, a large negative effect on the demand slope when moving from the estimates in Table 15.6 to the estimates with weak exogeneity imposed in Table 15.8. On the one hand, the test for weak exogeneity in (14.2.4) was marginal, giving some reason to believe that the regression estimate in Table 15.8 suffers from a simultaneity bias. On the other hand, the systems estimate in Table 15.6 is a complicated non-linear function of the data, so while it is consistent, a bias could arise in small samples due to the non-linearity.

15.5 INSTRUMENTAL VARIABLES ESTIMATION

Throughout this chapter, we have worked with various levels of identification of the demand function but have never actually identified the supply function. It turns out that the result depends only on certain aspects of the under-identified supply function. This property was discovered early in the history of econometrics and led to the development of a series of instrumental variables based regression estimators for structural equations. These methods are computationally simple, which was an important property at a time of limited computing power. We will start by noting the important aspects of the under-identified supply function, then review instrumental variables methods.

15.5.1 The specification of the under-identified structural equation

In §15.2.1 we analyzed a demand function of the type:

$$q_t = b_d + a_d p_t + u_{d,t}. \tag{15.5.1}$$

The supply function was specified as:

$$q_t = b_s + a_{d,s} p_t + b_{p,w} w_t + u_{d,t}.$$

We could actually have chosen any linear "supply function" of the form:

$$c_q q_t + c_p p_t = c + c_w w_t + v_t, \tag{15.5.2}$$

where the instrument has a non-zero coefficient, $c_w \neq 0$, and where the relationship between the endogenous variables, q_t, p_t, in the demand and "supply" functions are linearly independent, so $c_p + a_d c_q \neq 0$. An example would be the reduced-form equation for p_t or for q_t. After modifying the calculations in §15.2.1, it is seen that the reduced-form system will be of the same type with an intercept changing with w_t. While the reduced-form parameters will depend on both the demand and the "supply" parameters, the identified structural parameters will be precisely of the same form (15.2.2) as before (see Exercise 15.5). This indicates that it is not necessary to specify the supply function, and it suffices to justify that the "supply function" is of the form (15.5.2). We will review methods exploiting this finding.

In matrix notation, we can write the "structural" model as:

$$\begin{pmatrix} -a_d & 1 \\ c_p & c_q \end{pmatrix} \begin{pmatrix} p_t \\ q_t \end{pmatrix} = \begin{pmatrix} b_d & 0 \\ c & c_w \end{pmatrix} \begin{pmatrix} 1 \\ w_t \end{pmatrix} + \begin{pmatrix} u_{d,t} \\ u_{s,t} \end{pmatrix}.$$

The usual $\mathbf{A}$-matrix has now changed. The condition for linear independence between demand and "supply" function is simply that $\det(\mathbf{A}) \neq 0$, so $\mathbf{A}$ is invertible. The identification of the demand function is done precisely as before. To identify the supply function, therefore, at least one variable is needed to shift the demand function without entering the supply function, which would thereby provide the relevant instrument(s) for estimation.

15.5.2 Full-information maximum likelihood estimation

The maximum likelihood approach we have followed above is often called *full-information maximum likelihood* (FIML) estimation in the context of structural models. The approach begins with formulating the reduced-form system, by modeling the joint distribution of the endogenous variables, as was done for q and p_t in Chapter 14. The structural model is then formulated and identified. Any over-identifying restrictions can be imposed and tested at this stage.

In a program like PcGive, this approach is followed through a set of menus. First, the joint distribution is modeled using the "multiple-equation dynamic modeling" class. There are various graphical and statistical tools to test the congruence of the model as reviewed in Chapter 13. The structural model is then formulated using the "constrained simultaneous equations system" model setting. In the demand and supply example, two structural models need to be formulated. The first one would be the identified demand function, and the other could be any equation of the form (15.5.2), with a reduced-form equation as default. The second equation should contain the instrument(s), while the first should not. If more than one instrument has been specified, Sargan's test for over-identification, which approximates (14.2.3), will be reported. The routine is described in Doornik and Hendry (2006b) (§13 and in particular, §13.7). As a by-product of this approach, standard errors of estimates are reported.

In applications, one will typically be working with a larger number of structural equations than just two, and identify more than just one equation. With the higher dimensionality of such problems, it is harder to determine whether structural equations are identified. Computer programs like PcGive can determine the degree of identification numerically. This can also be worked out analytically. Two matrix algebraic criteria known as the *order-condition* and the *rank-condition* can help determine the degree of identification.

In a situation with two over-identified structural equations, the reduced-form matrix will contain two reduced-rank matrices. Full-information maximum likelihood methods will in that case have to be based on numerical optimization algorithms, which are already coded in software like PcGive. Alternatively, the problem can be solved by *limited-information maximum likelihood* (LIML) estimation, in which only one equation is estimated at the time. The chosen equation is then treated as over-identified, and the other equation is replaced by a reduced-form equation. In this case, the reduced-rank regression approach with its analytic expressions can be used, but the method is not a proper maximum likelihood method.

15.5.3 Two-stage least-squares estimation

The estimators for the slope of the identified demand equations found in §§15.2.2 and 15.3.2 can be approximated using two single-equation regressions, using the so-called *two-stage least-squares* (2SLS) approach. In general this will not give maximum likelihood estimators, but this estimator will be consistent. The advantage of this approach is that only the identified structural equation and the instruments are formulated. The step of estimating the reduced-form system is then avoided, but, of course, it will be impossible to tell whether the reduced-form system is congruent.

In the demand and supply function, the two-stage least-squares approach works as follows. It is specified that:

Demand function:	$q_{d,t} = b_d + a_d p_t + b_{d,p} p_{t-1} + b_{d,h} h_t + u_{d,t},$
Endogeneous variables:	$q_t, \; p_t,$
Instruments:	$s_t, \; m_t,$

where the demand shocks are assumed independent $N[0, \omega_{dd}]$-distributed. This formulation implicitly assumes that the "supply function" is of the form (15.5.2), and that the structural system satisfies assumptions like (a)–(h). The two-stage least-squares approach is then as follows:

First stage: Regress the endogenous regressor, p_t, on all the regressors in the reduced form: that is, the constant, the unrestricted regressors p_{t-1}, h_t, and the instruments, s_t, m_t. Keep the predictor $\hat{p}_t$ for p_t.

Second stage: Replace p_t by $\hat{p}_t$ in the demand equation and estimate this modified demand equation by regression.

In the case where only one additional instrument is chosen, the demand function will be exactly-identified. In that case, the two-stage least-squares estimator is called an *indirect least-squares* (ILS) estimator, and it is identical to the maximum likelihood estimator in (15.2.9); see Exercise 15.6. It can be shown that the two-stage least-squares estimator is consistent and approximately normally distributed in cross-sectional as well as stationary time-series models. Most econometric software can compute these estimators, along with standard errors, tests for over-identifying restrictions, and mis-specification tests applied directly to the residuals from the estimated demand function.

Table 15.9 reports two-stage least-squares estimation of the over-identified demand equation for the Fulton Fish Market. These estimates are seen to be only slightly different from the maximum likelihood estimates in Table 15.5. The difference between the two methods tends to increase with the number of instruments.

$$\hat{q}_t = 8.52 - 2.19 p_t + 1.83 p_{t-1} - 1.89 \, hol_t$$
$$\text{se} \quad (0.07) \quad (0.59) \quad (0.47) \quad (0.36)$$
$$\sqrt{\hat{\sigma}^2} = 0.61, \qquad T = 110, \qquad \text{no likelihood}$$

Table 15.9 Instrumental variables estimation of an over-identified demand function with p_t as the endogenous regressor and s_t, m_t as instruments

15.6 SUMMARY AND EXERCISES

Summary: Economic models often describe behavioral objects like a demand function or a supply function. This is usually called a structural model. The economic data describe actual outcomes, like the observed clearing price. A reduced-form econometric model seeks to describe the sample distribution of such data. The problem of identification is to match the structural model with the reduced-form model. Three cases are seen: under-identification; just- or exact-identification; and over-identification. A variety of estimation methods is described for such settings.

The empirical illustration of the past few chapters has been the demand for whiting using weather variables as instruments. While these instruments are binary, there are many situations in which continuous instruments are more appropriate. All the econometric techniques discussed above carry through to the continuous case.

Bibliography: The struggle to understand the joint issues of identification, simultaneity, and partial correlations—all of which play key roles above—is one of the major epics of econometrics, with many researchers contributing. Hendry and Morgan (1995) record that history and reprint many of the seminal papers. A lot of research has been undertaken on instrumental variables estimation methods for higher-dimensional systems. Hendry (1995a, Chapter 11) discusses an "estimator-generating equation" that provides an overview of all these methods. A recent exposition of instrumental variables estimation can be found in Wooldridge (2002).

Key questions:

- Discuss the difference between structural and reduced-form models.
- What roles do each of the assumptions (a)–(h) play in the formulation of a structural model?
- To what extent can the assumptions of a structural model be tested?

Exercise 15.1. *Verify the solution (15.1.2).*

Exercise 15.2. *Consider the demand and supply model in section 15.2.1. Prove that the supply equation is under-identified.*

Exercise 15.3. *Consider the structural model given in section 15.1.2. Define:*

$$\Omega = \begin{pmatrix} \omega_{dd} & \omega_{ds} \\ \omega_{sd} & \omega_{ss} \end{pmatrix}, \qquad \Sigma = \begin{pmatrix} \sigma_{pp} & \sigma_{pq} \\ \sigma_{qp} & \sigma_{qq} \end{pmatrix}, \qquad D = \frac{1}{a_s - a_d}.$$

Show that:
(a) $\sigma_{pp} = D^2(\omega_{dd} - 2\omega_{ds} + \omega_{ss})$.
(b) $\sigma_{pq} = D^2\{a_s\omega_{dd} - (a_s + a_d)\omega_{ds} + a_d\omega_{ss}\}$.
(c) $\sigma_{qq} = D^2(a_s^2\omega_{dd} - 2a_sa_d\omega_{ds} + a_d^2\omega_{ss})$.
(d) The covariance expressions for the identified models in section 15.2.2 and section 15.3.2 are the same.

Exercise 15.4. *Consider the structural model given by (15.2.3), (15.2.4), along with the expressions for Σ in Exercise 15.3. Show that the demand variance is identified by:* $\omega_{dd} = \sigma_{qq} - 2a_d\sigma_{pq} + a_d^2\sigma_{pp}$.

Exercise 15.5. *Consider the structural model given by (15.5.1), (15.5.2):*

$$q_t = b_d + a_d + u_{d,t}, \qquad c_q q_t + c_p p_t = c + c_w w_t + v_t,$$

so $c_w \neq 0$ *and* $c_p + a_d c_q \neq 0$*. Show that:*
(a) *The demand function is exactly-identified.*
(b) *The demand parameters relate to the reduced-form parameters as in (15.2.2).*

Exercise 15.6. *Show that the indirect least-squares estimator of* $a_{d,2}$ *described in section 15.5.3 is identical to the maximum likelihood estimator in section 15.2.2.*

Exercise 15.7. * *Consider the structural model given by (15.2.3), (15.2.4), with the additional* **covariance restriction** *that* $\omega_{ds} = \mathsf{Cov}(u_{d,t}, u_{s,t}) = 0$*. Show that:*
(a) *The demand function is exactly-identified.*
(b) *Use Exercise 15.4 to identify* ω_{dd}*.*
(c) *Use Exercise 15.3 to identify* ω_{ss} *from* σ_{pp}*.*
(d) *Use Exercise 15.3 to identify* a_s *from* σ_{pq}*.*
(e) *Express the supply parameters in terms of the reduced-form parameters.*

Exercise 15.8. *Consider the structural model:*

Demand:	$q_t^d = b_d + a_d p_t + b_{d,p} p_{t-1} + u_{d,t},$	$a_d < 0,$
Supply:	$q_t^s = b_s + a_s p_t + b_{s,q} q_{t-1}^d + u_{s,t},$	$a_s > 0, b_{s,q} > 0,$
Equilibrium:	$q_t^d = q_t^s.$	

(a) *Would you expect the sign of* $b_{d,p}$ *to be negative or positive?*
(b) *Show that both equations are exactly-identified.*
(c) * *Suppose* $\omega_{ds} = \mathsf{Cov}(u_{d,t}, u_{s,t}) = 0$*. Use Exercise 15.7 to show that the system is over-identified.*

Computing Task 15.9. *Table 15.9 is based on two-stage least-squares regression. Reproduce this by estimating the two regressions separately.*

Chapter Sixteen

Non-stationary time series

Many economic time series are better described as non-stationary than stationary, although the growth rates of such non-stationary time series are often closer to being stationary. In the following, we will look more closely at this type of non-stationarity, which is fundamental in modern macro-econometrics.

This chapter is organized by first describing properties of some economic time series in §16.1. The statistical analysis of the first-order autoregressive model is reviewed in §16.2 and then applied to a time series for UK total expenditure in §16.3. The properties of non-stationary time series with stationary increments are discussed in §16.4, while inference concerning such processes follows in §16.5.

16.1 MACROECONOMIC TIME-SERIES DATA

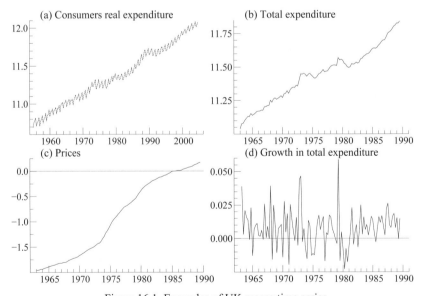

Figure 16.1 Examples of UK macro time series

Figure 16.1 reports examples of some quarterly macroeconomic time series for the UK: (a) log consumers real expenditure, (b) log real total final expenditure (denoted x_t), (c) log prices, px_t, measured by the total final expenditure deflator, and (d) the change in log total final expenditure, Δx_t.

When considering a time-series graph, a first characteristic is the scale of the data. We see that x_t rose by about $\exp(0.8) = 2.2$-fold over the period 1963 to 1989, while prices rose about $\exp(2.25) = 9.5$-fold. Another notable difference is the shape of the graphs, varying from the very smooth price series to the marked seasonality pattern in the consumption series, and to a highly varying growth rate. The growth rate appears similar to the time series for prices and quantities of whiting in Figures 12.1(b) and 13.2(b), while the other three series are more trending, which we will describe by a higher degree of temporal dependence.

Correlograms and partial correlograms are helpful tools for describing the temporal dependence of time series. Chapter 12 noted that econometric and statistical software rarely report these, but rather compute covariograms and partial covariograms. For time series like prices and quantities of whiting, which can be described as stationary, there is not much difference between correlograms and covariograms, but for trending variables, more care is needed. This is illustrated in Figure 16.2, showing all four functions for log expenditure and for log prices from panels (b) and (c) in Figure 16.1.

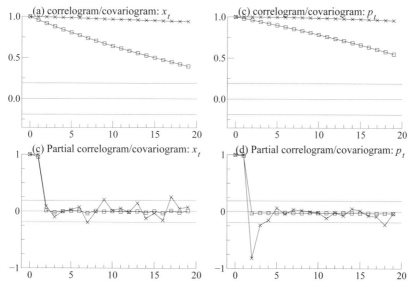

Figure 16.2 Correlograms and partial correlograms are shown with crosses; covariograms and partial covariograms are shown with boxes

For the log-expenditure series, the correlogram indicates strong temporal dependence, while the partial correlogram suggests that the second-order partial correlation is zero, so a first-order autoregression can be used to describe the temporal dependence. The covariogram and partial covariogram in panels (a) and (c) tell approximately the same story, although the temporal dependence shown in the covariogram is less pronounced than in the correlogram.

For the log-price series, the appearances of the correlogram and the covariogram in panel (b) are more or less like those for the log-expenditure series, despite the smoother and more persistent appearance of the log-price series There is, however, a remarkable difference for the partial correlogram and the partial covariogram in panel (d), with the former suggesting dependence of up to third order and the latter first-order dependence. If an autoregressive model was used to describe the data, lags of up to third order would probably be needed. The covariogram and partial covariograms are therefore harder to interpret. If we did interpret them as correlograms and partial correlograms, we would be led to think that this series could be described as a stationary first-order autoregression, which does not match the data, since this price series is even more trending than the UK expenditure series. More formally, the confidence intervals shown in the figure relate to the correlograms and partial correlograms, and cannot be used for the covariograms and partial covariograms; for a more detailed discussion, see Nielsen (2006). These features become even more extreme when considering exponentially rising data, such as log prices collected from hyper-inflation periods. In that case, the covariogram can be exponentially declining as for a stationary series.

16.2 FIRST-ORDER AUTOREGRESSIVE MODEL AND ITS ANALYSIS

In the following, we will review the first-order autoregressive model and the likelihood analysis as presented in Chapter 12. The simplest case without deterministic terms, like a constant, is discussed first.

The data set we have in mind is given by $X_0, \ldots, X_T$, where for simplicity $X_0 = 0$. The model is then given by the autoregressive equation:

$$X_t = \alpha X_{t-1} + \epsilon_t. \tag{16.2.1}$$

The conditional statistical model for the innovations given the initial value, $X_0 = 0$, is defined by:

(i) *independence*: $\epsilon_1, \ldots, \epsilon_T$ are independent;
(ii) *distribution*: $\epsilon_t \overset{\mathrm{D}}{=} \mathsf{N}[0, \sigma^2]$;
(iii) *parameter space*: $\alpha, \sigma^2 \in \mathbb{R} \times \mathbb{R}_+$.

In the interpretation presented in §12.6, assumption (c) that $|\alpha| < 1$ was needed for stationarity, although that assumption was not actually used when formulating the likelihood function nor maximizing it.

In line with (12.4.2) and Exercise 12.3, the log-likelihood function is:

$$\ell_{X_1, \ldots, X_T | X_0}(\alpha, \sigma^2) = -\frac{T}{2} \log\left(2\pi\sigma^2\right) - \frac{1}{2\sigma^2} \sum_{t=1}^{T} (X_t - \alpha X_{t-1})^2.$$

This likelihood corresponds to that of a two-variable model without intercept, so it is maximized by:

$$\widehat{\alpha} = \frac{\sum_{t=1}^{T} X_t X_{t-1}}{\sum_{t=1}^{T} X_{t-1}^2}, \qquad \widehat{\sigma}^2 = \frac{1}{T} \sum_{t=1}^{T} (X_t - \widehat{\alpha} X_{t-1})^2.$$

As pointed out above, this analysis applies regardless of the value of the unknown parameter α, provided the model describes the data.

16.3 EMPIRICAL MODELING OF UK EXPENDITURE

In the following, we will seek to develop autoregressive models for UK log expenditure, x_t, as well as for its growth rate, $\Delta x_t = x_t - x_{t-1}$.

An autoregressive fit to x_t is reported in Table 16.1. A linear trend is included in the model since Figure 16.1(b) indicated that x_t more or less follows a linear trend. Figure 16.3(a,c,e) reports graphical properties of the residuals from this model. We see that the model is not ideal, in that the innovations appear to be non-normal, although the temporal dependence seems to be captured. The non-normality can be seen both from the formal normality test, and from the Q-Q plot of the residuals.

$$\widehat{x}_t = \underset{(0.039)}{0.92} \, x_{t-1} + \underset{(0.43)}{0.91} + \underset{(0.00025)}{0.00051t}$$
se

$$\widehat{\sigma} = 0.014, \qquad \widehat{\ell} = 303.20 \qquad T = 106$$

$\chi^2_{\text{norm}}[2]$	$= 10.1$	$[\text{p}= 0.01]$	$F_{\text{ar}(1-5)}[5, 98] = 0.6$	$[\text{p}= 0.72]$
$F_{\text{het}}[5, 97]$	$= 1.1$	$[\text{p}= 0.27]$	$F_{\text{arch}(1-4)}[4, 95] = 2.0$	$[\text{p}= 0.10]$

Table 16.1 A first autoregressive model for expenditure, x_t

We will seek to address the non-normality by looking at the largest residuals. There are three positive residuals of more than 2.5 standard errors corresponding to 1972:4, 1973:1, and 1979:2. Economic history shows that these dates are consistent with expansionary fiscal policy shifts in 1972–1973 and in 1979. Such shifts are clearly seen in the graph of expenditure, x_t, in Figure 16.1(b). Unfortunately for the British economy, both expansions were followed by oil crises. We will adopt the same approach as Hendry and Mizon (1993) in extending the model by a dummy variable $D_{out,t}$ taking the value unity on these three dates, and zero otherwise. The extended model delivers the results reported in Table 16.2, with corresponding graphical tests in Figure 16.3(b,d,f). It can be seen that the dummy helps to address the non-normality, by removing "blips" of 4.6% in the 3 non-zero quarters.

In the model for log expenditure reported in Table 16.2, the coefficient of the lagged dependent variable, x_{t-1}, is about 0.9, which is close to unity. Figure

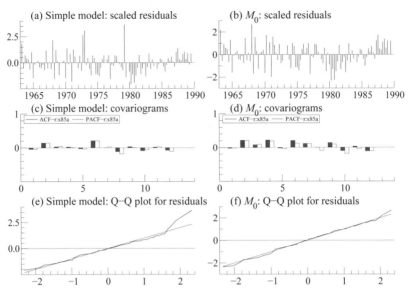

Figure 16.3 Properties of models for UK log expenditure with and without dummies as reported in Tables 16.1 and 16.2

16.4(a) shows how well the model fits the data. There is a pronounced tendency for the fitted time series $\widehat{x}_t$ to follow the lagged dependent variable, x_{t-1}.

$$\widehat{x}_t \;=\; \underset{(0.033)}{0.90}\,x_{t-1} + \underset{(0.36)}{1.14} + \underset{(0.00021)}{0.00064t} + \underset{(0.006)}{0.046\,D_{out,t}}$$

standard error

$\widehat{\sigma} = 0.012, \qquad \widehat{\ell}_0 = 321.79 \qquad R^2 = 0.996 \qquad T = 106$

$\chi^2_{\text{norm}}[2]$	$= \;0.1$	[p= 0.97]	$F_{\text{ar}(1-3)}[3,99] = 2.2$	[p= 0.10]
$F_{\text{het}}[5,96]$	$= \;1.6$	[p= 0.16]	$F_{\text{ar}(1-5)}[5,97] = 2.4$	[p= 0.05]
			$F_{\text{arch}(1-4)}[4,94] = 1.4$	[p= 0.22]

Table 16.2 M_0: autoregressive model for expenditure x_t with $D_{out,t}$

In the following, we will be interested in the hypothesis that the coefficient on the lagged dependent variable equals unity. It is, therefore, natural to reparametrize the model by simply subtracting x_{t-1} from both sides of the equation reported in Table 16.2. This delivers the results reported in Table 16.3. For such a reparametrization, the standard error, the likelihood function, and the mis-specification tests all remain the same. The fit for the growth rate Δx_t reported in Figure 16.4(b) appears much worse than that for the levels x_t reported in panel (a). This is a natural consequence of the strong temporal dependence. Correspondingly, the multiple correlation, R^2, between the dependent variable and the regressors falls, from 0.996 to 0.325 when moving from levels to differences. Nevertheless, the likelihood value is identical to that for the model in levels recorded in Table 16.2. This is in line with the lack of invariance of R^2 to the model specification, which was pointed out in §7.4.1.

$$\begin{aligned}
\widehat{\Delta x} &= -\underset{(0.033)}{0.10}\, x_{t-1} + \underset{(0.36)}{1.14} + \underset{(0.00021)}{0.00064t} + \underset{(0.006)}{0.046\, D_{out,t}} \\
\text{standard error} & \\
\widehat{\sigma} = 0.012, \quad & \widehat{\ell}_0 = 321.79 \quad R^2 = 0.325 \quad T = 106
\end{aligned}$$

Table 16.3 M_0: autoregressive model for growth of UK log expenditure, Δx_t with $D_{out,t}$

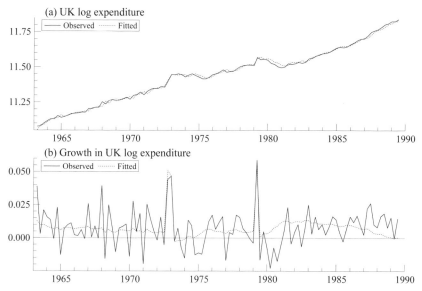

Figure 16.4 Observed time series and fitted model for UK log expenditure: panel (a) shows the levels of the variable, while panel (b) shows the growth rate

16.4 PROPERTIES OF UNIT-ROOT PROCESSES

We will now examine the properties of first-order autoregressions when the first-order autoregressive coefficient is unity. First, the simple process X_t given by equation (16.2.1) is studied, then deterministic terms are introduced, and finally we discuss why processes in this class are called unit-root processes.

16.4.1 The simple case without deterministic terms

Consider the time series $X_0, \ldots, X_T$ given by model equation (16.2.1):

$$X_t = \alpha X_{t-1} + \epsilon_t,$$

Solving this equation recursively as in §12.6.1 gives the solution:

$$X_t = \epsilon_t + \alpha \epsilon_{t-1} + \cdots + \alpha^{t-1} \epsilon_1 + \alpha^t X_0 = \sum_{j=1}^{t} \alpha^{t-j} \epsilon_j + \alpha^t X_0.$$

In particular, when $\alpha = 1$, the weighted sum reduces to:

$$X_t = \sum_{j=1}^{t} \epsilon_j + X_0. \tag{16.4.1}$$

We call such a process a random walk, since the increments, $\Delta X_t = X_t - X_{t-1} = \epsilon_t$ are independent and identically distributed.

It is now easy to find the marginal distribution of X_t, which is given by:

$$(X_t \mid X_0 = 0) \overset{D}{=} \mathsf{N}[0, \sigma^2 t].$$

In other words, the expectation is a constant, equal to the initial value, X_0, while the variance increases linearly with time. The latter entails that X_t is an example of a *non-stationary* time series. More precisely, we say that such a process is *integrated of order one*, denoted $\mathsf{I}(1)$, since $X_t - \mathsf{E}(X_t)$ is non-stationary, but the differences of $X_t - \mathsf{E}(X_t)$ are stationary. Note that the differences cumulate back to an $\mathsf{I}(1)$ process as in (16.4.1). Correspondingly, a stationary process that can be written as the difference of an $\mathsf{I}(1)$-process is said to be integrated of order zero, denoted $\mathsf{I}(0)$. This somewhat convoluted definition of an $\mathsf{I}(0)$-process rules out the process $\epsilon_t - \epsilon_{t-1}$, which is stationary, but cumulates to a stationary process.

Taking this finding for $\alpha = 1$, together with the results of §12.6 for $|\alpha| < 1$, we have the distinction:

Stationary case: $\qquad X_t \overset{D}{\approx} \mathsf{N}\left[0, \dfrac{\sigma^2}{1-\alpha^2}\right] \qquad$ if $|\alpha| < 1$,

Non-stationary case: $\qquad X_t \overset{D}{=} \mathsf{N}\left[X_0, \sigma^2 t\right] \qquad$ if $\alpha = 1$.

To illustrate the difference in interpretation, let X_t represent productivity. An innovation like the Internet can influence future productivity. Suppose this happens initially, so X_0 represents the level achieved thereby. In the unit-root case, productivity is shifted permanently whereas in the stationary case, the effect of the innovation will eventually die out.

16.4.2 Deterministic terms in unit-root processes

In the empirical illustration based on UK expenditure, we included deterministic terms. This issue will be discussed in the following.

As a start, consider data $Y_0, \ldots, Y_T$ that are modeled by an autoregression with an intercept:

$$Y_t = \beta_1 + \beta_2 Y_{t-1} + \epsilon_t.$$

When $\beta_2 = 1$, this equation reduces to:

$$Y_t = \beta_1 + Y_{t-1} + \epsilon_t,$$

or equivalently:

$$\Delta Y_t = \beta_1 + \epsilon_t.$$

The interpretation of this equation is that, on average, the change in the process ΔY_t equals β_1. These equivalent equations are solved by:

$$Y_t = \sum_{j=1}^{t} \epsilon_j + Y_0 + \beta_1 t.$$

In particular, when $\beta_2 = 1$ and $\beta_1 = 0$, this last equation reduces to:

$$Y_t = \sum_{j=1}^{t} \epsilon_j + Y_0,$$

which is the sum of a random walk, $\sum_{j=1}^{t} \epsilon_j$, and a constant level, Y_0.

It is useful to compare such results with the stationary case where $|\beta_2| < 1$. In that situation, the results of §12.6 show that the process Y_t is the sum of a stationary process and a constant level $\mu_Y = \beta_1/(1 - \beta_2)$. Combining the results for the non-stationary and the stationary case, we have:

$Y_t = $ constant level $+$ stationary process   if $|\beta_2| < 1$,

$Y_t = $ constant level $+$ non-stationary process   if $\beta_2 = 1, \beta_1 = 0$.

In applications, it is usually most appropriate to compare these two cases. When $\beta_2 = 1$ but $\beta_1 \neq 0$, we get a unit-root process with a linear trend, $Y_0 + \beta_1 t$, which is far removed from a stationary process around a constant level. More generally, for an autoregressive model with an intercept and a linear trend:

$$Y_t = \beta_1 + \beta_2 t + \beta_3 Y_{t-1} + \epsilon_t,$$

we have correspondingly:

$Y_t = $ linear trend $+$ stationary process   if $|\beta_3| < 1$,

$Y_t = $ linear trend $+$ non-stationary process   if $\beta_3 = 1, \beta_2 = 0$,

where the slope of the linear trend is given by $\beta_2/(1 - \beta_3)$ in the stationary case, and β_1 in the non-stationary case. Again, it seems reasonable to compare these alternatives, as opposed to the situation where $\beta_3 = 1$ and $\beta_2 \neq 0$.

Turning to the empirical model reported in Table 16.3, the additional dummy variable $D_{out,t}$ is included. For the purpose of interpretation, the dummy can be treated together with the innovations. In the model of Table 16.2, the autoregressive coefficient is about 0.9. When interpreting the series as stationary, the slope of the linear trend, which represents the deterministic component of the long-term quarterly growth rate, can then be computed as:

$$0.00064/(1 - 0.90) = 0.0063,$$

which corresponds to an annual rate of increase of about 0.0252 or about 2.5% per annum.

Imposing the restriction that the autoregressive coefficient is unity in the levels formulation, or equivalently zero in the growth formulation, as well as no linear trend component, yields the model reported in Table 16.4. The growth rate is seen to be the same in this model.

$$\begin{array}{cc} \widehat{\Delta x} & = 0.0063 + 0.043\,D_{out,t} \\ \text{standard error} & (0.0012) \quad (0.007) \end{array}$$

$$\widehat{\sigma} = 0.012, \qquad \widehat{\ell}_1 = 316.91 \qquad T = 106$$

Table 16.4 M_1: restricted autoregressive model for growth of UK log expenditure, Δx_t

16.4.3 Unit-root processes

Integrated processes of order one are also called unit-root processes. The term originates in the time-series literature. The idea is to write the model equation (12.6.1) as:

$$\epsilon_t = X_t - \alpha X_{t-1} = X_t - \alpha L X_t = (1 - \alpha L) X_t,$$

where L symbolizes the operation of lagging X_t once to get X_{t-1}. Here, $(1 - \alpha L)$ is a polynomial in L called the *characteristic polynomial*. We find the corresponding roots by solving the equation $1 - \alpha L = 0$. The polynomial $(1 - \alpha L)$, therefore, has a root of α^{-1}. When $\alpha = 1$, we say the polynomial has a unit root.

16.5 INFERENCE ABOUT UNIT ROOTS

Due to the temporal dependence, the distribution theory for estimators and test statistics is complicated. This is in contrast to the cross-sectional two-variable regression model, so detailed proofs for the unit-root autoregressive model are omitted here.

In §5.5, distribution theory was discussed for the two-variable model:

$$Y_i = \beta_1 + \beta_2 X_i + u_i.$$

The normalized estimator for β_2 is:

$$V = \frac{\widehat{\beta}_2 - \beta_2}{\{\sigma^2 / \sum_{j=1}^n (X_j - \overline{X})^2\}^{1/2}} = \frac{\sum_{i=1}^n u_i (X_i - \overline{X})}{\{\sigma^2 \sum_{j=1}^n (X_j - \overline{X})^2\}^{1/2}}.$$

Due to the strong exogeneity of the regressors X_i, we could condition on the regressors $X_1, \ldots, X_n$. We found the conditional distribution:

$$(V \mid X_1, \ldots, X_n) \overset{\text{D}}{=} \mathsf{N}\,[0, 1]\,.$$

Since this result does not depend on the conditioning variables, the unconditional distribution of V is standard normal $V \overset{D}{=} N[0,1]$.

For the autoregression with an intercept, (12.3.1) given by the equation:

$$Y_t = \beta_1 + \beta_2 Y_{t-1} + \epsilon_t, \tag{16.5.1}$$

we will once again be interested in the normalized estimator:

$$W = \frac{\widehat{\beta}_2 - \beta_2}{\{\sigma^2/\sum_{j=1}^{T}(Y_{t-1} - \overline{Y}_{(-)})^2\}^{1/2}} = \frac{\sum_{i=1}^{T} \epsilon_t(Y_{t-1} - \overline{Y}_{(-)})}{\{\sigma^2 \sum_{j=1}^{T}(Y_{t-1} - \overline{Y}_{(-)})^2\}^{1/2}}.$$

This argument cannot be repeated for the time-series regression (16.5.1) because of the serial dependence. The regressors $Y_0, \ldots, Y_{T-1}$ are not strongly exogenous. In fact, by conditioning on those lagged values, the dependent variable Y_t is also fixed. Nonetheless it can be proved that in the stationary case:

$$W \overset{D}{\approx} N[0,1] \qquad \text{if } |\beta_2| < 1.$$

The proof relies on a general type of Central Limit Theorem that allows for dependence that declines exponentially over time. The t-statistic is no longer t-distributed.

In the unit-root case, W has a different distribution, often called a Dickey–Fuller distribution after Dickey and Fuller (1979), so:

$$W \overset{D}{\approx} DF_c \qquad \text{if } \beta_2 = 1, \beta_1 = 0.$$

The subindex indicates that the process has a *c*onstant level. This asymptotic distribution also applies for the signed log-likelihood ratio test statistic ω for the hypothesis $\beta_2 = 0$, provided $\beta_1 = 0$. The most important quantiles are reported in Table 16.5. The joint hypothesis that $\beta_2 = 1$, $\beta_1 = 0$ can be tested using the log-likelihood ratio test statistic, which has an asymptotic distribution denoted by DF_c^2 and is reported in Table 16.6.

Distribution	2.5%	5%	10%	50%	90%	95%	97.5%
$N[0,1]$	-1.96	-1.64	-1.28	0	1.28	1.64	1.96
DF_c	-3.12	-2.86	-2.57		-0.44	-0.07	0.23
DF_l	-3.66	-3.41	-3.12		-1.25	-0.94	-0.66

Table 16.5 Asymptotic quantiles for one-sided Dickey–Fuller distributions. From Banerjee et al. (1993, Chapter 4)

For an autoregression with a trend given by:

$$Y_t = \beta_1 + \beta_2 t + \beta_3 Y_{t-1} + \epsilon_t,$$

the results are similar, except for using a different Dickey–Fuller distribution, DF_l, where the subindex indicates that the process has a *l*inear trend. Quantiles are reported in Table 16.5 for a signed log-likelihood ratio test for the one-sided test for $\beta_3 = 1$ assuming $\beta_2 = 0$, whereas quantiles for the distribution DF_l^2 used for testing the joint hypothesis $\beta_3 = 1, \beta_2 = 0$ are reported in Table 16.6. Both for the model with a constant and for the model with a trend, the required critical values to reject at a given significance level are rather different from the standard $N[0, 1]$- and χ^2-distributions that apply for the corresponding stationary processes.

Distribution	50%	90%	95%	97.5%
χ_2^2	1.39	4.61	5.99	7.38
DF_c^2	3.43	7.50	9.13	10.73
DF_l^2	5.62	10.56	12.39	14.13

Table 16.6 Asymptotic quantiles for two-sided Dickey–Fuller distributions. From Johansen (1995, Chapter 15)

16.5.1 Example: unit-root testing for total expenditure

Returning to the autoregressions for total expenditure, x_t, reported in Tables 16.3 and 16.4, we can now perform a unit-root test. The joint hypothesis $\beta_3 = 1$, $\beta_2 = 0$ can be tested by comparing the two values of the likelihood function, giving the log-likelihood ratio test statistic:

$$LR = -2(316.91 - 321.79) = 9.77.$$

When compared with the 95% quantile of the DF_l^2-distribution of 12.4, the unit-root hypothesis can be accepted. The unit-root restriction in Table 16.4, therefore, represents a valid reduction of the model in Table 16.3. However, had conventional χ^2-based critical values been used, a rejection decision would have been incorrectly made.

A one-sided test can be performed by computing the t-statistic, which is still called that, although it is no longer t-distributed:

$$(0.90 - 1)/0.033 = -3.13.$$

The corresponding signed log-likelihood ratio test statistic is $\omega = \sqrt{LR} = -3.13$. Comparing either test statistic with the 5% quantile of the DF_l-distribution, which is -3.41, we cannot reject the unit-root hypothesis. Note that the use of this one-sided test requires that $\beta_2 = 0$, which is most easily checked by testing the joint hypothesis $\beta_3 = 1, \beta_2 = 0$.

16.5.2 Example: unit-root testing for the price of whiting

When analyzing the whiting price series in Chapters 12–15, p_t was assumed to be stationary. We will show that the unit-root hypothesis can be rejected, indicating that it is valid to interpret the price series as I(0), as we did above.

$$
\begin{aligned}
\widehat{\Delta p_t} &= \underset{0.06}{-0.33} p_{t-1} - \underset{(0.04)}{0.17} + \underset{(0.06)}{0.25} s_t + \underset{(0.06)}{0.14} m_t \\
\text{se} \\
&= \underset{0.06}{-0.33} p_{t-1} - \underset{(0.026)}{0.055} + \underset{(0.06)}{0.25} (s_t - \bar{s}) + \underset{(0.06)}{0.14} (m_t - \bar{m})
\end{aligned}
$$

$\widehat{\sigma} = 0.24, \qquad \widehat{\ell}_{\text{fish},0} = 4.61 \qquad T = 110$

$\chi^2_{\text{norm}}[2]$	$= 2.0$	[p= 0.37]	$F_{\text{ar}(1-2)}[2, 104]$	$= 1.8$	[p= 0.18]
$F_{\text{het}}[4, 101]$	$= 0.7$	[p= 0.56]	$F_{\text{arch}(1-1)}[1, 104]$	$= 0.9$	[p= 0.35]

Table 16.7 $M_{\text{fish},0}$: unrestricted autoregressive model for price of whiting

$$
\widehat{\Delta p_t} = \underset{(0.06)}{0.15} (s_t - \bar{s}) + \underset{(0.06)}{0.09} (m_t - \bar{m})
$$
$$
\text{se}
$$

$\widehat{\sigma} = 0.26, \qquad \widehat{\ell}_{\text{fish},1} = -7.76 \qquad T = 110$

Table 16.8 $M_{\text{fish},1}$: restricted autoregressive model for price of whiting

The empirical model for prices that was reported in Table 13.2 is repeated in Table 16.7, now including both weather dummies. The model contains a constant, but no trend, as well as the two weather dummies. We have seen that in a model with a constant, the unit-root hypothesis involves the autoregressive parameter as well as the intercept, as the intercept otherwise cumulates to a trend in the presence of a unit root. Since the weather dummies take the values 0 and 1, their cumulative behavior looks more or less like a trend. To counter this effect, their mean values have been subtracted in the second line of Table 16.7. As this in effect orthogonalizes the weather variables with respect to the constant, the likelihood is not changed. The cumulative behavior of these "de-meaned" dummies will then be approximately constant rather than trending. Unit-root testing can therefore be done using the DF_c- and DF_c^2-distributions. A restricted model imposing the unit root and the absence of the constant is presented in Table 16.8. The log-likelihood ratio test for the unit-root hypothesis is therefore:

$$
\text{LR} = -2\{(-7.76) - 4.61\} = 24.73,
$$

which is large compared to 9.13, the 95% quantile of the DF_c^2-distribution. A one-sided test can be based on the t-type statistic:

$$
-0.33/0.06 = -5.15.
$$

This statistic is not t-distributed, but approximately DF_c-distributed, assuming that the constant is absent from the unit-root model. The 5% quantile of that distribution is -2.86, which also leads to a rejection of the unit-root hypothesis.

16.5.3 Models with stationary and unit roots

Sometimes more that just one lag is need to describe the dynamics of a time series. In this way in §13.3.3 we used the second-order autoregression:

$$Y_t = \beta_1 Y_{t-1} + \beta_2 Y_{t-2} + \mu + \epsilon_t.$$

In the context of a unit root, such a model can be reformulated in equilibrium-correction form as:

$$\Delta Y_t = \pi Y_{t-1} + \gamma \Delta Y_{t-2} + \mu + \epsilon_t,$$

where $\pi = \beta_1 + \beta_2 - 1$ and $\gamma = -\beta_2$. The characteristic polynomial is now $A(L) = (1 - L) - \pi L - \gamma L(1 - L)$. This can only have a unit root if $\pi = 0$. If indeed $\pi = 0$—and also $|\gamma| < 1$—then ΔY_t is stationary, so Y_t is I(1). In this situation a test for $\pi = 0$ in (16.5.3) would be based on the DF_c^2-distribution. The unit root test in this model is often referred to as an augmented Dickey–Fuller test. The same would actually apply as long as $\gamma \neq 1$ (Nielsen, 2001). When $\pi = 0$ and $\gamma = 1$ then Y_t is said to be I(2), and a different limit theory applies. The I(2)-theory is relevant in the analysis of nominal macro series, such as the log-prices seen in Figure 16.1(c); see Juselius (2006). As pointed out in §13.3.1 the test for $\gamma = 0$ in (16.5.3) would be based on the $\chi^2[1]$-distribution.

16.6 SUMMARY AND EXERCISES

Summary: Macroeconomic data are often better described as non-stationary than stationary. This was illustrated by modeling UK expenditure using a first-order autoregression. The autoregressive parameter was found to be close to unity. Autoregressions with unit roots were interpreted. Inference for the unit-root hypothesis was discussed, and both non-rejection and rejection illustrations noted.

Bibliography: The analysis of non-stationary processes dates from the early days of econometrics, as Hendry and Morgan (1995) show, but the modern resurgence starts in the mid-1970s (see Dickey and Fuller, 1979; Hendry, 1980), for reasons the next chapter will discuss.

Key questions:

- What are the characteristics of a unit-root process?
- When are Dickey–Fuller distributions used for inference?
- Why are the values for $\widehat{\sigma}^2$ and the log-likelihood function the same in Tables 16.1 and 16.2?
- Discuss the validity of the assumptions of the statistical models for the final expenditure data.

Computing Task 16.1. *We wish to analyze log GDP, y_t say. Data on quarterly US real GDP for the period 1947:1 to 2006:1 can be found in different formats in the files* USgdp.dat *and* USgdp.in7.

(a) *Check if the data are in log format already.*

(b) *As a start, fit an autoregression with many lags, 4 say. Look at mis-specification tests, both formal and graphical tests. Is it a good model? What could be the sources of potential problems?*

(c) *Fit an autoregression with four lags to the subsample 1947:1 to 1984:4. Does that provide a better model?*

(d) *Conduct a unit-root test and interpret the result.*

(e) *Fit an autoregression with four lags to the subsample 1986:1 to 2006:1. Is that model well-specified?*

(f) *Conduct a unit-root test and interpret the result.*

(g) *Compare the estimated models for the two subsamples. Does the outcome shed light on the results for the full sample analysis in* (b)?

Chapter Seventeen

Cointegration

In Chapter 12 the notion of a stationary time series was introduced, while in Chapter 16 we considered random walks as examples of non-stationary time series. Random walks are difference-stationary time series. We say that stationary and difference stationary time series are integrated of order zero and one, respectively, and write as a shorthand that they are $I(0)$ or $I(1)$. Economic theory usually leads us to think about more than one variable. While each of these variables could be $I(1)$, it may happen that they drift in the same way, so that a linear combination of them is $I(0)$. In that case, we say that the variables cointegrate, and in practice, such a cointegrating relation often has an economic interpretation. The idea of cointegration was due to Clive Granger, who was awarded the Nobel Prize for this contribution in 2003.

In the following, we will first consider a stylized example of cointegration, and then proceed to look at cointegration in a vector autoregressive model, with the demand for money as an example. Finally, we will comment on single-equation analyses of cointegration using autoregressive distributed-lag models.

17.1 STYLIZED EXAMPLE OF COINTEGRATION

To illustrate the idea of cointegration, we will consider two variables, v_t, C_t, that could represent the log of the velocity of money, v_t, and an interest rate, measuring the cost of holding money, C_t. Suppose these follow the vector autoregression:

$$\Delta v_t = C_{t-1} - v_{t-1} + \epsilon_{v,t}, \tag{17.1.1}$$

$$\Delta C_t = \epsilon_{C,t}. \tag{17.1.2}$$

In order to interpret this set of autoregressive equations, we need to express the variables v_t and C_t in terms of the current and past innovations.

The second equation shows that the variable C_t is a unit-root process. From §16.4.3, we have that:

$$C_t = \sum_{s=1}^{t} \epsilon_{C,s} + C_0,$$

so C_t is a random walk, and therefore an $I(1)$ process. Having solved for C_t, it is easy to get from (17.1.1), canceling v_{t-1}, so that:

$$v_t = C_{t-1} + \epsilon_{v,t} = \sum_{s=1}^{t} \epsilon_{C,s} + C_0 + \epsilon_{v,t} - \epsilon_{C,t}.$$

Combining these results, we have the solutions:

$$v_t = \sum_{s=1}^{t} \epsilon_{C,s} + C_0 + \epsilon_{v,t} - \epsilon_{C,t},$$

$$C_t = \sum_{s=1}^{t} \epsilon_{C,s} + C_0.$$

This is an example of the *Granger–Johansen* representation. Both variables are seen to have a random-walk component and are therefore $I(1)$. From the representation, we see that they have a *common stochastic trend*, $\sum_{s=1}^{t} \epsilon_{C,s}$, which can be eliminated by the linear combination:

$$e_t = v_t - C_t = \epsilon_{v,t} - \epsilon_{C,t}.$$

This linear combination is stationary and $I(0)$. Because of the common stochastic trend, we say the variables *cointegrate* and e_t is a *cointegrating relation*.

It is illuminating to write equations (17.1.1) and (17.1.2) in matrix notation:

$$\Delta \mathbf{X}_t = \mathbf{\Pi} \mathbf{X}_{t-1} + \boldsymbol{\epsilon}_t,$$

where the processes $\mathbf{X}_t$ and $\boldsymbol{\epsilon}_t$ are given by:

$$\mathbf{X}_t = \begin{pmatrix} v_t \\ C_t \end{pmatrix}, \qquad \boldsymbol{\epsilon}_t = \begin{pmatrix} \epsilon_{v,t} \\ \epsilon_{C,t} \end{pmatrix},$$

while the parameter matrix $\mathbf{\Pi}$ can be written using matrix algebra as follows:

$$\mathbf{\Pi} = \begin{pmatrix} -1 & 1 \\ 0 & 0 \end{pmatrix} = \begin{pmatrix} -1 \\ 0 \end{pmatrix} (1, -1) = \boldsymbol{\alpha}\boldsymbol{\beta}'.$$

This matrix therefore satisfies a reduced-rank restriction similar to that introduced in §14.2.3, which was interpreted as an over-identifying restriction in §15.3.2.

17.2 COINTEGRATION ANALYSIS OF VECTOR AUTOREGRESSIONS

We next consider a cointegration analysis, using the demand for narrow money in the UK as an illustration. The maximum likelihood analysis was suggested by Johansen (1988, 1995). We will consider the bivariate case, but the analysis can also be applied to systems of higher dimension. As a start, we will briefly review the relevant economic theories and introduce the data. The formal analysis then follows.

17.2.1 The demand for money

The basic economic theory will be taken as known, but briefly summarized. Most researchers postulate a relation of the form $M^d = f(P, C, X)$, where M^d is money demanded, and P, C, X are prices, the cost of holding money, and real income. Usually a log-linear relation is assumed, with C in levels. The main problem is measurement: what are M, P, C, and X? The choices range from very narrow to very broad money; prices can be measured by retail prices, consumer prices, or other deflators; the cost of holding money has to be an opportunity-cost measure; and income could, for instance, be gross domestic product or total final expenditure. Depending on the chosen information set, the empirical evidence can be quite different. We will consider the narrow money measure known as M1.

Narrow money is primarily used for transactions, but is also part of financial portfolios, and is held as a liquid reserve for contingencies. Thus, M^d depends on: P, measuring its real purchasing power; X, measuring the volume of real transactions to be financed; the opportunity cost of intertemporal holding, measured by inflation, $\dot{p}$; and both the own rate of interest R_m paid on money holdings and competing rates of return on alternative liquid assets, R_a. Since money demand should be unit free, the relation is usually assumed to be homogeneous of degree one in P, so we will look at real money demanded. It should be increasing in X, sometimes homogeneously as well, decreasing in both inflation and R_a, and increasing in R_m. If a log-linear form is assumed, the model is written schematically in steady state (i.e., ignoring adjustment to equilibrium) as:

$$m^d - p = \tau_0 + \tau_1 x - \tau_2 \dot{p} - \tau_3 R_a + \tau_4 R_m.$$

The coefficients $\tau_1, \ldots, \tau_4$ are anticipated to be positive, probably with $\tau_1 = 1$, and $\tau_3 = \tau_4$.

Dynamics are central to many theories of money demand: economic agents are assumed to have upper and lower targets for their desired real-money holdings and adjust balances toward their mean when such bands are exceeded; see, for example, Smith (1986). While the observed money stock also depends on the supply, on the basis of institutional knowledge we assume that the monetary authority controls the short-term interest rate and manipulates that to achieve its policy objectives, leaving private agents to hold the quantities of M1 that they desire.

For analyzing the quarterly, seasonally adjusted UK M1 for the period from 1963:1 to 1989:2, Hendry and Ericsson (1991b), in a long line of such studies, select the four variables:

   m: the logarithm of nominal, narrow money, M1, in million pounds;
   x: the logarithm of real total final expenditure (TFE), in million pounds, at 1985 prices;
   p: the logarithm of the TFE deflator;

R_n: a net interest rate measuring the cost of holding money measured as the difference between the three-month local authority interest rate, R_a, and a learning-adjusted own interest rate, R_m.

Two dummy variables are also included in the model:

D_{out}: which is 1 for 1972:4, 1973:1, 1979:2, and 0 otherwise, to represent the timing of major fiscal expansions in 1972 and 1979;

D_{oil}: which is 1 for 1973:3, 1973:4, 1979:3, and 0 otherwise, to represent the timing of the two oil crises in 1973 and 1979.

The dummy D_{out} entered the total expenditure series analyzed in Chapter 16, whereas D_{oil} is relevant for inflation and interest rates.

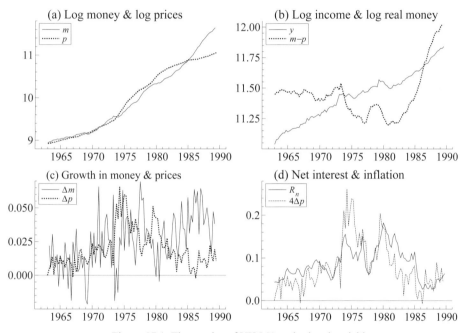

Figure 17.1 Time series of UK M1 and related variables

Figure 17.1 shows m with p; real M1 ($m - p$) with x; Δm_t with Δp_t; and $R_{n,t}$ with Δp_t at annual rates. Real M1 increased by more than 50% in the second half of the 1980s, despite "monetary control" under Mrs. Thatcher. The nominal series in (a) are strongly trended, smooth, and seem integrated: the low correlation between $m - p$ and its main determinant x seen in (b) is surprising and not immediately suggestive of cointegration. The changes, Δm_t and Δp_t, move rather differently over time (c): despite large increases in m_t from 1984 on, Δp_t falls. Lastly, in (d) the interest rate and inflation do not move closely in line either: their changing covariance shows $R_{n,t}$ could not have provided an equally good hedge against inflation at all times, so the nominal interest rate is not the only opportunity cost of holding money.

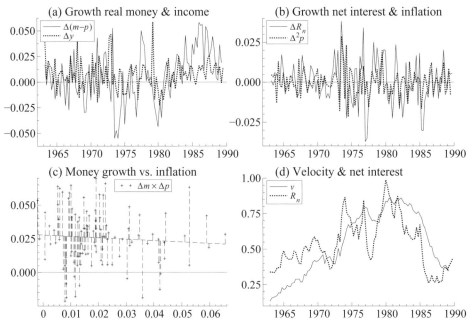

Figure 17.2 Differences of UK M1 and related series

Figure 17.2 records the behavior of $\Delta(m-p)$ with Δx in (a), and again there are marked departures between them, so transactions are not the only purpose of holding M1. Panel (b) shows that $\Delta^2 p_t$ (the inflation surprise) and $\Delta R_{n,t}$ do, however, share many features, although the latter is considerably more volatile. When Δm_t and Δp_t are cross plotted in (c), there is no correlation between them, in marked contrast to the levels, but neither graph throws much light on whether or not "money causes prices". Finally, the velocity of circulation of money $v = (x_t + p_t - m_t)$ is shown in (d) with $R_{n,t}$; velocity has varied considerably, but the two series are positively correlated over the sample, so could cointegrate.

Overall, the rather distinct behavior of the four series seems to offer an unpromising arena for developing a constant-parameter congruent model across the major financial innovation of introducing interest-bearing checking accounts in 1984. Fortunately, appearances can be deceptive, and our modeling efforts will be well rewarded.

17.3 A BIVARIATE MODEL FOR MONEY DEMAND

To simplify the empirical analysis, we will construct the variables:

$$v_t = x_t - m_t + p_t, \qquad C_t = \Delta p_t + R_{n,t} = \Delta p_t + R_{a,t} - R_{m,t}$$

and consider v_t together with C_t in a bivariate system. Here, $m_t - p_t$ is the log of real money, so $V_t = P_t X_t / M_t$ is often called the velocity of circulation of money.

We take C_t as a measure for the cost of holding money, although the homogeneity between inflation and the net interest rate does not have any economic founding. Computer Task 17.4 therefore analyzes a four-variable system, showing that this restriction can be justified empirically. For the moment, we will just accept it as a convenient simplification of the problem to sustain a bivariate analysis.

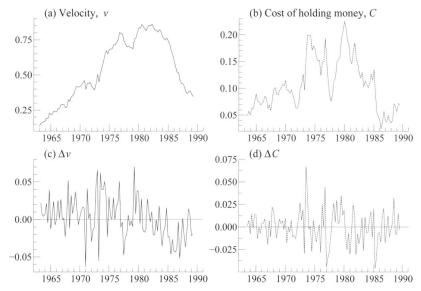

Figure 17.3 Velocity of money, v_t, and the cost of holding money, C_t, shown in levels and first differences

Figure 17.3 shows graphs of v_t and C_t both in levels and differences. The levels of these variables are drifting over time. In particular, for the cost of holding money, C_t, the high inflation in the 1970s and early 1980s is clearly evident. The differences of the time series seem to revert to the same average level of about zero. The graphs, therefore, suggest that v_t and C_t are both $\mathsf{I}(1)$ series.

We will analyze these two series using the bivariate second-order vector autoregressive model. In equilibrium-correction form this is:

$$\Delta v_t = \Pi_{vv} v_{t-1} + \Pi_{vC} C_{t-1} + \Pi_{vc}$$
$$+\Gamma_{vv}\Delta v_{t-1} + \Gamma_{vC}\Delta C_{t-1} + \Psi_{v,out} D_{out,t} + \Psi_{v,oil} D_{oil,t} + \epsilon_{v,t},$$
$$\Delta C_t = \Pi_{Cv} v_{t-1} + \Pi_{CC} C_{t-1} + \Pi_{Cc}$$
$$+\Gamma_{Cv}\Delta v_{t-1} + \Gamma_{CC}\Delta C_{t-1} + \Psi_{C,out} D_{out,t} + \Psi_{C,oil} D_{oil,t} + \epsilon_{C,t},$$

which can also be written in matrix form as:

$$\Delta \mathbf{X}_t = \mathbf{\Pi}\mathbf{X}_{t-1} + \mathbf{\Gamma}\Delta\mathbf{X}_{t-1} + \mathbf{\Psi}\mathbf{D}_t + \epsilon_t. \qquad (17.3.1)$$

A constant but no linear trend is included in the model since Figure 17.3 indicates that the variables do not have linear trends, and their differences have a level that is close to zero.

Table 17.1 reports the results from fitting this second-order autoregressive model to the data. From the estimated models, it is seen that the fiscal expansions mainly affect velocity, and this is probably through the expenditure variable as seen in Table 16.3. The oil crisis shocks mainly affect inflation, and therefore the interest rate, which is closely linked to inflation.

$$
\begin{aligned}
\widehat{\Delta v_t} &= \underset{(0.014)}{-0.097}\,v_{t-1} + \underset{(0.07)}{0.53}\,C_{t-1} - \underset{(0.0055)}{0.0036} \\
\text{standard error} &\quad \underset{(0.10)}{-0.34}\,\Delta v_{t-1} + \underset{(0.11)}{0.09}\,\Delta C_{t-1} + \underset{(0.012)}{0.051}\,D_{out,t} + \underset{(0.012)}{0.030}\,D_{oil,t} \\[4pt]
\widehat{\Delta C_t} &= \underset{(0.012)}{-0.005}\,v_{t-1} - \underset{(0.06)}{0.08}\,C_{t-1} + \underset{(0.0047)}{0.0094} \\
\text{standard error} &\quad \underset{(0.08)}{-0.05}\,\Delta v_{t-1} + \underset{(0.10)}{0.05}\,\Delta C_{t-1} + \underset{(0.010)}{0.013}\,D_{out,t} + \underset{(0.010)}{0.051}\,D_{oil,t}
\end{aligned}
$$

$$\sqrt{\widehat{\sigma}_{vv}} = 0.019, \quad \sqrt{\widehat{\sigma}_{CC}} = 0.016, \quad \widehat{\rho} = 0.51, \quad \widehat{\ell} = 559.31, \quad T = 103$$

Table 17.1 M_2: unrestricted vector autoregressive model for velocity of money, v_t, and the cost of holding money, C_t

Table 17.2 and Figure 17.4 show the mis-specification analysis of the model in Table 17.1. While the velocity equation seems well-specified, there is some problem with the equation for the cost of holding money. This is most clearly seen in the test for autoregressive conditional heteroskedasticity, but it is also found in the break-point Chow test in panel (l) of Figure 17.4. Interest rates and inflation are typically difficult to describe by autoregressions, and this is what motivated Engle (1982) to develop the autoregressive conditional heteroskedasticity model. While the suggested model is not an ideal description of the data, it can be argued that the subsequent analysis is somewhat robust to this type of deviation from a well-specified, or congruent, specification (§11.4 and Chapter 20 define congruence).

Test	$\widehat{v}$	$\widehat{C}$	Test	$(\widehat{v}, \widehat{C})$
$\chi^2_{norm}[2]$	2.2 [p=0.33]	1.9 [p=0.39]	$\chi^2_{norm}[4]$	4.0 [p=0.41]
$F_{ar(1-5)}[5,91]$	0.4 [p=0.86]	1.9 [p=0.10]	$F_{ar(1-5)}[20,170]$	0.7 [p=0.84]
$F_{arch(1)}[1,94]$	0.7 [p=0.41]	7.4 [p=0.01]		
$F_{het}[8,87]$	0.6 [p=0.77]	1.6 [p=0.13]	$F_{het}[24,247]$	1.0 [p=0.46]

Table 17.2 Mis-specification tests for the unrestricted model M_2

In the cointegration analysis, we will focus on the matrix:

$$\Pi = \begin{pmatrix} \Pi_{vv} & \Pi_{vC} & \Pi_{vc} \\ \Pi_{Cv} & \Pi_{CC} & \Pi_{Cc} \end{pmatrix}$$

of coefficients for the lagged dependent variables, v_{t-1} and C_{t-1}, as well as the constant. From Table 17.1 we see that these are estimated by:

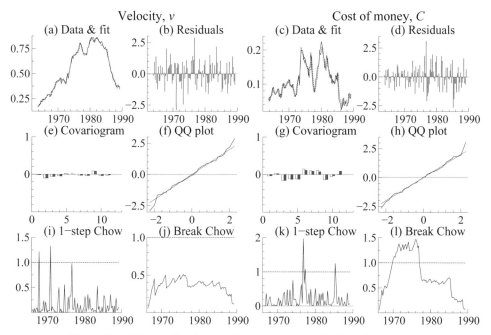

Figure 17.4 Mis-specification graphics for the unrestricted model of Table 17.1

$$\widehat{\Pi} = \begin{pmatrix} \underset{(0.014)}{-0.097} & \underset{(0.07)}{+0.53} & \underset{(0.0055)}{-0.0036} \\ \underset{(0.012)}{+0.005} & \underset{(0.06)}{-0.08} & \underset{(0.0047)}{+0.0094} \end{pmatrix}$$

The standard errors indicate that the second row of numbers and the third column of numbers are both insignificant, rendering a matrix that is very much of the same structure as seen in the stylized example of §17.1. In other words, it looks as if:

$$\Pi_{vc} = \Pi_{Cv} = \Pi_{CC} = \Pi_{Cc} = 0. \tag{17.3.2}$$

We impose these restrictions in several stages in order to treat unit roots correctly. The first stage consists of imposing the restriction:

$$\Pi = \begin{pmatrix} \alpha_v\beta_v & \alpha_v\beta_C & \alpha_v\beta_c \\ \alpha_C\beta_v & \alpha_C\beta_C & \alpha_C\beta_c \end{pmatrix}.$$

In terms of matrix algebra, this can be written as the matrix product:

$$\Pi = \begin{pmatrix} \alpha_v \\ \alpha_C \end{pmatrix} (\beta_v, \beta_C, \beta_c), \tag{17.3.3}$$

showing that the restriction is a reduced-rank restriction just as in §14.2.3. In the present setting, it is called a cointegration rank restriction. Once this restriction has been established, we can, in the second stage, impose the restrictions $\alpha_C = 0$ and $\beta_c = 0$ to obtain the desired restricted model.

17.3.1 Interpreting a cointegrated model

Before actually testing the restrictions given by (17.3.3), and ultimately (17.3.2), it is useful to discuss the interpretation of the vector autoregression (17.3.1) when it satisfies the restriction (17.3.3).

The vector autoregression satisfying the restriction (17.3.3) can be interpreted through the Granger–Johansen representation. This was stated for a stylized situation in §17.1. Ignoring the dummy variables $D_{out,t}$ and $D_{oil,t}$ by setting the Ψ-parameters to zero, that representation is:

$$v_t \approx \mathbf{G}_{vv} \sum_{s=1}^{t} \epsilon_{v,s} + \mathbf{G}_{vC} \sum_{s=1}^{t} \epsilon_{C,s} + S_{v,t} + \tau_v,$$

$$C_t \approx \mathbf{G}_{Cv} \sum_{s=1}^{t} \epsilon_{v,s} + \mathbf{G}_{CC} \sum_{s=1}^{t} \epsilon_{C,s} + S_{C,t} + \tau_C,$$

where $S_{v,t}$ and $S_{C,t}$ are stationary processes with zero expectations. The G- and τ-parameters depend on the original parameters in such a way that:

$$\beta_v v_t + \beta_C C_t + \beta_c \approx \beta_v S_{v,t} + \beta_C S_{C,t}$$

is stationary, and therefore:

$$e_t = \beta_v v_t + \beta_C C_t + \beta_c$$

is a cointegrating relation, with the notation e used for equilibrium as in §14.4. Any other linear combination of v_t and C_t is non-stationary. As in the stylized example §17.1, there is one common stochastic trend driving that non-stationarity. This common stochastic trend can be expressed as a linear combination of the random walks $\sum_{s=1}^{t} \epsilon_{v,s}$ and $\sum_{s=1}^{t} \epsilon_{C,s}$. The proof of this result is more complicated than for the stylized example in §17.1 and can be found in Johansen (1995, Chapter 4).

For completeness, we will also present the Granger–Johansen representation using matrix notation. This can be done in the more compact equation:

$$\mathbf{X}_t \approx \mathbf{G} \sum_{s=1}^{t} \epsilon_s + \mathbf{S}_t + \tau,$$

where $\mathbf{G}$ and τ satisfy $\beta' \mathbf{G} = \mathbf{0}$ and $\beta' \tau + \beta_c = \mathbf{0}$ when $\beta' = (\beta_v, \beta_R)$.

Table 17.1 indicates that the relation:

$$e_t = v_t - 6.24 C_t + 0.11 \tag{17.3.4}$$

is a candidate for a cointegrating relation. To illustrate the Granger–Johansen representation, Figure 17.5 shows different aspects of e_t.

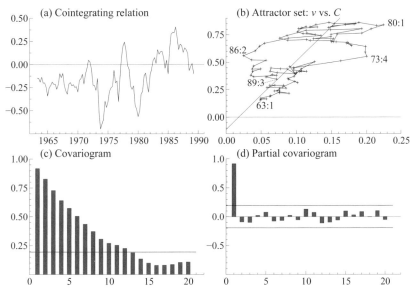

Figure 17.5 Cointegrating relation: $e_t = v_t - 6.24C_t + 0.11$

Panel (a) shows e_t as a time series. In comparison with the time series for v_t in Figure 17.3(a), e_t is seen to revert more frequently to its expected value, but as seen by the covariogram in panel (c), this reversion only happens slowly. Panel (b) shows a cross plot of v_t against C_t. The plot also shows the line $v_t = 6.24C_t - 0.11$, which represents the cointegrating relation and is called the attractor set. The cross-plot curve crosses that line when e_t zero. However, the crossing happens in a new place every time, because the bivariate process is driven up and down the line by the common trend. Whenever the process departs from the equilibrium given by $e_t = 0$, there is a tendency to converge back toward the equilibrium, a tendency that is larger the larger is the disequilibrium. For this reason, the parametrization of the form (17.3.1) is often called an equilibrium-correction model.

The long-run effect from the cost of holding money on velocity is very large: the data values of C_t have changed from 0.05 to 0.20 back to 0.07, a range of approximately 0.15, so the induced change in v_t from (17.3.4) is almost unity, roughly doubling log velocity. This large response accounts for the "flight from and return to money" seen in Figure 17.3(a), as well as revealing substantial "portfolio" adjustment effects on transactions demand. If (17.3.4) is a cointegration relation, then e_t should be I(0), in which case, $\mathsf{E}(\Delta e_t) = 0$ so that:

$$\mathsf{E}\left(-\Delta e_t\right) = \mathsf{E}\left(\Delta m_t - \Delta p_t - \Delta x_t + 6.24\Delta p_t + 6.24\Delta R_{n,t}\right) = 0.$$

Since Δp_t and $R_{n,t}$ may be I(1), but should not drift then $\mathsf{E}(\Delta p_t) = \mathsf{E}(\Delta R_{n,t}) = 0$, whereas $\mathsf{E}(\Delta x_t) = g$, which is the real growth, we deduce that $\mathsf{E}(\Delta m_t - \Delta p_t) = g$. Thus, in steady state, real money should grow at the same rate as real expenditure; the huge variations around that path manifest in Figure 17.1(b) are due to changes in the opportunity cost of holding money.

Since we have established the framework for identification in Chapter 15, we should give thought to whether the cointegrating relation can be identified as a money demand function. Given our discussion of the technical sense of identification in Chapter 15, it may be anticipated that the answer should be clear: either the reported equation is unique, or it is not. In practice, however, the meaning of "identified" is ambiguous and could refer to any or all of three important aspects. The first is indeed that of "uniqueness" as discussed in Chapter 15, so that no linear combination with another equation (or equations) "looks like" the reported model. If it is not unique, it is clearly not identified.

However, two other aspects underlie the question, even when the reported model is unique. The second concerns whether the reported equation "satisfies the theoretical interpretation of a money demand function". This questions whether the reported equation is indeed interpretable as a demand equation, as opposed to some other unique—but by implication uninteresting—function. The third is whether it "corresponds to the actual demand function in the economy". This is an issue of the goodness of the specification, so the three aspects map naturally onto "uniqueness", "interpretation" and "specification" of any postulated relationship.

As an example, consider simply regressing a quantity on a lagged price. This will always deliver a unique function of the data second moments, but need not correspond to any underlying demand behavior, and could be incorrectly interpreted as a supply schedule if there happened to be a positive sign on prices.

Here we have discussed estimating the demand function for money and have used several features to "identify" the result as such. First, there is considerable UK institutional knowledge that economic agents freely control their holdings of narrow money: they can deposit and withdraw money as they wish, and the Bank of England cannot control the quantities involved. On the other hand, the Bank of England can control the interest rate that comprises a major component of the opportunity cost of holding money, and it did so in the past to influence how much money was held. Currently, the main focus of interest-rate policy is direct control of inflation. Thus, the equation has an institutional basis.

Second, the reported equation is interpretable on the basis of modern theories of money demand such as those discussed in §17.2.1: raising the opportunity cost lowers holdings; demand is for real money in the long run and is proportional to real expenditure; and adjustment to equilibrium is relatively slow (Akerlof, 1982).

Third, there have been numerous policy regime changes over the sample, of which the most dramatic was the Banking Act of 1984, which permitted payment of interest on narrow-money (checking) accounts. This greatly shifted the opportunity-cost measure, yet left the parameters of the demand equation unaltered: an impressive invariance. That change can be crudely modeled by a shift variable, zero before the change in the law and the own rate of interest after. This is captured by the learning-adjusted own interest rate, R_m, which is zero prior to 1984 and positive thereafter. Since $C_t = \Delta p_t + R_{n,t} = \Delta p_t + R_{a,t} + R_{m,t}$, the cost of holding money is shifted by R_m, but R_m does not directly enter the demand model. In the language of Chapter 15, the own interest rate, R_m, is an instrument, identifying the cointegrating relation. For all these reasons, we interpret the reported equation as a demand for money function.

17.3.2 Test for cointegration rank

In the first stage, we will test the reduced-rank restriction (17.3.3). In line with §14.2.3, we can use numerical methods to maximize the likelihood under this restriction. The result is reported in Table 17.3. The log-likelihood ratio statistic for this restriction is given by:

$$\text{LR}\,(\mathsf{M}_1 \mid \mathsf{M}_2) = -2(556.25 - 559.31) = 6.13, \qquad [\mathsf{p} = 0.19].$$

Since the restricted model M_1 imposes one common stochastic trend, or unit-root component, while the unrestricted model M_2 imposes none, this test statistic is approximately DF_c^2-distributed. Comparing the test statistic with the 95% quantile of 9.13 reported in Table 16.6 indicates that the restriction cannot be rejected.

$$
\begin{aligned}
\widehat{\Delta v_t} &= -\underset{(0.011)}{0.085}\{v_{t-1} - \underset{(0.41)}{6.24}\,C_{t-1} + \underset{(0.05)}{0.11}\,\} \\
\text{standard error} & \\
&\quad - \underset{(0.10)}{0.35}\,\Delta v_{t-1} + \underset{(0.12)}{0.11}\,\Delta C_{t-1} + \underset{(0.011)}{0.051}\,D_{out,t} + \underset{(0.011)}{0.028}\,D_{oil,t} \\
\widehat{\Delta C_t} &= +\underset{(0.010)}{0.011}\{v_{t-1} - \underset{(0.41)}{6.24}\,C_{t-1} + \underset{(0.05)}{0.11}\,\} \\
\text{standard error} & \\
&\quad - \underset{(0.08)}{0.06}\,\Delta v_{t-1} + \underset{(0.10)}{0.08}\,\Delta C_{t-1} + \underset{(0.010)}{0.011}\,D_{out,t} + \underset{(0.010)}{0.049}\,D_{oil,t} \\
\sqrt{\widehat{\sigma}_{vv}} &= 0.019, \quad \sqrt{\widehat{\sigma}_{CC}} = 0.017, \quad \widehat{\rho} = 0.53, \quad \widehat{\ell} = 556.25, \quad T = 103
\end{aligned}
$$

Table 17.3 M_1: vector autoregressive model with reduced-rank restriction

r	$\widehat{\ell}$	$LR(\text{rank}\Pi \leq r \mid \text{rank}\Pi \leq 2)$	p-value
0	521.90	74.82	$[\mathsf{p} = 0.00]$
1	556.25	6.13	$[\mathsf{p} = 0.19]$
2	559.31		

Table 17.4 Cointegration analysis: rank determination

As a slight technicality, the β-parameters in (17.3.3) are defined only if the α-parameters are different from zero and vice versa. Johansen therefore suggests testing the model M_0, say, subject to the restriction that $\boldsymbol{\Pi} = \mathbf{0}$, prior to testing M_1. This test will be based on yet another DF-type distribution. This is tabulated by Johansen (1995, Chapter 15), and also embedded in software like PcGive. In terms of matrix algebra, the models M_0, M_1, and M_2 impose that the rank r of $\boldsymbol{\Pi}$ is at most 0, 1, and 2 respectively. A cointegration rank determination will, therefore, be based on results like those reported in Table 17.4. It is seen that the model M_0: $\Pi = 0$ is rejected when compared with M_2, while M_1 is not rejected.

17.3.3 Tests on cointegrating relations and adjustment parameters

Once the number of cointegrating relations is known, restrictions can be imposed on the α- and β-parameters using standard χ^2-inference, as the system is now $\mathsf{I}(0)$.

$$
\begin{aligned}
\widehat{\Delta v_t} &= \underset{(0.010)}{-0.094} \{v_{t-1} \underset{(0.40)}{-6.09\,C_{t-1}} + \underset{(0.05)}{0.10}\} \\
\text{standard error} \quad & \\
&\quad \underset{(0.09)}{-0.38\,\Delta v_{t-1}} + \underset{(0.11)}{0.09\,\Delta C_{t-1}} + \underset{(0.011)}{0.050\,D_{out,t}} + \underset{(0.011)}{0.028\,D_{oil,t}} \\
\widehat{\Delta C_t} &= \underset{(0.07)}{-0.11\,\Delta v_{t-1}} + \underset{(0.10)}{0.06\,\Delta C_{t-1}} + \underset{(0.010)}{0.011\,D_{out,t}} + \underset{(0.010)}{0.048\,D_{oil,t}} \\
\text{standard error} \quad & \\
\sqrt{\widehat{\sigma}_{vv}} &= 0.019, \quad \sqrt{\widehat{\sigma}_{CC}} = 0.017, \quad \widehat{\rho} = 0.53, \quad \widehat{\ell} = 555.58, \quad T = 103
\end{aligned}
$$

Table 17.5 M_α: reduced-rank vector autoregression for velocity of money, v_t, and the cost of holding money, R_t, with the restriction $\alpha_C = 0$

First, we will impose the restriction that $\alpha_C = 0$. The results are reported in Table 17.5. The log-likelihood ratio statistic for testing this model within the model M_1 of Table 17.3 is given by:

$$\mathsf{LR}(\mathsf{M}_\alpha \mid \mathsf{M}_1) = -2(555.57 - 556.25) = 1.34,$$

with $\mathsf{p} = 0.25$ using a $\chi^2[1]$-distribution. The hypothesis $\alpha_C = 0$ is in fact a weak exogeneity hypothesis. While the model M_1 has a cross-equation restriction, since the β-parameters appear in both equations and the likelihood cannot be maximized using least-squares regression, the model where $\alpha_C = 0$ removes the cross-equation restriction, so the likelihood is maximized by least-squares regression, which we will do in the single-equation analysis of §17.4 below.

Second, the final restriction $\beta_c = 0$ is imposed. Due to the restriction $\alpha_C = 0$, weak exogeneity is preserved. The log-likelihood ratio statistics for testing this model against the models M_α and M_1 respectively are:

$$
\begin{aligned}
\mathsf{LR}(\mathsf{M}_\beta \mid \mathsf{M}_\alpha) &= -2(553.62 - 555.57) = 3.92, \qquad [\mathsf{p} = 0.05], \\
\mathsf{LR}(\mathsf{M}_\beta \mid \mathsf{M}_1) &= -2(553.62 - 556.25) = 5.26, \qquad [\mathsf{p} = 0.07],
\end{aligned}
$$

compared with $\chi^2[1]$- and $\chi^2[2]$-distributions, respectively. Any decision to impose the restriction would be marginal. The hypothesis actually has no substantive interpretation, in that the cointegrating relation involves a price index, which has an arbitrary level. We will therefore refrain from pursuing this hypothesis.

17.4 SINGLE-EQUATION ANALYSIS OF COINTEGRATION

As an alternative to the systems analysis just presented, we could adopt a single-equation approach. The idea is then to analyze the conditional equation of v_t given C_t and the lagged variables, which will amount to an autoregressive distributed-lag model as in (14.1.3). The results for the cointegrating relation will be the same when the conditioning variable C_t is weakly exogenous. This was demonstrated above, so we will find that a single-equation analysis gives the same results here.

$$\widehat{v}_t = \underset{(0.09)}{0.59}\, v_{t-1} + \underset{(0.08)}{0.31}\, v_{t-2} + \underset{(0.10)}{0.61}\, C_t + \underset{(0.15)}{0.03}\, C_{t-1} - \underset{(0.10)}{0.06}\, C_{t-2}$$
$$\text{standard error}$$
$$- \underset{(0.005)}{0.009} + \underset{(0.010)}{0.044}\, D_{out,t} + \underset{(0.011)}{0.001}\, D_{oil,t}$$

$$\sqrt{\widehat{\sigma}^2} = 0.017, \quad \widehat{\ell} = 278.87, \quad T = 103$$

$\chi^2_{norm}[2]$	$=$	6.6	$[p = 0.04]$	$F_{ar(1-5)}[5, 90]$ = 0.6 $[p = 0.71]$
$F_{het}[12, 82]$	$=$	1.1	$[p = 0.34]$	$F_{arch(1-4)}[4, 87]$ = 0.2 $[p = 0.96]$

Table 17.6 Autoregressive distributed-lag model for velocity of money, v_t, given the cost of holding money, C_t

Table 17.6 reports an unrestricted autoregressive distributed-lag model. In the system modeling, we saw that the velocity equation was well-specified, and in the same way this conditional equation appears well-specified, apart from some indication of non-normality. To help interpret the results, it is convenient to reparametrize the equation to an equilibrium-correction form as in §14.4 to find the candidate for the cointegrating relation. This in done in Table 17.7, and the cointegrating relation of model M_α in Table 17.5 is recognized.

$$\widehat{\Delta v}_t = \underset{(0.012)}{0.094}\, (v_{t-1} - 6.09\, C_{t-1} + 0.10) + \underset{(0.10)}{0.61}\, \Delta C_t$$
$$\text{standard error}$$
$$- \underset{(0.08)}{0.31}\, \Delta v_{t-1} - \underset{(0.10)}{0.06}\, \Delta C_{t-1} + \underset{(0.010)}{0.044}\, D_{out,t} - \underset{(0.011)}{0.001}\, D_{oil,t}$$

$$\sqrt{\widehat{\sigma}^2} = 0.017, \quad \widehat{\ell} = 278.87, \quad T = 103$$

Table 17.7 Autoregressive distributed-lag model for velocity of money, v_t, given the cost of holding money, C_t, in equilibrium-correction form

While the analysis of the single-equation model is simpler than a system analysis, it is valid only under the weak exogeneity assumption, $\alpha_C = 0$. For this particular data set, weak exogeneity was found to be a valid restriction, but that will not be the case in general. In addition, when considering situations with more than just two variables of interest, there may be several cointegrating relations, and a single-equation analysis will then pick a linear combination of these, which may have a misleading interpretation. It is, therefore, more reliable to model all the variables as endogenous through a system analysis and to condition only when weak exogeneity is satisfied.

17.5 SUMMARY AND EXERCISES

Summary: If two (or more) integrated variables have a common stochastic trend, so a linear combination has no stochastic trend, then they cointegrate. Cointegration analysis was presented for a system of equations. The system was interpreted using the Granger–Johansen Representation. Cointegration analysis is conducted in two steps. First, the number of cointegrating relations, or the cointegration rank, is determined. This is done using test statistics with Dickey–Fuller type distributions. Second, the system is reduced to I(0), after which restrictions can be imposed on the remaining parameters using χ^2-inference.

Bibliography: Cointegration analysis arose in the mid-1980s as a single-equation method following the work of Granger (1986) and Engle and Granger (1987) but rapidly advanced to a systems approach following Johansen (1988). Hendry (2004) reviews the developments leading to cointegration.

Key questions:
- Discuss the notions of cointegration and common trends.
- Discuss the validity of the assumptions of the system analysis presented in §17.2.
- Discuss the validity of the assumptions of the single-equation analysis presented in §17.4.

Exercise 17.1. *The data-generating process for the log of velocity of narrow money (v_t) and the cost of holding money (C_t) in a certain economy is:*

$$\Delta v_t = -\alpha_1 \left(v_{t-1} - \beta C_{t-1} \right) + \varepsilon_{v,t} \tag{17.5.1}$$

$$\Delta C_t = +\alpha_2 \left(v_{t-1} - \beta C_{t-1} \right) + \varepsilon_{C,t} \tag{17.5.2}$$

for $t = 1, \ldots, T$, where the pairs $(\varepsilon_{v,t}, \varepsilon_{C,t})$ are independent and $N_2[0, \Sigma]$-distributed. The parameters $\alpha_1, \alpha_2, \beta$ are all positive and less than unity.
(a) Show that $c_t = v_t - \beta C_t$ is integrated of order 0.
(b) Show that $z_t = \alpha_2 v_t + \alpha_1 C_t$ is integrated of order 1.
(c) Discuss the degree of integration of the two series v_t and C_t. Do v_t and C_t cointegrate? If so, what is the long-run equilibrium?
(d) Is it legitimate to estimate the Δv_t and ΔC_t equations, (17.5.1) and (17.5.2), by regression?
(e) Suppose $\alpha_2 = 0$. Does that change the answer in (d)?

Exercise 17.2. *Consider the autoregressive distributed-lag model:*

$$y_t = \beta_1 z_t + \beta_2 y_{t-1} + \beta_3 z_{t-1} + \epsilon_{1,t} \tag{17.5.3}$$

where $|\beta_2| < 1$, z_t is generated by:

$$z_t = z_{t-1} + \epsilon_{2,t}$$

and:

$$\begin{pmatrix} \epsilon_{1,t} \\ \epsilon_{2,t} \end{pmatrix} \overset{D}{=} \mathsf{N}_2 \left[\begin{pmatrix} 0 \\ 0 \end{pmatrix}, \begin{pmatrix} \sigma_{11} & 0 \\ 0 & \sigma_{22} \end{pmatrix} \right]$$

with all parameters constant.
(a) Is z_t stationary or not?
(b) Express (17.5.3) in equilibrium-correction form.
(c) Is y_t stationary or not, and does it depend on your answer to (a)?
(d) Are y_t and z_t cointegrated?
(e) What happens to the cointegrating relation when $\beta_1 + \beta_2 + \beta_3 = 1$?
(f) Interpret the model as the demand for money (so y_t is velocity and z_t the cost of holding money).

Exercise 17.3. *Starting from the model in Table 17.6 derive the equilibrium form in Table 17.7 along the lines of section 14.4.*

Computing Task 17.4. *Analyze the four variable system $m_t - p_t$, x_t, Δp_t, $R_{n,t}$ with a constant, a linear trend, $D_{out,t}$, and $D_{oil,t}$.*
(a) Establish the number of cointegrating relationships.
(b) Find a parsimonious congruent model where all transformed variables are $\mathsf{I}(0)$.
(c) Are all of the resulting equations interpretable?

Chapter Eighteen

Monte Carlo simulation experiments

We have already encountered models where analytical derivations of the distributions of estimators and tests cannot be easily undertaken. Indeed, so far we have explicitly obtained such distributions only for simple, and not very realistic, data generation processes. Once data generation processes are non-stationary, from either unit roots or structural breaks, derivations of asymptotic distributions are often the only possible route. That leaves open how well such results will describe smaller samples of the size typically available in macroeconomics.

One widely applicable "solution" is to use computer simulation methods to obtain approximations to the distributions of statistics in complicated data generation processes. This chapter describes Monte Carlo methods for doing so, mainly focused on distribution sampling, where random numbers are used to mimic the behavior of the random errors assumed in the statistical theory.

18.1 MONTE CARLO SIMULATION

A Monte Carlo experiment involves mimicking the real-life process of interest on a computer. For example, we might create an artificial data-generating process like:

$$Y_t = \alpha + Y_{t-1} + \epsilon_t, \tag{18.1.1}$$

beginning from $Y_0 = 0$, and a given value of α, say zero, while standard normally distributed random numbers are used for the sequence of innovations, ϵ_t. A sample of size T is drawn from that data generation process, and the modeling methods, or statistics of interest, are calculated from the resulting sample of artificial data. This process is then repeated M times (called replications) to create a large simulation sample. The distributions based on the artificial data simulate the actual, but unknown, distributions we seek to derive. For example, one can plot the histogram of the replications to investigate the shape of the distribution of the statistic. This particular approach is termed distribution sampling and was used, for example, by Student (1908) to check his hypothesized distribution for the t-statistic.

For each of $i = 1, \ldots, M$ replications of the data-generating process, we compute a statistic, W_i, based on the simulated sample. This could for instance be a test statistic or an estimator. Providing the simulation is correctly formulated, the Law of Large Numbers (see Theorem 2.1) ensures that the sample mean of the replications, $\overline{W}$, for any statistic, W, will approximate the unknown population mean of that statistic, $\mathsf{E}(W) = \mu$, so $\widehat{\mu} = \overline{W}$. Likewise, the Central Limit Theorem (see Theorem 2.2), will give information about the precision of $\overline{W}$ as an estimator for $\mathsf{E}(W) = \mu$. A common use of Monte Carlo is when it is difficult to derive $\mathsf{E}(W)$ analytically, as often occurs in econometrics. We discuss such uses below.

18.1.1 Simulating expected values

The basic Monte Carlo setup is that M replications of an artificial sample are drawn. From each replication we can compute, for instance, a t-statistic or an estimator, resulting in an observation W_i. Based on the M replications, we then have the variables $W_1, \ldots, W_M$, which are drawn independently from the same distribution, and their expectation, $\mathsf{E}(W_i) = \mu$, and variance, $\mathsf{Var}(W_i) = \sigma^2$, will match those of the statistic of interest. In short:

$$W_i \overset{\mathrm{D}}{=} \mathsf{IID}\left[\mu, \omega^2\right] \quad \text{where} \quad \mu, \, \omega^2 \in \mathbb{R} \times \mathbb{R}_+, \tag{18.1.2}$$

where the symbol IID means independent, identically distributed according to a particular, but unspecified, distribution with expectation μ, and variance ω^2.

We now have two types of distributions in play. There is the distribution from the econometric model, and the distribution from the Monte Carlo. To distinguish these we use $\mathsf{E}(\cdot)$ for the expectation in the econometric model and $\mathcal{E}(\cdot)$ for the expectation in the Monte Carlo. Similarly, we use $\mathsf{Var}(\cdot)$ and $\mathcal{V}(\cdot)$ for the variances. When the experiment is correctly implemented, then $\mathcal{E}(W_i) = \mu$ and $\mathcal{V}(W_i) = \omega^2$.

The simulated sample mean is simply:

$$\overline{W} = \frac{1}{M} \sum_{j=1}^{M} W_j, \tag{18.1.3}$$

so taking expectations over the simulation replications:

$$\mathcal{E}\left(\overline{W}\right) = \mathcal{E}\left(\frac{1}{M} \sum_{j=1}^{M} W_j\right) = \frac{1}{M} \sum_{j=1}^{M} \mathcal{E}\left(W_j\right) = \mu. \tag{18.1.4}$$

Thus the simulation average provides an unbiased estimate of the unknown mean of the statistic. Also, given (18.1.2), we can prove:

$$\mathcal{V}\left(\overline{W}\right) = \frac{\omega^2}{M}, \tag{18.1.5}$$

and the Central Limit Theorem (see Theorem 2.2), yields:

$$\overline{W} \overset{\mathrm{D}}{\approx} \mathsf{N}\left[\mu, \frac{\omega^2}{M}\right]. \tag{18.1.6}$$

The Monte Carlo sample mean $\overline{W}$ of a set of drawings from (18.1.2) is, therefore, an unbiased estimator of the unknown population mean μ, with a variance of ω^2/M, and is normally distributed around μ when M is large. Further, letting the across-experiment sample variance be:

$$\overline{\omega}^2 = \frac{1}{M-1} \sum_{j=1}^{M} \left(W_j - \overline{W}\right)^2, \tag{18.1.7}$$

then:

$$\mathcal{E}\left(\overline{\omega}^2\right) = \omega^2 \quad \text{with} \quad \mathcal{V}\left(\overline{W}\right) = \mathcal{E}\left(\frac{\overline{\omega}^2}{M}\right) = \frac{\omega^2}{M}. \tag{18.1.8}$$

From (18.1.8), the simulation sample variance, denoted $\overline{\omega}^2$, is an unbiased estimator of the unknown population variance. Also, when divided by the sample size, as in $\overline{\omega}^2/M$, then (18.1.8) shows that it delivers an unbiased estimator of the variance of the sample mean, $\overline{W}$, around μ. This measures the precision of the simulation. Consequently, from the variability across replications, we can calculate measures of the uncertainty due to the experiment itself. Then $\overline{\omega}$ in (18.1.7) is called the Monte Carlo standard deviation (MCSD), whereas $M^{-1/2}\overline{\omega}$ is the Monte Carlo standard error (MCSE). This is the same distinction as that between the standard deviation of a data set and the standard error of an estimator.

18.1.2 Simulating rejection frequencies and quantiles

It is not just expectations that can be simulated. Various other aspects of the distribution can be simulated too. Suppose the simulated variables, W_i, have density $f(\cdot)$. Having the replications $W_1, \ldots, W_M$ at hand, a histogram of these will approximate the density $f(\cdot)$. Smoothed versions of histograms based on kernel density estimator are readily available in most software packages (see Figure 9.2).

Often it is of interest to simulate p-values. In the case of test statistics, these are rejection frequencies. They can be simulated as follows. The p-value for a quantile q is given by $p = P(W_i > q)$. Using the indicator function defined in (4.4.1), we can construct the binary variable $X_i = 1_{(W_i > q)}$ satisfying $X_i \overset{D}{=} \text{Bernoulli}[p]$. The sample average of these binary variables, namely $\overline{X} = M^{-1} \sum_{j=1}^{M} X_i$ will then approximate p. Since $\overline{X}$ is indeed a sample average, the results derived in §18.1.1 can be used straight away. The expectation and the variance of the Bernoulli distribution were found in §2.1.3 to be $\mathcal{E}(W_i) = p$ and $\mathcal{V}(W_i) = p(1-p)$. Inserting these in the results of §18.1.1 gives:

$$\overline{X} \overset{D}{\approx} \mathsf{N}\left[p, \frac{p(1-p)}{M}\right]. \tag{18.1.9}$$

The variance $p(1-p)$ can be approximated through the Monte Carlo standard error given by $\overline{\omega}_p^2 = (M-1)^{-1} \sum_{j=1}^{M}(X_j - \overline{X})^2$ as before, or directly by $\overline{X}(1 - \overline{X})$.

Approximating a quantile is also possible, although done somewhat differently. Suppose we are interested in the 95% quantile, q say. This will have p-value of $p = 5\%$ and satisfy $\mathsf{P}(W_i > q) = p$. To approximate this, we sort the replications $W_1, \ldots, W_M$ in descending order according to size, creating the ordered sample $W_{(1)} \geq \cdots \geq W_{(M)}$, where the *order statistic* $W_{(\cdot)}$ is referred to as "W-round". The Mp largest observation will then approximate q. If Mp is not an integer, we will round it toward zero giving the integer part, $\mathrm{int}(Mp)$. Thus, $\widehat{q} = W_{(\mathrm{int}(Mp))}$ is the Monte Carlo estimator for the quantile q. The asymptotic theory for this estimator requires some manipulation beyond the scope of this book, so we will just quote a result from Davidson and MacKinnon (1981, p. 255):

$$\widehat{q} \stackrel{\mathsf{D}}{\approx} \mathsf{N}\left[q, \frac{p(1-p)}{\{\mathsf{f}(q)\}^2 M}\right]. \qquad (18.1.10)$$

Here $\mathsf{f}(q)$ is the density of W_i evaluated at q and can be approximated using the histogram discussed above, while p and M are known at the outset.

18.2 TESTING IN CROSS-SECTIONAL REGRESSIONS

In a first Monte Carlo experiment, we will consider the properties of the t-test on the intercept in the simple regression on a constant introduced in §3.3. First, we investigate the situation where the null hypothesis is true. This will largely confirm the results of §3.4.2. Second, we turn to the situation where the hypothesis is false. This could be derived analytically but would be complicated. We can, however, get a good understanding from a Monte Carlo experiment.

18.2.1 Testing when the hypothesis is true

The simple regression on a constant was introduced in §3.3 and is given by:

$$Y_i = \beta + u_i, \quad \text{with} \quad u_i \stackrel{\mathsf{D}}{=} \mathsf{N}[0, \sigma^2], \qquad (18.2.1)$$

where $\beta, \sigma^2 \in \mathbb{R} \times \mathbb{R}_+$, for $i = 1, \ldots, n$. Then data can be generated as a function of the parameters β, σ^2, as well as the sample size, n. We will be interested in analyzing the t-statistic for testing the hypothesis that $\beta = 0$. This was defined as:

$$Z = \frac{\widehat{\beta} - \beta}{\sqrt{s^2/n}} \quad \text{where} \quad \widehat{\beta} = \overline{Y}, \quad s^2 = \frac{1}{n-1}\sum_{i=1}^{n}\left(Y_i - \overline{Y}\right)^2 : \qquad (18.2.2)$$

see (3.4.8). To limit the scope of the simulation experiment, it is useful to analyze the invariance properties of the t-statistic. Indeed, it is scale-invariant, in the sense that t-statistics computed from an outcome $y_1, \ldots, y_n$ and from the scaled outcome $y_1/\sigma, \ldots, y_n/\sigma$ are identical. As long as we are interested only in the distribution of this t-statistic, we can therefore normalize σ^2 at unity without loss.

As an "experimenter", one chooses the numerical value of the parameter β, as well as n, to generate a specific set of data; but as an "econometrician", one observes only the samples of Ys and pretends not to know the data-generating process parameter values. First, choose a particular value for the parameters β, as well as n, say $\beta = 0$, so the hypothesis is true, and set the sample size n, such as $n = 10$. The pair $(\beta, n) = (0, 10)$ defines one experiment, and other experiments can be conducted at other parameter values. Generate a set of random variables $(u_1, \ldots, u_{10})$ using a standard normal random-number generator, and create a sample $(Y_1, \ldots, Y_{10})$ using (18.2.1). Calculate the t-statistic, Z, which we will denote $t(0)$, noting that the hypothesis is true here. The outcome of this first replication is our $W_1 = t(0)$, which is a function of $(Y_1, \ldots, Y_{10})$ and hence of $(u_1, \ldots, u_{10})$. Independently replicate this whole process M times, $M = 1000$ say, to generate a random sample $(W_1, \ldots, W_M)$, each of which is based on 10 u_i. This collection provides M trials of the experiment, where $\mathcal{E}(W_j) = \mathsf{E}\{t(0)\}$ by construction. As before, let:

$$\overline{W} = \frac{1}{1000} \sum_{j=1}^{1000} W_j \qquad \text{and} \qquad \overline{\omega}^2 = \frac{1}{999} \sum_{j=1}^{1000} \left(W_j - \overline{W} \right)^2,$$

then:

$$\overline{W} \stackrel{\mathrm{D}}{\approx} \mathsf{N} \left[\mathsf{E}\{t(0)\}, \frac{\overline{\omega}^2}{M} \right].$$

Thus, $\overline{W}$ estimates the unknown $\mathsf{E}\{t(0)\}$, and the Monte Carlo standard error of $\overline{W}$ will decrease toward zero as the number of Monte Carlo trials, M, increases, so the result becomes as accurate as desired. Likewise, the 95% quantile of $t(0)$ can be estimated by the order statistic $W_{(50)}$.

To see what actually happens using $\overline{W}$ as an estimator of $\mathsf{E}\{t(0)\}$, we conduct an experiment on the computer program PcNaive, which is an acronym from numerical analysis of instrumental variables estimators (see Doornik and Hendry, 2006d). An experiment of $M = 1000$ replications where $\beta = 0$ and n increases from 10 to 100 by steps of 5 allows us to investigate the impact of changes in sample size. At $n = 100$, this yields:

$$\overline{W} = -0.028, \quad \text{with MCSD}\left(\overline{W}\right) = 1.00, \quad \text{so MCSE}\left(\overline{W}\right) = 0.032, \quad (18.2.3)$$

recalling that $\mathrm{MCSE} = M^{-1/2}\mathrm{MCSD}$. An approximate 95% confidence interval for the simulated expectation of $t(0)$ can be computed from twice the Monte Carlo standard error, giving $[-0.006, 0.006]$. This confidence range is small, so the Monte Carlo is reasonably precise, but could of course be narrowed by increasing the number of replications.

Figure 18.1 illustrates the results graphically. Panel (a) shows the Monte Carlo standard deviation of $\widehat{\beta}$ as a function of n. This falls roughly as $n^{-1/2}$,

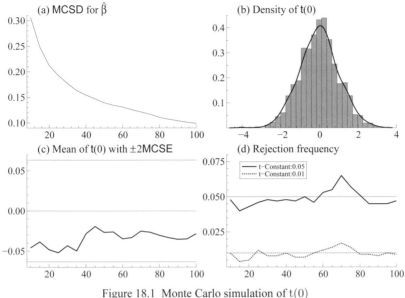

Figure 18.1 Monte Carlo simulation of $t(0)$

thereby illustrating that $n^{1/2}(\widehat{\beta} - \beta)$ is standard normal; see (3.4.7). At $n = 100$, the statistic $t(0)$ is $t[99]$-distributed. The simulated density is shown in panel (b) and appears to be close to standard normal, as expected for a t-distribution with a large degrees-of-freedom parameter. In panel (c), the simulated expectation of the t-statistic is shown as a function of n, and this is close to zero for all values of n. Correspondingly, the variance is close to one, so the 95% Monte Carlo standard error bands for the sample average is given by values close to $\pm 2M^{-1/2}$ as shown. The mean value of $t(0)$ is seen to behave a bit like a random walk. Finally, panel (d) analyzes the rejection frequency of t-tests at 5% and 1% levels, comparing $t(0)$ with $t[n-1]$-distributions. The rejection frequencies from such tests are shown in panel (d), again as a function of n. It is seen that they are close to their nominal values of 5% and 1%, with deviation due to the Monte Carlo sampling error.

18.2.2 Testing when the hypothesis is false

We now turn to the properties of the t-test when the hypothesis is not satisfied. As before, we will look at the restriction $\beta = 0$ in the simple regression model (18.2.1). The t-statistic, Z, is defined in (18.2.2) precisely as before, but we will investigate its properties when in fact $\beta \neq 0$.

When deriving the critical values of tests, we always use the distribution of the test statistic under the assumption that the restriction, $\beta = 0$, is satisfied. To get a test of level α of 5%, say, we choose a critical value c_α so $P_{\beta=0,n}(Z > c_\alpha) = \alpha$. With the present model, c_α is chosen from a $t[n-1]$-distribution, or up to an approximation, from a standard normal distribution. By fixing the level, the probability of a type I error of rejecting a true hypothesis is fixed. If the restriction is not satisfied, so $\beta \neq 0$, we will be interested in the probability of not committing a type II error of accepting a false hypothesis, $P_{\beta,n}(Z > c_\alpha)$, which we refer to as the power.

Even in simple situations, like here, it is complicated to give detailed analytic descriptions of power functions. To outline the idea, rewrite the t-statistic for the hypothesis $\beta = 0$ as:

$$Z = \frac{\widehat{\beta} - 0}{\sqrt{s^2/n}} = \frac{\widehat{\beta} - \beta}{\sqrt{s^2/n}} + \frac{(\beta - 0)\sqrt{n}}{\sqrt{s^2}}.$$

Whatever the value of β, the first term is always $t[n-1]$-distributed, whereas the second term determines a location shift of the distribution, which is of course zero, if indeed the hypothesis $\beta = 0$ is true. Since s^2 is a unbiased estimator for $\sigma^2 = 1$, the new location will be at $\psi = n^{1/2}\beta/\sigma$, and Z is said to have a non-central t-distribution with $n - 1$ degrees of freedom and non-centrality parameter ψ. In shorthand, we write $Z \overset{\text{D}}{=} t[n-1, \psi]$.

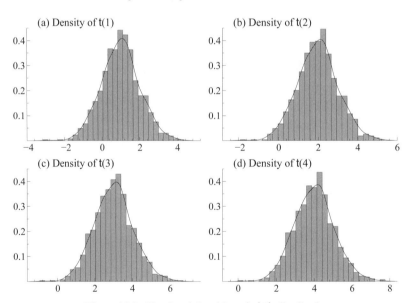

Figure 18.2 Simulated densities of $t(\psi)$-distributions

Using a Monte Carlo simulation, we can illustrate the properties of the t-test when the hypothesis is not satisfied. We will now have to vary the pairs (ψ, n), where $\psi = n^{1/2}\beta$ to describe the properties. In each of $M = 1000$ replications, we can generate data, $Y_1, \ldots, Y_n$, from (18.2.1) and calculate the t-statistic, Z, which we will now denote by $t(\psi)$, to emphasize the non-central element. Figure 18.2 shows the simulated densities of $t(\psi)$ for $n = 100$ and $\psi = 1, 2, 3, 4$. The densities are close to a normal distribution in shape, centered at ψ, but with a slight skewness to the right, which increases with ψ. Table 18.1 shows rejection frequencies for a one-sided test of $\beta = 0$ at a 5% level for the different values of ψ, so the critical value is 2.0. As can be seen both from Table 18.1 and Figure 18.2(b), there is a 50–50 chance of rejecting a false hypothesis when $\psi = 2$. For higher values of ψ, the probability of rejecting a false hypothesis increases toward unity, whereas for small values of ψ it is hard to reject the false hypothesis that $\beta = 0$.

ψ	0	1	2	3	4
$P_{\psi,n}\{t(\psi) > c_{5\%}\}$	0.05	0.16	0.51	0.84	0.98

Table 18.1 Rejection frequencies for t-tests

18.3 AUTOREGRESSIONS

We will now look at a stationary autoregression. First, we consider the properties of the so-called t-test that the intercept of a stationary autoregressive process is zero. Thereafter, the estimator of the autoregressive coefficient is investigated.

The data-generating process is now an autoregression:

$$Y_t = \phi + \rho Y_{t-1} + \epsilon_t \quad \text{with} \quad \epsilon_t \overset{D}{=} \mathsf{IN}\left[0, \sigma^2\right], \qquad (18.3.1)$$

where ρ, ϕ, $\sigma^2 \in \mathbb{R}^2 \times \mathbb{R}_+$, and $Y_0 \in \mathbb{R}$, for $t = 1, \ldots, T$. Then the simulation experiment is determined by specifying the set $(\rho, \phi, \sigma^2, Y_0, T)$.

18.3.1 Tests on the intercept

In a first experiment, we will be interested in analyzing the properties of the so-called t-statistic for the hypothesis that the intercept is zero, $\phi = 0$. Calculate the usual t-test of the hypothesis that $\phi = 0$, which we will denote by $t_{\phi=0}$, noting that the hypothesis is true here. As before the t-ratio is scale invariant, so we may normalize σ^2 at unity; see Exercise 18.1. Figure 18.3 illustrates the results from simulating with $M = 1000$ replications. Even though the t-statistic is not t-distributed, it is approximately standard normal, and the results of Figure 18.3 turn out to be similar to those of Figure 18.1. Panel (a) shows the Monte Carlo standard deviation of $\widehat{\phi}$ as a function of T, which is again falling roughly as $T^{-1/2}$, illustrating that $T^{1/2}(\widehat{\phi} - \phi)$ is asymptotically normal (see §12.7). The density of $t_{\phi=0}$ at $T = 100$ is shown in panel (b) and appears to be close to standard normal. In panel (c), the expectation of the simulated t-statistic is shown as a function of T, and it is seen to be close to zero for all values of T. Finally, panel (d) analyzes the rejection frequency of a t-test. The distribution of the t-statistic is not exactly a t-distribution, due to the time-series structure. Yet, we can still compare the t-statistic with a critical value stemming from a t-distribution and investigate the deviation by simulation. The rejection frequencies from such tests are shown in panel (d), again as a function of T. It is seen that they are reasonably close to their nominal values of 5% and 1%, converging as the sample size increases.

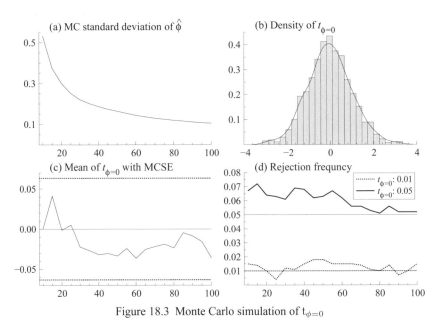

Figure 18.3 Monte Carlo simulation of $t_{\phi=0}$

18.3.2 Estimation of the autoregressive coefficient

In a second experiment, we will study the properties of the estimator for the autoregressive coefficient, $\widehat{\rho}$, using the same autoregressive model in (18.3.1). Here we consider the stationary case when $|\rho| < 1$, and below the unit-root case, $\rho = 1$. In large samples, when $|\rho| < 1$ it can be shown that:

$$\sqrt{T}\,(\widehat{\rho} - \rho) \stackrel{D}{\approx} \mathsf{N}\left[0, 1 - \rho^2\right]. \tag{18.3.2}$$

While the details of this argument are omitted, it is illustrative to compare the sample expressions in (12.7.1) with the population variance in (12.6.5). We can, however, check the result in (18.3.2) by a simple Monte Carlo, doing the same experiment as in §18.3 of $M = 1000$ replications at $(\rho, \phi, \sigma^2, Y_0, T) = (0.5, 0, 1, 0, T)$ with T increasing from 10 to 100 by steps of 5.

Figure 18.4 reports the results. Panel (a) records the density of $\widehat{\rho}$ for $T = 100$: this is no longer symmetric, although $M = 1000$ replications is rather small to reveal that very clearly. However, panel (b) shows that $E(\widehat{\rho})$ is about 0.25 at $T = 10$ and 0.47 ± 0.005 at $T = 100$, so in small samples, $\widehat{\rho}$ is far from ρ. Next, the t-test for the false hypothesis $\rho = 0$ is investigated. Panel (c) shows that the density of $t_{\rho=0}$ is more symmetric than that of ρ. As the hypothesis is false, it is centered on a value different from zero. This value is about 6, which is roughly $T^{1/2}\rho/(1 - \rho^2)^{1/2}$. To see this write:

$$t_{\rho=0} = t_{\rho=\rho} + \tau \qquad \text{where} \qquad t_{\rho=\rho} = \frac{\widehat{\rho} - \rho}{\text{se}\,(\widehat{\rho})}, \qquad \tau = \frac{\rho - 0}{\text{se}\,(\widehat{\rho})}, \tag{18.3.3}$$

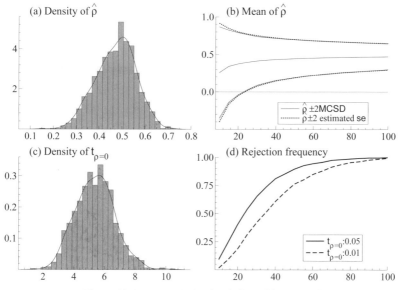

Figure 18.4 Monte Carlo simulation of $\widehat{\rho}$ and $t_{\rho=0}$

where $\widehat{\rho}$ and $se(\widehat{\rho})$ are given in (12.5.1) and (12.7.1), respectively. Since the t-statistic $t_{\rho=\rho}$ is approximately standard normally distributed, the expectation of $t_{\rho=0}$ will be close to the parameter τ. As indicated in (18.3.2), the standard error of $\widehat{\rho}$ is approximately $\{(1 - \rho^2)/T\}^{-1/2}$, rendering $\tau \approx T^{1/2}\rho/(1 - \rho^2)^{1/2}$ as desired. Finally, panel (d) shows that the rejection frequency of the false hypothesis that $\rho = 0$ rises rapidly with T, and is higher for a 5% than a 1% significance level.

18.3.3 Testing for a unit root

We next turn to the unit-root case where $\rho = 1$ in the autoregressive model (18.3.1). The asymptotic theory is now non-standard and involves Dickey–Fuller distributions rather than normal distributions, as discussed in §16.5, but can be illustrated using simulation.

The "t-statistic", $t_{\rho=1}$, for testing the unit-root hypothesis $\rho = 1$ now has a Dickey–Fuller DF$_c$-distribution. The standardized estimator $T(\widehat{\rho} - 1)$ can also be shown to have a Dickey–Fuller distribution, which will, however, be different from those Dickey–Fuller distributions reviewed in §16.5. Note that $(\widehat{\rho} - 1)$ needs to be scaled by T, rather than the usual $T^{1/2}$, to obtain a non-degenerate asymptotic distribution. We, therefore, refer to $\widehat{\rho}$ as being T-consistent, or super-consistent, in the I(1)–case where $\rho = 1$, and $T^{1/2}$-consistent in the I(0)–case where $|\rho| < 1$, respectively; but even after appropriate scaling, the form of the limiting distribution is different from that holding under stationarity. We now explore that difference.

Continuing with a Monte Carlo experiment for $M = 1000$ replications, but now at $(\rho, \phi, \sigma^2, Y_0, T) = (1, 0, 1, 0, T)$ with T increasing from 10 to 100 by steps of 5, we obtain the results shown in Figure 18.5. Panel (a) reveals that the density of $\hat{\rho}$ for $T = 100$ is definitely not symmetric, with a long left tail and few values greater than 1.0. The density of $\hat{\phi}$ in panel (b) has a very wide range, so outliers are quite likely. When discussing testing for a unit root, it is convenient to reparametrize (18.3.1) as:

$$\Delta Y_t = \phi + \pi Y_{t-1} + \epsilon_t, \qquad (18.3.4)$$

where $\pi = \rho - 1$. The density of the "t-statistic", $t_{\rho=1} = t_{\pi=0}$, which is referred to as the Dickey–Fuller t-statistic, is analyzed in panel (c). This distribution has most of its mass to the left of zero, even though the hypothesis is true—hence its different critical values, as reported in Table 16.5. Finally, panel (d) shows the density of a t-statistic for the intercept parameter, $t_{\phi=0}$. This is bimodal, and nothing like a t-distribution any longer, though again the null is true.

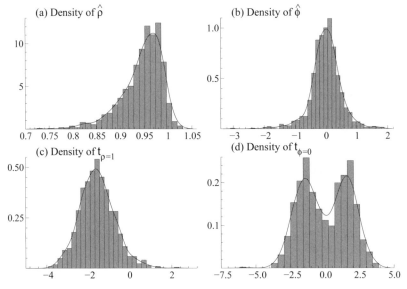

Figure 18.5 Monte Carlo simulations for a unit root

Panels (a) and (b) in Figure 18.6 record the coefficient of determination, R^2, when the regression is carried out in levels as in (18.3.1) and for the reparametrized model in (18.3.4). This emphasizes the point made earlier that R^2 is not invariant to reparametrization. High values are found for the specification in levels, where the regressand and the regressors are near colinear whereas lower values are found when applying the differenced regressand. Similar values for R^2 were found in the empirical models in Table 16.2 and Table 16.3.

Panels (c) and (d) in Figure 18.6 record the distributions of $\hat{\rho}$ for $\rho = 1$ and $\rho = 0.5$ as T increases from 25 to 100, to show the comparative behavior. The collapse toward a spike in $\hat{\rho}$ when $\rho = 1$ corresponds to the need to normalize its distribution by T rather than $T^{1/2}$. It is clear that unit-root non-stationarity

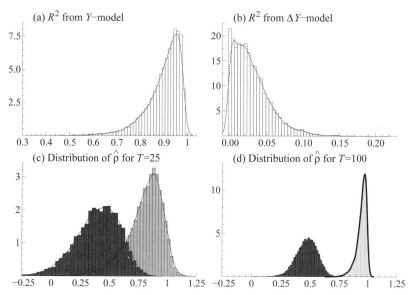

Figure 18.6 (a)/(b) Distribution of R^2 arising from (18.3.1)/(18.3.4) specifications. (c)/(d) Distributions of $\hat{\rho}$ for $\rho = 0.5$ (left) and $\rho = 1$ for $T = 25/100$

substantively changes the distributions of estimators and tests.

18.4 TESTING FOR COINTEGRATION

In Chapter 17, tests for cointegration rank were discussed in the context of a vector autoregression. The absence of cointegration can also be tested in a univariate autoregressive distributed-lag model. The properties of such tests can be investigated easily by Monte Carlo. The inspiration for cointegration came from the "nonsense regressions" of Yule (1926). These are considered at first.

18.4.1 Nonsense regressions

Relating two unrelated variable Y_t to Z_t by regression:

$$Y_t = \beta_0 + \beta_1 Z_t + u_t, \tag{18.4.1}$$

can induce what Yule (1926) called a "nonsense regression". That is, if the variables are non-stationary, but the non-stationarity is ignored, a "significant" relation is usually found, even though the variables have in fact no direct link. The simplest situation where this is the case is for the following bivariate $I(1)$ process:

$$\begin{aligned} \Delta Y_t &= \epsilon_{1,t}, \\ \Delta Z_t &= \epsilon_{2,t}, \end{aligned} \tag{18.4.2}$$

with $(\epsilon_{1,t}\ \epsilon_{2,t})$ having an independent bivariate standard normal distribution. Note that Y_t and Z_t are not cointegrated so are unrelated in levels or changes.

Using Monte Carlo we can check that the data-generating process (18.4.2) results in a "nonsense regression" when applying (18.4.1): Hendry (2004) offers a recent review. The fitted regression is likely to be severely mis-specified. Since Y_t is $I(1)$, under the hypothesis $H_0: \beta_1 = 0$ in (18.4.1), the error term u_t must be $I(1)$, and there is a massive violation of the regression assumptions of independent errors for the levels regression (18.4.1). But if u_t is $I(1)$, conventional "t-tests" will not have the correct distributions, namely it is not true that $P(|t_{\beta_1=0}| \geq 2.0|H_0) \simeq 0.05$. Phillips (1986) provides the correct distribution and shows that the "t-test" of $\beta_1 = 0$ has approximately a zero mean, but a diverging variance, so that $P(|t_{\beta_1=0}| \geq 2.0|H_0)$ converges to unity: in large samples, one is almost certain to reject the null, even though the series are unrelated! This lay behind the "rainfall causes inflation" spoof result in Hendry (1980).

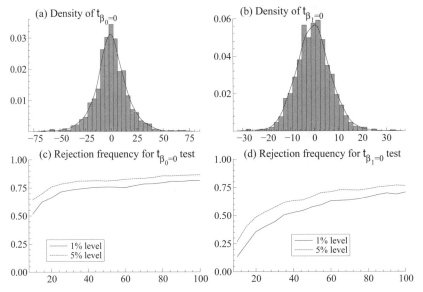

Figure 18.7 Monte Carlo simulations for a nonsense regression

Figure 18.7 illustrates the nonsense regression using Monte Carlo, with $T = 100$ and 1000 repetitions. Panels (a) and (c) record the density and rejection frequency for the "t-test" of the null that $\beta_0 = 0$. The former shows the very large values that result even under the null, the latter that the correct null is rejected about 80% of the time. Similar findings recur in panels (b) and (d) for testing $\beta_1 = 0$: a relationship would be claimed to exist about 75% of the time between Y_t and Z_t even though they are unrelated. The R^2 of the regression is also distorted (see Computer Task 18.2).

18.4.2 Cointegration testing

To check that a "nonsense regression" has not been estimated in (18.4.1), or, equivalently, test the hypothesis of no cointegration, one could test that the residuals

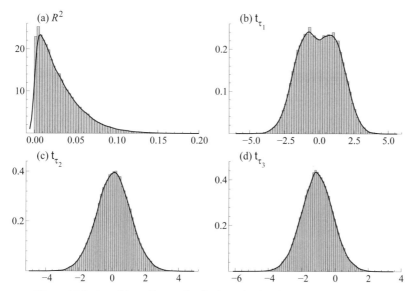

Figure 18.8 Densities of t-tests for the hypothesis of no relation in (18.4.4)

from the levels regression were $I(1)$ using a unit root. Let $\widehat{u}_t = Y_t - \widehat{\beta}_0 - \widehat{\beta}_1 Z_t$ denote residuals from fitting (18.4.1) and compute a t-test statistic for $\rho = 0$ in:

$$\Delta\widehat{u}_t = \rho\widehat{u}_{t-1} + \omega_t, \qquad\qquad (18.4.3)$$

possibly augmented with lags of $\Delta\widehat{u}_t$. The test distribution is of Dickey–Fuller-type but differs from those in Table 16.5, so its critical values need separate tabulation. This is the test for no cointegration suggested originally by Engle and Granger (1987). The distribution requires that the variable Z_t is weakly exogenous. It is also required that Y_t and Z_t are $I(1)$, so this test would have to be combined with unit root tests on Y_t and Z_t. This is in contrast to the cointegration analysis presented in Chapter 17, that is invariant to linear transformations of the variables. If Z_t were replaced a by k-dimensional vector of variables the distribution would alter with k. Only one cointegrating relation would be allowed among these variables, which is a non-trivial assumption when $k > 1$.

There are a number of alternatives to the Engle–Granger test. The one implemented in PcGive is based directly on an autoregressive distributed-lag model as in (14.4.4):

$$\Delta Y_t = \tau_1 + \tau_2\Delta Z_t + \tau_3 Y_{t-1} + \tau_4 Z_{t-1} + \epsilon_t. \qquad\qquad (18.4.4)$$

When $\tau_3 \neq 0$, the cointegrating vector can be obtained by solving (18.4.4) for $(1, \tau_4/\tau_3)$. Kremers, Ericsson and Dolado (1992) and Kiviet and Phillips (1992) show that the hypothesis of no cointegration can be tested using a t-test statistic for $\tau_3 = 0$. This is the "unit-root" test computed using the relevant distributions in PcGive when "analyzing the lag structure". This test requires the same set of assumptions as the Engle–Granger test. Banerjee et al. (1993) find the power of this test is higher than that of the Engle–Granger test when conditioning is valid. Harbo, Johansen, Nielsen and Rahbek (1998) discuss tests for the joint hypothesis $\tau_3 = \tau_4 = 0$, and present generalizations to cases where Y_t and Z_t are multivariate.

Again we can easily investigate this problem by Monte Carlo. We use the data-generating process in (18.4.2) and analyze it using (18.4.4) with the restriction $\tau_4 = -\tau_3$. Figure 18.8 shows that the difficulties observed for the "nonsense regression" are largely removed by using autoregressive distributed-lag model in equilibrium-correction form as in (18.4.4). Panel (a) shows the distribution of R^2 where small values now prevail. Compared with the "nonsense regression", the departure from normality is modest for the three t-tests. The distributions in (b,c) relating to the constant and the unit root are, however, of Dickey–Fuller type and somewhat similar to those seen in Figure 18.5(c,d). Such distributions are well-understood and implemented in econometric software. Thus, by always using a well-specified model, an investigator need not be fooled into estimating nonsense relations.

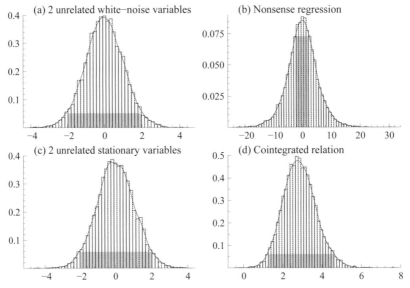

Figure 18.9 Frequency distributions of t-tests

As a final comparison, Figure 18.9 shows the frequency distributions of various t-tests for relationships between: (a) 2 unrelated series of independent observations, also called white-noise series; (b) 2 unrelated random-walk series: so this repeats Figure 18.7(b); (c) 2 unrelated stationary autoregressive series; and (d) 2 cointegrated I(1) series. The shaded region approximates the 95% confidence interval. In all but the 2 unrelated random-walk series, the interval is about ± 2 on either side of the mean, which is zero for (a) and (c), but not for the cointegrated series in (d). We can reasonably conclude that the large sample approximations to t-tests work well when the model is well-specified and in an equilibrium-correction or $I(0)$ form.

18.5 SUMMARY AND EXERCISES

Summary: The chapter describes the widely applicable technique of computer simulation experiments, called Monte Carlo methods, to obtain approximations to the distributions of statistics in complicated data-generating processes. We focus on distribution sampling, where random numbers replace the random errors assumed in the statistical model. Experiments are described for autoregressive coefficient estimation, testing for a unit root and testing for cointegration.

Bibliography: Distribution sampling has a long history in statistics, including such famous studies as Student (1908), who checked his analytical results for the t-distribution, and Yule (1926), who used it to explain the occurrence of nonsense regressions. More sophisticated methods of Monte Carlo were developed of the following decades, and Hammersley and Handscomb (1964) discuss many of these.

Key questions:

- Explain how averages of random numbers can be used to estimate the distributions of statistics such as estimators and tests.
- What do you think the major advantages and disadvantages of simulation experiments are compared to deriving distributions analytically?

Exercise 18.1. *Scale invariance. Consider the model given by (18.3.1) and the t-ratio for testing $\phi = 0$. Let $Y_0, Y_1, \ldots Y_T$ be a sample generated from (18.3.1) for a certain set of parameters $(\rho, 0, \sigma^2, Y_0, T)$. Let $\widetilde{Y}_t = Y_t/\sigma$ for $t = 0, 1, \ldots T$. (a) Argue that the t-ratios computed from $Y_0, Y_1, \ldots Y_T$ and $\widetilde{Y}_0, \widetilde{Y}_1, \ldots \widetilde{Y}_T$ are the same.*
(b) Argue that the distribution of the t-statistic is the same when the data generating process is given by the parameters $(\rho, 0, \sigma^2, Y_0, T)$ and $(\rho, 0, 1, Y_0/\sigma, T)$.

Computing Task 18.2. *Nonsense regression. Conduct a Monte Carlo experiment for the data-generating process in (18.4.2) when fitting the linear model in (18.4.1), to check the claim that the model is a "nonsense regression", namely, the variables Y and Z have no direct link, but an apparently significant relation between them will usually be found. Also, investigate R^2 of the regression.*

Computing Task 18.3. *Cointegrating regression. Conduct a Monte Carlo experiment where now (18.4.1) is the data-generating process with $\beta_0 = \beta_1 = 1$, when $Z_t = Z_{t-1} + v_t$ with u_t and v_t being independent and standard normal. Fit the linear model (18.4.1) to check the claim that the model is a "cointegrating relation", namely, the variables Y and Z have a well-defined link even though Z_t is non-stationary.*

Chapter Nineteen

Automatic model selection

The empirical analyses discussed so far have been relatively simple. Statistical models have been postulated and justified using a range of mis-specification tests and economic reasoning. These general models have then been simplified using testing, typically using likelihood ratio tests, resulting in the selection of simpler models. Among the major recent developments that will, in due course, almost certainly revolutionize this selection process are computer algorithms that aim to automate this process.

Several different approaches to automatic model selection are currently being researched, but as usual in this book, we will focus on methods using the approach to econometric modeling we have developed here. Initially, economists were skeptical of the properties of such methods, sometimes referring pejoratively to them as data mining, or "garbage in, garbage out" routines, but research has now demonstrated their excellent performance. We will briefly review what has been established in a regression framework, noting that the principles can be generalized to other models (see Campos, Ericsson and Hendry, 2005, for an overview and reprints of many of the key papers).

19.1 THE MODEL

Consider a large number, N, of candidate explanatory variables, where the general linear model is postulated to be:

$$Y_t = \sum_{i=1}^{N} \gamma_i Z_{i,t} + u_t, \qquad (19.1.1)$$

when the conditional data-generating equation is in fact nested in (19.1.1) as:

$$Y_t = \sum_{j=1}^{n} \beta_j Z_{(j),t} + \epsilon_t, \qquad (19.1.2)$$

with $\epsilon_t \overset{D}{=} \text{IN}\left[0, \sigma_\epsilon^2\right]$, independently of all the $\{Z_{i,t}\}$ in (19.1.1) for $n \leq N$. The variables that actually matter in (19.1.2) are denoted by $Z_{(j),t}$ to reflect that, say, only the first, third, and eighth of the original set might be relevant. The objective is to select these relevant regressors, namely the n different $Z_{(j),t}$ where $\beta_j \neq 0$ in (19.1.2), and to eliminate the irrelevant regressors, which are all the other $N - n$ variables, when all N are initially thought to be potentially relevant. A selection process will then select a model, with m, say, variables:

$$Y_t = \sum_{r=1}^{m} \delta_r Z_{\{r\},t} + \eta_t,
\qquad (19.1.3)$$

where $Z_{\{r\},t}$ again denotes some subset of the initial N candidate regressors. The key issue concerns the average "closeness" of the selected model (19.1.3) to the generating process (19.1.2). For simplicity, we consider the case where all the regressors in (19.1.1) are mutually orthogonal, and only discuss selection based on individual t-tests; a more advanced analysis is given in Hendry and Krolzig (2005).

The objective of locating (19.1.2) when commencing from (19.1.1) in a general-to-specific (Gets) approach can be analyzed in five main stages. The next section, §19.2, sketches the first two steps of model formulation and congruence testing leading to (19.1.1), then §19.3 considers how to eliminate its irrelevant variables. Section 19.4 discusses the issues involved in keeping the variables that matter, which is the other main problem to be solved if (19.1.3) is to be close to (19.1.2). The algorithm itself is described in §19.5. Properties of that algorithm, and the fifth stage of how to obtain nearly unbiased estimates, are noted in §19.6. Finally, §19.7 describes a variant that also makes a number of decisions about the formulation of (19.1.1).

19.2 MODEL FORMULATION AND MIS-SPECIFICATION TESTING

We will start with the formulation of (19.1.1), which is the most general, statistical model that can reasonably be postulated initially, given the available sample of data, previous empirical and theoretical research, and any institutional and measurement information available. We call this a *general unrestricted model* (GUM).

The general unrestricted model should embed as a special case the parsimonious, interpretable, and invariant econometric model at which the modeling exercise aims. For example, in analyzing quarterly money demand as in Chapter 17, the general unrestricted model might comprise the current values and five lags of each of nominal money and prices, income, inflation, and the opportunity cost of holding money, indices of taxation structure, proxies for major financial innovations, and so on. Because of the interdependence of variables in economics, and the resulting invalidity of models that omit relevant variables, one should allow at the outset for everything that might matter, at least logically, if not necessarily empirically. The general unrestricted model must be structured by a careful theoretical analysis, as mindlessly modeling the contents of a large data bank is rarely helpful. One helpful step is taking appropriate data transformations, such as logs or differences, or possible cointegrating relations, in order to form near orthogonal variables. The parameters should be formulated such that they are likely to be constant over the sample (we will return to this issue in Chapter 20), and possibly interpretable as propensities or elasticities. The parametrization may perhaps evolve with changes in financial regulation, and so on. Many of these issues can be resolved only by empirical evidence.

We test that (19.1.1) is consistent with the data by conducting k independent mis-specification tests based on statistics $t_1, \dots t_k$, as discussed in §9.5. Each test is conducted at significance level α, say 1%, with critical values c_α, where rejection occurs when $|t_i| > c_\alpha$. Then, under the null that (19.1.2) is correctly specified, the probability that none of the tests will reject (19.1.1) can be computed as in (9.5.1):

$$ \mathsf{P}\left(|t_i| \le c_\alpha, i = 1, \dots, k\right) = (1 - \alpha)^k \simeq 1 - \alpha k, \qquad (19.2.1) $$

giving an overall level of approximately αk. Thus, if $\alpha = 0.01$ and $k = 5$, roughly 95% of the time no tests will reject, and (19.1.1) will be retained when it should be. The probability calculation in (19.2.1) is typical of model selection based on repeated testing, and similar formulas will recur below. Here, we note that more tests lead to a higher probability of falsely rejecting specification (19.1.1) when it is correct, in the sense that it is not mis-specified and nests the data-generating process (19.1.2). Thus, a small number of tests directed at the most likely mis-specifications is desirable. However, more sophisticated rules than a simple accept/reject decision could be used, though we will not investigate those here.

Assuming that a congruent general unrestricted model has been selected, the objective is to simplify it without significant loss of information about the parameters of interest. We would like to select (19.1.2), but of course, do not actually know which are the relevant and which the irrelevant regressors. After simplification, we should check that the choice remains congruent, then test it by encompassing any alternative models not already embedded in the general unrestricted model. This used to be an art, requiring experience, practice and skill, but as we will discuss in the next sections model selection can been computerized to automatically implement many of these steps.

19.3 REMOVING IRRELEVANT VARIABLES

With N candidate explanatory variables in (19.1.1), there are 2^N possible models, corresponding to the inclusion or exclusion of each variable. When $N = 40$, that is $2^{40} \simeq 10^{12}$ possible models—rather too many for any human to consider manually. Consider using t-tests to select which are the relevant variables, using a significance level α and associated critical value c_α. If (19.2.1) determined the outcome of such a large number of tests as 2^N, it may be thought that the situation would be hopeless, since even a tiny null rejection frequency per test would lead to almost certain rejection of the data-generating process. Fortunately, the practical situation is quite different, partly because selection does not necessarily involve fitting all the submodels. Indeed, in the orthogonal regressor case that we are considering for the moment, compute the t-test statistics after fitting (19.1.1). Square them to avoid considering their signs, and rank them in the order, say, $t^2_{(1)} \geq t^2_{(2)} \geq \cdots \geq t^2_{(N)}$, where $t^2_{(1)}$ denotes whichever happens to be largest. To select a submodel like (19.1.3), let m be such that $t^2_{(m)} \geq c^2_\alpha > t^2_{(m+1)}$ so $t^2_{(m)}$ defines the smallest, but still significant, t-value. Retain the regressors corresponding to the m largest t-values and discard the rest. Thus, only one decision is needed, not many, and especially not 2^N, to select equation (19.1.3). The obvious question is how close (19.1.3) is likely to be to (19.1.2).

Because every test statistic has a distribution, different outcomes will occur in different samples, and these are determined by the specification of the unrestricted general model in (19.1.1) and the data-generating process in (19.1.2). For the irrelevant regressors, their number, M, matters, whereas for the relevant regressors the non-centrality parameters, introduced in §18.2 matter. First, consider the situation where all the variables are in fact irrelevant and independent. For each variable, the decision to retain it can be described as a Bernoulli$[\alpha]$-distributed variable. With N independent irrelevant variables, the average number of retained variables will then be αN even though none really matters. For example, if $\alpha = 0.01$ and $N = 40$ as before, then $\alpha N = 0.4$: roughly, from every five times one tries to select significant variables out of 40 irrelevant regressors, then on three occasions none will be retained, so all 40 will be correctly eliminated, and on two occasions out of five times, 1 irrelevant variable out of the 40 will be kept, with 39 correctly eliminated. Thus, even in such an extreme scenario, almost every irrelevant variable will be correctly eliminated almost every time, and in that sense (19.1.3) is likely to be close to (19.1.2). A large increase in knowledge results from discovering that almost every candidate variable can be ignored.

The same outcome can be represented using (19.2.1) to calculate the probability that no test will reject, which delivers $(1 - 0.01)^{40} \simeq 0.67$, with the implication that the wrong model is selected 33% of the time. The difference between this probability of 0.33 and the average number of retained variables of 0.4, described above, comes about as occasionally 2 or more variables might be retained by chance, which was omitted in the rough heuristic above. It sounds poor that the wrong model is selected 33% of the time. However, that summary fails to reflect how successful the reduction is from 40 variables to almost none most of the time.

In the implementation of this approach to selection, it is important to realize that, under the hypothesis that all variables are irrelevant, the largest test statistic, $t^2_{(1)}$, will typically have a value close to the chosen critical value c^2_α. For example, when $\alpha = 0.01$, using a 2-sided test for $T = 100$, then $c_\alpha \simeq 2.6$ (see Table 2.1), whereas an observed t-statistic outside the interval ± 3 will occur only 0.34% of the time, and one outside ± 4 only 0.01%, which is once for every 10000 irrelevant variables tried. Hendry and Krolzig (2005) conclude that although eliminating the irrelevant variables is often deemed to be problematic, in practice that is not the case, and the real difficulty is retaining the variables that matter, so we now consider that issue.

19.4 KEEPING VARIABLES THAT MATTER

This is the obverse problem to be solved if (19.1.3) is to be close to (19.1.2). To progress, we must first consider how often (19.1.2) would be found if it was in fact the general model from which we commenced, so $N = n$, with all candidate variables relevant. We draw on the analysis in Hendry and Krolzig (2001) and consider $n = 1$. The equations (19.1.1) and (19.1.2) now reduce to:

$$Y_t = \beta Z_t + \epsilon_t, \tag{19.4.1}$$

with $\beta \neq 0$ and $\epsilon \overset{D}{=} N[0, \sigma_\epsilon^2]$. In the selection procedure, we will seek to test the false hypothesis that $\beta = 0$. Since the hypothesis is false, the non-central t-distribution introduced in §18.2 is relevant to describe the outcome from testing. The t-test statistic for the hypothesis $\beta = 0$ will have the non-central t$[T - 1, \psi]$-distribution (see §18.2.2), where $\psi = T^{1/2}\beta/\sigma_\epsilon$ is the non-centrality parameter. As in Chapter 18, we will denote the t-test statistic by t(ψ). A two-sided test is used, so $P_{\psi=0,T-1}(|t(0)| \geq c_\alpha) = \alpha$. When the null is false, such a test will reject with a probability that varies with ψ, c_α, and the degrees of freedom $T - 1$. At a practical level, variables with very small non-centralities will be similar to irrelevant variables, and almost never detected by the algorithm, or by an empirical investigator. When information about the likely sign of a parameter exists, a 1-sided test would deliver somewhat higher power.

ψ	0	1	2	3	4	5
$\alpha = 0.05$	0.05	0.168	0.508	0.843	0.977	0.998
$\alpha = 0.01$	0.01	0.057	0.271	0.648	0.913	0.989
$\alpha = 0.001$	0.001	0.010	0.092	0.352	0.730	0.942

Table 19.1 Rejection frequencies $P_{\psi,T-1}\{t^2(\psi) > c_\alpha^2\}$ for the t-statistic for $\beta = 0$ in (19.4.1) with $T = 100$; simulated using $M = 10^4$ repetitions

We will be interested in calculating the probability of rejecting the false hypothesis, $\beta = 0$, when $\psi \neq 0$, also called the power. In this case, these powers are found by comparing the non-central t$[T - 1, \psi]$-distribution, when $\psi = T^{1/2}\beta/\sigma_\epsilon$ with the quantiles of the standard t$[T - 1]$-distribution. This is easy to simulate, as reported in Table 18.1 in §18.2.2. In this way, Table 19.1 is based on simulating from (19.4.1) with $Z_t = 1$, so Z_t is strongly exogenous, and calculating rejection frequencies for the t-statistic for $\beta = 0$. The table reveals that there is little chance of retaining a variable when $\psi = 1$: consequently, power must be

even lower for smaller non-centralities, which is a property of statistical inferen-
ceper se, not model selection. For $\psi = 2$ there is only a 51% chance of retaining
a variable using a 5% level test, when the critical value is 2, and that probability
falls to 27% for a 1%-level test with critical value 2.6. When $\psi = 3$, the power of
detection is sharply higher at the 5%-level, but still leads to 35% misclassifications
when $\alpha = 0.01$. Finally, when $\psi \geq 4$, a variable will almost always be retained,
even at more stringent significance levels. One may conclude that despite knowing the correct distribution, using exact rather than asymptotic critical values, and
only testing once, there is a probability in excess of 35% of not finding a variable
significant for $\psi \leq 3$. This is roughly the same probability as retaining by chance
1 of 40 irrelevant variables.

ψ	1	2	3	4	5	6
$\alpha = 0.05$	0.000	0.014	0.322	0.848	0.986	1.000
$\alpha = 0.01$	0.000	0.000	0.055	0.521	0.921	0.995
$\alpha = 0.001$	0.000	0.000	0.001	0.109	0.635	0.943

Table 19.2 Overall frequencies for rejecting $\beta_j = 0$ for all $j = 1, \ldots, 6$, based on simulating $p = P_{\psi, T-6}\{t^2(\psi) > c_\alpha^2\}$ for $T = 100$ using $M = 10^4$ repetitions; the reported numbers are the 6th powers, p^6

Turning to a situation with $n = 6$ orthogonal and relevant regressors, we
may want to test each of the hypotheses $\beta_j = 0$ for $j = 1, \ldots, 6$, and compute
the overall frequency of rejecting all hypotheses. In this case, the powers of the
individual tests are found by comparing the non-central $t[T - 6, \psi]$-distribution,
where $\psi = T^{1/2}\beta/\sigma_\epsilon$, to the quantiles of the standard $t[T - 6]$-distribution. These
can be simulated as above. Due to the orthogonality, the $n = 6$ test statistics are
independent, so the overall rejection frequency is found by taking the 6th power of
the individual rejection frequencies. Table 19.2 reports the results for $T = 100$ and
$M = 10^4$. As can be seen, the probability of retaining all six relevant variables is
essentially negligible for a wide range of non-centralities, $\psi < 5$, and levels, α.

The figures reported in Table 19.2 are close to the 6th powers of the figures
in Table 19.1, since T and $T - n$ are close. Settings with mixed values of ψ can be
derived simply by multiplying the probabilities in Table 19.1. For instance, if $n =
3$ and $\alpha = 5\%$ and the non-centralities are $\psi = 2, 3, 4$, the joint rejection frequency
is approximately $0.505 \times 0.846 \times 0.979 = 0.418$. Such combined probabilities
are most influenced by variables with small non-centralities. Even if one knew
the specification of the data-generating process equation, but had to test the null
hypothesis that each variable was indeed relevant, it is unlikely that every variable
would be correctly retained unless all had large non-centralities. This reveals a lack
of power in statistical inference, not a problem with search algorithms.

In evaluating a search algorithm, therefore, there are two aspects to keep in
mind: the elimination of irrelevant variables and the retention of relevant variables.

The cost of eliminating the irrelevant variables, which could be called the cost of search, is low, whereas the cost of retaining relevant variables is high, associated with the cost of making inference. When commencing from (19.1.1), with $N-n=$ 10 irrelevant variables and $n=6$ relevant variables, say, the outcome in (19.1.3), should be judged against the baseline of how often the data-generating process equation itself would be retained when commencing from (19.1.1), with only the $n=6$ relevant variables, to focus on the cost of search. A comparison with a benchmark where it was known a priori which variables are relevant as in (19.1.2) so no testing was needed, would mix the costs of search and inference. On that basis, Hendry and Krolzig (2005) conclude that general-to-specific (Gets) searches from a congruent initial model are successful.

19.5 A GENERAL-TO-SPECIFIC ALGORITHM

We have shown that repeated testing to sort relevant from irrelevant variables will correctly eliminate most of the latter, but cannot retain more of the former than when starting from the data-generating process equation. Hendry and Krolzig (2005) show for their program PcGets that with orthogonal regressors, (19.1.3) chosen from (19.1.1) will be close to the equation selected by the same rules when commencing from (19.1.2). Their particular algorithm is discussed in Hendry and Krolzig (2001), but we can summarize the main features of general-to-specific model selection matching the stages of selection noted in §19.1 above.

First, the specification of the general unrestricted model (19.1.1) must be made by the investigator based on the substantive context. Next, (19.1.1) is tested for mis-specification, usually that the residuals are well behaved in terms of being approximately normal, homoskedastic and independent, and that the parameters are constant. If so, the third stage of model reduction commences. Since all 2^N paths cannot be investigated in reasonable time for a large N, even on a computer, any algorithm would have to focus on some of these paths only. Such a subselection of paths can be chosen efficiently though. The PcGets algorithm checks whether the least significant variable can be eliminated given a critical value c_α, and if so, whether the simplified equation remains congruent. The path of successive elimination of each least-significant variable is explored, checking that congruence is maintained at every step, until either no variables can be eliminated, or a diagnostic test rejects. The last non-rejected model is stored as a terminal equation. The search recommences from (19.1.1), but now checking if the next least-significant variable can be eliminated, and so on until all initially feasible paths are explored, and a set of terminal models has been collected. This multipath search procedure, related to that proposed by Hoover and Perez (1999), has been a crucial element in the development of operationally successful Gets algorithms.

A new stage is testing between these terminal selections using encompassing to ascertain if there is a single dominant model in the set that encompasses all the others. If so, this becomes the selected model. If not, dominated models are eliminated, the union of the remainder is formed as a new starting point, and the multipath search procedure recommences. This complete sequence continues until either a unique selection emerges or a set of mutually encompassing, well-specified, and undominated terminal models is located. It can often be an advantage to be confronted with a few good models, as this may given an investigator a better chance of understanding the nuances of the econometric problem. An investigator can select between these on economic grounds leading to a congruent model. Alternatively, the selection can be guided by information criteria, which are likelihood values penalized by the number of parameters. A selection based exclusively on information criteria without any regard to the subject matter is, however, not necessarily optimal.

19.6 SELECTION BIAS

Once a final selection has been made as in (19.1.3), the issue arises as to what the distribution of the resulting estimators should be. In §7.6.2, a "conditional interpretation" was put forward. According to that interpretation, the selected model (19.1.3) is viewed as the starting point, and estimators of this model are considered normally distributed. With automatic selection of submodels, the substantive context is, however, largely ignored. This in itself is not necessarily a problem, in that the automatically selected submodel could be evaluated and modified according to the substantive context. The other issue brought forward in §7.6.2 was that marginal decisions would enlarge selection bias effects. We will now look more systematically at that issue.

A more formalistic interpretation than the "conditional interpretation" arises when analyzing the distribution of the estimators in the submodel in the context of the general model. To clarify the effects of selection, we will initially consider the situation where the data-generating process equation (19.1.2) is the starting point, then turn to the case of a general unrestricted model (19.1.1) as the starting point, which seems more realistic since an economy is too complicated and evolving to ever anticipate a perfect initial model specification.

Starting from (19.1.2), we will consider the impact of a selection rule such as "retain $Z_{(j),t}$ in (19.1.2) if and only if $|t_{\beta_j=0}| > c_\alpha$". With this selection rule, which does not involve the substantive context, the selected model (19.1.3) will have estimates, $\widetilde{\beta}_j$, which are large relative to their estimated standard error, because regressors with small t-statistics have been eliminated. Since the estimators, $\widehat{\beta}_j$, obtained from the initial model (19.1.2) would be unbiased, conditionally on (19.1.2) being the data-generating process equation, the selected estimator, $\widetilde{\beta}_j$, must be upward biased conditional on retaining $Z_{(j),t}$. Conversely, unselected variables will have downward biased estimators, but one could not tell if their elimination was correct, in the sense of the hypothesis being true, or "bad luck" in that an insignificant draw occurred. Indeed, Tables 19.1 and 19.2 rejection frequencies showed that incorrect omission was quite likely to occur. We will now focus on the upward selection bias after retention. This will be done by allowing a general specification like (19.1.1) to be the starting point.

We can investigate the magnitude of the selection bias using simulation. The general unrestricted model is of the form in (19.1.1) with $N = 4$ variables, of which 2 are irrelevant, and 2 relevant with coefficients of $(0.2,\ 0.3)$, so the data-generating process is:

$$Y_t = \gamma_1 + \gamma_2 Z_{2,t} + \gamma_3 Z_{3,t} + \gamma_4 Z_{4,t} + u_t \qquad (19.6.1)$$

for $t = 1, \ldots, T$, with $T = 100$ and $u_t \overset{D}{=} \mathsf{IN}[0, \sigma^2]$. The regressors $Z_{j,t}$ in (19.6.1) are generated from $Z_{j,t} \overset{D}{=} \mathsf{IN}[0, 1]$ and renewed in each replication of the simulation study. The regressors are, therefore, not orthogonal, but will have modest sample correlations. The data-generating process is then defined by:

$$\gamma_1 = 0, \qquad \gamma_2 = 0.2, \qquad \gamma_3 = 0.3, \qquad \gamma_4 = 0, \qquad \sigma^2 = 1.$$

The relevant regressors are $Z_{2,t}$ and $Z_{3,t}$, while the intercept and $Z_{4,t}$ are irrelevant. The corresponding non-centrality parameters, $\psi = T^{1/2} \beta / \sigma$, are 2, 3, 0, 0 respectively. The data-generating process (19.6.1) resembles that of Krolzig and Hendry (2001). They conducted an experiment with $N = 22$ orthogonal variables or which 5 are relevant with coefficients $(0.2,\ 0.3,\ 0.4,\ 0.6,\ 0.8)$. To simplify, we report a subset of their result. Because all the variables are nearly orthogonal, the distributions of these 4 are not much affected by the fact that selected models involved more variables.

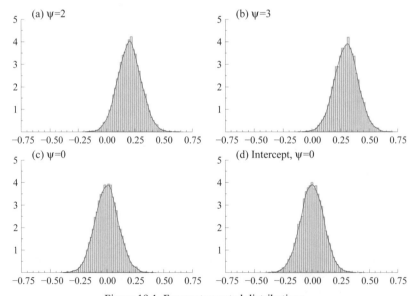

Figure 19.1 Four untruncated distributions

Figure 19.1 illustrates the distributional outcomes for the four coefficients from direct least-squares estimates of the unrestricted model (19.6.1). The figures are based on a simulation with $M = 10000$ replications. The outcomes are relatively uncertain, with all the ranges well in excess of 0.5, but each distribution is correctly centered at the value of the corresponding parameter in (19.6.1) and appears to be normal, as we saw in §7.5. We call these the untruncated distributions.

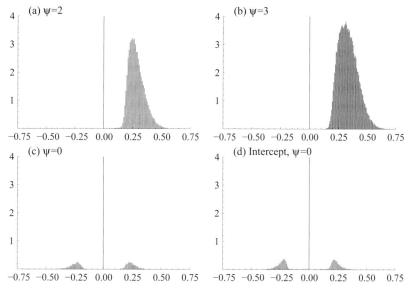

Figure 19.2 Four unconditional distributions; the point masses at zero are not to scale

Figure 19.2 reports the results of selection at $c_\alpha = 2$. In each replication, the general model is estimated. Regressors with t-statistics smaller than $c_\alpha = 2$ are eliminated, and the remaining regressors retained. This results in selecting one of $2^4 = 16$ submodels of (19.6.1). A new regression is performed for the selected submodel with the retained variables only. For instance, if the t-statistics associated with $Z_{3,t}$ and $Z_{4,t}$ were small, a new regression would be performed with just $Z_{1,t}$ and $Z_{2,t}$ as regressors. The coefficients γ_3 and γ_4 would then be estimated as zero, contributing to the point masses at zero in Figure 19.2. We refer to these as the unconditional distributions. The coefficients of the irrelevant regressors, shown in (c,d) are seen to be close to zero for most replications, whereas in (a,b) the distributions of relevant regressors are skewed relatively to those in Figure 19.1.

In Figure 19.3, the point masses at zero have been eliminated and the densities normalized so as to integrate to unity. This then shows the sampling distributions of the estimators, conditionally on selecting the associated regressors. We refer to these as the conditional distributions. Figure 19.3(c,d) shows more clearly that the distributions of the coefficients for the irrelevant variables are bimodal, because all values with small t-statistics have been eliminated. These panels, therefore, reflect a situation of type I errors. This situation is relatively rare; is controlled by the testing level, which is 5% here; and results in test statistics for irrelevant variables that are retained by chance, which tend to be close to the critical value. Panels (a,b) show the different extents of truncation for non-zero non-centralities. This is roughly 50% when the non-centrality equals the critical value of two, and much smaller, at 15% for the larger non-centrality parameter. This also matches the calculations in Table 19.1 above. In actual practice, we could not observe these non-centralities, but merely estimate them. The results indicate that the selection bias will be largest in marginal cases, where the corresponding test statistics would be close to the critical value.

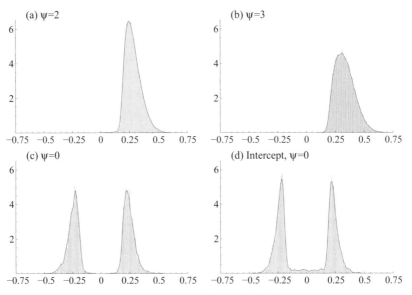

Figure 19.3 Four conditional distributions

From a statistical viewpoint, the shift in relevant variable distributions due to selecting only significant outcomes entails that the final selected estimators are biased estimators of the true parameter. For some purposes, such as economic policy analysis, such a bias is undesirable and would suggest a stronger absolute reaction than will in fact occur. A natural response is to bias-correct the outcome, and for normally distributed outcomes, it is relatively easy to derive approximate corrections based on knowing the degree of truncation, which in turn is determined by c_α. Hendry and Krolzig (2005) present the relevant formulas, closely related to the corrections for sample selection proposed by Heckman (1976). Figure 19.4 illustrates the post-correction distributions for the same four variables as in (19.6.1). The bias correction brings the distributions closer to the origin. The impact is more marked for $\psi = 2$ than $\psi = 3$, and even more so for the irrelevant variables, whose distributions are sharply shifted toward the origin. Thus, not only are the resulting estimates for non-zero β_j nearly unbiased, but those for irrelevant variables are considerably attenuated. This occurs because the bias corrections are largest for estimates with $|t|$-values closest to c_α, becoming smaller as $|t|$-values rise; there is, therefore, little effect on highly significant estimates and a large effect on marginal estimates, which could be significant by chance. Such an outcome is again beneficial in a policy context, since the impacts of irrelevant variables are attenuated.

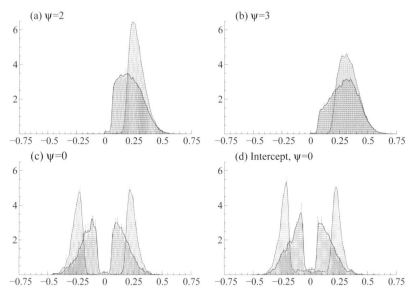

Figure 19.4 Bias-corrected distributions; the darker distributions are the corrected ones; the lighter are taken from Figure 19.3 for comparison

In this Monte Carlo simulation, the regressors $Z_{j,t}$ in (19.6.1) have been constructed to be independent. With near collinearity between relevant and irrelevant regressors, it would become difficult to correctly eliminate irrelevant regressors. This can, however, be avoided through orthogonalization. The order of the orthogonalization will matter, however, and result in different selected models, which could be compared using encompassing and evaluated in the substantive context.

To summarize, using the correction formulas, unbiased estimates of parameters of relevant variables can be obtained, with considerable attenuation in the coefficients of variables that have been retained by chance sampling. Hendry and Krolzig (2005) also demonstrate that the estimated equation standard error, $\widehat{\sigma}_\epsilon$ in (19.1.2), is approximately unbiased, perhaps even upward biased when $\alpha = 0.01$ by omitting relevant variables, so that the selected model does not "overfit" despite selecting from 40 candidate regressors. Consequently, when the relevant variables are retained, their estimated standard errors are close to those that would have been obtained from estimating (19.1.2).

In practical econometric modeling, a wide range of information is of course used. A formal statistical model is set up and analyzed. At every stage in the analysis, inferences are evaluated in light of the economic context and related economic studies as well as the data evidence. The simplification of the model can be done manually or by using an automated model selection program like PcGets or "autometrics" in PcGive, but in the end, the result from automatic model selection should be evaluated in the substantive context, and any variables that have been eliminated may be reentered. The largest selection bias arises from marginal test statistics and strongly correlated regressors, in which case statistics alone cannot provide a clear guide. When these cases are treated with caution, the "conditional interpretation" can be applied.

19.7 ILLUSTRATION USING UK MONEY DATA

To illustrate the automatic model selection, we return to the UK money data analyzed in Chapter 17. There we looked at time series for the velocity of circulation of narrow money, $v_t = x_t - (m_t - p_t)$, and the opportunity cost of holding money C_t. The primary tool for analysis was a systems-based cointegration analysis. In principle, it would be possible to construct software for automatic model selection in that situation, but that is not available at present. We will, instead, go through a single equation analysis using the software PcGets; see Hendry and Krolzig (2001).

There will be two stages of the analysis, reflecting the cointegration properties of the data. In a first step, the data are entered in levels to find the cointegrating relationship. For that stage, PcGets, has a "quick modeler", where only the variable names are entered. Entering the variables (v_t, C_t, $D_{oil,t}$, $D_{out,t}$) with v_t as the only endogenous variable, PcGets initially allows for up to five lags of all variables, corresponding to a year of quarterly data plus an additional lag. Mis-specification tests are conducted, and then a model selection algorithm is used, resulting in the model presented in Table 19.3.

$$\widehat{v}_t = \underset{(0.07)}{0.62}\,v_{t-1} + \underset{(0.07)}{0.28}\,v_{t-2} + \underset{(0.05)}{0.55}\,C_t + \underset{(0.01)}{0.04}\,D_{out,t} - \underset{(0.02)}{0.06}\,D_{71:1,t}$$

standard error

$$\sqrt{\widehat{\sigma}^2} = 0.0156, \quad \widehat{\ell} = 275.5, \quad T = 100, \quad 1964{:}3\text{--}1989{:}2$$

$\chi^2_{norm}[2] = 1.3 \quad [p = 0.53]$	$F_{ar(1-4)}[4, 91] = 0.7 \quad [p = 0.60]$
$F_{het}[8, 86] = 0.7 \quad [p = 0.68]$	$F_{arch(1-4)}[4, 87] = 0.7 \quad [p = 0.56]$

Table 19.3 Initially selected model, using the "quick modeling" option of PcGets

Using an outlier detection procedure, the observation for 1971:1 has been singled out and a dummy variable inserted. Overall, the selected model should be interpreted with a grain of salt. We have previously found from testing and from graphing that the variables are non-stationary. Two important consequences are that t-ratios will have non-standard distributions, and there can be near collinearity among the regressors. PcGets has a collinearity tool that indicates the presence of near collinearity. An orthogonalization of the regressors is called for. Cointegration gives a means of orthogonalizing the variables. The long-run solution can be determined as in §17.4, using the dynamic analysis option of PcGets:

$$e_t = v_t - 5.30C_t.$$

If we assume that there is one cointegrating vector and that C_t is weakly exogenous, which we established in Chapter 17 (also see Computing Task 19.1), this long-run solution will be a consistent estimate of the cointegrating relation. Indeed, it is not much different from what was found in Chapter 17.

In the second step of the analysis, the variables are orthogonalized by taking differences and using the long-run solution, giving $(\Delta v, \ \Delta C, \ e)$, which are $I(0)$-variables. The "quick modeling" device can no longer be used, as there is perfect collinearity among the variables $(\Delta v_t, \ \Delta C_t, \ e_t, \ e_{t-1})$. We now use the "advanced modeling" device and specify the general unrestricted model explicitly:

$$\Delta v_t = \beta_0 + \sum_{j=1}^{k} \beta_{v,j} \Delta v_{t-j} + \sum_{j=0}^{k} \beta_{C,j} \Delta C s_{t-j}$$

$$+ \beta_e e_{t-1} + \beta_{out} D_{out,t} + \beta_{oil} D_{oil,t} + u_t,$$

with $k = 4$ chosen as the initial lag length, in the light of the previous analysis. There is a choice of two strategies that, respectively, minimize the risks of deleting relevant variables (liberal strategy) and of keeping irrelevant variables (conservative strategy). In this case, the choice does not make a difference. PcGets then selects the model in Table 19.4. This model is identical to the model in Table 19.3. A careful inspection reveals minor differences in the numerical rounding errors, since the near collinearity in the first model makes it slightly less reliable. The fact that these reduced models are all the same stems from the few variables involved, but this will not generally be the case, as illustrated by Computing Task 19.3.

$$\widehat{\Delta v}_t = \underset{(0.01)}{-0.10}\, e_{t-1} - \underset{(0.07)}{0.27}\, \Delta v_{t-1} + \underset{(0.08)}{0.58}\, \Delta C_t + \underset{(0.01)}{0.04}\, D_{out,t} - \underset{(0.02)}{0.07}\, D_{71:1,t}$$
$$\text{se}$$

$$\sqrt{\widehat{\sigma}^2} = 0.0158, \quad \widehat{\ell} = 275.6, \quad T = 100, \quad 1964{:}3\text{--}1989{:}2$$

$\chi^2_{\text{norm}}[2] = 1.5 \quad [\text{p} = 0.47]$	$F_{\text{ar}(1-4)}[4, 91] = 0.6 \quad [\text{p} = 0.64]$
$F_{\text{het}}[8, 86] = 0.8 \quad [\text{p} = 0.58]$	$F_{\text{arch}(1-4)}[4, 87] = 0.7 \quad [\text{p} = 0.58]$

Table 19.4 Final selected model, using the "advanced modeling" option of PcGets

The model in Table 19.4 can be interpreted as follows. The lack of intercept indicates that velocity does not have an "autonomous" growth rate over the period. The negative coefficient on the lagged dependent variable, v_{-1}, suggests some "overshooting", consistent with some theories of money demand, such as Smith (1986). The impact effects on $\widehat{\Delta v}_t$ from changes in the cost of holding money, C_t, are much smaller than their long-run effects, suggesting relatively slow adjustment. The feedback coefficient for e_{t-1} is very significant and suggests that about 10% of any disequilibrium is removed each quarter (see Akerlof, 1982). Finally, the dummy in 1971:1 picks up an outlier when decimalization occurred in the UK (15 February 1971). Banks were closed for four days before decimalization day to convert accounts, machinery, clear old currency checks, and so on: anticipating that closure, individuals may reasonably have held rather more money than usual.

To gather information about how many marginal decisions have been made in the process of eliminating variables Table 19.5 reports tests for omitted variables. These are constructed by reentering the variables one by one. The most marginal cases come from the longest lags, suggesting a slight seasonal effect even though the data are seasonally adjusted. An overall test against the general unrestricted model can be based on the reduction in likelihood value from 273.8 to 271.4, giving a likelihood ratio statistic of 4.8. A $\chi^2[9]$ gives a p-value of 0.85. Finally, note that the non-centrality parameters implied from Table 19.4 are all at least 3 in absolute value, so a correction for selection bias would have a modest impact.

Constant	-0.15	$[\text{p} = 0.88]$	ΔC_{t-1}	0.33	$[\text{p} = 0.75]$
Δv_{t-2}	-0.64	$[\text{p} = 0.52]$	ΔC_{t-2}	0.02	$[\text{p} = 0.98]$
Δv_{t-3}	-0.14	$[\text{p} = 0.89]$	ΔC_{t-3}	-0.40	$[\text{p} = 0.69]$
Δv_{t-4}	-0.48	$[\text{p} = 0.63]$	ΔC_{t-4}	-1.08	$[\text{p} = 0.28]$
$D_{oil,t}$	0.01	$[\text{p} = 0.99]$			

Table 19.5 Tests for omitted variables

19.8 SUMMARY AND EXERCISES

Summary: The objective of general-to-specific (Gets) model selection is to locate a good approximation to the unknown data-generating process, commencing from a general unrestricted model (GUM) intended to nest the data-generating process. Automatic model selection lets the computer take the strain. The Gets approach was analyzed in the five main stages of model formulation, congruence testing, eliminating irrelevant variables, keeping the variables that matter, and obtaining nearly unbiased estimates of the parameters of the selected model. The algorithm was described and its properties sketched. A labor-saving variant that makes decisions about the formulation of the GUM for I(1) time-series data was illustrated.

Bibliography: The selection bias discussed here has long been a concern in econometrics and statistics. It is related to the "pre-test bias" discussed in, say, Judge, Griffiths, Hill, Lütkepohl and Lee (1985), and "post-model-selection estimators" discussed by Leeb and Pötscher (2005). Together with criticisms of "data mining", as in Lovell (1983), these all contributed to a rather negative attitude toward data-based model selection in the econometric literature. This was changed by the study of Hoover and Perez (1999), which has led to the development of a range of automatic model selection algorithms such as PcGets and "autometrics" in PcGive.

Key questions:

- What are the costs of search and of inference?
- What is selection bias?

Computing Task 19.1. *Consider the UK Money data and the two data series v_t, C_t, along with the dummy variables $D_{out,t}$, $D_{oil,t}$. The model in Table 19.4 represents a conditional model for v_t given C_t.*
(a) Construct a general marginal model for ΔC_t including the long-run equilibrium variable e_t. Apply PcGets to this model.
(b) Does this reduced model support the claim that C_t is weakly exogenous?

Computing Task 19.2. *Re-estimate the model reported in Table 19.4, for instance in PcGive. Investigate graphical mis-specification tests and recursive estimation plots. Do they support the model?*

Computing Task 19.3. *Consider the UK money data and the four data series $m_t - p_t$, x_t, Δp_t, $R_{n,t}$, along with the dummy variables $D_{out,t}$, $D_{oil,t}$.*
(a) Analyze the variables in levels using "quick modeler" in PcGets. Look at collinearity. Find the long-run solution. What assumptions are made?
(b) Transform the variables to $\mathsf{I}(0)$-variables. Re-analyze the variables using "advanced modeling" in PcGets. Use both conservative and liberal strategies.
(c) Interpret and discuss the three estimated models.

Chapter Twenty

Structural breaks

So far, we have assumed constant parameters in all the models considered. In practice, few models maintain the same parameters over long historical time periods, so econometricians need to test for, and model, structural breaks. Shifts in the means and variances of time series are a source of non-stationarity additional to unit roots, but their analysis is less well developed. Shifts in means, often called location shifts, are especially pernicious for forecasting, as Chapter 21 will show. Moreover, the occurrence of unanticipated location shifts also affects the ability of economic agents to form useful expectations of future events.

In the following, we first consider how two important aspects of congruence are more easily tested using the natural ordering of time series, specifically, dependence in errors, and parameter constancy over time. We next look more closely at structural breaks as an additional source of non-stationarity in economic time series and introduce the notion of co-breaking. Finally, rational expectations will be discussed.

20.1 CONGRUENCE IN TIME SERIES

Time series are naturally ordered from $1, \ldots, T$, and that ordering can be exploited to test two important aspects of congruence, namely dependence in the errors, and parameter constancy. Tests of serial correlation and autoregressive conditional heteroskedasticity have been described in §13.3 for the former, and constancy tests and recursive analyses in §13.4 for the latter. We now consider these more formally.

Conceptually partition the data used in modeling into three information sets, namely past, present, and future data, where the classification is relative to every t, that is Y_{t-1}, Y_t, Y_{t+1} for each $t = 1, \ldots, T$. Additional information includes economic theory, measurement, and the data used in rival models, as described in §11.4 for cross sections. As before, evaluation proceeds by formulating a null hypothesis, then testing against relevant alternatives, where the following null hypotheses correspond to these six classes of information:

(1) homoskedastic, innovation errors, so matching past information;

(2) weakly-exogenous conditioning variables for the parameters of interest, so matching present information;

(3) constant, invariant parameters of interest, so matching future information;

(4) theory-consistent, identifiable structures, so matching theory information;

(5) data-admissible formulations on accurate observations, so matching measurement information; and

(6) encompassing rival models, so matching data information outside the present model.

As noted in §11.4, a model must satisfy the first three conditions to be well-specified, and the first five conditions to be congruent, so any failure is sufficient to reject a congruency claim. The application of encompassing to competing models of time series follows the same principles as explained in §11.5, although tests no longer have exactly t- or F-distributions.

We now consider the first three conditions in more detail. These need to be satisfied to have a well-specified description of the sample distribution.

First, to "match" the past, a model's fit should not deviate from the observations systematically (hence are innovations) and should not behave differently in different periods (hence are homoskedastic). These are all testable claims, and appropriate tests have been described in earlier chapters; see §9.3 for heteroskedasticity tests, and §13.3 for temporal-dependence tests. Such tests can now be seen as part of checking congruence against past data. Equally, not rejecting the hypotheses of homoskedastic, innovation errors validates having simplified the model relative to a potentially more general specification that allowed for additional dependencies.

Second, to "match" the present data, contemporaneous variables should be exogenous—determined outside the model under consideration (see Chapter 10). Because of possible lagged feedbacks between variables in time series, in that contemporaneous values of regressor variables are affected by past values of the regressand (often called Granger causality), strong exogeneity is unlikely to hold, and needs to be weakened to weak exogeneity (see §14.1). There are two requirements for weak exogeneity: that the parameters of interest can be obtained uniquely from the conditional model, and that these parameters are not related to the parameters of the model for the regressor, z_t. The second condition often fails in cointegrated systems, where a feedback enters several relations. Tests of weak exogeneity usually require additional information beyond that in a regression. One possibility is to find additional variables that are known to be valid instruments, such as $stormy_t$ in Chapter 15. In time series, lagged values of regressors can sometimes also play this role, if they occur in the system but not in the conditional equation to be tested for weak exogeneity. Also, structural breaks in the equations for the conditioning variables which do not induce breaks in the conditional model provide additional identifying information which will prove invaluable in §20.4.

Third, to "match" the future, the parameters of interest must be constant and invariant. Constancy is essential in a time-series model, as previous parameters cease to be relevant after a break, so forecasts would fail. Constancy over time is easily tested using that as an ordering, whereas constancy is hard to test in a cross section where no natural order may exist. Section 13.4 showed the application of recursive estimation and evaluation to investigating parameter constancy, but many other tests have been developed for this crucial hypothesis. Section 20.2 will consider structural breaks in more detail.

Invariance means that parameters do not change when Z_t changes and that requirement would fail if the conditional model parameters altered when the parameters of the Z_t process changed. Thus, constancy is invariance over time. Weak exogeneity plus invariance of the parameters of interest gives super exogeneity; see (11.4.2) and (14.1.5). Super exogeneity is needed to sustain economic policy when regime changes occur. This relates to the so-called Lucas critique, which will be discussed in §20.4 below. Technically, invariance does not require constancy: for example, a sine wave is invariant but not constant. However, the parameters of that sine wave need to be constant, and hence invariance is usually tested only after parameter constancy has not been rejected.

The discussion above links closely back to the analysis of structure in §5.3.1, where the necessary conditions for a parameter of an econometric model to be structural were:

(1) invariance to an extension of the sample, so constancy over time;
(2) invariance to regime shifts, so constancy despite changing distributions of conditioning variables; and
(3) invariance to adding variables to the analysis, so constancy despite extending the information set.

The first two are aspects tested under by the constancy tests, and the third is tested by encompassing. Hence our emphasis on developing congruent, encompassing models as sustainable relationships. Given the importance of constancy in policy analysis and forecasting, we examine its converse, of structural breaks, in detail in the next section.

20.2 STRUCTURAL BREAKS AND CO-BREAKING

A major source of non-stationarity in economics derives from structural breaks, namely, changes in the parameters of processes generating the data. Whereas intercepts, regression coefficients, and error variances all could change, the primary problems for econometric modeling, and especially forecasting, derive from shifts in the coefficients of deterministic terms such as long-run means, growth rates, and trends, called location shifts (see Clements and Hendry, 1999). We consider a simple case as an illustration.

Suppose the intercept in a stationary first-order autoregression (12.3.1) is non-constant:

$$Y_t = \beta_{1,t} + \beta_2 Y_{t-1} + \epsilon_t, \qquad (20.2.1)$$

where the innovations ϵ_t are assumed independent $N[0, \sigma^2]$-distributed, and $|\beta_2| < 1$. The expectation $E(Y_t)$ is now non-constant and hard to derive analytically, so we consider a single shift from $\beta_{1,1}$ to $\beta_{1,2}$ after a time T_1, where $T_1 < T$. In practice, to detect the shift, a parameter-constancy test is usually required.

To model such a shift requires knowing when it happened, and creating an indicator variable $1_{(t>T_1)}$, which is zero up to and including T_1 then unity, as defined in (4.4.1):

$$Y_t = \beta_{1,1} + (\beta_{1,2} - \beta_{1,1}) \, 1_{(t>T_1)} + \beta_2 Y_{t-1} + \epsilon_t. \qquad (20.2.2)$$

Then we have from (12.6.6) that:

$$E(Y_t) \approx \begin{pmatrix} \mu_1 \\ \mu_2 \end{pmatrix} = \begin{cases} \dfrac{\beta_{1,1}}{1 - \beta_2} & \text{for } t \leq T_1, \\[2mm] \dfrac{\beta_{1,2}}{1 - \beta_2} & \text{for } t > T_1, \end{cases}$$

noting that dynamic adjustment from μ_1 to the new level μ_2 can be rather slow. The exact trajectory of Y_t following the shift can be calculated from (20.2.2). At time $T_1 + 1$ it holds:

$$E(Y_{T_1+1}) = \beta_{1,2} + \beta_2 E(Y_{T_1}) + E(\epsilon_{T_1+1}) \approx \beta_{1,2} + \beta_2 \mu_1,$$

and at $T_1 + 2$:

$$\begin{aligned} E(Y_{T_1+2}) &= \beta_{1,2} + \beta_2 E(Y_{T_1+1}) + E(\epsilon_{T_1+2}) \\ &\approx \beta_{1,2} + \beta_2 (\beta_{1,2} + \beta_2 \mu_1) = \beta_{1,2}(1 + \beta_2) + \beta_2^2 \mu_1. \end{aligned}$$

From this result, the pattern is clear: at time $T_1 + t$ the expectation $E(Y_{T_1+t})$ will have two terms. The first term is the geometric series $\beta_{1,2} \sum_{s=0}^{t-1} \beta_2^s$, which converges toward μ_2 as in (12.6.4), while the second term vanishes. Thus, the expectation of Y_t has undergone a location shift starting at μ_1 and ending at μ_2, assuming no further breaks. The expectation is non-constant throughout the process, so Y_t is indeed non-stationary for reasons other than a unit root. Clements and Hendry (1999) argue that such forms of non-stationary are common in practice and propose some solutions, one of which we address below.

20.2.1 Location shifts

The simplest illustration of a location shift is when $\beta_2 = 0$ and Y_{t-1} is correctly excluded as a regressor, but the step shift in (20.2.2) is not modeled. The equation to be estimated is then just:

$$Y_t = \beta + u_t. \qquad (20.2.3)$$

Because regression is based on minimizing the sum of squared errors, the intercept estimate $\widehat{\beta}$ removes as much as possible of the break. Letting $k = T^{-1}T_1$ denote the proportion of the sample before the break, the full-sample intercept in (20.2.3) will be roughly $\widetilde{\beta} = k\beta_{1,1} + (1 - k)\,\beta_{1,2}$. The residual sum of squared deviations, $\min_{\beta\in\mathbb{R}} \sum_{t=1}^{T}(Y_t - \beta)^2 = \sum_{t=1}^{T}(Y_t - \overline{Y})^2$, from the regression (20.2.3) is, therefore, as derived in Exercises 20.1, 20.2, approximately:

$$\mathsf{E}\left\{\sum_{t=1}^{T}(Y_t - \widetilde{\beta})^2\right\} = T_1\left(\beta_{1,1} - \widetilde{\beta}\right)^2 + (T - T_1)\left(\beta_{1,2} - \widetilde{\beta}\right)^2 + T\sigma_\epsilon^2$$

$$= Tk\,(1 - k)\,(\beta_{1,2} - \beta_{1,1})^2 + T\sigma_\epsilon^2, \qquad (20.2.4)$$

which could be very large. The residuals will be autocorrelated, on average being systematically positive, then negative, or vice versa, depending on the direction of the shift. Potentially, a very poor data description could result from using (20.2.3).

Consider, instead, differencing (20.2.2) when $\beta_2 = 0$, so that the intercept is zero except at the break-point $T_1 + 1$:

$$\Delta Y_t = (\beta_{1,2} - \beta_{1,1})\,1_{(t=T_1+1)} + \Delta\epsilon_t. \qquad (20.2.5)$$

The error variance of (20.2.5) is approximately double that of σ_ϵ^2, since at $t \neq T_1 + 1$:

$$\mathsf{E}\left\{(\Delta\epsilon_t)^2\right\} = \mathsf{E}\left\{(\epsilon_t - \epsilon_{t-1})^2\right\} = 2\sigma_\epsilon^2.$$

However, the whole-sample impact on (20.2.5) from the break is just the term $(\beta_{1,2} - \beta_{1,1})^2$. Thus, combining the effects of $2T\sigma_\epsilon^2 + (\beta_{1,2} - \beta_{1,1})^2$ could be much smaller than from (20.2.4), depending on:

$$Tk\,(1 - k)\,(\beta_{1,2} - \beta_{1,1})^2 + T\sigma_\epsilon^2 \lessgtr (\beta_{1,2} - \beta_{1,1})^2 + 2T\sigma_\epsilon^2,$$

or:

$$\frac{|\beta_{1,2} - \beta_{1,1}|}{\sigma_\epsilon} \lessgtr \frac{1}{\sqrt{k\,(1 - k) - 1/T}}.$$

When $T = 100$ and $k = 0.5$ say, then it will pay to difference for any step shift larger than 2 standard deviations of the error, or for $k = 0.1$, a $3.5\sigma_\epsilon$ shift. Notice that in both cases, the model in (20.2.3) will almost always fail a parameter constancy test, although (20.2.5) will rarely do so; and that the residuals in (20.2.5) are now negatively autocorrelated. These results will prove useful in Chapter 21 when we consider forecasting.

When $\beta_2 \neq 0$, if (20.2.1) is estimated with Y_{t-1} included as a regressor, it can approximate (20.2.5) by writing it as:

$$Y_t = (\beta_{1,2} - \beta_{1,1})\,1_{(t=T_1+1)} + Y_{t-1} + \{\beta_2\Delta Y_{t-1} + \Delta\epsilon_t\} \qquad (20.2.6)$$

where $\{\cdot\}$ is an autocorrelated error. In words, to remove the effect of the step change, the estimated coefficient of Y_{t-1} will be close to unity, thereby differencing the intercept. We will use Monte Carlo methods to illustrate this result in §20.3.

20.2.2 Co-breaking

Co-breaking occurs when there are breaks in several series, but a linear combination of those series has no break. Such an occurrence is similar to cointegration using a linear combination to remove unit-root non-stationarities. For example, consider two variables (Y_t, Z_t) that have the joint density:

$$\begin{pmatrix} Y_t \\ Z_t \end{pmatrix} \stackrel{\mathsf{D}}{=} \mathsf{N}_2 \left[\begin{pmatrix} \mu_{y,t} \\ \mu_{z,t} \end{pmatrix}, \begin{pmatrix} \sigma_{yy} & \sigma_{yz} \\ \sigma_{zy} & \sigma_{zz} \end{pmatrix} \right], \qquad (20.2.7)$$

where the expectations depend on time, whereas the variances do not. Then the conditional distribution of Y_t given Z_t has expectation $\mu_{y \cdot z, t} = \mu_{y,t} - \beta_2 \mu_{z,t}$, for $\beta_2 = \sigma_{yz}/\sigma_{zz}$ (see §10.2.2). If this conditional expectation is constant over time, so $\mu_{y \cdot z, t} = \mu_{y \cdot z}$ say, then $Y_t - \beta_2 Z_t$ is a *co-breaking* combination of Y_t and Z_t, leading to the constant-parameter conditional model:

$$Y_t = \mu_{y \cdot z} + \beta_2 Z_t + v_t. \qquad (20.2.8)$$

The analogy with cointegration removing unit roots, or common trends, is close. In fact, co-breaking between changing growth rates looks like a cointegrating combination of the associated variables, whereas the shifting expectations of those variables looks like a common trend; see Hendry and Massmann (2007).

The example in (20.2.8) also highlights the relationship between super exogeneity and co-breaking. If the conditional model of Y_t given Z_t has β_2 as a parameter of interest, and the parameters of the Z_t process are not dependent on β_2, then Z_t is super exogenous for β_2, the co-breaking parameter. Consequently, tests of super exogeneity based on co-breaking have been formalized.

20.3 LOCATION SHIFTS REVISITED

The most valuable use of simulation is for problems that prove intractable analytically, such as that of structural breaks as in §20.2, but now in an autoregressive context.

The data-generating process (20.2.2) is an autoregression, now with a shift in the intercept from $\beta_{1,1} = 1$ to $\beta_{1,2} = 4$, setting the innovation standard deviation to unity, $\sigma = 1$, so that the shift is 3 standard deviations of the error. Using simulations we can easily analyze the situation of a non-zero autoregressive parameter: $\beta_2 = 0.5$. The break happens at $T_1 = 40$ when $T = 100$.

We will see what happens when analyzing such data using a mis-specified model ignoring the break:

$$Y_t = \alpha_1 + \alpha_2 Y_{t-1} + u_t. \qquad (20.3.1)$$

In §20.2.1 we could analyze such a situation analytically since the autoregressive parameter was left out both from the data-generating process and from the econometric model. Now, an analytic approach is difficult but can be replaced by a simulation study. Figure 20.1 reports the results. Panels (a) and (b) show the densities of the estimators for the autoregressive parameter, $\widehat{\alpha}_2$, and for the intercept $\widehat{\alpha}_1$, based on the full sample with $T = 100$ observations. Panels (c) and (d) show recursive estimates with 95% bands based on the Monte Carlo standard deviation. The estimate of the autoregressive parameter, $\widehat{\alpha}_2$, jumps toward unity after the break, and the intercept estimate falls, even though the true value increased. This matches the observation, that if the autoregressive parameter became unity, the intercept would have to be near zero because the data have no trend. The result shows that the non-stationarity in the data-generating process arising from the shift in the intercept would be interpreted as a random walk in a model like (20.3.1) that does not allow for changing parameters.

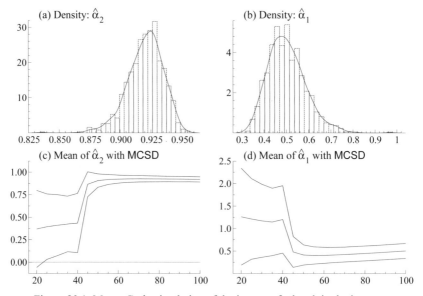

Figure 20.1 Monte Carlo simulation of the impact of a break in the intercept

A more surprising outcome occurs when there are breaks in the autoregressive parameter. This is left as a computer exercise (see Computer Task 20.6).

20.4 RATIONAL EXPECTATIONS AND THE LUCAS CRITIQUE

Conditional equations assume an underlying contingent plan theory, rather than a behavioral model. As we noted, a behavioral model requires expectations to be modeled. Expectations are often assumed to be rational, meaning that agents use the correct conditional expectations. It is unclear how agents could form such expectations in a non-stationary world, and the regularity of forecast failure publicly reveals that expert economists cannot. Nevertheless, Lucas (1976, p.41) (building on earlier work reviewed by Favero and Hendry, 1992) criticized econometric models that failed to handle expectations explicitly since:

> Given that the structure of an econometric model consists of optimal decision rules for economic agents, and that optimal decision rules vary systematically with changes in the structure of series relevant to the decision maker, it follows that any change in policy will systematically alter the structure of econometric models.

The case of particular interest to Lucas was when agents' plans depended on expectations formed about policy variables. The behavioral model in §11.3.5 is an example when z_t is a policy variable. In that case, changes to the c_i parameters in (11.3.14) will occur after policy changes, rendering the 2-equation system (11.3.13) and (11.3.14) non-constant. Moreover, the derived conditional model will also be non-constant, as the π_i are functions of the c_i. The solved equation (11.3.21) will, therefore, change with policy. Thus, all the possible representations other than models with explicit and correct expectations are no longer constant. At first sight, such a critique may be thought to seriously damage empirical econometric models.

However, Lucas's formulation is testable by testing whether the parameters of the various econometric equations are invariant, or not, to policy-rule changes. The class of tests proposed by Engle and Hendry (1993) for super exogeneity (see §14.1) models breaks in the structure of the series relevant to agents, and then tests if there are statistically significant matching breaks in the conditional model. Alternatively, Hendry (1988) proposed an encompassing test between the expectations and conditional models by testing the equivalent of (11.3.20) against (11.3.21); as we saw, the π_i should alter when the c_i change, whereas the b_i could be constant. Conversely, if the c_i change, but the π_i do not, then the Lucas critique is refuted.

Ericsson and Irons (1995) find little empirical evidence for the Lucas critique. Since agents do make intertemporal plans (life insurance, pension provision, and house purchase are all examples) and must form expectations about the future to do so, yet structural breaks are relatively common, how can we reconcile the evidence? The answer lies in recent developments in the theory of economic forecasting discussed in Chapter 21: there exist relatively simple methods of forecasting that deliver unbiased forecasts when there are no breaks, yet are also robust to previous structural breaks. In practice, such devices often beat forecasts based on the best causal (econometric) models. If agents used such forecasting devices, they would not need to discover complicated data-generating processes to form their conditional expectations; moreover, the use of robust forecasts would lead to conditional models that actually had an expectations interpretation, yet were immune to the Lucas critique. What are these methods, and why would they overcome the problems of structural breaks in econometric models?

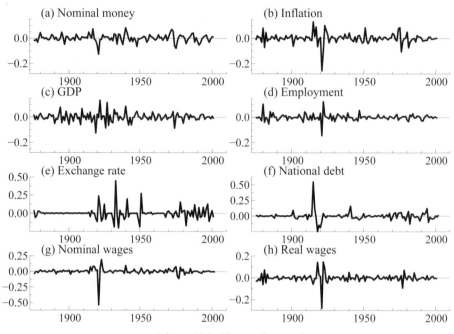

Figure 20.2 Changes in growth rates

First, we note that few economic time series continuously accelerate, at least after log transforms (many do in levels). Thus, the unconditional expectation of the second difference of most economic variables should be zero, namely:

$$E\left(\Delta^2 x_t\right) = 0. \tag{20.4.1}$$

Notable exceptions are that UK industrial production did accelerate in the first half of the 1800s—so (20.4.1) would not have worked well then. Similarly for output growth in 1990s China, or during hyperinflations. Apart from these few cases of acceleration, (20.4.1) is a good first approximation for many economic time series. Figure 20.2 illustrates for a number of UK data series from 1860 on.

The second key to the success of double differencing is its effect on deterministic terms. We saw in §20.2 that differencing reduces the impacts of breaks in intercepts: similarly, second differencing offsets breaks in trends as well. Thus, second differencing removes two unit roots (building on Chapter 16), as well as any intercepts and linear trends. Also, second differencing reduces location shifts to blips, and converts breaks in trends to impulses. Figure 20.3 illustrates.

Translate (20.4.1) into the forecasting rule at time T:

$$\Delta \widehat{x}_{T+1} = \Delta x_T. \tag{20.4.2}$$

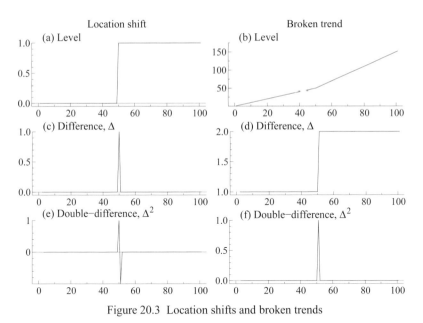

Figure 20.3 Location shifts and broken trends

Then (20.4.1) entails that $\Delta\widehat{x}_{T+1}$ will be unbiased for Δx_{T+1}. If agents were to forecast this way, then Δx_T (a current conditioning variable) is really an expectations variable (namely $\Delta\widehat{x}_{T+1}$) but is immune to the Lucas critique because it involves no parameters that could change. Thus, the robustness that agents achieve using (20.4.2) is reflected in the robustness to breaks of the resulting conditional model. We return to this issue in Chapter 21 in the context of macro-econometric forecasts.

20.5 EMPIRICAL TESTS OF THE LUCAS CRITIQUE

We now illustrate tests of the Lucas critique for UK narrow-money demand using the analysis of Chapters 17 and 19. Money-demand equations were once thought to be important because it was believed they could be inverted to determine prices, p, as a function of nominal money, m_t, assuming m_t was exogenous in some sense. However, no agency actually controls the money stock, and most central banks explicitly use interest rates as their policy instrument, so an exogenous money stock seems unlikely. Conversely, having individuals acting contingently on prices, p, and interest rates, R_t, is feasible, especially given the explanation in the previous section for current changes possibly acting as forecasts. If any of the processes for inflation, interest rates, or expenditure are not constant, the reverse regressions of inflation on money should be non-constant—regression is not invariant to renormalization. This can be seen by noting that $R^2 = \widehat{\beta}\widehat{\gamma}$ where $\widehat{\beta}$ is from regressing Y_t on Z_t (say), and $\widehat{\gamma}$ from Z_t on Y_t, see (5.4.4). When $\widehat{\beta}$ is found to be constant, while the process undergoes shifts, then R^2 must change, so $\widehat{\gamma}$ cannot be constant as well. We therefore start by reconsidering the conditional model of Table 19.4

for velocity, $v_t = x_t - m_t + p_t$, given the joint opportunity cost of holding money, $C_t = R_{n,t} + \Delta p_t$. Then, we investigate the constancy of an autoregressive model for C_t and show it is not constant. Finally, we invert the money demand equation to explain C_t and show that the resulting relationship is not constant.

$$\widehat{\Delta v_t} = \underset{(0.01)}{-0.10\,e_{t-1}} - \underset{(0.07)}{0.27\,\Delta v_{t-1}} + \underset{(0.08)}{0.58\,\Delta C_t} + \underset{(0.01)}{0.04\,D_{out,t}} - \underset{(0.02)}{0.07\,D_{71:1,t}}$$
$$\text{se}$$

$$e_t = v_t - 5.30 C_t$$

$$\sqrt{\widehat{\sigma}^2} = 0.0158, \quad \widehat{\ell} = 275.6, \quad T = 100, \quad 1964{:}3{-}1989{:}2$$

Table 20.1 Model for velocity given cost of holding money from Table 19.4

First, Table 20.1 reproduces the model for velocity, $v_t = x_t - m_t + p_t$, given the joint opportunity cost of holding money, $C_t = R_{n,t} + \Delta p_t$, that was presented in Table 19.4. None of the mis-specification tests in Table 19.4 were rejected. Likewise the graphical mis-specification tests and recursive estimation plots of Computer Task 19.2 were found to support the model. The model also has a sensible interpretation. There is a large impact from changes in the opportunity cost, a strong feedback from past equilibrium errors, and a smaller but significant influence from past changes in velocity. From (20.4.1) above, ΔC_t is a robust predictor, $\Delta \widehat{C}_{t+1}$ say, of ΔC_{t+1}, confirming that there is an expectations interpretation but one that is not subject to the Lucas critique (see §20.4). Interpreting ΔC_t as $\Delta \widehat{C}_{t+1}$, then inverse velocity falls by almost $\frac{2}{3}$% for every percentage point increase in expected interest rates or (quarterly) inflation combined. This initial impact rises to 6.1% in equilibrium, with an adjustment speed of about 10% per quarter. Alternatively, acting contingently on C_t is sensible for a short-term liquid asset. Finally, the dummies have are interpretable as explained earlier with $D_{out,t}$ relating to the fiscal expansions in 1973 and 1979 and $D_{71:1,t}$ relating to the decimalization of the pound. Overall, therefore, the model in Table 20.1 provides a constant-parameter congruent representation, consistent with the economic analysis of a contingent demand model.

Second, we turn to the inversion of the money demand model. It is illustrative to start by collecting contemporaneous outcomes of inflation, Δp_t, on the left-hand side of the model equation in Table 20.1. Note that the increment in velocity is $\Delta v_t = \Delta x_t - \Delta m_t + \Delta p_t$ whereas the increment in the cost of holding money is $\Delta C_t = \Delta R_{n,t} + \Delta p_t - \Delta p_{t-1}$, so subtracting $0.58 \Delta C_t$ from both sides, the left-hand side becomes:

$$\Delta v_t - 0.58\Delta C_t = \Delta x_t - \Delta m_t + \Delta p_t - 0.58\Delta R_{n,t} - 0.58\Delta p_t + 0.58\Delta p_{t-1}$$
$$= \Delta x_t - \Delta m_t + 0.42\Delta p_t + 0.58\Delta p_{t-1} - 0.58\Delta R_{n,t}. \ (20.5.1)$$

Thus, the resulting coefficient of Δp_t is modest. The model equation in Table 20.1 is, in effect, an equation in *nominal* money in the short run—almost not dependent on contemporary prices or inflation—although real money is demanded in the long run, as the cointegrating relation in Table 20.1 confirms. In fact, as seen in Hendry and Ericsson (1991b), if the elements of C_t are entered unrestrictedly, the coefficient of Δp_t in (20.5.1) is even closer to zero (see Exercise 20.7). Thus, inverting the relationship in Table 20.1 to determine inflation is rather meaningless. Nevertheless, by doing so, the inverted model based on the variables identified in Table 20.1 and in (20.5.1) is reported in Table 20.2.

$$\widehat{\Delta p_t} = 0.0049 + 0.77\,\Delta p_{t-1} + 0.02\,\Delta m_t - 0.13\,\Delta x_t + 0.23\,\Delta R_t$$
$$\text{se} \quad (0.0019) \quad (0.08) \quad\quad (0.06) \quad\quad (0.07) \quad\quad (0.06)$$
$$-\,0.007\,e_{t-1} - 0.039\,\Delta v_{t-1} + 0.008\,D_{out,t} - 0.0006\,D_{71:1,t}$$
$$(0.008) \quad\quad (0.038) \quad\quad (0.006) \quad\quad (0.0083)$$
$$\sqrt{\widehat{\sigma}^2} = 0.0076, \quad \widehat{\ell} = 350.5, \quad R^2 = 0.73, \quad T = 100, \quad 1964{:}3{-}1989{:}2$$
$$\chi^2_{\text{norm}}[2] = 16 \quad [\text{p} < 0.001] \quad F_{\text{ar}(1-5)}[5,86] = 2.7 \quad [\text{p} = 0.03]$$
$$F_{\text{het}}[14,76] = 2.8 \quad [\text{p} = 0.002] \quad F_{\text{arch}(1-4)}[4,83] = 2.1 \quad [\text{p} = 0.08]$$

Table 20.2 Inverted money demand model based on the variables in Table 20.1 and (20.5.1)

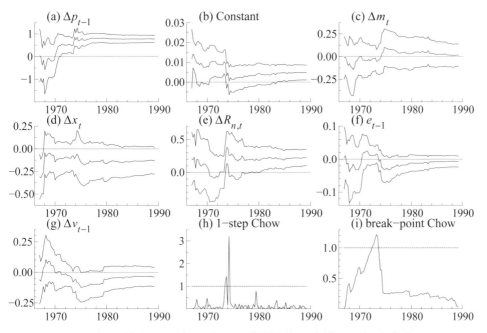

Figure 20.4 Recursive estimates of UK M1 model inverted to inflation

The explanation in the re-estimated inverted model is mainly due to lagged inflation. Indeed, contemporaneous money growth is insignificant, and most diagnostic tests reject, though Figure 20.4 shows that constancy is only marginally rejected (but that test is invalidated by others rejecting—can you see why?). On every count, this evidence is against "money causes inflation" interpretations, and in favor of individuals determining the money holdings they want, given inflation, interest rates, and expenditure.

Third, we develop in Table 20.3 a representation for C_t using only lagged information. Three features of Table 20.3 deserve comment. First, e_{t-1} was insignificant, supporting C_t being weakly exogenous in the conditional equation of v_t given C_t, which includes e_{t-1}. In addition, v_{t-1} is insignificant, indicating that C_t is actually strongly exogenous. Second, C_{t-1} is not very important either, and little is lost by treating C_t as a unit-root process. Finally, seven dummies were detected, but none coincides with $D_{71:1,t}$ or $D_{out,t} = D_{72:4,t} + D_{73:1,t} + D_{79:2,t}$. Had some of the dummies been in common, then the conditional model of q given C_t would not have been free of changes in the marginal model, prima facie evidence against super exogeneity of C_t. Thus, an alternative test of the super exogeneity of ΔC_t in Table 20.1 is an F-test from adding the dummies in Table 20.1, and this yields $F[7, 93] = 1.33$ with $p = 0.25$, which is insignificant (although $D_{73:2,t}$ had a t-value of 2.5 with $p = 0.02$).

$$\widehat{\Delta C_t} = \underset{se}{0.0082} - \underset{(0.0035)}{0.074} C_{t-1} - \underset{(0.014)}{0.036} D_{73:2,t} + \underset{(0.014)}{0.063} D_{73:3,t} + \underset{(0.014)}{0.051} D_{76:4,t}$$
$$- \underset{(0.015)}{0.036} D_{77:1,t} + \underset{(0.014)}{0.035} D_{79:3,t} - \underset{(0.014)}{0.043} D_{85:2,t} - \underset{(0.014)}{0.035} D_{85:3,t}$$

$$\sqrt{\widehat{\sigma^2}} = 0.015, \quad R^2 = 0.76$$

$\chi^2_{norm}[2] = 2.6 \quad [p = 0.27]$	$F_{ar(1-4)}[4, 94] = 2.0 \quad [p = 0.81]$
$F_{het}[14, 83] = 0.7 \quad [p = 0.00]$	$F_{arch(1-4)}[4, 90] = 0.6 \quad [p = 0.64]$
$F_{reset}[1, 97] = 0.1 \quad [p = 0.73]$	

Table 20.3 Marginal model for cost of holding money, C, selected using PcGets

Similar results to these are found for broad money demand (M4). Following the analysis in Friedman and Schwartz (1982), Hendry and Ericsson (1991a) developed a constant-parameter, congruent model for the period 1878–1975. This was first successfully updated to 1993 by Ericsson et al. (1998), and then to 2000 by Escribano (2004). That model therefore maintained constancy for a quarter century of data after first being proposed, despite numerous financial innovations, and major redefinitions of the banking sector caused by building societies converting their status from cooperatives to public companies in 1989. Indeed, that last event is why UK M1 data terminate in 1989: following the conversion to a bank by Abbey National, its retail sight deposits suddenly became part of M1, inducing a large increase therein, although neither money demand nor money supply had changed. Finally, inverting even a broad money equation to determine inflation proves unsuccessful.

20.6 RATIONAL EXPECTATIONS AND EULER EQUATIONS

The example we consider is consumers' expenditure, which is the largest single component of GNP, and has been a subject of intensive study since John Maynard Keynes's *General Theory*. Both the economic theoretical and empirical literatures on consumers' expenditure are now vast. We will discuss the Euler equation approach here, which is based on the marginal conditions necessary for optimal consumers' behavior. The discussion emphasizes the need to test the assumptions underlying any empirical study.

The Euler equation approach in (say) Hall (1978) assumes an intertemporal optimizing consumer with a concave utility function. Such a consumer will seek to equate the marginal utility of consumption at all points in time, since falls in consumption by a given amount will lower utility more than it is raised by corresponding rises in consumption. Such a theory generates a smooth flow of consumption. In effect, equating marginal utility over time is like having a powerful habit, which entails smoothing consumption. Thus, all changes in consumption become unanticipated given past consumption.

However, to implement their aspirations, such a consumer needs either the appropriate income flows or a substantial borrowing capability in a world where early-age income is usually lower than later, and real incomes generally are rising over time from technical progress. This is formalized in the concept of permanent income, which is the income that can be consumed indefinitely without affecting wealth, $Y^p = \lambda W$ say, where wealth in turn is the sum of the initial endowment W_0 and expected discounted future earnings, and λ is the permanent rate of return.

Hall (1978) assumes the validity of a version of the permanent income hypothesis, whereby permanent consumption, C^p, is proportional to permanent income, Y^p:

$$C_t^p = \kappa Y_t^p, \qquad (20.6.1)$$

where κ is the proportion of income consumed. Since Y^p is the rational expected value over all future income flows, it should reflect all information available to consumers, and hence only change when information changes. Thus, if $\mathcal{I}_{t-1}$ is used to denote available information at time $t-1$, then changes in next period's permanent income should be unpredictable:

$$\mathsf{E}\left(Y_t^p \mid \mathcal{I}_{t-1}\right) = Y_{t-1}^p. \qquad (20.6.2)$$

Substituting (20.6.1) into (20.6.2) then leads to the prediction that the change in permanent consumption should also be unpredictable:

$$\mathsf{E}\left(C_t^p \mid \mathcal{I}_{t-1}\right) = C_{t-1}^p. \qquad (20.6.3)$$

Finally, if consumers' plans are rational, then actual consumption should only deviate randomly from permanent consumption, so:

$$\mathsf{E}\,(C_t) = C_t^p. \tag{20.6.4}$$

Unfortunately, consumption is not observed, so C_t has to be related to consumers' expenditure, which necessitates a range of additional assumptions about usage of durables and semi-durables, or treats non-durables and services expenditure as a proxy, neither of which is very satisfactory.

The functional form of the econometric model is not fully specified by equation (20.6.3) as both subtraction and division are valid operations. The former leads to the claim that absolute changes are random, and while some studies have adopted that form, we will see below that it creates a highly heteroskedastic time series (see figure 20.6). The latter entails that the ratio or, more tractably, the log change, should be unpredictable. In its simplest form, the theory can be thought of as specifying $\mathsf{E}(\Delta c_t) = 0$, so the unconditional growth rate of consumers' expenditure (Δc) in constant prices is zero.

Expressing (20.6.3)–(20.6.4) as a model after taking logs:

$$\Delta c_t = \epsilon_t \ \text{ where } \ \mathsf{E}\,(\epsilon_t \mid \mathcal{I}_{t-1}) = 0. \tag{20.6.5}$$

Two immediate implications are that consumption should have a unit root, and that all lagged information should be irrelevant in predicting Δc_t. In practice, various puzzles arise as Deaton (1992) discusses: there is an "excess sensitivity" of consumption reactions to income changes if income is a stationary process, but "excess smoothness" if income is a random walk, in which case, permanent income need not be smoother than actual.

Figure 20.5 records the time series from 1955:2 to 2004:2 for aggregate UK log real quarterly consumers' expenditure (c) and constant-price log personal disposable income (y), their difference (approximately the savings ratio minus unity), and quarterly and annual changes. Both c and y have trended, with the former much more seasonal than the latter (panel a). That behavior induces both seasonality and substantial cycles in $c - y$ (panel b). The quarter-on-quarter changes in c, that is $\Delta c_t = c_t - c_{t-1}$, are as large as $\pm 10\%$ and far larger than those in y, not suggestive of any form of smoothing (panel c). The behavior of the year-on-year changes $\Delta_4 c_t = c_t - c_{t-4}$ and $\Delta_4 y_t = y_t - y_{t-4}$ more closely matches the theory in that there is more smoothing (panel d), and usually consumption fluctuates less than income.

Table 20.4 records various sample means and standard deviations. The whole sample standard deviation of Δc_t is twice that of Δy_t and is highly variable over subsamples. The means ($\overline{\Delta_4 c_t}$) and standard deviations ($s_{\Delta_4 c_t}$) of $\Delta_4 c_t$ and of $\Delta_4 y_t$ also both change considerably over subsamples and their magnitude order is

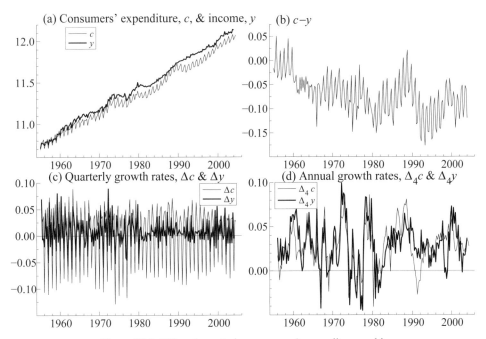

Figure 20.5 UK real quarterly consumers' expenditure and income

Period	$\overline{\Delta_4 c_t}$	$\overline{\Delta_4 y_t}$	$s_{\Delta_4 c_t}$	$s_{\Delta_4 y_t}$	$s_{\Delta c_t}$	$s_{\Delta y_t}$
1956:1–1979:4	2.5%	2.9%	2.4%	3.1%	6.0%	3.3%
1979:4–1992:4	2.5%	2.8%	2.9%	2.4%	5.1%	1.8%
1992:4–2004:1	3.2%	2.8%	1.9%	1.1%	4.7%	2.1%
1956:1–2004:1	2.7%	2.8%	2.3%	2.6%	5.4%	2.7%

Table 20.4 Means and standard deviations of changes in c and y

sometimes reversed. Thus, even the annual changes are not stationary, exhibiting changing moments. Moreover, any analysis of such data based on smoothing consumption over time has to postulate either a seasonally dependent utility function or a seasonally varying relation between expenditure and consumption. Although not shown in the table, the standard deviation of $(c - y)$ is large at 4.3%, and even removing seasonality by a four-period moving average, is still 3.2%, compared to mean annual growth in real expenditure of only 2.7%.

Figure 20.6 graphs the actual changes ΔC_t (panel a), highlighting its considerable increase in variability over the period as the scale of the economy expanded. The data densities of Δc_t and Δy_t (in panel b) are visibly dramatically different, whereas those for $\Delta_4 c_t$ and $\Delta_4 y_t$ (in panel c) are similar. Finally, inflation, $\Delta_4 p_t$ has changed greatly (panel d). Several of the features in figures 20.5 and 20.6 are at odds with life-cycle theory: specifically in the mid- to late 1980s, $\Delta_4 c_t$ exceeded $\Delta_4 y_t$ during the upswing, and fell more in the subsequent downturn, including going negative while income growth was positive in the late 1980s to early 1990s.

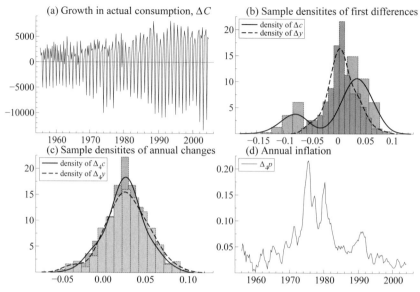

Figure 20.6 UK real quarterly consumers' expenditure and income

Since our data have not been seasonally adjusted, we translate the Euler equation (20.6.5) into:

$$\Delta_4 c_t = \gamma + \epsilon_t \quad \text{where} \quad \mathsf{E}\left(\epsilon_t \mid \mathcal{I}_{t-1}\right) = 0, \tag{20.6.6}$$

where γ is the unconditional annual growth rate of c. We first test for a unit root in the level of real consumers' expenditure (anticipating one at the seasonal frequency), and if that is not rejected, test whether lagged information matters. Then, if we allow for up to five lags of c_{t-i} with a constant, seasonal indicator variables, and a linear deterministic trend, the null hypothesis of a unit root cannot be rejected at the 5% level, or in the corresponding equation for y, consistent with (20.6.2). Thus, that aspect is not rejected.

$$\widehat{\Delta_4 c_t} = \underset{\text{hacse}}{0.014} + \underset{(0.07)}{0.63} \Delta_4 c_{t-1} + \underset{(0.08)}{0.19} \Delta_4 c_{t-2} - \underset{(0.12)}{0.35} \Delta_4 c_{t-4}$$

$$+ \underset{(0.07)}{0.35} \Delta_4 c_{t-5} - \underset{(0.05)}{0.18} \Delta_4 y_{t-4} - \underset{(0.024)}{0.069} \Delta_4 p_{t-1}$$

$$\sqrt{\widehat{\sigma}^2} = 0.0141, \quad R^2 = 0.64, \quad T = 186: \quad 1958{:}2\text{–}2004{:}3$$

$\chi^2_{\text{norm}}[2] = 61 \quad [\text{p} < 0.001]$		$F_{\text{ar}(1-5)}[5, 177] = 3.7 \quad [\text{p} = 0.003]$
$F_{\text{het}}[12, 169] = 4.0 \quad [\text{p} < 0.001]$		$F_{\text{arch}(1-4)}[4, 174] = 4.9 \quad [\text{p} = 0.001]$
$F_{\text{GUM}}[6, 182] = 55 \quad [\text{p} < 0.001]$		$F_{\text{Chow}}[19, 163] = 0.4 \quad [\text{p} = 0.99 \,]$

Table 20.5 Consumption model selected using PcGets

Imposing that unit root by reformulating in fourth differences, we next test the other main implication of unpredictability, namely that $\mathsf{E}\left(\epsilon_t \mid \mathcal{I}_{t-1}\right) = 0$ in (20.6.6), by including five lagged values of $\Delta_4 c_{t-i}$, $\Delta_4 y_{t-i}$, and $\Delta_4 p_{t-i}$ (where

$\Delta_4 p$ is annual consumer price inflation), as well as a constant, seasonal indicator variables, and a linear deterministic trend. Doing so leads PcGets to select the model in Table 20.5.

The F-test of the joint significance of all the added variables rejects at any reasonable significance level (denoted F_{GUM}), although the significance of most mis-specification tests reveals noncongruency. Consequently, the standard errors are corrected for heteroskedasticity and autocorrelation (see §13.3.3). The second implication is strongly rejected in Table 20.5, with 6 significant lagged regressors. It should be noted that the use of overlapping data deriving from the use of fourth differences is valid. The issue is that $\Delta_4 c_t$ and $\Delta_4 c_{t-1}$ share some intermediate values of $\Delta_1 c_{t-i}$. However, the model in Table 20.5 is simply a transformation of a model of order 9 with certain restrictions giving the fourth-differences without changing the error term. A fourth-difference operator, which multiplied each variable and the error term by Δ_4, would indeed induce fourth-order residual autocorrelation. In any case, even with five lags or longer imposed, we find the model in Table 20.6, which still rejects the hypothesis of the irrelevance of lagged information, albeit that model is far from congruent.

$$\widehat{\Delta_4 c_t} = \underset{(0.005)}{0.043} + \underset{(0.13)}{0.32}\,\Delta_4 c_{t-5} - \underset{(0.08)}{0.34}\,\Delta_4 y_{t-5} - \underset{(0.04)}{0.16}\,\Delta_4 p_{t-5} - \underset{(0.07)}{0.21}\,\Delta_4 y_{t-9}$$

hacse

$$\sqrt{\widehat{\sigma}^2} = 0.0203, \quad R^2 = 0.27, \quad T = 186: \quad 1958{:}2\text{--}2004{:}3$$

$\chi^2_{\mathsf{norm}}[2] = 6.0$	$[\mathsf{p} = 0.05\,]$	$F_{\mathsf{ar}(1-5)}[5, 176] = 30$	$[\mathsf{p} < 0.001]$
$F_{\mathsf{het}}[8, 172] = 2.1$	$[\mathsf{p} = 0.04\,]$	$F_{\mathsf{arch}(1-4)}[4, 173] = 6.5$	$[\mathsf{p} < 0.001]$
$F_{\mathsf{GUM}}[4, 181] = 17$	$[\mathsf{p} < 0.001]$	$F_{\mathsf{Chow}}[19, 162] = 0.4$	$[\mathsf{p} = 0.99\,]$

Table 20.6 Consumption model selected using PcGets with all lags longer than five

The models in Table 20.5 and Table 20.6 are inconsistent with the initial assumptions in (20.6.1)–(20.6.2). Indeed, over this sample, c_t and y_t are not cointegrated on standard tests, in conflict with (20.6.1). The Monte Carlo experiment in §20.3 suggests one possible explanation: if the mean of $\Delta_4 c_t$ had shifted insample, but that effect was not modeled, then the autoregressive representation would be driven toward an additional unit root. The major financial innovations of the mid-1980s that radically changed credit rationing in the UK offer one possibility and coincide with the biggest changes noted in Table 20.4 (see Muellbauer, 1996). Thus, despite the considerable theoretical analysis that lies behind Euler equations and rational expectations, the resulting model provides an incomplete picture of the behavior of consumers' expenditure in the UK.

20.7 SUMMARY AND EXERCISES

Summary: Time-series data have a natural ordering that can be exploited to test assumptions about independence and parameter constancy. The chapter describes congruence testing in greater detail for time series, and emphasizes the need for invariant parameters if structural models are desired. Structural breaks, therefore, need careful consideration, as does testing of invariance, especially against the Lucas Critique. The rejection of Euler-equation models of consumers' expenditure based on rational expectations and intertemporal optimization may be due to unmodeled major shifts in credit rationing.

Bibliography: Disputes about how to undertake economic research in general, and empirical economics in particular, long predate the formal creation of econometrics in the 1930s. Hendry and Morgan (1995) discuss much of the early history and reprint many of the salient contributions. They also note important precursors of the "Lucas Critique".

Key questions:

- Discuss the roles of theory and data in empirical econometric modeling.
- Discuss the possibility of economic agents forming rational expectations when the data-generating process is subject to structural breaks.
- Discuss testing of congruence for models of time series.
- How would you try to ascertain the causes underlying a theory model being rejected by data evidence?

Exercise 20.1. *Prove (20.2.4) in the following steps.*
(a) Argue that $\sum_{t=1}^{T}(Y_t - \widetilde{\beta})^2 = \sum_{t=1}^{T_1}(Y_t - \widetilde{\beta})^2 + \sum_{t=T_1+1}^{T}(Y_t - \widetilde{\beta})^2$.
(b) Argue that $\sum_{t=1}^{T_1}(Y_t - \widetilde{\beta})^2$ is equal to $\sum_{t=1}^{T_1}(Y_t - \beta_{1,1})^2 + T_1(\beta_{1,1} - \widetilde{\beta})^2 + 2(\beta_{1,1} - \widetilde{\beta})\sum_{t=1}^{T_1}(Y_t - \beta_{1,1})$.
(c) Argue that $E\{\sum_{t=1}^{T_1}(Y_t - \widetilde{\beta})^2\} = T_1\sigma_\epsilon^2 + T_1(\beta_{1,1} - \widetilde{\beta})^2$.
(d) Argue that $T_1(\beta_{1,1} - \widetilde{\beta})^2 = Tk(1-k)^2(\beta_{1,1} - \beta_{1,2})^2$.
(e) Argue in a similar way that $E\{\sum_{t=T_1+1}^{T}(Y_t - \widetilde{\beta})^2\}$ is equal to $(T - T_1)\sigma_\epsilon^2 + Tk^2(1-k)(\beta_{1,1} - \beta_{1,2})^2$.
(f) Finish by combining the above results.

Exercise 20.2. * *Consider the setup in section 20.2.1. It is to be argued that, as $T \to \infty$, while k is fixed:*

$$T^{-1}\sum_{t=1}^{T}(Y_t - \overline{Y})^2 \xrightarrow{P} E\left\{T^{-1}\sum_{t=1}^{T}(Y_t - \widetilde{\beta})^2\right\}. \qquad (20.7.1)$$

(a) Argue that $\sum_{t=1}^{T}(Y_t - \overline{Y})^2 = \sum_{t=1}^{T}(Y_t - \widetilde{\beta})^2 - T(\overline{Y} - \widetilde{\beta})^2$.
(b) Argue that $\overline{Y} = kT_1^{-1}\sum_{t=1}^{T_1}Y_t + (1-k)(T - T_1)^{-1}\sum_{t=T_1+1}^{T}Y_t$.
(c) Use the Law of Large Numbers in Theorem 2.1 to argue $\overline{Y} - \widetilde{\beta} \xrightarrow{P} 0$.
(d) Argue that $E\{T^{-1}\sum_{t=1}^{T}(Y_t - \widetilde{\beta})^2\} = kE\{(Y_1 - \widetilde{\beta})^2\} + (1-k)E\{(Y_{T_1+1} - \widetilde{\beta})^2\}$.
(e) Argue that $T^{-1}\sum_{t=1}^{T}(Y_t - \widetilde{\beta})^2$ equals the sum of $kT_1^{-1}\sum_{t=1}^{T_1}(Y_t - \widetilde{\beta})^2$ and

$(1 - k)(T - T_1)^{-1} \sum_{t=T_1+1}^{T} (Y_t - \tilde{\beta})^2$.

(f) *Finish using the Law of Large Numbers to argue* $T^{-1} \sum_{t=1}^{T} (Y_t - \tilde{\beta})^2 \xrightarrow{P}$
$E\{T^{-1} \sum_{t=1}^{T} (Y_t - \tilde{\beta})^2\}$.

Exercise 20.3. * *In Exercise 20.2 it is assumed that k is fixed as $T \to \infty$.*
(*a*) *How would the result in (20.7.1) change if it is assumed that T_1 is fixed as*
$T \to \infty$?
(*b*) *Discuss the practical implications of these assumptions.*

Exercise 20.4. *An economic agent has a desired value y_t^* for a random variable*
y at time t, related to a variable z_t by:

$$y_t^* = \beta z_t \qquad \text{for } \beta \in \mathbb{R}. \tag{20.7.2}$$

In each period, the agent plans to reduce by a fraction $0 < \gamma < 1$ the previous
disequilibrium between the outcome y and her target y^* using:

$$\Delta y_t^p = \Delta y_t^* + \gamma(y_{t-1}^* - y_{t-1}), \tag{20.7.3}$$

where Δy_t^p is the planned change and $\Delta x_t = x_t - x_{t-1}$ for any x_t. However, the
outcome change deviates randomly from her plan:

$$\Delta y_t = \Delta y_t^p + \epsilon_t, \tag{20.7.4}$$

where $\epsilon_t \overset{D}{=} \mathsf{IIN}[0, \sigma_\epsilon^2]$. The process $\{z_t\}$ is determined outside of the agent's control
by:

$$z_t = \lambda z_{t-1} + u_t, \tag{20.7.5}$$

where $u_t \overset{D}{=} \mathsf{IIN}[0, \sigma_u^2]$ with $\lambda \in [-1, 1]$. The processes $\{\epsilon_t\}$ and $\{u_t\}$ are indepen-
dent.
(*a*) *Use (20.7.2) and (20.7.4) to express (20.7.3) as a relation between y_t and z_t*
and their lagged values (i.e., eliminate the unobservable variables y_t^p and y^*).
(*b*) *Discuss the properties of the resulting model when z_t is stationary, including*
deriving its static equilibrium solution.
(*c*) *How would you estimate the parameters of your derived equation given the*
assumptions above?
(*d*) *Carefully discuss how the system's properties are affected by z_t being $\mathsf{I}(1)$,*
rather than $\mathsf{I}(0)$.
(*e*) *Explain how to test the claim that y_t and z_t are cointegrated when z_t is known*
to be $\mathsf{I}(1)$?

Exercise 20.5. *The data-generating process for the logs of real consumers' ex-*
penditure, c_t, and real disposable income, y_t, in a certain economy is:

$$\Delta c_t = \gamma_1 - \alpha_1 (c_{t-1} - y_{t-1} - \mu) + \epsilon_{1,t}, \tag{20.7.6}$$
$$\Delta y_t = \gamma_2 + \alpha_2 (c_{t-1} - y_{t-1} - \mu) + \epsilon_{2,t}, \tag{20.7.7}$$

where:

$$\left(\begin{array}{c} \epsilon_{1,t} \\ \epsilon_{2,t} \end{array} \right) \stackrel{D}{=} \mathsf{IN}_2 \left[\left(\begin{array}{c} 0 \\ 0 \end{array} \right), \left(\begin{array}{cc} \sigma_{11} & 0 \\ 0 & \sigma_{22} \end{array} \right) \right]. \tag{20.7.8}$$

All of the parameters (γ_1, α_1, μ, σ_{11}, γ_2, α_2, σ_{22}) in (20.7.6)–(20.7.8) are positive and less than unity.

(a) What model type is each equation (20.7.6) and (20.7.7)?

(b) Interpret all of their parameters, commenting on any economic or statistical implications.

(c) Discuss the degree of integration of the two series c_t and y_t. Do c_t and y_t cointegrate? If so, what is the long-run equilibrium?

(d) When $\mathsf{E}(c_t - y_t) = \mu$, how would you interpret the parameters γ_1 and γ_2? Does this suggest any other restriction that should be imposed?

(e) Is it legitimate to estimate the Δc_t and Δy_t equations by regression?

(f) Which assumptions would you consider to be the most restrictive in (20.7.6)–(20.7.8) given the interpretation of the variables?

Computing Task 20.6. *Break in autoregressive parameter. Consider the data-generating process:*

$$Y_t = \beta_1 + \left\{ \beta_{2,1} 1_{(t \leq T_1)} + \beta_{2,2} 1_{(t > T_1)} \right\} Y_{t-1} + \epsilon_t, \tag{20.7.9}$$

where $\epsilon_t \stackrel{D}{=} \mathsf{IN}[0,1]$. Let $\beta_{2,1} = 0.9$, $\beta_{2,2} = 0.45$ with $T_1 = 50$, $T = 100$, while $Y_0 = 0$. Simulate using $M = 1000$ replications.

(a) Analyze the properties of the estimators of the model in (20.3.1), namely:

$$Y_t = \alpha_1 + \alpha_2 Y_{t-1} + u_t,$$

when $\beta_1 = 0$ in (20.7.9).

(b) Discuss the results. Are you surprised by the outcome?

(c) Analyze the properties of the estimators of the model (20.3.1), when $\beta_1 = 2$ in (20.7.9).

(d) Compare the two outcomes. Can you explain why they differ so much?

Computing Task 20.7. *(a) Reestimate Table 19.4 where the coefficients of $R_{n,t}$ and Δp_t are unrestricted. This can be done either using PcGets or directly by estimating a second-order autoregressive distributed-lag model with $m_t - p_t$ as regressand and x_t, $R_{n,t}$, Δp_t, $D_{out,t}$, $D_{71:1,t}$ as regressors.*

(b) Write the model in equilibrium correction form.

(c) Redo the argument in (20.5.1).

Chapter Twenty One

Forecasting

So far we have been concerned with the development of statistical models. Within such models, inferences can be made about economic phenomena. Policy-relevant equations are often put together in economy-wide macroeconomic systems (e.g., the published models in Bank of England, 1999). However, these can comprise 100+ equations, so will not be discussed in this book. Instead, we focus on forecasting, without being explicit about the role of macroeconomic models therein, although to date they do not have a particularly good forecasting track record.

Clements and Hendry (1998, 1999) present a general theory of economic forecasting, much of which is summarized non-technically in Hendry and Ericsson (2001). The choice of forecasting methods needs to be based on such a general theory to avoid episodes of systematic forecast failure. The causes of such failure are reasonably well understood—specifically, shifts in coefficients of deterministic terms, also called location shifts in §20.2—and there are techniques for "fixing" that problem. Section 21.1 sketches an earlier theoretical background. Unfortunately, despite its mathematical elegance and the simplicity of its prescriptions, the evidence against that framework providing a useful theory for economic forecasting cannot be ignored. A more viable framework based on Clements and Hendry (1999) is therefore proposed in §21.2, while §21.3 explains that theory and illustrates its operation for an autoregressive model. §21.4 proposes a taxonomy of sources of forecast error to understand which mistakes are most pernicious; and §21.5 illustrates the analysis for UK M1 data.

21.1 BACKGROUND

We will start by giving an overview of the uncertainties met by forecasters. Subsequently a traditional approach to forecasting and its failure to address these uncertainties are discussed.

21.1.1 The uncertainties of forecasting

A forecast is any statement about the future, so economic forecasting is a vast subject. To be successful at forecasting, one really requires a "crystal ball" to reveal the future: unfortunately, "crystal balls" appear to be unavailable—as the *Washington Post* headlined in relation to the probability of a recession in the USA, "Never a crystal ball when you need one" (Robert J. Samuelson, 16 June, 2001, p. A23). Consequently, economists focus on extrapolating from present information using systematic forecasting rules. Many such extrapolative methods exist, but all face the difficulty that the future is uncertain—for two reasons. The first is uncertainty where the probabilities involved are understood and can be used to calculate forecast uncertainty. The second reason involves uncertainty that is not currently understood and is the more serious problem, particularly in economics where non-stationary data are the norm—to quote Singer (1997, p. 39):

> Because of the things we don't know we don't know, the future is largely unpredictable.

Empirical models can take into account the effects of earlier events, even when these were unanticipated at the time, and so explain the past quite well. However, new unpredictable events will occur in the future, so the future will always appear more uncertain than the past. Any operational theory of economic forecasting must allow for such contingencies, especially as the levels and variability of l(0) transformations of economic variables might alter because of changes in technology, legislation, politics, climate, and society; Stock and Watson (1996) document the pervasiveness of structural change in macroeconomic time series.

Regular persistent changes are now modeled by stochastic trends, so unit roots are pandemic in econometric and forecasting models. Structural breaks—defined as sudden large changes, almost invariably unanticipated—are a major source of forecast failure, namely a significant deterioration in forecast performance relative to the anticipated outcome, usually based on the historical performance of a model. To date, no generic approaches to modeling such breaks have evolved, although considerable effort is being devoted to regime-switching and non-linear models. Thus, in practice, economic forecasts end up being a mixture of science, based on econometric systems that embody consolidated economic knowledge and have been carefully evaluated, and art, namely judgments about perturbations from recent unexpected events.

21.1.2 An "optimality theory" for forecasting

Historically, the theory of economic forecasting has relied on two key assumptions (see, e.g., Klein, 1971). We refer to this approach as "optimality theory" following Makridakis and Hibon (2000):

(1) The empirical model is a good representation of the economy.

(2) The structure of the economy will remain relatively unchanged.

Given these assumptions, a number of important theorems can be proved, each with many testable implications. We will list six general properties.

First, forecasts from such models will closely approximate the conditional expectation of the data, so the best in-sample model generally produces the best forecasts. Hence, an in-sample congruent encompassing model will dominate in forecasting.

Second, the only judgments that should improve forecasts are those based on advance warnings of events to come. These could be announcements of future tax changes or strikes.

Third, it should not pay to pool forecasts across several models—indeed, the need to pool refutes encompassing by any of the models—since adding biased forecasts or those from a badly-fitting model, should merely serve to worsen forecast errors from the best model.

Fourth, forecast accuracy should decline as the forecast horizon increases, because more innovation errors accrue and so predictability falls. Interval forecasts calculated from in-sample estimates reflect this property.

Fifth, in-sample based interval forecasts should be a good guide to the likely variations in the forecast errors. Monte Carlo simulation evidence from studies embodying the above two assumptions corroborate this finding (see, e.g., Calzolari, 1981).

Finally, while adding causally relevant variables should improve forecasts, adding irrelevant variables should generally worsen forecasts from unnecessary parameter-estimation uncertainty.

Given such a strong foundation, one might anticipate a successful history of economic forecasting. The facts are otherwise.

21.1.3 The failure of "optimality theory" in changing environments

Unfortunately, empirical experience in economic forecasting has highlighted the inadequacy of the above two assumptions. Such an outcome should not be a surprise; in practice, econometric models are mis-specified, and economies have been subject to important unanticipated shifts. As one of many examples, Barrell (2001) discusses six episodes of structural change during the 1990s. Also, Clements and Hendry (2001b) note the historical prevalence of forecast failure in output forecasts for the UK and the association of such poor forecasts with major economic events. Since the future is rarely like the past in economics, forecast failure has been all too common.

There is also a vast literature evaluating the forecast performance of models; Mills (1999) reprints most of the key papers. Early forecast-evaluation exercises compared econometric model forecasts to those of naive time-series models such as "no-change" predictors; see, for instance, Theil (1966), Mincer and Zarnowitz

(1969), Dhrymes et al. (1972), and Cooper and Nelson (1975), with findings that were not favorable to large econometric systems. More recently, Wallis (1989) and McNees (1990) survey UK and US evidence respectively, and the former concludes that "published model forecasts generally outperform their time series competitors", which should be understood in the context that published model forecasts often embody judgmental adjustments. In assessing the track record of the UK Treasury, its past chief economic advisor Burns (1986) saw little improvement in forecast accuracy over time, despite improvements in the underlying models.

The major empirical forecasting competitions, such as Makridakis, Andersen, Carbone, Fildes et al. (1982) and Makridakis and Hibon (2000), reviewed respectively by Fildes and Makridakis (1995) and Clements and Hendry (2001a), produce results across many models on numerous time series: their general findings are inconsistent with the implications of the two assumptions above. Although which model does best in a forecasting competition depends on how the forecasts are evaluated and what horizons and samples are selected, simple extrapolative methods tend to outperform econometric systems, and pooling forecasts often pays. Stock and Watson (1999) strongly confirm that last finding, but report that simple methods, such as no-change forecasts, do relatively poorly.

Even within the present generation of equilibrium-correction economic forecasting models, there is no evidence that the best in-sample model is the best at forecasting, as shown by the results in Eitrheim, Husebø and Nymoen (1999). They find that at short horizons, up to four quarters ahead, simple extrapolative devices outperform the Norges Bank econometric system, although the Norges Bank model wins over longer horizons such as 12 quarters ahead, primarily because the greater forecast-error variances of the simpler devices offset their smaller biases.

The final conflicting evidence is that judgment has value added in economic forecasting (see Turner, 1990; and Wallis and Whitley, 1991). One might surmise that forecasters have fore knowledge which contributes to that finding, but the widespread use of forecasts extrapolating directly from data suggests that existing estimated macroeconomic models do not provide a good approximation to conditional expectations over relevant forecast horizons. The next section explores the consequences of abandoning these two "optimality" assumptions. Instead, we allow for models that provide a mis-specified description of the data-generating process when that data-generating process changes over time.

21.2 FORECASTING IN CHANGING ENVIRONMENTS

The forecasting theory in Clements and Hendry (1999) makes two matching, but far less stringent, assumptions:

(1) Models are simplified representations which are incorrect in many ways.
(2) Economies both evolve and suddenly shift.

In this more realistic setting, none of the properties discussed in §21.1.2 holds. Econometric equations have three main components: deterministic terms such as intercepts and linear trends whose future values are known; observed stochastic variables with unknown future values, like consumers' expenditure or prices; and unobserved errors, all of whose values in the past, the present, and the future are unknown, though perhaps estimable in the context of a model. The relationships between any of these three components could be inappropriately formulated, inaccurately estimated, or change in unanticipated ways. Each of the resulting nine types of mistake could induce poor forecast performance, either from inaccuracy in the sense of bias or imprecision in the sense of high variance of the forecasts. Instead, theory suggests that some mistakes have pernicious effects on forecasts, whereas others are relatively less important in most settings. Surprisingly, the key to understanding systematic forecast failure depends on the behavior of the deterministic terms, even though their future values are known, rather than on the behavior of variables with unknown future values. A hint of this was seen in §20.3 on estimation in the context of location shifts.

When shifts in the coefficients of deterministic terms occur, the best model in-sample need not produce the best forecasts. Indeed, models with no causally relevant variables can outperform. Further, pooling of forecasts may pay dividends by averaging offsetting biases. Also, longer-term forecasts may be more accurate than short-term ones. Judgment can improve forecasting performance. Finally, calculated forecast intervals can be misleading about actual forecast uncertainty, although the increase in reporting of fan charts to represent known uncertainties is welcome; Ericsson (2001) provides an exposition.

Thus, almost the opposite implications now hold compared to the previous theory, and do match empirical findings. In particular, since differencing lowers the degree of a polynomial in time by one degree, intercepts and linear trends can be eliminated by double differencing, so devices based on that idea might be expected to avoid forecast failure despite fitting badly in-sample.

21.3 FORECASTING FROM AN AUTOREGRESSION

Consider a time series $X_1, \ldots, X_T$, where the conditional distribution of X_t given X_{t-1} has density $f_\theta(x_t|x_1, \ldots, x_{t-1})$ for some parameter $\theta \in \Theta \subseteq \mathbb{R}^k$. An *h-step ahead forecast* for period $T+h$, conditional on information up to time T, is defined by $\widetilde{X}_{T+h|T} = \psi_h(X_1, \ldots, X_T)$ where $\psi_h(\cdot)$ may depend on a prior estimate of θ and may vary with the forecast horizon h. Forecast errors are often measured in terms of mean square forecast error (MSFE):

$$\mathsf{M}\left(\widetilde{X}_{T+h|T}\middle| X_1, \ldots, X_T\right) = \mathsf{E}\left\{\left(X_{T+h} - \widetilde{X}_{T+h|T}\right)^2\middle| X_1, \ldots, X_T\right\}.$$

With that measure as a guideline, a forecast $\widehat{X}_{T+h|T}$ is said to be efficient, or optimal, if no other predictor has a smaller mean square forecast error, so:

$$\mathsf{M}\left(\widetilde{X}_{T+h|T}\Big|X_1,\ldots,X_T\right) \geq \mathsf{M}\left(\widehat{X}_{T+h|T}\Big|X_1,\ldots,X_T\right), \qquad (21.3.1)$$

for any forecast $\widetilde{X}_{T+h|T}$. In Exercise 21.1, it is found that the conditional expectation $\widehat{X}_{T+h|T} = \mathsf{E}(X_{T+h}|X_1,\ldots,X_T)$ is unbiased and efficient. In practice, any forecast $\widehat{X}_{T+h|T}$ is based on an estimated model $\widetilde{\psi}_h\,(X_1,\ldots,X_T)$, which is itself an approximation to the in-sample data-generating process. More importantly, the relevant future density may be $f_{\theta^*}(x_{T+h}|x_1,\ldots,x_T)$, where the parameter θ^* may be different from θ, as in the event of a structural break in the forecast period.

   We now list the ten issues that structure the analysis of economic forecasting. First, there are six issues relating to the in-sample density, $f_\theta(x_t|x_1,\ldots,x_{t-1})$, and the in-sample parameter, θ, which introduce in-sample uncertainties:

  (1) the *specification* of the set of relevant variables, x_t;
  (2) the *measurement* of the xs;
  (3) the *formulation* of $f_\theta(x_t|x_1,\ldots,x_{t-1})$;
  (4) the *modeling* of the relationships;
  (5) the *estimation* of θ;
  (6) the *properties* of $f_\theta(x_t|x_1,\ldots,x_{t-1})$ determining the intrinsic uncertainty.

Next there are four difficulties associated with the forecast horizon:

  (7) the *properties* of $f_\theta(x_{T+h}|x_1,\ldots,x_T)$ determining the forecast uncertainty;
  (8) *which grows* as h increases;
  (9) especially for *integrated* data;
 (10) increased by *changes* in $f_\theta(x_{T+h}|x_1,\ldots,x_T)$, or θ to θ^*.

   To illustrate these, and their consequences, we consider a stationary scalar first-order autoregressive example. A sample $X_1,\ldots,X_T$ is available. The distribution of this and future observations is given by:

$$X_t = \rho X_{t-1} + \epsilon_t \qquad t = 2,\ldots,T,T+1,\ldots \qquad (21.3.2)$$

given X_1, where $\epsilon_t \stackrel{\mathrm{D}}{=} \mathsf{IN}\left[0,\sigma_\epsilon^2\right]$ and $|\rho| < 1$. The 1-step ahead forecast from the model equation (21.3.2) is:

$$\widehat{X}_{T+1|T} = \rho X_T.$$

This is the conditional expectation of X_{T+1} given the past, so it produces an unbiased forecast when ρ is known and constant:

$$\mathsf{E}\left(X_{T+1} - \widehat{X}_{T+1|T}\Big|X_1,\ldots,X_T\right) = \mathsf{E}\left\{(\rho - \rho)\,X_T + \nu_T|\,X_1,\ldots,X_T\right\} = 0,$$

with the smallest possible variance determined by $f_\theta(x_{T+1}|x_1,\ldots,x_T)$:

$$\mathsf{Var}\left(X_{T+1} - \widehat{X}_{T+1|T}\Big|X_1,\ldots,X_T\right) = \sigma_\epsilon^2.$$

Thus $(X_{T+1}|X_1, \ldots, X_T) \overset{\mathrm{D}}{=} \mathsf{N}\left[\rho X_T, \sigma_\epsilon^2\right]$. In effect, all the issues (1)–(10) have been assumed away.

Now reconsider all ten potential problems in a setting where matters go awry:

(1) The specification could be incomplete: e.g., a vector $\mathbf{X}_t$ might be needed, not a scalar.

(2) Measurements could be incorrect, if, e.g., we observed $\widetilde{X}_t$ not X_t.

(3) The formulation could be inadequate, if, e.g., an intercept was needed.

(4) Modeling could go wrong, if, e.g., the data variation happened to lead to X_{t-2} being selected.

(5) Estimating ρ adds a bias, $\{\rho - \mathsf{E}(\widehat{\rho})\}X_T$, as well as a variance component $\mathsf{Var}(\widehat{\rho})X_T^2$ to the forecast variance denoted σ_f^2.

(6) The properties of ϵ_t determine $\mathsf{Var}(X_t)$, but $\epsilon_t \overset{\mathrm{D}}{=} \mathsf{IN}[0, \sigma_\epsilon^2]$ may be incorrect.

(7) We assumed $\epsilon_{T+1} \overset{\mathrm{D}}{=} \mathsf{IN}[0, \sigma_\epsilon^2]$, but $\mathsf{Var}(\epsilon_{T+1})$ could differ from $\mathsf{Var}(\epsilon_T)$.

(8) The h-step forecast error $\sum_{i=1}^{h} \rho^{i-1}\epsilon_{T+i}$ has variance $\sigma_\epsilon^2(1-\rho^{2h})/(1-\rho^2)$.

(9) If $\rho = 1$, the forecast error variance is $h\sigma_\epsilon^2$, so trends.

(10) If ρ changes, the forecaster could experience forecast failure.

Forecasters must be prepared for all of (1)–(10) to occur. Fortunately, many of the possible problems do not lead to forecast failure, as Figure 21.1 illustrates. Panel (c) shows a time series generated from (21.3.2) with $(\rho, \ \sigma_\epsilon^2, \ X_1, \ T) = (0.8, 10, 0, 46)$, with the forecast starting after period 41, leaving five observations for comparison. Panel (a) shows the five 1-step ahead forecasts, where X_{T+h-1} is recursively updated over the period 42–46, for both known ρ and when using the in-sample estimate $\widehat{\rho}$, together with interval forecasts shown as bars and bands respectively at $\pm 2\widehat{\sigma}_f$. As can be seen, estimation by itself has had only a small impact on forecast accuracy and uncertainty. More surprisingly, the same comments apply to the sequence of 1- through 5-step ahead forecasts shown in panel (b): estimation barely changes the outcomes. The lower right panel shows the effects of forecasting after a break in ρ to $\rho^* = 0.4$ at $T = 42$, which is the beginning of the forecast period. The simulation study described in Computer Task 21.4 shows that this structural change would be hard to pick up with the Chow (1960) test introduced in §13.4. That simulation looks at 5%-level Chow tests for constancy in the two situations where $\rho = 0.8$ remains constant, and where it changes to $\rho^* = 0.4$ after $t = 41$ so that the constancy hypothesis is violated. The rejection frequency of a 5% test is about 10%, so that the type II error of accepting a false hypothesis of constancy is about 90%. Correspondingly, panel (d) shows that the forecasts based on $\rho = 0.8$, but for data generated by $\rho^* = 0.4$, lie well within the anticipated interval.

Such problems hardly seem disastrous: there is only a small increase in the forecast uncertainty from estimating ρ; forecast intervals grow quite slowly as h increases; there is little noticeable impact even from halving ρ at the beginning of the forecast period; and the constancy test hardly ever rejects the false null.

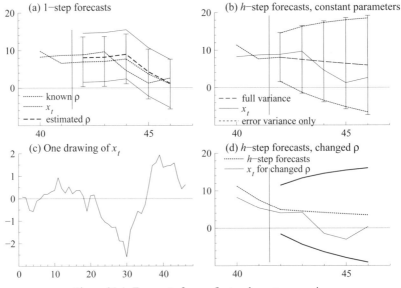

Figure 21.1 Forecasts from a first-order autoregression

But, a slight change to the model has a dramatic effect. Change (21.3.2) to:

$$X_t = \alpha + \rho X_{t-1} + \epsilon_t \text{ where } \epsilon_t \overset{\mathsf{D}}{=} \mathsf{IN}\left[0, \sigma_\epsilon^2\right] \text{ and } |\rho| < 1, \qquad (21.3.3)$$

where a constant $\alpha \neq 0$ is added. It must be stressed that the intercept in an econometric equation is often dependent on the units of measurement, with no intrinsic value. We hold everything else the same, including the size and timing of the break in ρ, but set $\alpha = 10$ instead of $\alpha = 0$. Now the data and forecasts differ greatly, as Figure 21.2 reveals, leading to a large increase in the forecast errors.

The simulation in Computer Task 21.4 shows that the rejection frequency of a 5%-level Chow test which was about 10% when the intercept was zero now jumps to 100% in the presence of the same size of break. Panels (a) and (b) show clear forecast failure on the 1- through 5-step ahead forecasts. Indeed, the 5-step ahead forecasts are for a rise in x_t, even though the break leads to a large fall in the outcomes, a typical finding for this situation.

The radical differences between Figures 21.1 and 21.2 resulting from simply altering the value of the intercept α from 0 to 10 might at first seem puzzling. The changes are due to the indirect effect of the shift in ρ on $\mathsf{E}(X_t)$, which is the equilibrium in this simple example. Equation (21.3.3) can be written as:

$$\Delta X_t = (\rho - 1)\left(X_{t-1} - \frac{\alpha}{1 - \rho}\right) + \epsilon_t. \qquad (21.3.4)$$

In the first case, where $\alpha = 0$, the equilibrium is $\mathsf{E}(X_t) = 0$ both before and after the shift in ρ; but in the second, where $\alpha = 10$, $\mathsf{E}(X_t) = \alpha/(1 - \rho)$, which shifts

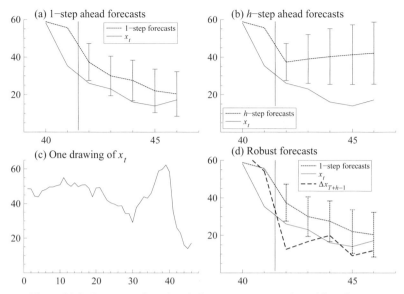

Figure 21.2 Forecasts after a break from an autoregression with an intercept

the equilibrium markedly from 50 to 17. Any model that "corrects" to $E(X_t)$ will suffer from forecast failure when $E(X_{T+h})$ shifts relative to $E(X_t)$.

Unfortunately, almost all econometric models are members of the class of equilibrium-correction mechanisms (EqCMs), including regressions, autoregressions, most simultaneous systems, and vector autoregressions. Even autoregressive conditional heteroskedastic models (ARCH) and generalized ARCH (GARCH) equilibrium correct to their long-run variances. Such models systematically fail in forecasting when $E(\cdot)$ changes such that the in-sample model is mis-specified for the non-stationary data-generating process over the forecast horizon.

The preceding example highlights the flaw with the earlier claim that the conditional expectation delivers the smallest mean square forecasting error: it does so only if written as $\widehat{X}_{T+h|T} = E_{T+h}(X_{T+h}|X_1 \ldots X_T)$. Thus, the expectation evaluated at time $T + h$ must be the integral over the distribution from which the data will be drawn. Using the expectation $E_T(\cdot)$ evaluated at time T assumes a stationary world, such that $E_{T+h}(\cdot) = E_T(\cdot)$. But if the distribution is not constant, then, paradoxically, one must know the whole future distribution to derive the optimal mean forecast.

An empirically relevant forecasting theory needs to allow for the model being mis-specified for the data-generating process, with parameters estimated from inaccurate observations on an integrated-cointegrated system, which intermittently alters unexpectedly from structural breaks. Only a magician can take account of breaks that may or may not happen in a future still to be determined. The focus therefore switches from finding an optimal forecasting model, to finding one that is robust to breaks after they have occurred. Since the source of the forecast failure above was due to a shift in $E(x_{T+h})$, a natural strategy is to consider forecasting methods that adapt rapidly to such shifts and so are not equilibrium-correction mechanisms. This approach was presaged in §20.4 in the context of the Lucas critique, where agents faced an identical problem of forecasting after a break. One simple example is the constant-change forecasting device discussed there, namely:

$$\widehat{\Delta^2 x}_{T+1|T} = 0. \tag{21.3.5}$$

Written in a more extensive form, (21.3.5) corresponds to:

$$\widehat{\Delta x}_{T+1|T} = \Delta x_T. \tag{21.3.6}$$

Such an equation does not equilibrium correct, and indeed has no natural level. Rather, it tracks the data on a 1-step ahead basis, but becomes increasingly poor for larger values of the step ahead h. Moreover, conventional interval forecasts as reported by standard computer software are inappropriate.

For the realization of the artificial data reported in Figure 21.2(c), the derived sequence of 1-step ahead forecasts $\widehat{X}_{T+h|T+h-1}$ from (21.3.5) is shown in Figure 21.2(d) in comparison with those from the estimated in-sample data-generating process. Notice that (21.3.6) is neither using data-generating process variables nor estimating any parameters. Nevertheless, there is no evidence of systematic misforecasting as occurred when using the estimated in-sample data-generating process equation, although the forecast variability is clear.

21.4 A FORECAST-ERROR TAXONOMY

The aim of a taxonomy is to decompose a forecast error into all potential sources to understand which components affect the mean and which the variance, and to establish their relative importance. The taxonomy can yield important insights into the comparative properties of forecasting models, and how to mitigate systematic forecast failures. Here we will explain the principles of constructing a taxonomy, using as an example the first-order autoregressive process. The analysis follows from the taxonomies in Clements and Hendry (1998).

Let X_t denote the variable to be forecast, determined by an I(0) autoregression with constant parameters when the in-sample DGP is:

$$X_t = \alpha + \rho X_{t-1} + \epsilon_t \text{ for } t = 1, \dots, T, \tag{21.4.1}$$

with $|\rho| < 1$ where $\epsilon_t \sim \text{IID}\left[0, \sigma_\epsilon^2\right]$. Taking expectations in (21.4.1) under in-sample stationarity:

$$E\left(X_t\right) = \alpha + \rho E\left(X_{t-1}\right) = \alpha + \rho\phi = \phi,$$

where:

$$\phi = (1 - \rho)^{-1} \alpha, \qquad (21.4.2)$$

as $|\rho| < 1$, and hence:

$$X_t - \phi = \rho (X_{t-1} - \phi) + \epsilon_t. \qquad (21.4.3)$$

This reformulation expresses (21.4.1) as an equilibrium-correction model, where $E(X_t) = \phi$ is the equilibrium. The investigator wishes to forecast X_{T+1}. To do so, the parameters of (21.4.1) must be estimated from the in-sample data, and we also allow for an uncertain measured value, $\widehat{X}_T$, at the forecast origin, which together entail forecasting X_{T+1} by:

$$\widehat{X}_{T+1|T} = \widehat{\phi} + \widehat{\rho} \left(\widehat{X}_T - \widehat{\phi} \right). \qquad (21.4.4)$$

21.4.1 Post-break outcomes

However, there is a break in the parameter values at the forecast origin T so that:

$$X_{T+1} = \alpha^* + \rho^* X_T + \epsilon_{T+1}, \qquad (21.4.5)$$

although the process stays I(0), in that $|\rho^*| < 1$. Such a change reflects the prevalence of forecast failure in economics. We construct a taxonomy of the forecast errors from using (21.4.4) when the forecast period is determined by (21.4.5). Because of the breaks in the parameters at the forecast origin, all expectations of data moments will change over the forecast horizon, generating considerable non-stationarity even though the dynamic parameter lies inside the unit interval. We calculate these expectations now, to derive the first moments. From (21.4.5):

$$E(X_{T+1}) = \alpha^* + \rho^* E(X_T) = \alpha^* + \rho^* \phi, \qquad (21.4.6)$$

since $E(X_T) = \phi$. But $E(X_{T+1}) \neq \phi$ and $E(X_{T+1}) \neq \phi^* = (1 - \rho^*)^{-1} \alpha^*$, the post-break equilibrium mean. Nevertheless, from the expression for ϕ^*, we can express (21.4.5) as:

$$X_{T+1} - \phi^* = \rho^* (X_T - \phi^*) + \epsilon_{T+1}, \qquad (21.4.7)$$

so the deviation from equilibrium of the forecast period outcome, $(X_{T+1} - \phi^*)$, depends on how far the forecast-origin value happened to deviate from the *post-break* equilibrium mean. Thus, (21.4.6) can be rewritten as:

$$E(X_{T+1}) = \phi^* + \rho^* (\phi - \phi^*). \qquad (21.4.8)$$

Consequently, we obtain our first important implication: when the equilibrium mean stays constant, $\phi = \phi^*$, then shifts in α and ρ have no impact on the first moment, $E(X_{T+1})$.

21.4.2 The forecast error

At $T + 1$, the forecast error that will result is $\widehat{\epsilon}_{T+1|T} = X_{T+1} - \widehat{X}_{T+1|T}$, so subtracting (21.4.4) from (21.4.7):

$$\widehat{\epsilon}_{T+1|T} = \left(\phi^* - \widehat{\phi}\right) + \rho^*\left(X_T - \phi^*\right) - \widehat{\rho}\left(\widehat{X}_T - \widehat{\phi}\right) + \epsilon_{T+1}. \qquad (21.4.9)$$

The forecast-error taxonomy now follows by decomposing each of the first three terms in (21.4.9) into its shift, mis-specification, and estimation components.

Since models will rarely coincide with the DGP, we cannot assume that parameter estimates will coincide on average with the in-sample population values, so we let $\mathsf{E}\left(\widehat{\rho}\right) = \rho_e$ and $\mathsf{E}(\widehat{\phi}) = \phi_e$, where the subscript denotes the expected value and allows for the possibility that $\rho_e \neq \rho$ and $\phi_e \neq \phi$. An example of when $\phi_e \neq \phi$ was noted in §2.2.1. A correctly-specified model with unbiased estimates will have $\rho_e = \rho$, but that is unlikely in dynamic models. To simplify notation in the taxonomy table, we let $\widehat{\rho} = \rho_e + \delta_\rho$, $\widehat{\phi} = \phi_e + \delta_\phi$, and $\widehat{X}_T = X_T + \delta_x$, so δ_z denotes an estimation error with an expected value of zero.

To illustrate the construction of the taxonomy, consider the first term in (21.4.9), written as:

$$\phi^* - \widehat{\phi} \equiv (\phi^* - \phi) + (\phi - \phi_e) - \delta_\phi. \qquad (21.4.10)$$

The expression in (21.4.10) is achieved by first subtracting ϕ and adding it; then subtracting ϕ_e and adding it; and finally using the notation that $\delta_\phi = \widehat{\phi} - \phi_e$ for the estimation error. Doing so separates the initial difference into components on the right-hand side that are logically independent: $(\phi^* - \phi) = 0$ if there is no break; $(\phi - \phi_e) = 0$ when the estimator is unbiased for the population parameter; and $\delta_\phi \to 0$ as the sample size grows, whatever is happening to the other two terms. The full taxonomy is reported in Table 21.1 below. We will now interpret the taxonomy, then return to consider the details of how it was constructed.

There are eight interesting findings from Table 21.1. First, the impact of a location shift is in italics as it is the only term that is always non-zero on average. It is possible that $\mathsf{E}(\delta_x) \neq 0$ when the forecast-origin is systematically mis-measured, but that seems unlikely, and we assume it does not occur. Hence, $\mathsf{E}\left(\widehat{\epsilon}_{T+1|T}\right) = (1 - \rho^*)(\phi^* - \phi)$. Surprisingly, therefore, changes in, and biases to, all other terms and estimates have no impact on the mean forecast error. Second, the slope change is multiplied by $(X_T - \phi)$ which is zero on average. Thus, its effect is mainly on the variance of the forecast error, and perhaps its autocorrelation if several 1-step ahead forecasts are made in succession. Third, the equilibrium-mean mis-specification will usually be non-zero only when there has been an unmodeled location shift in-sample since the sample mean would otherwise be an unbiased estimator. Next, the slope mis-specification is again zero on average even if $\rho_e \neq \rho$, but could induce an increase in the forecast-error variance. Fifth and sixth, both equilibrium-mean and slope-estimation effects are of a smaller order than the earlier terms, in that they decrease as the sample size grows, here at the rate $T^{-1/2}$ (a four-fold increase in T halves the estimation standard error). Seventh, we have noted the impact of δ_x above, which adds to the error variance. Finally, the innovation error has a one-for-one effect on the forecast error.

$\widehat{\epsilon}_{T+1\|T} \approx$		
$(1 - \rho^*)(\phi^* - \phi)$	(ia)	equilibrium-mean shift
$+ (\rho^* - \rho)(X_T - \phi)$	(ib)	slope change
$+ (1 - \rho_e)(\phi - \phi_e)$	(iia)	equilibrium-mean mis-specification
$+ (\rho - \rho_e)(X_T - \phi)$	(iib)	slope mis-specification
$- (1 - \rho_e)\delta_\phi$	$(iiia)$	equilibrium-mean estimation
$- (X_T - \phi_e)\delta_\rho$	$(iiib)$	slope estimation
$- \rho_e\delta_x$	(iv)	forecast origin uncertainty
$+ \epsilon_{T+1}$	(v)	innovation error.

Table 21.1 Forecast-error taxonomy from (21.4.9)

Many forecasters are interested in the properties of conditional forecasts, taking X_T as fixed. We can also calculate the conditional mean error from Table 21.1 as:

$$\mathsf{E}\left(\widehat{\epsilon}_{T+1|T} \mid X_T\right) = (1 - \rho^*)(\phi^* - \phi) + (\rho^* - \rho_e)(X_T - \phi). \qquad (21.4.11)$$

A possible third right-hand side term, namely $(1 - \rho_e)(\phi - \phi_e)$, should be zero in a congruent model, as $\phi = \phi_e$, so is omitted. A biased parameter estimate only matters when $X_T \neq \phi$. Moreover:

$$\widehat{\epsilon}_{T+1|T} - \mathsf{E}\left(\widehat{\epsilon}_{T+1|T} \mid X_T\right) \approx -(1 - \rho_e)\delta_\phi - (X_T - \phi)\delta_\rho - \rho_e\delta_x + \epsilon_{T+1}, \qquad (21.4.12)$$

from which we can obtain the conditional forecast-error variance. We assume that the components in (21.4.12) are sufficiently independent that covariances between them should be negligible, so that:

$$\mathsf{Var}\left(\widehat{\epsilon}_{T+1|T} \mid X_T\right) \approx (1 - \rho_e)^2\,\mathsf{Var}\left(\delta_\phi\right) + (X_T - \phi)^2\,\mathsf{Var}\left(\delta_\rho\right) + \rho_e^2\mathsf{Var}\left(\delta_x\right) + \sigma_\epsilon^2.$$

Both $\mathsf{Var}\left(\delta_\phi\right)$ and $\mathsf{Var}\left(\delta_\rho\right)$ decrease proportionately as T increases, but little is known about $\mathsf{Var}\left(\delta_x\right)$ except from later data revisions, which suggest it can be an important contributor to forecast error variances.

Another important implication from Table 21.1 is that if we held the parameter estimates unchanged at their in-sample values, and then tried to forecast X_{T+2} from the next forecast origin at $T+1$, updating all the time subscripts by unity, precisely the same forecast error components would recur. Thus, the mistakes shown are systematic, which is a forecasting problem endemic to equilibrium-correction models. Proving this claim is left as an exercise.

21.4.3 Constructing the taxonomy

Equation (21.4.10) showed the general approach for the equilibrium mean, and we now do similar calculations for the autoregressive component, first collecting terms in ϕ, then ρ and finally in δ_ρ etc., proceeding as shown. First:

$$\begin{aligned}
\rho^* \left(X_T - \phi^* \right) = {} & \rho^* \left(X_T - \phi^* \right) - \rho^* \left(X_T - \phi \right) \\
& + \rho^* \left(X_T - \phi \right) - \rho \left(X_T - \phi \right) \\
& + \rho \left(X_T - \phi \right) - \rho_e \left(X_T - \phi \right) \\
& + \rho_e \left(X_T - \phi \right)
\end{aligned}$$

where the first and second lines subtract then add $\rho^* \left(X_T - \phi \right)$; then the same operation for $\rho \left(X_T - \phi \right)$; and finally, we subtract then add $\rho_e \left(X_T - \phi \right)$. Collecting terms in the pairs shown on each line:

$$\begin{aligned}
\rho^* \left(X_T - \phi^* \right) = {} & -\rho^* \left(\phi^* - \phi \right) \\
& + \left(\rho^* - \rho \right) \left(X_T - \phi \right) \\
& + \left(\rho - \rho_e \right) \left(X_T - \phi \right) \\
& + \rho_e \left(X_T - \phi \right) .
\end{aligned} \tag{21.4.13}$$

Turning our attention to $\widehat{\rho}(\widehat{X}_T - \widehat{\phi})$, we write that as:

$$\begin{aligned}
\widehat{\rho} \left(\widehat{X}_T - \widehat{\phi} \right) = {} & \widehat{\rho} \left(\widehat{X}_T - \widehat{\phi} \right) - \widehat{\rho} \left(X_T - \widehat{\phi} \right) \\
& + \widehat{\rho} \left(X_T - \widehat{\phi} \right) - \widehat{\rho} \left(X_T - \phi_e \right) \\
& + \widehat{\rho} \left(X_T - \phi_e \right) - \rho_e \left(X_T - \phi_e \right) \\
& + \rho_e \left(X_T - \phi_e \right)
\end{aligned}$$

then again collecting terms line by line:

$$\begin{aligned}
\widehat{\rho} \left(\widehat{X}_T - \widehat{\phi} \right) = {} & \widehat{\rho} \left(\widehat{X}_T - X_T \right) \\
& - \widehat{\rho} \left(\widehat{\phi} - \phi_e \right) \\
& + \left(\widehat{\rho} - \rho_e \right) \left(X_T - \phi_e \right) \\
& + \rho_e \left(X_T - \phi_e \right) .
\end{aligned}$$

To separate off the estimation terms, we next use $\widehat{\rho} = \rho_e + \delta_\rho$, $\widehat{X}_T = X_T + \delta_x$ and $\widehat{\phi} = \phi_e + \delta_\phi$, and reformulate $\left(X_T - \phi_e \right)$ as $\left(X_T - \phi \right) - \left(\phi_e - \phi \right)$ so that:

$$\begin{aligned}
\widehat{\rho} \left(\widehat{X}_T - \widehat{\phi} \right) = {} & \rho_e \delta_x + \delta_\rho \delta_x \\
& - \rho_e \delta_\phi - \delta_\rho \delta_\phi \\
& + \delta_\rho \left(X_T - \phi \right) - \delta_\rho \left(\phi_e - \phi \right) \\
& + \rho_e \left(X_T - \phi \right) - \rho_e \left(\phi_e - \phi \right) .
\end{aligned} \tag{21.4.14}$$

Finally, collecting all the components in (21.4.10), (21.4.13) and (21.4.14):

$$
\begin{aligned}
\widehat{\epsilon}_{T+1|T} = {} & (\phi^* - \phi) + (\phi - \phi_e) - \delta_\phi \\
& -\rho^* (\phi^* - \phi) + (\rho^* - \rho)(X_T - \phi) \\
& + (\rho - \rho_e)(X_T - \phi) + \rho_e (X_T - \phi) \\
& -\rho_e (X_T - \phi) + \rho_e (\phi_3 - \phi) \\
& -\rho_e \delta_x + \rho_e \delta_\phi - \delta_\rho (X_T - \phi) + \delta_\rho (\phi_e - \phi) \\
& -\delta_\rho \delta_x + \delta_\rho \delta_\phi \\
& +\epsilon_{T+1}.
\end{aligned}
$$

Dropping the term $\delta_\rho (\delta_\phi - \delta_x)$ as of smaller order, and simplifying by collecting like terms, leads to the results in Table 21.1.

21.4.4 Updating estimates

A natural question concerns what happens if we re-estimate the parameters including the data now available at $T + 1$. If all parameters stay constant, then the estimation errors decrease as the sample size grows larger. However, if some parameters change, an analytic answer is difficult, although a simulation study is easy, and highlights the main features. Computer Task 21.5 focuses on two possible types of change: (a) when ϕ shifts to ϕ^*; and (b) when α shifts to α^* and ρ shifts to ρ^* but in such a way that $\phi = \phi^*$.

21.5 ILLUSTRATION USING UK MONEY DATA

The potential problems with forecasting can be neatly illustrated using the data set for UK narrow money introduced in §17.2.1. An institutional change in 1984 led to a significant rise in narrow money. We will explore the impact on forecasting.

Prior to 1984, checking accounts were not interest bearing. As a result, agents kept less money in such accounts in the high-inflation period of the 1970s and early 1980s than in the 1960s. In 1984, interest payments were allowed for checking accounts, and their level changed radically. This can be seen in the graph of real money, $m_t - p_t$, in Figure 17.1(b) as well as in the graph of velocity, $v_t = x_t - m_t + p_t$, in Figure 21.3(a). Prior to 1984, the cost of holding narrow money would simply be the interest rate on a broad liquid asset, measured as the three-month local authority interest rate, $R_{a,t}$. With the introduction of own interest rates, the cost of holding narrow money changed to the difference between $R_{a,t}$ and the interest rate on narrow money, R_{m_t}, measured as $R_{n,t} = R_{a,t} - R_{m,t}$. These interest rates are shown in Figure 21.3(b).

To investigate the influence of this institutional change, we revisit the data previously analyzed in Chapter 17. Only the period until 1984:2 is considered, for

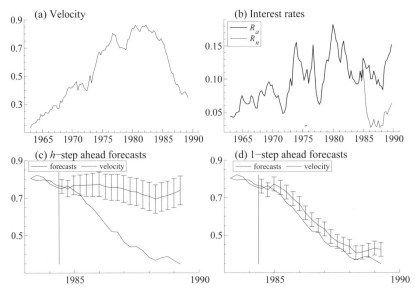

Figure 21.3 Forecasts of velocity using the local authority interest rate

which $R_{n,t} = R_{a,t}$. The results from estimating an autoregressive distributed-lag model are reported in Table 21.2. The results are very similar to the results seen for the full sample in Table 17.6. This is hardly surprising as recursive investigations supported the congruence of the full model.

$$\widehat{v}_t = \underset{(0.10)}{0.63}\,v_{t-1} + \underset{(0.09)}{0.27}\,v_{t-2} + \underset{(0.17)}{0.70}\,R_{a,t} - \underset{(0.26)}{0.08}\,R_{a,t-1}$$

$$\text{standard error} \qquad + \underset{(0.18)}{0.08}\,R_{a,t-2} - \underset{(0.006)}{0.009} + \underset{(0.011)}{0.048}\,D_{out,t} + \underset{(0.012)}{0.009}\,D_{oil,t}$$

$$\sqrt{\widehat{\sigma}^2} = 0.019, \quad \widehat{\ell} = 220.14, \quad T = 84$$

$\chi^2_{\text{norm}}[2] = 3.3 \quad [\text{p} = 0.19]$	$F_{\text{ar}(1-5)}[5, 71] = 0.8 \quad [\text{p} = 0.95]$
$F_{\text{het}}[12, 63] = 1.0 \quad [\text{p} = 0.46]$	$F_{\text{arch}(1-4)}[4, 68] = 0.2 \quad [\text{p} = 0.95]$

Table 21.2 Autoregressive distributed-lag model for velocity of money, v_t, given the local authority interest rate, $R_{a,t}$

The model reported in Table 21.2 turns out to have disastrous forecasting properties. Figure 21.3(c) shows 1- through to 20-step ahead forecasts of velocity. Velocity plummets, while the forecasts stay flat. But even dynamically updated 1-step ahead forecasts, $\widehat{X}_{T+h|T+h-1}$, are poor as seen in panel (d). Given the institutional change in 1984, the forecast failure can be explained easily by economics. The problem could be picked up by an investigator who had a few more observations, until 1985:3 say, either through a 1-step ahead forecast or a 1-step ahead Chow test as introduced in §13.4. That investigator would then realize the lack of congruency of a model involving $R_{a,t}$. Knowledge of economics and the recent institutional change may then lead to a change in the measure for the opportunity cost of holding money.

Alternatively, a more robust forecasting device could be used, such as an intercept correction, or one could use the differences of all the variables in the initial congruent model. We consider these briefly.

An intercept correction adds the latest in-sample residual to the forecast, or a short average of recent residuals, to reflect any recent unmodeled location shift. The simplest implementation is to create a dummy variable equal to unity over the suspected break period and the forecast horizon, and zero otherwise. Exercise 21.2 asks you to derive the properties of such an intercept correction for known parameter values for a first-order autoregression and establish both that the resulting forecast is unbiased and that an intercept correction is beneficial to offset even a relatively small location shift. Figure 21.4(a) shows the marked improvement in multistep forecast accuracy for velocity relative to 21.3(c) using a dummy set to unity from 1985:1 on—when large residuals first appear—to forecast from 1985:4.

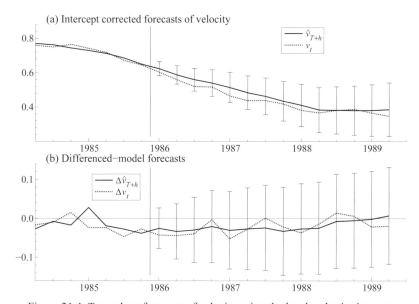

Figure 21.4 Two robust forecasts of velocity using the local authority interest rate

$$\widehat{\Delta v}_{T+h|T} = 0.63\Delta v_{T+h-1} + 0.27\Delta v_{T+h-2} + 0.70\Delta R_{a,T+h}$$
$$-0.08\Delta R_{a,T+h-1} + 0.08\Delta R_{a,T+h-2}$$
$$+0.048\Delta D_{out,T+h} + 0.009\Delta D_{oil,T+h}$$

Table 21.3 Differenced version of the autoregressive distributed-lag model in Table 21.2 for velocity of money, v_t, given the local authority interest rate, $R_{a,t}$

Differencing the congruent model does precisely that: when the estimated model is the one shown in Table 21.2, then the forecasting equation is as shown in Table 21.3. The outcomes for forecasting the change in velocity using the model reported in Table 21.3 are shown in figure 21.4(b) (although the forecast-error bars are no longer correct, since the equation is not congruent after differencing). Again, a marked improvement results, removing the earlier forecast failure.

In both cases, there is an increase in the forecast error variance by making the forecast robust to a location shift. Nevertheless, for even moderate location shifts, a reduction in the mean square forecast error can result. It is, of course, more satisfying to understand and to take account of shifts, but in the absence of that level of knowledge, relatively good forecasts are at least feasible.

21.6 SUMMARY AND EXERCISES

Summary: Many econometric analyses have an element of forecasting. When an econometric model is a good description of the sample at hand, and the structure of the economy does not change much, out-of-sample forecasting from the econometric model will be optimal. There is, however, a prevalence of structural changes in the economy, which makes forecast failure all too common. A taxonomy of forecast errors clarifies which sources have the most pernicious effects on forecast accuracy. Even when the sources of such forecast failures can be identified, robust forecasting devices can be useful in a changing environment.

Key questions:
- Discuss what assumptions are needed for a theory of forecasting to be relevant to practical experience. Present evidence that supports your argument.
- Explain why equilibrium-correction models will systematically misforecast if there is a shift in the equilibrium over the forecast period.
- Discuss how to avoid forecast failure due to an equilibrium shift that happens just prior to forecasting.

Exercise 21.1. *Prove the inequality (21.3.1) when the data-generating process is stationary across both the sample and the forecast horizons. This can be done in the following steps. Let $A = X_{T+h|T} - \widetilde{X}_{T+h|T}$, $B = X_{T+h|T} - \widehat{X}_{T+h|T}$, and $C = \widehat{X}_{T+h|T} - \widetilde{X}_{T+h|T}$.*
(a) Write A as $B + C$.
(b) Argue that $\mathsf{E}\{C^2 \mid X_1, \ldots, X_T\} = C^2$.
(c) Argue that $\mathsf{E}\{BC \mid X_1, \ldots, X_T\} = 0$, and finish the proof of (21.3.1).

Exercise 21.2. *Intercept correction.* *Consider the stationary first-order autoregression in (21.3.4):*

$$\Delta X_t = (\rho - 1)\left(X_{t-1} - \frac{\alpha}{1-\rho}\right) + \epsilon_t.$$

A researcher wishes to forecast X_{T+1} using:

$$\widehat{X}_{T+1|T} = X_T + (\rho - 1)\left(X_T - \frac{\alpha}{1-\rho}\right).$$

(a) *Derive the forecast error when in fact* α *shifted to* α^* *at time* $T - 1$, *unknown to the researcher, so that for* $h = 0, 1, \ldots$:

$$X_{T+h} = X_{T+h-1} + (\rho - 1) \left(X_{T+h-1} - \frac{\alpha^*}{1 - \rho} \right) + \epsilon_{T+h}.$$

(b) *Show that adding the last in-sample residual* $\widehat{\epsilon}_T = X_T - \widehat{X}_T$ *to forecast by:*

$$\widetilde{X}_{T+1|T} = \widehat{X}_{T+1|T} + \widehat{\epsilon}_T$$

produces a zero-mean forecast error. This is an intercept correction.
(c) *Compare the mean square forecast errors in these two cases, and hence derive a condition for when it is beneficial to intercept correct.*

Exercise 21.3. *Redo Table 21.1 from a forecast origin at* $T + 1$ *to forecast* X_{T+2} *using the in-sample parameter estimates based on data up to* T.

Computing Task 21.4. *Simulate the distribution of the 1-step ahead Chow test for the following data-generating processes. PcNaive can be used.*
(a) *Use (21.3.2), with* $(\rho, \sigma_\epsilon^2, X_1, T) = (0.8, 10, 0, 46)$.
(b) *Let* ρ *change to* $\rho^* = 0.4$ *after* $t = 41$ *in the process in* (a).
(c) *Use (21.3.3), with* $(\alpha, \rho, \sigma_\epsilon^2, X_1, T) = (10, 0.8, 10, 50, 46)$.
(d) *Let* ρ *change to* $\rho^* = 0.4$ *after* $t = 41$ *in the process in* (c).
(e) *Discuss your simulation results.*

Computing Task 21.5. *Consider two possible changes in (21.4.6):*
(a) *when* ϕ *shifts to* ϕ^*; *and*
(b) *when* α *shifts to* α^* *and* ρ *shifts to* ρ^* *but in such a way that* $\phi = \phi^*$.
Undertake a Monte Carlo simulation to see what you can discover about the detectablility of these two types of break using recursive estimation and testing.

Chapter Twenty Two

The way ahead

The main idea of this book has been to construct econometric models with the dual aim of matching the data and learning about the economy. While we have been selective in terms of the econometric theory, economic models, and data types discussed, we hope this introduction has inspired you to use econometrics and to learn more about econometrics. We will finish by giving a few suggestions for further study in econometrics.

We have presented a likelihood-based approach to econometric modeling. This combines an investigation of the sample distribution of the data, leading to a likelihood function, with information from economic theory and previous econometric studies. Hendry (1995a) gives a more detailed exposition of this approach than has been given here. The likelihood approach is followed in many areas of econometrics. The logit model is often applied this way, for a binary dependent variable; see Cramer (2003), and Hosmer and Lemeshow (2000). Likelihood-based analysis of cointegrated systems is proposed by Johansen (1995), focusing on the statistical theory, and by Juselius (2006) focusing on applications. While these authors consider systems of relatively low dimension, Bårdsen, Eitrheim, Jansen and Nymoen (2005) provide an account of the analysis of larger systems.

An extensive general likelihood theory is available (see Cox and Hinkley, 1974). In non-stationary cases, maximum likelihood estimators can be shown to be approximately normal distributed under rather general assumptions. The likelihood ratio test can be shown to be optimal in specialized settings, but for general cases of more relevance, there is no clear optimality theory. For many likelihood functions, the maximum cannot be found analytically. Ruud (2000) and Hendry (1995a) discuss ways of finding the maximum by numerical methods.

There is an abundance of distributions that can be used in modeling as alternatives to the Bernoulli and normal distributions that have been the focus here. Many tricks are needed to manipulate such distributions. Some can be found in introductory probability texts such as Hoel et al. (1971). An overview of important classes of distributions and their known properties can be found in the volumes by Johnson, Kotz and Kemp (1993), & Johnson, Kotz and Balakrishnan (1994, 1995).

For inference, we need approximate, and preferably exact, distributions for estimators and test statistics. *Asymptotic theory* is used extensively in econometric theory to derive such approximations. After an introductory text like Hoel et al. (1971), one can proceed to books like those of White (2001) or Davidson (1994).

An important mathematical tool in econometrics is *matrix algebra*. Using matrix formulations, the derivations in Chapter 7 can be simplified, as we illustrated in Chapters 6 and 8; see, for instance, Ruud (2000). Matrix notation also comes in handy in the discussion of the multivariate normal distribution and of systems of equations; see, for example, Johnston and DiNardo (1997).

The distributional assumptions of the likelihood approach have both advantages and drawbacks. One advantage is that those assumptions are explicit, and so can be tested with relative ease, allowing the possibility of refuting an inappropriate model (although a likelihood approach is not essential for testing). A disadvantage of the likelihood approach is that distributional assumptions can be restrictive. One response to that issue is to develop econometric methods with flexible assumptions. There is a tendency for such methods to work less well than likelihood methods when the likelihood assumptions are satisfied, but better when the likelihood assumptions are not satisfied. Examples of flexible methods are: *pseudo-* or *quasi-likelihood*, where, for instance, least-squares regression is used even though the errors are not normal; *methods of moments* and *generalized methods of moments* (GMM), where expectations are specified instead of entire densities; and *semi-* and *non-parametric* methods, where (e.g.) the linear form of the regression equation is replaced by a general, unknown function. *Simulated likelihoods* and *simulated methods of moments* can be used when a specified likelihood, or method of moments, model is not analytically tractable. These are often used when the model is formulated directly from an economic theory, rather than from the sample distribution. A general reference for these flexible methods is the textbook by Greene (2003); Wooldridge (2006) gives a methods-of-moments-based introduction to econometrics; and Gourieroux and Monfort (1996) describe simulation estimation.

The above-mentioned methods are frequentist in their nature; parameters are given, and have a "true" value, which can be estimated more precisely the more data are available. An alternative paradigm is *Bayesian statistics*. This is also based on the likelihood function, but with stochastic parameters. "Prior" distributions for the parameters are specified, which express subjective uncertainties about them. A recent Bayesian account in econometrics is given by Lancaster (2004). Cox (2006) contrasts the principles of frequentist and Bayesian approaches.

Last, but not least, there are many types of economic data that we have not discussed. There are many other models for *time series* than autoregressive models. Hamilton (1994) gives a general introduction, while Durbin and Koopman (2001) cover state space models. *Panel data*, also called longitudinal data, consist of cross sections of time series, typically following individuals or firms over time, but it could also be countries. Arellano (2003) gives an overview of panel data methods. The resulting models often have different intercepts for different individuals. Maximum likelihood does not work well in that situation, so the method of moments approach dominates in that literature. *Duration data*, or point processes, are used for instance in labor economics to model the time that individuals are unemployed before getting a job. When the dependent variable is *categorical* with two or perhaps a few states, *count data* analysis can be used. Cameron and Trivedi (2005) and Wooldridge (2002) discuss the use of panel data methods, duration models, and count models in micro-econometrics. *Contingency tables* occur when the joint distribution of categorical variables is of interest (see Andersen, 1997). *Financial data* for prices of assets or currencies can come in the form of time-series, or point, processes; see Taylor (2005) for an introduction. There is plenty to explore.

References

Akerlof, G. A. (1982). The short-run demand for money: A new look at an old problem. *American Economic Review*, **72**, 35–39.

Andersen, E. B. (1997). *Introduction to the Statistical Analysis of Categorical Data*. Heidelberg: Springer-Verlag.

Anderson, T. W. (1951). Estimating linear restrictions on regression coefficients for multivariate normal distributions. *Annals of Mathematical Statistics*, **22**, 327–351.

Anderson, T. W. (1984). *An Introduction to Multivariate Statistical Analysis,* 2nd ed. New York: John Wiley & Sons.

Angrist, J. D., Graddy, K., and Imbens, G. W. (2000). The interpretation of instrumental variables estimators in simultaneous equations models with an application to the demand for fish. *Review of Economic Studies*, **67**, 499–527.

Arellano, M. (2003). *Panel Data Econometrics*. Oxford: Oxford University Press.

Ashenfelter, O., Harmon, C., and Oosterbeek, H. (1999). A review of estimates of the schooling/earnings relationship, with tests for publication bias. *Labour Economics*, **6**, 453–470.

Banerjee, A., Dolado, J. J., Galbraith, J. W., and Hendry, D. F. (1993). *Co-integration, Error Correction and the Econometric Analysis of Non-Stationary Data*. Oxford: Oxford University Press.

Bank of England (1999). *Economic Models at the Bank of England*. London: Bank of England.

Bårdsen, G., Eitrheim, Ø., Jansen, E. S., and Nymoen, R. (2005). *The Econometrics of Macroeconomic Modelling*. Oxford: Oxford University Press.

Barrell, R. (2001). Forecasting the world economy. In Hendry and Ericsson (2001), pp. 149–169.

Bartlett, M. S. (1938). Further aspects of the theory of multiple regression. *Proceedings of the Cambridge Philosophical Society*, **34**, 33–40.

Becker, G. S. (1964). *Human Capital*. Chicago: University of Chicago Press.

Belzil, C., and Hansen, J. (2002). Unobserved ability and the returns to schooling. *Econometrica*, **70**, 2075–2091.

Blundell, R., and Stoker, T. M. (2005). Heterogeneity and aggregation. *Journal of Economic Literature*, **43**, 347–391.

Burns, T. (1986). The interpretation and use of economic predictions. *Proceedings of the Royal Society of London*, A, **407**, 103–125.

Caceres, C., and Nielsen, B. (2007). On the distribution of tests for cointegration rank. Working paper, Nuffield College, Oxford.

Calzolari, G. (1981). A note on the variance of ex post forecasts in econometric models. *Econometrica*, **49**, 1593–1596.

Cameron, A. C., and Trivedi, P. K. (2005). *Microeconometrics: Methods and Applications*. Cambridge: Cambridge University Press.

Campbell, J. Y., and Mankiw, N. G. (1991). The response of consumption to income. A cross-country investigation. *European Economic Review*, **35**, 723–767.

Campos, J., Ericsson, N. R., and Hendry, D. F. (eds.)(2005). *Readings on General-to-Specific Modeling*. Cheltenham: Edward Elgar.

Card, D. (1999). The causal effect of education on earnings. In Ashenfelter, O., and Card, D. (eds.), *Handbook of Labor Economics*, vol 3A, pp. 1801–1863. Amsterdam: North-Holland.

Census Bureau, U.S. (2005). *Statistical Abstract of the United States: 2006*. Washington, D.C.: U.S. Census Bureau.

Central Statistical Office, U.K. (1993). *Economic Trends Annual Supplement*. London: H.M.S.O.

Chow, G. C. (1960). Tests of equality between sets of coefficients in two linear regressions. *Econometrica*, **28**, 591–605.

Clements, M. P., and Hendry, D. F. (1998). *Forecasting Economic Time Series*. Cambridge: Cambridge University Press.

Clements, M. P., and Hendry, D. F. (1999). *Forecasting Non-stationary Economic Time Series*. Cambridge, Mass.: MIT Press.

Clements, M. P., and Hendry, D. F. (2001a). Explaining the results of the M3 forecasting competition. *International Journal of Forecasting*, **17**, 550–554.

Clements, M. P., and Hendry, D. F. (2001b). An historical perspective on forecast errors. *National Institute Economic Review*, **177**, 100–112.

Cooper, J. P., and Nelson, C. R. (1975). The ex ante prediction performance of the St. Louis and FRB-MIT-PENN econometric models and some results on composite predictors. *Journal of Money, Credit, and Banking*, **7**, 1–32.

Cox, D. R. (1961). Tests of separate families of hypotheses. In *Proceedings of the Fourth Berkeley Symposium on Mathematical Statistics and Probability*, vol 1, pp. 105–123. Berkeley California: University of California Press.

Cox, D. R. (2006). *Principles of Statistical Inference*. Cambridge: Cambridge University Press.

Cox, D. R., and Hinkley, D. V. (1974). *Theoretical Statistics*. London: Chapman and Hall.

Crafts, N. F. R., and Harley, C. K. (1992). Output growth and the British Industrial Revolution: A restatement of the Crafts–Harley view. *Economic History Review*, **45**, 703–730.

Cramer, J. S. (2003). *Logit Models from Economics and other Fields*. Cambridge: Cambridge University Press.

Davidson, J. E. H. (1994). *Stochastic Limit Theory*. Oxford: Oxford University Press.

Davidson, J. E. H., Hendry, D. F., Srba, F., and Yeo, J. S. (1978). Econometric modelling of the aggregate time-series relationship between consumers' expenditure and income in the United Kingdom. *Economic Journal*, **88**, 661–692.

Davidson, R., and MacKinnon, J. G. (1981). Several tests for model specification in the presence of alternative hypotheses. *Econometrica*, **49**, 781–793.

Deaton, A. S. (1992). *Understanding Consumption*. Oxford: Oxford University Press.

Dhrymes, P. J., et al. (1972). Criteria for evaluation of econometric models. *Annals of Economic and Social Measurement*, **1**, 291–324.

Dickey, D. A., and Fuller, W. A. (1979). Distribution of the estimators for autoregressive time series with a unit root. *Journal of the American Statistical Association*, **74**, 427–431.

Doornik, J. A. (2006). *An Introduction to OxMetrics*. London: Timberlake Consultants Press.

Doornik, J. A., and Hendry, D. F. (2006a). *Empirical Econometric Modelling using PcGive: Volume I*. London: Timberlake Consultants Press.

Doornik, J. A., and Hendry, D. F. (2006b). *Modelling Dynamic Systems using PcGive: Volume II*. London: Timberlake Consultants Press.

Doornik, J. A., and Hendry, D. F. (2006c). *Econometric Modelling using PcGive: Volume III*. London: Timberlake Consultants Press.

Doornik, J. A., and Hendry, D. F. (2006d). *Interactive Monte Carlo Experimentation in Econometrics using PcNaive. PcGive 11: Volume IV*. London: Timberlake Consultants Press.

Doornik, J. A., and O'Brien, R. J. (2002). Numerically stable cointegration analysis. *Computational Statistics & Data Analysis*, **41**, 185–193.

Dougherty, C. (2002). *Introduction to Econometrics*. Oxford: Oxford University Press.

Durbin, J. (1954). Errors in variables. *Review of the Institute of International Statistics*, **22**, 23–54.

Durbin, J., and Koopman, S. J. (2001). *Time Series Analysis by State Space Methods*. Oxford: Oxford University Press.

Eitrheim, Ø., Husebø, T. A., and Nymoen, R. (1999). Equilibrium-correction versus differencing in macroeconometric forecasting. *Economic Modelling*, **16**, 515–544.

Engle, R. F. (1982). Autoregressive conditional heteroscedasticity, with estimates of the variance of United Kingdom inflation. *Econometrica*, **50**, 987–1007.

Engle, R. F., and Granger, C. W. J. (1987). Cointegration and error correction: Representation, estimation and testing. *Econometrica*, **55**, 251–276.

Engle, R. F., and Hendry, D. F. (1993). Testing super exogeneity and invariance in regression models. *Journal of Econometrics*, **56**, 119–139.

Engle, R. F., Hendry, D. F., and Richard, J.-F. (1983). Exogeneity. *Econometrica*, **51**, 277–304.

Engler, E., and Nielsen, B. (2007). The empirical process of autoregressive residuals. Working paper, Nuffield College, University of Oxford.

Ericsson, N. R. (2001). Forecast uncertainty in economic modeling. In Hendry and Ericsson (2001), pp. 68–92.

Ericsson, N. R., Hendry, D. F., and Prestwich, K. M. (1998). The demand for broad money in the United Kingdom, 1878–1993. *Scandinavian Journal of Economics*, **100**, 289–324.

Ericsson, N. R., and Irons, J. S. (1994). *Testing Exogeneity*. Oxford: Oxford University Press.

Ericsson, N. R., and Irons, J. S. (1995). The Lucas critique in practice: Theory without measurement. In K. D. Hoover (ed.), *Macroeconometrics: Developments, Tensions and Prospects*, pp. 263–312. Dordrecht: Kluwer Academic Press.

Escribano, A. (2004). Nonlinear error correction: The case of money demand in the UK (1878–2000). *Macroeconomic Dynamics*, **8**, 76–116.

Favero, C., and Hendry, D. F. (1992). Testing the Lucas critique: A review. *Econometric Reviews*, **11**, 265–306.

Fildes, R. A., and Makridakis, S. (1995). The impact of empirical accuracy studies on time series analysis and forecasting. *International Statistical Review*, **63**, 289–308.

Fisher, R. A. (1915). Frequency distribution of the values of the correlation coefficient in samples from an indefinitely large population. *Biometrika*, **10**, 507–521.

Fisher, R. A. (1922). On the mathematical foundations of theoretical statistics. *Philosophical Transactions of the Royal Society*, A, **222**, 309–368.

Friedman, M., and Schwartz, A. J. (1982). *Monetary Trends in the United States and the United Kingdom: Their Relation to Income, Prices, and Interest Rates, 1867–1975*. Chicago: University of Chicago Press.

Frisch, R. (1934). *Statistical Confluence Analysis by means of Complete Regression Systems*. Oslo: University Institute of Economics.

Frisch, R., and Waugh, F. V. (1933). Partial time regression as compared with individual trends. *Econometrica*, **1**, 221–223.

Galton, F. (1886). Regression towards mediocrity in hereditary stature. *Journal of the Anthropological Institute of Great Britain and Ireland*, **15**, 246–263.

Galton, F. (1889). Co-relations and their measurement, chiefly from anthropometric data. *Proceedings of the Royal Society of London*, **45**, 135–145.

Goldberger, A. S. (1991). *A Course in Econometrics*: Cambridge, Mass.: Harvard University Press.

Goldberger, A. S. (1998). *Introductory Econometrics*. Cambridge, Mass: Harvard University Press.

Golub, G. H., and Van Loan, C. F. (1996). *Matrix Computations*. 3rd ed. Baltimore, Maryland: Johns Hopkins University Press.

Gourieroux, C., and Monfort, A. (1996). *Simulation Based Econometric Methods*. Oxford: Oxford University Press.

Graddy, K. (1995). Testing for imperfect competition at the Fulton Fish Market. *RAND Journal of Economics*, **26**, 75–92.

Graddy, K. (2006). The Fulton Fish Market. *Journal of Economic Perspectives*, **20**, 207–220.

Granger, C. W. J. (1986). Developments in the study of cointegrated economic variables. *Oxford Bulletin of Economics and Statistics*, **48**, 213–228.

Greene, W. H. (2003). *Econometric Analysis*. 5th ed. Englewood Cliffs, N.J.: Prentice-Hall.

Gujarati, D. N. (2003). *Basic Econometrics*. 4th ed. New York: McGraw-Hill.

Hall, R. E. (1978). Stochastic implications of the life cycle-permanent income hypothesis: Evidence. *Journal of Political Economy*, **86**, 971–987.

Hamilton, J. D. (1994). *Time Series Analysis*. Princeton, NJ: Princeton University Press.

Hammersley, J. M., and Handscomb, D. C. (1964). *Monte Carlo Methods*. London: Chapman and Hall.

Harbo, I., Johansen, S., Nielsen, B., and Rahbek, A. (1998). Asymptotic inference on cointegrating rank in partial systems. *Journal of Business and Economic Statistics*, **16**, 388–399.

Hausman, J. A. (1978). Specification tests in econometrics. *Econometrica*, **46**, 1251–1271.

Heckman, J. J. (1976). The common structure of statistical models of truncation, sample selection and limited dependent variables and a simple estimator for such models. *Annals of Economic and Social Measurement*, **5**, 475–492.

Heckman, J. J. (2005). The scientific model of causality. *Sociological Methodology*, **35**, 1–98.

Hendry, D. F. (1980). Econometrics: Alchemy or science? *Economica*, **47**, 387–406.

Hendry, D. F. (1988). The encompassing implications of feedback versus feedforward mechanisms in econometrics. *Oxford Economic Papers*, **40**, 132–149.

Hendry, D. F. (1995a). *Dynamic Econometrics*. Oxford: Oxford University Press.

Hendry, D. F. (1995b). On the interactions of unit roots and exogeneity. *Econometric Reviews*, **14**, 383–419.

Hendry, D. F. (2001). How economists forecast. In Hendry and Ericsson (2001), pp. 15–41.

Hendry, D. F. (2004). The Nobel Memorial Prize for Clive W. J. Granger. *Scandinavian Journal of Economics*, **106**, 187–213.

Hendry, D. F., and Ericsson, N. R. (1991a). An econometric analysis of UK money demand in "Monetary Trends in the United States and the United Kingdom" by Milton Friedman and Anna J. Schwartz. *American Economic Review*, **81**, 8–38.

Hendry, D. F., and Ericsson, N. R. (1991b). Modeling the demand for narrow money in the United Kingdom and the United States. *European Economic Review*, **35**, 833–886.

Hendry, D. F., and Ericsson, N. R. (eds.) (2001). *Understanding Economic Forecasts*. Cambridge, Mass.: MIT Press.

Hendry, D. F., and Krolzig, H.-M. (2001). *Automatic Econometric Model Selection*. London: Timberlake Consultants Press.

Hendry, D. F., and Krolzig, H.-M. (2005). The properties of automatic Gets modelling. *Economic Journal*, **115**, C32–C61.

Hendry, D. F., and Massmann, M. (2007). Co-breaking: Recent advances and a synopsis of the literature. forthcoming, *Journal of Business and Economic Statistics*, Special Issue.

Hendry, D. F., and Mizon, G. E. (1993). Evaluating dynamic econometric models by encompassing the VAR. In P. C. B. Phillips (ed.), *Models, Methods and Applications of Econometrics*, pp. 272–300. Oxford: Basil Blackwell.

Hendry, D. F., and Morgan, M. S. (1995). *The Foundations of Econometric Analysis*. Cambridge: Cambridge University Press.

Hendry, D. F., and Santos, C. (2005). Regression models with data-based indicator variables. *Oxford Bulletin of Economics and Statistics*, **67**, 571–595.

Hoel, P. G., Port, S. C., and Stone, C. J. (1971). *Introduction to Probability Theory*. New York: Houghton Mifflin.

Hoover, K. D., and Perez, S. J. (1999). Data mining reconsidered: Encompassing and the general-to-specific approach to specification search. *Econometrics Journal*, **2**, 167–191.

Hosmer, D. W., and Lemeshow, S. (2000). *Applied Logistic Regression*. 2nd ed. New York: John Wiley & Sons.

Hotelling, H. (1936). Relations between two sets of variates. *Biometrika*, **28**, 321–377.

Jarque, C. M., and Bera, A. K. (1980). Efficient tests for normality, homoscedasticity and serial independence of regression residuals. *Economics Letters*, **6**, 255–259.

Jarque, C. M., and Bera, A. K. (1987). A test for normality of observations and regression residuals. *International Statistical Review*, **55**, 163–172.

Johansen, S. (1988). Statistical analysis of cointegration vectors. *Journal of Economic Dynamics and Control*, **12**, 231–254.

Johansen, S. (1995). *Likelihood-based Inference in Cointegrated Vector Autoregressive Models*. Oxford: Oxford University Press.

Johnson, N. L., Kotz, S., and Balakrishnan, N. (1994). *Continuous Univariate Distributions – 1*. 2nd ed. New York: John Wiley.

Johnson, N. L., Kotz, S., and Balakrishnan, N. (1995). *Continuous Univariate Distributions – 2*. 2nd ed. New York: John Wiley.

Johnson, N. L., Kotz, S., and Kemp, A. W. (1993). *Univariate Discrete Distributions*. New York: John Wiley.

Johnston, J., and DiNardo, J. (1997). *Econometric Methods*. 4th ed. New York: McGraw-Hill.

Judge, G. G., Griffiths, W. E., Hill, R. C., Lütkepohl, H., and Lee, T.-C. (1985). *The Theory and Practice of Econometrics*. 2nd ed. New York: John Wiley.

Juselius, K. (2006). *The Cointegrated VAR Model: Methodology and Applications*. Oxford: Oxford University Press.

Kennedy, P. E. (2003). *A Guide to Econometrics*. 5th ed. Oxford: Basil Blackwell.

Kilian, L., and Demiroglu, U. (2000). Residual-based tests for normality in autoregressions: Asymptotic theory and simulation evidence. *Journal of Business and Economic Statistics*, **18**, 40–50.

King, G. (1989). *Unifying Political Methodology: The Likelihood Theory of Statistical Inference*. Cambridge: Cambridge University Press.

Kiviet, J. F. (1986). On the rigor of some mis-specification tests for modelling dynamic relationships. *Review of Economic Studies*, **53**, 241–261.

Kiviet, J. F., and Phillips, G. D. A. (1992). Exact similar tests for unit roots and cointegration. *Oxford Bulletin of Economics and Statistics*, **54**, 349–367.

Klein, L. R. (1971). *An Essay on the Theory of Economic Prediction*. Chicago: Markham Publishing Company.

Kremers, J. J. M., Ericsson, N. R., and Dolado, J. J. (1992). The power of cointegration tests. *Oxford Bulletin of Economics and Statistics*, **54**, 325–348.

Krolzig, H.-M., and Hendry, D. F. (2001). Computer automation of general-to-specific model selection procedures. *Journal of Economic Dynamics and Control*, **25**, 831–866.

Lancaster, A. (2004). *An Introduction to Modern Bayesian Econometrics*. Oxford: Blackwell.

Lauritzen, S. L. (2002). *Thiele: Pioneer in Statistics*. Oxford: Oxford University Press.

Leeb, H., and Pötscher, B. M. (2005). Model selection and inference: Facts and fiction. *Econometric Theory*, **21**, 21–59.

Lindley, D. V., and Scott, W. F. (1995). *New Cambridge Statistical Tables*. 2nd ed. Cambridge: Cambridge University Press.

Lovell, M. C. (1983). Data mining. *Review of Economics and Statistics*, **65**, 1–12.

Lucas, R. E. (1976). Econometric policy evaluation: A critique. In K. Brunner, and A. Meltzer (eds.), *The Phillips Curve and Labor Markets*, vol 1 of *Carnegie-Rochester Conferences on Public Policy*, pp. 19–46. Amsterdam: North-Holland.

Maddala, G. S. (1983). *Limited Dependent and Qualitative Variables in Econometrics*. Cambridge: Cambridge University Press.

Maddala, G. S., Rao, C. R., and Vinod, H. D. (eds.) (1992). *Handbook of Statistics*. Amsterdam: North-Holland.

Magnus, J. R., and Neudecker, H. (1999). *Matrix Differential Calculus with Applications in Statistics and Econometrics*. 2nd ed. New York: John Wiley.

Makridakis, S., Andersen, A., Carbone, R., Fildes, R., et al. (1982). The accuracy of extrapolation (time series) methods: Results of a forecasting competition. *Journal of Forecasting*, **1**, 111–153.

Makridakis, S., and Hibon, M. (2000). The M3-competition: Results, conclusions and implications. *International Journal of Forecasting*, **16**, 451–476.

McNees, S. K. (1990). The accuracy of macroeconomic forecasts. In P. A. Klein (ed.), *Analyzing Modern Business Cycles*, pp. 143–173. London: M. E. Sharpe Inc.

Mills, T. C. (ed.) (1999). *Economic Forecasting*. Cheltenham, UK: Edward Elgar.

Mincer, J. (ed.) (1974). *Schooling, Experience and Earnings*. New York: National Bureau of Economic Research.

Mincer, J., and Zarnowitz, V. (1969). The evaluation of economic forecasts. In J. Mincer (ed.), *Economic Forecasts and Expectations: Analysis of Forecasting Behavior and Performance*, pp. 3–46. New York: National Bureau of Economic Research.

Mitchell, B. R. (1988). *British Historical Statistics*. Cambridge: Cambridge University Press.

Muellbauer, J. N. J. (1996). Consumer expenditure. In T. Jenkinson (ed.), *Readings in Macroeconomics*, pp. 92–125. Oxford: Oxford University Press.

Newey, W. K., and West, K. D. (1987). A simple positive semi-definite heteroskedasticity and autocorrelation-consistent covariance matrix. *Econometrica*, **55**, 703–708.

Nielsen, B. (2001). The asymptotic distribution of unit root tests of unstable autoregressive processes. *Econometrica*, **69**, 211–219.

Nielsen, B. (2006). Correlograms for non-stationary autoregressions. *Journal of the Royal Statistical Society, B*, **68**, 707–720.

Nielsen, B. (2007). Order determination in general vector autoregressions. In Ho, H.-C., Ing, C.-K., and Lai, T. L. (eds.), *Time Series and Related Topics: In Memory of Ching-Zong Wei*, pp. 93–112. New York: IMS Lecture Notes and Monograph Series, 52. forthcoming.

Nymoen, R. (2002). Faulty watch towers –"structural" models in Norwegian monetary policy analysis. Unpublished paper, University of Oslo.

Office for National Statistics (2005). *Key Population and Vital Statistics, 2003*. London: Her Majesty's Stationery Office. Series VS no 30, PP1 no 26.

Office for National Statistics (2006). *Key Population and Vital Statistics, 2004*. London: Her Majesty's Stationery Office. Series VS no 31, PP1 no 27.

Pearson, K. (1902). On the mathematical theory of errors of judgment, with special reference to the personal equation. *Philosophical Transactions of the Royal Society of London*, A, **198**, 235–299.

Pesaran, M. H. (1974). On the general problem of model selection. *Review of Economic Studies*, **41**, 153–171.

Phillips, P. C. B. (1986). Understanding spurious regressions in econometrics. *Journal of Econometrics*, **33**, 311–340.

R Development Core Team (2006). *R: A Language and Environment for Statistical Computing*. R Foundation for Statistical Computing, Vienna, Austria. ISBN 3-900051-07-0.

Ramsey, J. B. (1969). Tests for specification errors in classical linear least squares regression analysis. *Journal of the Royal Statistical Society*, B, **31**, 350–371.

Ruud, P. A. (2000). *An Introduction to Classical Econometric Theory*. Oxford: Oxford University Press.

Sargan, J. D. (1964). Wages and prices in the United Kingdom: A study in econometric methodology (with discussion). In Hart, P. E., Mills, G., and Whitaker, J. K. (eds.), *Econometric Analysis for National Economic Planning*, vol. 16 of *Colston Papers*, pp. 25–63. London: Butterworth Co.

Savin, N. E. (1984). Multiple hypothesis testing. In Z. Griliches and M. D. Intriligator (eds.), *Handbook of Econometrics*, vol 2, Ch. 14. Amsterdam: North-Holland.

Singer, M. (1997). Thoughts of a nonmillenarian. *Bulletin of the American Academy of Arts and Sciences*, **51**(2), 36–51.

Slutsky, E. (1937). The summation of random causes as the source of cyclic processes. *Econometrica*, **5**, 105–146. (Translation from the Russian version of 1927).

Smith, G. W. (1986). A dynamic Baumol–Tobin model of money demand. *Review of Economic Studies*, **53**, 465–469.

Söderbom, M., Teal, F., Wambugu, A., and Kahyarara, G. (2004). The dynamics of returns to education in Kenyan and Tanzanian manufacturing. Working paper, Department of Economics, University of Oxford.

Stock, J. H., and Watson, M. W. (1996). Evidence on structural instability in macroeconomic time series relations. *Journal of Business and Economic Statistics*, **14**, 11–30.

Stock, J. H., and Watson, M. W. (1999). A comparison of linear and nonlinear models for forecasting macroeconomic time series. In R. F. Engle and H. White (eds.), *Cointegration, Causality and Forecasting*, pp. 1–44. Oxford: Oxford University Press.

Student (1908). On the probable error of the mean. *Biometrika*, **6**, 1–25.

Svensson, L. E. O., Houg, K., Solheim, H. O. A., and Steigum, E. (2002). Norges Bank Watch, 2002. An independent review of monetary policy and institutions in Norway. Technical report, Centre for Monetary Economics at the Norwegian School of Management, BI.

Taylor, S. J. (2005). *Asset Price Dynamics, Volatitility, and Prediction*. Princeton: Princeton University Press.

Theil, H. (1966). *Applied Economic Forecasting*. Amsterdam: North-Holland.

Thiele, T. N. (1886). *Almindelig Iagttagelseslære: Sandsynlighedsregning og mindste Kvadraters Methode*. Copenhagen: C. A. Reitzel.

Train, K. E. (2003). *Discrete Choice Methods with Simulation*. Cambridge: Cambridge University Press.

Turner, D. S. (1990). The role of judgement in macroeconomic forecasting. *Journal of Forecasting*, **9**, 315–345.

Verbeek, M. (2000). *A Guide to Modern Econometrics*. New York: John Wiley & Sons.

Wallis, K. F. (1989). Macroeconomic forecasting: A survey. *Economic Journal*, **99**, 28–61.

Wallis, K. F., and Whitley, J. D. (1991). Sources of error in forecasts and expectations: UK economic models, 1984–1988. *Journal of Forecasting*, **10**, 231–253.

White, H. (1980). A heteroskedastic-consistent covariance matrix estimator and a direct test for heteroskedasticity. *Econometrica*, **48**, 817–838.

White, H. (2001). *Asymptotic Theory for Econometricians*. San Diego, CA: Academic Press.

Wooldridge, J. M. (2002). *Econometric Analysis of Cross Section and Panel Data*. Cambridge Mass.: MIT Press.

Wooldridge, J. M. (2006). *Introductory Econometrics – A Modern Approach*. 3rd ed. New York: South-Western College Publishing.

Yule, G. U. (1926). Why do we sometimes get nonsense-correlations between time-series? A study in sampling and the nature of time series (with discussion). *Journal of the Royal Statistical Society*, **89**, 1–64.

Yule, G. U. (1927). On a method of investigating periodicities in disturbed series, with special reference to Wolfer's sunspot numbers. *Philosophical Transactions of the Royal Society*, A, **226**, 267–298.

Author index

Subject index

R^2: multiple correlation, 107
χ^2-distribution, 24, 62
2SLS, 236

Affine restriction, 116
Analysis of variance (ANOVA), 83
Ancillarity, 55
Asymptotic
— theory, 279
Asymptotic theory, 19, 343
  Central Limit Theorem, 22
  Law of Large Numbers, 19
  Stationary processes, 187
  Unit-root processes, 249
Autocorrelation, 176, 184
— function, 177
Partial —, *see* Partial
Test for —, 192
Automatic model selection, 113, 286
  Encompassing, 292
  Gets, 287, 292
  Multipath search, 292
Autoregression
Linear trend, *see* Linear
Autoregression (AR), 175–188
  First-order model, 178
  Forecast taxonomy, 332
  Forecasting, 327
  Intercept, 186, 277
  Second-order, 252
  Structural breaks, 304–308
  Unconditional distribution, 182
Autoregressive conditional heteroskedasticity

(ARCH), 193
Autoregressive
distributed-lag (ADL), 204, 213
  Cointegration, 267
  Equilibrium-correction, 214
Auxiliary regression, 132, 134, 192, 193

Bayesian statistics, 343
Behavioral
— equation, 167, 218
— model, 164, 217, 308
Bernoulli distribution, 6
  Expectation and variance, 17
Bernoulli model, 7
Bias
  Omitted variable —, *see* Omitted variable bias
  Pre-test —, *see* Pre-test
  Selection —, *see* Selection bias
  Simultaneity —, *see* Simultaneity bias
Bivariate normal distribution, 142
  Addition, 144
  Conditioning, 143
  Correlation and independence, 144
  Expectation and variance, 144
  Marginalization, 143
  Matrix formulation, 153
Box plot, 67

Cauchy–Schwarz inequality, 65, 86
Causality, 59, 168

Censored regression model, 43
Central Limit Theorem, 22
Characteristic polynomial, 248, 252
Chow test, *see* Test
Closed model, *see* Model
Co-breaking, 307
Cobb–Douglas production functions, 117
Coefficient of determination, 108
Cointegrating relation, 255, 262
Cointegration, 255, 342
— rank, 265
— rank test, 265
  and weak exogeneity, 266
  Interpretation, 262
  Single equation, 267, 283
Collinearity
  and estimation, 110
  and testing, 113
  Near —, 106, 297
  Perfect —, 106
Common factor, 168
Common trend, 255, 262
Concentrated likelihood, 37
Conditional
— density, 52
— inference, 85, 150, 155
— interpretation, 112, 293
— likelihood, 56, 180, 204
— model, 55, 141
— model and identification, 231
— sample distribution, 49